THE BEST OF BATTLE

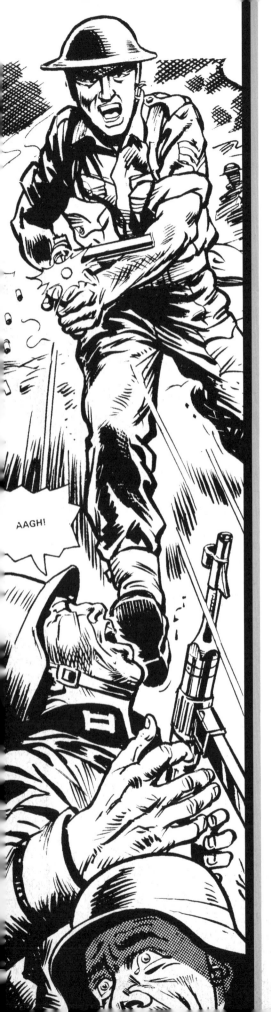

AAGH!

THE BEST OF

BATTLE

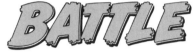

This book is dedicated to Gerry Finley-Day, John Wagner and Pat Mills.

ISBN: 9781848560253

Published by Titan Books,
A division of Titan Publishing Group Ltd.
144 Southwark Street
London SE1 0UP

A CIP catalogue record for this title is available from the British Library.

First published: October 2009
10 9 8 7 6 5 4 3 2 1
Printed in Italy.

Special thanks to Pat Mills, Dave Hunt, Gerry Finley-Day, Steve MacManus, Carl Alexander, Melanie Leggett and Martin Morgan for their help and support in the production of this book.

What did you think of this book? We love to hear from our readers. Please email us at: **readerfeedback@titanemail.com**, or write to us at the above address.

To receive advance information, news, competitions, and exclusive Titan offers online, please register as a member by clicking the "sign up" button on our website: **www.titanbooks.com**

This book is a work of fiction. Characters may have views and use language which some of today's readers may find offensive. The publisher and copyright holder in no way endorse the views expressed or language used.

Much of the comic strip source material used by Titan Books in this edition is exceedingly rare. As such, we hope that readers appreciate that the quality of reproduction achievable can vary.

THE BEST OF BATTLE

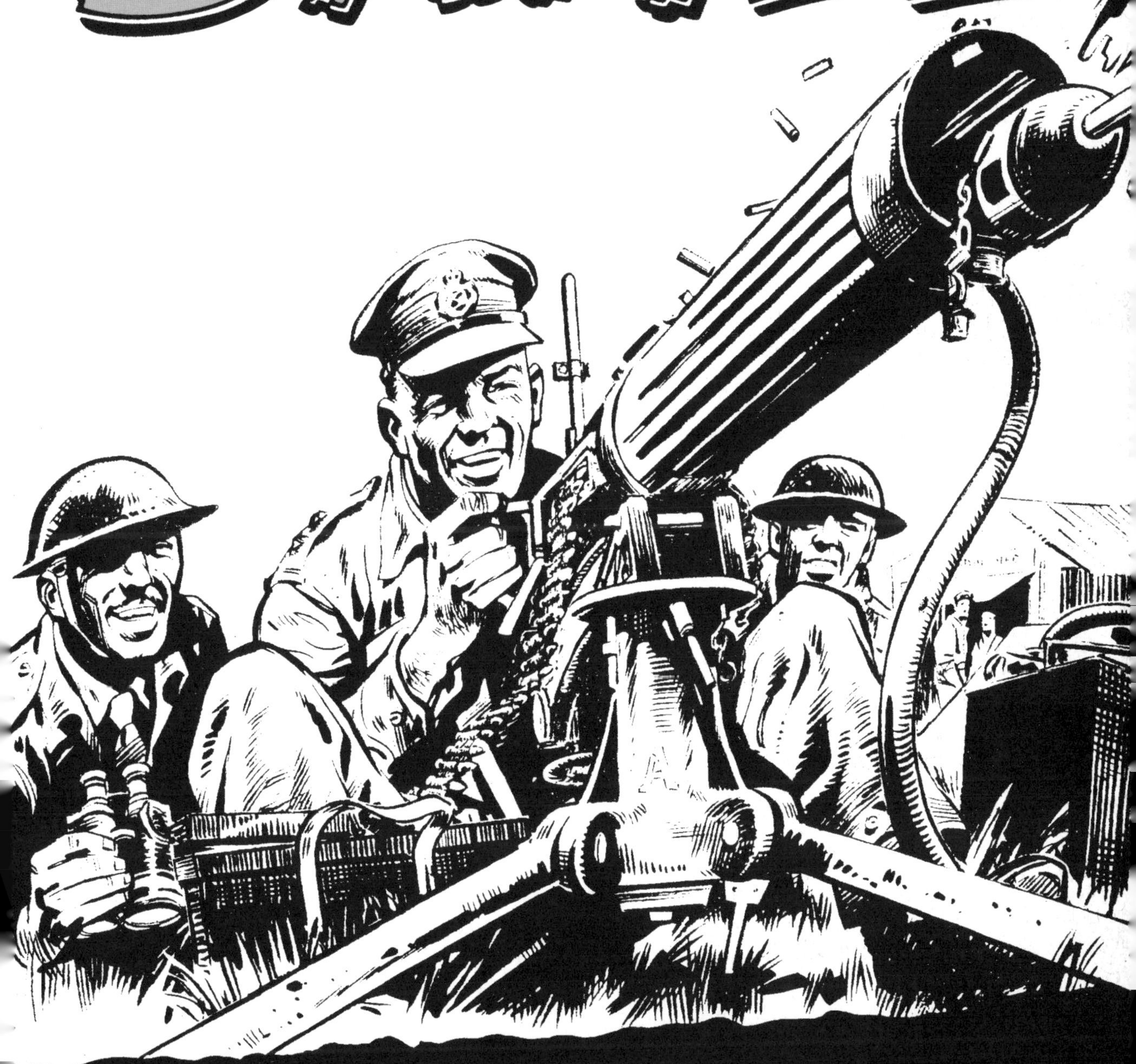

TITAN BOOKS

ROLL CALL

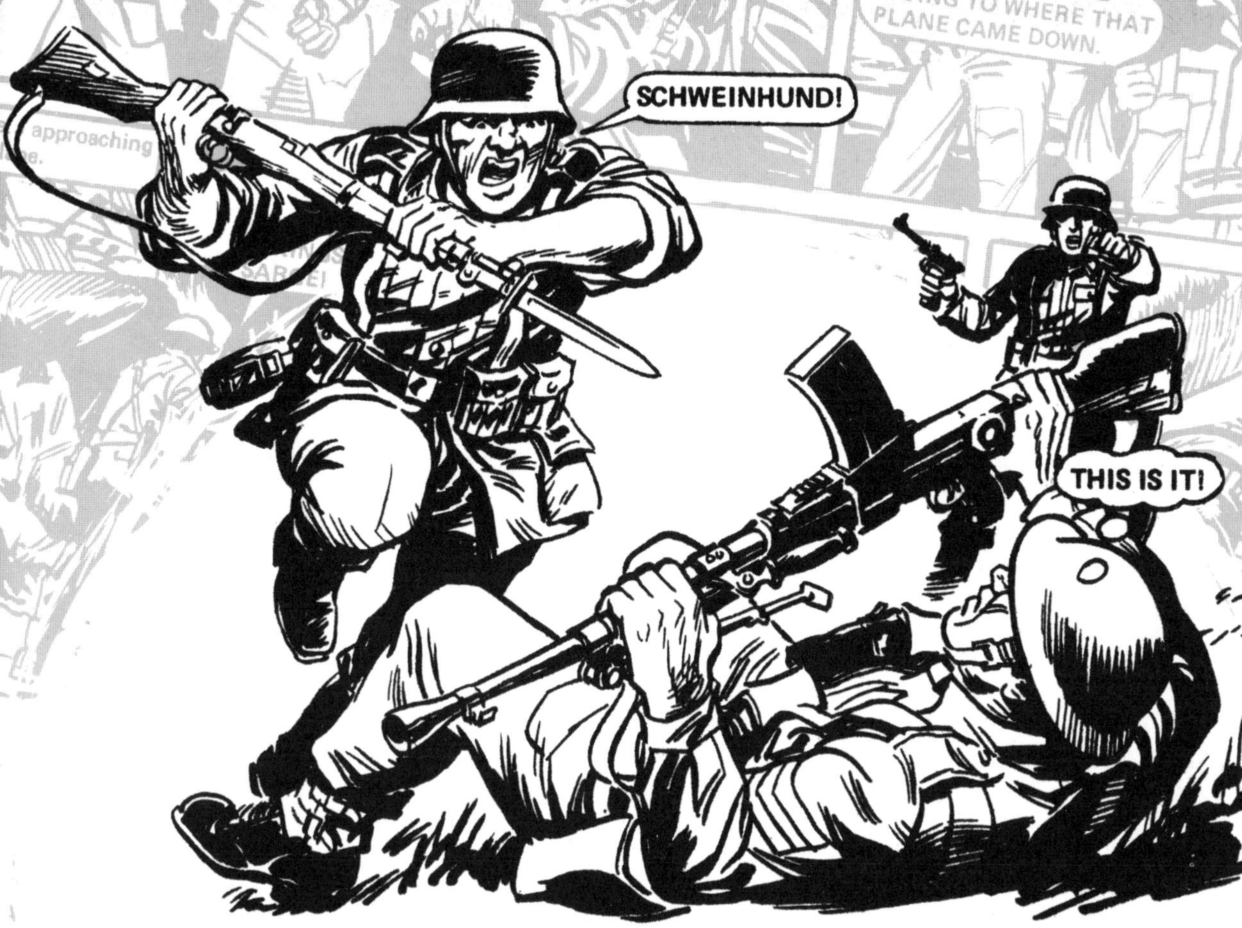
SCHWEINHUND!
THIS IS IT!

D-DAY DAWSON

"THAT'S THE WAY I WANT TO GO OUT – FIGHTING!"

Nothing was going to stop Sgt Steve Dawson from fighting alongside his men — not even the German bullet lodged close to his heart which had given him just a year left to live, and nothing to lose.

Now, there's no mission too daring, no odds too small: he's going to fight the Hun 'til his last breath, or die trying!

During its run of two series and nearly two years, from 8 March 1975 to 22 January 1977, 'D-Day Dawson' regularly fought the 'Rat Pack' for top dog status in *Battle's* Reader's Poll. Gerry Finley-Day and Ron Carpenter wrote the majority of the first series while Colin Page supplied most of the artwork.

NOTES FROM THE FRONTLINE:

"We did have a lot of fun coming up with the characters and although D-Day Dawson wasn't the very first created, he was certainly one of the earliest. We wanted a very archetypal comic character, which D-Day Dawson clearly is, and then we needed to give him an original spin and I think the idea of a guy with only a limited period of time to live seemed to fit the bill.

We knew it would be very popular with the readers and that's why it was *Battle*'s lead story.

We rather naively thought that twelve months would be enough for 'Dawson', but the managing editor said: 'No, this character is phenomenally popular, you've got to keep him going forever!'" — **Pat Mills**

WRITTEN BY Gerry Finley-Day & Ron Carpenter
DRAWN BY Colin Page

THE BRITISH SOLDIER WHO HAS A DATE WITH DEATH!

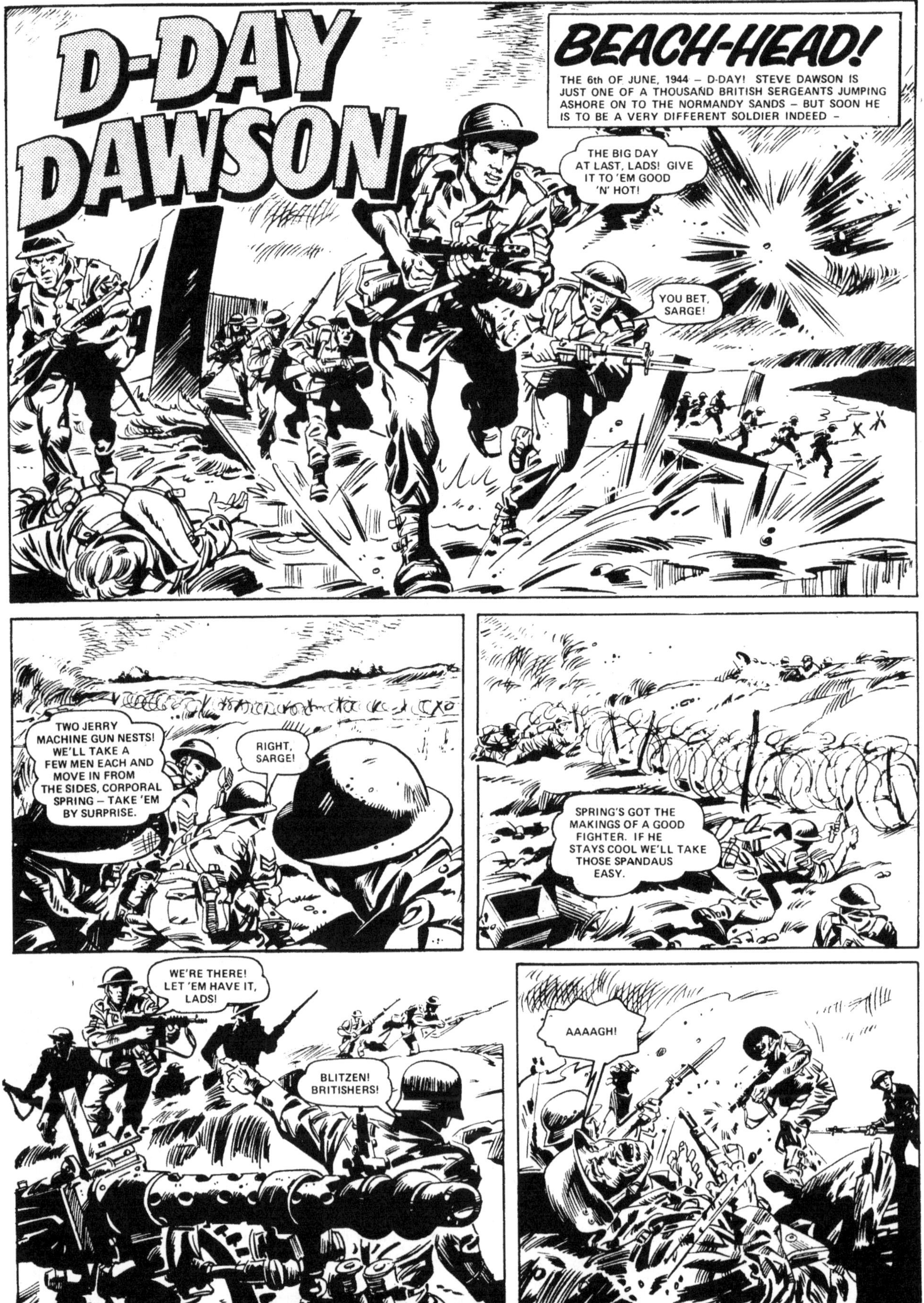
D-DAY DAWSON
BEACH-HEAD!
THE 6th OF JUNE, 1944 – D-DAY! STEVE DAWSON IS JUST ONE OF A THOUSAND BRITISH SERGEANTS JUMPING ASHORE ON TO THE NORMANDY SANDS – BUT SOON HE IS TO BE A VERY DIFFERENT SOLDIER INDEED –
THE BIG DAY AT LAST, LADS! GIVE IT TO 'EM GOOD 'N' HOT!
YOU BET, SARGE!
TWO JERRY MACHINE GUN NESTS! WE'LL TAKE A FEW MEN EACH AND MOVE IN FROM THE SIDES, CORPORAL SPRING – TAKE 'EM BY SURPRISE.
RIGHT, SARGE!
SPRING'S GOT THE MAKINGS OF A GOOD FIGHTER. IF HE STAYS COOL WE'LL TAKE THOSE SPANDAUS EASY.
WE'RE THERE! LET 'EM HAVE IT, LADS!
BLITZEN! BRITISHERS!
AAAAGH!

"THERE'S NOTHING WE CAN DO FOR YOU."

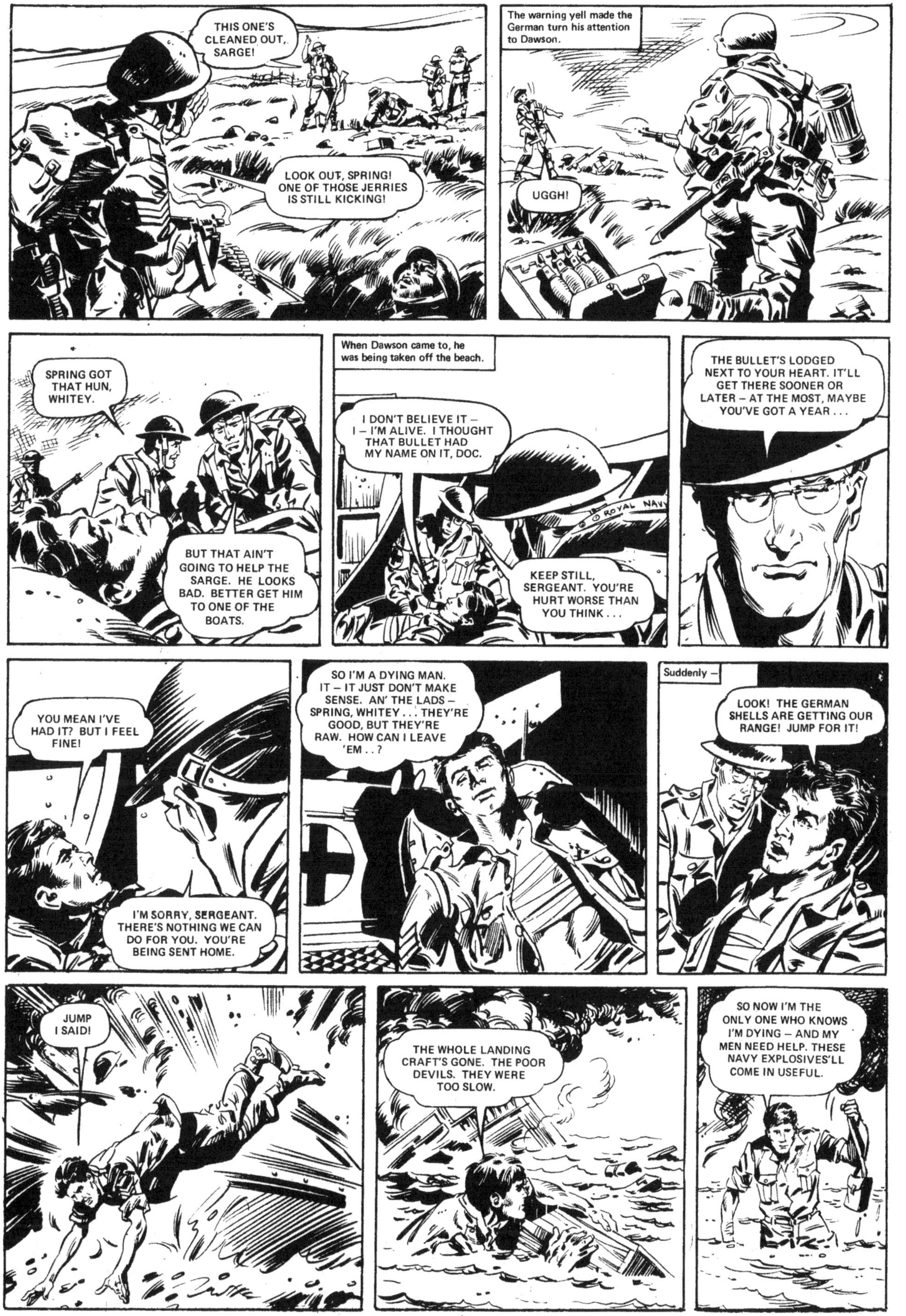

THIS ONE'S CLEANED OUT, SARGE!
LOOK OUT, SPRING! ONE OF THOSE JERRIES IS STILL KICKING!
The warning yell made the German turn his attention to Dawson.
UGGH!
SPRING GOT THAT HUN, WHITEY.
BUT THAT AIN'T GOING TO HELP THE SARGE. HE LOOKS BAD. BETTER GET HIM TO ONE OF THE BOATS.
When Dawson came to, he was being taken off the beach.
I DON'T BELIEVE IT – I – I'M ALIVE. I THOUGHT THAT BULLET HAD MY NAME ON IT, DOC.
ROYAL NAVY
KEEP STILL, SERGEANT. YOU'RE HURT WORSE THAN YOU THINK . . .
THE BULLET'S LODGED NEXT TO YOUR HEART. IT'LL GET THERE SOONER OR LATER – AT THE MOST, MAYBE YOU'VE GOT A YEAR . . .
YOU MEAN I'VE HAD IT? BUT I FEEL FINE!
I'M SORRY, SERGEANT. THERE'S NOTHING WE CAN DO FOR YOU. YOU'RE BEING SENT HOME.
SO I'M A DYING MAN. IT – IT JUST DON'T MAKE SENSE. AN' THE LADS – SPRING, WHITEY . . . THEY'RE GOOD, BUT THEY'RE RAW. HOW CAN I LEAVE 'EM . . ?
Suddenly –
LOOK! THE GERMAN SHELLS ARE GETTING OUR RANGE! JUMP FOR IT!
JUMP I SAID!
THE WHOLE LANDING CRAFT'S GONE. THE POOR DEVILS. THEY WERE TOO SLOW.
SO NOW I'M THE ONLY ONE WHO KNOWS I'M DYING – AND MY MEN NEED HELP. THESE NAVY EXPLOSIVES'LL COME IN USEFUL.

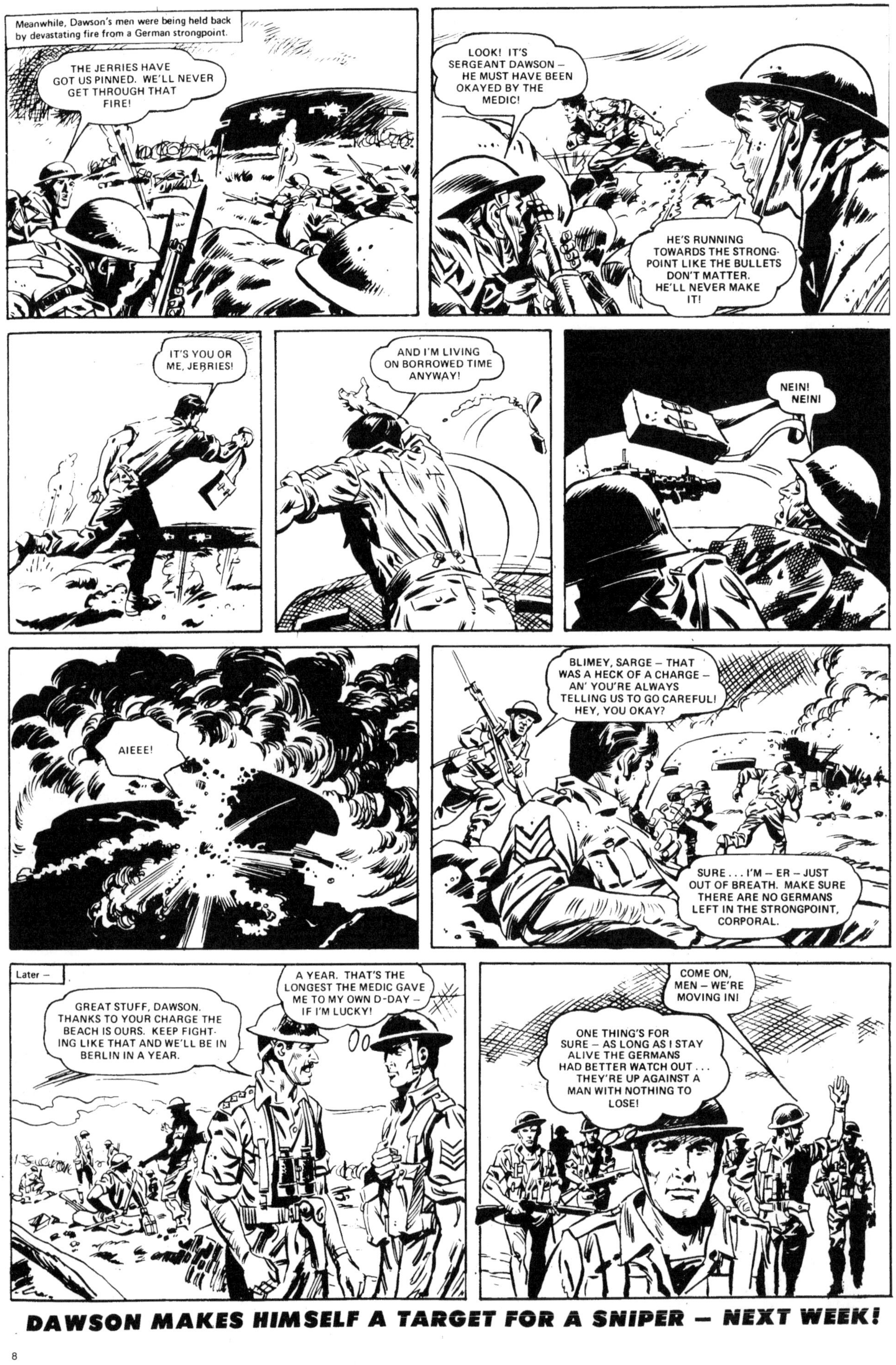

Meanwhile, Dawson's men were being held back by devastating fire from a German strongpoint.
THE JERRIES HAVE GOT US PINNED. WE'LL NEVER GET THROUGH THAT FIRE!
LOOK! IT'S SERGEANT DAWSON — HE MUST HAVE BEEN OKAYED BY THE MEDIC!
HE'S RUNNING TOWARDS THE STRONG-POINT LIKE THE BULLETS DON'T MATTER. HE'LL NEVER MAKE IT!
IT'S YOU OR ME, JERRIES!
AND I'M LIVING ON BORROWED TIME ANYWAY!
NEIN! NEIN!
AIEEE!
BLIMEY, SARGE — THAT WAS A HECK OF A CHARGE — AN' YOU'RE ALWAYS TELLING US TO GO CAREFUL! HEY, YOU OKAY?
SURE . . . I'M — ER — JUST OUT OF BREATH. MAKE SURE THERE ARE NO GERMANS LEFT IN THE STRONGPOINT, CORPORAL.
Later —
GREAT STUFF, DAWSON. THANKS TO YOUR CHARGE THE BEACH IS OURS. KEEP FIGHT-ING LIKE THAT AND WE'LL BE IN BERLIN IN A YEAR.
A YEAR. THAT'S THE LONGEST THE MEDIC GAVE ME TO MY OWN D-DAY — IF I'M LUCKY!
COME ON, MEN — WE'RE MOVING IN!
ONE THING'S FOR SURE — AS LONG AS I STAY ALIVE THE GERMANS HAD BETTER WATCH OUT . . . THEY'RE UP AGAINST A MAN WITH NOTHING TO LOSE!

DAWSON MAKES HIMSELF A TARGET FOR A SNIPER — NEXT WEEK!

EXPLOSIVE ACTION FROM THE MAN WHO HAS A DATE WITH DEATH!

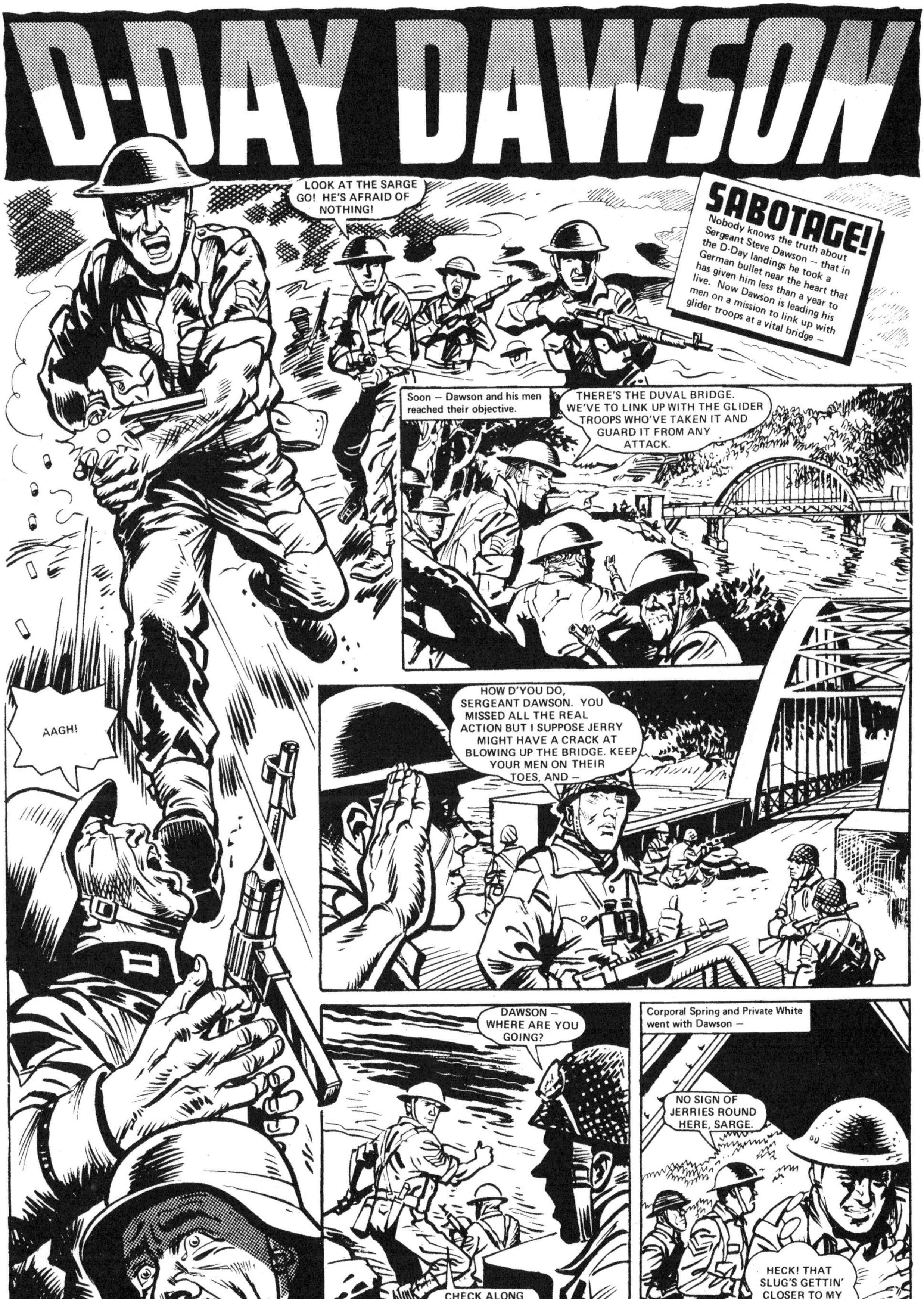

D-DAY DAWSON
SABOTAGE!
Nobody knows the truth about Sergeant Steve Dawson – that in the D-Day landings he took a German bullet near the heart that has given him less than a year to live. Now Dawson is leading his men on a mission to link up with glider troops at a vital bridge –
LOOK AT THE SARGE GO! HE'S AFRAID OF NOTHING!
AAGH!
Soon – Dawson and his men reached their objective.
THERE'S THE DUVAL BRIDGE. WE'VE TO LINK UP WITH THE GLIDER TROOPS WHO'VE TAKEN IT AND GUARD IT FROM ANY ATTACK.
HOW D'YOU DO, SERGEANT DAWSON. YOU MISSED ALL THE REAL ACTION BUT I SUPPOSE JERRY MIGHT HAVE A CRACK AT BLOWING UP THE BRIDGE. KEEP YOUR MEN ON THEIR TOES, AND –
DAWSON – WHERE ARE YOU GOING?
CHECK ALONG THE RIVERBANK, SIR – JUST IN CASE.
Corporal Spring and Private White went with Dawson –
NO SIGN OF JERRIES ROUND HERE, SARGE.
HECK! THAT SLUG'S GETTIN' CLOSER TO MY HEART.

"THEY'RE SABOTEURS–"

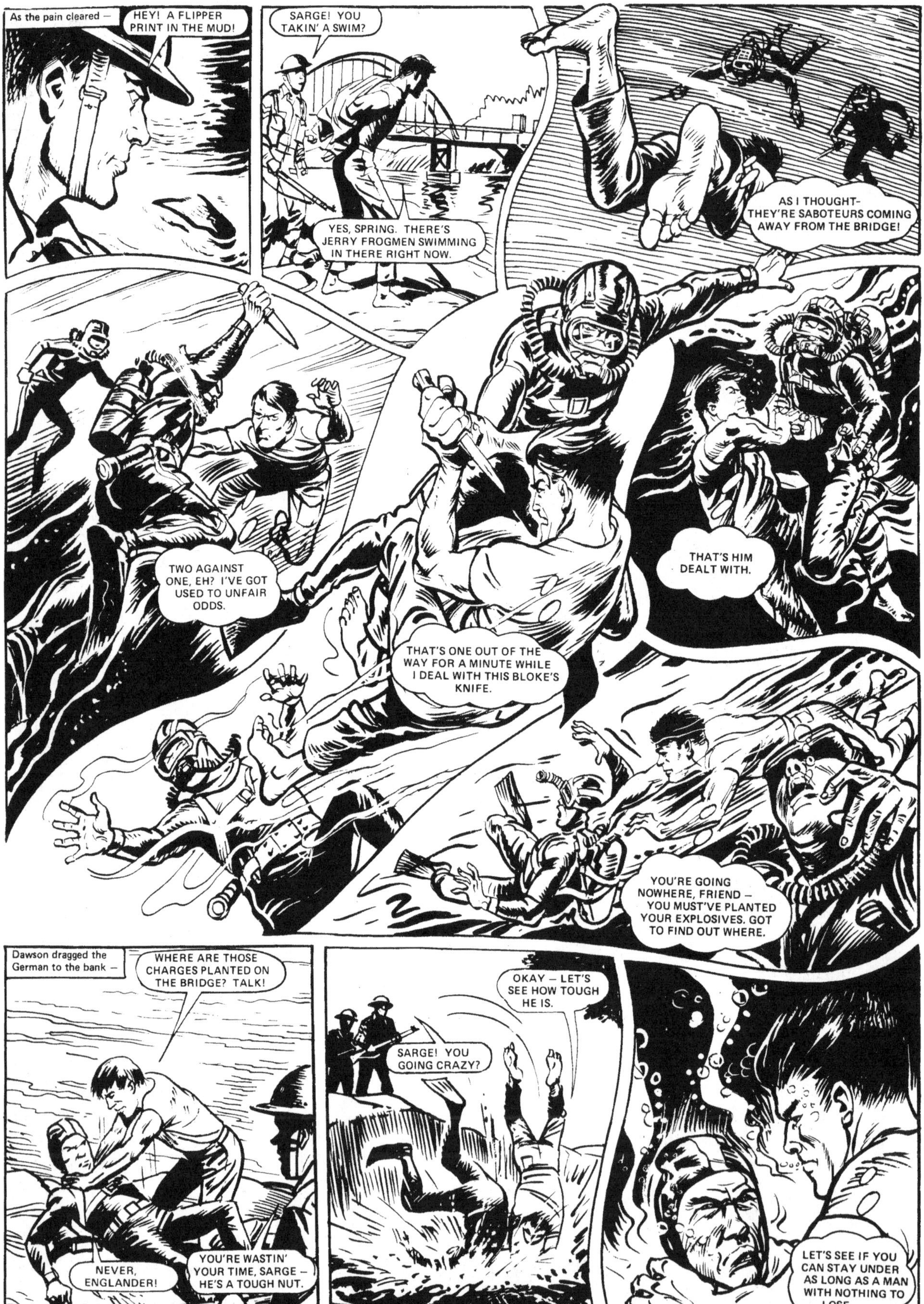

As the pain cleared –
HEY! A FLIPPER PRINT IN THE MUD!
SARGE! YOU TAKIN' A SWIM?
YES, SPRING. THERE'S JERRY FROGMEN SWIMMING IN THERE RIGHT NOW.
AS I THOUGHT- THEY'RE SABOTEURS COMING AWAY FROM THE BRIDGE!
TWO AGAINST ONE, EH? I'VE GOT USED TO UNFAIR ODDS.
THAT'S HIM DEALT WITH.
THAT'S ONE OUT OF THE WAY FOR A MINUTE WHILE I DEAL WITH THIS BLOKE'S KNIFE.
YOU'RE GOING NOWHERE, FRIEND – YOU MUST'VE PLANTED YOUR EXPLOSIVES. GOT TO FIND OUT WHERE.
Dawson dragged the German to the bank –
WHERE ARE THOSE CHARGES PLANTED ON THE BRIDGE? TALK!
NEVER, ENGLANDER!
YOU'RE WASTIN' YOUR TIME, SARGE – HE'S A TOUGH NUT.
OKAY – LET'S SEE HOW TOUGH HE IS.
SARGE! YOU GOING CRAZY?
LET'S SEE IF YOU CAN STAY UNDER AS LONG AS A MAN WITH NOTHING TO LOSE –

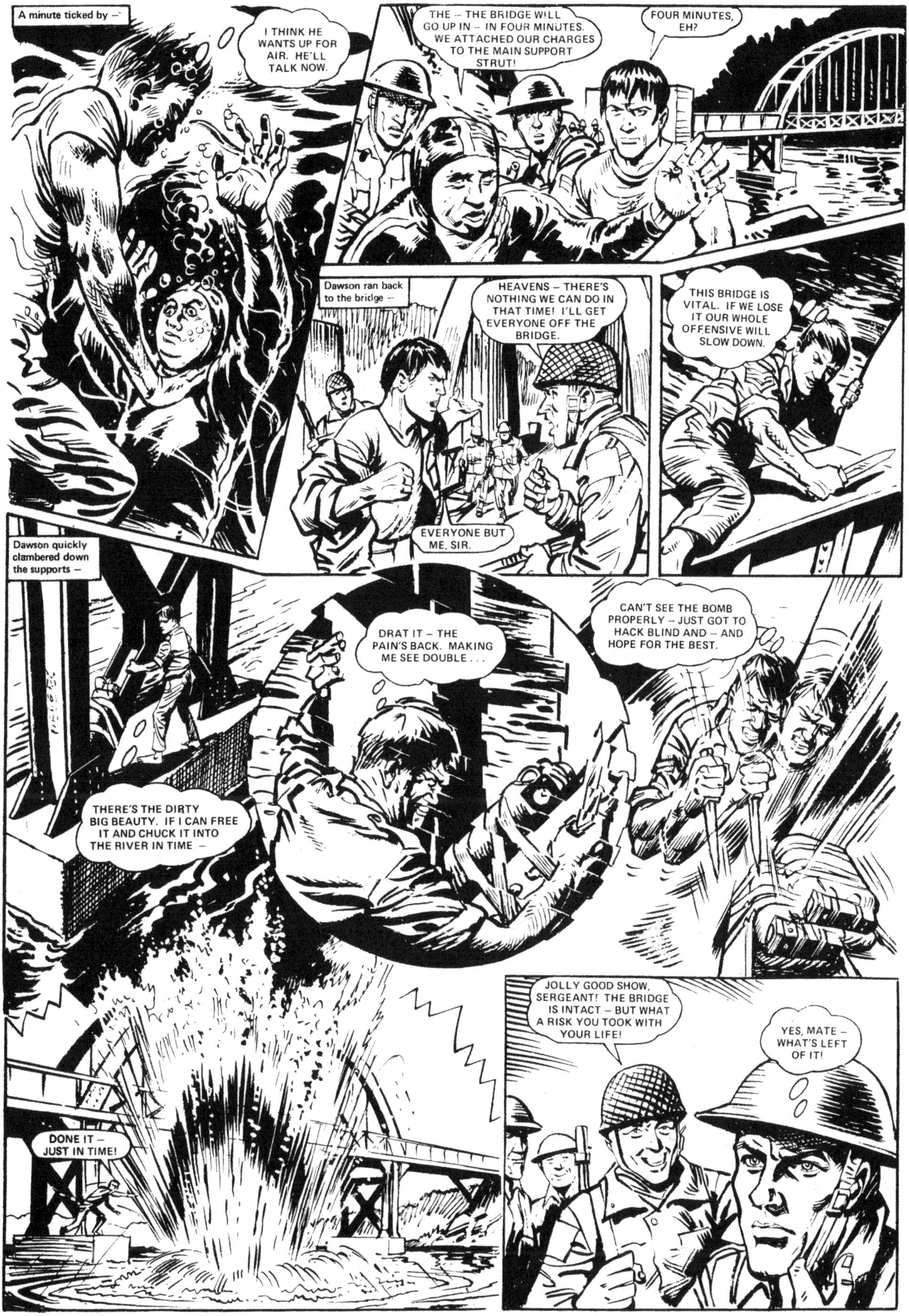
A minute ticked by –
I THINK HE WANTS UP FOR AIR. HE'LL TALK NOW.
THE – THE BRIDGE WILL GO UP IN – IN FOUR MINUTES. WE ATTACHED OUR CHARGES TO THE MAIN SUPPORT STRUT!
FOUR MINUTES, EH?
Dawson ran back to the bridge –
HEAVENS – THERE'S NOTHING WE CAN DO IN THAT TIME! I'LL GET EVERYONE OFF THE BRIDGE.
EVERYONE BUT ME, SIR.
THIS BRIDGE IS VITAL. IF WE LOSE IT OUR WHOLE OFFENSIVE WILL SLOW DOWN.
Dawson quickly clambered down the supports –
THERE'S THE DIRTY BIG BEAUTY. IF I CAN FREE IT AND CHUCK IT INTO THE RIVER IN TIME –
DRAT IT – THE PAIN'S BACK. MAKING ME SEE DOUBLE . . .
CAN'T SEE THE BOMB PROPERLY – JUST GOT TO HACK BLIND AND – AND HOPE FOR THE BEST.
DONE IT – JUST IN TIME!
JOLLY GOOD SHOW, SERGEANT! THE BRIDGE IS INTACT – BUT WHAT A RISK YOU TOOK WITH YOUR LIFE!
YES, MATE – WHAT'S LEFT OF IT!

NEXT WEEK – DAWSON UNDER FIRE FROM A FLAME THROWER!

THE MONTHS PASS RAPIDLY FOR DAWSON AND HIS DATE WITH DEATH!

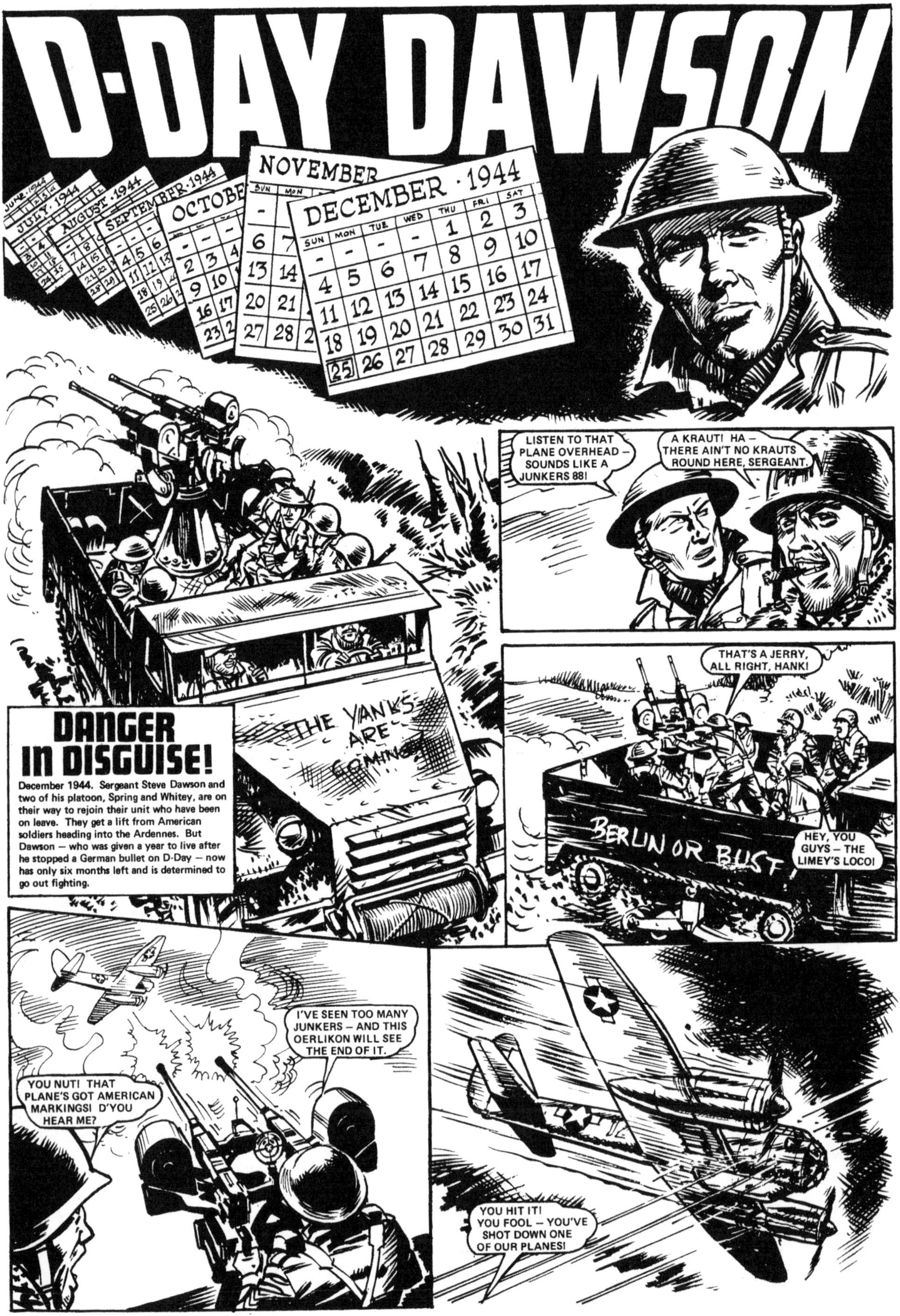
D-DAY DAWSON
NOVEMBER
DECEMBER · 1944
DANGER IN DISGUISE!
December 1944. Sergeant Steve Dawson and two of his platoon, Spring and Whitey, are on their way to rejoin their unit who have been on leave. They get a lift from American soldiers heading into the Ardennes. But Dawson — who was given a year to live after he stopped a German bullet on D-Day — now has only six months left and is determined to go out fighting.
THE YANKS ARE COMING
LISTEN TO THAT PLANE OVERHEAD — SOUNDS LIKE A JUNKERS 88!
A KRAUT! HA — THERE AIN'T NO KRAUTS ROUND HERE, SERGEANT.
THAT'S A JERRY, ALL RIGHT, HANK!
BERLIN OR BUST!
HEY, YOU GUYS — THE LIMEY'S LOCO!
I'VE SEEN TOO MANY JUNKERS — AND THIS OERLIKON WILL SEE THE END OF IT.
YOU NUT! THAT PLANE'S GOT AMERICAN MARKINGS! D'YOU HEAR ME?
YOU HIT IT! YOU FOOL — YOU'VE SHOT DOWN ONE OF OUR PLANES!

"GERMANY WILL HAVE HER REVENGE!"

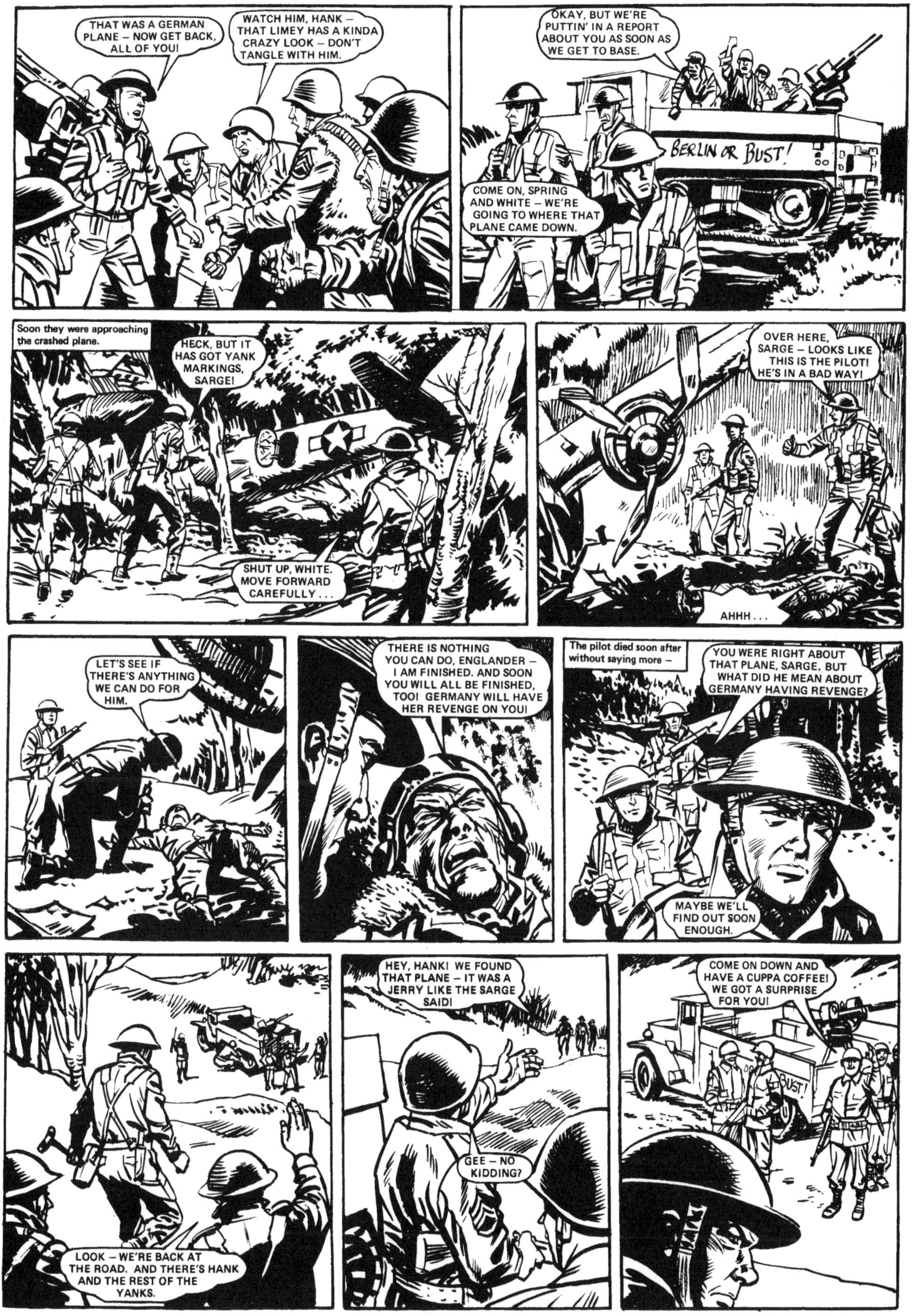

THAT WAS A GERMAN PLANE – NOW GET BACK, ALL OF YOU!
WATCH HIM, HANK – THAT LIMEY HAS A KINDA CRAZY LOOK – DON'T TANGLE WITH HIM.
OKAY, BUT WE'RE PUTTIN' IN A REPORT ABOUT YOU AS SOON AS WE GET TO BASE.
BERLIN OR BUST!
COME ON, SPRING AND WHITE – WE'RE GOING TO WHERE THAT PLANE CAME DOWN.
Soon they were approaching the crashed plane.
HECK, BUT IT HAS GOT YANK MARKINGS, SARGE!
SHUT UP, WHITE. MOVE FORWARD CAREFULLY . . .
OVER HERE, SARGE – LOOKS LIKE THIS IS THE PILOT! HE'S IN A BAD WAY!
AHHH . . .
LET'S SEE IF THERE'S ANYTHING WE CAN DO FOR HIM.
THERE IS NOTHING YOU CAN DO, ENGLANDER – I AM FINISHED. AND SOON YOU WILL ALL BE FINISHED, TOO! GERMANY WILL HAVE HER REVENGE ON YOU!
The pilot died soon after without saying more –
YOU WERE RIGHT ABOUT THAT PLANE, SARGE. BUT WHAT DID HE MEAN ABOUT GERMANY HAVING REVENGE?
MAYBE WE'LL FIND OUT SOON ENOUGH.
LOOK – WE'RE BACK AT THE ROAD. AND THERE'S HANK AND THE REST OF THE YANKS.
HEY, HANK! WE FOUND THAT PLANE – IT WAS A JERRY LIKE THE SARGE SAID!
GEE – NO KIDDING?
COME ON DOWN AND HAVE A CUPPA COFFEE! WE GOT A SURPRISE FOR YOU!
BUST!

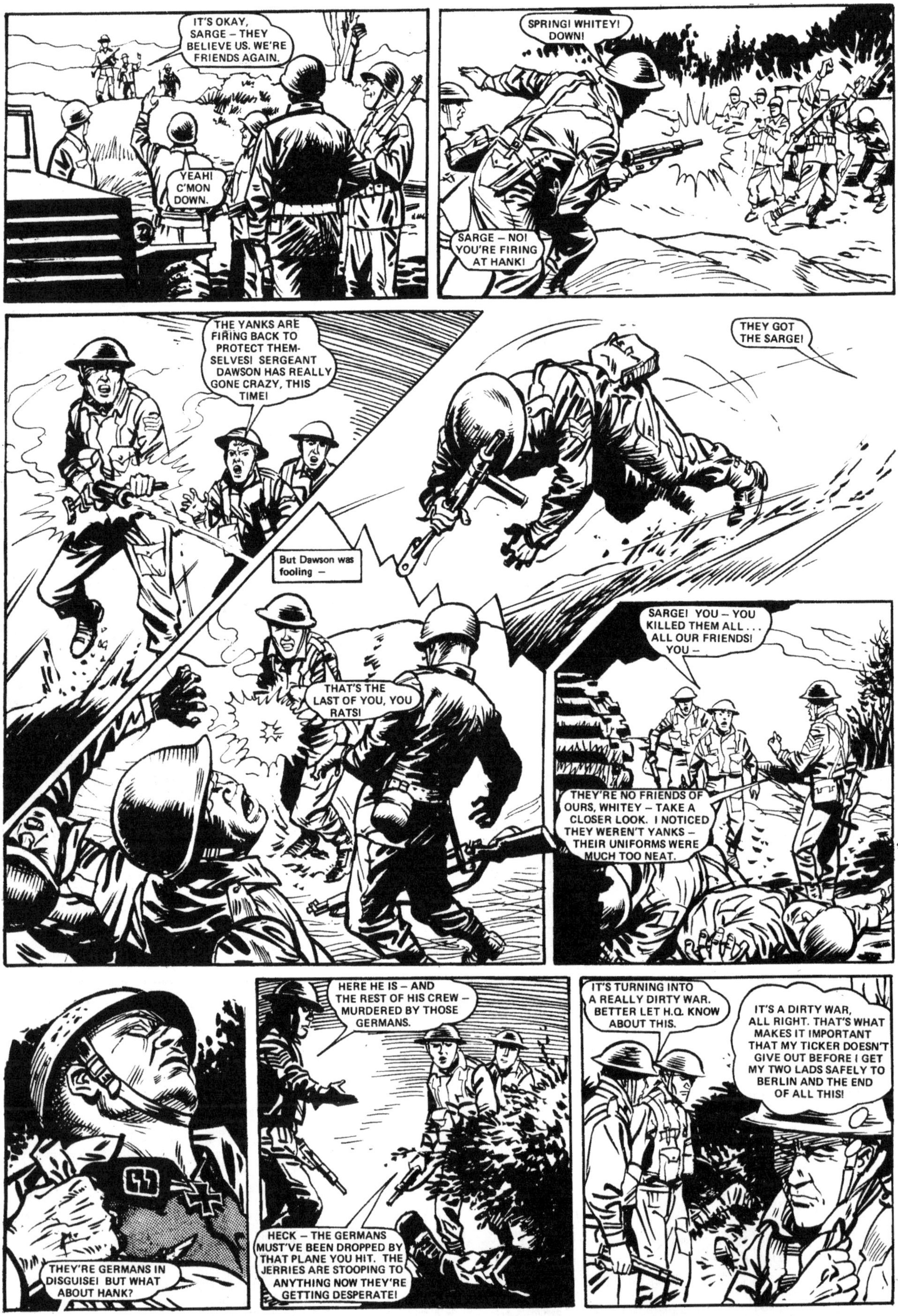
IT'S OKAY, SARGE – THEY BELIEVE US. WE'RE FRIENDS AGAIN.
YEAH! C'MON DOWN.
SPRING! WHITEY! DOWN!
SARGE – NO! YOU'RE FIRING AT HANK!
THE YANKS ARE FIRING BACK TO PROTECT THEM-SELVES! SERGEANT DAWSON HAS REALLY GONE CRAZY, THIS TIME!
THEY GOT THE SARGE!
But Dawson was fooling –
THAT'S THE LAST OF YOU, YOU RATS!
SARGE! YOU – YOU KILLED THEM ALL . . . ALL OUR FRIENDS! YOU –
THEY'RE NO FRIENDS OF OURS, WHITEY – TAKE A CLOSER LOOK. I NOTICED THEY WEREN'T YANKS – THEIR UNIFORMS WERE MUCH TOO NEAT.
THEY'RE GERMANS IN DISGUISE! BUT WHAT ABOUT HANK?
HERE HE IS – AND THE REST OF HIS CREW – MURDERED BY THOSE GERMANS.
HECK – THE GERMANS MUST'VE BEEN DROPPED BY THAT PLANE YOU HIT. THE JERRIES ARE STOOPING TO ANYTHING NOW THEY'RE GETTING DESPERATE!
IT'S TURNING INTO A REALLY DIRTY WAR. BETTER LET H.Q. KNOW ABOUT THIS.
IT'S A DIRTY WAR, ALL RIGHT. THAT'S WHAT MAKES IT IMPORTANT THAT MY TICKER DOESN'T GIVE OUT BEFORE I GET MY TWO LADS SAFELY TO BERLIN AND THE END OF ALL THIS!

NEXT WEEK — DAWSON IN THE BATTLE OF THE BULGE!

AFRAID OF NOTHING OR NO-ONE — DAWSON FACES A FIRING SQUAD!

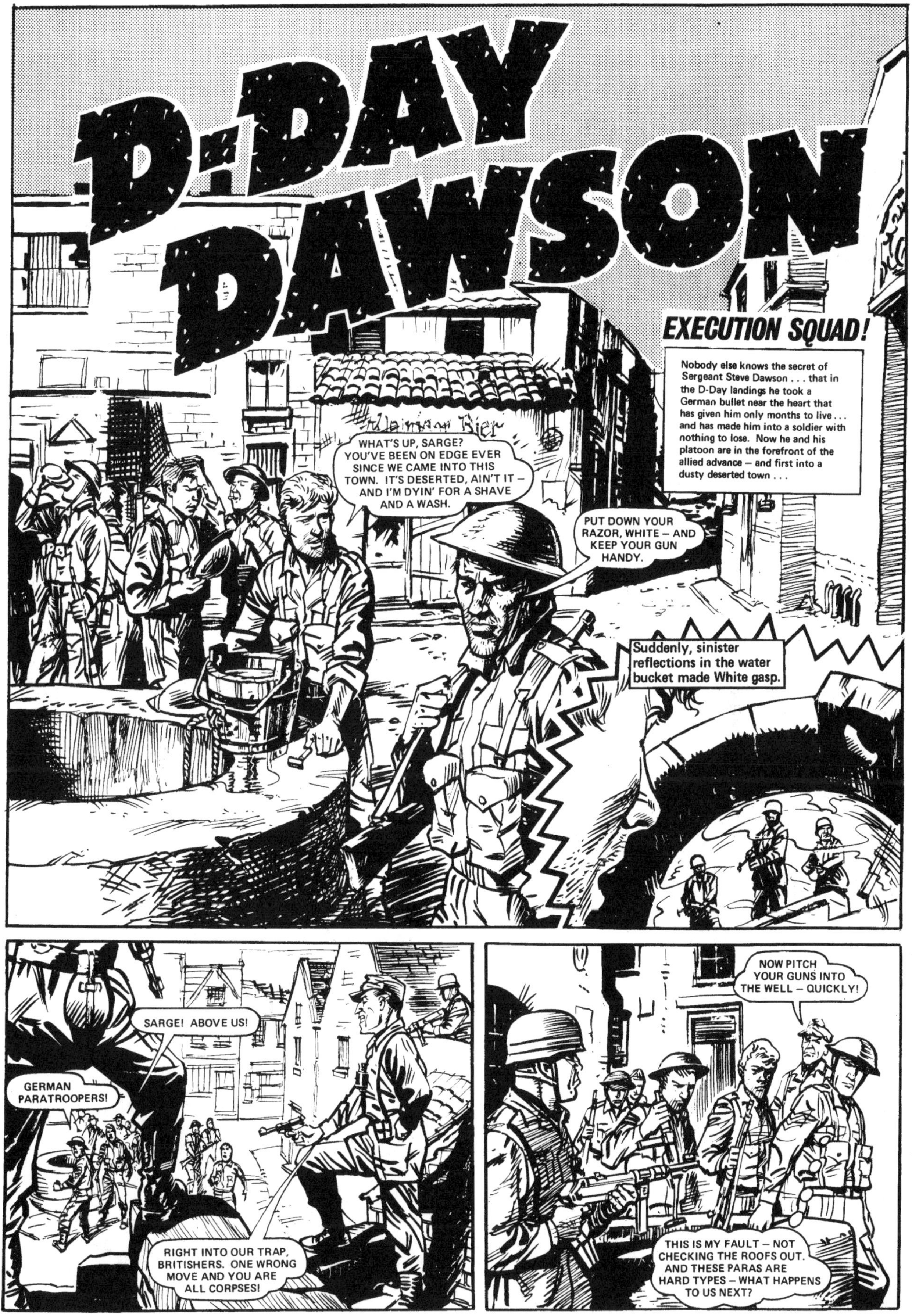

D-DAY DAWSON
EXECUTION SQUAD!
Nobody else knows the secret of Sergeant Steve Dawson . . . that in the D-Day landings he took a German bullet near the heart that has given him only months to live . . . and has made him into a soldier with nothing to lose. Now he and his platoon are in the forefront of the allied advance – and first into a dusty deserted town . . .
WHAT'S UP, SARGE? YOU'VE BEEN ON EDGE EVER SINCE WE CAME INTO THIS TOWN. IT'S DESERTED, AIN'T IT – AND I'M DYIN' FOR A SHAVE AND A WASH.
PUT DOWN YOUR RAZOR, WHITE – AND KEEP YOUR GUN HANDY.
Suddenly, sinister reflections in the water bucket made White gasp.
SARGE! ABOVE US!
GERMAN PARATROOPERS!
RIGHT INTO OUR TRAP, BRITISHERS. ONE WRONG MOVE AND YOU ARE ALL CORPSES!
NOW PITCH YOUR GUNS INTO THE WELL – QUICKLY!
THIS IS MY FAULT – NOT CHECKING THE ROOFS OUT. AND THESE PARAS ARE HARD TYPES – WHAT HAPPENS TO US NEXT?

"THIS LOOKS LIKE MY D-DAY AT LAST."

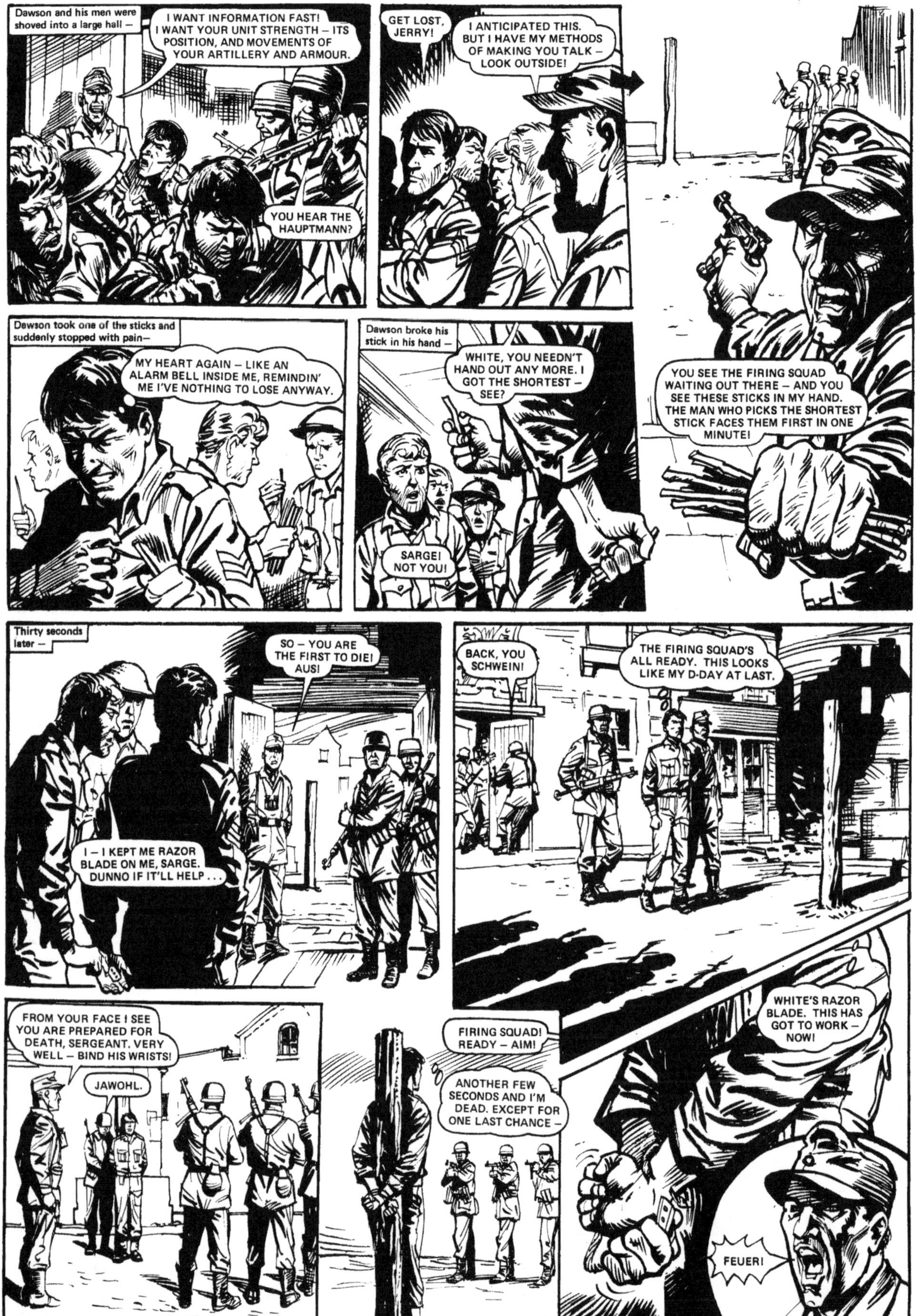

Dawson and his men were shoved into a large hall –
I WANT INFORMATION FAST! I WANT YOUR UNIT STRENGTH – ITS POSITION, AND MOVEMENTS OF YOUR ARTILLERY AND ARMOUR.
YOU HEAR THE HAUPTMANN?
GET LOST, JERRY!
I ANTICIPATED THIS. BUT I HAVE MY METHODS OF MAKING YOU TALK – LOOK OUTSIDE!
YOU SEE THE FIRING SQUAD WAITING OUT THERE – AND YOU SEE THESE STICKS IN MY HAND. THE MAN WHO PICKS THE SHORTEST STICK FACES THEM FIRST IN ONE MINUTE!
Dawson took one of the sticks and suddenly stopped with pain–
MY HEART AGAIN – LIKE AN ALARM BELL INSIDE ME, REMINDIN' ME I'VE NOTHING TO LOSE ANYWAY.
Dawson broke his stick in his hand –
WHITE, YOU NEEDN'T HAND OUT ANY MORE. I GOT THE SHORTEST – SEE?
SARGE! NOT YOU!
Thirty seconds later –
SO – YOU ARE THE FIRST TO DIE! AUS!
I – I KEPT ME RAZOR BLADE ON ME, SARGE. DUNNO IF IT'LL HELP . . .
BACK, YOU SCHWEIN!
THE FIRING SQUAD'S ALL READY. THIS LOOKS LIKE MY D-DAY AT LAST.
FROM YOUR FACE I SEE YOU ARE PREPARED FOR DEATH, SERGEANT. VERY WELL – BIND HIS WRISTS!
JAWOHL.
FIRING SQUAD! READY – AIM!
ANOTHER FEW SECONDS AND I'M DEAD. EXCEPT FOR ONE LAST CHANCE –
WHITE'S RAZOR BLADE. THIS HAS GOT TO WORK – NOW!
FEUER!

Next instant Dawson had slashed out of his ropes and was diving sideways.

ACHTUNG! HE IS FREE!

DONE IT — MISSED THE WHOLE BURST. GOTTA FIND COVER FAST.

KILL THE SCHWEIN!

DOWN THIS WELL'S MY ONLY CHANCE! GOTTA DIVE DEEP.

But —

WE HAVE PUT TWO MAGAZINES DOWN THE WELL, HERR HAUPTMANN! HE MUST BE DEAD!

WE HAVE WASTED ENOUGH TIME! THE REST OF THE BRITISHERS — GET THEM OUT HERE.

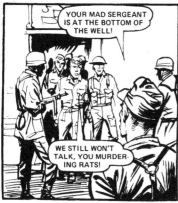

YOUR MAD SERGEANT IS AT THE BOTTOM OF THE WELL!

WE STILL WON'T TALK, YOU MURDER-ING RATS!

VERY WELL — WIPE THEM ALL OUT! THESE ARE THEIR LAST SECONDS ON THIS EARTH!

NO . . . THEY'RE YOURS!

THE SARGE! HE'S ALIVE AN' GOT A GUN FROM THE WELL! LET'S TAKE 'EM!

COME ON! IT'S THEM OR US!

Fighting like desperate wildcats, Dawson's men soon overran the paratroopers —

THAT — THAT'S THE LOT, WHITE. NOW WE CAN PUT OUR GUNS DOWN.

NO, SARGE! THAT PARA OFFICER — WATCH OUT!

White desperately tossed his Schmeisser to Dawson —

THIS TIME I EXECUTE YOU MYSELF!

MISSED, YOU RAT! AND THIS TIME —

AIEEEE!

IT'S YOUR D-DAY TODAY — NOT MINE!

YOU GOT HIM, SARGE. HE WON'T COME BACK FROM THE DEAD LIKE YOU DID!

BACK FROM THE DEAD — BUT I'M STILL LIVING ON BORROWED TIME, WHITE!

NEXT WEEK — DAWSON IN A SUICIDE ATTACK!

THE FIGHTING SERGEANT WITH A TERRIBLE SECRET IN HIS HEART!

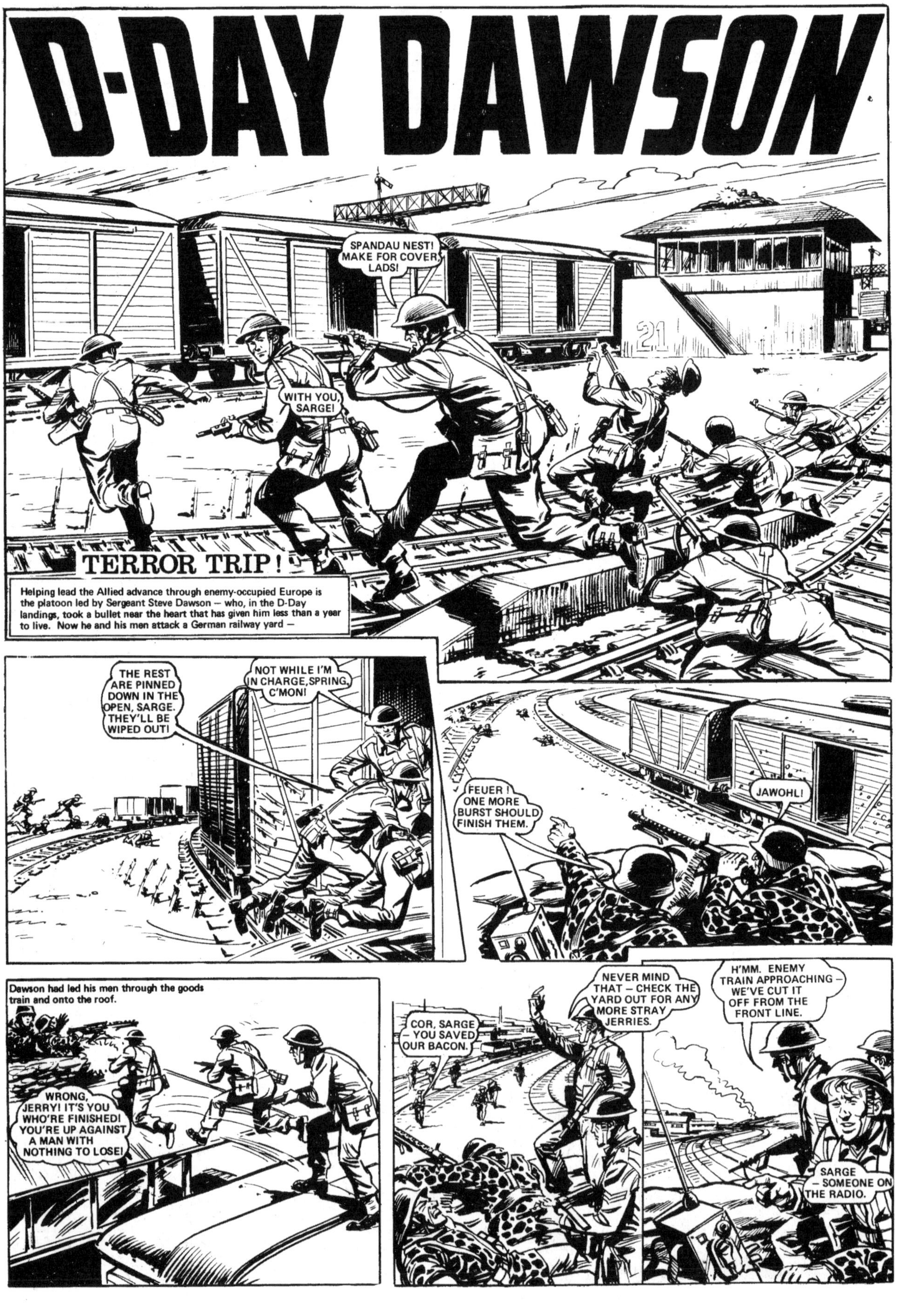

D-DAY DAWSON
SPANDAU NEST! MAKE FOR COVER, LADS!
WITH YOU, SARGE!
TERROR TRIP!
Helping lead the Allied advance through enemy-occupied Europe is the platoon led by Sergeant Steve Dawson — who, in the D-Day landings, took a bullet near the heart that has given him less than a year to live. Now he and his men attack a German railway yard —
THE REST ARE PINNED DOWN IN THE OPEN, SARGE. THEY'LL BE WIPED OUT!
NOT WHILE I'M IN CHARGE, SPRING, C'MON!
FEUER! ONE MORE BURST SHOULD FINISH THEM.
JAWOHL!
Dawson had led his men through the goods train and onto the roof.
WRONG, JERRY! IT'S YOU WHO'RE FINISHED! YOU'RE UP AGAINST A MAN WITH NOTHING TO LOSE!
COR, SARGE — YOU SAVED OUR BACON.
NEVER MIND THAT — CHECK THE YARD OUT FOR ANY MORE STRAY JERRIES.
H'MM. ENEMY TRAIN APPROACHING — WE'VE CUT IT OFF FROM THE FRONT LINE.
SARGE — SOMEONE ON THE RADIO.

"TRUST THE S.S. — THE RATS!"

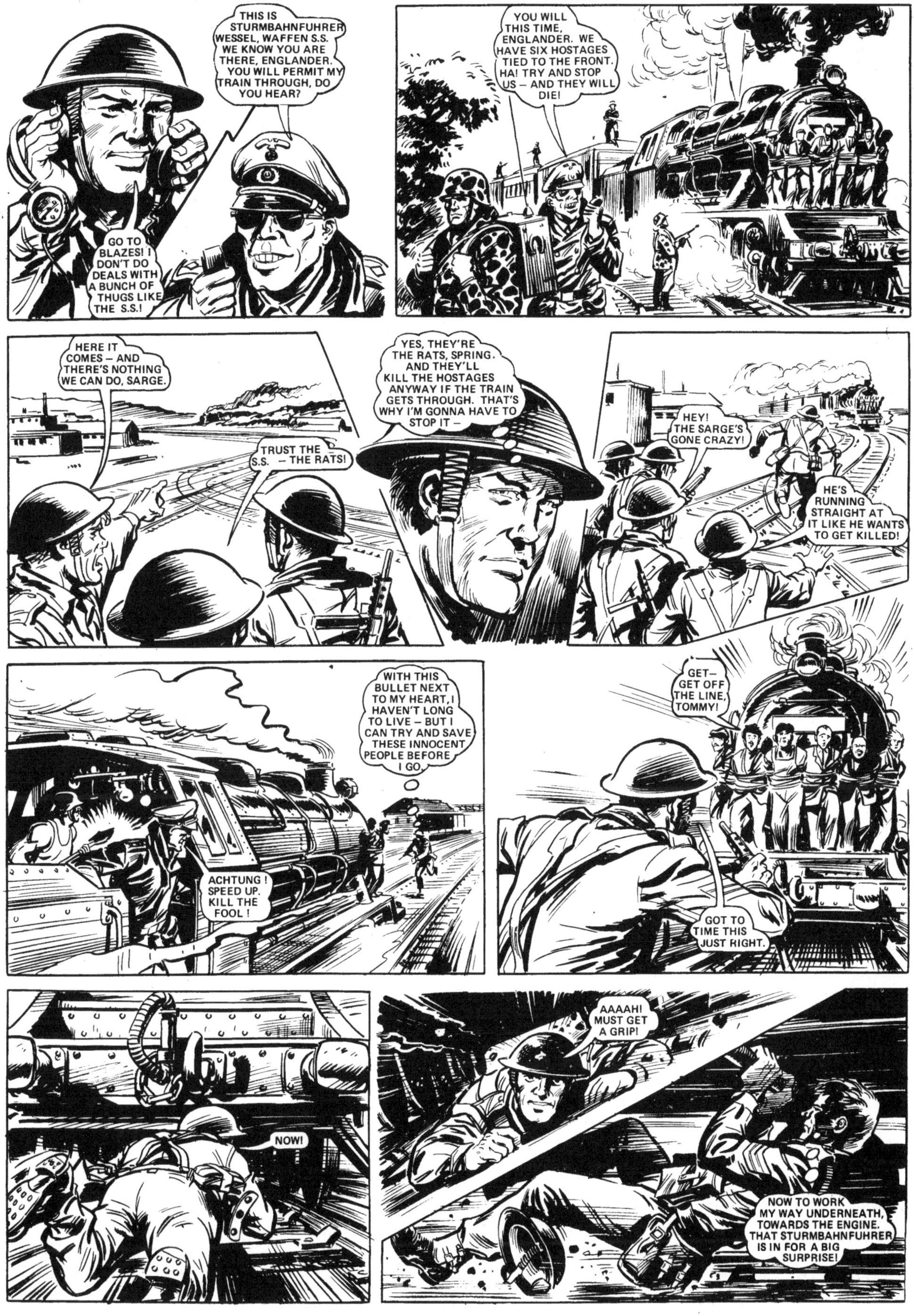
THIS IS STURMBAHNFUHRER WESSEL, WAFFEN S.S. WE KNOW YOU ARE THERE, ENGLANDER. YOU WILL PERMIT MY TRAIN THROUGH, DO YOU HEAR?
GO TO BLAZES! I DON'T DO DEALS WITH A BUNCH OF THUGS LIKE THE S.S.!
YOU WILL THIS TIME, ENGLANDER. WE HAVE SIX HOSTAGES TIED TO THE FRONT. HA! TRY AND STOP US – AND THEY WILL DIE!
HERE IT COMES – AND THERE'S NOTHING WE CAN DO, SARGE.
TRUST THE S.S. – THE RATS!
YES, THEY'RE THE RATS, SPRING. AND THEY'LL KILL THE HOSTAGES ANYWAY IF THE TRAIN GETS THROUGH. THAT'S WHY I'M GONNA HAVE TO STOP IT –
HEY! THE SARGE'S GONE CRAZY!
HE'S RUNNING STRAIGHT AT IT LIKE HE WANTS TO GET KILLED!
WITH THIS BULLET NEXT TO MY HEART, I HAVEN'T LONG TO LIVE – BUT I CAN TRY AND SAVE THESE INNOCENT PEOPLE BEFORE I GO.
ACHTUNG ! SPEED UP. KILL THE FOOL !
GET— GET OFF THE LINE, TOMMY!
GOT TO TIME THIS JUST RIGHT.
NOW!
AAAAH! MUST GET A GRIP!
NOW TO WORK MY WAY UNDERNEATH, TOWARDS THE ENGINE. THAT STURMBAHNFUHRER IS IN FOR A BIG SURPRISE!

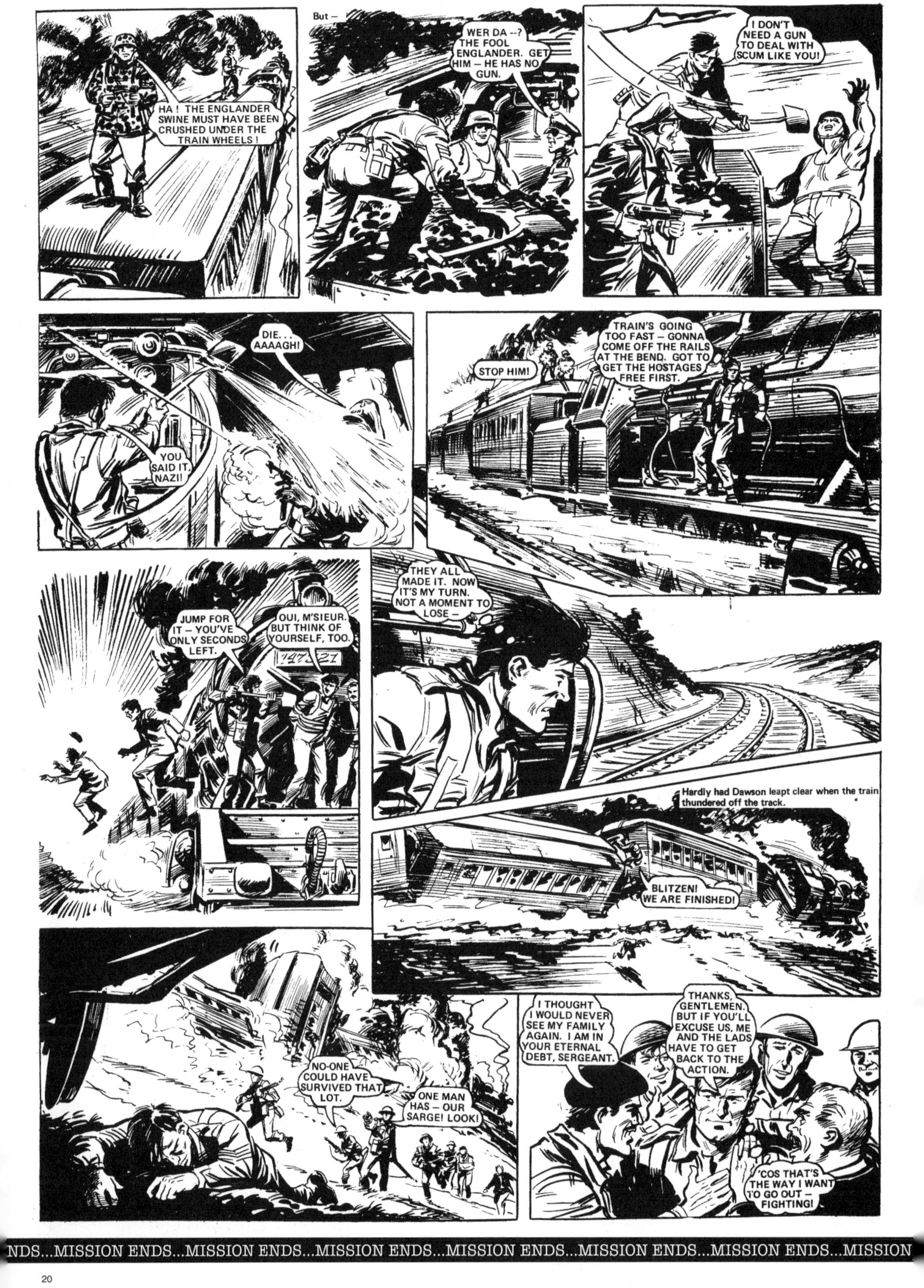
HA ! THE ENGLANDER SWINE MUST HAVE BEEN CRUSHED UNDER THE TRAIN WHEELS !
But –
WER DA --? THE FOOL ENGLANDER. GET HIM – HE HAS NO GUN.
I DON'T NEED A GUN TO DEAL WITH SCUM LIKE YOU!
DIE... AAAAGH!
YOU SAID IT, NAZI!
STOP HIM!
TRAIN'S GOING TOO FAST – GONNA COME OFF THE RAILS AT THE BEND. GOT TO GET THE HOSTAGES FREE FIRST.
JUMP FOR IT – YOU'VE ONLY SECONDS LEFT.
OUI, M'SIEUR. BUT THINK OF YOURSELF, TOO.
THEY ALL MADE IT. NOW IT'S MY TURN. NOT A MOMENT TO LOSE –
Hardly had Dawson leapt clear when the train thundered off the track.
BLITZEN! WE ARE FINISHED!
NO-ONE COULD HAVE SURVIVED THAT LOT.
ONE MAN HAS – OUR SARGE! LOOK!
I THOUGHT I WOULD NEVER SEE MY FAMILY AGAIN. I AM IN YOUR ETERNAL DEBT, SERGEANT.
THANKS, GENTLEMEN. BUT IF YOU'LL EXCUSE US, ME AND THE LADS HAVE TO GET BACK TO THE ACTION.
'COS THAT'S THE WAY I WANT TO GO OUT – FIGHTING!

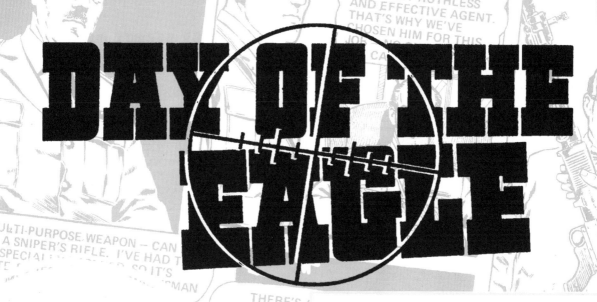

DAY OF THE EAGLE

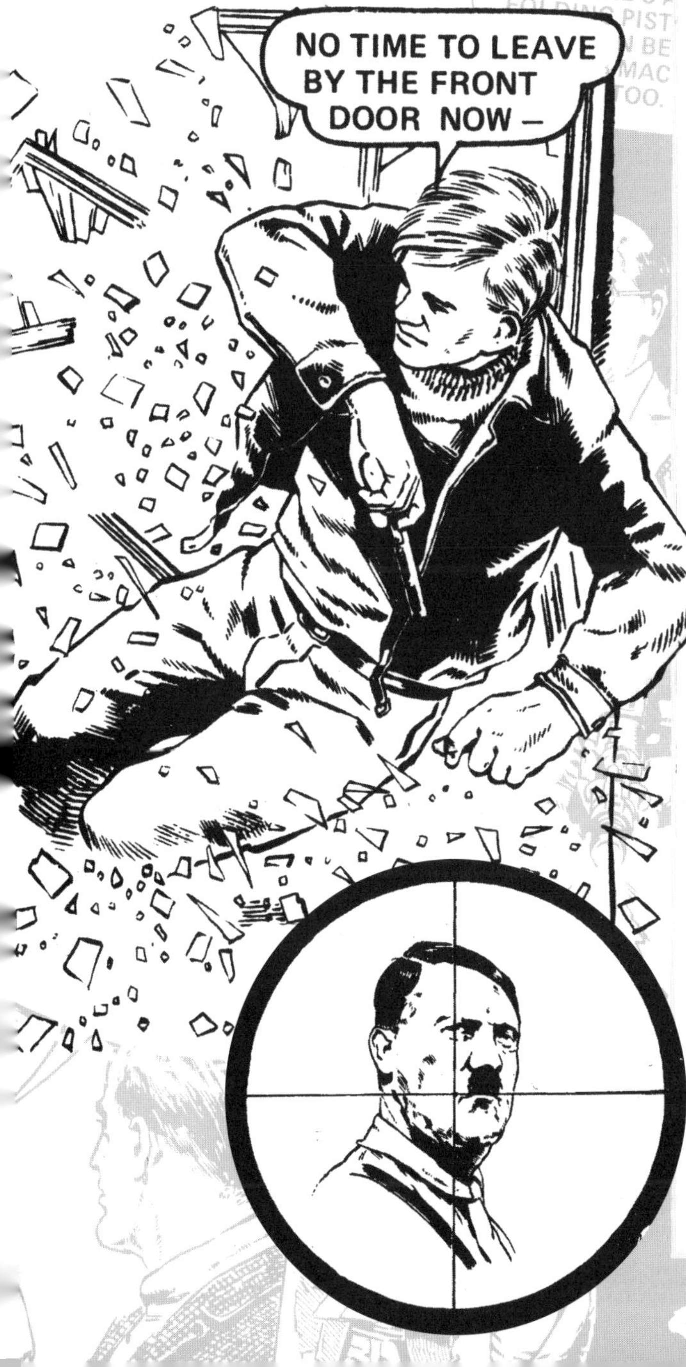
NO TIME TO LEAVE BY THE FRONT DOOR NOW –

"MY MISSION REMAINS ON UNTIL MY TARGET IS KILLED – OR I AM!"

He is Mike Nelson — Codename: The Eagle — the Gestapo's worst nightmare and the S.O.E's (Special Operations Executive) top agent. He's a master of disguise, unarmed combat, espionage and assassination.

Now armed with a specially-adapted S.S. paratrooper sniper rifle, the Eagle's on a mission that might just end the war: TO KILL ADOLF HITLER!

'Day of the Eagle' first appeared on March 8 1973 and quickly proved to be one of *Battle*'s most popular strips. Nelson's first adventure, part presented here, spawned several sequels and a prequel written by writers such as John Wagner, Gerry Finley-Day, Pat Mills, Alan Hebden and Eric Hebden and artists like Pat Wright, Barrie Mitchell, Mike Dorey and Jim Watson.

NOTES FROM THE FRONTLINE:

"We went for writers who had some experience of the war. The difficulty was finding someone who had interesting war memoirs; knew how to adapt them; and who could get on with these long-haired hippy types like John, Gerry and myself.

'Day of the Eagle' was written by Major Eric Hebden who'd come in and delight us with his tales of the war; in particular he was an expert on covert warfare and we thought he'd be perfect. He knew all the S.O.E. procedures, so we'd draw that out of him and rewrite it to give it that James Bond feeling. If you look at 'Day Of The Eagle', it has all this technical stuff on the weapons... that's Eric. Then you'll see a scene where the Eagle is driving a motorbike into a lift and jumping it off a building — no prizes for guessing who wrote that bit!" — **Pat Mills**

WRITTEN by Eric Hebden • DRAWN by Pat Wright

MEET MIKE NELSON – BRITAIN'S DEADLIEST SECRET AGENT!

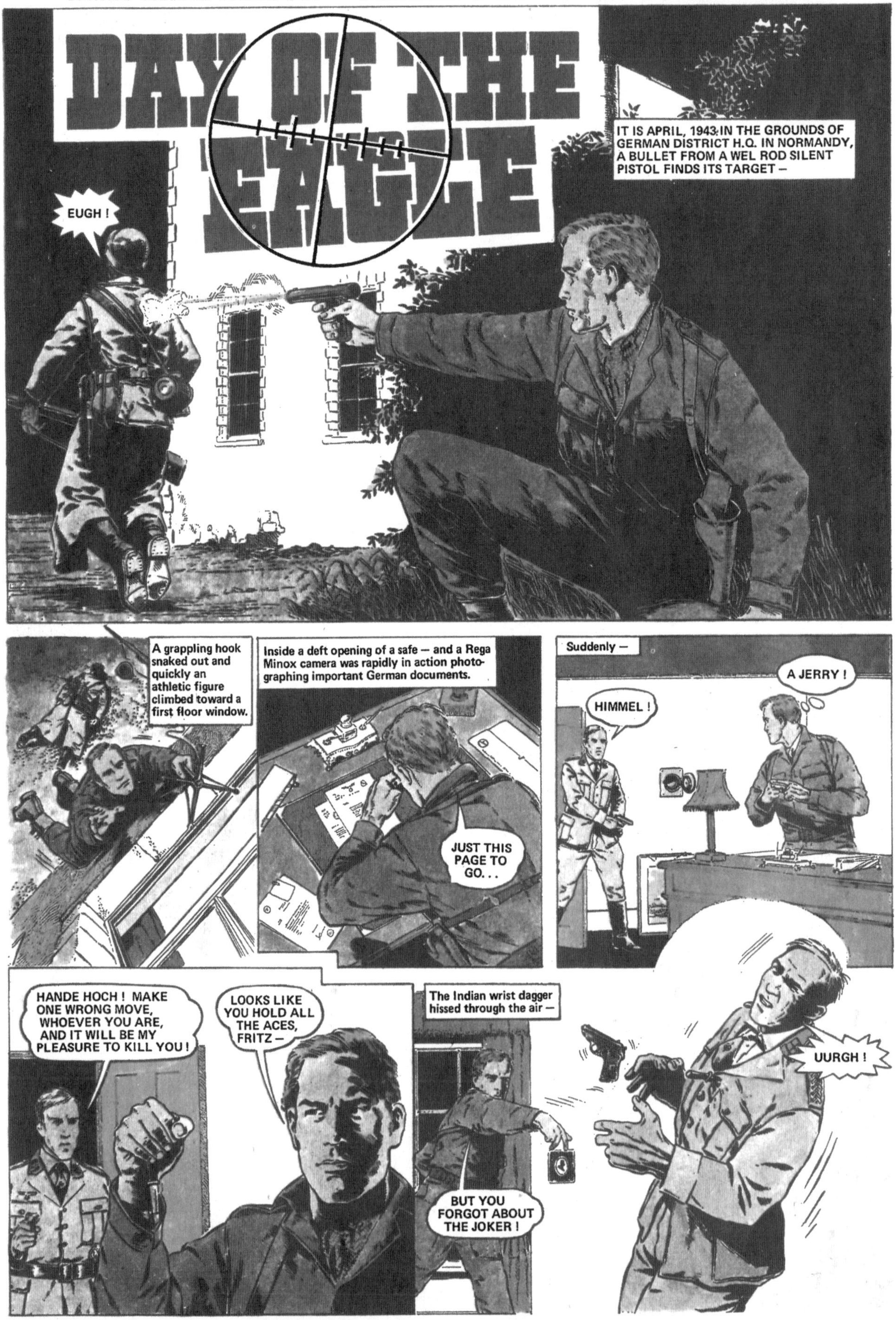
DAY OF THE EAGLE
IT IS APRIL, 1943. IN THE GROUNDS OF GERMAN DISTRICT H.Q. IN NORMANDY, A BULLET FROM A WEL ROD SILENT PISTOL FINDS ITS TARGET –
EUGH !
A grappling hook snaked out and quickly an athletic figure climbed toward a first floor window.
Inside a deft opening of a safe – and a Rega Minox camera was rapidly in action photographing important German documents.
JUST THIS PAGE TO GO. . .
Suddenly –
HIMMEL !
A JERRY !
HANDE HOCH ! MAKE ONE WRONG MOVE, WHOEVER YOU ARE, AND IT WILL BE MY PLEASURE TO KILL YOU !
LOOKS LIKE YOU HOLD ALL THE ACES, FRITZ –
The Indian wrist dagger hissed through the air –
BUT YOU FORGOT ABOUT THE JOKER !
UURGH !

"THIS LIMPET BOMB HAS A TEN SECOND DELAYED ACTION!"

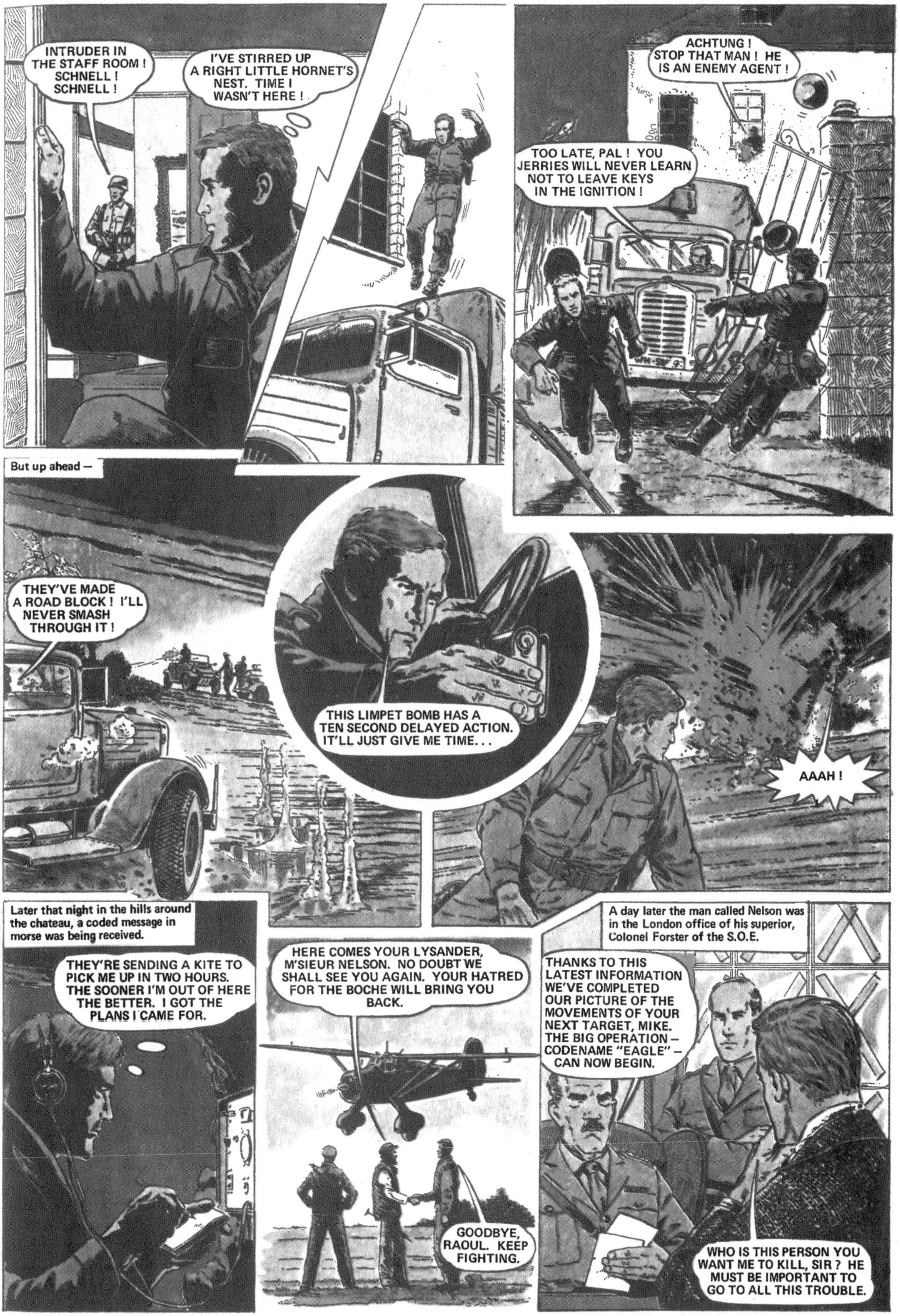

INTRUDER IN THE STAFF ROOM ! SCHNELL ! SCHNELL !
I'VE STIRRED UP A RIGHT LITTLE HORNET'S NEST. TIME I WASN'T HERE !
ACHTUNG ! STOP THAT MAN ! HE IS AN ENEMY AGENT !
TOO LATE, PAL ! YOU JERRIES WILL NEVER LEARN NOT TO LEAVE KEYS IN THE IGNITION !
But up ahead —
THEY'VE MADE A ROAD BLOCK ! I'LL NEVER SMASH THROUGH IT !
THIS LIMPET BOMB HAS A TEN SECOND DELAYED ACTION. IT'LL JUST GIVE ME TIME. . .
AAAH !
Later that night in the hills around the chateau, a coded message in morse was being received.
THEY'RE SENDING A KITE TO PICK ME UP IN TWO HOURS. THE SOONER I'M OUT OF HERE THE BETTER. I GOT THE PLANS I CAME FOR.
HERE COMES YOUR LYSANDER, M'SIEUR NELSON. NO DOUBT WE SHALL SEE YOU AGAIN. YOUR HATRED FOR THE BOCHE WILL BRING YOU BACK.
GOODBYE, RAOUL. KEEP FIGHTING.
A day later the man called Nelson was in the London office of his superior, Colonel Forster of the S.O.E.
THANKS TO THIS LATEST INFORMATION WE'VE COMPLETED OUR PICTURE OF THE MOVEMENTS OF YOUR NEXT TARGET, MIKE. THE BIG OPERATION – CODENAME "EAGLE" – CAN NOW BEGIN.
WHO IS THIS PERSON YOU WANT ME TO KILL, SIR ? HE MUST BE IMPORTANT TO GO TO ALL THIS TROUBLE.

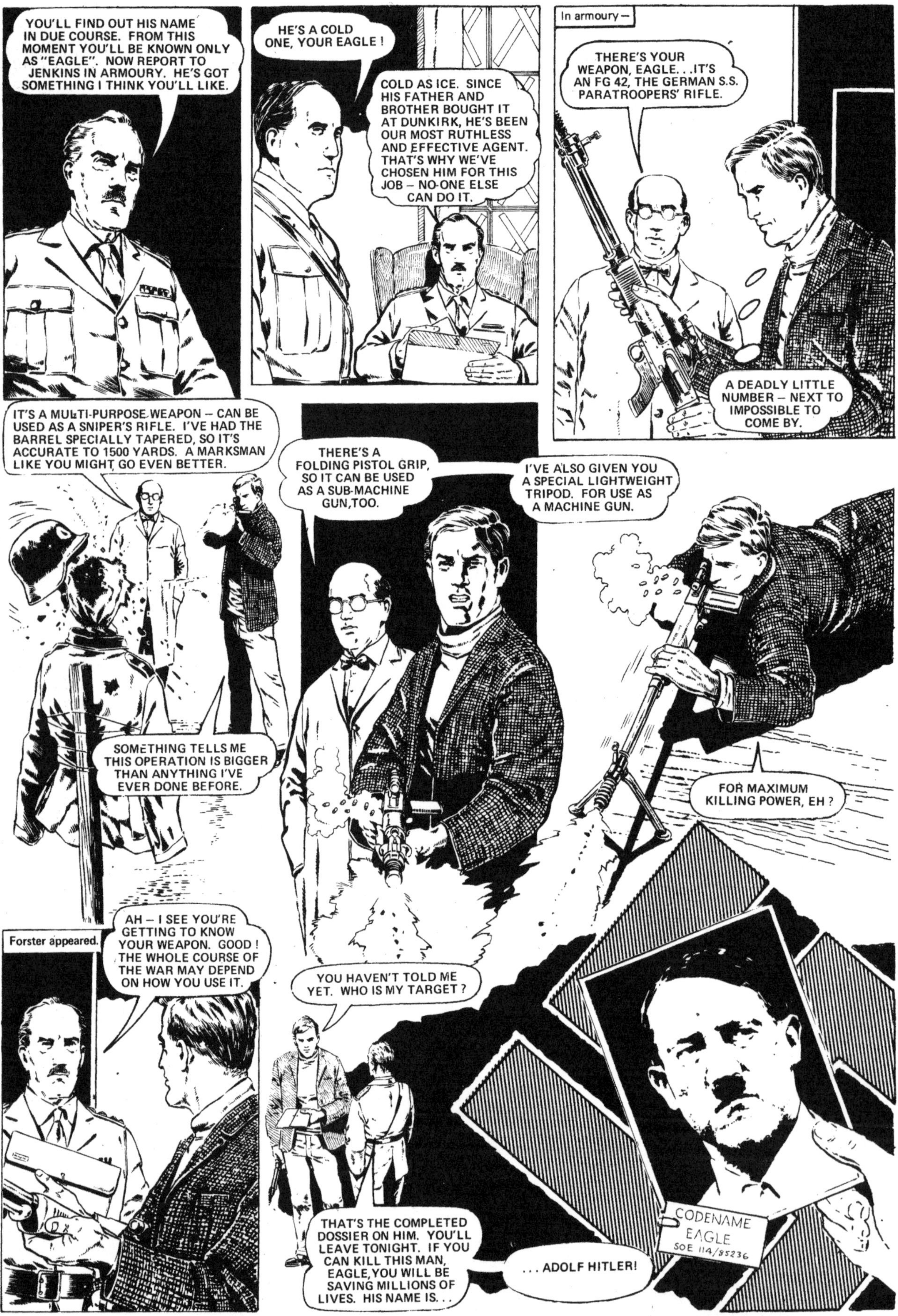
YOU'LL FIND OUT HIS NAME IN DUE COURSE. FROM THIS MOMENT YOU'LL BE KNOWN ONLY AS "EAGLE". NOW REPORT TO JENKINS IN ARMOURY. HE'S GOT SOMETHING I THINK YOU'LL LIKE.
HE'S A COLD ONE, YOUR EAGLE !
COLD AS ICE. SINCE HIS FATHER AND BROTHER BOUGHT IT AT DUNKIRK, HE'S BEEN OUR MOST RUTHLESS AND EFFECTIVE AGENT. THAT'S WHY WE'VE CHOSEN HIM FOR THIS JOB – NO-ONE ELSE CAN DO IT.
In armoury –
THERE'S YOUR WEAPON, EAGLE. . .IT'S AN FG 42, THE GERMAN S.S. PARATROOPERS' RIFLE.
A DEADLY LITTLE NUMBER – NEXT TO IMPOSSIBLE TO COME BY.
IT'S A MULTI-PURPOSE WEAPON – CAN BE USED AS A SNIPER'S RIFLE. I'VE HAD THE BARREL SPECIALLY TAPERED, SO IT'S ACCURATE TO 1500 YARDS. A MARKSMAN LIKE YOU MIGHT GO EVEN BETTER.
SOMETHING TELLS ME THIS OPERATION IS BIGGER THAN ANYTHING I'VE EVER DONE BEFORE.
THERE'S A FOLDING PISTOL GRIP, SO IT CAN BE USED AS A SUB-MACHINE GUN,TOO.
I'VE ALSO GIVEN YOU A SPECIAL LIGHTWEIGHT TRIPOD. FOR USE AS A MACHINE GUN.
FOR MAXIMUM KILLING POWER, EH ?
Forster appeared.
AH – I SEE YOU'RE GETTING TO KNOW YOUR WEAPON. GOOD ! THE WHOLE COURSE OF THE WAR MAY DEPEND ON HOW YOU USE IT.
YOU HAVEN'T TOLD ME YET. WHO IS MY TARGET ?
THAT'S THE COMPLETED DOSSIER ON HIM. YOU'LL LEAVE TONIGHT. IF YOU CAN KILL THIS MAN, EAGLE, YOU WILL BE SAVING MILLIONS OF LIVES. HIS NAME IS. . .
. . . ADOLF HITLER!
CODENAME
EAGLE
SOE 114/85236

NEXT WEEK – THE EAGLE RUNS INTO A GESTAPO TRAP!

AGENT MIKE NELSON – WITH THE WAR'S MOST IMPORTANT MISSION!

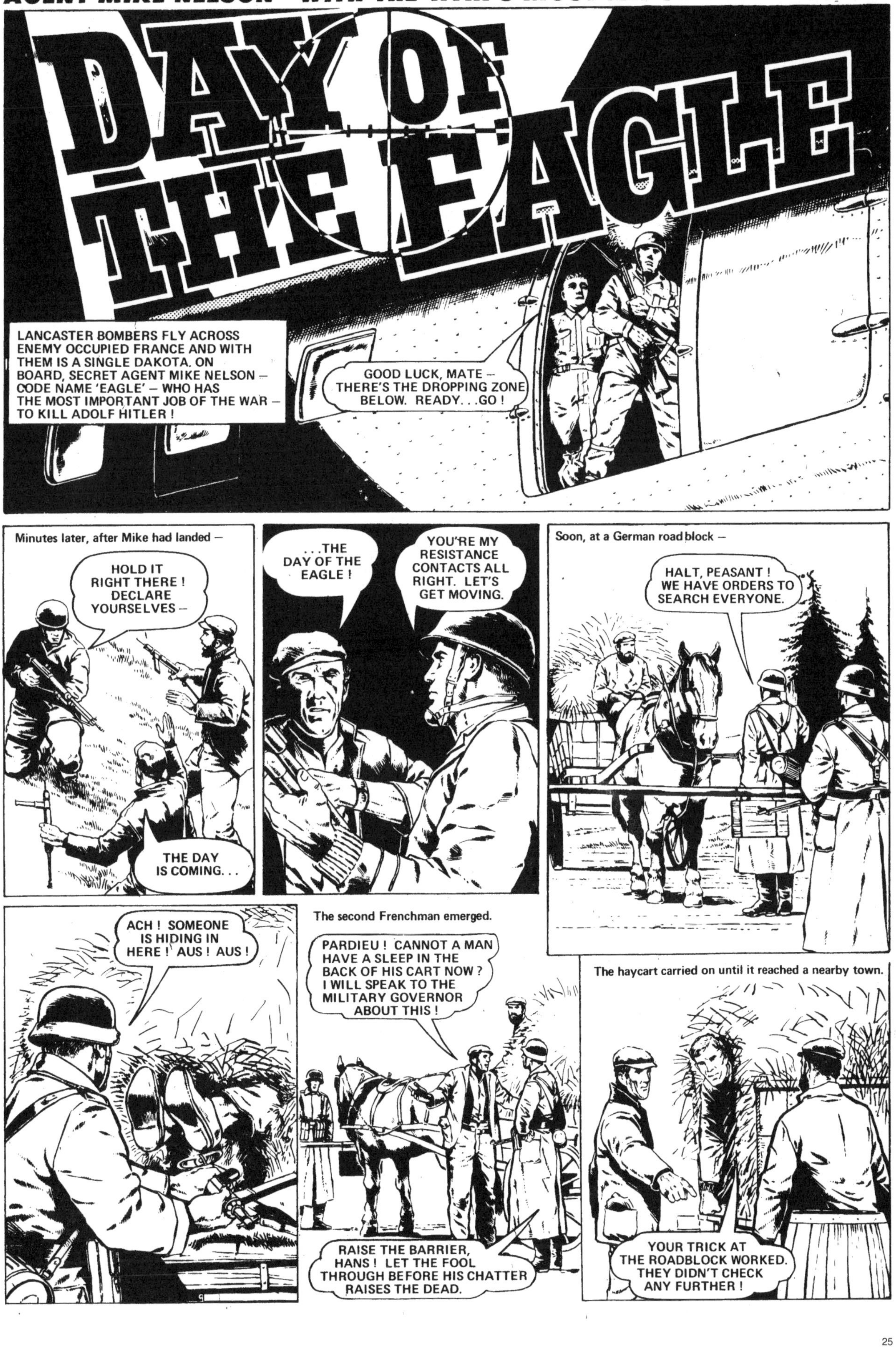
DAY OF THE EAGLE
LANCASTER BOMBERS FLY ACROSS ENEMY OCCUPIED FRANCE AND WITH THEM IS A SINGLE DAKOTA. ON BOARD, SECRET AGENT MIKE NELSON – CODE NAME 'EAGLE' – WHO HAS THE MOST IMPORTANT JOB OF THE WAR – TO KILL ADOLF HITLER !
GOOD LUCK, MATE – THERE'S THE DROPPING ZONE BELOW. READY. . . GO !
Minutes later, after Mike had landed –
HOLD IT RIGHT THERE ! DECLARE YOURSELVES –
THE DAY IS COMING. . .
. . .THE DAY OF THE EAGLE !
YOU'RE MY RESISTANCE CONTACTS ALL RIGHT. LET'S GET MOVING.
Soon, at a German road block –
HALT, PEASANT ! WE HAVE ORDERS TO SEARCH EVERYONE.
ACH ! SOMEONE IS HIDING IN HERE ! AUS ! AUS !
The second Frenchman emerged.
PARDIEU ! CANNOT A MAN HAVE A SLEEP IN THE BACK OF HIS CART NOW ? I WILL SPEAK TO THE MILITARY GOVERNOR ABOUT THIS !
RAISE THE BARRIER, HANS ! LET THE FOOL THROUGH BEFORE HIS CHATTER RAISES THE DEAD.
The haycart carried on until it reached a nearby town.
YOUR TRICK AT THE ROADBLOCK WORKED. THEY DIDN'T CHECK ANY FURTHER !

"EXTERMINATE HIM!"

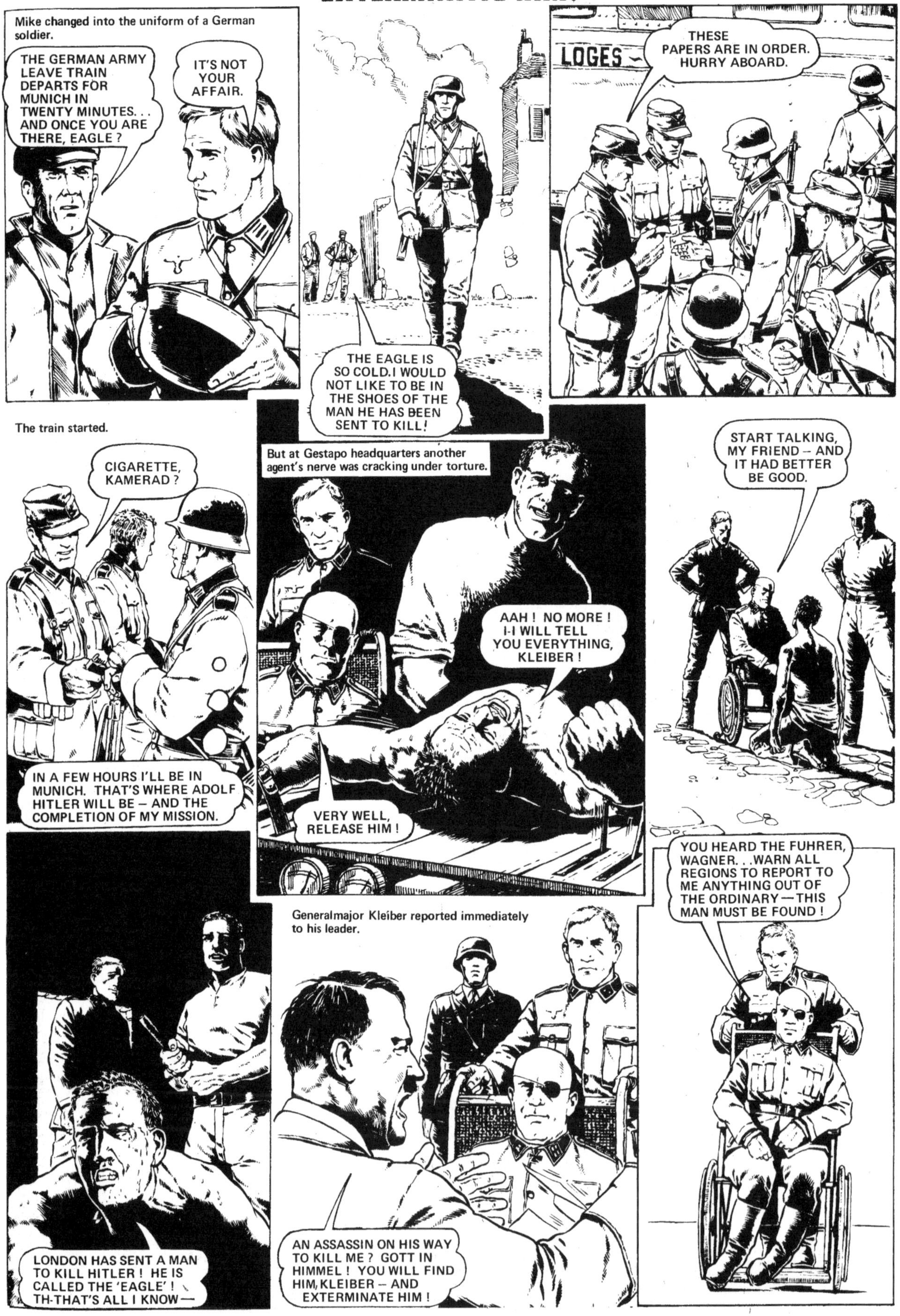

Mike changed into the uniform of a German soldier.
THE GERMAN ARMY LEAVE TRAIN DEPARTS FOR MUNICH IN TWENTY MINUTES. . . AND ONCE YOU ARE THERE, EAGLE ?
IT'S NOT YOUR AFFAIR.
THE EAGLE IS SO COLD. I WOULD NOT LIKE TO BE IN THE SHOES OF THE MAN HE HAS BEEN SENT TO KILL!
LOGES
THESE PAPERS ARE IN ORDER. HURRY ABOARD.
The train started.
CIGARETTE, KAMERAD ?
IN A FEW HOURS I'LL BE IN MUNICH. THAT'S WHERE ADOLF HITLER WILL BE – AND THE COMPLETION OF MY MISSION.
But at Gestapo headquarters another agent's nerve was cracking under torture.
AAH ! NO MORE ! I-I WILL TELL YOU EVERYTHING, KLEIBER !
VERY WELL, RELEASE HIM !
START TALKING, MY FRIEND – AND IT HAD BETTER BE GOOD.
LONDON HAS SENT A MAN TO KILL HITLER ! HE IS CALLED THE 'EAGLE' ! TH-THAT'S ALL I KNOW –
Generalmajor Kleiber reported immediately to his leader.
AN ASSASSIN ON HIS WAY TO KILL ME ? GOTT IN HIMMEL ! YOU WILL FIND HIM, KLEIBER – AND EXTERMINATE HIM !
YOU HEARD THE FUHRER, WAGNER. . .WARN ALL REGIONS TO REPORT TO ME ANYTHING OUT OF THE ORDINARY — THIS MAN MUST BE FOUND !

"YOU ARE UNDER ARREST!"

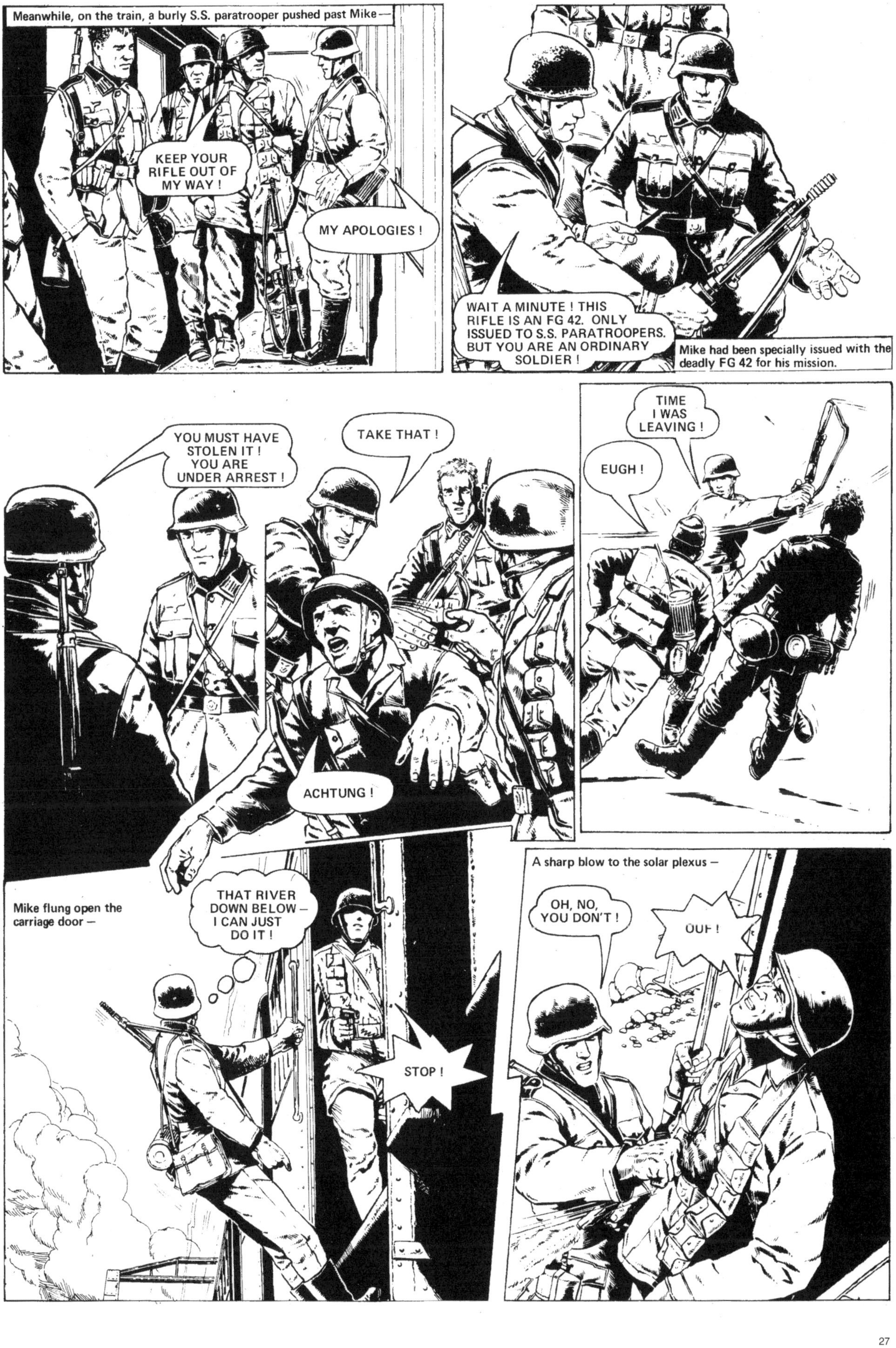

Meanwhile, on the train, a burly S.S. paratrooper pushed past Mike—
KEEP YOUR RIFLE OUT OF MY WAY !
MY APOLOGIES !
WAIT A MINUTE ! THIS RIFLE IS AN FG 42. ONLY ISSUED TO S.S. PARATROOPERS. BUT YOU ARE AN ORDINARY SOLDIER !
Mike had been specially issued with the deadly FG 42 for his mission.
YOU MUST HAVE STOLEN IT ! YOU ARE UNDER ARREST !
TAKE THAT !
ACHTUNG !
TIME I WAS LEAVING !
EUGH !
Mike flung open the carriage door—
THAT RIVER DOWN BELOW— I CAN JUST DO IT !
STOP !
A sharp blow to the solar plexus—
OH, NO, YOU DON'T !
OUF !

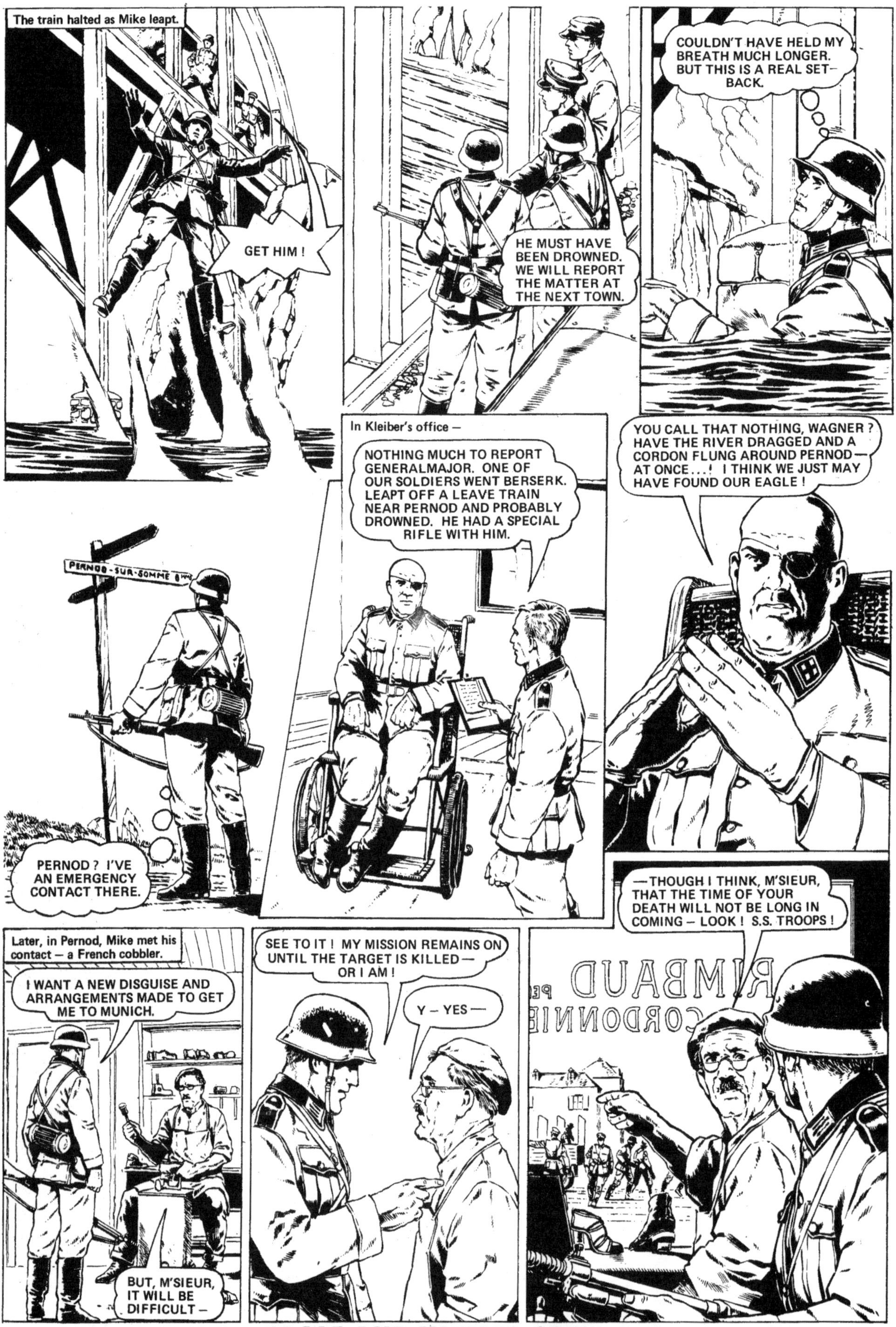

The train halted as Mike leapt.
GET HIM !
HE MUST HAVE BEEN DROWNED. WE WILL REPORT THE MATTER AT THE NEXT TOWN.
COULDN'T HAVE HELD MY BREATH MUCH LONGER. BUT THIS IS A REAL SET-BACK.
PERNOD-SUR-SOMME
PERNOD ? I'VE AN EMERGENCY CONTACT THERE.
In Kleiber's office —
NOTHING MUCH TO REPORT GENERALMAJOR. ONE OF OUR SOLDIERS WENT BERSERK. LEAPT OFF A LEAVE TRAIN NEAR PERNOD AND PROBABLY DROWNED. HE HAD A SPECIAL RIFLE WITH HIM.
YOU CALL THAT NOTHING, WAGNER ? HAVE THE RIVER DRAGGED AND A CORDON FLUNG AROUND PERNOD — AT ONCE . . . ! I THINK WE JUST MAY HAVE FOUND OUR EAGLE !
Later, in Pernod, Mike met his contact — a French cobbler.
I WANT A NEW DISGUISE AND ARRANGEMENTS MADE TO GET ME TO MUNICH.
BUT, M'SIEUR, IT WILL BE DIFFICULT —
SEE TO IT ! MY MISSION REMAINS ON UNTIL THE TARGET IS KILLED — OR I AM !
Y — YES —
—THOUGH I THINK, M'SIEUR, THAT THE TIME OF YOUR DEATH WILL NOT BE LONG IN COMING — LOOK ! S.S. TROOPS !

NEXT WEEK — EAGLE AND KLEIBER COME FACE TO FACE!

THE GERMANS CLOSE IN – CAN MIKE NELSON BREAK OUT?

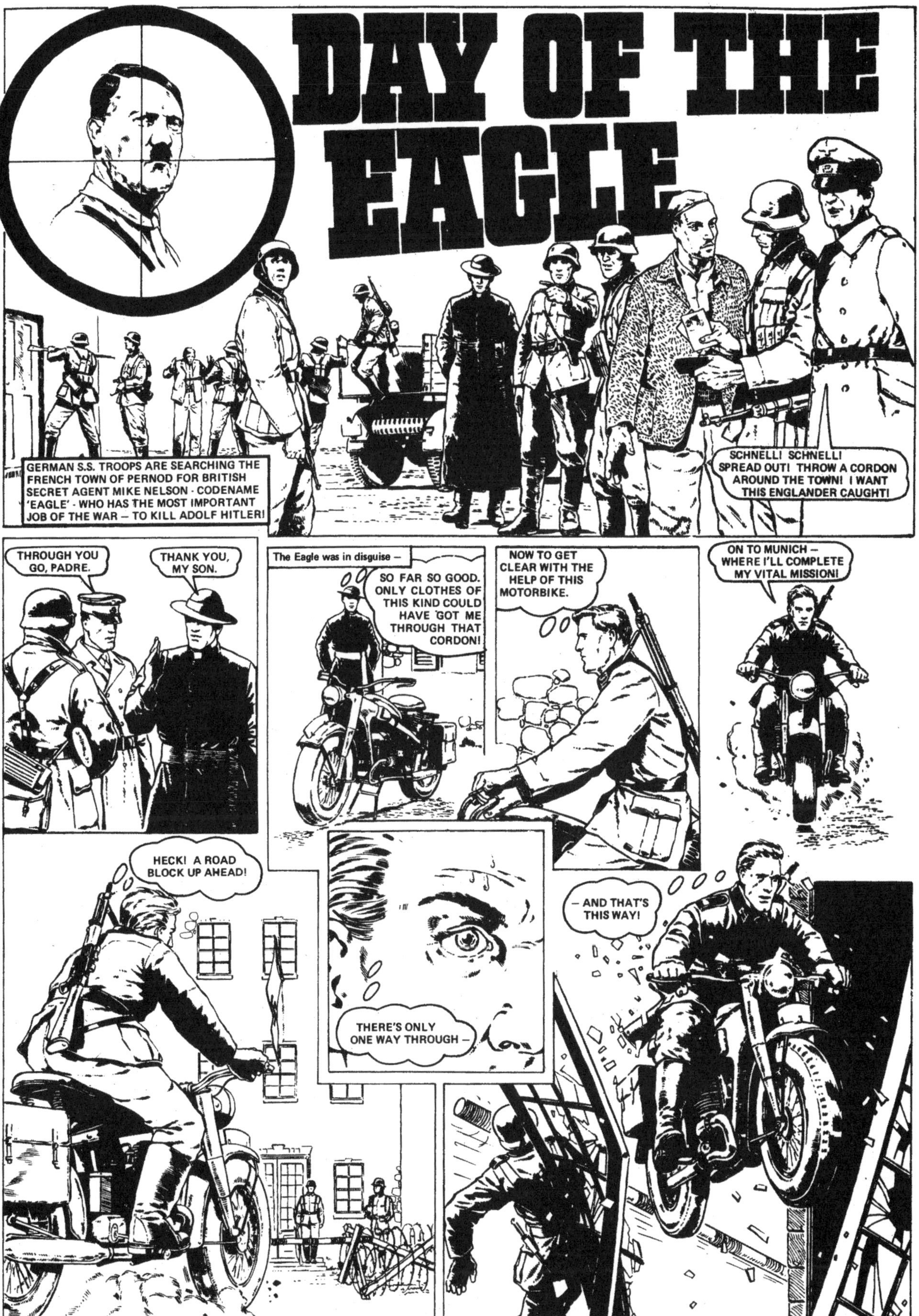
DAY OF THE EAGLE
GERMAN S.S. TROOPS ARE SEARCHING THE FRENCH TOWN OF PERNOD FOR BRITISH SECRET AGENT MIKE NELSON - CODENAME 'EAGLE' - WHO HAS THE MOST IMPORTANT JOB OF THE WAR – TO KILL ADOLF HITLER!
SCHNELL! SCHNELL! SPREAD OUT! THROW A CORDON AROUND THE TOWN! I WANT THIS ENGLANDER CAUGHT!
THROUGH YOU GO, PADRE.
THANK YOU, MY SON.
The Eagle was in disguise –
SO FAR SO GOOD. ONLY CLOTHES OF THIS KIND COULD HAVE GOT ME THROUGH THAT CORDON!
NOW TO GET CLEAR WITH THE HELP OF THIS MOTORBIKE.
ON TO MUNICH – WHERE I'LL COMPLETE MY VITAL MISSION!
HECK! A ROAD BLOCK UP AHEAD!
THERE'S ONLY ONE WAY THROUGH –
– AND THAT'S THIS WAY!

"THE BRITISHER IS TRAPPED!"

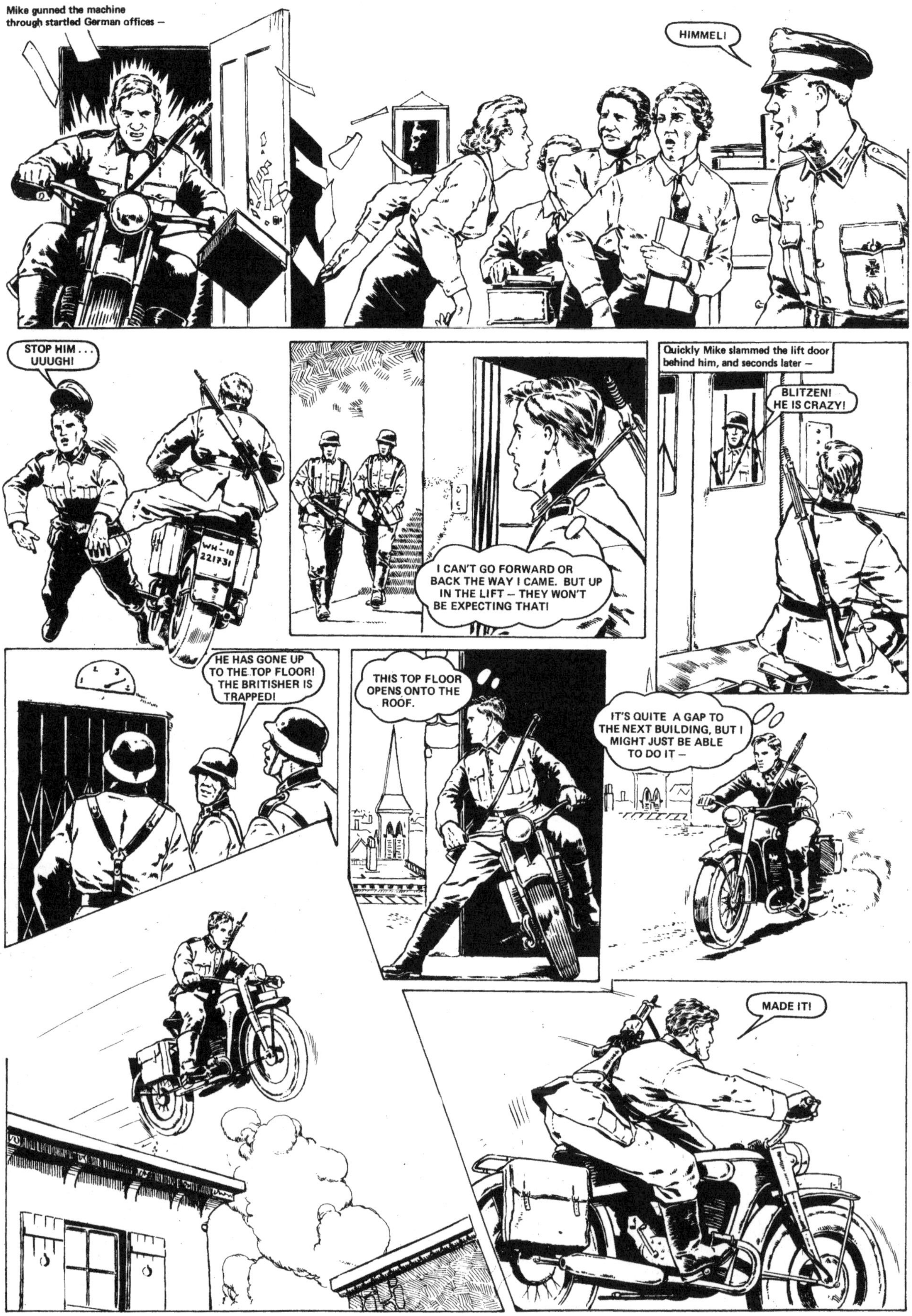

Mike gunned the machine through startled German offices –
HIMMEL!
STOP HIM . . . UUUGH!
I CAN'T GO FORWARD OR BACK THE WAY I CAME. BUT UP IN THE LIFT – THEY WON'T BE EXPECTING THAT!
Quickly Mike slammed the lift door behind him, and seconds later –
BLITZEN! HE IS CRAZY!
HE HAS GONE UP TO THE TOP FLOOR! THE BRITISHER IS TRAPPED!
THIS TOP FLOOR OPENS ONTO THE ROOF.
IT'S QUITE A GAP TO THE NEXT BUILDING, BUT I MIGHT JUST BE ABLE TO DO IT –
MADE IT!

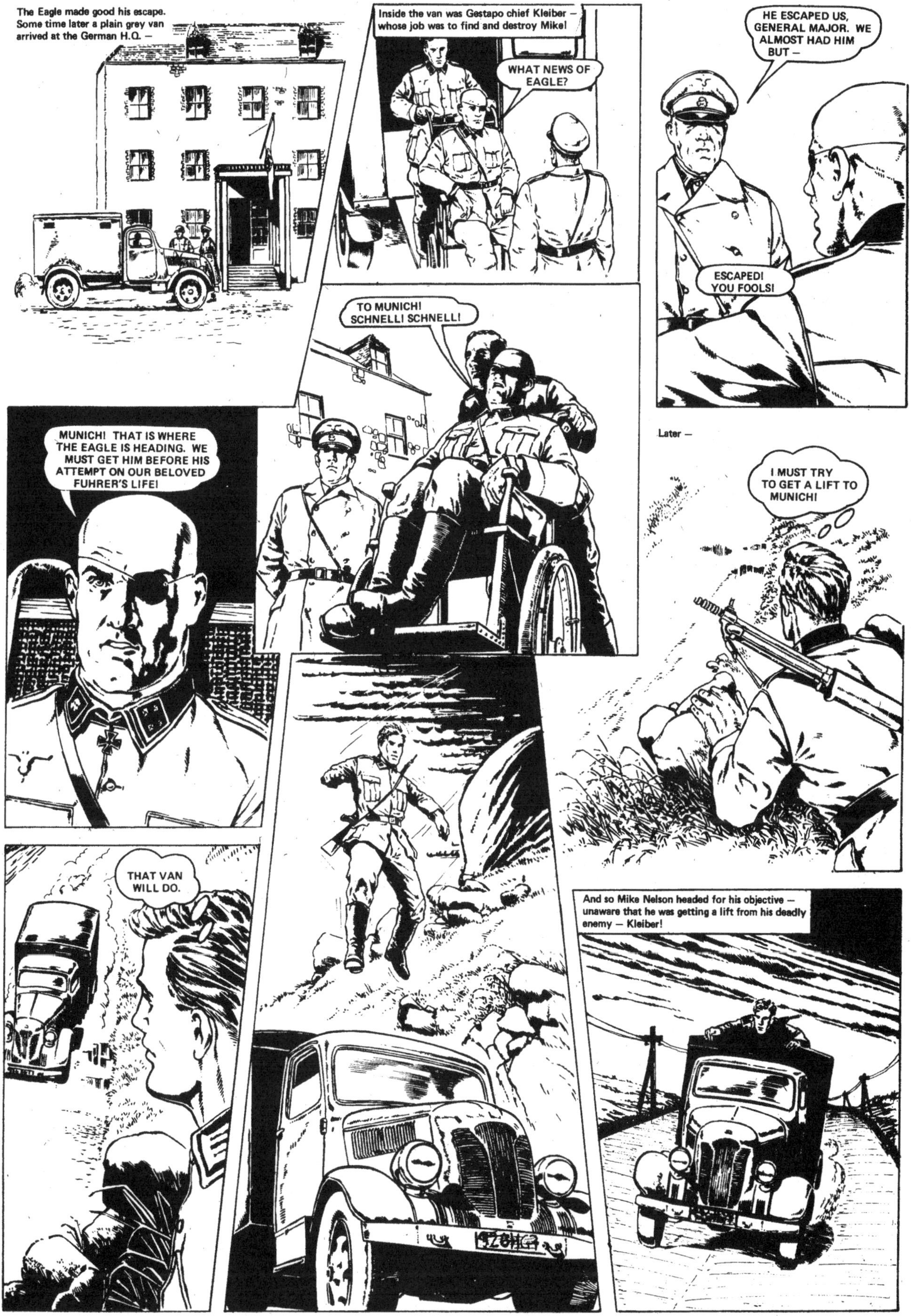
The Eagle made good his escape. Some time later a plain grey van arrived at the German H.Q. –
Inside the van was Gestapo chief Kleiber – whose job was to find and destroy Mike!
WHAT NEWS OF EAGLE?
HE ESCAPED US, GENERAL MAJOR. WE ALMOST HAD HIM BUT –
ESCAPED! YOU FOOLS!
TO MUNICH! SCHNELL! SCHNELL!
MUNICH! THAT IS WHERE THE EAGLE IS HEADING. WE MUST GET HIM BEFORE HIS ATTEMPT ON OUR BELOVED FUHRER'S LIFE!
Later –
I MUST TRY TO GET A LIFT TO MUNICH!
THAT VAN WILL DO.
And so Mike Nelson headed for his objective – unaware that he was getting a lift from his deadly enemy – Kleiber!

NEXT WEEK – TARGET HITLER!

THE EAGLE CLOSES ON HIS TARGET!

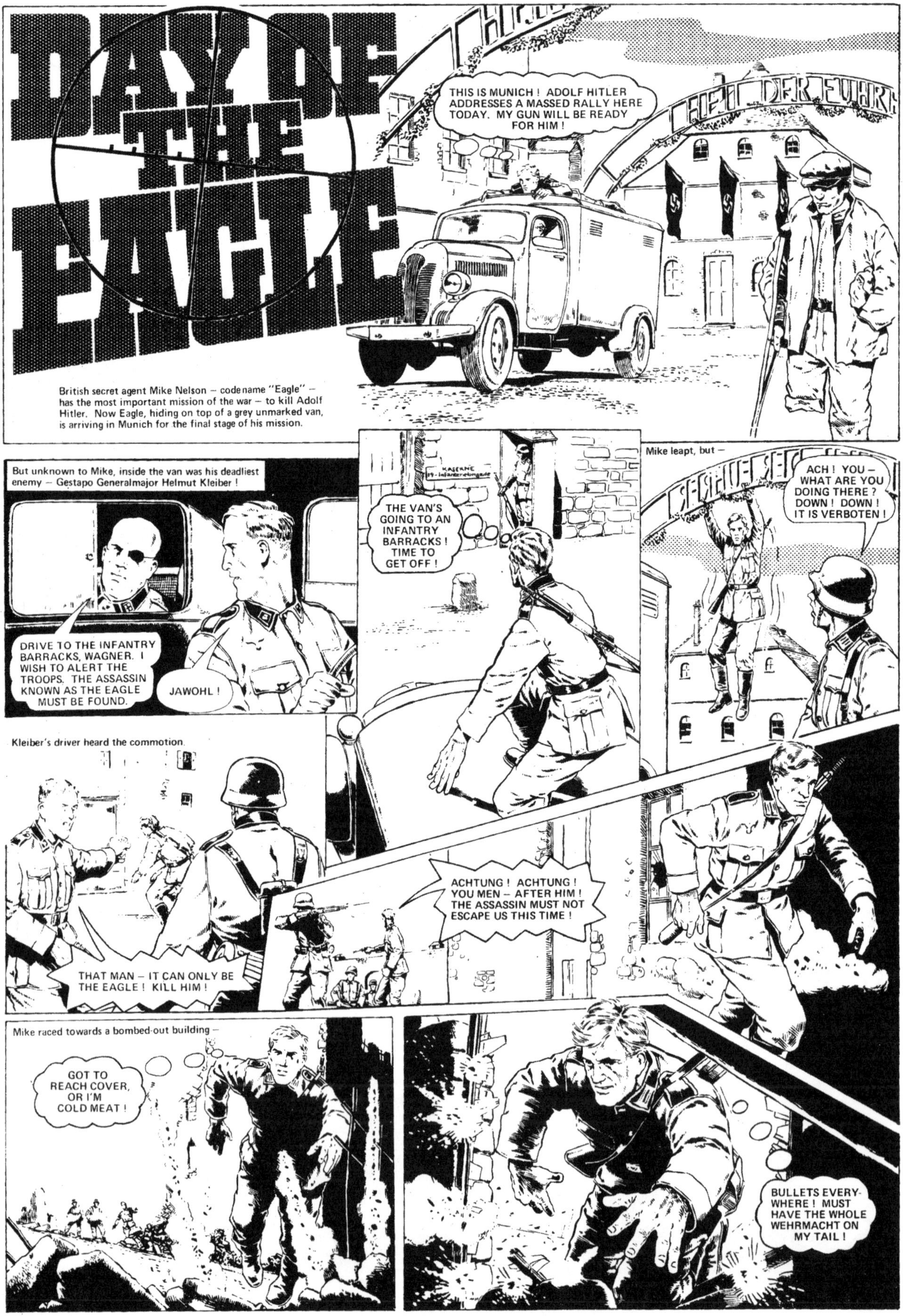

DAY OF THE EAGLE
THIS IS MUNICH ! ADOLF HITLER ADDRESSES A MASSED RALLY HERE TODAY. MY GUN WILL BE READY FOR HIM !
British secret agent Mike Nelson – codename "Eagle" – has the most important mission of the war – to kill Adolf Hitler. Now Eagle, hiding on top of a grey unmarked van, is arriving in Munich for the final stage of his mission.
But unknown to Mike, inside the van was his deadliest enemy – Gestapo Generalmajor Helmut Kleiber !
DRIVE TO THE INFANTRY BARRACKS, WAGNER. I WISH TO ALERT THE TROOPS. THE ASSASSIN KNOWN AS THE EAGLE MUST BE FOUND.
JAWOHL !
THE VAN'S GOING TO AN INFANTRY BARRACKS ! TIME TO GET OFF !
Mike leapt, but –
ACH ! YOU – WHAT ARE YOU DOING THERE ? DOWN ! DOWN ! IT IS VERBOTEN !
Kleiber's driver heard the commotion.
THAT MAN – IT CAN ONLY BE THE EAGLE ! KILL HIM !
ACHTUNG ! ACHTUNG ! YOU MEN – AFTER HIM ! THE ASSASSIN MUST NOT ESCAPE US THIS TIME !
Mike raced towards a bombed-out building –
GOT TO REACH COVER, OR I'M COLD MEAT !
BULLETS EVERY-WHERE ! MUST HAVE THE WHOLE WEHRMACHT ON MY TAIL !

"THE FUHRER'S ASSASSIN IS DEAD!"

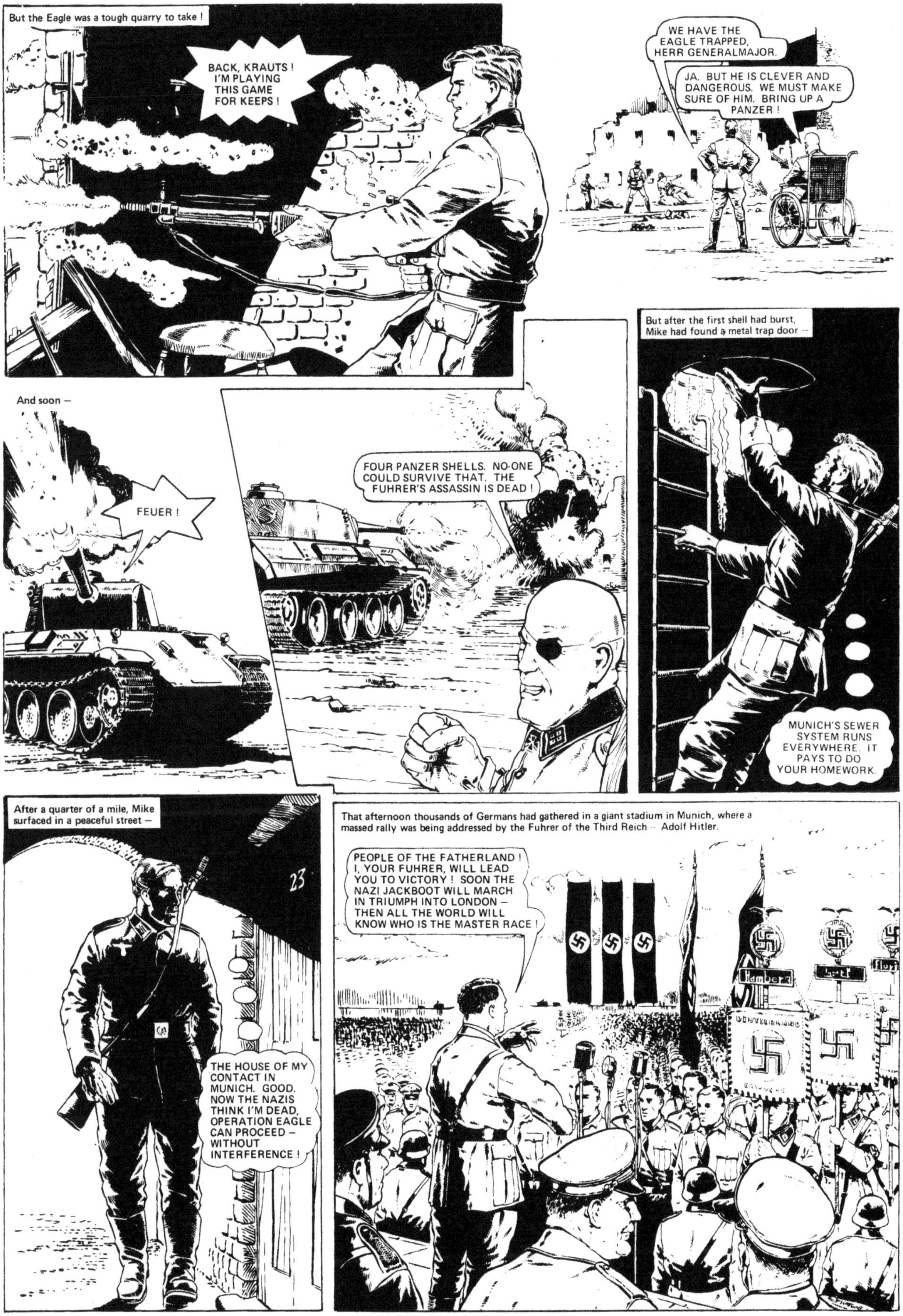

But the Eagle was a tough quarry to take !
BACK, KRAUTS ! I'M PLAYING THIS GAME FOR KEEPS !
WE HAVE THE EAGLE TRAPPED, HERR GENERALMAJOR.
JA. BUT HE IS CLEVER AND DANGEROUS. WE MUST MAKE SURE OF HIM. BRING UP A PANZER !
And soon –
FEUER !
FOUR PANZER SHELLS. NO-ONE COULD SURVIVE THAT. THE FUHRER'S ASSASSIN IS DEAD !
But after the first shell had burst, Mike had found a metal trap door –
MUNICH'S SEWER SYSTEM RUNS EVERYWHERE. IT PAYS TO DO YOUR HOMEWORK.
After a quarter of a mile, Mike surfaced in a peaceful street –
23
THE HOUSE OF MY CONTACT IN MUNICH. GOOD. NOW THE NAZIS THINK I'M DEAD, OPERATION EAGLE CAN PROCEED – WITHOUT INTERFERENCE !
That afternoon thousands of Germans had gathered in a giant stadium in Munich, where a massed rally was being addressed by the Fuhrer of the Third Reich – Adolf Hitler.
PEOPLE OF THE FATHERLAND ! I, YOUR FUHRER, WILL LEAD YOU TO VICTORY ! SOON THE NAZI JACKBOOT WILL MARCH IN TRIUMPH INTO LONDON – THEN ALL THE WORLD WILL KNOW WHO IS THE MASTER RACE !

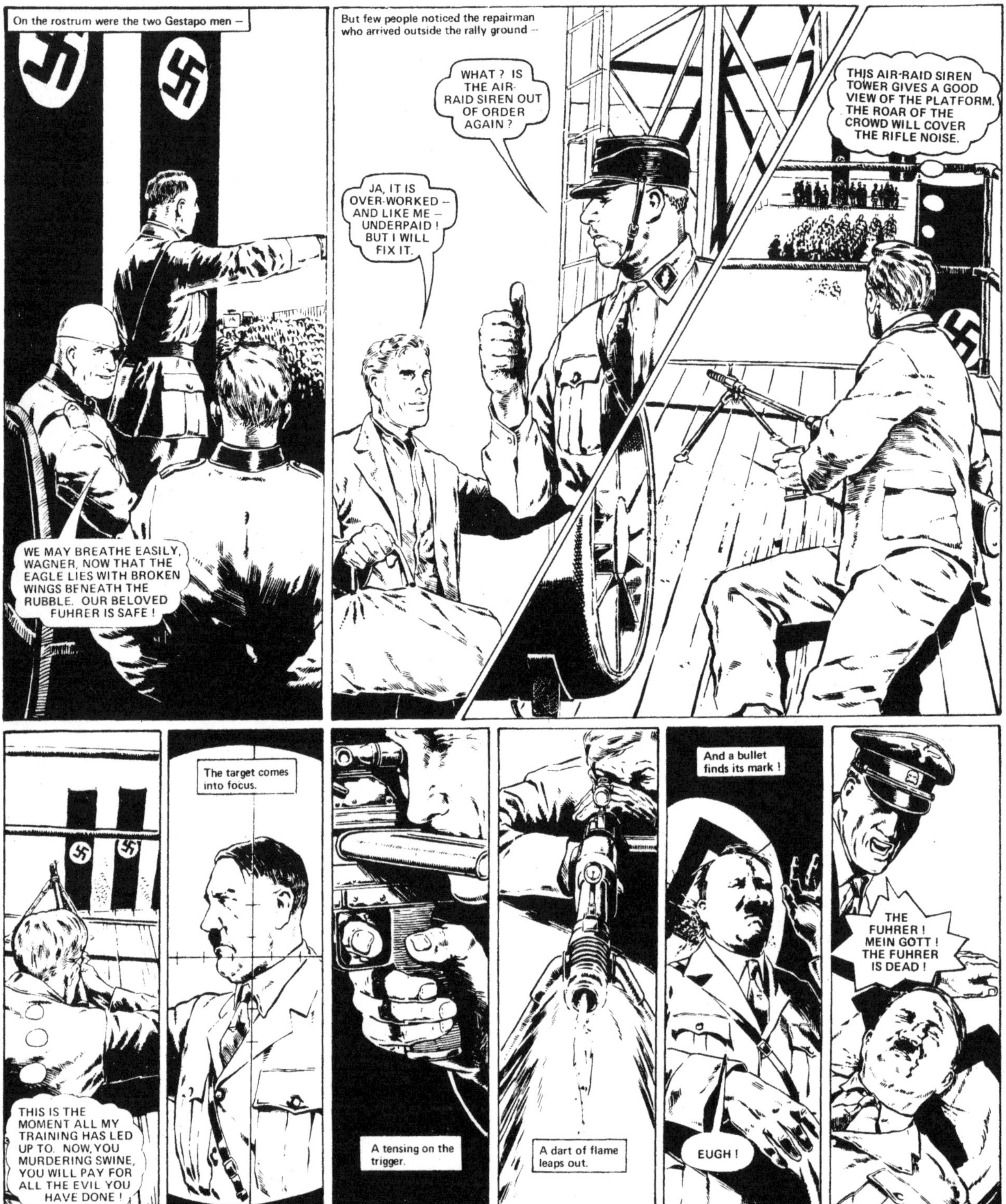

On the rostrum were the two Gestapo men —
WE MAY BREATHE EASILY, WAGNER, NOW THAT THE EAGLE LIES WITH BROKEN WINGS BENEATH THE RUBBLE. OUR BELOVED FUHRER IS SAFE !
But few people noticed the repairman who arrived outside the rally ground —
WHAT ? IS THE AIR-RAID SIREN OUT OF ORDER AGAIN ?
JA, IT IS OVER-WORKED — AND LIKE ME — UNDERPAID ! BUT I WILL FIX IT.
THIS AIR-RAID SIREN TOWER GIVES A GOOD VIEW OF THE PLATFORM. THE ROAR OF THE CROWD WILL COVER THE RIFLE NOISE.
THIS IS THE MOMENT ALL MY TRAINING HAS LED UP TO. NOW, YOU MURDERING SWINE, YOU WILL PAY FOR ALL THE EVIL YOU HAVE DONE !
The target comes into focus.
A tensing on the trigger.
A dart of flame leaps out.
And a bullet finds its mark !
EUGH !
THE FUHRER ! MEIN GOTT ! THE FUHRER IS DEAD !

SSION ENDS...MISSION ENDS...MISSION ENDS...MISSION ENDS...MISSION ENDS...MISSION ENDS...MISSION ENDS...I

The BOOTNECK BOY

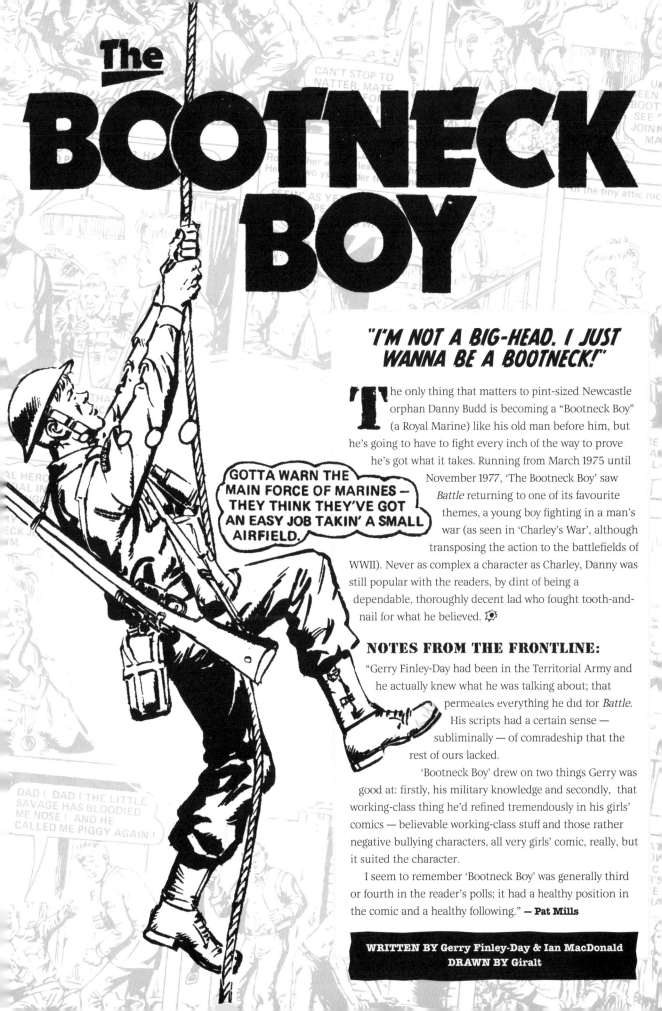

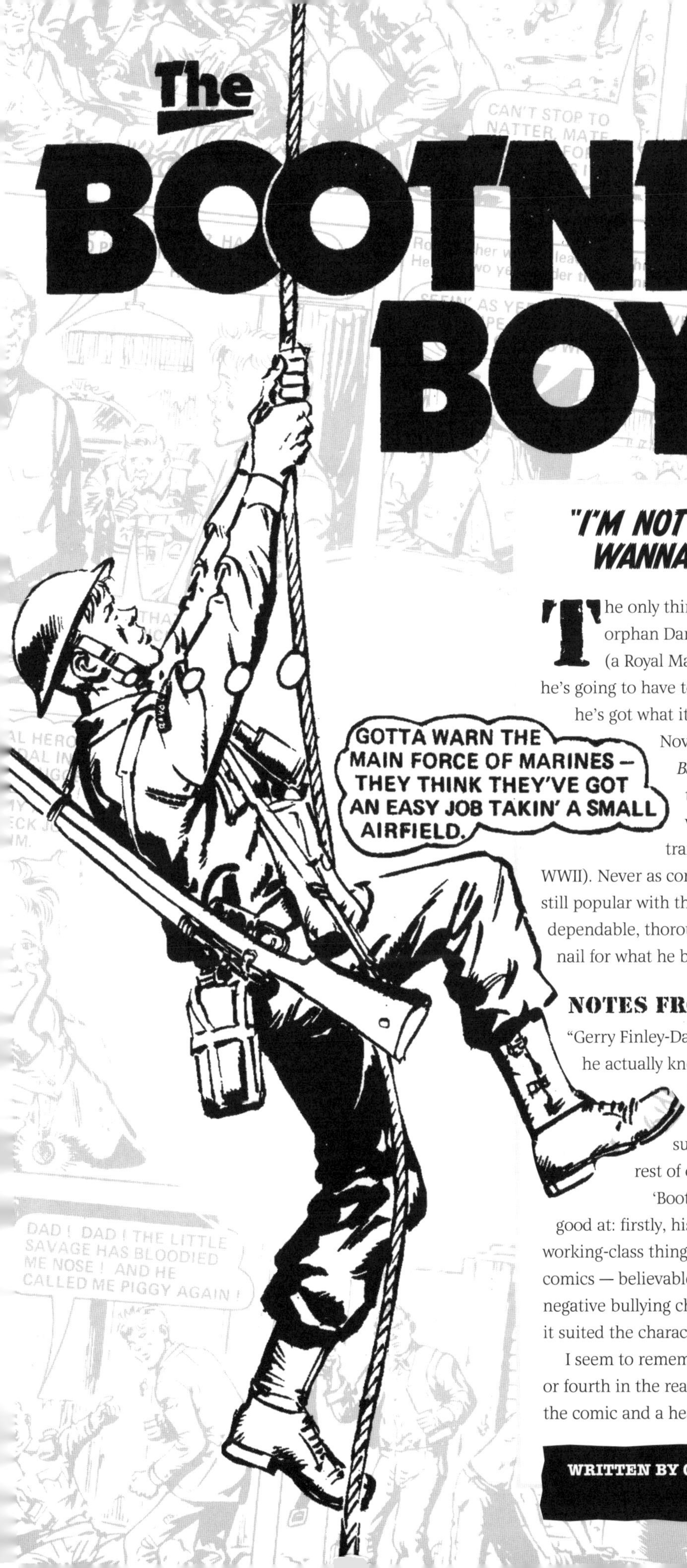
GOTTA WARN THE MAIN FORCE OF MARINES – THEY THINK THEY'VE GOT AN EASY JOB TAKIN' A SMALL AIRFIELD.

"I'M NOT A BIG-HEAD. I JUST WANNA BE A BOOTNECK!"

The only thing that matters to pint-sized Newcastle orphan Danny Budd is becoming a "Bootneck Boy" (a Royal Marine) like his old man before him, but he's going to have to fight every inch of the way to prove he's got what it takes. Running from March 1975 until November 1977, 'The Bootneck Boy' saw *Battle* returning to one of its favourite themes, a young boy fighting in a man's war (as seen in 'Charley's War', although transposing the action to the battlefields of WWII). Never as complex a character as Charley, Danny was still popular with the readers, by dint of being a dependable, thoroughly decent lad who fought tooth-and-nail for what he believed.

NOTES FROM THE FRONTLINE:

"Gerry Finley-Day had been in the Territorial Army and he actually knew what he was talking about; that permeates everything he did for *Battle*. His scripts had a certain sense — subliminally — of comradeship that the rest of ours lacked.

'Bootneck Boy' drew on two things Gerry was good at: firstly, his military knowledge and secondly, that working-class thing he'd refined tremendously in his girls' comics — believable working-class stuff and those rather negative bullying characters, all very girls' comic, really, but it suited the character.

I seem to remember 'Bootneck Boy' was generally third or fourth in the reader's polls; it had a healthy position in the comic and a healthy following." **— Pat Mills**

WRITTEN BY Gerry Finley-Day & Ian MacDonald
DRAWN BY Giralt

THE EXCITING ADVENTURES OF A LAD WHO WANTS TO BE A MARINE!

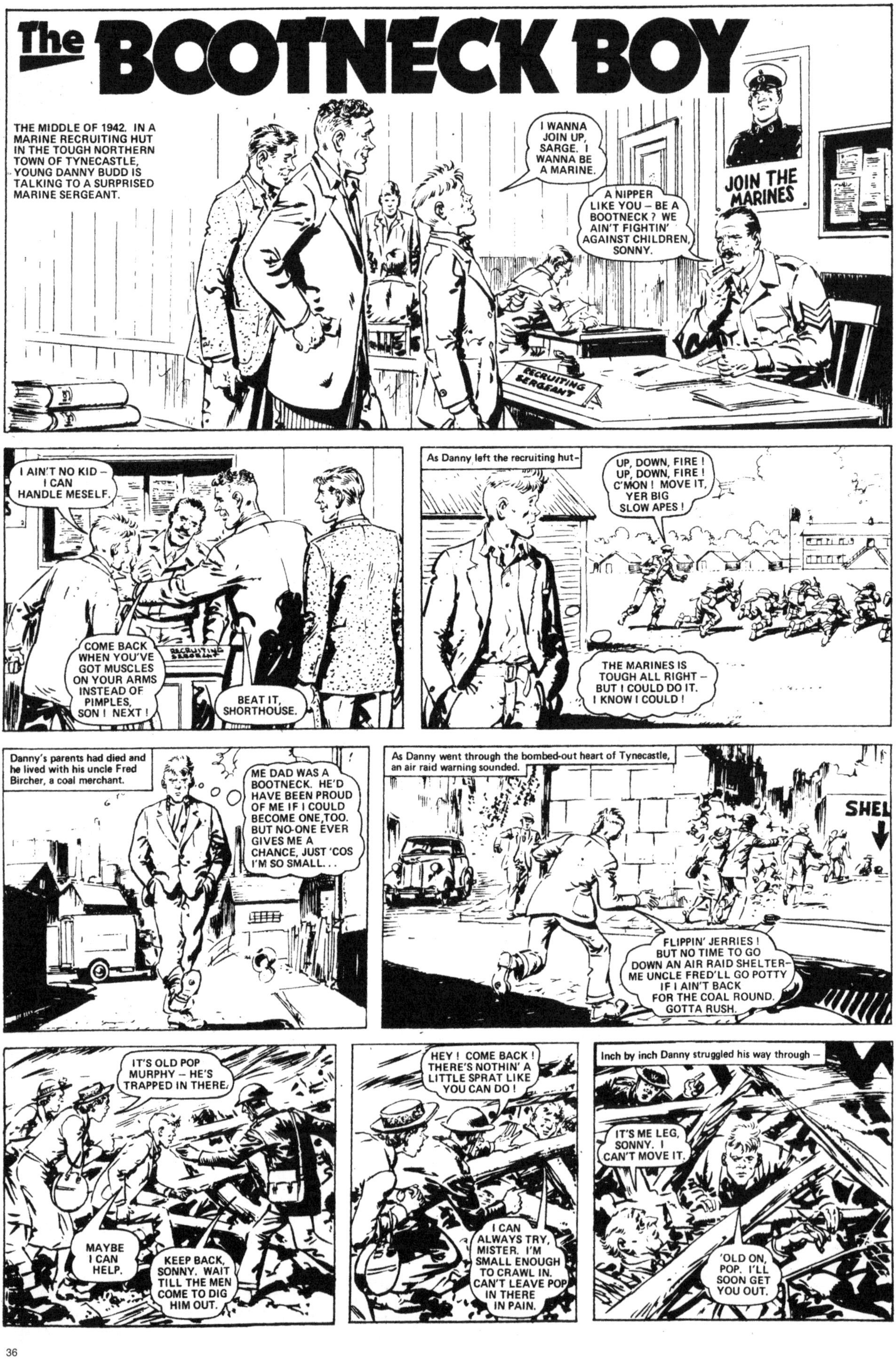

The BOOTNECK BOY
THE MIDDLE OF 1942. IN A MARINE RECRUITING HUT IN THE TOUGH NORTHERN TOWN OF TYNECASTLE, YOUNG DANNY BUDD IS TALKING TO A SURPRISED MARINE SERGEANT.
I WANNA JOIN UP, SARGE. I WANNA BE A MARINE.
A NIPPER LIKE YOU – BE A BOOTNECK? WE AIN'T FIGHTIN' AGAINST CHILDREN, SONNY.
JOIN THE MARINES
RECRUITING SERGEANT
I AIN'T NO KID – I CAN HANDLE MESELF.
COME BACK WHEN YOU'VE GOT MUSCLES ON YOUR ARMS INSTEAD OF PIMPLES, SON! NEXT!
BEAT IT, SHORTHOUSE.
As Danny left the recruiting hut–
UP, DOWN, FIRE! UP, DOWN, FIRE! C'MON! MOVE IT, YER BIG SLOW APES!
THE MARINES IS TOUGH ALL RIGHT – BUT I COULD DO IT. I KNOW I COULD!
Danny's parents had died and he lived with his uncle Fred Bircher, a coal merchant.
ME DAD WAS A BOOTNECK. HE'D HAVE BEEN PROUD OF ME IF I COULD BECOME ONE,TOO. BUT NO-ONE EVER GIVES ME A CHANCE, JUST 'COS I'M SO SMALL...
As Danny went through the bombed-out heart of Tynecastle, an air raid warning sounded.
SHEL
FLIPPIN' JERRIES! BUT NO TIME TO GO DOWN AN AIR RAID SHELTER– ME UNCLE FRED'LL GO POTTY IF I AIN'T BACK FOR THE COAL ROUND. GOTTA RUSH.
IT'S OLD POP MURPHY – HE'S TRAPPED IN THERE.
MAYBE I CAN HELP.
KEEP BACK, SONNY. WAIT TILL THE MEN COME TO DIG HIM OUT.
HEY! COME BACK! THERE'S NOTHIN' A LITTLE SPRAT LIKE YOU CAN DO!
I CAN ALWAYS TRY, MISTER. I'M SMALL ENOUGH TO CRAWL IN. CAN'T LEAVE POP IN THERE IN PAIN.
Inch by inch Danny struggled his way through –
IT'S ME LEG, SONNY. I CAN'T MOVE IT.
'OLD ON, POP. I'LL SOON GET YOU OUT.

"GET YOUR HANDS OFF!"

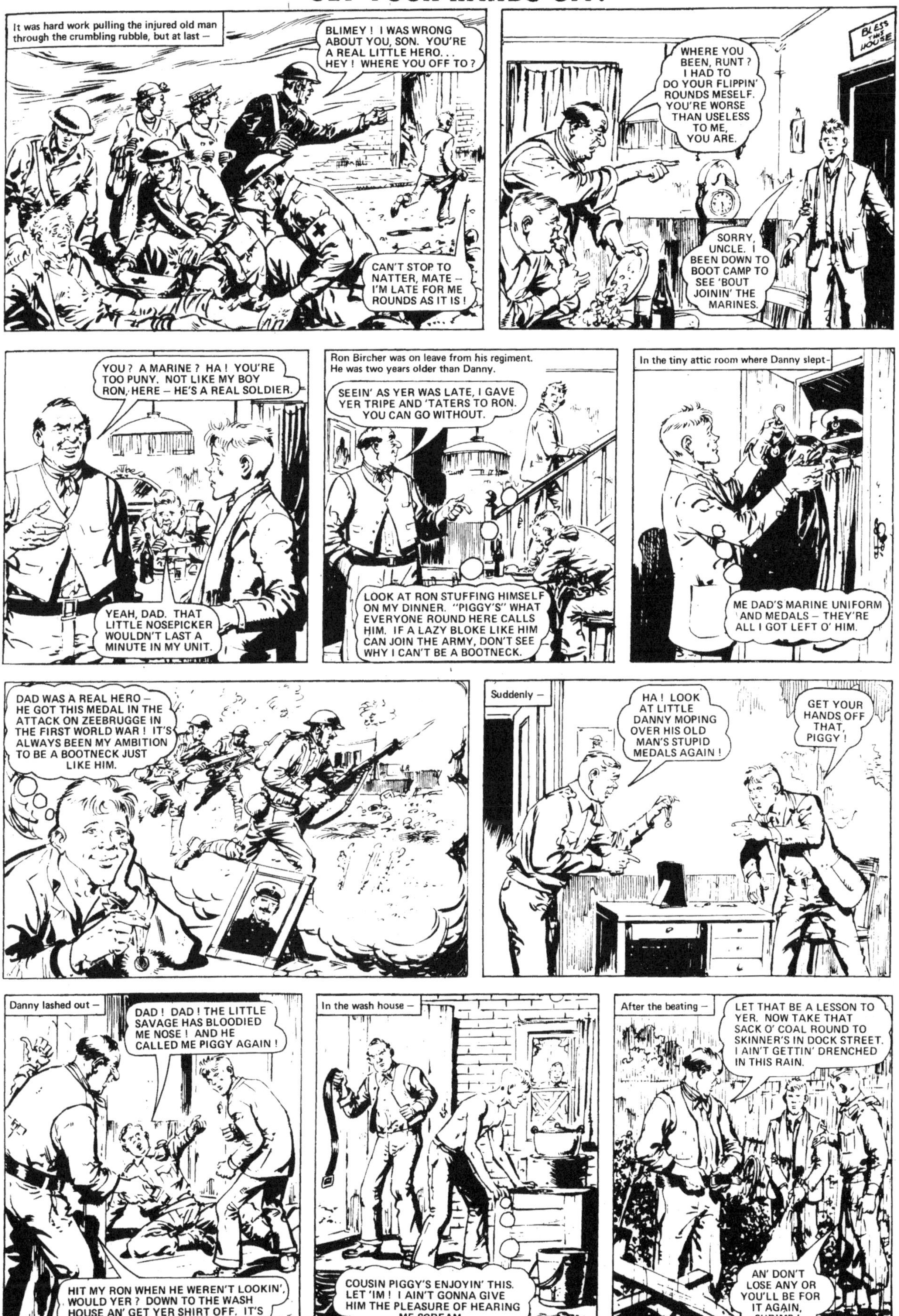

It was hard work pulling the injured old man through the crumbling rubble, but at last –
BLIMEY ! I WAS WRONG ABOUT YOU, SON. YOU'RE A REAL LITTLE HERO. . . HEY ! WHERE YOU OFF TO ?
CAN'T STOP TO NATTER, MATE – I'M LATE FOR ME ROUNDS AS IT IS !
BLESS THIS HOUSE
WHERE YOU BEEN, RUNT ? I HAD TO DO YOUR FLIPPIN' ROUNDS MESELF. YOU'RE WORSE THAN USELESS TO ME, YOU ARE.
SORRY, UNCLE. I BEEN DOWN TO BOOT CAMP TO SEE 'BOUT JOININ' THE MARINES.
YOU ? A MARINE ? HA ! YOU'RE TOO PUNY. NOT LIKE MY BOY RON, HERE – HE'S A REAL SOLDIER.
YEAH, DAD. THAT LITTLE NOSEPICKER WOULDN'T LAST A MINUTE IN MY UNIT.
Ron Bircher was on leave from his regiment. He was two years older than Danny.
SEEIN' AS YER WAS LATE, I GAVE YER TRIPE AND 'TATERS TO RON. YOU CAN GO WITHOUT.
LOOK AT RON STUFFING HIMSELF ON MY DINNER. "PIGGY'S" WHAT EVERYONE ROUND HERE CALLS HIM. IF A LAZY BLOKE LIKE HIM CAN JOIN THE ARMY, DON'T SEE WHY I CAN'T BE A BOOTNECK.
In the tiny attic room where Danny slept–
ME DAD'S MARINE UNIFORM AND MEDALS – THEY'RE ALL I GOT LEFT O' HIM.
DAD WAS A REAL HERO – HE GOT THIS MEDAL IN THE ATTACK ON ZEEBRUGGE IN THE FIRST WORLD WAR ! IT'S ALWAYS BEEN MY AMBITION TO BE A BOOTNECK JUST LIKE HIM.
Suddenly –
HA ! LOOK AT LITTLE DANNY MOPING OVER HIS OLD MAN'S STUPID MEDALS AGAIN !
GET YOUR HANDS OFF THAT, PIGGY !
Danny lashed out –
DAD ! DAD ! THE LITTLE SAVAGE HAS BLOODIED ME NOSE ! AND HE CALLED ME PIGGY AGAIN !
HIT MY RON WHEN HE WEREN'T LOOKIN', WOULD YER ? DOWN TO THE WASH HOUSE AN' GET YER SHIRT OFF. IT'S TIME I TOOK ME BELT TO YER !
In the wash house –
COUSIN PIGGY'S ENJOYIN' THIS. LET 'IM ! I AIN'T GONNA GIVE HIM THE PLEASURE OF HEARING ME SCREAM.
After the beating –
LET THAT BE A LESSON TO YER. NOW TAKE THAT SACK O' COAL ROUND TO SKINNER'S IN DOCK STREET. I AIN'T GETTIN' DRENCHED IN THIS RAIN.
AN' DON'T LOSE ANY OR YOU'LL BE FOR IT AGAIN, SHRIMP !

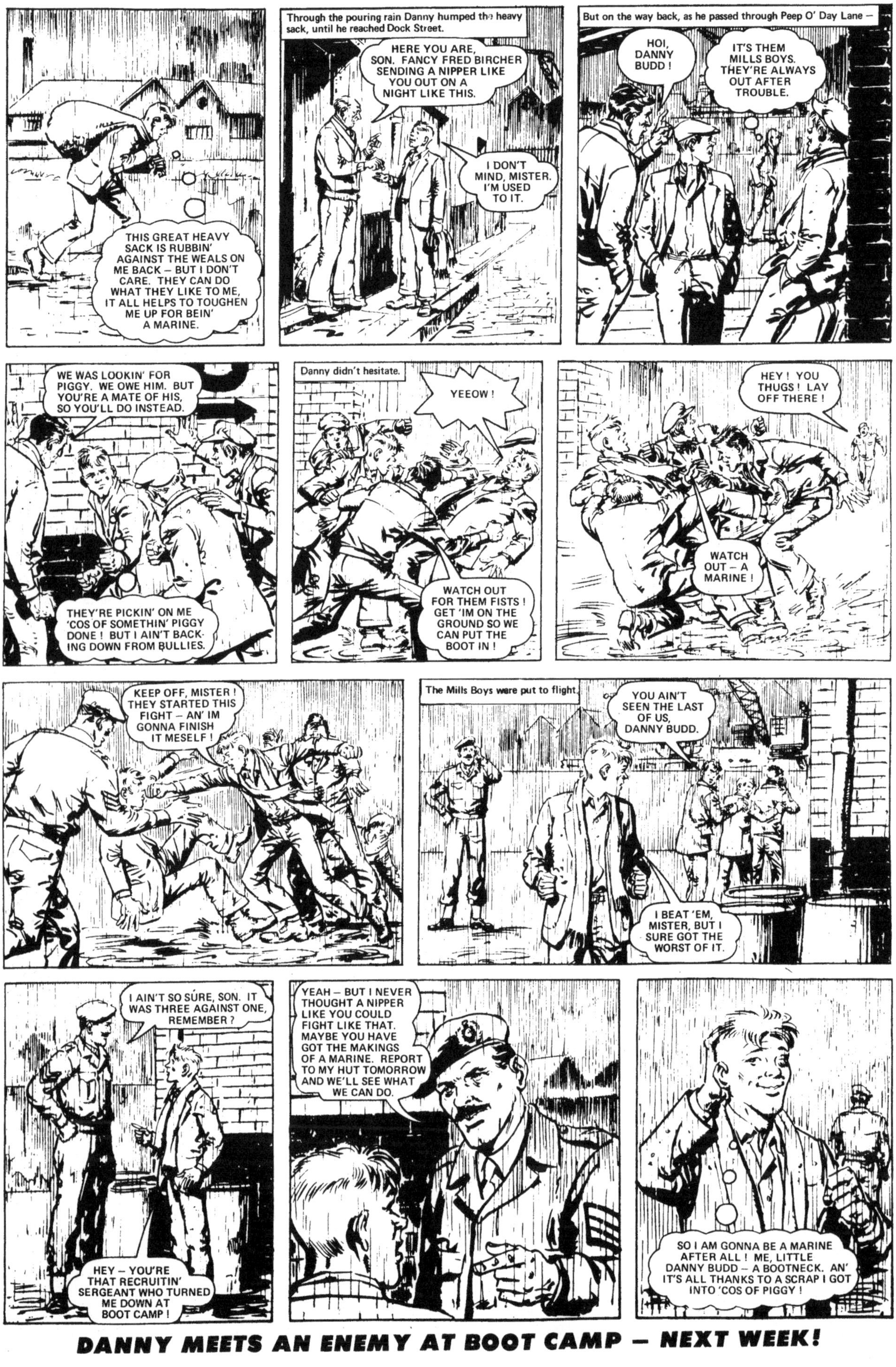
THIS GREAT HEAVY SACK IS RUBBIN' AGAINST THE WEALS ON ME BACK – BUT I DON'T CARE. THEY CAN DO WHAT THEY LIKE TO ME, IT ALL HELPS TO TOUGHEN ME UP FOR BEIN' A MARINE.
Through the pouring rain Danny humped the heavy sack, until he reached Dock Street.
HERE YOU ARE, SON. FANCY FRED BIRCHER SENDING A NIPPER LIKE YOU OUT ON A NIGHT LIKE THIS.
I DON'T MIND, MISTER. I'M USED TO IT.
But on the way back, as he passed through Peep O' Day Lane –
HOI, DANNY BUDD !
IT'S THEM MILLS BOYS. THEY'RE ALWAYS OUT AFTER TROUBLE.
WE WAS LOOKIN' FOR PIGGY. WE OWE HIM. BUT YOU'RE A MATE OF HIS, SO YOU'LL DO INSTEAD.
THEY'RE PICKIN' ON ME 'COS OF SOMETHIN' PIGGY DONE ! BUT I AIN'T BACKING DOWN FROM BULLIES.
Danny didn't hesitate.
YEEOW !
WATCH OUT FOR THEM FISTS ! GET 'IM ON THE GROUND SO WE CAN PUT THE BOOT IN !
HEY ! YOU THUGS ! LAY OFF THERE !
WATCH OUT – A MARINE !
KEEP OFF, MISTER ! THEY STARTED THIS FIGHT – AN' IM GONNA FINISH IT MESELF !
The Mills Boys were put to flight.
YOU AIN'T SEEN THE LAST OF US, DANNY BUDD.
I BEAT 'EM, MISTER, BUT I SURE GOT THE WORST OF IT.
I AIN'T SO SURE, SON. IT WAS THREE AGAINST ONE, REMEMBER ?
HEY – YOU'RE THAT RECRUITIN' SERGEANT WHO TURNED ME DOWN AT BOOT CAMP !
YEAH – BUT I NEVER THOUGHT A NIPPER LIKE YOU COULD FIGHT LIKE THAT. MAYBE YOU HAVE GOT THE MAKINGS OF A MARINE. REPORT TO MY HUT TOMORROW AND WE'LL SEE WHAT WE CAN DO.
SO I AM GONNA BE A MARINE AFTER ALL ! ME, LITTLE DANNY BUDD – A BOOTNECK. AN' IT'S ALL THANKS TO A SCRAP I GOT INTO 'COS OF PIGGY !

DANNY MEETS AN ENEMY AT BOOT CAMP – NEXT WEEK!

DANNY'S DIVE INTO DEADLY PERIL!

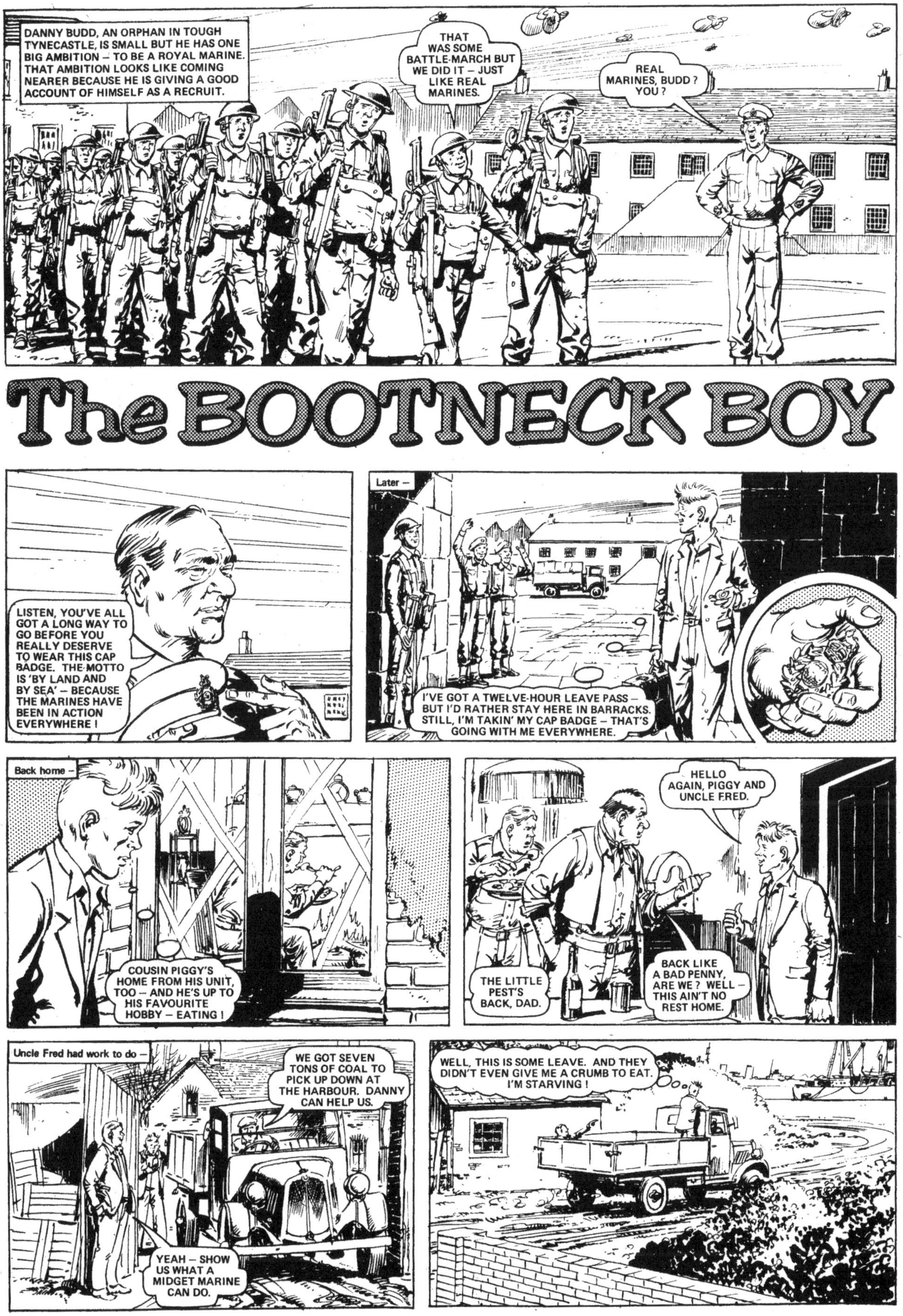

DANNY BUDD, AN ORPHAN IN TOUGH TYNECASTLE, IS SMALL BUT HE HAS ONE BIG AMBITION – TO BE A ROYAL MARINE. THAT AMBITION LOOKS LIKE COMING NEARER BECAUSE HE IS GIVING A GOOD ACCOUNT OF HIMSELF AS A RECRUIT.
THAT WAS SOME BATTLE-MARCH BUT WE DID IT – JUST LIKE REAL MARINES.
REAL MARINES, BUDD? YOU?
The BOOTNECK BOY
LISTEN, YOU'VE ALL GOT A LONG WAY TO GO BEFORE YOU REALLY DESERVE TO WEAR THIS CAP BADGE. THE MOTTO IS 'BY LAND AND BY SEA' – BECAUSE THE MARINES HAVE BEEN IN ACTION EVERYWHERE!
Later –
I'VE GOT A TWELVE-HOUR LEAVE PASS – BUT I'D RATHER STAY HERE IN BARRACKS. STILL, I'M TAKIN' MY CAP BADGE – THAT'S GOING WITH ME EVERYWHERE.
Back home –
COUSIN PIGGY'S HOME FROM HIS UNIT, TOO – AND HE'S UP TO HIS FAVOURITE HOBBY – EATING!
HELLO AGAIN, PIGGY AND UNCLE FRED.
THE LITTLE PEST'S BACK, DAD.
BACK LIKE A BAD PENNY, ARE WE? WELL – THIS AIN'T NO REST HOME.
Uncle Fred had work to do –
WE GOT SEVEN TONS OF COAL TO PICK UP DOWN AT THE HARBOUR. DANNY CAN HELP US.
YEAH – SHOW US WHAT A MIDGET MARINE CAN DO.
WELL, THIS IS SOME LEAVE. AND THEY DIDN'T EVEN GIVE ME A CRUMB TO EAT. I'M STARVING!

"IT'S A MINE!"

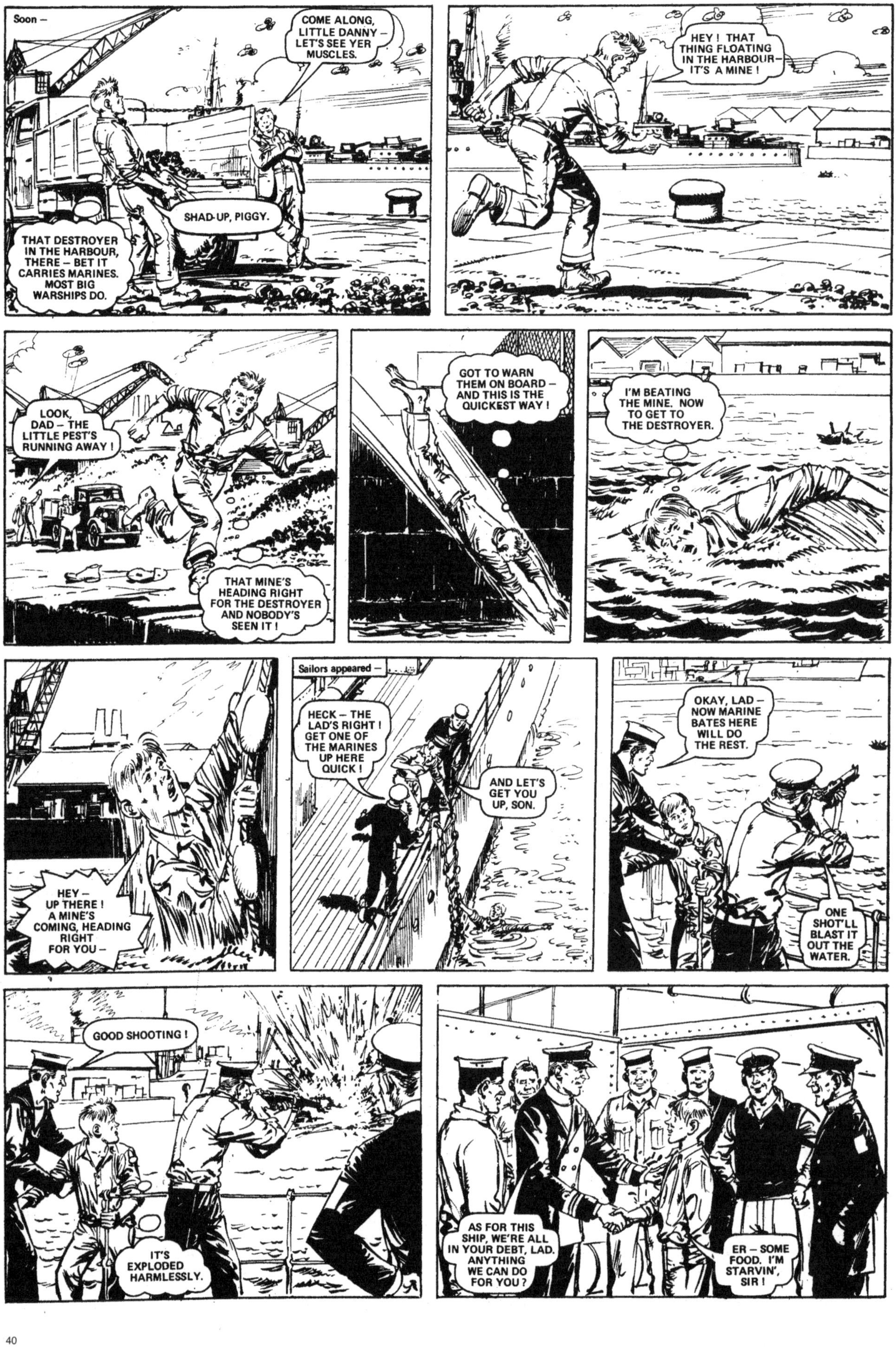

Soon –
COME ALONG, LITTLE DANNY – LET'S SEE YER MUSCLES.
SHAD-UP, PIGGY.
THAT DESTROYER IN THE HARBOUR, THERE – BET IT CARRIES MARINES. MOST BIG WARSHIPS DO.
HEY ! THAT THING FLOATING IN THE HARBOUR – IT'S A MINE !
LOOK, DAD – THE LITTLE PEST'S RUNNING AWAY !
THAT MINE'S HEADING RIGHT FOR THE DESTROYER AND NOBODY'S SEEN IT !
GOT TO WARN THEM ON BOARD – AND THIS IS THE QUICKEST WAY !
I'M BEATING THE MINE. NOW TO GET TO THE DESTROYER.
HEY – UP THERE ! A MINE'S COMING, HEADING RIGHT FOR YOU –
Sailors appeared –
HECK – THE LAD'S RIGHT ! GET ONE OF THE MARINES UP HERE QUICK !
AND LET'S GET YOU UP, SON.
OKAY, LAD – NOW MARINE BATES HERE WILL DO THE REST.
ONE SHOT'LL BLAST IT OUT THE WATER.
GOOD SHOOTING !
IT'S EXPLODED HARMLESSLY.
AS FOR THIS SHIP, WE'RE ALL IN YOUR DEBT, LAD. ANYTHING WE CAN DO FOR YOU ?
ER – SOME FOOD. I'M STARVIN', SIR !

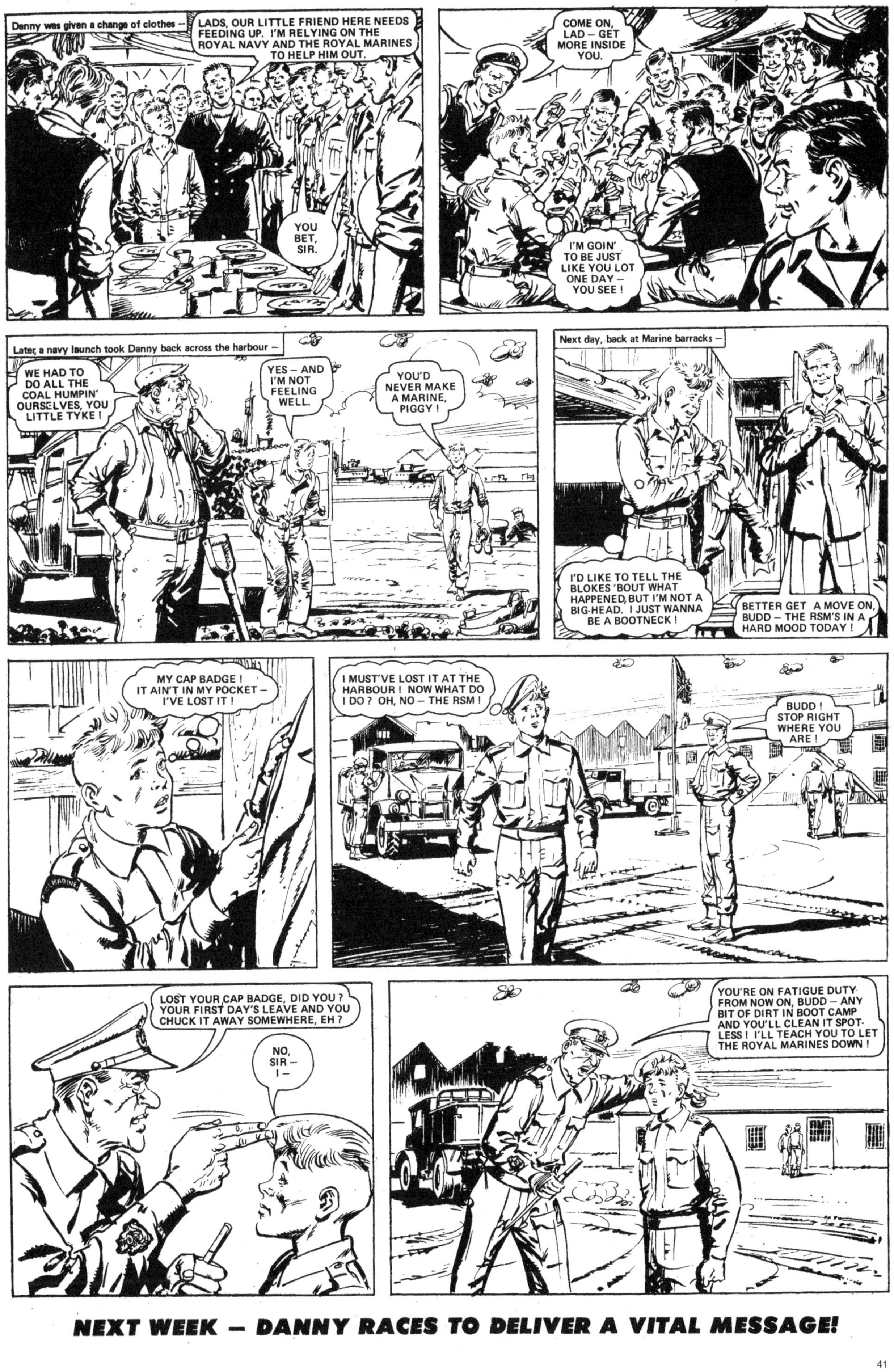
Danny was given a change of clothes –
LADS, OUR LITTLE FRIEND HERE NEEDS FEEDING UP. I'M RELYING ON THE ROYAL NAVY AND THE ROYAL MARINES TO HELP HIM OUT.
YOU BET, SIR.
COME ON, LAD – GET MORE INSIDE YOU.
I'M GOIN' TO BE JUST LIKE YOU LOT ONE DAY – YOU SEE !
Later, a navy launch took Danny back across the harbour –
WE HAD TO DO ALL THE COAL HUMPIN' OURSELVES, YOU LITTLE TYKE !
YES – AND I'M NOT FEELING WELL.
YOU'D NEVER MAKE A MARINE, PIGGY !
Next day, back at Marine barracks –
I'D LIKE TO TELL THE BLOKES 'BOUT WHAT HAPPENED, BUT I'M NOT A BIG-HEAD. I JUST WANNA BE A BOOTNECK !
BETTER GET A MOVE ON, BUDD – THE RSM'S IN A HARD MOOD TODAY !
MY CAP BADGE ! IT AIN'T IN MY POCKET – I'VE LOST IT !
I MUST'VE LOST IT AT THE HARBOUR ! NOW WHAT DO I DO ? OH, NO – THE RSM !
BUDD ! STOP RIGHT WHERE YOU ARE !
LOST YOUR CAP BADGE, DID YOU ? YOUR FIRST DAY'S LEAVE AND YOU CHUCK IT AWAY SOMEWHERE, EH ?
NO, SIR – I –
YOU'RE ON FATIGUE DUTY FROM NOW ON, BUDD – ANY BIT OF DIRT IN BOOT CAMP AND YOU'LL CLEAN IT SPOTLESS ! I'LL TEACH YOU TO LET THE ROYAL MARINES DOWN !

NEXT WEEK – DANNY RACES TO DELIVER A VITAL MESSAGE!

YOUNG DANNY BUDD IN A DESPERATE RACE AGAINST TIME!

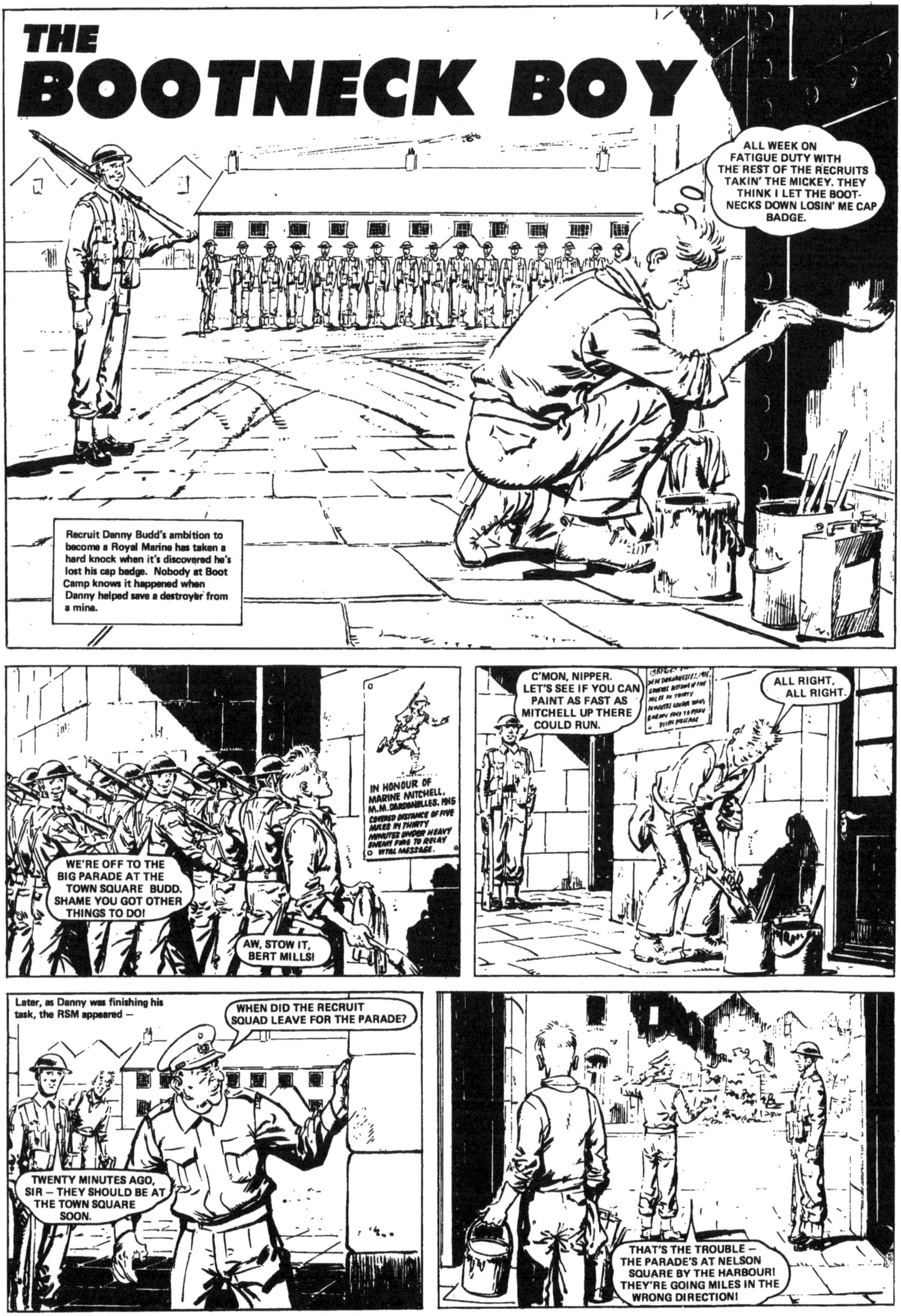
THE BOOTNECK BOY
ALL WEEK ON FATIGUE DUTY WITH THE REST OF THE RECRUITS TAKIN' THE MICKEY. THEY THINK I LET THE BOOT-NECKS DOWN LOSIN' ME CAP BADGE.
Recruit Danny Budd's ambition to become a Royal Marine has taken a hard knock when it's discovered he's lost his cap badge. Nobody at Boot Camp knows it happened when Danny helped save a destroyer from a mine.
IN HONOUR OF MARINE MITCHELL, M.M. DARDANELLES, 1915 COVERED DISTANCE OF FIVE MILES IN THIRTY MINUTES UNDER HEAVY ENEMY FIRE TO RELAY VITAL MESSAGE.
WE'RE OFF TO THE BIG PARADE AT THE TOWN SQUARE BUDD. SHAME YOU GOT OTHER THINGS TO DO!
AW, STOW IT, BERT MILLS!
C'MON, NIPPER. LET'S SEE IF YOU CAN PAINT AS FAST AS MITCHELL UP THERE COULD RUN.
ALL RIGHT, ALL RIGHT.
Later, as Danny was finishing his task, the RSM appeared —
WHEN DID THE RECRUIT SQUAD LEAVE FOR THE PARADE?
TWENTY MINUTES AGO, SIR — THEY SHOULD BE AT THE TOWN SQUARE SOON.
THAT'S THE TROUBLE — THE PARADE'S AT NELSON SQUARE BY THE HARBOUR! THEY'RE GOING MILES IN THE WRONG DIRECTION!

"DON'T LISTEN TO HIM, CORP – HE'S LYIN'!"

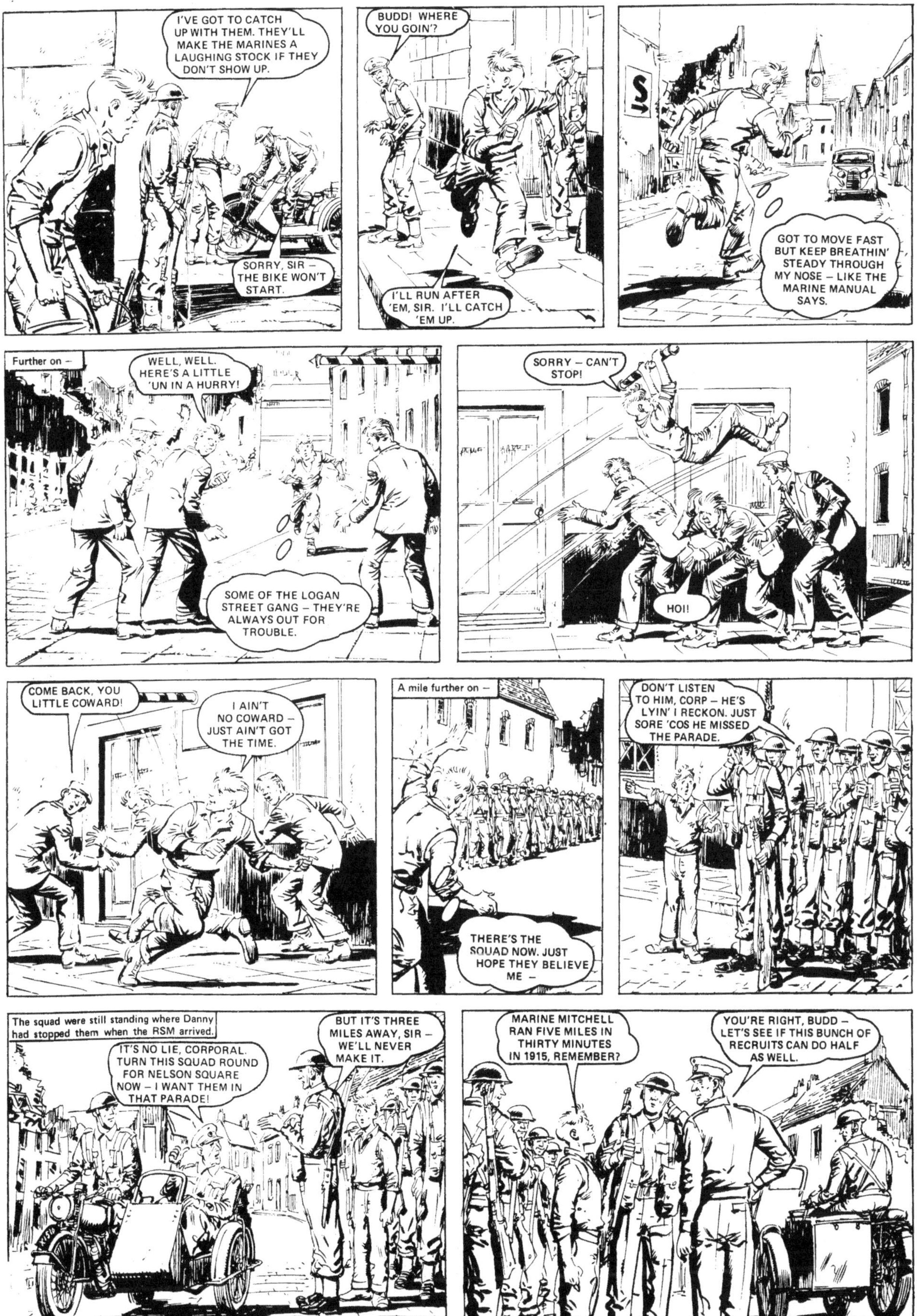
I'VE GOT TO CATCH UP WITH THEM. THEY'LL MAKE THE MARINES A LAUGHING STOCK IF THEY DON'T SHOW UP.
SORRY, SIR – THE BIKE WON'T START.
BUDD! WHERE YOU GOIN'?
I'LL RUN AFTER 'EM, SIR. I'LL CATCH 'EM UP.
GOT TO MOVE FAST BUT KEEP BREATHIN' STEADY THROUGH MY NOSE – LIKE THE MARINE MANUAL SAYS.
Further on –
WELL, WELL. HERE'S A LITTLE 'UN IN A HURRY!
SOME OF THE LOGAN STREET GANG – THEY'RE ALWAYS OUT FOR TROUBLE.
SORRY – CAN'T STOP!
HOI!
COME BACK, YOU LITTLE COWARD!
I AIN'T NO COWARD – JUST AIN'T GOT THE TIME.
A mile further on –
THERE'S THE SQUAD NOW. JUST HOPE THEY BELIEVE ME –
DON'T LISTEN TO HIM, CORP – HE'S LYIN' I RECKON. JUST SORE 'COS HE MISSED THE PARADE.
The squad were still standing where Danny had stopped them when the RSM arrived.
IT'S NO LIE, CORPORAL. TURN THIS SQUAD ROUND FOR NELSON SQUARE NOW – I WANT THEM IN THAT PARADE!
BUT IT'S THREE MILES AWAY, SIR – WE'LL NEVER MAKE IT.
MARINE MITCHELL RAN FIVE MILES IN THIRTY MINUTES IN 1915, REMEMBER?
YOU'RE RIGHT, BUDD – LET'S SEE IF THIS BUNCH OF RECRUITS CAN DO HALF AS WELL.

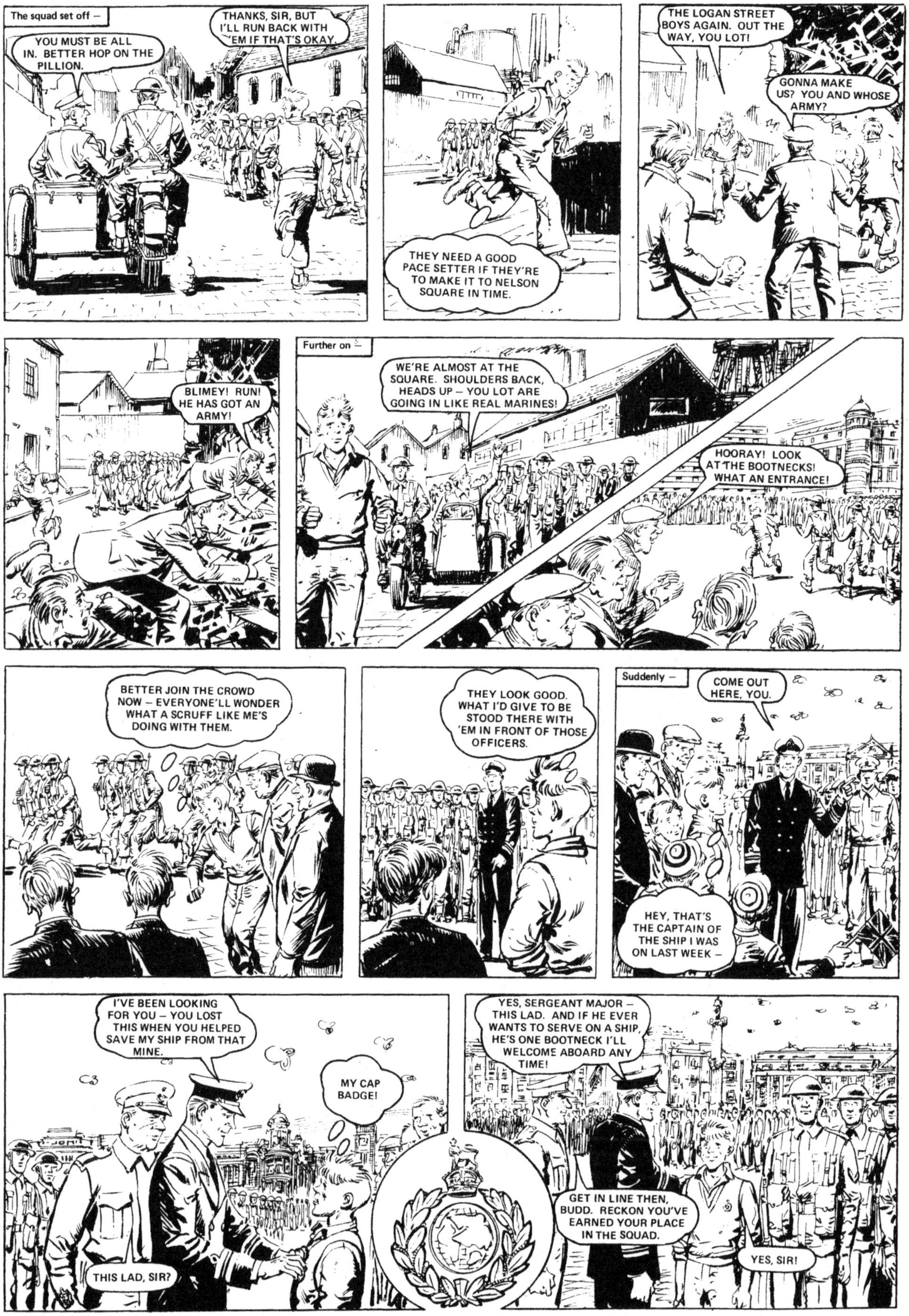

The squad set off –
YOU MUST BE ALL IN. BETTER HOP ON THE PILLION.
THANKS, SIR, BUT I'LL RUN BACK WITH 'EM IF THAT'S OKAY.
THEY NEED A GOOD PACE SETTER IF THEY'RE TO MAKE IT TO NELSON SQUARE IN TIME.
THE LOGAN STREET BOYS AGAIN. OUT THE WAY, YOU LOT!
GONNA MAKE US? YOU AND WHOSE ARMY?
BLIMEY! RUN! HE HAS GOT AN ARMY!
Further on –
WE'RE ALMOST AT THE SQUARE. SHOULDERS BACK, HEADS UP – YOU LOT ARE GOING IN LIKE REAL MARINES!
HOORAY! LOOK AT THE BOOTNECKS! WHAT AN ENTRANCE!
BETTER JOIN THE CROWD NOW – EVERYONE'LL WONDER WHAT A SCRUFF LIKE ME'S DOING WITH THEM.
THEY LOOK GOOD. WHAT I'D GIVE TO BE STOOD THERE WITH 'EM IN FRONT OF THOSE OFFICERS.
Suddenly –
COME OUT HERE, YOU.
HEY, THAT'S THE CAPTAIN OF THE SHIP I WAS ON LAST WEEK –
I'VE BEEN LOOKING FOR YOU – YOU LOST THIS WHEN YOU HELPED SAVE MY SHIP FROM THAT MINE.
MY CAP BADGE!
THIS LAD, SIR?
YES, SERGEANT MAJOR – THIS LAD. AND IF HE EVER WANTS TO SERVE ON A SHIP, HE'S ONE BOOTNECK I'LL WELCOME ABOARD ANY TIME!
GET IN LINE THEN, BUDD. RECKON YOU'VE EARNED YOUR PLACE IN THE SQUAD.
YES, SIR!

NEXT WEEK – DANNY GOES ON A RAID!

DANNY BUDD OFF TO WAR — AND INTO DANGER!

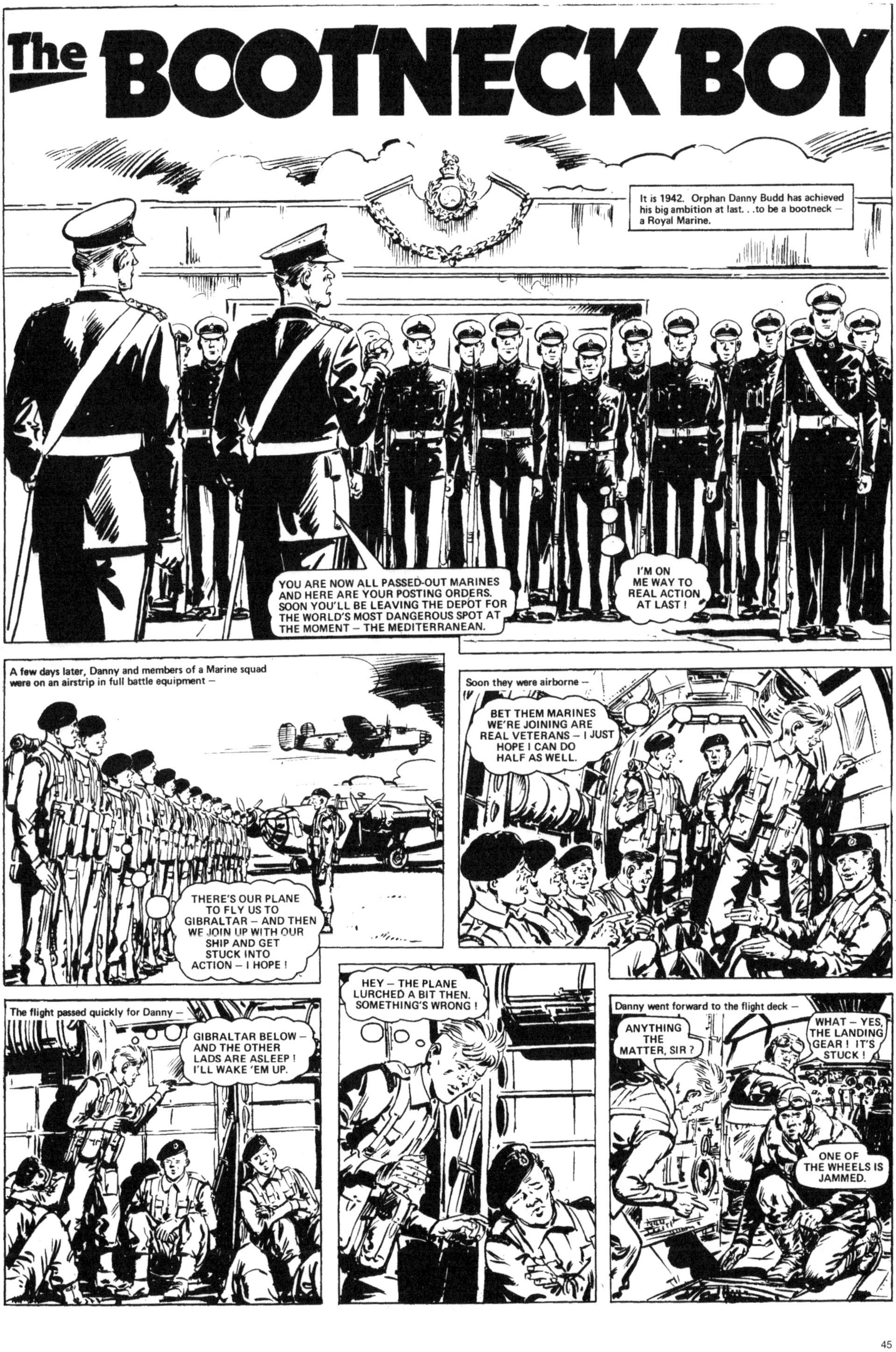
The BOOTNECK BOY
It is 1942. Orphan Danny Budd has achieved his big ambition at last. . .to be a bootneck — a Royal Marine.
YOU ARE NOW ALL PASSED-OUT MARINES AND HERE ARE YOUR POSTING ORDERS. SOON YOU'LL BE LEAVING THE DEPOT FOR THE WORLD'S MOST DANGEROUS SPOT AT THE MOMENT — THE MEDITERRANEAN.
I'M ON ME WAY TO REAL ACTION AT LAST !
A few days later, Danny and members of a Marine squad were on an airstrip in full battle equipment —
THERE'S OUR PLANE TO FLY US TO GIBRALTAR — AND THEN WE JOIN UP WITH OUR SHIP AND GET STUCK INTO ACTION — I HOPE !
Soon they were airborne —
BET THEM MARINES WE'RE JOINING ARE REAL VETERANS — I JUST HOPE I CAN DO HALF AS WELL.
The flight passed quickly for Danny —
GIBRALTAR BELOW — AND THE OTHER LADS ARE ASLEEP ! I'LL WAKE 'EM UP.
HEY — THE PLANE LURCHED A BIT THEN. SOMETHING'S WRONG !
Danny went forward to the flight deck —
ANYTHING THE MATTER, SIR ?
WHAT — YES, THE LANDING GEAR ! IT'S STUCK !
ONE OF THE WHEELS IS JAMMED.

"THAT'S A LIE, SOLDIER!"

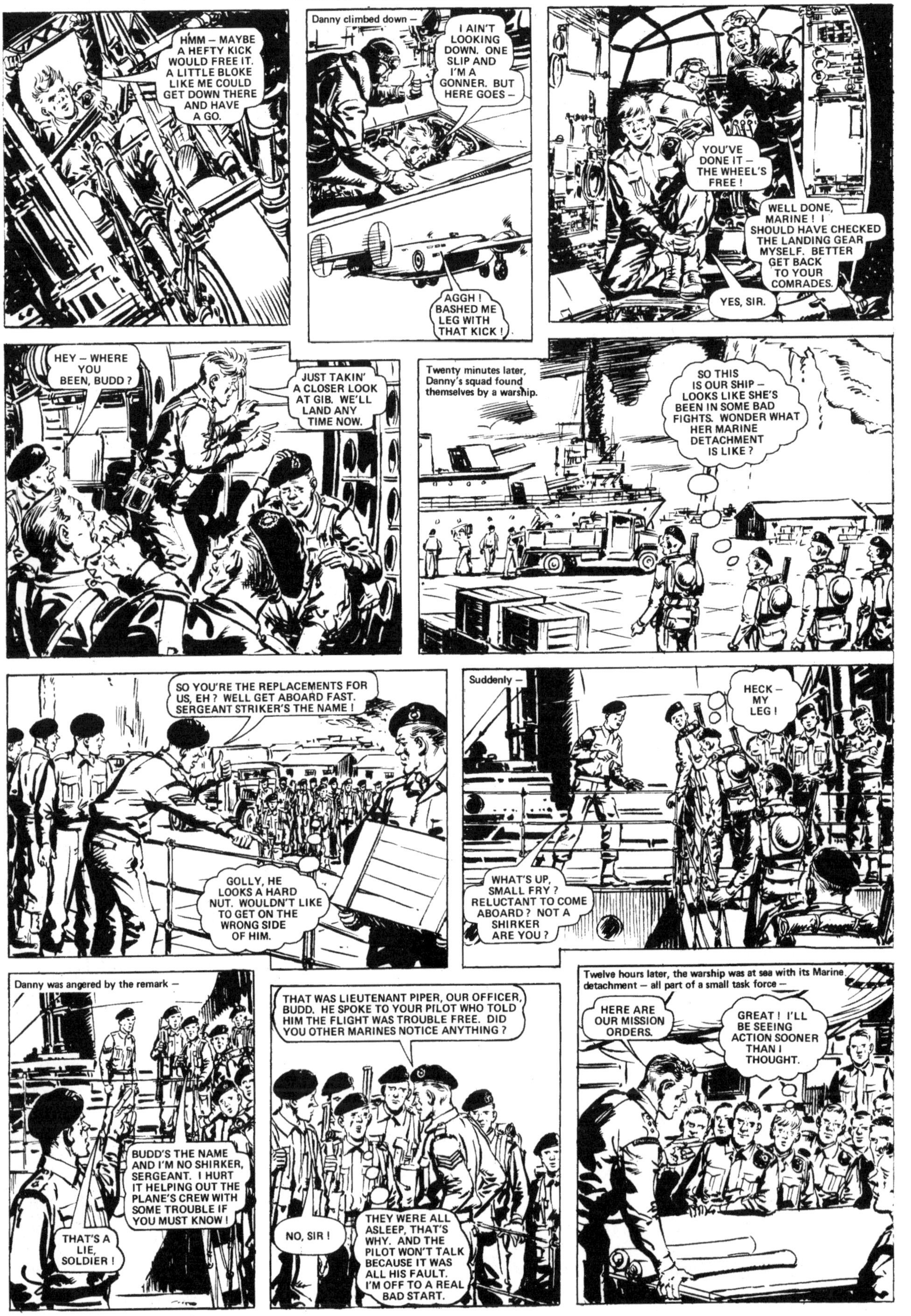
HMM – MAYBE A HEFTY KICK WOULD FREE IT. A LITTLE BLOKE LIKE ME COULD GET DOWN THERE AND HAVE A GO.
Danny climbed down –
I AIN'T LOOKING DOWN. ONE SLIP AND I'M A GONNER. BUT HERE GOES –
AGGH! BASHED ME LEG WITH THAT KICK!
YOU'VE DONE IT – THE WHEEL'S FREE!
WELL DONE, MARINE! I SHOULD HAVE CHECKED THE LANDING GEAR MYSELF. BETTER GET BACK TO YOUR COMRADES.
YES, SIR.
HEY – WHERE YOU BEEN, BUDD?
JUST TAKIN' A CLOSER LOOK AT GIB. WE'LL LAND ANY TIME NOW.
Twenty minutes later, Danny's squad found themselves by a warship.
SO THIS IS OUR SHIP – LOOKS LIKE SHE'S BEEN IN SOME BAD FIGHTS. WONDER WHAT HER MARINE DETACHMENT IS LIKE?
SO YOU'RE THE REPLACEMENTS FOR US, EH? WELL GET ABOARD FAST. SERGEANT STRIKER'S THE NAME!
GOLLY, HE LOOKS A HARD NUT. WOULDN'T LIKE TO GET ON THE WRONG SIDE OF HIM.
Suddenly –
HECK – MY LEG!
WHAT'S UP, SMALL FRY? RELUCTANT TO COME ABOARD? NOT A SHIRKER ARE YOU?
Danny was angered by the remark –
BUDD'S THE NAME AND I'M NO SHIRKER, SERGEANT. I HURT IT HELPING OUT THE PLANE'S CREW WITH SOME TROUBLE IF YOU MUST KNOW!
THAT'S A LIE, SOLDIER!
THAT WAS LIEUTENANT PIPER, OUR OFFICER, BUDD. HE SPOKE TO YOUR PILOT WHO TOLD HIM THE FLIGHT WAS TROUBLE FREE. DID YOU OTHER MARINES NOTICE ANYTHING?
NO, SIR!
THEY WERE ALL ASLEEP, THAT'S WHY. AND THE PILOT WON'T TALK BECAUSE IT WAS ALL HIS FAULT. I'M OFF TO A REAL BAD START.
Twelve hours later, the warship was at sea with its Marine detachment – all part of a small task force –
HERE ARE OUR MISSION ORDERS.
GREAT! I'LL BE SEEING ACTION SOONER THAN I THOUGHT.

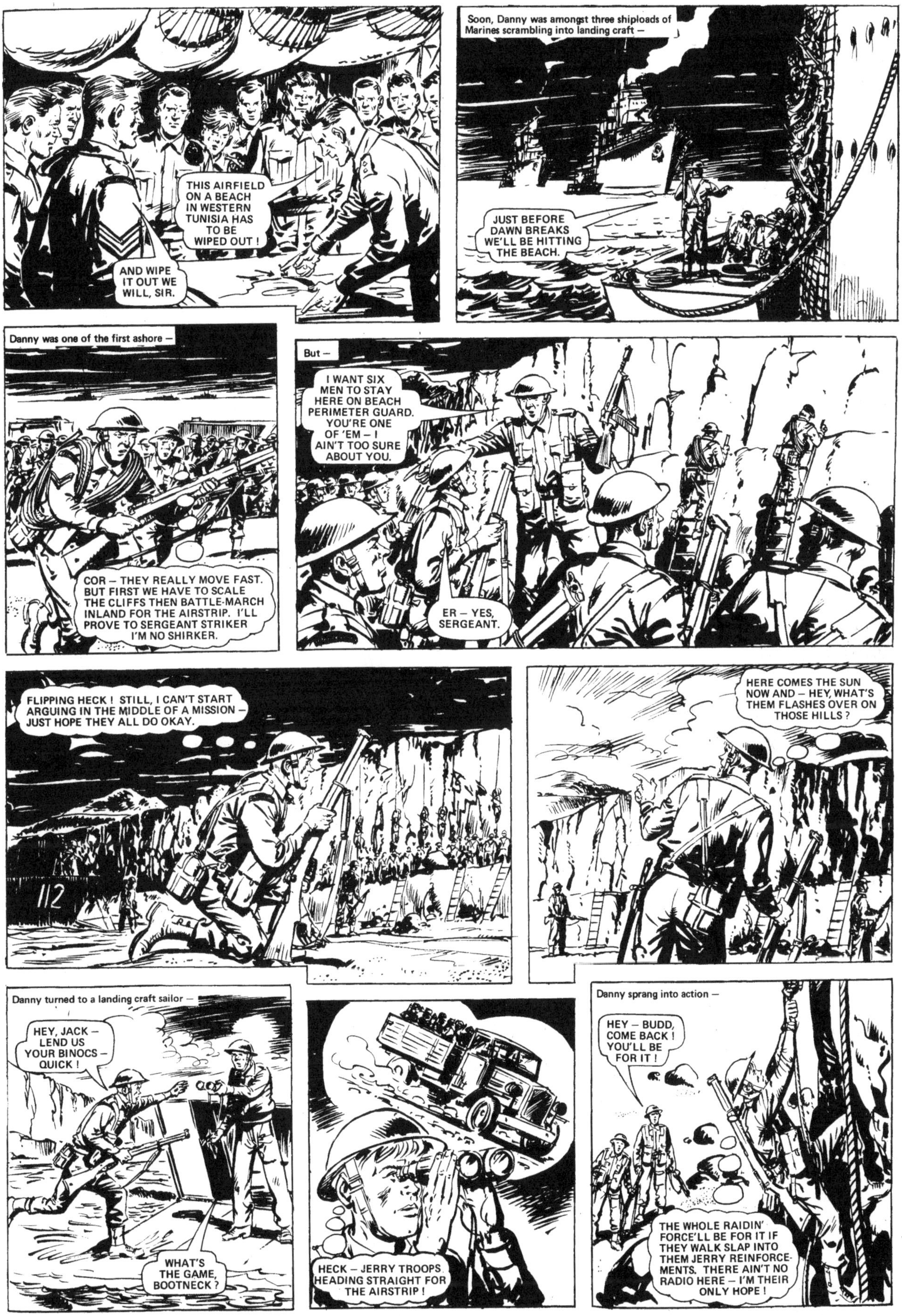
THIS AIRFIELD ON A BEACH IN WESTERN TUNISIA HAS TO BE WIPED OUT !
AND WIPE IT OUT WE WILL, SIR.
Soon, Danny was amongst three shiploads of Marines scrambling into landing craft –
JUST BEFORE DAWN BREAKS WE'LL BE HITTING THE BEACH.
Danny was one of the first ashore –
COR – THEY REALLY MOVE FAST. BUT FIRST WE HAVE TO SCALE THE CLIFFS THEN BATTLE-MARCH INLAND FOR THE AIRSTRIP. I'LL PROVE TO SERGEANT STRIKER I'M NO SHIRKER.
But –
I WANT SIX MEN TO STAY HERE ON BEACH PERIMETER GUARD. YOU'RE ONE OF 'EM – I AIN'T TOO SURE ABOUT YOU.
ER – YES, SERGEANT.
FLIPPING HECK ! STILL, I CAN'T START ARGUING IN THE MIDDLE OF A MISSION – JUST HOPE THEY ALL DO OKAY.
112
HERE COMES THE SUN NOW AND – HEY, WHAT'S THEM FLASHES OVER ON THOSE HILLS ?
Danny turned to a landing craft sailor –
HEY, JACK – LEND US YOUR BINOCS – QUICK !
WHAT'S THE GAME, BOOTNECK ?
HECK – JERRY TROOPS HEADING STRAIGHT FOR THE AIRSTRIP !
Danny sprang into action –
HEY – BUDD, COME BACK ! YOU'LL BE FOR IT !
THE WHOLE RAIDIN' FORCE'LL BE FOR IT IF THEY WALK SLAP INTO THEM JERRY REINFORCEMENTS. THERE AIN'T NO RADIO HERE – I'M THEIR ONLY HOPE !

CAN DANNY SAVE HIS MATES? SEE THE DRAMATIC DEVELOPMENTS!

DANNY BUDD AGAINST A SQUAD OF CRACK JERRY TROOPS!

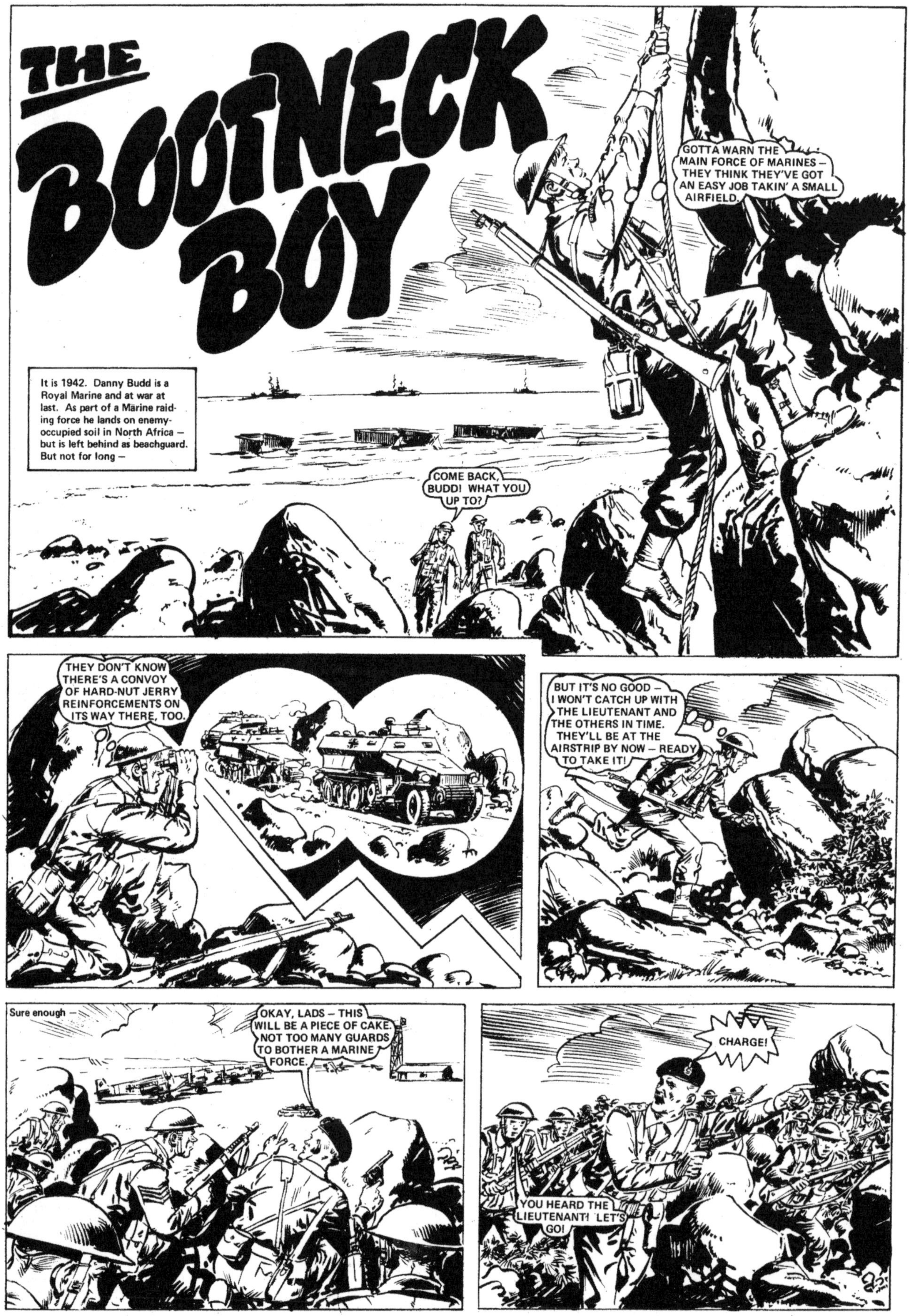
THE BOOTNECK BOY
GOTTA WARN THE MAIN FORCE OF MARINES – THEY THINK THEY'VE GOT AN EASY JOB TAKIN' A SMALL AIRFIELD.
It is 1942. Danny Budd is a Royal Marine and at war at last. As part of a Marine raiding force he lands on enemy-occupied soil in North Africa – but is left behind as beachguard. But not for long –
COME BACK, BUDD! WHAT YOU UP TO?
THEY DON'T KNOW THERE'S A CONVOY OF HARD-NUT JERRY REINFORCEMENTS ON ITS WAY THERE, TOO.
BUT IT'S NO GOOD – I WON'T CATCH UP WITH THE LIEUTENANT AND THE OTHERS IN TIME. THEY'LL BE AT THE AIRSTRIP BY NOW – READY TO TAKE IT!
Sure enough –
OKAY, LADS – THIS WILL BE A PIECE OF CAKE. NOT TOO MANY GUARDS TO BOTHER A MARINE FORCE.
CHARGE!
YOU HEARD THE LIEUTENANT! LET'S GO!

"IT'S UP TO ME AND THIS LEE-ENFIELD TO PIN THEM DOWN!"

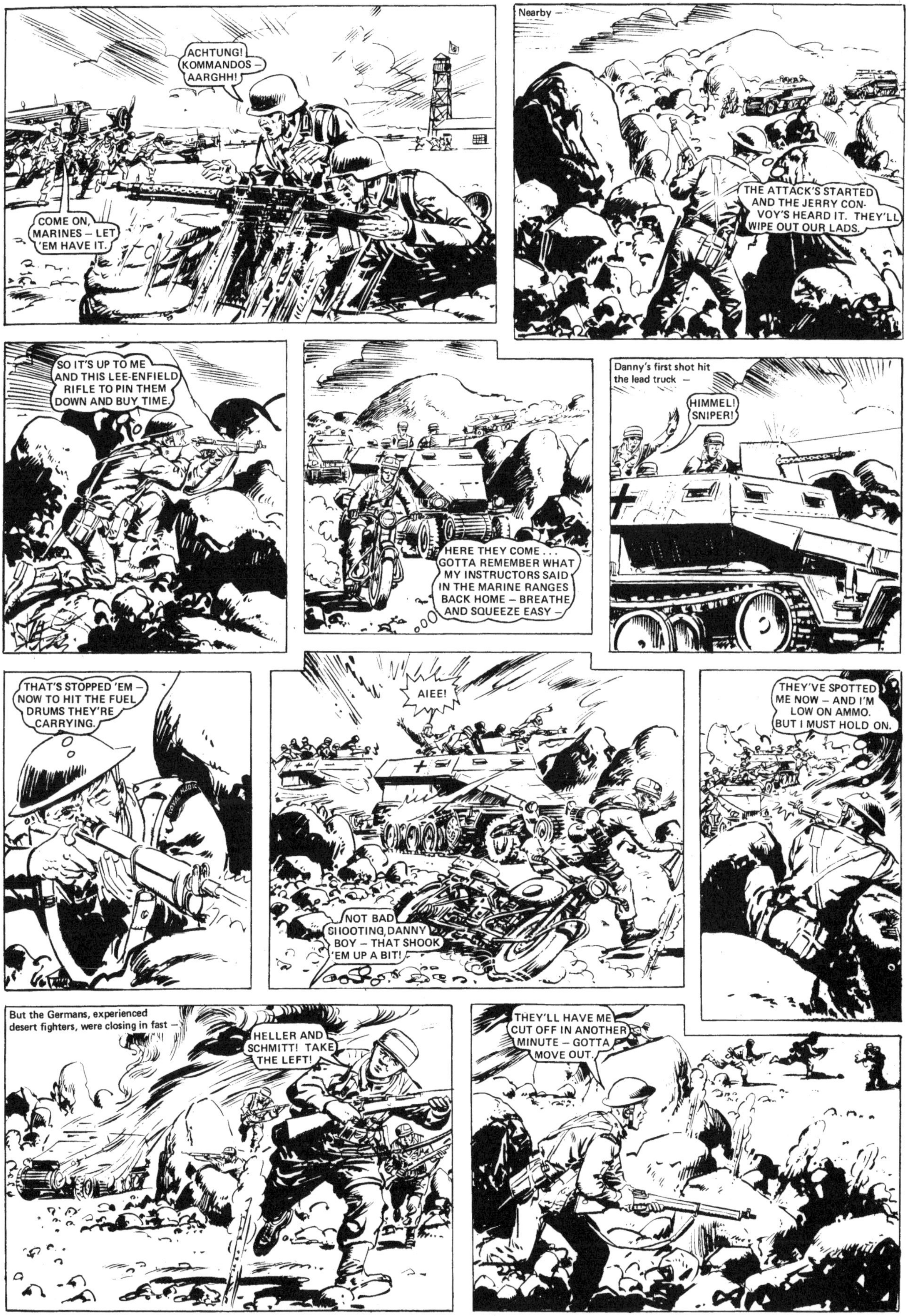

ACHTUNG! KOMMANDOS – AARGHH!
COME ON, MARINES – LET 'EM HAVE IT.
Nearby –
THE ATTACK'S STARTED AND THE JERRY CON-VOY'S HEARD IT. THEY'LL WIPE OUT OUR LADS.
SO IT'S UP TO ME AND THIS LEE-ENFIELD RIFLE TO PIN THEM DOWN AND BUY TIME.
HERE THEY COME . . . GOTTA REMEMBER WHAT MY INSTRUCTORS SAID IN THE MARINE RANGES BACK HOME – BREATHE AND SQUEEZE EASY –
Danny's first shot hit the lead truck –
HIMMEL! SNIPER!
THAT'S STOPPED 'EM – NOW TO HIT THE FUEL DRUMS THEY'RE CARRYING.
AIEE!
NOT BAD SHOOTING, DANNY BOY – THAT SHOOK 'EM UP A BIT!
THEY'VE SPOTTED ME NOW – AND I'M LOW ON AMMO. BUT I MUST HOLD ON.
But the Germans, experienced desert fighters, were closing in fast –
HELLER AND SCHMITT! TAKE THE LEFT!
THEY'LL HAVE ME CUT OFF IN ANOTHER MINUTE – GOTTA MOVE OUT.

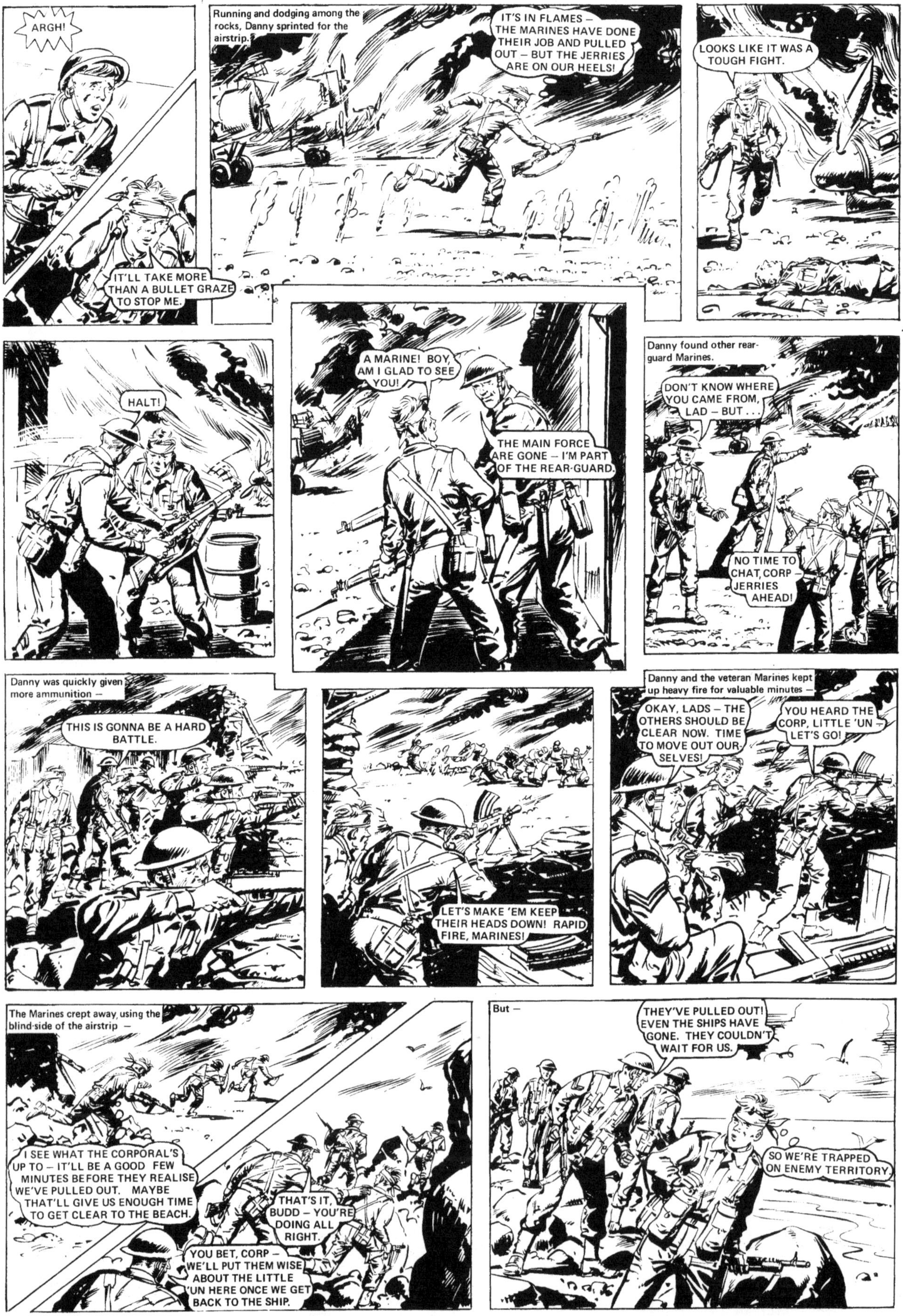

ARGH!
IT'LL TAKE MORE THAN A BULLET GRAZE TO STOP ME.
Running and dodging among the rocks, Danny sprinted for the airstrip.
IT'S IN FLAMES — THE MARINES HAVE DONE THEIR JOB AND PULLED OUT — BUT THE JERRIES ARE ON OUR HEELS!
LOOKS LIKE IT WAS A TOUGH FIGHT.
HALT!
A MARINE! BOY, AM I GLAD TO SEE YOU!
THE MAIN FORCE ARE GONE — I'M PART OF THE REAR-GUARD.
Danny found other rear-guard Marines.
DON'T KNOW WHERE YOU CAME FROM, LAD — BUT . . .
NO TIME TO CHAT, CORP — JERRIES AHEAD!
Danny was quickly given more ammunition —
THIS IS GONNA BE A HARD BATTLE.
LET'S MAKE 'EM KEEP THEIR HEADS DOWN! RAPID FIRE, MARINES!
Danny and the veteran Marines kept up heavy fire for valuable minutes —
OKAY, LADS — THE OTHERS SHOULD BE CLEAR NOW. TIME TO MOVE OUT OURSELVES!
YOU HEARD THE CORP, LITTLE 'UN — LET'S GO!
The Marines crept away, using the blind-side of the airstrip —
I SEE WHAT THE CORPORAL'S UP TO — IT'LL BE A GOOD FEW MINUTES BEFORE THEY REALISE WE'VE PULLED OUT. MAYBE THAT'LL GIVE US ENOUGH TIME TO GET CLEAR TO THE BEACH.
THAT'S IT, BUDD — YOU'RE DOING ALL RIGHT.
YOU BET, CORP — WE'LL PUT THEM WISE ABOUT THE LITTLE 'UN HERE ONCE WE GET BACK TO THE SHIP.
But —
THEY'VE PULLED OUT! EVEN THE SHIPS HAVE GONE. THEY COULDN'T WAIT FOR US.
SO WE'RE TRAPPED ON ENEMY TERRITORY.

...MISSION ENDS...MISSION ENDS...MISSION ENDS...MISSION ENDS...MISSION ENDS...MISSION ENDS...MISSION E

RAT PACK

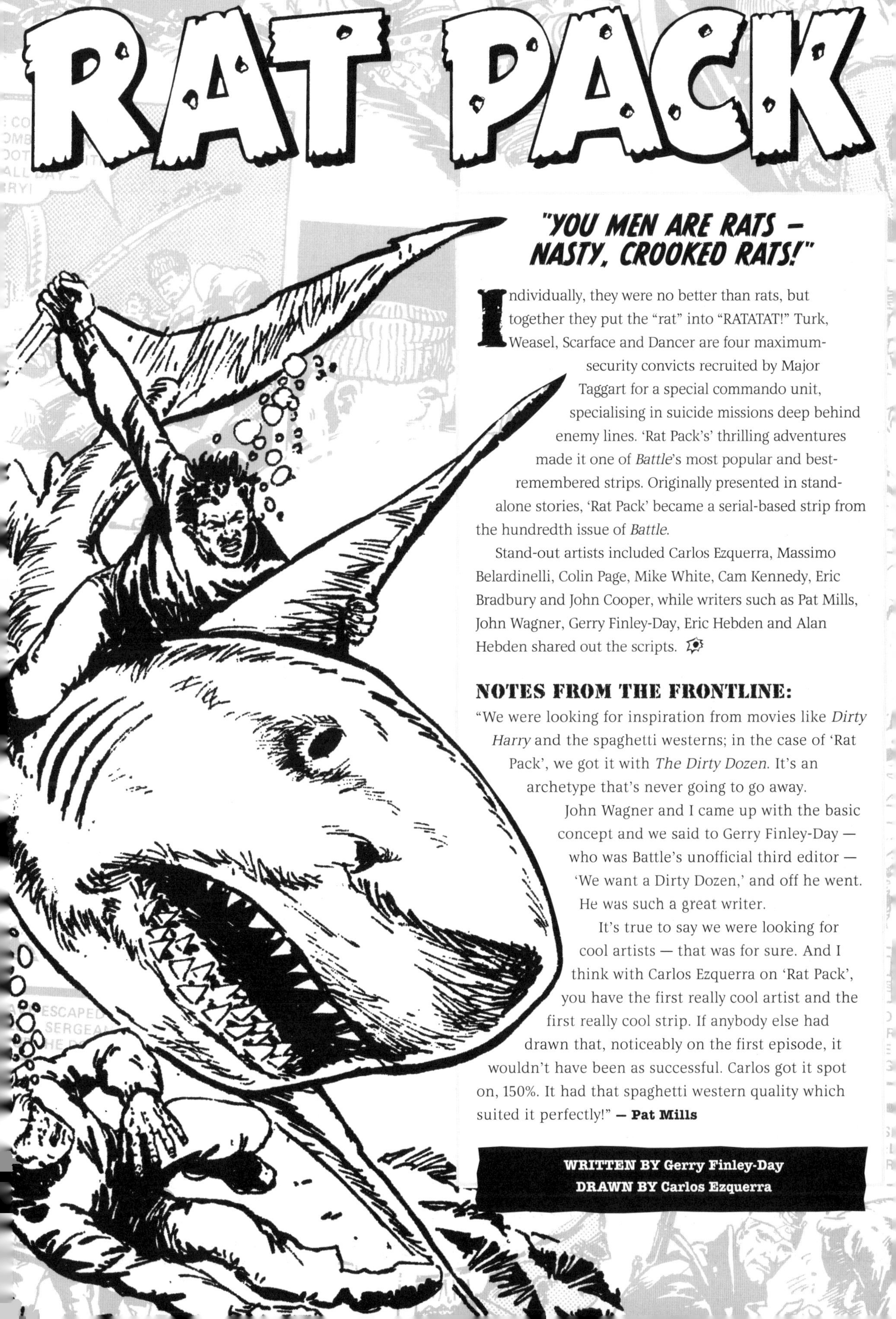

"YOU MEN ARE RATS – NASTY, CROOKED RATS!"

Individually, they were no better than rats, but together they put the "rat" into "RATATAT!" Turk, Weasel, Scarface and Dancer are four maximum-security convicts recruited by Major Taggart for a special commando unit, specialising in suicide missions deep behind enemy lines. 'Rat Pack's' thrilling adventures made it one of *Battle*'s most popular and best-remembered strips. Originally presented in stand-alone stories, 'Rat Pack' became a serial-based strip from the hundredth issue of *Battle*.

Stand-out artists included Carlos Ezquerra, Massimo Belardinelli, Colin Page, Mike White, Cam Kennedy, Eric Bradbury and John Cooper, while writers such as Pat Mills, John Wagner, Gerry Finley-Day, Eric Hebden and Alan Hebden shared out the scripts.

NOTES FROM THE FRONTLINE:

"We were looking for inspiration from movies like *Dirty Harry* and the spaghetti westerns; in the case of 'Rat Pack', we got it with *The Dirty Dozen*. It's an archetype that's never going to go away.

John Wagner and I came up with the basic concept and we said to Gerry Finley-Day — who was Battle's unofficial third editor — 'We want a Dirty Dozen,' and off he went. He was such a great writer.

It's true to say we were looking for cool artists — that was for sure. And I think with Carlos Ezquerra on 'Rat Pack', you have the first really cool artist and the first really cool strip. If anybody else had drawn that, noticeably on the first episode, it wouldn't have been as successful. Carlos got it spot on, 150%. It had that spaghetti western quality which suited it perfectly!" — **Pat Mills**

WRITTEN BY Gerry Finley-Day
DRAWN BY Carlos Ezquerra

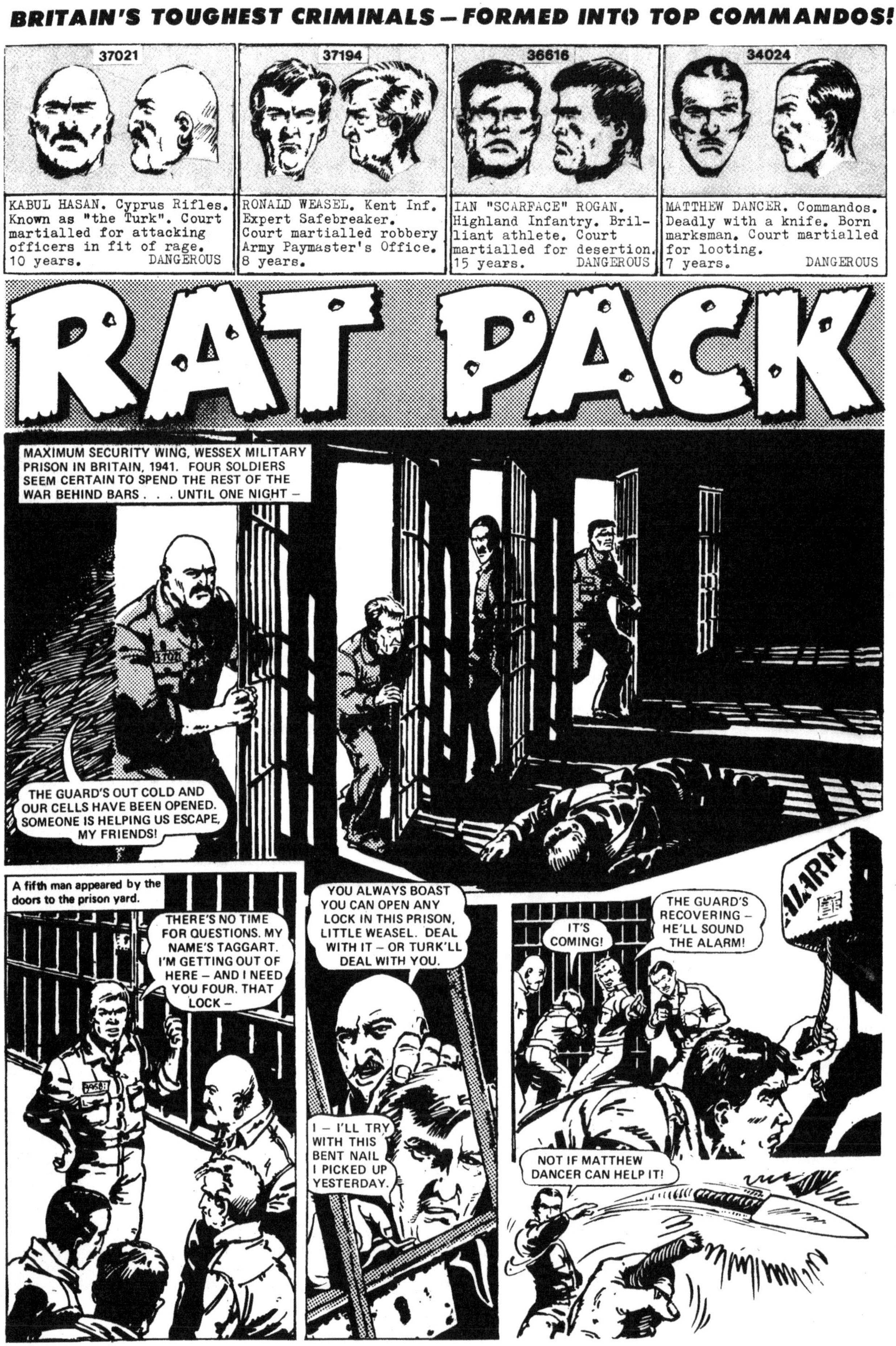
BRITAIN'S TOUGHEST CRIMINALS – FORMED INTO TOP COMMANDOS!
37021
KABUL HASAN. Cyprus Rifles. Known as "the Turk". Court martialled for attacking officers in fit of rage. 10 years. DANGEROUS
37194
RONALD WEASEL. Kent Inf. Expert Safebreaker. Court martialled robbery Army Paymaster's Office. 8 years.
36616
IAN "SCARFACE" ROGAN. Highland Infantry. Brilliant athlete. Court martialled for desertion. 15 years. DANGEROUS
34024
MATTHEW DANCER. Commandos. Deadly with a knife. Born marksman. Court martialled for looting. 7 years. DANGEROUS
RAT PACK
MAXIMUM SECURITY WING, WESSEX MILITARY PRISON IN BRITAIN, 1941. FOUR SOLDIERS SEEM CERTAIN TO SPEND THE REST OF THE WAR BEHIND BARS . . . UNTIL ONE NIGHT –
THE GUARD'S OUT COLD AND OUR CELLS HAVE BEEN OPENED. SOMEONE IS HELPING US ESCAPE, MY FRIENDS!
A fifth man appeared by the doors to the prison yard.
THERE'S NO TIME FOR QUESTIONS. MY NAME'S TAGGART. I'M GETTING OUT OF HERE – AND I NEED YOU FOUR. THAT LOCK –
YOU ALWAYS BOAST YOU CAN OPEN ANY LOCK IN THIS PRISON, LITTLE WEASEL. DEAL WITH IT – OR TURK'LL DEAL WITH YOU.
I – I'LL TRY WITH THIS BENT NAIL I PICKED UP YESTERDAY.
IT'S COMING!
THE GUARD'S RECOVERING – HE'LL SOUND THE ALARM!
ALARM
NOT IF MATTHEW DANCER CAN HELP IT!

"THE IMPORTANT THING IS WE ARE FREE!"

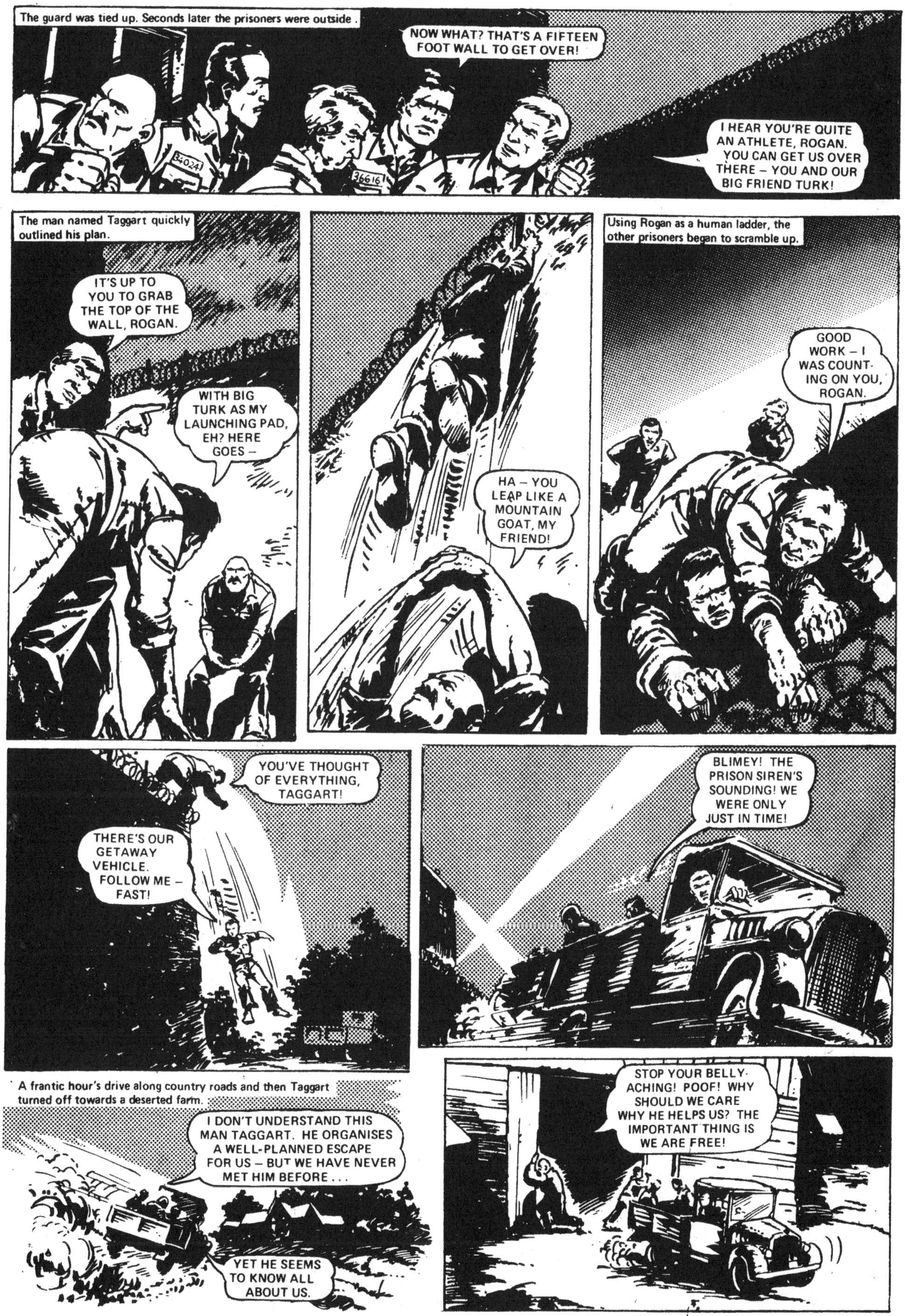

The guard was tied up. Seconds later the prisoners were outside .
NOW WHAT? THAT'S A FIFTEEN FOOT WALL TO GET OVER!
34024
36616
I HEAR YOU'RE QUITE AN ATHLETE, ROGAN. YOU CAN GET US OVER THERE – YOU AND OUR BIG FRIEND TURK!
The man named Taggart quickly outlined his plan.
IT'S UP TO YOU TO GRAB THE TOP OF THE WALL, ROGAN.
WITH BIG TURK AS MY LAUNCHING PAD, EH? HERE GOES –
HA – YOU LEAP LIKE A MOUNTAIN GOAT, MY FRIEND!
Using Rogan as a human ladder, the other prisoners began to scramble up.
GOOD WORK – I WAS COUNTING ON YOU, ROGAN.
YOU'VE THOUGHT OF EVERYTHING, TAGGART!
THERE'S OUR GETAWAY VEHICLE. FOLLOW ME – FAST!
BLIMEY! THE PRISON SIREN'S SOUNDING! WE WERE ONLY JUST IN TIME!
A frantic hour's drive along country roads and then Taggart turned off towards a deserted farm.
I DON'T UNDERSTAND THIS MAN TAGGART. HE ORGANISES A WELL-PLANNED ESCAPE FOR US – BUT WE HAVE NEVER MET HIM BEFORE . . .
YET HE SEEMS TO KNOW ALL ABOUT US.
STOP YOUR BELLY-ACHING! POOF! WHY SHOULD WE CARE WHY HE HELPS US? THE IMPORTANT THING IS WE ARE FREE!

"YOU MEN ARE RATS — "

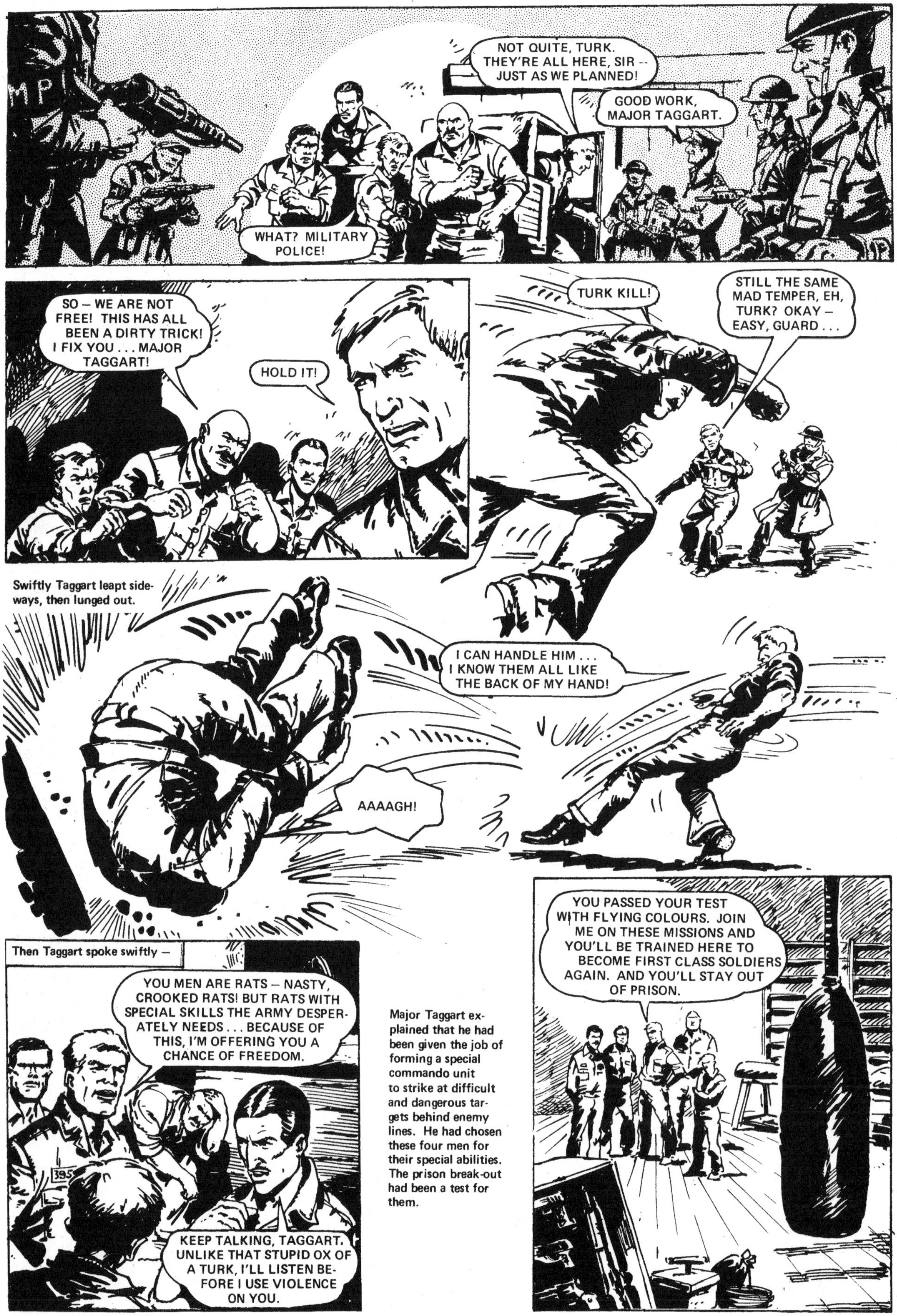

NOT QUITE, TURK. THEY'RE ALL HERE, SIR -- JUST AS WE PLANNED!
GOOD WORK, MAJOR TAGGART.
WHAT? MILITARY POLICE!
MP
SO — WE ARE NOT FREE! THIS HAS ALL BEEN A DIRTY TRICK! I FIX YOU . . . MAJOR TAGGART!
HOLD IT!
TURK KILL!
STILL THE SAME MAD TEMPER, EH, TURK? OKAY — EASY, GUARD . . .
Swiftly Taggart leapt sideways, then lunged out.
I CAN HANDLE HIM . . . I KNOW THEM ALL LIKE THE BACK OF MY HAND!
AAAAGH!
Then Taggart spoke swiftly —
YOU MEN ARE RATS — NASTY, CROOKED RATS! BUT RATS WITH SPECIAL SKILLS THE ARMY DESPERATELY NEEDS . . . BECAUSE OF THIS, I'M OFFERING YOU A CHANCE OF FREEDOM.
KEEP TALKING, TAGGART. UNLIKE THAT STUPID OX OF A TURK, I'LL LISTEN BEFORE I USE VIOLENCE ON YOU.
Major Taggart explained that he had been given the job of forming a special commando unit to strike at difficult and dangerous targets behind enemy lines. He had chosen these four men for their special abilities. The prison break-out had been a test for them.
YOU PASSED YOUR TEST WITH FLYING COLOURS. JOIN ME ON THESE MISSIONS AND YOU'LL BE TRAINED HERE TO BECOME FIRST CLASS SOLDIERS AGAIN. AND YOU'LL STAY OUT OF PRISON.

"THIS JOB COULD BE SUICIDE."

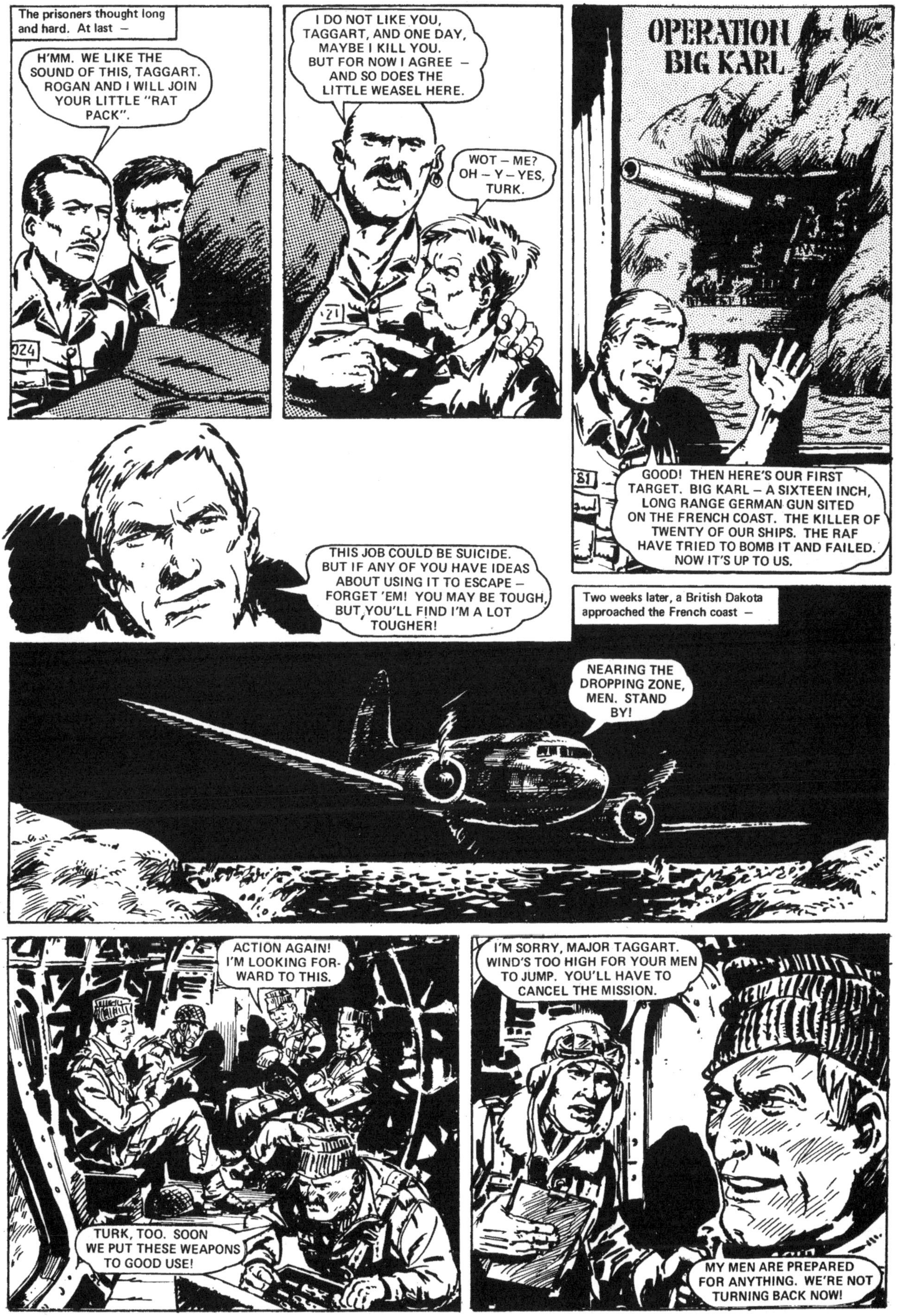

The prisoners thought long and hard. At last –
H'MM. WE LIKE THE SOUND OF THIS, TAGGART. ROGAN AND I WILL JOIN YOUR LITTLE "RAT PACK".
024
I DO NOT LIKE YOU, TAGGART, AND ONE DAY, MAYBE I KILL YOU. BUT FOR NOW I AGREE – AND SO DOES THE LITTLE WEASEL HERE.
WOT – ME? OH – Y – YES, TURK.
21
OPERATION BIG KARL
81
GOOD! THEN HERE'S OUR FIRST TARGET. BIG KARL – A SIXTEEN INCH, LONG RANGE GERMAN GUN SITED ON THE FRENCH COAST. THE KILLER OF TWENTY OF OUR SHIPS. THE RAF HAVE TRIED TO BOMB IT AND FAILED. NOW IT'S UP TO US.
THIS JOB COULD BE SUICIDE. BUT IF ANY OF YOU HAVE IDEAS ABOUT USING IT TO ESCAPE – FORGET 'EM! YOU MAY BE TOUGH, BUT YOU'LL FIND I'M A LOT TOUGHER!
Two weeks later, a British Dakota approached the French coast –
NEARING THE DROPPING ZONE, MEN. STAND BY!
ACTION AGAIN! I'M LOOKING FORWARD TO THIS.
TURK, TOO. SOON WE PUT THESE WEAPONS TO GOOD USE!
I'M SORRY, MAJOR TAGGART. WIND'S TOO HIGH FOR YOUR MEN TO JUMP. YOU'LL HAVE TO CANCEL THE MISSION.
MY MEN ARE PREPARED FOR ANYTHING. WE'RE NOT TURNING BACK NOW!

"I'LL BE KILLED!"

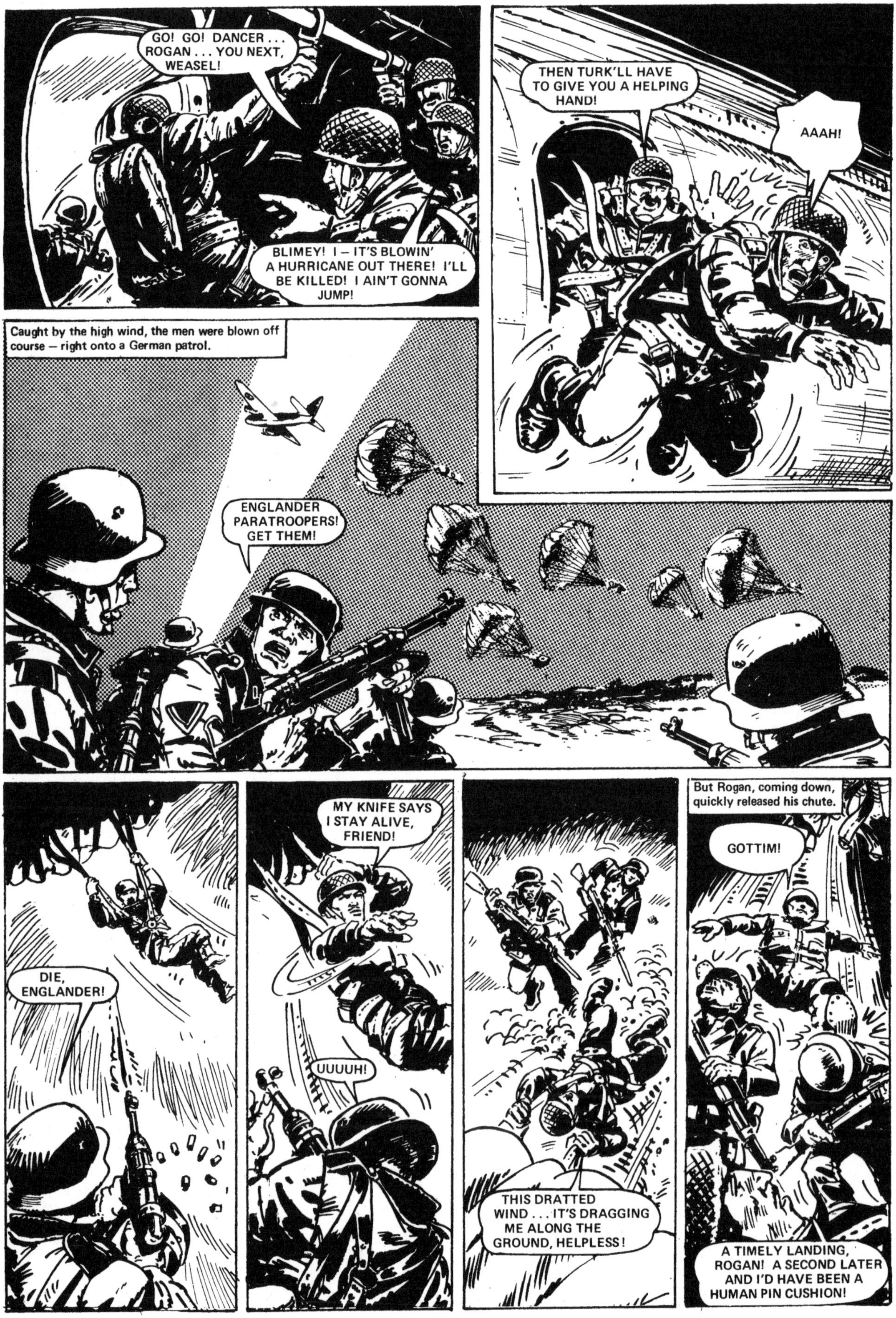
GO! GO! DANCER . . . ROGAN . . . YOU NEXT, WEASEL!
BLIMEY! I – IT'S BLOWIN' A HURRICANE OUT THERE! I'LL BE KILLED! I AIN'T GONNA JUMP!
THEN TURK'LL HAVE TO GIVE YOU A HELPING HAND!
AAAH!
Caught by the high wind, the men were blown off course – right onto a German patrol.
ENGLANDER PARATROOPERS! GET THEM!
DIE, ENGLANDER!
MY KNIFE SAYS I STAY ALIVE, FRIEND!
UUUUH!
THIS DRATTED WIND . . . IT'S DRAGGING ME ALONG THE GROUND, HELPLESS!
But Rogan, coming down, quickly released his chute.
GOTTIM!
A TIMELY LANDING, ROGAN! A SECOND LATER AND I'D HAVE BEEN A HUMAN PIN CUSHION!

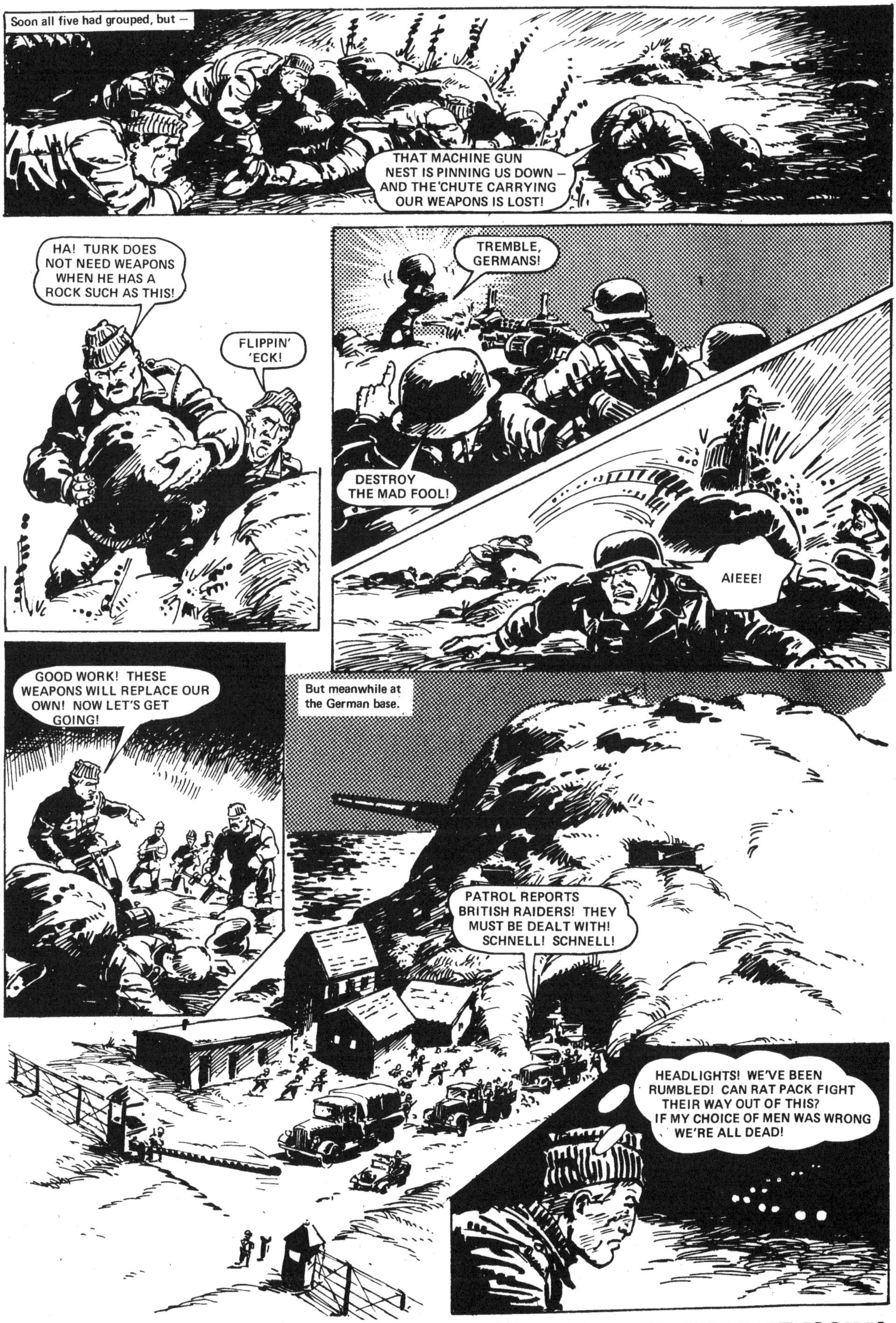
Soon all five had grouped, but —
THAT MACHINE GUN NEST IS PINNING US DOWN — AND THE 'CHUTE CARRYING OUR WEAPONS IS LOST!
HA! TURK DOES NOT NEED WEAPONS WHEN HE HAS A ROCK SUCH AS THIS!
FLIPPIN' 'ECK!
TREMBLE, GERMANS!
DESTROY THE MAD FOOL!
AIEEE!
GOOD WORK! THESE WEAPONS WILL REPLACE OUR OWN! NOW LET'S GET GOING!
But meanwhile at the German base.
PATROL REPORTS BRITISH RAIDERS! THEY MUST BE DEALT WITH! SCHNELL! SCHNELL!
HEADLIGHTS! WE'VE BEEN RUMBLED! CAN RAT PACK FIGHT THEIR WAY OUT OF THIS? IF MY CHOICE OF MEN WAS WRONG WE'RE ALL DEAD!

GREAT ACTION FROM THE RAT PACK IN THE NEXT FREE GIFT ISSUE!

BEHIND ENEMY LINES WITH THE MEN KNOWN AS –

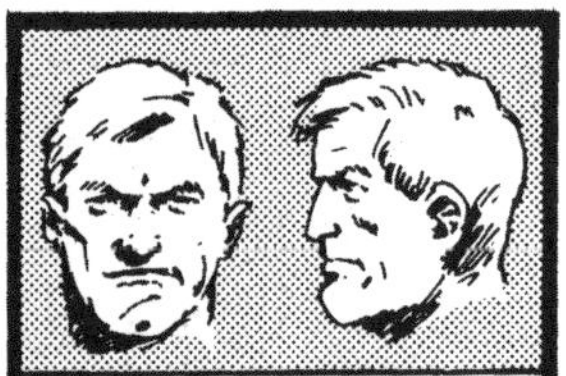

MAJOR TAGGART. Special Services Commando. Leader and founder of RAT.PACK. No mission too dangerous for this man.

RAT PACK

THE CONVICT COMMANDOS ON A SUICIDE MISSION–TO DESTROY A HUGE GERMAN GUN... OR DIE!

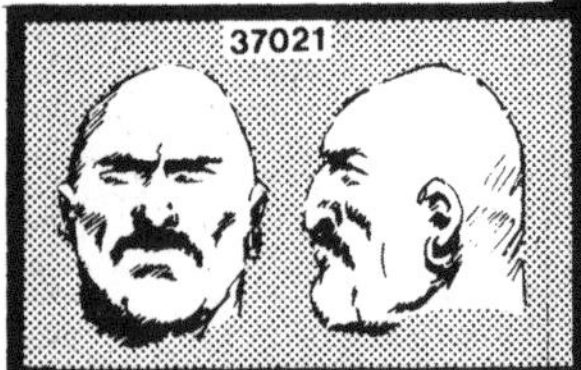
37021

KABUL HASAN. Cyprus Rifles. Known as "the Turk". Court martialled for attacking officers in fit of rage. 10 years. DANGEROUS

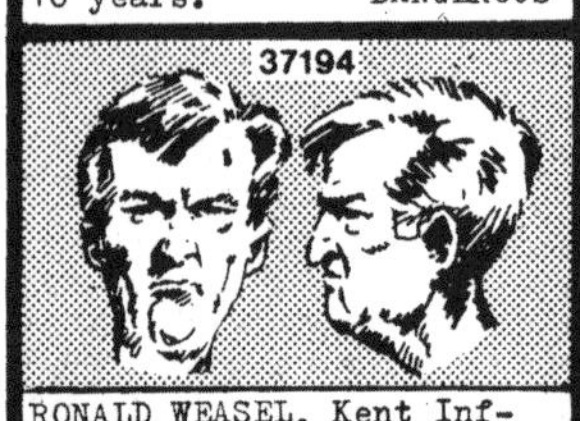
37194

RONALD WEASEL. Kent Infantry. Expert Safebreaker. Court martialled robbery Army Paymaster's Office. 8 years.

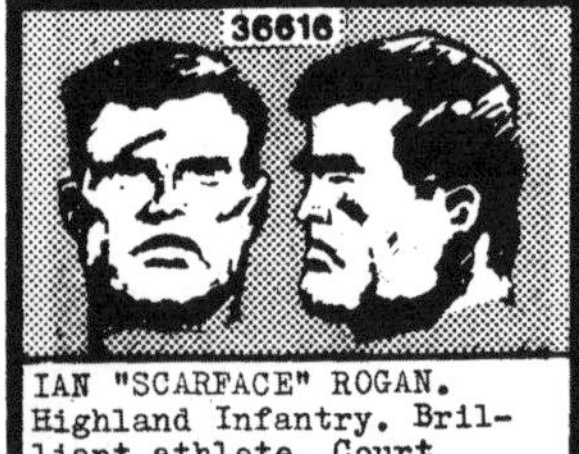
36616

IAN "SCARFACE" ROGAN. Highland Infantry. Brilliant athlete. Court martialled for desertion. 15 years. DANGEROUS

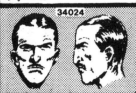

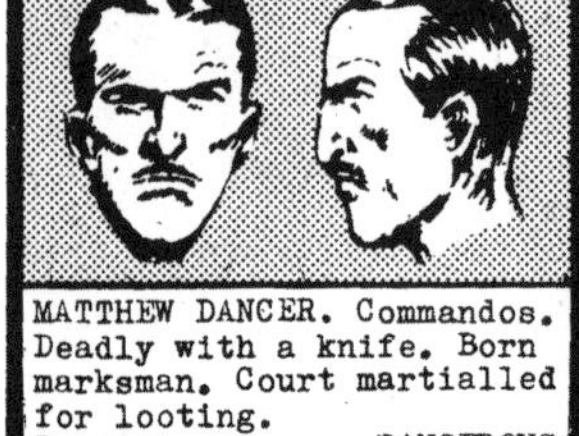
34024

MATTHEW DANCER. Commandos. Deadly with a knife. Born marksman. Court martialled for looting. 7 years. DANGEROUS

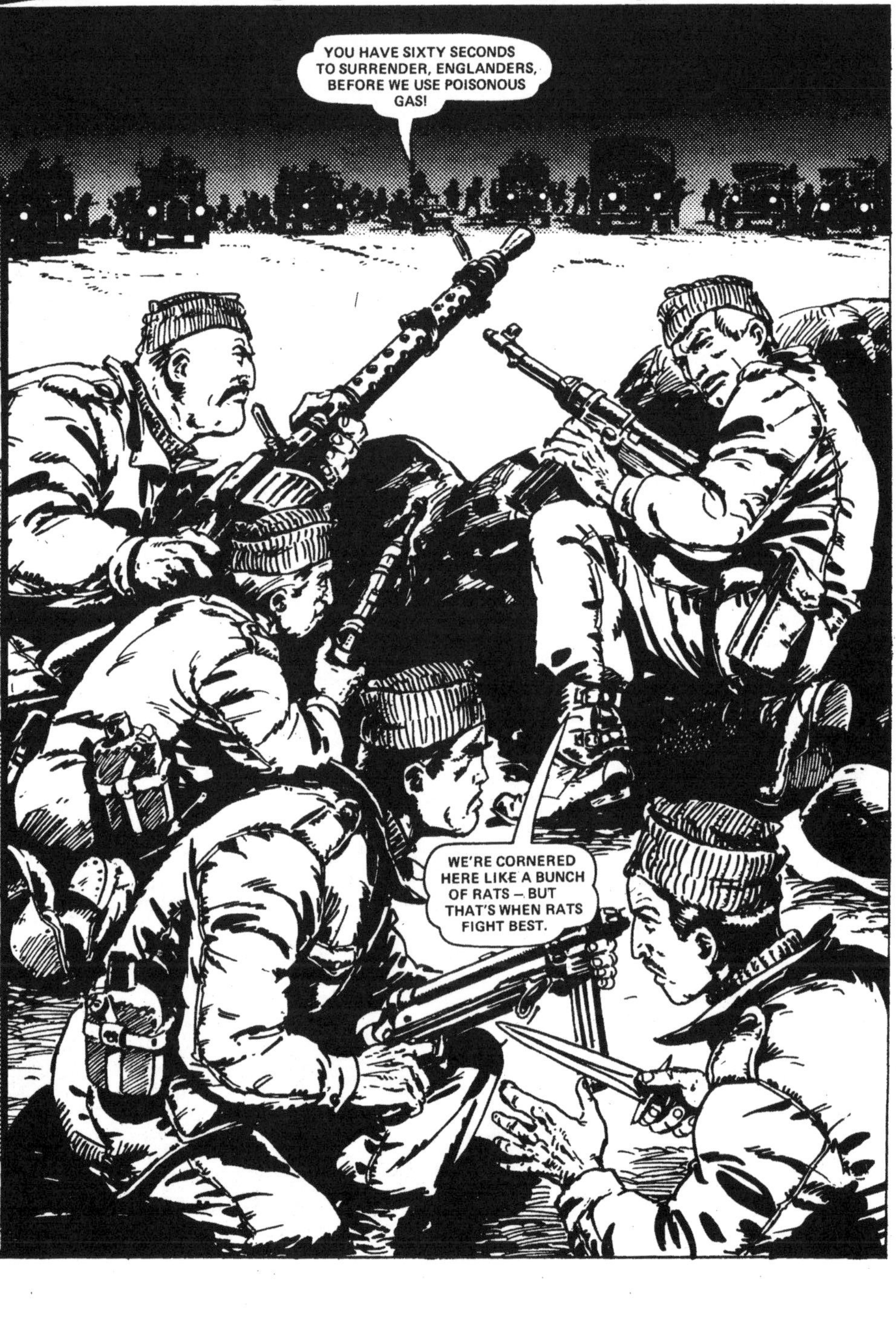
YOU HAVE SIXTY SECONDS TO SURRENDER, ENGLANDERS, BEFORE WE USE POISONOUS GAS!
WE'RE CORNERED HERE LIKE A BUNCH OF RATS – BUT THAT'S WHEN RATS FIGHT BEST.

"HERE COME THE GAS BOMBS!"

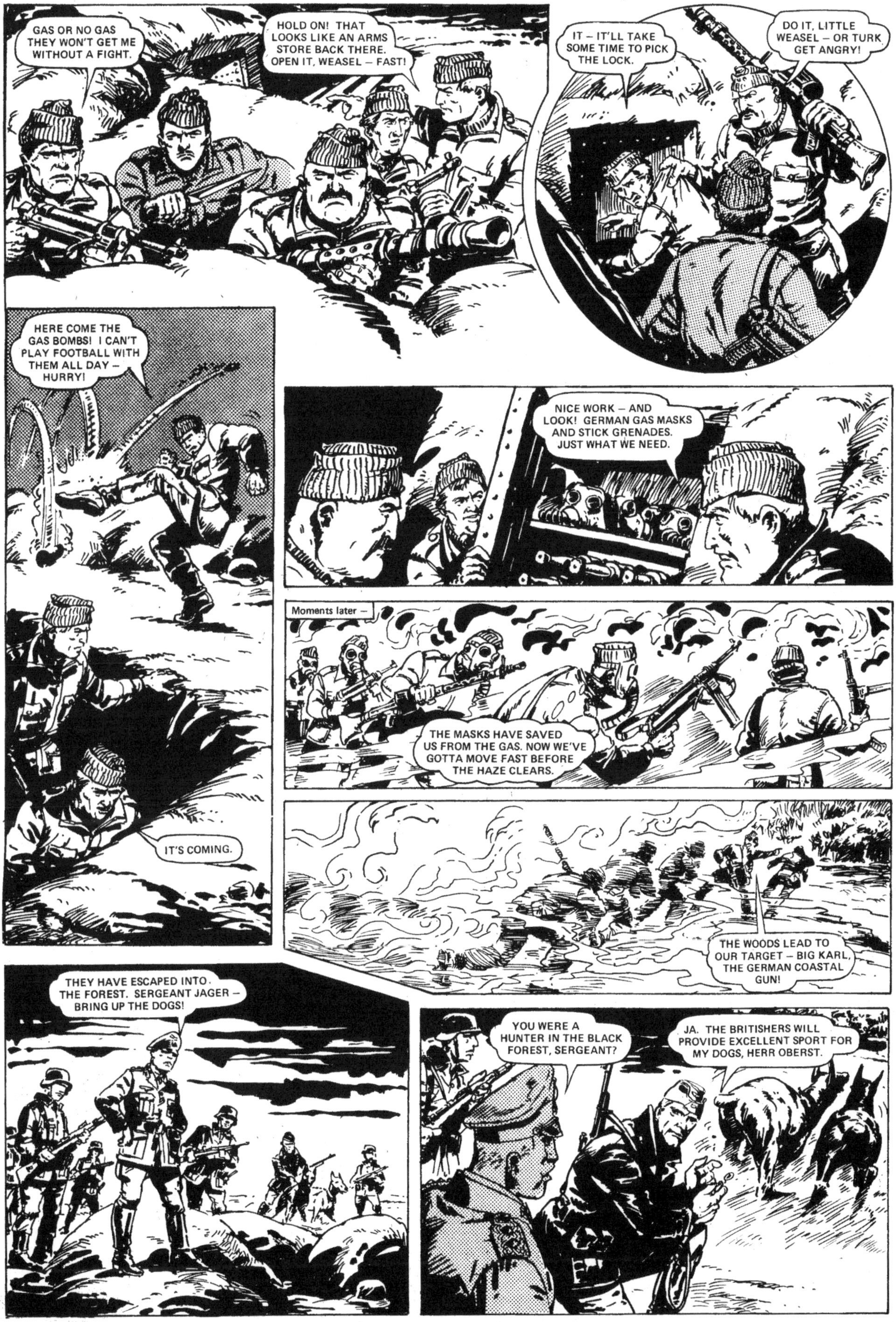

GAS OR NO GAS THEY WON'T GET ME WITHOUT A FIGHT.
HOLD ON! THAT LOOKS LIKE AN ARMS STORE BACK THERE. OPEN IT, WEASEL – FAST!
IT – IT'LL TAKE SOME TIME TO PICK THE LOCK.
DO IT, LITTLE WEASEL – OR TURK GET ANGRY!
HERE COME THE GAS BOMBS! I CAN'T PLAY FOOTBALL WITH THEM ALL DAY – HURRY!
IT'S COMING.
NICE WORK – AND LOOK! GERMAN GAS MASKS AND STICK GRENADES. JUST WHAT WE NEED.
Moments later –
THE MASKS HAVE SAVED US FROM THE GAS. NOW WE'VE GOTTA MOVE FAST BEFORE THE HAZE CLEARS.
THE WOODS LEAD TO OUR TARGET – BIG KARL, THE GERMAN COASTAL GUN!
THEY HAVE ESCAPED INTO THE FOREST. SERGEANT JAGER – BRING UP THE DOGS!
YOU WERE A HUNTER IN THE BLACK FOREST, SERGEANT?
JA. THE BRITISHERS WILL PROVIDE EXCELLENT SPORT FOR MY DOGS, HERR OBERST.

"THE TURK'S HAD IT."

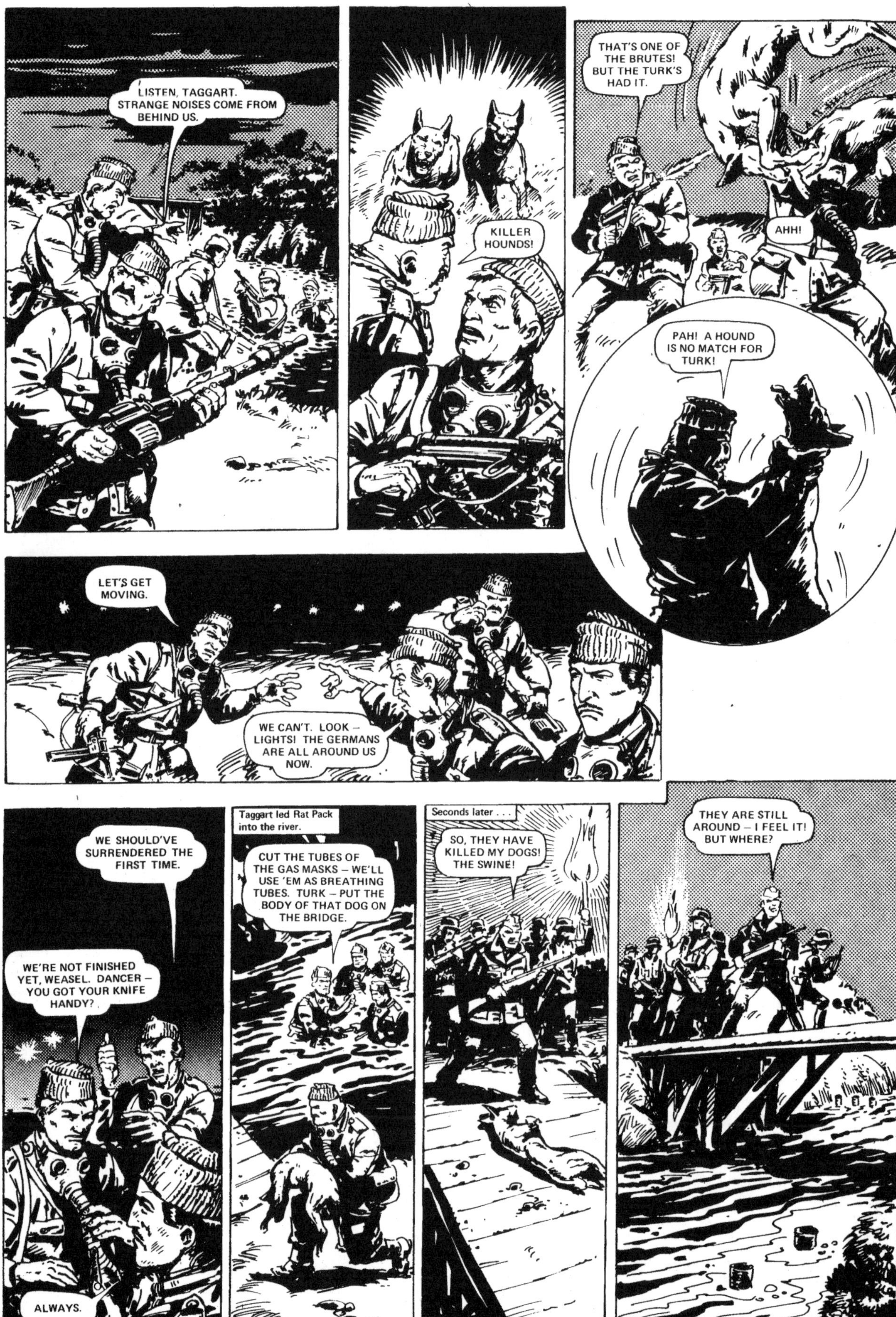

LISTEN, TAGGART. STRANGE NOISES COME FROM BEHIND US.
KILLER HOUNDS!
THAT'S ONE OF THE BRUTES! BUT THE TURK'S HAD IT.
AHH!
PAH! A HOUND IS NO MATCH FOR TURK!
LET'S GET MOVING.
WE CAN'T. LOOK – LIGHTS! THE GERMANS ARE ALL AROUND US NOW.
WE SHOULD'VE SURRENDERED THE FIRST TIME.
WE'RE NOT FINISHED YET, WEASEL. DANCER – YOU GOT YOUR KNIFE HANDY?
ALWAYS.
Taggart led Rat Pack into the river.
CUT THE TUBES OF THE GAS MASKS – WE'LL USE 'EM AS BREATHING TUBES. TURK – PUT THE BODY OF THAT DOG ON THE BRIDGE.
Seconds later . . .
SO, THEY HAVE KILLED MY DOGS! THE SWINE!
THEY ARE STILL AROUND – I FEEL IT! BUT WHERE?

"MAKE EVERY SHOT COUNT!"

Suddenly

HIMMEL!

AAAGHH!

WE'VE CAUGHT 'EM ON THE HOP! MAKE EVERY SHOT COUNT!

THE WATER'S JAMMED MY GUN!

NOW YOU WILL DIE!

NO YOU DON'T, LADDIE - TIME FOR YOUR EVENING BATH!

CRUDE BUT EFFECTIVE, ROGAN! I OWE YOU!

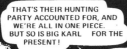

THAT'S THEIR HUNTING PARTY ACCOUNTED FOR, AND WE'RE ALL IN ONE PIECE. BUT SO IS BIG KARL FOR THE PRESENT!

ONE MOMENT, TAGGART

THE GERMANS KNOW WE'RE HERE. TO GO AFTER THE GUN NOW WILL BE SUICIDE.

YES, THIS MISSION COULD BE SUICIDE. THAT'S WHY CONVICTS WERE CHOSEN YOUR DEATHS WOULD BE NO LOSS TO ANYONE! BUT IF YOU PULL OUT, I'LL MAKE YOU SPEND THE REST OF YOUR LIVES BEHIND BARS!

HMMM . . . I'D RATHER DIE FIGHTING THAN ROT IN A PRISON.

YOU HOLD THE CARDS, TAGGART. FOR NOW I KILL GERMANS. BUT BEWARE - ONE DAY MAYBE I KILL YOU!

Soon Taggart and his men were on the hill overlooking Big Karl —

THE ENTRANCE DOWN THERE IS BUZZING WITH JERRIES. BUT THERE'S ANOTHER WAY TO GET TO IT — OVER THE TOP!

"ROGAN MOVES LIKE A CAT!"

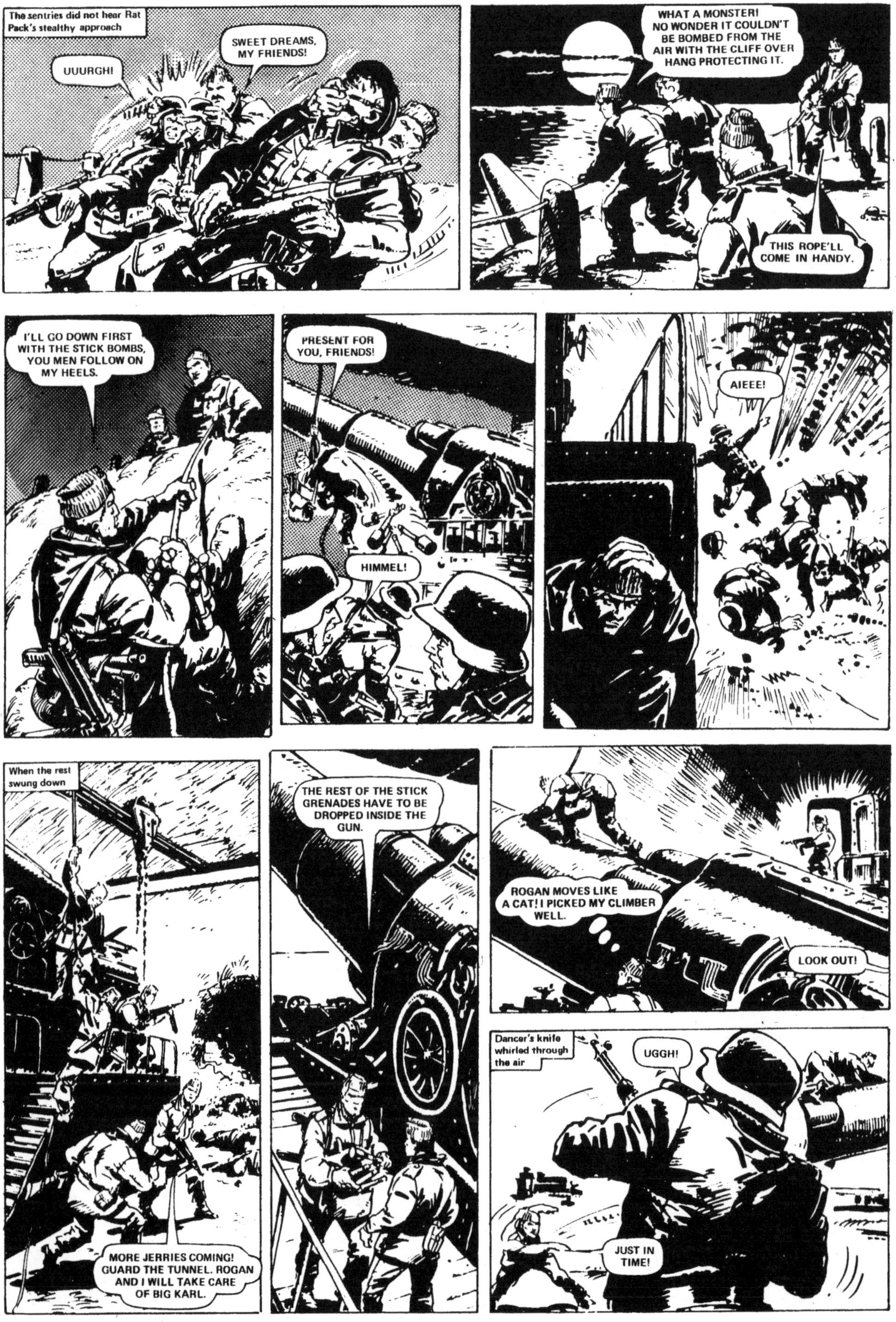

The sentries did not hear Rat Pack's stealthy approach
UUURGH!
SWEET DREAMS, MY FRIENDS!
WHAT A MONSTER! NO WONDER IT COULDN'T BE BOMBED FROM THE AIR WITH THE CLIFF OVER HANG PROTECTING IT.
THIS ROPE'LL COME IN HANDY.
I'LL GO DOWN FIRST WITH THE STICK BOMBS, YOU MEN FOLLOW ON MY HEELS.
PRESENT FOR YOU, FRIENDS!
HIMMEL!
AIEEE!
When the rest swung down
MORE JERRIES COMING! GUARD THE TUNNEL. ROGAN AND I WILL TAKE CARE OF BIG KARL.
THE REST OF THE STICK GRENADES HAVE TO BE DROPPED INSIDE THE GUN.
ROGAN MOVES LIKE A CAT! I PICKED MY CLIMBER WELL.
LOOK OUT!
Dancer's knife whirled through the air
UGGH!
JUST IN TIME!

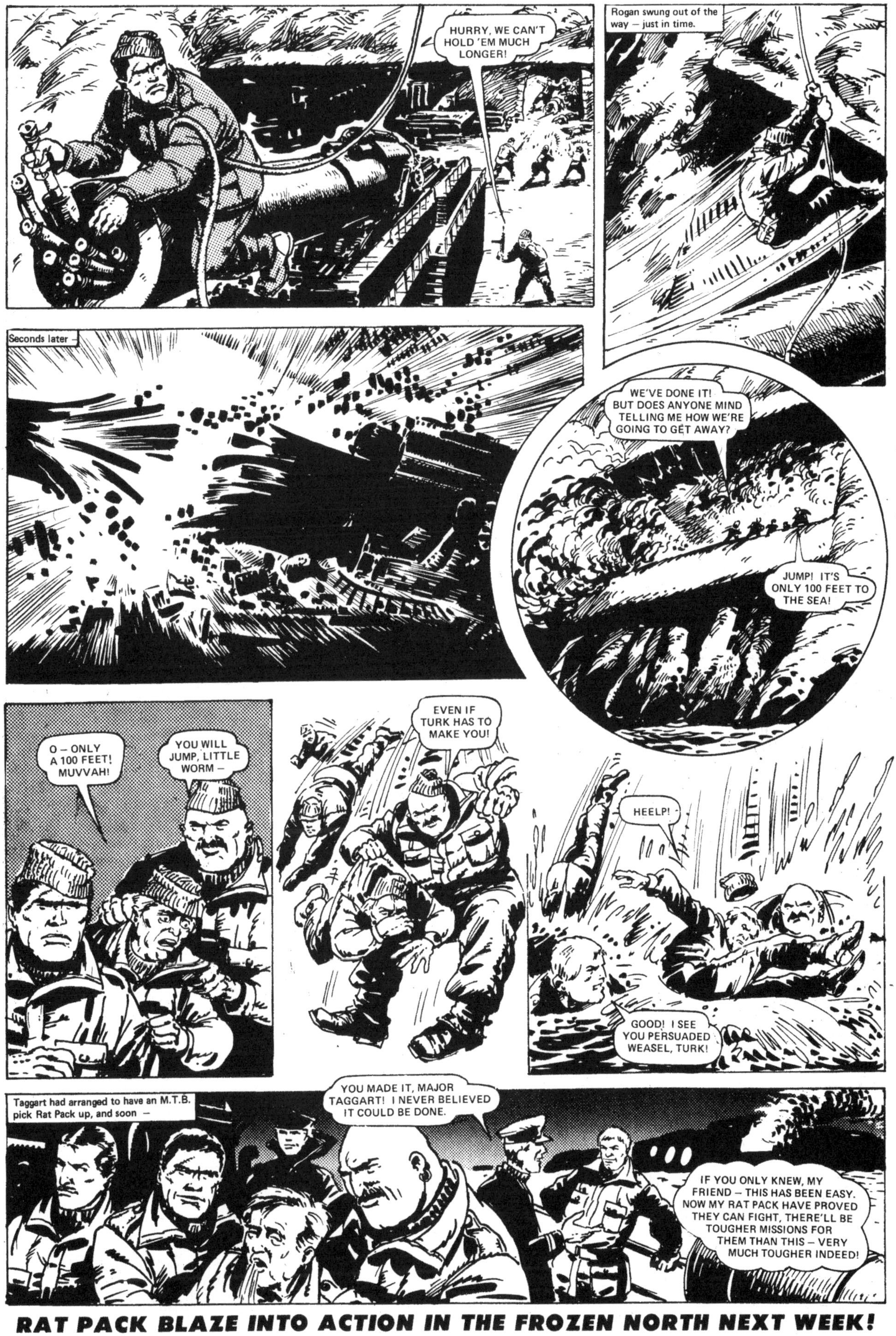

HURRY, WE CAN'T HOLD 'EM MUCH LONGER!
Rogan swung out of the way – just in time.
Seconds later –
WE'VE DONE IT! BUT DOES ANYONE MIND TELLING ME HOW WE'RE GOING TO GET AWAY?
JUMP! IT'S ONLY 100 FEET TO THE SEA!
O – ONLY A 100 FEET! MUVVAH!
YOU WILL JUMP, LITTLE WORM –
EVEN IF TURK HAS TO MAKE YOU!
HEELP!
GOOD! I SEE YOU PERSUADED WEASEL, TURK!
Taggart had arranged to have an M.T.B. pick Rat Pack up, and soon –
YOU MADE IT, MAJOR TAGGART! I NEVER BELIEVED IT COULD BE DONE.
IF YOU ONLY KNEW, MY FRIEND – THIS HAS BEEN EASY. NOW MY RAT PACK HAVE PROVED THEY CAN FIGHT, THERE'LL BE TOUGHER MISSIONS FOR THEM THAN THIS – VERY MUCH TOUGHER INDEED!

RAT PACK BLAZE INTO ACTION IN THE FROZEN NORTH NEXT WEEK!

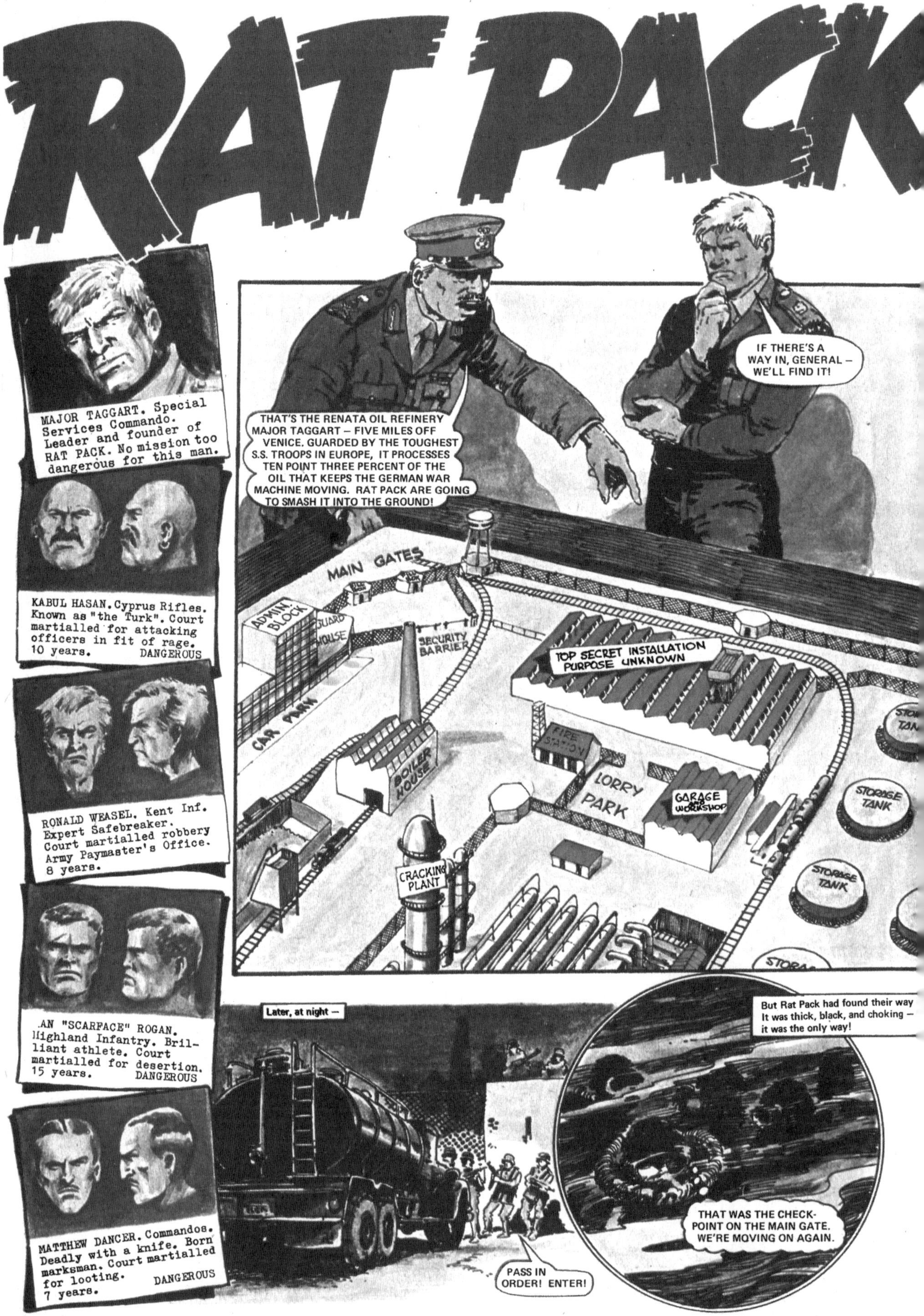

RAT PACK
MAJOR TAGGART. Special Services Commando. Leader and founder of RAT PACK. No mission too dangerous for this man.
KABUL HASAN. Cyprus Rifles. Known as "the Turk". Court martialled for attacking officers in fit of rage. 10 years. DANGEROUS
RONALD WEASEL. Kent Inf. Expert Safebreaker. Court martialled robbery Army Paymaster's Office. 8 years.
AN "SCARFACE" ROGAN. Highland Infantry. Brilliant athlete. Court martialled for desertion. 15 years. DANGEROUS
MATTHEW DANCER. Commandos. Deadly with a knife. Born marksman. Court martialled for looting. 7 years. DANGEROUS
THAT'S THE RENATA OIL REFINERY MAJOR TAGGART – FIVE MILES OFF VENICE. GUARDED BY THE TOUGHEST S.S. TROOPS IN EUROPE, IT PROCESSES TEN POINT THREE PERCENT OF THE OIL THAT KEEPS THE GERMAN WAR MACHINE MOVING. RAT PACK ARE GOING TO SMASH IT INTO THE GROUND!
IF THERE'S A WAY IN, GENERAL – WE'LL FIND IT!
MAIN GATES
ADMIN BLOCK
GUARD HOUSE
SECURITY BARRIER
TOP SECRET INSTALLATION PURPOSE UNKNOWN
CAR PARK
FIRE STATION
BOILER HOUSE
LORRY PARK
GARAGE AND WORKSHOP
STORAGE TANK
STORAGE TANK
CRACKING PLANT
Later, at night –
PASS IN ORDER! ENTER!
But Rat Pack had found their way It was thick, black, and choking – it was the only way!
THAT WAS THE CHECK-POINT ON THE MAIN GATE. WE'RE MOVING ON AGAIN.

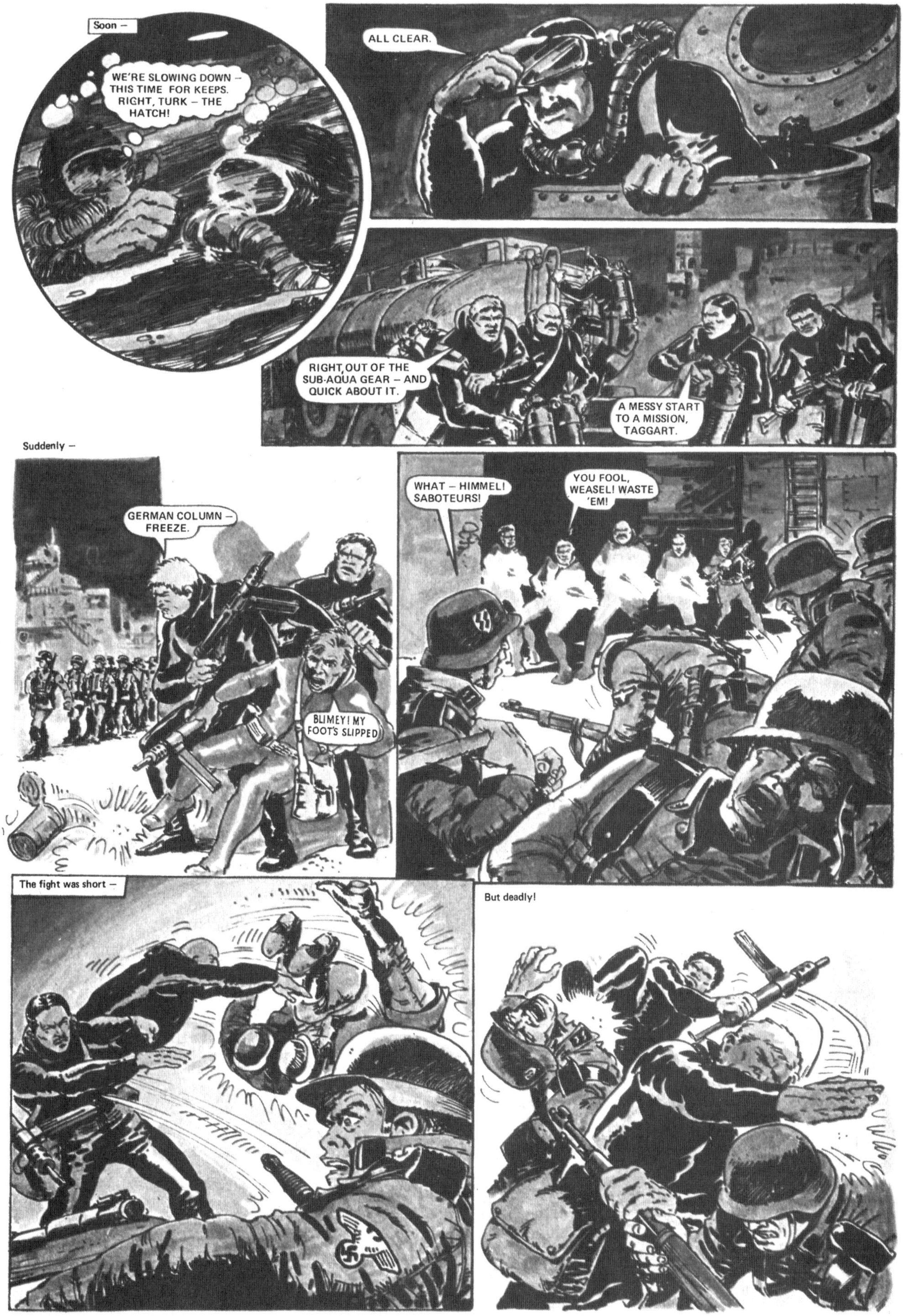
Soon –
WE'RE SLOWING DOWN – THIS TIME FOR KEEPS. RIGHT, TURK – THE HATCH!
ALL CLEAR.
RIGHT, OUT OF THE SUB-AQUA GEAR – AND QUICK ABOUT IT.
A MESSY START TO A MISSION, TAGGART.
Suddenly –
GERMAN COLUMN – FREEZE.
BLIMEY! MY FOOT'S SLIPPED
WHAT – HIMMEL! SABOTEURS!
YOU FOOL, WEASEL! WASTE 'EM!
The fight was short –
But deadly!

"ENEMY SABOTEURS HAVE PENETRATED THE REFINERY"

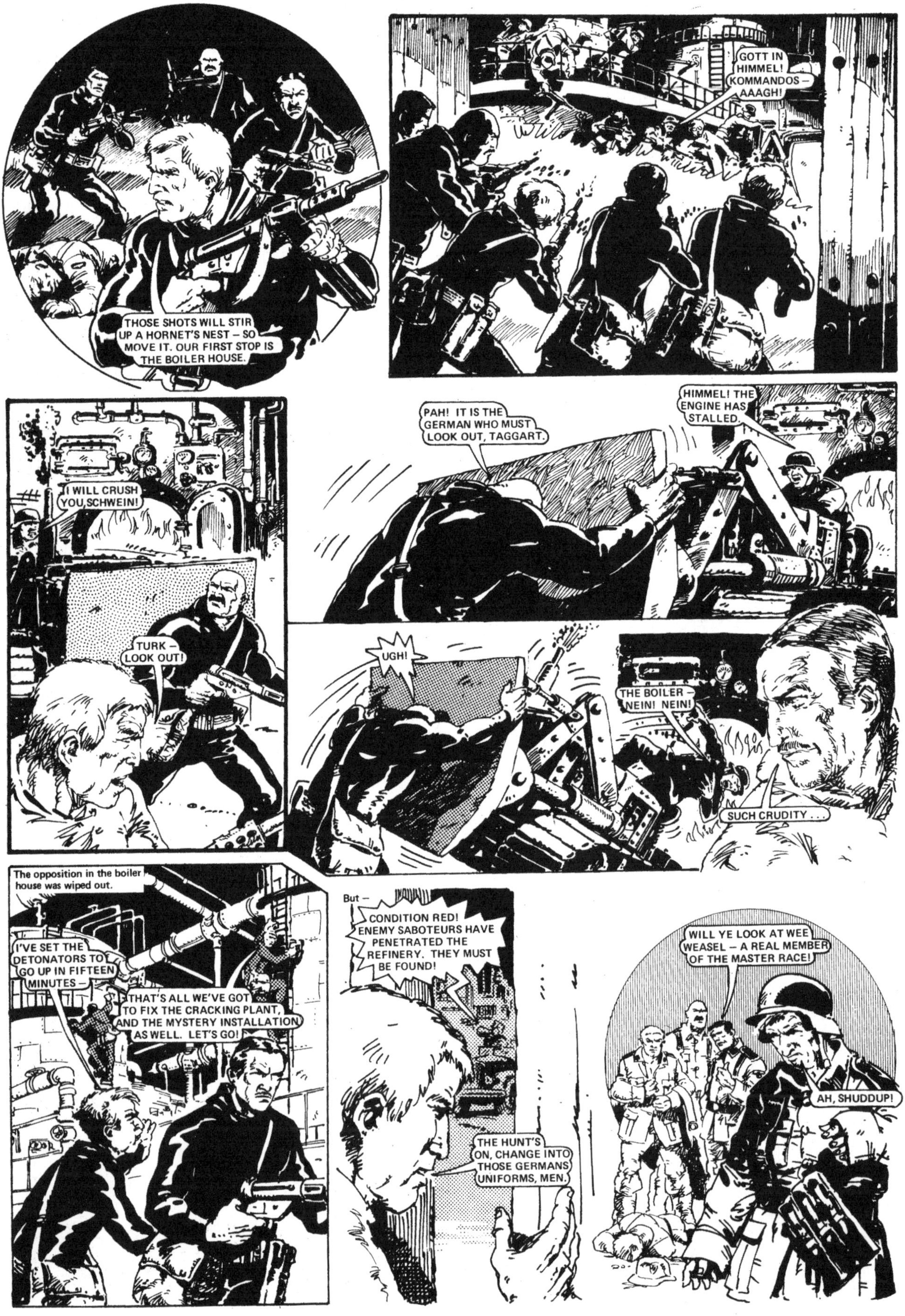

THOSE SHOTS WILL STIR UP A HORNET'S NEST – SO MOVE IT. OUR FIRST STOP IS THE BOILER HOUSE.
GOTT IN HIMMEL! KOMMANDOS – AAAGH!
I WILL CRUSH YOU,SCHWEIN!
TURK – LOOK OUT!
PAH! IT IS THE GERMAN WHO MUST LOOK OUT, TAGGART.
HIMMEL! THE ENGINE HAS STALLED.
UGH!
THE BOILER – NEIN! NEIN!
SUCH CRUDITY . . .
The opposition in the boiler house was wiped out.
I'VE SET THE DETONATORS TO GO UP IN FIFTEEN MINUTES –
THAT'S ALL WE'VE GOT TO FIX THE CRACKING PLANT, AND THE MYSTERY INSTALLATION AS WELL. LET'S GO!
But –
CONDITION RED! ENEMY SABOTEURS HAVE PENETRATED THE REFINERY. THEY MUST BE FOUND!
THE HUNT'S ON, CHANGE INTO THOSE GERMANS UNIFORMS, MEN.
WILL YE LOOK AT WEE WEASEL – A REAL MEMBER OF THE MASTER RACE!
AH, SHUDDUP!

"SLAP YOUR BOMBS ON THE SIDE, RATS."

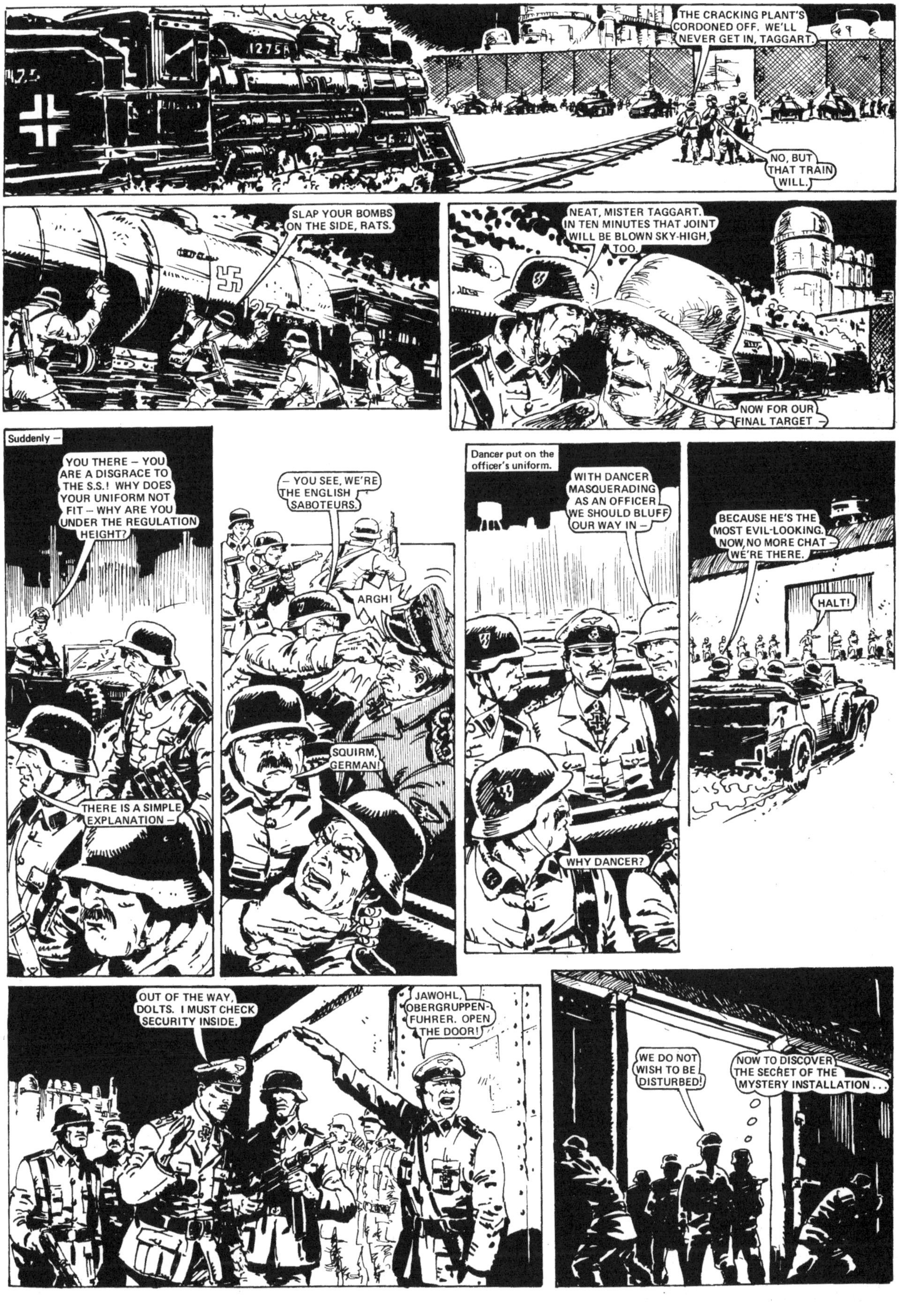

THE CRACKING PLANT'S CORDONED OFF. WE'LL NEVER GET IN, TAGGART.
NO, BUT THAT TRAIN WILL.
SLAP YOUR BOMBS ON THE SIDE, RATS.
NEAT, MISTER TAGGART. IN TEN MINUTES THAT JOINT WILL BE BLOWN SKY-HIGH, TOO.
NOW FOR OUR FINAL TARGET –
Suddenly –
YOU THERE – YOU ARE A DISGRACE TO THE S.S.! WHY DOES YOUR UNIFORM NOT FIT – WHY ARE YOU UNDER THE REGULATION HEIGHT?
THERE IS A SIMPLE EXPLANATION –
– YOU SEE, WE'RE THE ENGLISH SABOTEURS.
ARGH!
SQUIRM, GERMAN!
Dancer put on the officer's uniform.
WITH DANCER MASQUERADING AS AN OFFICER WE SHOULD BLUFF OUR WAY IN –
WHY DANCER?
BECAUSE HE'S THE MOST EVIL-LOOKING. NOW, NO MORE CHAT – WE'RE THERE.
HALT!
OUT OF THE WAY, DOLTS. I MUST CHECK SECURITY INSIDE.
JAWOHL, OBERGRUPPEN-FUHRER. OPEN THE DOOR!
WE DO NOT WISH TO BE DISTURBED!
NOW TO DISCOVER THE SECRET OF THE MYSTERY INSTALLATION . . .

"THE KRAUTS MUST HAVE A BATTERING RAM."

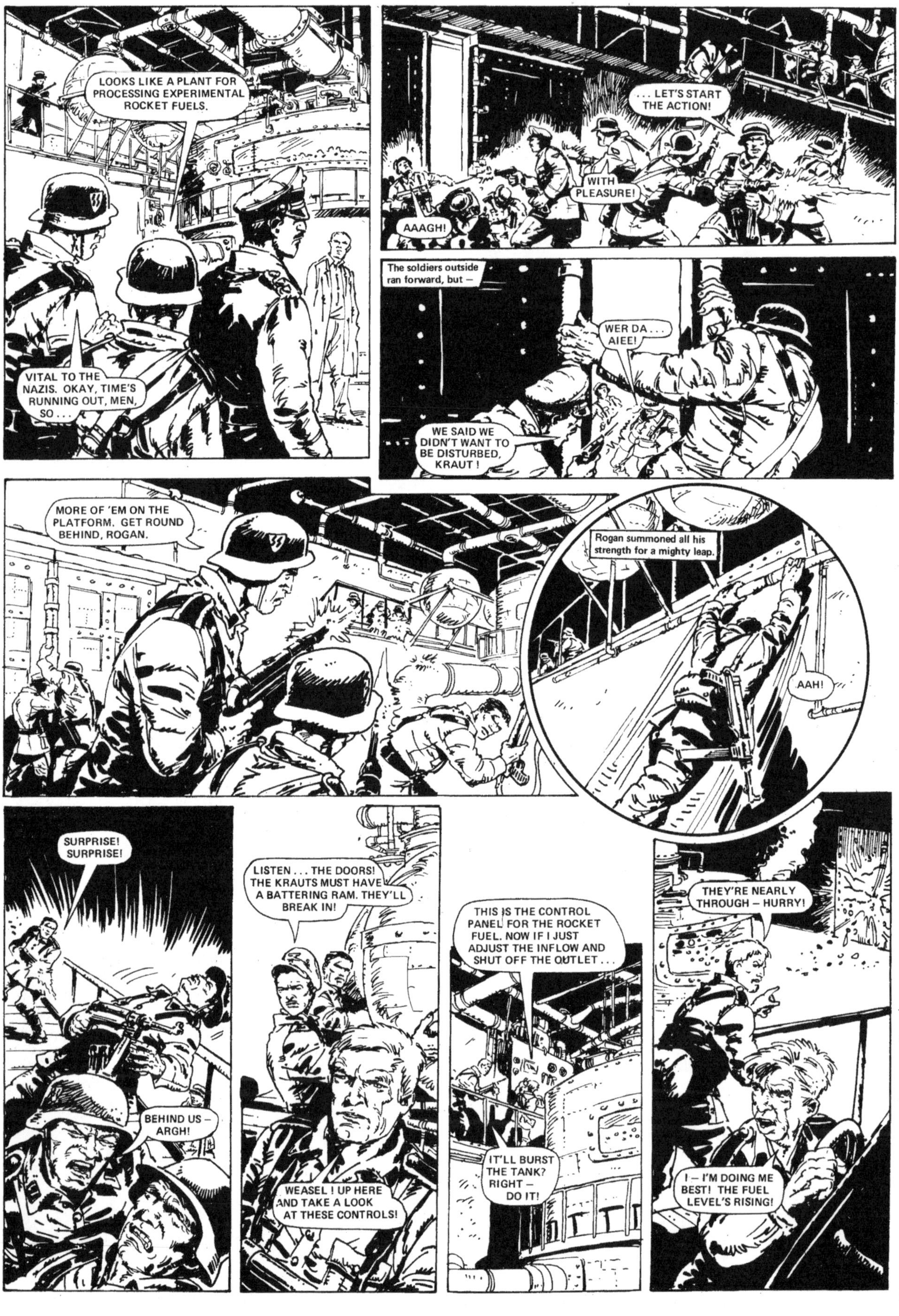
LOOKS LIKE A PLANT FOR PROCESSING EXPERIMENTAL ROCKET FUELS.
VITAL TO THE NAZIS. OKAY, TIME'S RUNNING OUT, MEN, SO . . .
. . . LET'S START THE ACTION!
WITH PLEASURE!
AAAGH!
The soldiers outside ran forward, but –
WER DA . . . AIEE!
WE SAID WE DIDN'T WANT TO BE DISTURBED, KRAUT !
MORE OF 'EM ON THE PLATFORM. GET ROUND BEHIND, ROGAN.
Rogan summoned all his strength for a mighty leap.
AAH!
SURPRISE! SURPRISE!
BEHIND US – ARGH!
LISTEN . . . THE DOORS! THE KRAUTS MUST HAVE A BATTERING RAM. THEY'LL BREAK IN!
WEASEL ! UP HERE AND TAKE A LOOK AT THESE CONTROLS!
THIS IS THE CONTROL PANEL FOR THE ROCKET FUEL. NOW IF I JUST ADJUST THE INFLOW AND SHUT OFF THE OUTLET . . .
IT'LL BURST THE TANK? RIGHT – DO IT!
THEY'RE NEARLY THROUGH – HURRY!
I – I'M DOING ME BEST! THE FUEL LEVEL'S RISING!

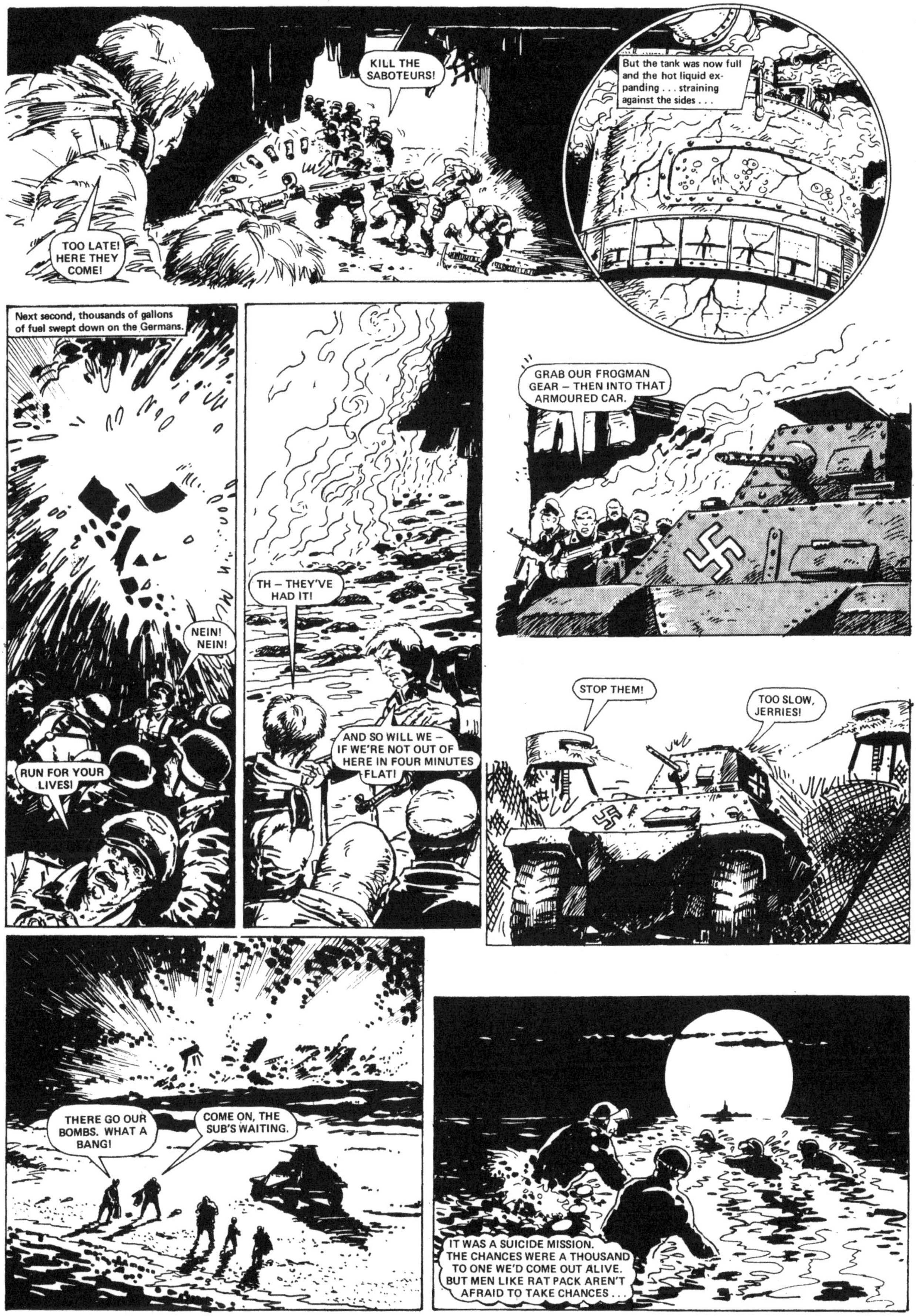

KILL THE SABOTEURS!
TOO LATE! HERE THEY COME!
But the tank was now full and the hot liquid expanding . . . straining against the sides . . .
Next second, thousands of gallons of fuel swept down on the Germans.
NEIN! NEIN!
RUN FOR YOUR LIVES!
TH – THEY'VE HAD IT!
AND SO WILL WE – IF WE'RE NOT OUT OF HERE IN FOUR MINUTES FLAT!
GRAB OUR FROGMAN GEAR – THEN INTO THAT ARMOURED CAR.
STOP THEM!
TOO SLOW, JERRIES!
THERE GO OUR BOMBS. WHAT A BANG!
COME ON, THE SUB'S WAITING.
IT WAS A SUICIDE MISSION. THE CHANCES WERE A THOUSAND TO ONE WE'D COME OUT ALIVE. BUT MEN LIKE RAT PACK AREN'T AFRAID TO TAKE CHANCES . . .

SION ENDS...MISSION ENDS...MISSION ENDS...MISSION ENDS...MISSION ENDS...MISSION ENDS...MISSION ENDS...M

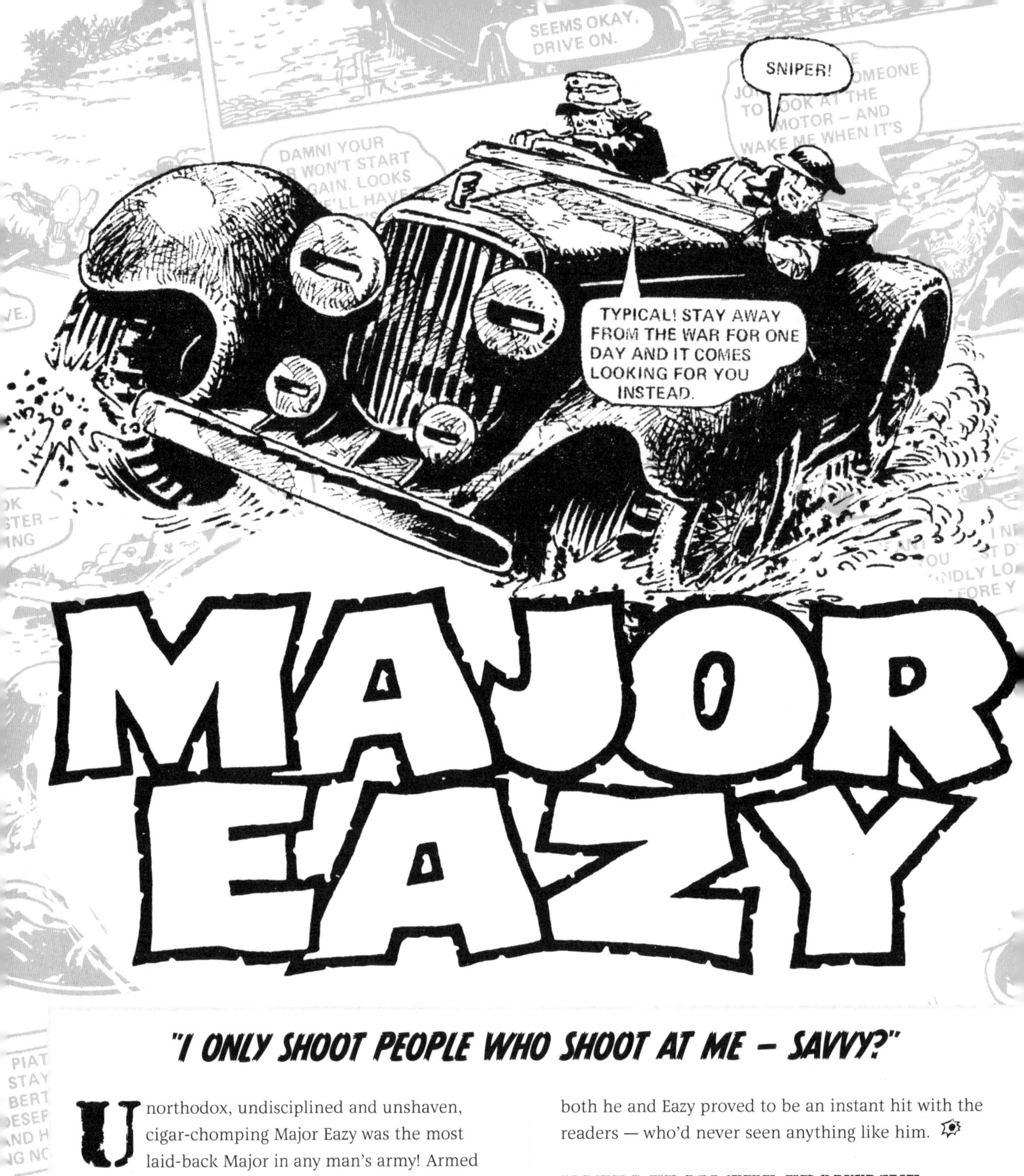
SEEMS OKAY, DRIVE ON.
SNIPER!
TYPICAL! STAY AWAY FROM THE WAR FOR ONE DAY AND IT COMES LOOKING FOR YOU INSTEAD.

MAJOR EAZY

"I ONLY SHOOT PEOPLE WHO SHOOT AT ME – SAVVY?"

Unorthodox, undisciplined and unshaven, cigar-chomping Major Eazy was the most laid-back Major in any man's army! Armed with a high-velocity rifle, a pair of six-shooters and a belt's worth of grenades, Eazy didn't so much burst onto the scene as calmly drive up to it in his own camouflaged Bentley sports car.

'Major Eazy' became Carlos Ezquerra's first full-time character for IPC. It had taken *Battle* editor Dave Hunt over a year to finally secure the services of the talented Spanish artist, who'd been working for *Battle*'s main competition, *Warlord*. 'Major Eazy' suited Carlos' rough-and-ready drawing style to a tee and both he and Eazy proved to be an instant hit with the readers — who'd never seen anything like him.

NOTES FROM THE FRONTLINE:

"Eazy was the classic, cool, anti-establishment anti-hero, who had to have things his own way, and it went very much against all the other stereotypes we'd been running up 'til then really. Alan Hebden, who was a very easy scriptwriter to work with, had based him on that Clint Eastwood type of character. 'Eazy' broke the mould and proved to be immensely popular with the readers. We had great fun with him, all the way along."
— Dave Hunt

WRITTEN BY Alan Hebden • **DRAWN BY** Carlos Ezquerra

STARTS TODAY! HE'S TOUGH . . . HE'S COOL . . . HE'S MAJOR EAZY!

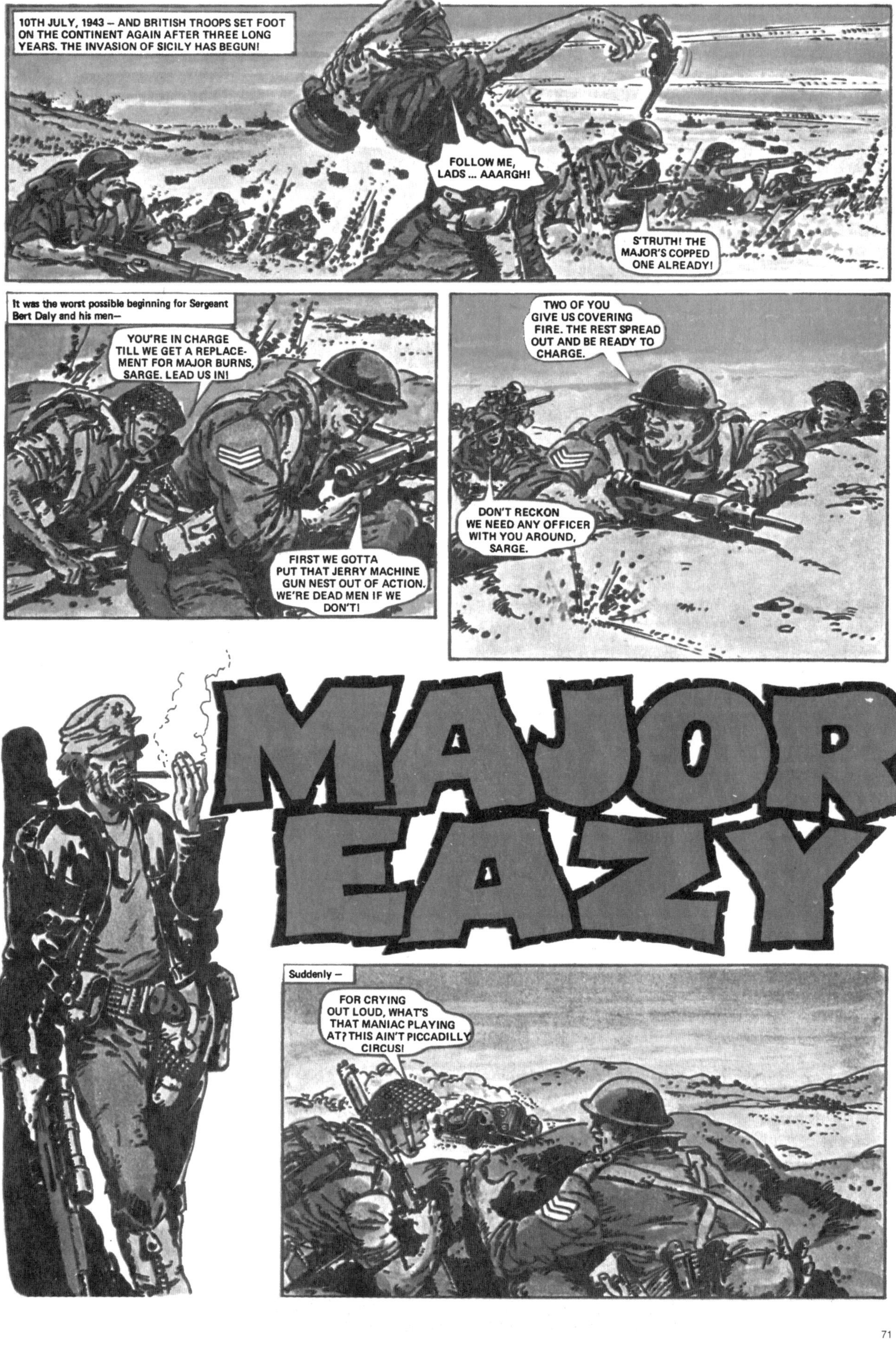

10TH JULY, 1943 – AND BRITISH TROOPS SET FOOT ON THE CONTINENT AGAIN AFTER THREE LONG YEARS. THE INVASION OF SICILY HAS BEGUN!
FOLLOW ME, LADS ... AAARGH!
S'TRUTH! THE MAJOR'S COPPED ONE ALREADY!
It was the worst possible beginning for Sergeant Bert Daly and his men–
YOU'RE IN CHARGE TILL WE GET A REPLACE-MENT FOR MAJOR BURNS, SARGE. LEAD US IN!
FIRST WE GOTTA PUT THAT JERRY MACHINE GUN NEST OUT OF ACTION. WE'RE DEAD MEN IF WE DON'T!
TWO OF YOU GIVE US COVERING FIRE. THE REST SPREAD OUT AND BE READY TO CHARGE.
DON'T RECKON WE NEED ANY OFFICER WITH YOU AROUND, SARGE.
MAJOR EAZY
Suddenly –
FOR CRYING OUT LOUD, WHAT'S THAT MANIAC PLAYING AT? THIS AIN'T PICCADILLY CIRCUS!

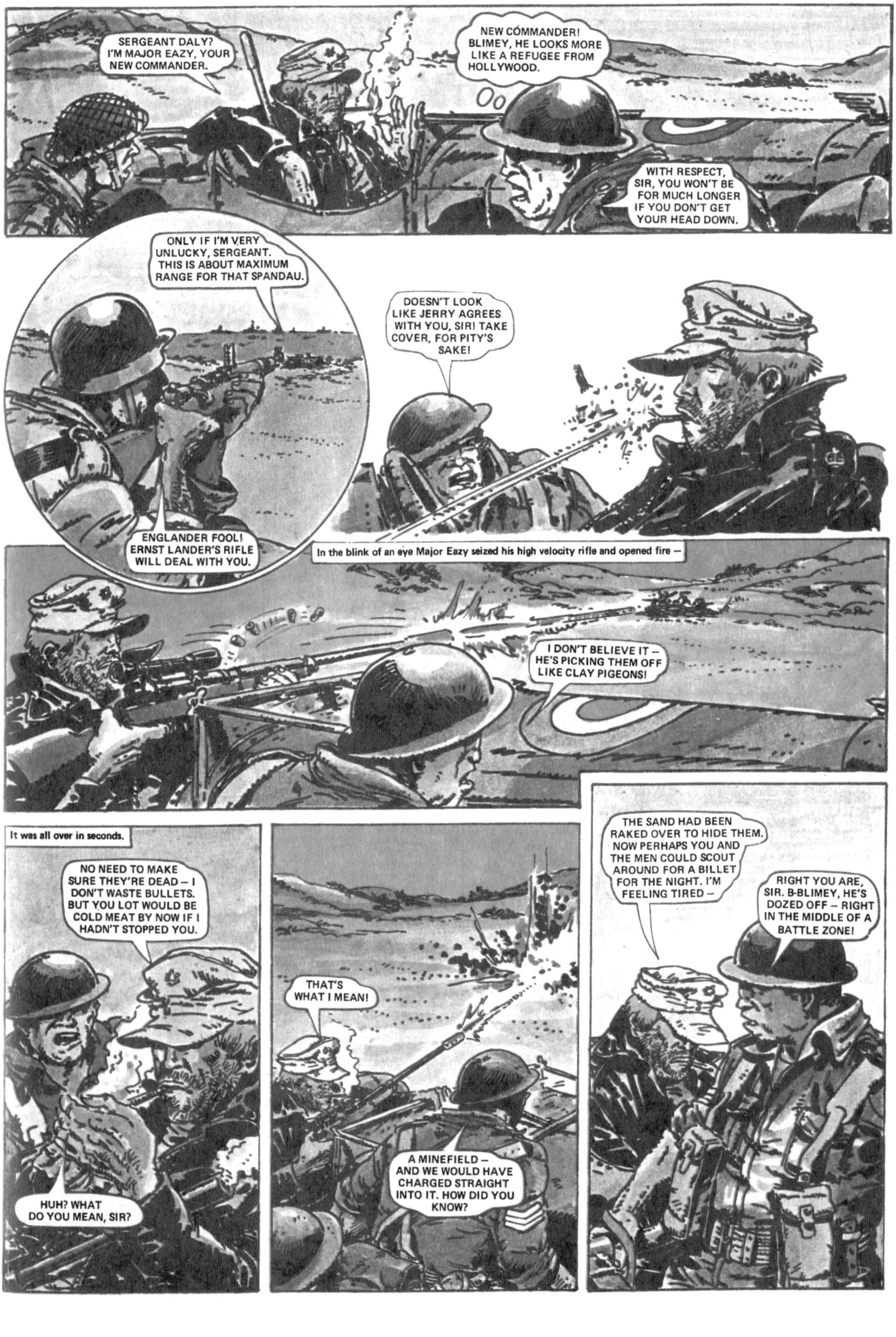
SERGEANT DALY? I'M MAJOR EAZY, YOUR NEW COMMANDER.
NEW COMMANDER! BLIMEY, HE LOOKS MORE LIKE A REFUGEE FROM HOLLYWOOD.
WITH RESPECT, SIR, YOU WON'T BE FOR MUCH LONGER IF YOU DON'T GET YOUR HEAD DOWN.
ONLY IF I'M VERY UNLUCKY, SERGEANT. THIS IS ABOUT MAXIMUM RANGE FOR THAT SPANDAU.
ENGLANDER FOOL! ERNST LANDER'S RIFLE WILL DEAL WITH YOU.
DOESN'T LOOK LIKE JERRY AGREES WITH YOU, SIR! TAKE COVER, FOR PITY'S SAKE!
In the blink of an eye Major Eazy seized his high velocity rifle and opened fire –
I DON'T BELIEVE IT – HE'S PICKING THEM OFF LIKE CLAY PIGEONS!
It was all over in seconds.
NO NEED TO MAKE SURE THEY'RE DEAD – I DON'T WASTE BULLETS. BUT YOU LOT WOULD BE COLD MEAT BY NOW IF I HADN'T STOPPED YOU.
HUH? WHAT DO YOU MEAN, SIR?
THAT'S WHAT I MEAN!
A MINEFIELD – AND WE WOULD HAVE CHARGED STRAIGHT INTO IT. HOW DID YOU KNOW?
THE SAND HAD BEEN RAKED OVER TO HIDE THEM. NOW PERHAPS YOU AND THE MEN COULD SCOUT AROUND FOR A BILLET FOR THE NIGHT. I'M FEELING TIRED –
RIGHT YOU ARE, SIR. B-BLIMEY, HE'S DOZED OFF – RIGHT IN THE MIDDLE OF A BATTLE ZONE!

"YOU'RE CRAZY! ONE MAN AGAINST A KING TIGER —"

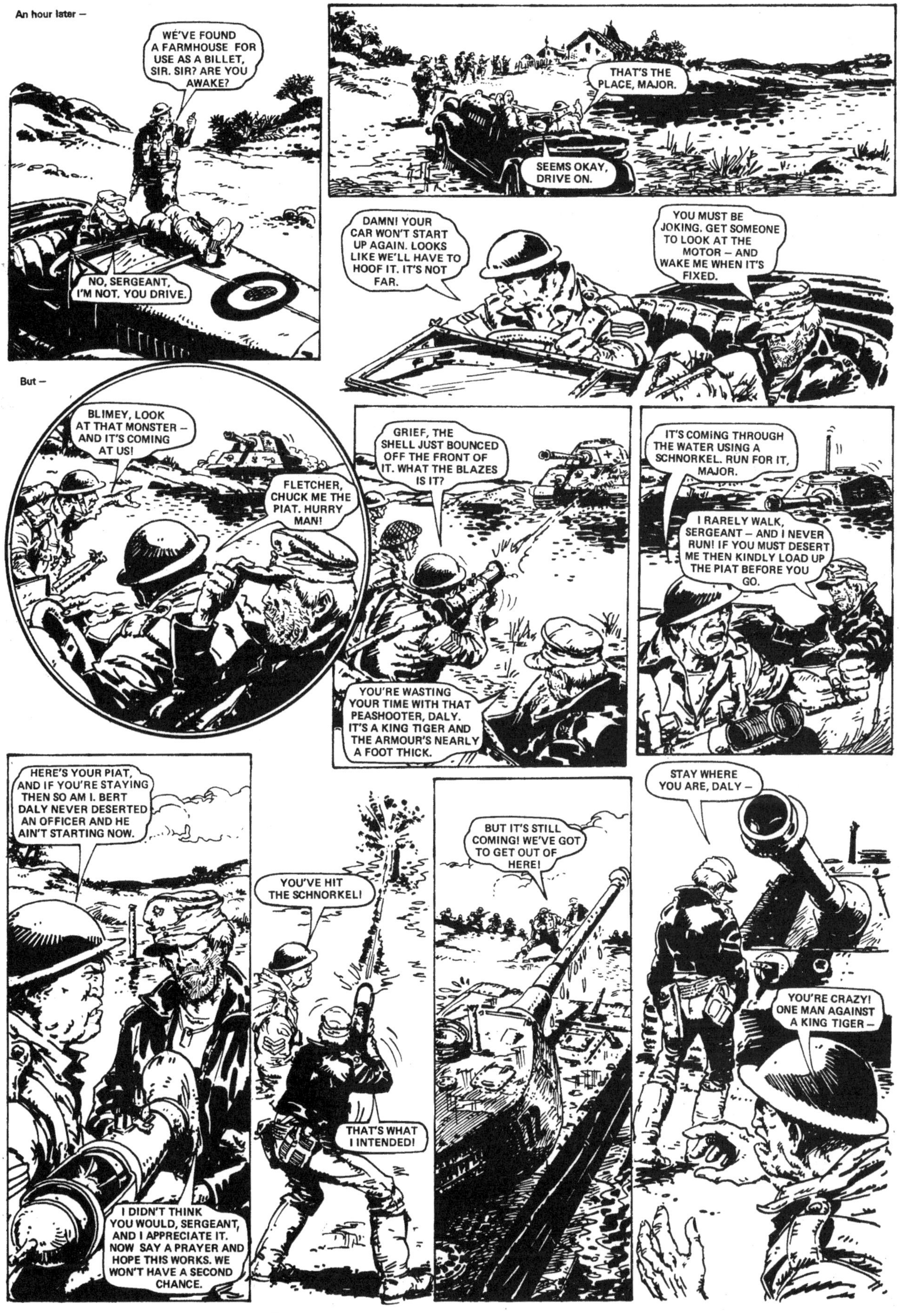

An hour later –
WE'VE FOUND A FARMHOUSE FOR USE AS A BILLET, SIR. SIR? ARE YOU AWAKE?
NO, SERGEANT, I'M NOT. YOU DRIVE.
THAT'S THE PLACE, MAJOR.
SEEMS OKAY, DRIVE ON.
DAMN! YOUR CAR WON'T START UP AGAIN. LOOKS LIKE WE'LL HAVE TO HOOF IT. IT'S NOT FAR.
YOU MUST BE JOKING. GET SOMEONE TO LOOK AT THE MOTOR – AND WAKE ME WHEN IT'S FIXED.
But –
BLIMEY, LOOK AT THAT MONSTER – AND IT'S COMING AT US!
FLETCHER, CHUCK ME THE PIAT. HURRY MAN!
GRIEF, THE SHELL JUST BOUNCED OFF THE FRONT OF IT. WHAT THE BLAZES IS IT?
YOU'RE WASTING YOUR TIME WITH THAT PEASHOOTER, DALY. IT'S A KING TIGER AND THE ARMOUR'S NEARLY A FOOT THICK.
IT'S COMING THROUGH THE WATER USING A SCHNORKEL. RUN FOR IT, MAJOR.
I RARELY WALK, SERGEANT – AND I NEVER RUN! IF YOU MUST DESERT ME THEN KINDLY LOAD UP THE PIAT BEFORE YOU GO.
HERE'S YOUR PIAT, AND IF YOU'RE STAYING THEN SO AM I. BERT DALY NEVER DESERTED AN OFFICER AND HE AIN'T STARTING NOW.
I DIDN'T THINK YOU WOULD, SERGEANT, AND I APPRECIATE IT. NOW SAY A PRAYER AND HOPE THIS WORKS. WE WON'T HAVE A SECOND CHANCE.
YOU'VE HIT THE SCHNORKEL!
THAT'S WHAT I INTENDED!
BUT IT'S STILL COMING! WE'VE GOT TO GET OUT OF HERE!
STAY WHERE YOU ARE, DALY –
YOU'RE CRAZY! ONE MAN AGAINST A KING TIGER –

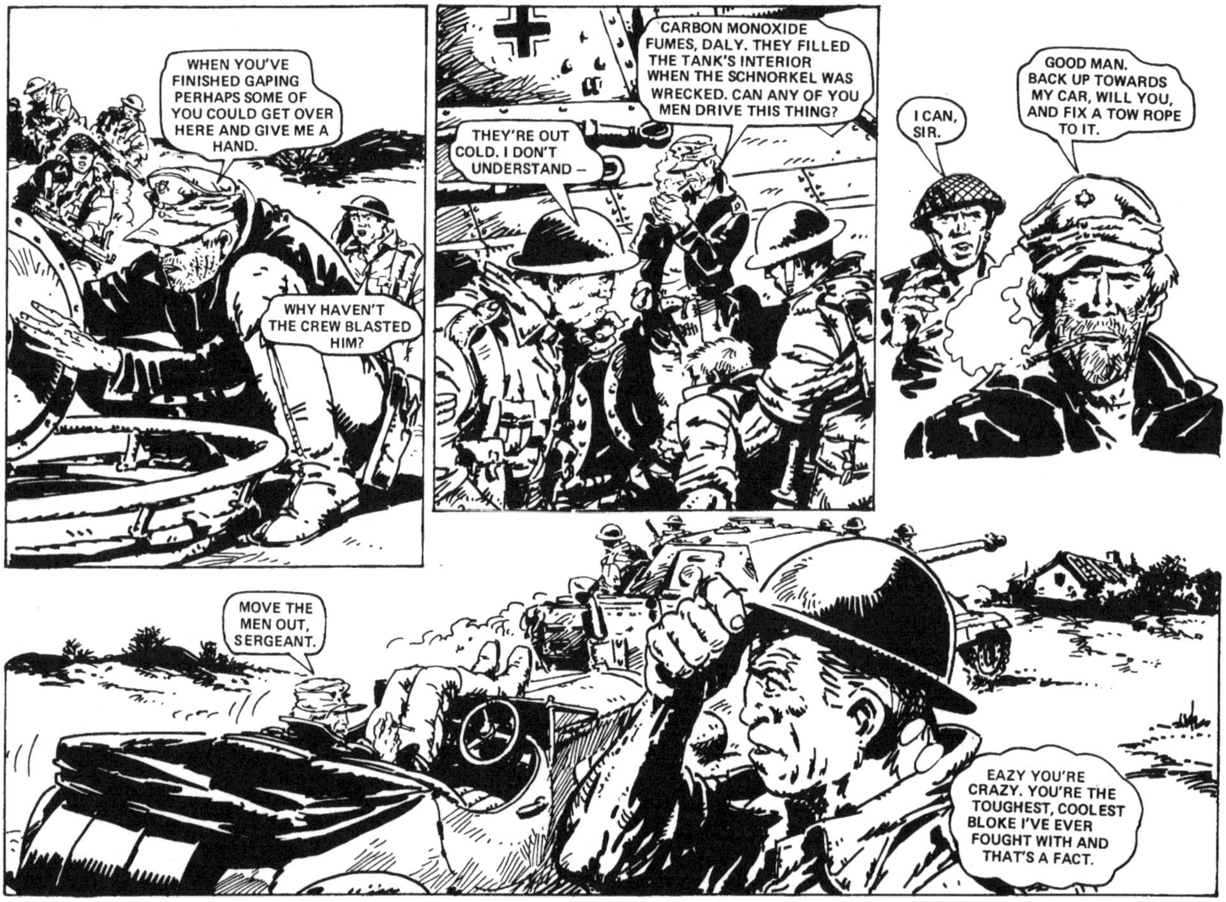
WHEN YOU'VE FINISHED GAPING PERHAPS SOME OF YOU COULD GET OVER HERE AND GIVE ME A HAND.
WHY HAVEN'T THE CREW BLASTED HIM?
THEY'RE OUT COLD. I DON'T UNDERSTAND –
CARBON MONOXIDE FUMES, DALY. THEY FILLED THE TANK'S INTERIOR WHEN THE SCHNORKEL WAS WRECKED. CAN ANY OF YOU MEN DRIVE THIS THING?
I CAN, SIR.
GOOD MAN. BACK UP TOWARDS MY CAR, WILL YOU, AND FIX A TOW ROPE TO IT.
MOVE THE MEN OUT, SERGEANT.
EAZY YOU'RE CRAZY. YOU'RE THE TOUGHEST, COOLEST BLOKE I'VE EVER FOUGHT WITH AND THAT'S A FACT.

NEXT WEEK — EAZY HAS A 'CLOSE SHAVE' WITH DEATH!

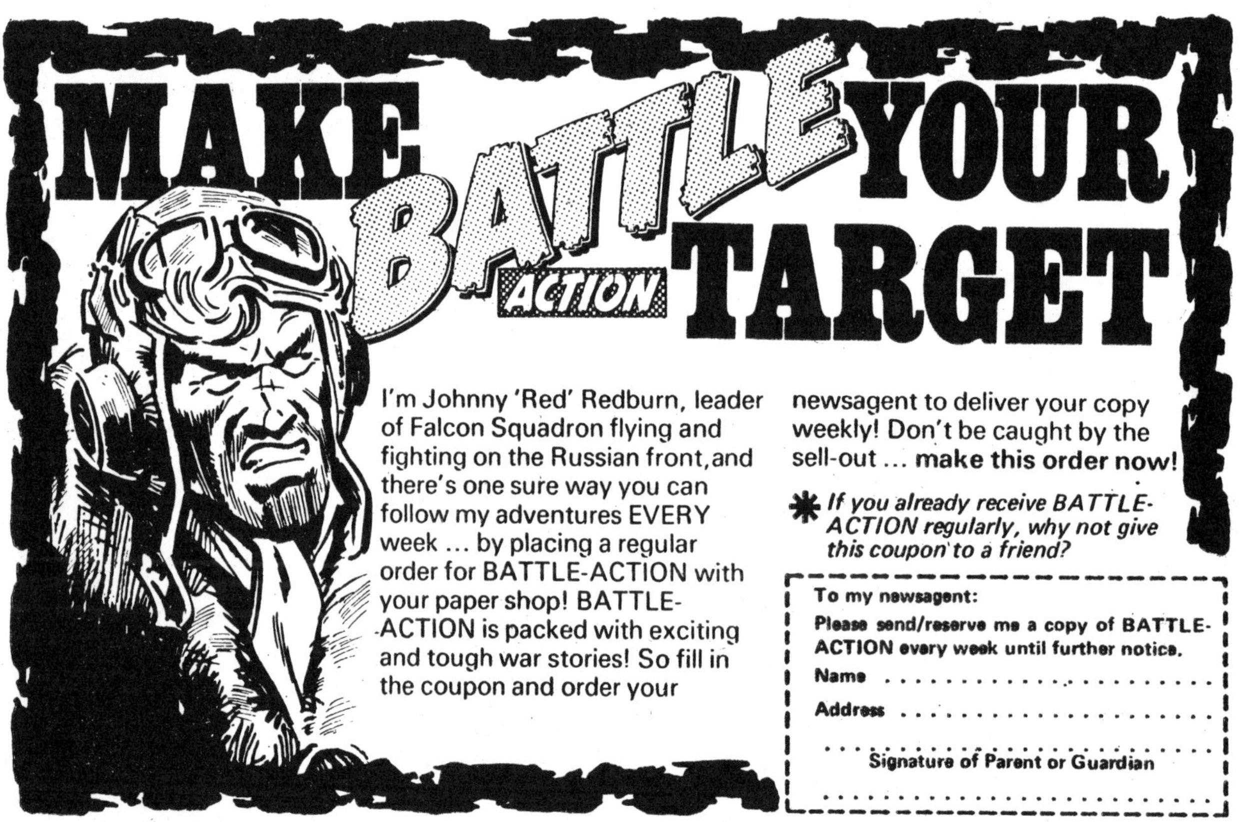
MAKE
BATTLE
ACTION
YOUR TARGET
I'm Johnny 'Red' Redburn, leader of Falcon Squadron flying and fighting on the Russian front, and there's one sure way you can follow my adventures EVERY week ... by placing a regular order for BATTLE-ACTION with your paper shop! BATTLE-ACTION is packed with exciting and tough war stories! So fill in the coupon and order your newsagent to deliver your copy weekly! Don't be caught by the sell-out ... make this order now!
* If you already receive BATTLE-ACTION regularly, why not give this coupon to a friend?
To my newsagent:
Please send/reserve me a copy of BATTLE-ACTION every week until further notice.
Name
Address
Signature of Parent or Guardian

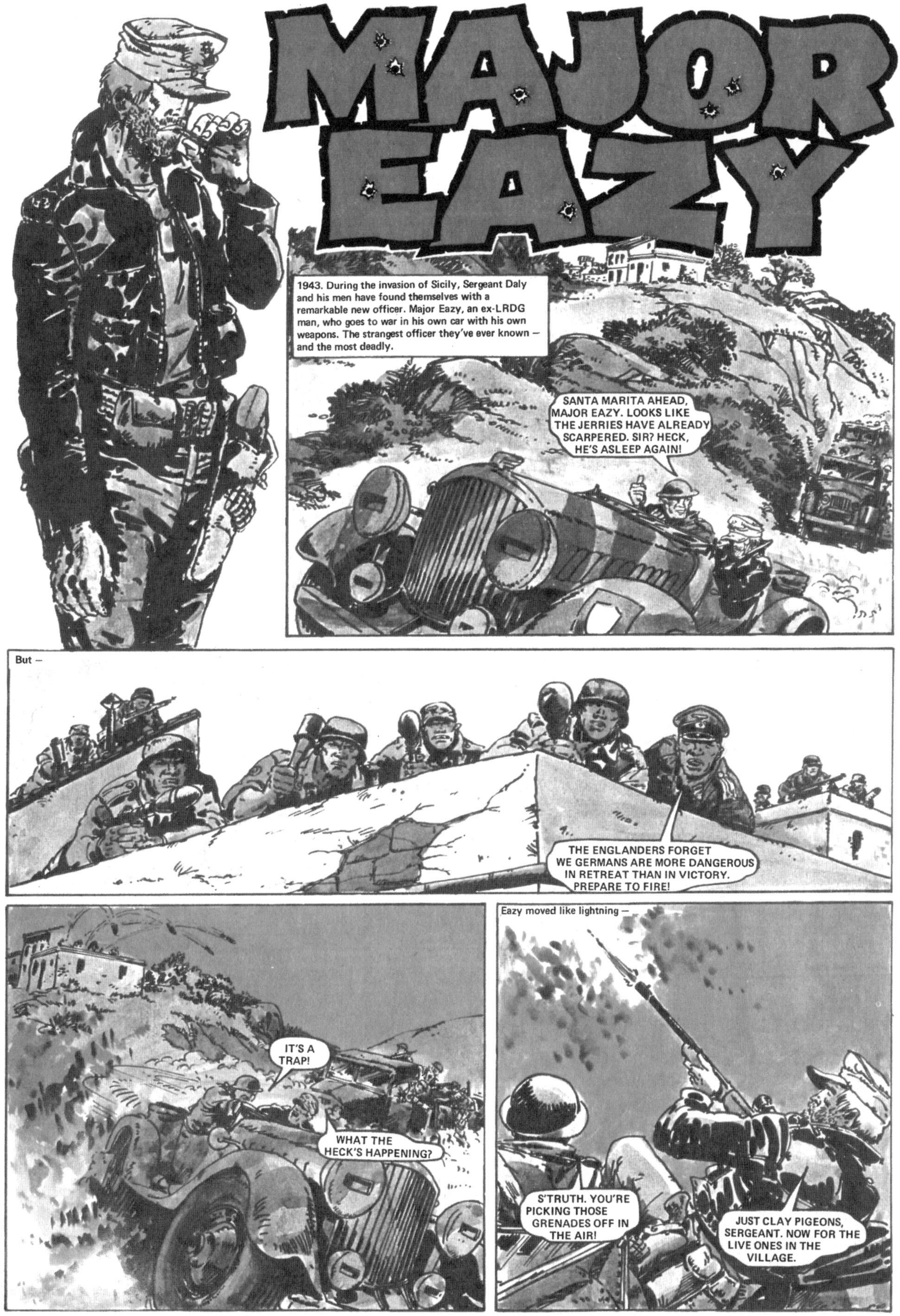
MAJOR EAZY
1943. During the invasion of Sicily, Sergeant Daly and his men have found themselves with a remarkable new officer. Major Eazy, an ex-LRDG man, who goes to war in his own car with his own weapons. The strangest officer they've ever known — and the most deadly.
SANTA MARITA AHEAD, MAJOR EAZY. LOOKS LIKE THE JERRIES HAVE ALREADY SCARPERED. SIR? HECK, HE'S ASLEEP AGAIN!
But —
THE ENGLANDERS FORGET WE GERMANS ARE MORE DANGEROUS IN RETREAT THAN IN VICTORY. PREPARE TO FIRE!
IT'S A TRAP!
WHAT THE HECK'S HAPPENING?
Eazy moved like lightning —
S'TRUTH. YOU'RE PICKING THOSE GRENADES OFF IN THE AIR!
JUST CLAY PIGEONS, SERGEANT. NOW FOR THE LIVE ONES IN THE VILLAGE.

"LET THE SCHWEINHUNDS HAVE THIS ACCURSED VILLAGE!"

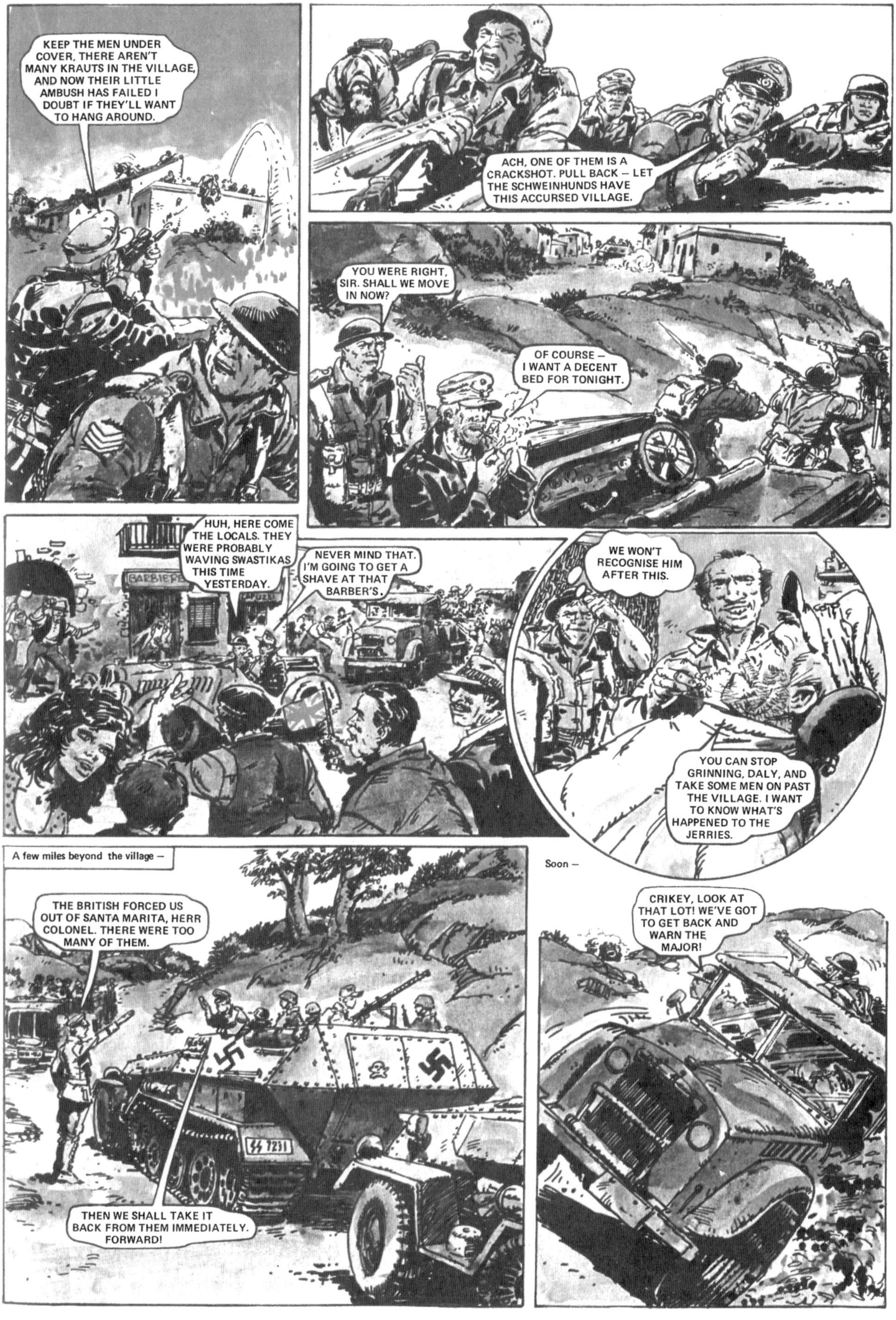

KEEP THE MEN UNDER COVER, THERE AREN'T MANY KRAUTS IN THE VILLAGE, AND NOW THEIR LITTLE AMBUSH HAS FAILED I DOUBT IF THEY'LL WANT TO HANG AROUND.
ACH, ONE OF THEM IS A CRACKSHOT. PULL BACK – LET THE SCHWEINHUNDS HAVE THIS ACCURSED VILLAGE.
YOU WERE RIGHT, SIR. SHALL WE MOVE IN NOW?
OF COURSE – I WANT A DECENT BED FOR TONIGHT.
BARBIERE
HUH, HERE COME THE LOCALS. THEY WERE PROBABLY WAVING SWASTIKAS THIS TIME YESTERDAY.
NEVER MIND THAT. I'M GOING TO GET A SHAVE AT THAT BARBER'S.
WE WON'T RECOGNISE HIM AFTER THIS.
YOU CAN STOP GRINNING, DALY, AND TAKE SOME MEN ON PAST THE VILLAGE. I WANT TO KNOW WHAT'S HAPPENED TO THE JERRIES.
A few miles beyond the village –
THE BRITISH FORCED US OUT OF SANTA MARITA, HERR COLONEL. THERE WERE TOO MANY OF THEM.
THEN WE SHALL TAKE IT BACK FROM THEM IMMEDIATELY. FORWARD!
Soon –
CRIKEY, LOOK AT THAT LOT! WE'VE GOT TO GET BACK AND WARN THE MAJOR!

"— STRAIGHT INTO A HERD OF JERRIES!"

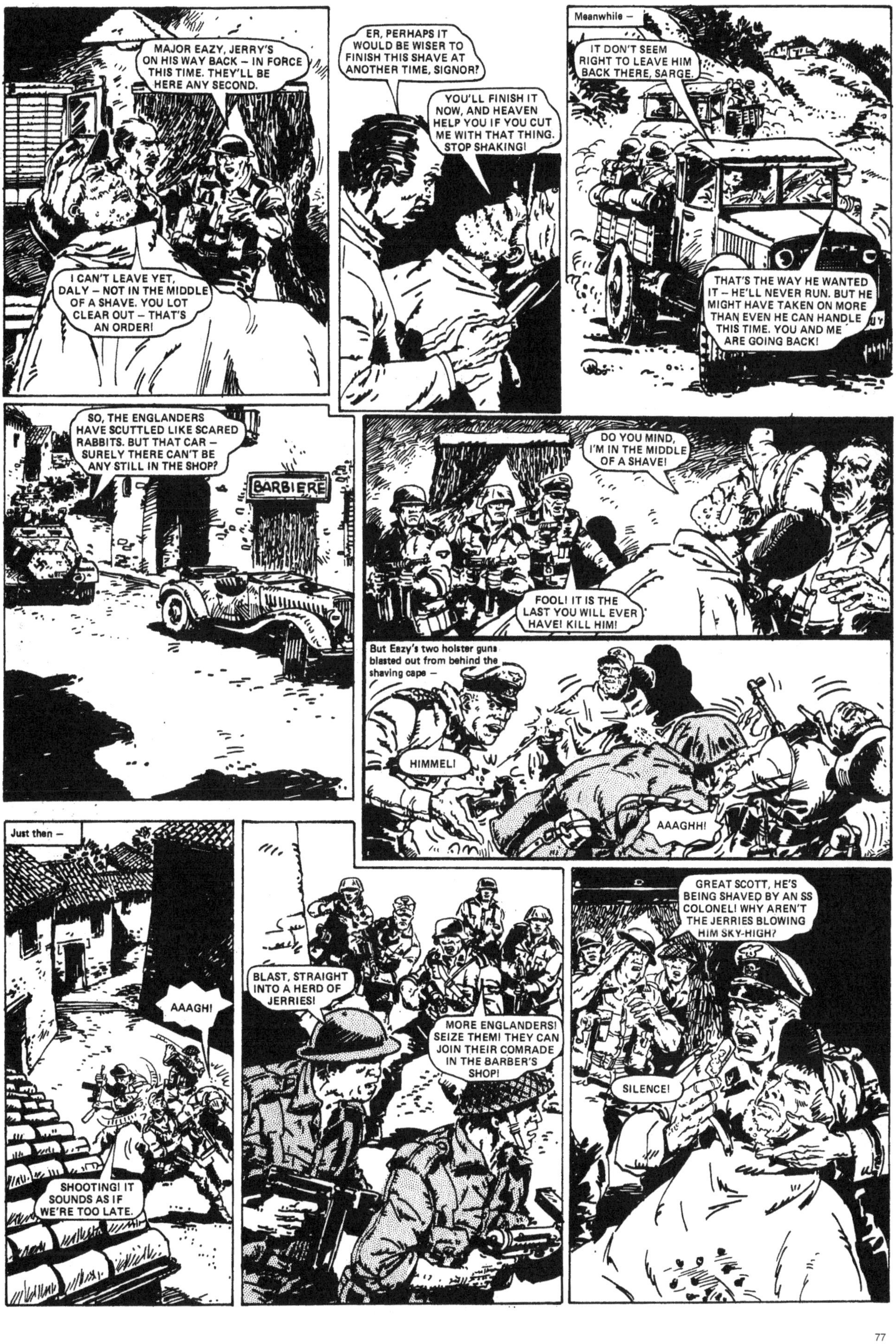
MAJOR EAZY, JERRY'S ON HIS WAY BACK – IN FORCE THIS TIME. THEY'LL BE HERE ANY SECOND.
I CAN'T LEAVE YET, DALY – NOT IN THE MIDDLE OF A SHAVE. YOU LOT CLEAR OUT – THAT'S AN ORDER!
ER, PERHAPS IT WOULD BE WISER TO FINISH THIS SHAVE AT ANOTHER TIME, SIGNOR?
YOU'LL FINISH IT NOW, AND HEAVEN HELP YOU IF YOU CUT ME WITH THAT THING. STOP SHAKING!
Meanwhile –
IT DON'T SEEM RIGHT TO LEAVE HIM BACK THERE, SARGE.
THAT'S THE WAY HE WANTED IT – HE'LL NEVER RUN. BUT HE MIGHT HAVE TAKEN ON MORE THAN EVEN HE CAN HANDLE THIS TIME. YOU AND ME ARE GOING BACK!
SO, THE ENGLANDERS HAVE SCUTTLED LIKE SCARED RABBITS. BUT THAT CAR – SURELY THERE CAN'T BE ANY STILL IN THE SHOP?
BARBIERE
DO YOU MIND, I'M IN THE MIDDLE OF A SHAVE!
FOOL! IT IS THE LAST YOU WILL EVER HAVE! KILL HIM!
But Eazy's two holster guns blasted out from behind the shaving cape –
HIMMEL!
AAAGHH!
Just then –
AAAGH!
SHOOTING! IT SOUNDS AS IF WE'RE TOO LATE.
BLAST, STRAIGHT INTO A HERD OF JERRIES!
MORE ENGLANDERS! SEIZE THEM! THEY CAN JOIN THEIR COMRADE IN THE BARBER'S SHOP!
GREAT SCOTT, HE'S BEING SHAVED BY AN SS COLONEL! WHY AREN'T THE JERRIES BLOWING HIM SKY-HIGH?
SILENCE!

I THOUGHT I TOLD YOU TO SCARPER, DALY. NEVER MIND, YOU CAN DRIVE ME AND THE COLONEL OUT OF HERE NOW THAT HE'S FINISHED SHAVING ME.
JA, JA. DO AS HE SAYS.
A PRIMED GRENADE . . . SO THAT'S IT! IF YOU LOOSENED YOUR GRIP FOR A MOMENT THE THING'D EXPLODE AND TAKE FRITZ ALONG WITH YOU.
RIGHT! YOU DON'T THINK THE COLONEL WOULD HAVE AGREED TO FINISH MY SHAVE JUST BECAUSE I ASKED HIM?
NOW MOVE, SERGEANT. WE CAN CALL UP SOME REINFORCEMENTS AND CLEAR THE JERRIES OUT OF SANTA MARITA FOR GOOD.
RIGHT YOU ARE, SIR. BUT WHAT ABOUT THE COLONEL HERE – IS HE A HOSTAGE OR A PRISONER?
AAARGH!
NEITHER! – HE'S JUST EXCESS BAGGAGE, TAKING UP TOO MUCH ROOM!
. . . AND I NEED THAT ROOM FOR SLEEPING! DRIVE ON, AND MIND THE BUMPS!
YES SIR!

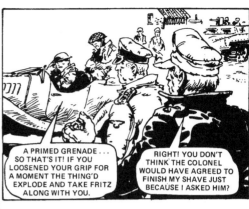

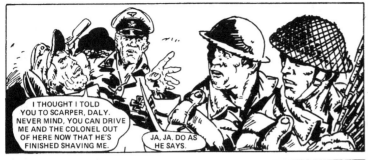

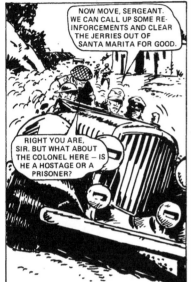

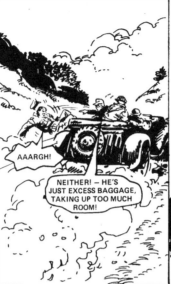

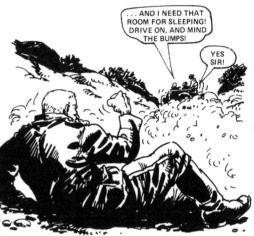

NEXT WEEK — MAJOR EAZY RIDDLES MILITARY POLICE WITH LEAD!

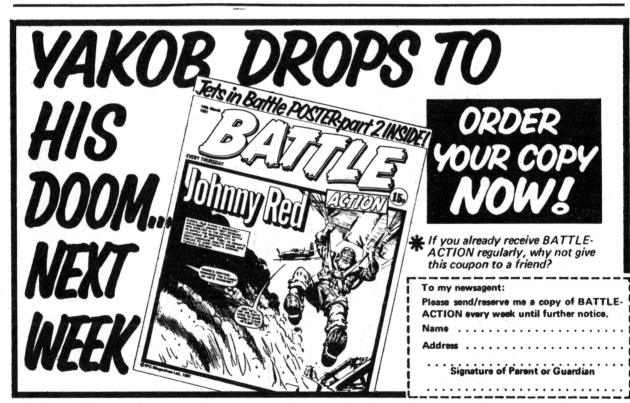

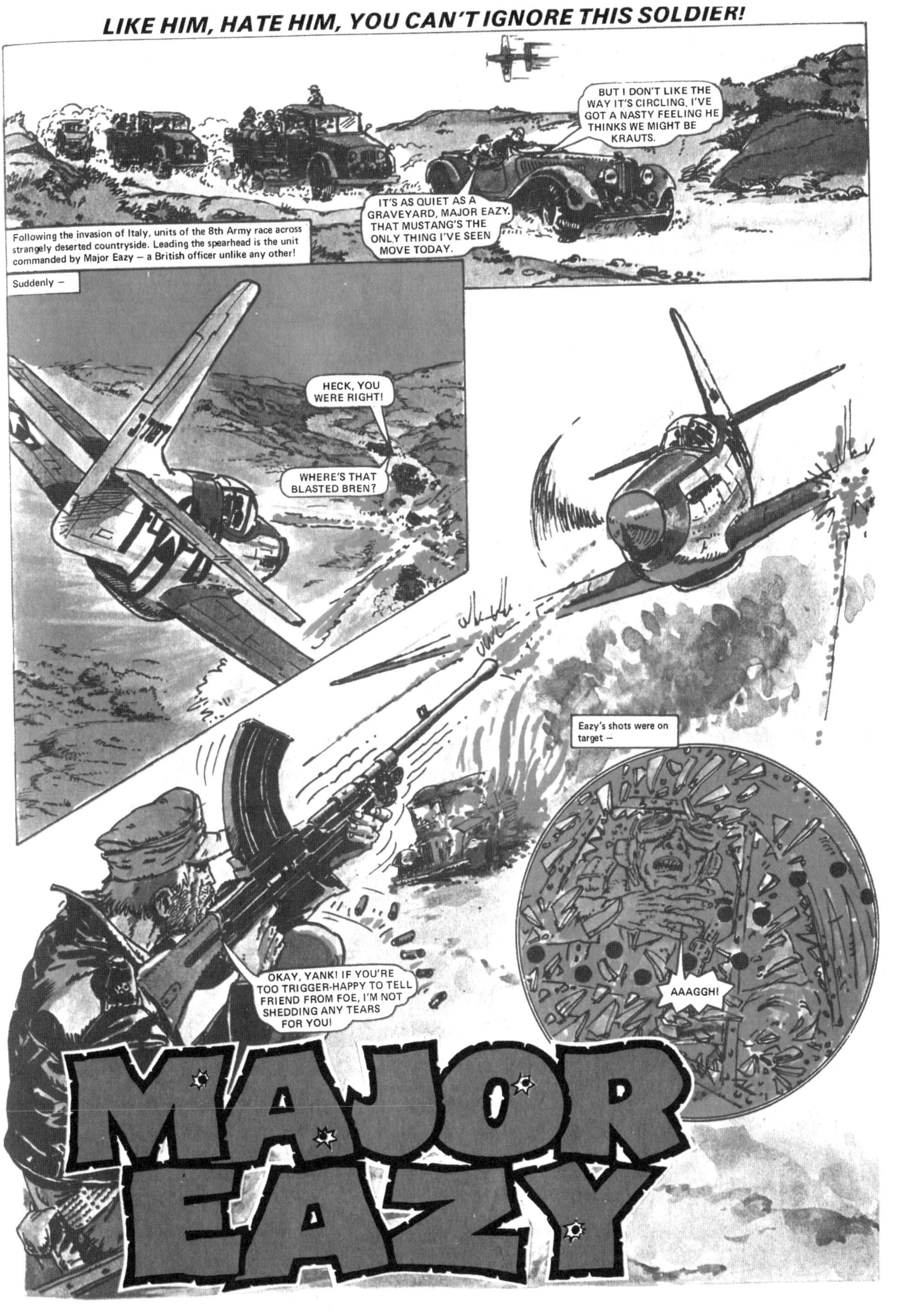

LIKE HIM, HATE HIM, YOU CAN'T IGNORE THIS SOLDIER!
Following the invasion of Italy, units of the 8th Army race across strangely deserted countryside. Leading the spearhead is the unit commanded by Major Eazy — a British officer unlike any other!
IT'S AS QUIET AS A GRAVEYARD, MAJOR EAZY. THAT MUSTANG'S THE ONLY THING I'VE SEEN MOVE TODAY.
BUT I DON'T LIKE THE WAY IT'S CIRCLING. I'VE GOT A NASTY FEELING HE THINKS WE MIGHT BE KRAUTS.
Suddenly —
HECK, YOU WERE RIGHT!
WHERE'S THAT BLASTED BREN?
OKAY, YANK! IF YOU'RE TOO TRIGGER-HAPPY TO TELL FRIEND FROM FOE, I'M NOT SHEDDING ANY TEARS FOR YOU!
Eazy's shots were on target —
AAAGGH!
MAJOR EAZY

"IT WAS ATTEMPTED MURDER!"

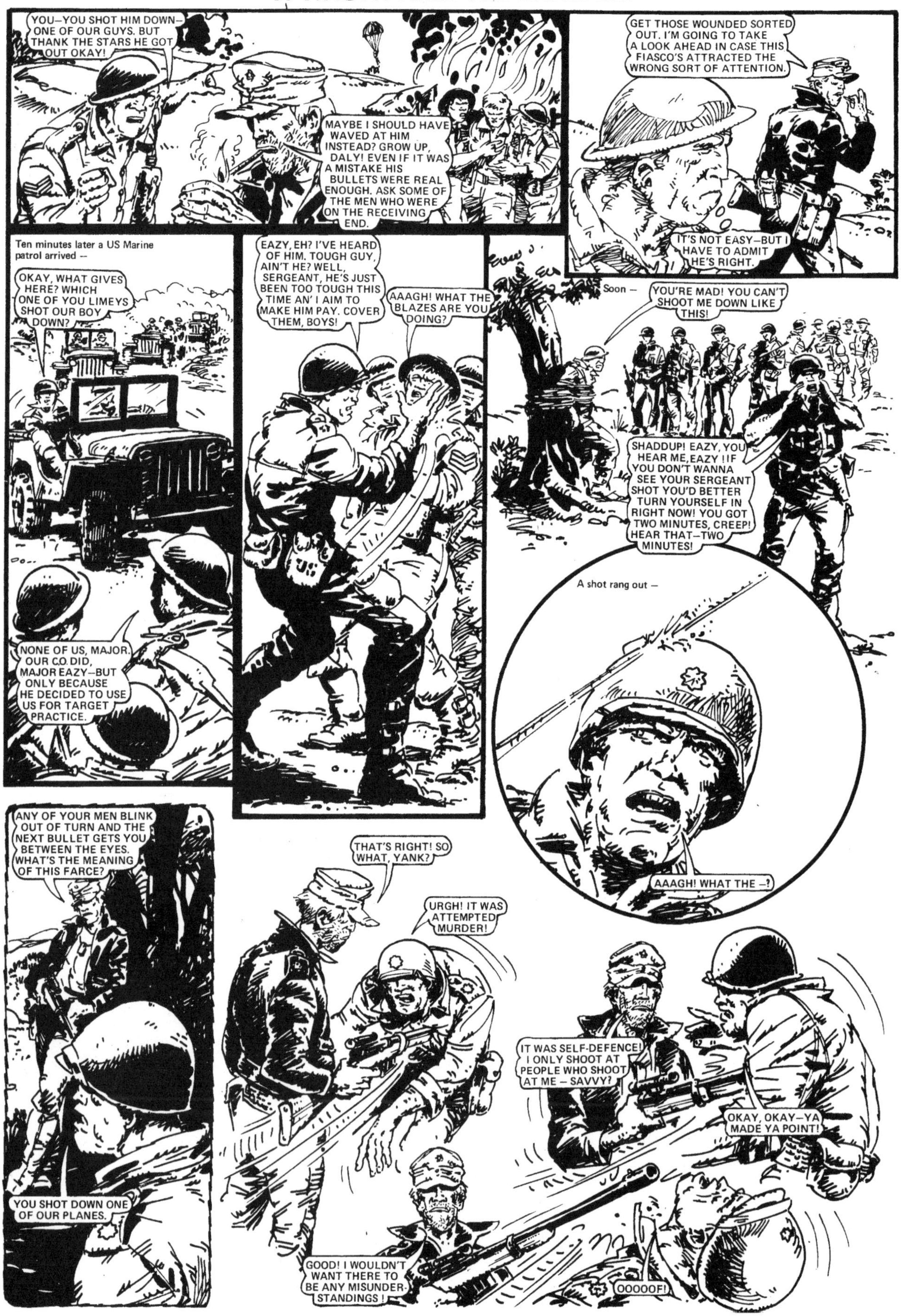

YOU—YOU SHOT HIM DOWN—ONE OF OUR GUYS. BUT THANK THE STARS HE GOT OUT OKAY!
MAYBE I SHOULD HAVE WAVED AT HIM INSTEAD? GROW UP, DALY! EVEN IF IT WAS A MISTAKE HIS BULLETS WERE REAL ENOUGH. ASK SOME OF THE MEN WHO WERE ON THE RECEIVING END.
GET THOSE WOUNDED SORTED OUT. I'M GOING TO TAKE A LOOK AHEAD IN CASE THIS FIASCO'S ATTRACTED THE WRONG SORT OF ATTENTION.
IT'S NOT EASY—BUT I HAVE TO ADMIT HE'S RIGHT.
Ten minutes later a US Marine patrol arrived —
OKAY, WHAT GIVES HERE? WHICH ONE OF YOU LIMEYS SHOT OUR BOY DOWN?
NONE OF US, MAJOR. OUR C.O. DID, MAJOR EAZY—BUT ONLY BECAUSE HE DECIDED TO USE US FOR TARGET PRACTICE.
EAZY, EH? I'VE HEARD OF HIM. TOUGH GUY, AIN'T HE? WELL, SERGEANT, HE'S JUST BEEN TOO TOUGH THIS TIME AN' I AIM TO MAKE HIM PAY. COVER THEM, BOYS!
AAAGH! WHAT THE BLAZES ARE YOU DOING?
Soon —
YOU'RE MAD! YOU CAN'T SHOOT ME DOWN LIKE THIS!
SHADDUP! EAZY, YOU HEAR ME, EAZY !IF YOU DON'T WANNA SEE YOUR SERGEANT SHOT YOU'D BETTER TURN YOURSELF IN RIGHT NOW! YOU GOT TWO MINUTES, CREEP! HEAR THAT—TWO MINUTES!
A shot rang out —
AAAGH! WHAT THE —?
ANY OF YOUR MEN BLINK OUT OF TURN AND THE NEXT BULLET GETS YOU BETWEEN THE EYES. WHAT'S THE MEANING OF THIS FARCE?
YOU SHOT DOWN ONE OF OUR PLANES.
THAT'S RIGHT! SO WHAT, YANK?
URGH! IT WAS ATTEMPTED MURDER!
IT WAS SELF-DEFENCE! I ONLY SHOOT AT PEOPLE WHO SHOOT AT ME – SAVVY?
OKAY, OKAY—YA MADE YA POINT!
GOOD! I WOULDN'T WANT THERE TO BE ANY MISUNDER-STANDINGS !
OOOOOF!

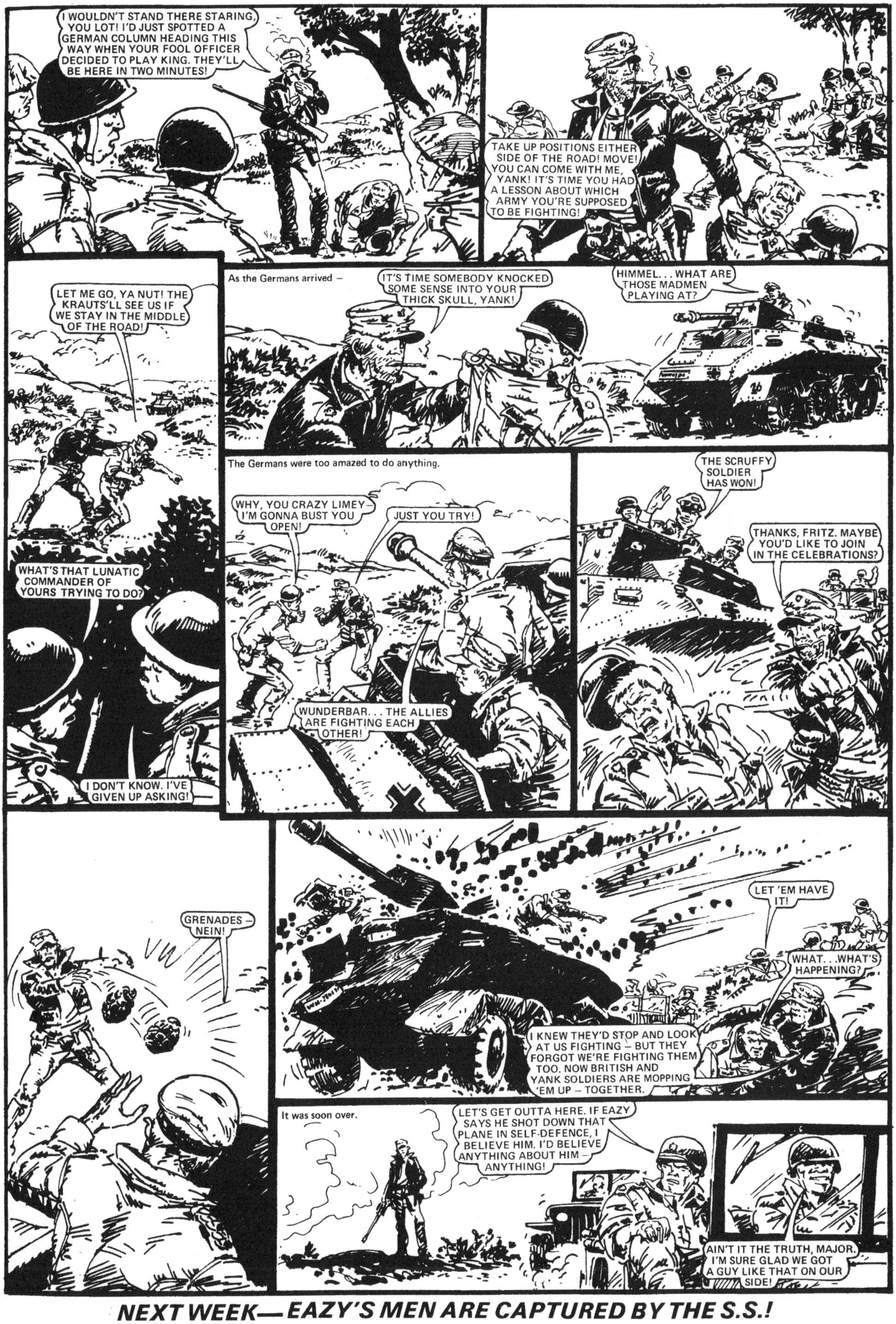
I WOULDN'T STAND THERE STARING, YOU LOT! I'D JUST SPOTTED A GERMAN COLUMN HEADING THIS WAY WHEN YOUR FOOL OFFICER DECIDED TO PLAY KING. THEY'LL BE HERE IN TWO MINUTES!
TAKE UP POSITIONS EITHER SIDE OF THE ROAD! MOVE! YOU CAN COME WITH ME, YANK! IT'S TIME YOU HAD A LESSON ABOUT WHICH ARMY YOU'RE SUPPOSED TO BE FIGHTING!
LET ME GO, YA NUT! THE KRAUTS'LL SEE US IF WE STAY IN THE MIDDLE OF THE ROAD!
WHAT'S THAT LUNATIC COMMANDER OF YOURS TRYING TO DO?
I DON'T KNOW. I'VE GIVEN UP ASKING!
As the Germans arrived –
IT'S TIME SOMEBODY KNOCKED SOME SENSE INTO YOUR THICK SKULL, YANK!
HIMMEL... WHAT ARE THOSE MADMEN PLAYING AT?
The Germans were too amazed to do anything.
WHY, YOU CRAZY LIMEY– I'M GONNA BUST YOU OPEN!
JUST YOU TRY!
WUNDERBAR... THE ALLIES ARE FIGHTING EACH OTHER!
THE SCRUFFY SOLDIER HAS WON!
THANKS, FRITZ. MAYBE YOU'D LIKE TO JOIN IN THE CELEBRATIONS?
GRENADES – NEIN!
LET 'EM HAVE IT!
WHAT... WHAT'S HAPPENING?
I KNEW THEY'D STOP AND LOOK AT US FIGHTING – BUT THEY FORGOT WE'RE FIGHTING THEM TOO. NOW BRITISH AND YANK SOLDIERS ARE MOPPING 'EM UP – TOGETHER.
It was soon over.
LET'S GET OUTTA HERE. IF EAZY SAYS HE SHOT DOWN THAT PLANE IN SELF-DEFENCE, I BELIEVE HIM. I'D BELIEVE ANYTHING ABOUT HIM – ANYTHING!
AIN'T IT THE TRUTH, MAJOR. I'M SURE GLAD WE GOT A GUY LIKE THAT ON OUR SIDE!

NEXT WEEK— EAZY'S MEN ARE CAPTURED BY THE S.S.!

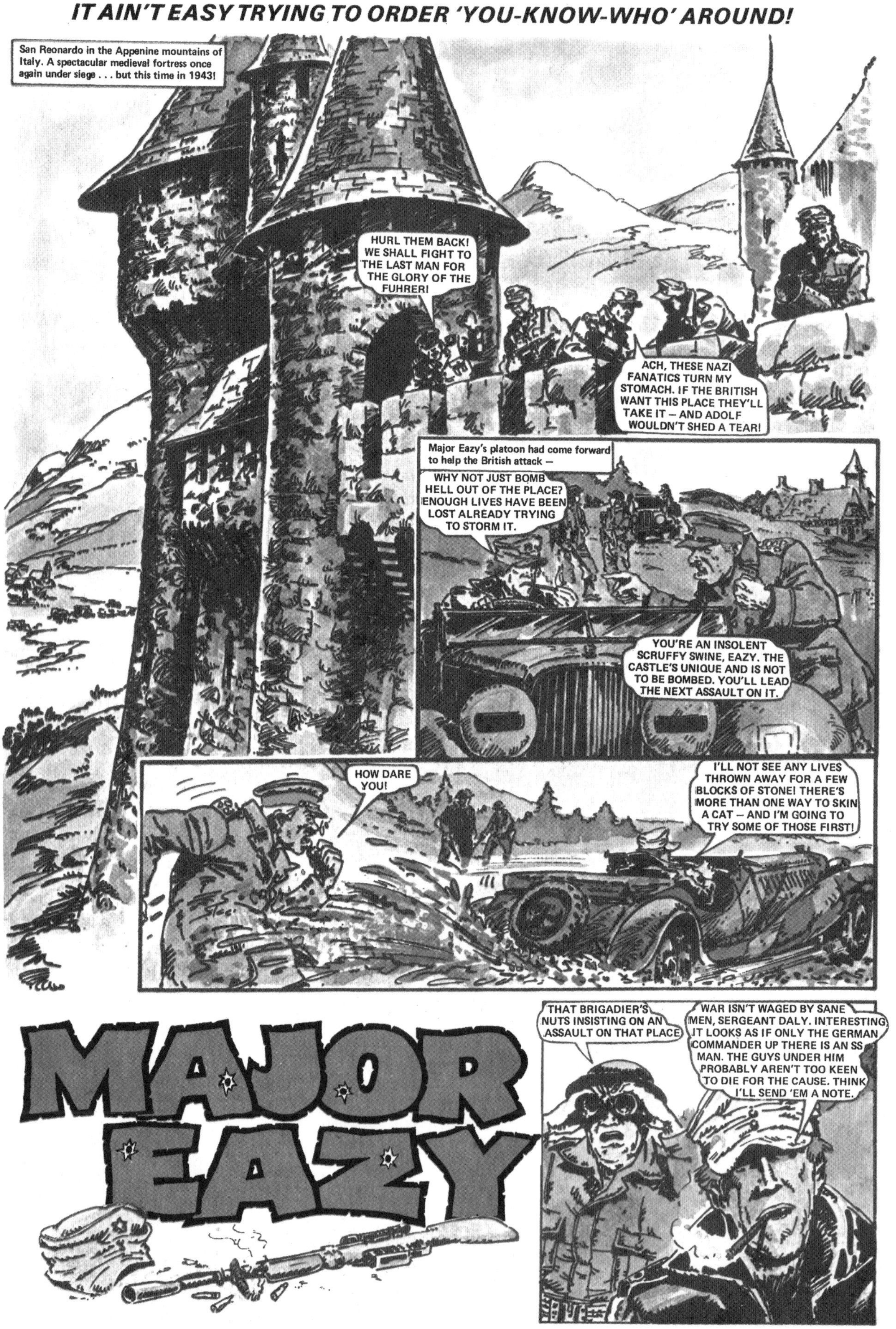
IT AIN'T EASY TRYING TO ORDER 'YOU-KNOW-WHO' AROUND!
San Reonardo in the Appenine mountains of Italy. A spectacular medieval fortress once again under siege . . . but this time in 1943!
HURL THEM BACK! WE SHALL FIGHT TO THE LAST MAN FOR THE GLORY OF THE FUHRER!
ACH, THESE NAZI FANATICS TURN MY STOMACH. IF THE BRITISH WANT THIS PLACE THEY'LL TAKE IT – AND ADOLF WOULDN'T SHED A TEAR!
Major Eazy's platoon had come forward to help the British attack –
WHY NOT JUST BOMB HELL OUT OF THE PLACE? ENOUGH LIVES HAVE BEEN LOST ALREADY TRYING TO STORM IT.
YOU'RE AN INSOLENT SCRUFFY SWINE, EAZY. THE CASTLE'S UNIQUE AND IS NOT TO BE BOMBED. YOU'LL LEAD THE NEXT ASSAULT ON IT.
HOW DARE YOU!
I'LL NOT SEE ANY LIVES THROWN AWAY FOR A FEW BLOCKS OF STONE! THERE'S MORE THAN ONE WAY TO SKIN A CAT – AND I'M GOING TO TRY SOME OF THOSE FIRST!
MAJOR EAZY
THAT BRIGADIER'S NUTS INSISTING ON AN ASSAULT ON THAT PLACE.
WAR ISN'T WAGED BY SANE MEN, SERGEANT DALY. INTERESTING. IT LOOKS AS IF ONLY THE GERMAN COMMANDER UP THERE IS AN SS MAN. THE GUYS UNDER HIM PROBABLY AREN'T TOO KEEN TO DIE FOR THE CAUSE. THINK I'LL SEND 'EM A NOTE.

"I WON'T LEAD AN ASSAULT ON THAT CASTLE, SIR."

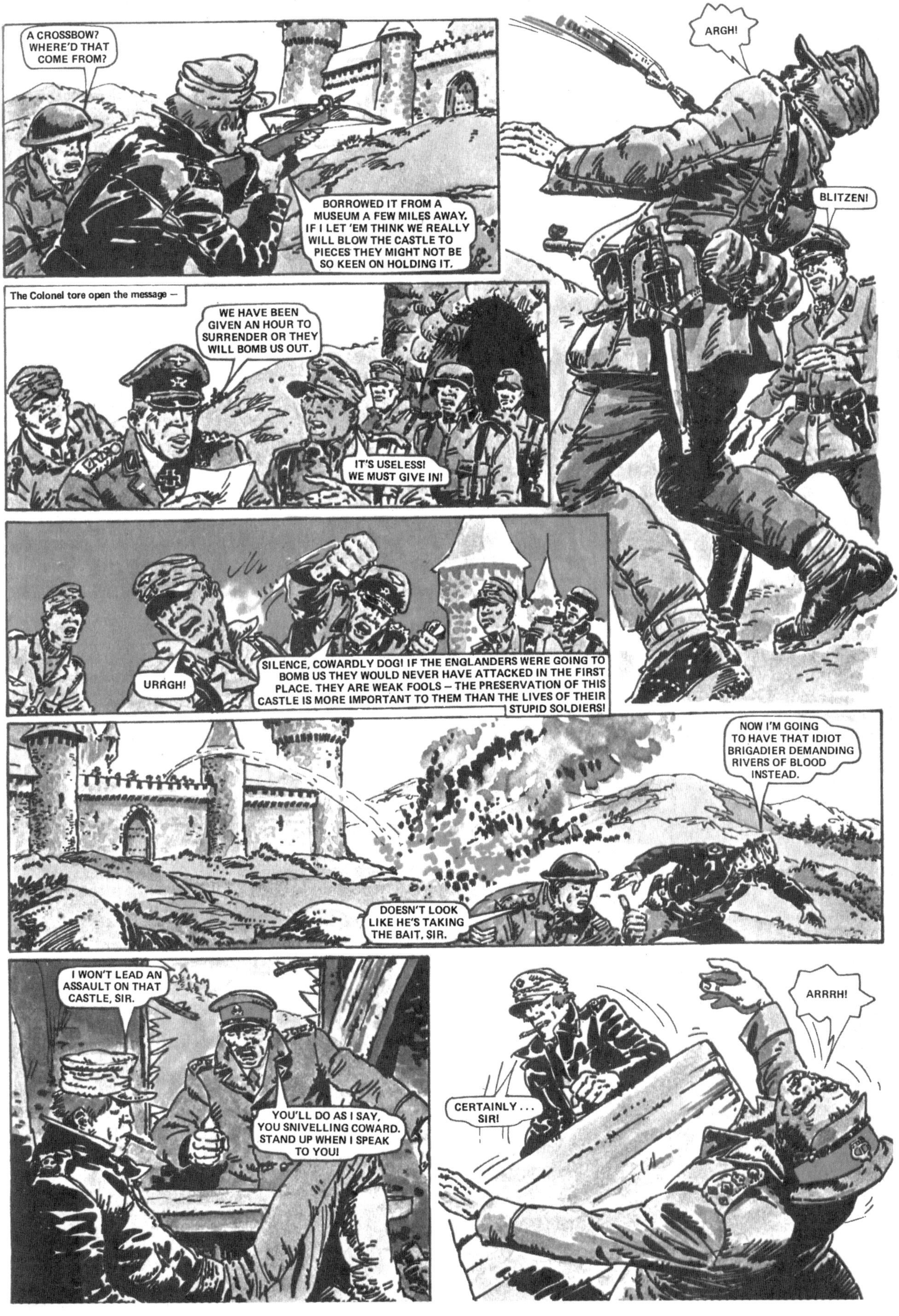

A CROSSBOW? WHERE'D THAT COME FROM?
BORROWED IT FROM A MUSEUM A FEW MILES AWAY. IF I LET 'EM THINK WE REALLY WILL BLOW THE CASTLE TO PIECES THEY MIGHT NOT BE SO KEEN ON HOLDING IT.
ARGH!
BLITZEN!
The Colonel tore open the message —
WE HAVE BEEN GIVEN AN HOUR TO SURRENDER OR THEY WILL BOMB US OUT.
IT'S USELESS! WE MUST GIVE IN!
URRGH!
SILENCE, COWARDLY DOG! IF THE ENGLANDERS WERE GOING TO BOMB US THEY WOULD NEVER HAVE ATTACKED IN THE FIRST PLACE. THEY ARE WEAK FOOLS – THE PRESERVATION OF THIS CASTLE IS MORE IMPORTANT TO THEM THAN THE LIVES OF THEIR STUPID SOLDIERS!
NOW I'M GOING TO HAVE THAT IDIOT BRIGADIER DEMANDING RIVERS OF BLOOD INSTEAD.
DOESN'T LOOK LIKE HE'S TAKING THE BAIT, SIR.
I WON'T LEAD AN ASSAULT ON THAT CASTLE, SIR.
YOU'LL DO AS I SAY, YOU SNIVELLING COWARD. STAND UP WHEN I SPEAK TO YOU!
CERTAINLY . . . SIR!
ARRRH!

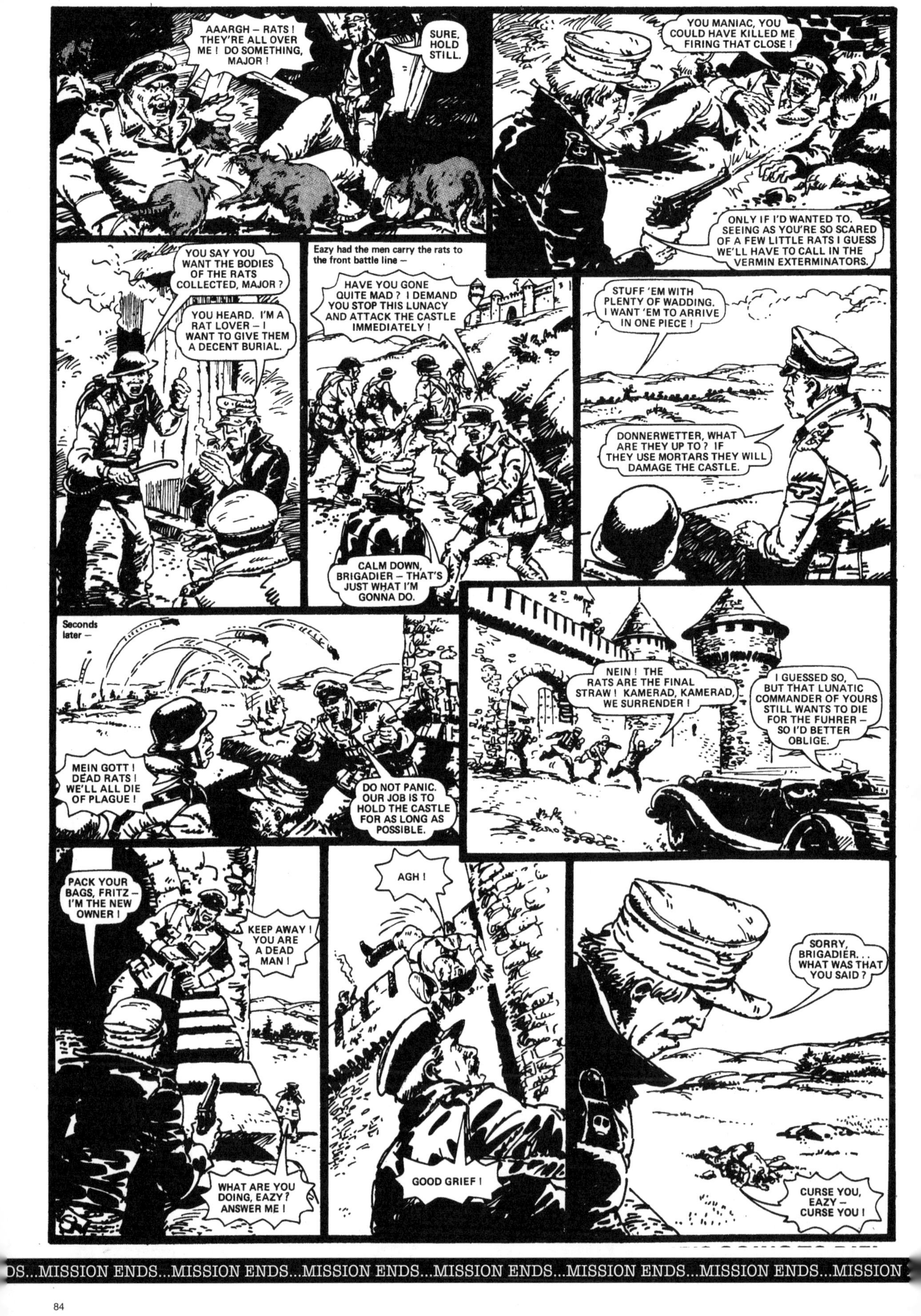

AAARGH – RATS! THEY'RE ALL OVER ME! DO SOMETHING, MAJOR!
SURE, HOLD STILL.
YOU MANIAC, YOU COULD HAVE KILLED ME FIRING THAT CLOSE!
ONLY IF I'D WANTED TO. SEEING AS YOU'RE SO SCARED OF A FEW LITTLE RATS I GUESS WE'LL HAVE TO CALL IN THE VERMIN EXTERMINATORS.
YOU SAY YOU WANT THE BODIES OF THE RATS COLLECTED, MAJOR?
YOU HEARD. I'M A RAT LOVER – I WANT TO GIVE THEM A DECENT BURIAL.
Eazy had the men carry the rats to the front battle line –
HAVE YOU GONE QUITE MAD? I DEMAND YOU STOP THIS LUNACY AND ATTACK THE CASTLE IMMEDIATELY!
CALM DOWN, BRIGADIER – THAT'S JUST WHAT I'M GONNA DO.
STUFF 'EM WITH PLENTY OF WADDING. I WANT 'EM TO ARRIVE IN ONE PIECE!
DONNERWETTER, WHAT ARE THEY UP TO? IF THEY USE MORTARS THEY WILL DAMAGE THE CASTLE.
Seconds later –
MEIN GOTT! DEAD RATS! WE'LL ALL DIE OF PLAGUE!
DO NOT PANIC. OUR JOB IS TO HOLD THE CASTLE FOR AS LONG AS POSSIBLE.
NEIN! THE RATS ARE THE FINAL STRAW! KAMERAD, KAMERAD, WE SURRENDER!
I GUESSED SO, BUT THAT LUNATIC COMMANDER OF YOURS STILL WANTS TO DIE FOR THE FUHRER – SO I'D BETTER OBLIGE.
PACK YOUR BAGS, FRITZ – I'M THE NEW OWNER!
KEEP AWAY! YOU ARE A DEAD MAN!
WHAT ARE YOU DOING, EAZY? ANSWER ME!
AGH!
GOOD GRIEF!
SORRY, BRIGADIER... WHAT WAS THAT YOU SAID?
CURSE YOU, EAZY – CURSE YOU!

DS...MISSION ENDS...MISSION ENDS...MISSION ENDS...MISSION ENDS...MISSION ENDS...MISSION ENDS...MISSION ENDS...MISSION

FIGHTER from the SKY

"I'LL MAKE SURE THEY DON'T FORGET THE NAME FALLMAN!"

German paratrooper Paul Fallman has fallen a long way since the invasion of Poland: his Nazi-hating father has been killed by the Gestapo, his family arrested, his ancestral home razed to the ground — and he's been busted down to the rank of ordinary solider.

Now he's fighting back; not just against the Allies, but also fellow paratrooper and Nazi loyalist Lieutenant Hung, to reclaim his honour and clear his family reputation... that's if the Allies leave him alive long enough to land! Never averse to showing war from the enemy's perspective, *Battle*'s German characters were invariably vehemently anti-Nazi, against the war and usually from the officer class. This short-lived series only lasted from April 1976 until August 1976.

NOTES FROM THE FRONTLINE:

"The introduction of German characters is one of my real successes; I'd kicked it off in *Action* with 'Hellman' [of Hammer Force], which Gerry Finley-Day wrote for me in 1976. Although John Sanders [then IPC comics Publisher] said 'You can't have a German hero!' I said, 'We've got to move on, John — the war's been over for a long time!' Despite his concerns, he agreed. So having fought really very, very hard to get a German character into *Action* I came away really delighted and commissioned Gerry to write it. Dave Hunt, *Battle*'s editor at the time, heard about this and he very quickly brought out 'Fighter from the Sky'; after that a whole number of other German heroes followed suit." — **Pat Mills**

WRITTEN BY Gerry Finley-Day
DRAWN BY Geoff Campion

WAR ACTION WITH FALLMAN – CRACK GERMAN PARATROOPER !

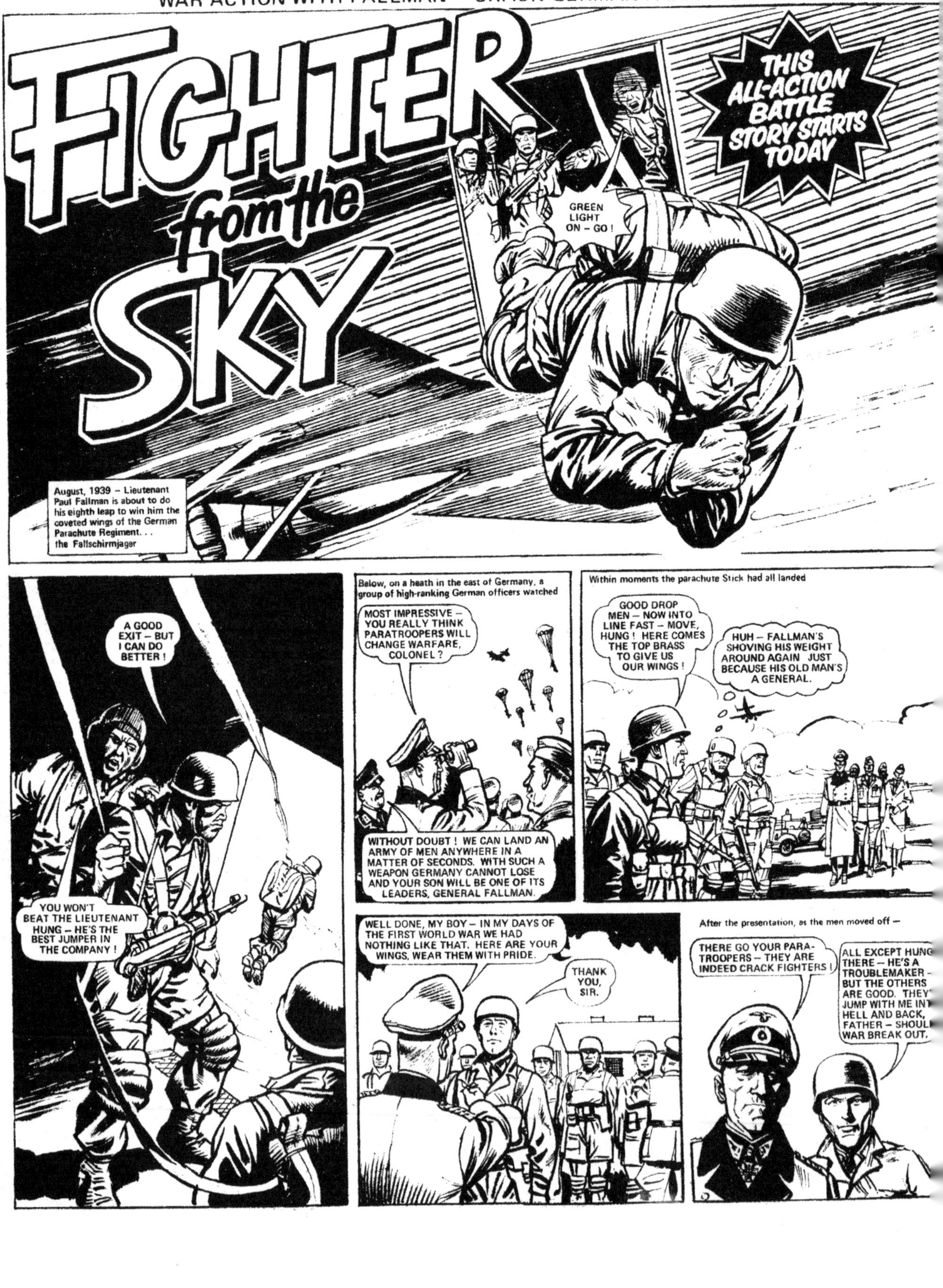
FIGHTER from the SKY
THIS ALL-ACTION BATTLE STORY STARTS TODAY
GREEN LIGHT ON – GO !
August, 1939 – Lieutenant Paul Fallman is about to do his eighth leap to win him the coveted wings of the German Parachute Regiment. . . the Fallschirmjager
A GOOD EXIT – BUT I CAN DO BETTER !
YOU WON'T BEAT THE LIEUTENANT HUNG – HE'S THE BEST JUMPER IN THE COMPANY !
Below, on a heath in the east of Germany, a group of high-ranking German officers watched
MOST IMPRESSIVE – YOU REALLY THINK PARATROOPERS WILL CHANGE WARFARE, COLONEL ?
WITHOUT DOUBT ! WE CAN LAND AN ARMY OF MEN ANYWHERE IN A MATTER OF SECONDS. WITH SUCH A WEAPON GERMANY CANNOT LOSE AND YOUR SON WILL BE ONE OF ITS LEADERS, GENERAL FALLMAN.
Within moments the parachute Stick had all landed
GOOD DROP MEN – NOW INTO LINE FAST – MOVE, HUNG ! HERE COMES THE TOP BRASS TO GIVE US OUR WINGS !
HUH – FALLMAN'S SHOVING HIS WEIGHT AROUND AGAIN JUST BECAUSE HIS OLD MAN'S A GENERAL.
WELL DONE, MY BOY – IN MY DAYS OF THE FIRST WORLD WAR WE HAD NOTHING LIKE THAT. HERE ARE YOUR WINGS, WEAR THEM WITH PRIDE.
THANK YOU, SIR.
After the presentation, as the men moved off –
THERE GO YOUR PARA-TROOPERS – THEY ARE INDEED CRACK FIGHTERS !
ALL EXCEPT HUNG THERE – HE'S A TROUBLEMAKER – BUT THE OTHERS ARE GOOD. THEY JUMP WITH ME INT HELL AND BACK, FATHER – SHOUL WAR BREAK OUT.

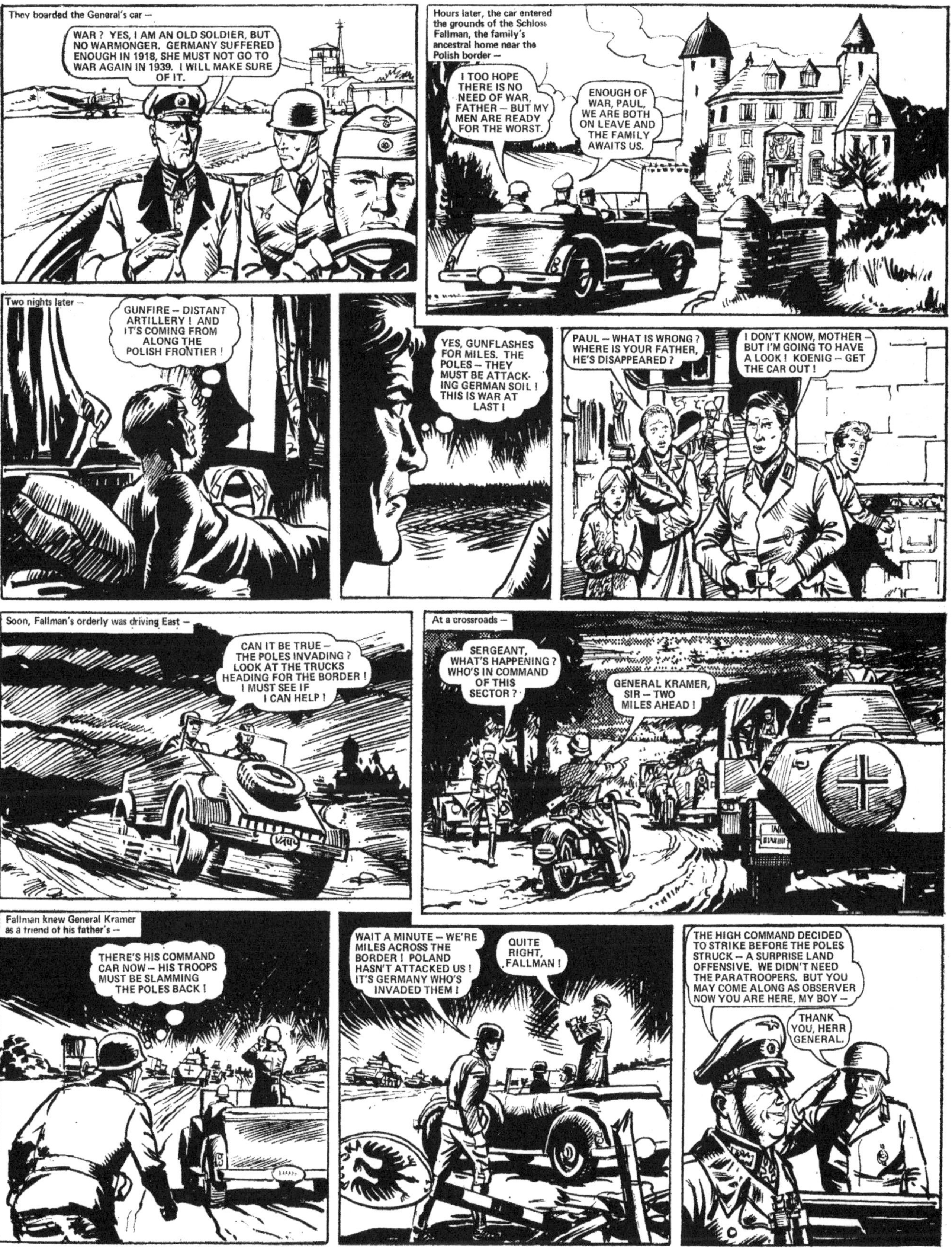
They boarded the General's car —
WAR ? YES, I AM AN OLD SOLDIER, BUT NO WARMONGER. GERMANY SUFFERED ENOUGH IN 1918, SHE MUST NOT GO TO WAR AGAIN IN 1939. I WILL MAKE SURE OF IT.
Hours later, the car entered the grounds of the Schloss Fallman, the family's ancestral home near the Polish border —
I TOO HOPE THERE IS NO NEED OF WAR, FATHER — BUT MY MEN ARE READY FOR THE WORST.
ENOUGH OF WAR, PAUL, WE ARE BOTH ON LEAVE AND THE FAMILY AWAITS US.
Two nights later —
GUNFIRE — DISTANT ARTILLERY ! AND IT'S COMING FROM ALONG THE POLISH FRONTIER !
YES, GUNFLASHES FOR MILES. THE POLES — THEY MUST BE ATTACKING GERMAN SOIL ! THIS IS WAR AT LAST !
PAUL — WHAT IS WRONG ? WHERE IS YOUR FATHER, HE'S DISAPPEARED ?
I DON'T KNOW, MOTHER — BUT I'M GOING TO HAVE A LOOK ! KOENIG — GET THE CAR OUT !
Soon, Fallman's orderly was driving East —
CAN IT BE TRUE — THE POLES INVADING ? LOOK AT THE TRUCKS HEADING FOR THE BORDER ! I MUST SEE IF I CAN HELP !
At a crossroads —
SERGEANT, WHAT'S HAPPENING ? WHO'S IN COMMAND OF THIS SECTOR ?
GENERAL KRAMER, SIR — TWO MILES AHEAD !
Fallman knew General Kramer as a friend of his father's —
THERE'S HIS COMMAND CAR NOW — HIS TROOPS MUST BE SLAMMING THE POLES BACK !
WAIT A MINUTE — WE'RE MILES ACROSS THE BORDER ! POLAND HASN'T ATTACKED US ! IT'S GERMANY WHO'S INVADED THEM !
QUITE RIGHT, FALLMAN !
THE HIGH COMMAND DECIDED TO STRIKE BEFORE THE POLES STRUCK — A SURPRISE LAND OFFENSIVE. WE DIDN'T NEED THE PARATROOPERS. BUT YOU MAY COME ALONG AS OBSERVER NOW YOU ARE HERE, MY BOY —
THANK YOU, HERR GENERAL.

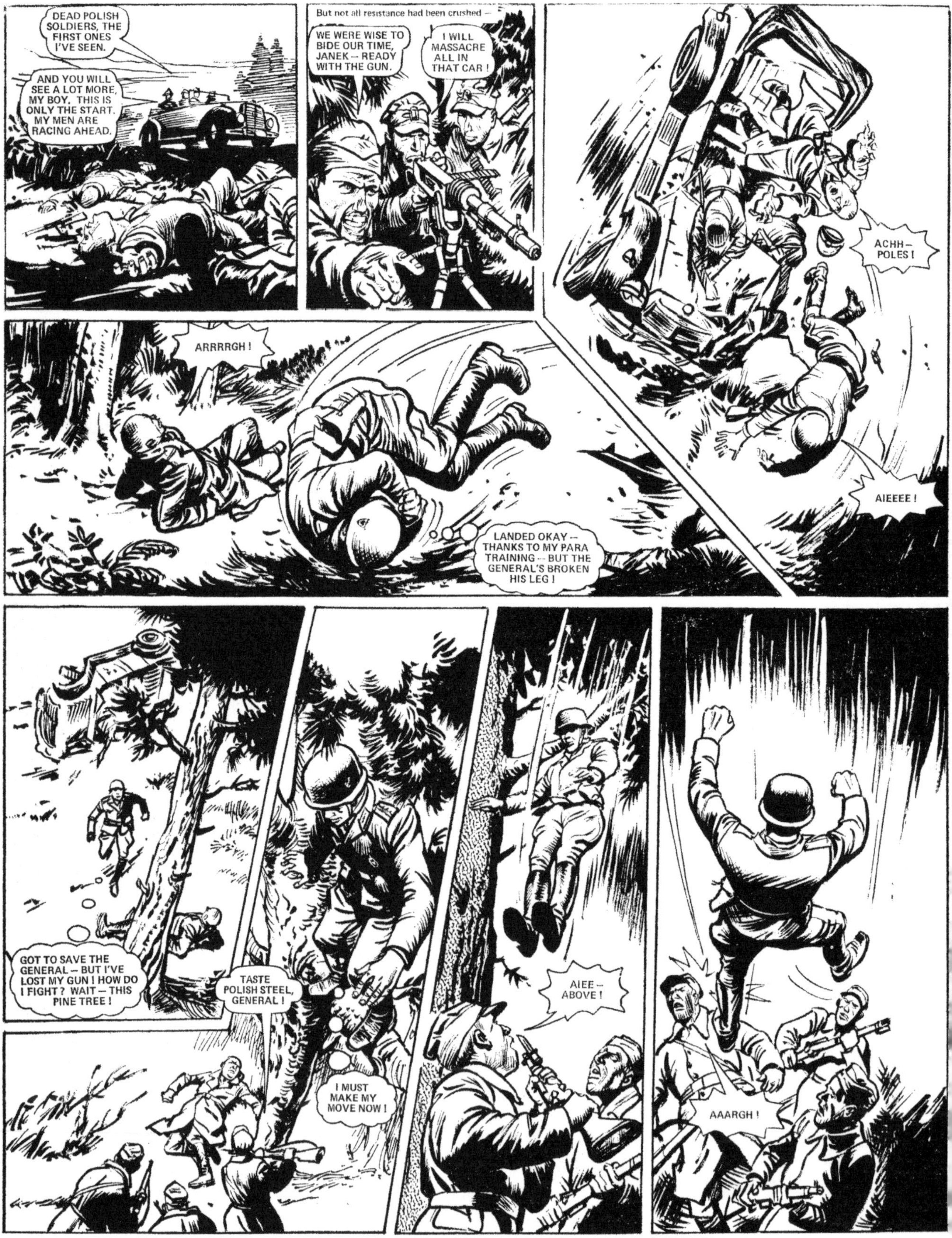
DEAD POLISH SOLDIERS, THE FIRST ONES I'VE SEEN.
AND YOU WILL SEE A LOT MORE, MY BOY, THIS IS ONLY THE START. MY MEN ARE RACING AHEAD.
But not all resistance had been crushed —
WE WERE WISE TO BIDE OUR TIME, JANEK -- READY WITH THE GUN.
I WILL MASSACRE ALL IN THAT CAR !
ACHH– POLES !
AIEEE !
ARRRRGH !
LANDED OKAY -- THANKS TO MY PARA TRAINING -- BUT THE GENERAL'S BROKEN HIS LEG !
GOT TO SAVE THE GENERAL – BUT I'VE LOST MY GUN ! HOW DO I FIGHT ? WAIT – THIS PINE TREE !
TASTE POLISH STEEL, GENERAL !
I MUST MAKE MY MOVE NOW !
AIEE – ABOVE !
AAARGH !

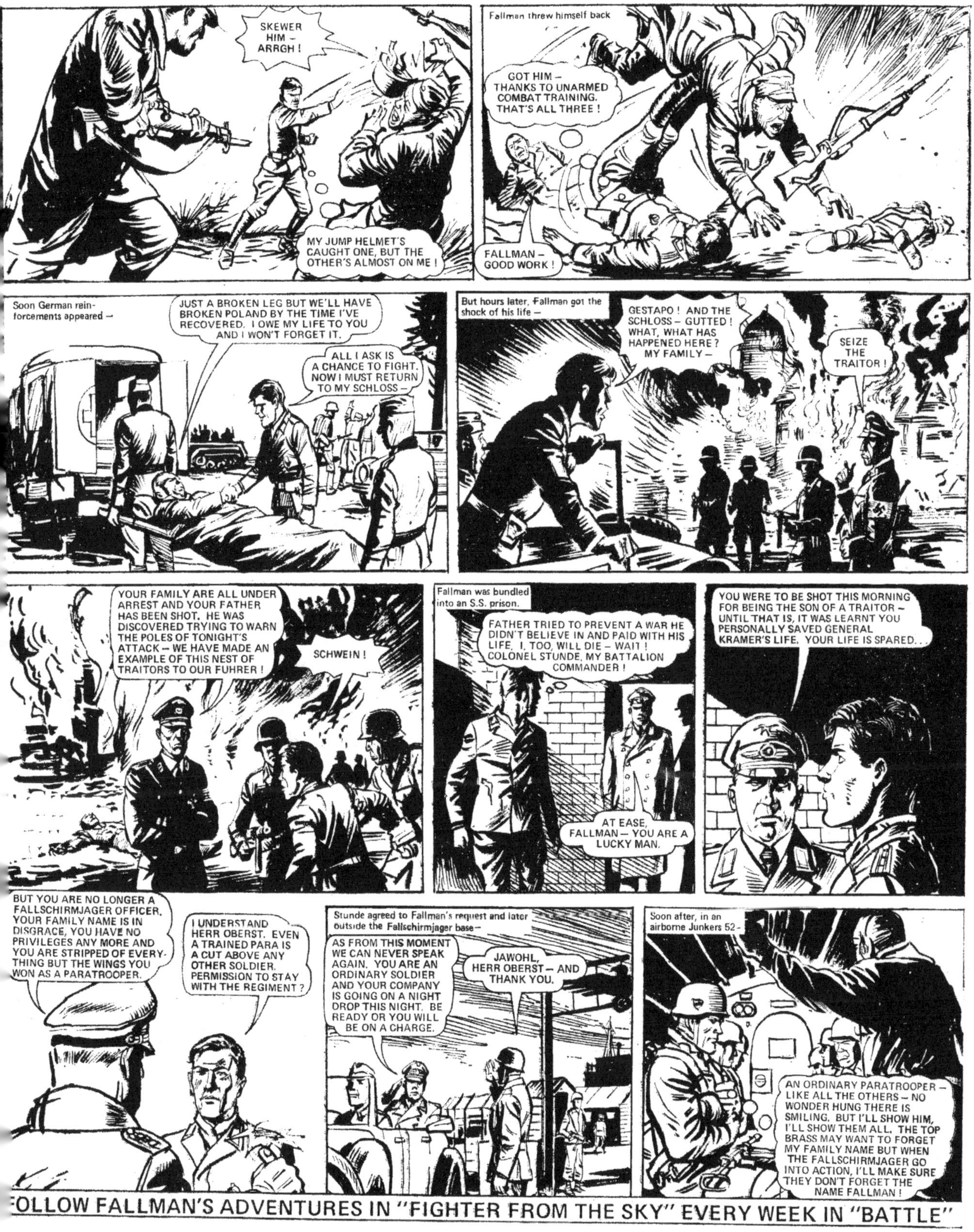
SKEWER HIM – ARRGH!
MY JUMP HELMET'S CAUGHT ONE, BUT THE OTHER'S ALMOST ON ME!
Fallman threw himself back
GOT HIM – THANKS TO UNARMED COMBAT TRAINING. THAT'S ALL THREE!
FALLMAN – GOOD WORK!
Soon German reinforcements appeared –
JUST A BROKEN LEG BUT WE'LL HAVE BROKEN POLAND BY THE TIME I'VE RECOVERED. I OWE MY LIFE TO YOU AND I WON'T FORGET IT.
ALL I ASK IS A CHANCE TO FIGHT. NOW I MUST RETURN TO MY SCHLOSS –
But hours later, Fallman got the shock of his life –
GESTAPO! AND THE SCHLOSS – GUTTED! WHAT, WHAT HAS HAPPENED HERE? MY FAMILY –
SEIZE THE TRAITOR!
YOUR FAMILY ARE ALL UNDER ARREST AND YOUR FATHER HAS BEEN SHOT. HE WAS DISCOVERED TRYING TO WARN THE POLES OF TONIGHT'S ATTACK – WE HAVE MADE AN EXAMPLE OF THIS NEST OF TRAITORS TO OUR FUHRER!
SCHWEIN!
Fallman was bundled into an S.S. prison.
FATHER TRIED TO PREVENT A WAR HE DIDN'T BELIEVE IN AND PAID WITH HIS LIFE. I, TOO, WILL DIE – WAIT! COLONEL STUNDE, MY BATTALION COMMANDER!
AT EASE, FALLMAN – YOU ARE A LUCKY MAN.
YOU WERE TO BE SHOT THIS MORNING FOR BEING THE SON OF A TRAITOR – UNTIL THAT IS, IT WAS LEARNT YOU PERSONALLY SAVED GENERAL KRAMER'S LIFE. YOUR LIFE IS SPARED...
BUT YOU ARE NO LONGER A FALLSCHIRMJAGER OFFICER. YOUR FAMILY NAME IS IN DISGRACE, YOU HAVE NO PRIVILEGES ANY MORE AND YOU ARE STRIPPED OF EVERYTHING BUT THE WINGS YOU WON AS A PARATROOPER.
I UNDERSTAND HERR OBERST. EVEN A TRAINED PARA IS A CUT ABOVE ANY OTHER SOLDIER. PERMISSION TO STAY WITH THE REGIMENT?
Stunde agreed to Fallman's request and later outside the Fallschirmjager base –
AS FROM THIS MOMENT WE CAN NEVER SPEAK AGAIN. YOU ARE AN ORDINARY SOLDIER AND YOUR COMPANY IS GOING ON A NIGHT DROP THIS NIGHT. BE READY OR YOU WILL BE ON A CHARGE.
JAWOHL, HERR OBERST – AND THANK YOU.
Soon after, in an airborne Junkers 52 –
AN ORDINARY PARATROOPER – LIKE ALL THE OTHERS – NO WONDER HUNG THERE IS SMILING. BUT I'LL SHOW HIM, I'LL SHOW THEM ALL. THE TOP BRASS MAY WANT TO FORGET MY FAMILY NAME BUT WHEN THE FALLSCHIRMJAGER GO INTO ACTION, I'LL MAKE SURE THEY DON'T FORGET THE NAME FALLMAN!

FOLLOW FALLMAN'S ADVENTURES IN "FIGHTER FROM THE SKY" EVERY WEEK IN "BATTLE"

IF GALE FORCE WINDS DIDN'T KILL FALLMAN – GROUND TROOPS WOULD !

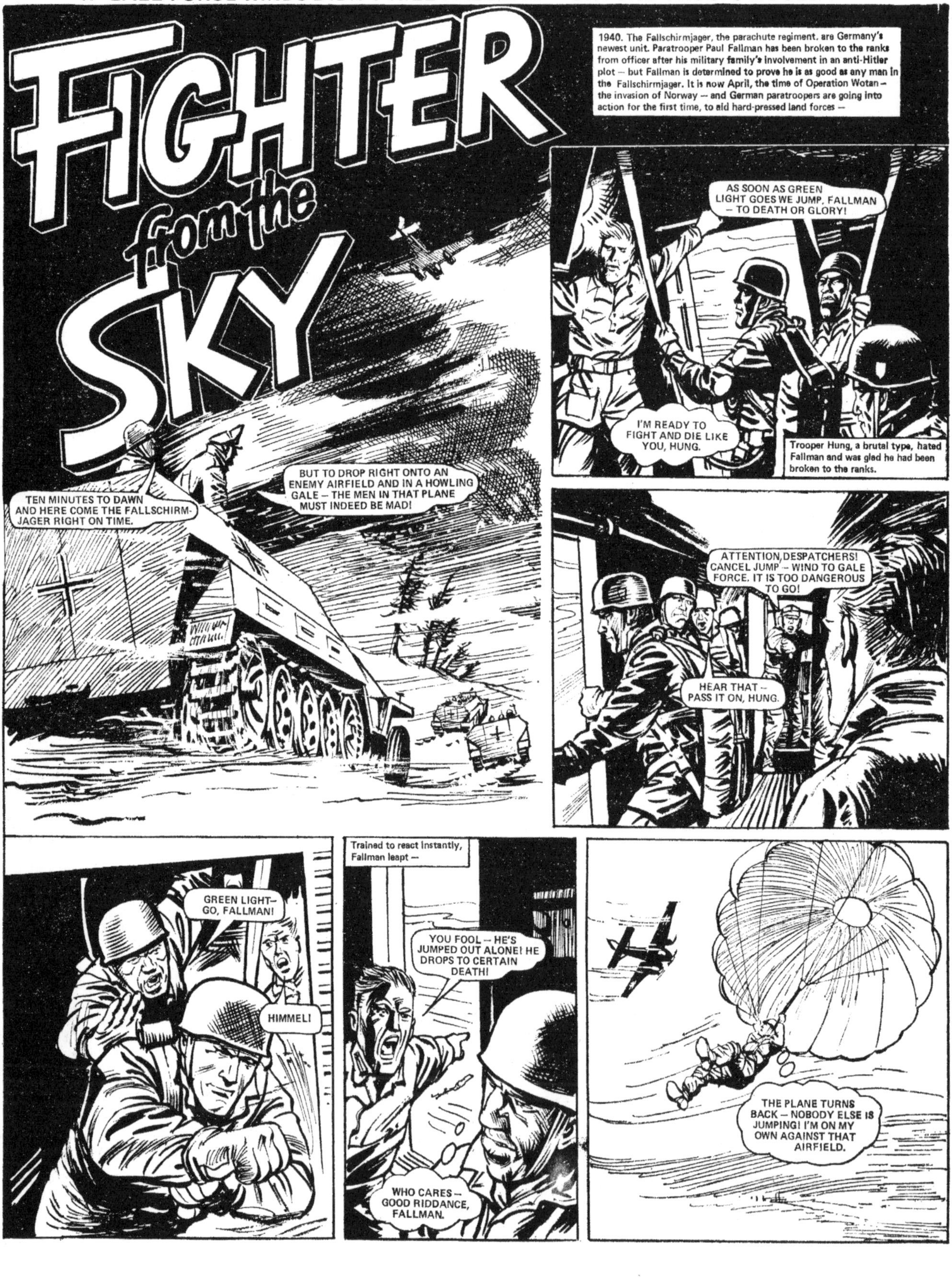
FIGHTER from the SKY
1940. The Fallschirmjager, the parachute regiment, are Germany's newest unit. Paratrooper Paul Fallman has been broken to the ranks from officer after his military family's involvement in an anti-Hitler plot – but Fallman is determined to prove he is as good as any man in the Fallschirmjager. It is now April, the time of Operation Wotan – the invasion of Norway – and German paratroopers are going into action for the first time, to aid hard-pressed land forces –
TEN MINUTES TO DAWN AND HERE COME THE FALLSCHIRM-JAGER RIGHT ON TIME.
BUT TO DROP RIGHT ONTO AN ENEMY AIRFIELD AND IN A HOWLING GALE – THE MEN IN THAT PLANE MUST INDEED BE MAD!
AS SOON AS GREEN LIGHT GOES WE JUMP, FALLMAN – TO DEATH OR GLORY!
I'M READY TO FIGHT AND DIE LIKE YOU, HUNG.
Trooper Hung, a brutal type, hated Fallman and was glad he had been broken to the ranks.
ATTENTION, DESPATCHERS! CANCEL JUMP – WIND TO GALE FORCE. IT IS TOO DANGEROUS TO GO!
HEAR THAT – PASS IT ON, HUNG.
GREEN LIGHT–GO, FALLMAN!
HIMMEL!
Trained to react instantly, Fallman leapt –
YOU FOOL – HE'S JUMPED OUT ALONE! HE DROPS TO CERTAIN DEATH!
WHO CARES – GOOD RIDDANCE, FALLMAN.
THE PLANE TURNS BACK – NOBODY ELSE IS JUMPING! I'M ON MY OWN AGAINST THAT AIRFIELD.

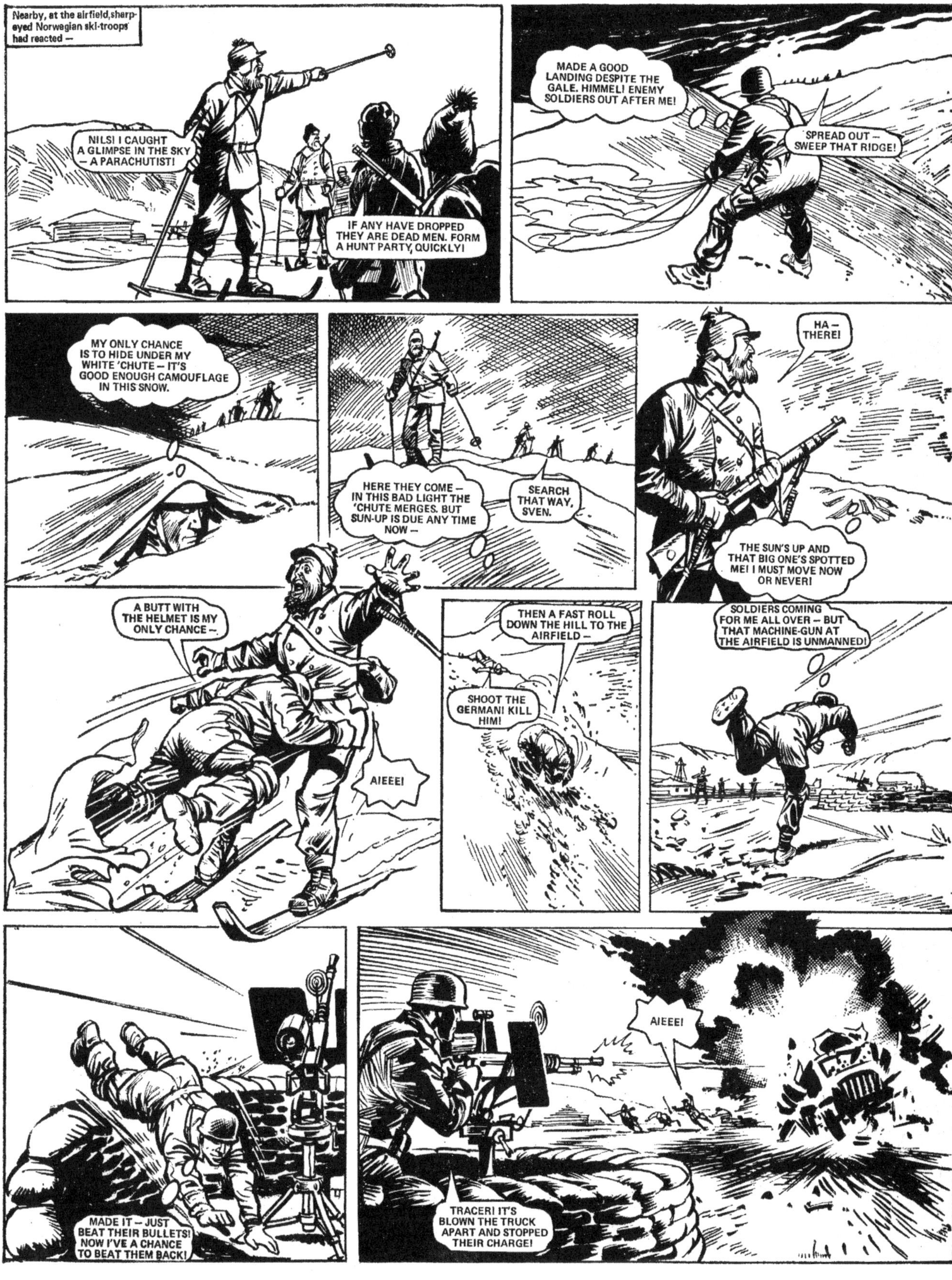
Nearby, at the airfield, sharp-eyed Norwegian ski-troops had reacted –
NILS! I CAUGHT A GLIMPSE IN THE SKY – A PARACHUTIST!
IF ANY HAVE DROPPED THEY ARE DEAD MEN. FORM A HUNT PARTY, QUICKLY!
MADE A GOOD LANDING DESPITE THE GALE. HIMMEL! ENEMY SOLDIERS OUT AFTER ME!
SPREAD OUT – SWEEP THAT RIDGE!
MY ONLY CHANCE IS TO HIDE UNDER MY WHITE 'CHUTE – IT'S GOOD ENOUGH CAMOUFLAGE IN THIS SNOW.
HERE THEY COME – IN THIS BAD LIGHT THE 'CHUTE MERGES. BUT SUN-UP IS DUE ANY TIME NOW –
SEARCH THAT WAY, SVEN.
HA – THERE!
THE SUN'S UP AND THAT BIG ONE'S SPOTTED ME! I MUST MOVE NOW OR NEVER!
A BUTT WITH THE HELMET IS MY ONLY CHANCE –.
AIEEE!
THEN A FAST ROLL DOWN THE HILL TO THE AIRFIELD –
SHOOT THE GERMAN! KILL HIM!
SOLDIERS COMING FOR ME ALL OVER – BUT THAT MACHINE-GUN AT THE AIRFIELD IS UNMANNED!
MADE IT – JUST BEAT THEIR BULLETS! NOW I'VE A CHANCE TO BEAT THEM BACK!
AIEEE!
TRACER! IT'S BLOWN THE TRUCK APART AND STOPPED THEIR CHARGE!

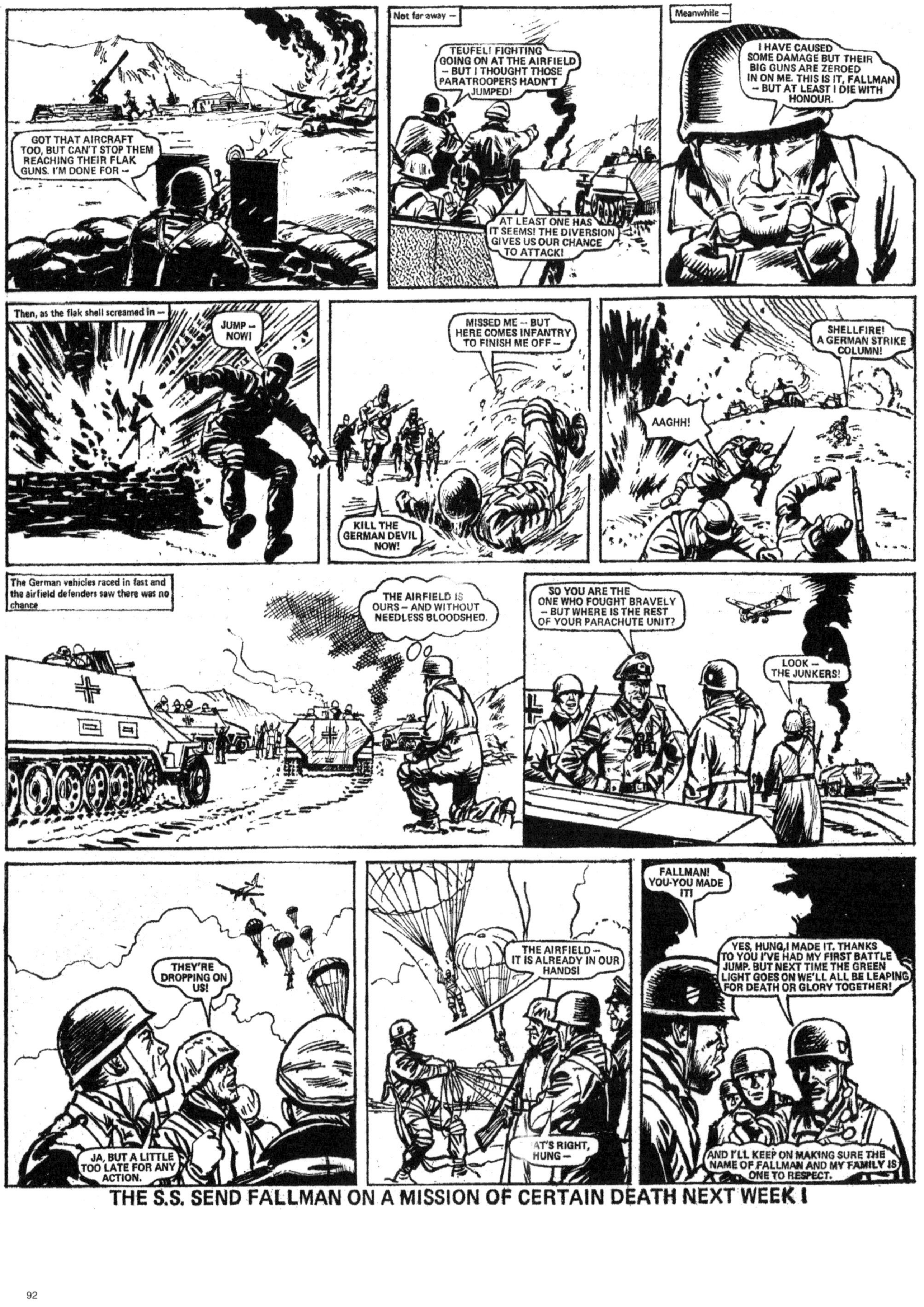
GOT THAT AIRCRAFT TOO, BUT CAN'T STOP THEM REACHING THEIR FLAK GUNS. I'M DONE FOR –
Not far away –
TEUFEL! FIGHTING GOING ON AT THE AIRFIELD – BUT I THOUGHT THOSE PARATROOPERS HADN'T JUMPED!
AT LEAST ONE HAS IT SEEMS! THE DIVERSION GIVES US OUR CHANCE TO ATTACK!
Meanwhile –
I HAVE CAUSED SOME DAMAGE BUT THEIR BIG GUNS ARE ZEROED IN ON ME. THIS IS IT, FALLMAN – BUT AT LEAST I DIE WITH HONOUR.
Then, as the flak shell screamed in –
JUMP – NOW!
MISSED ME – BUT HERE COMES INFANTRY TO FINISH ME OFF –
KILL THE GERMAN DEVIL NOW!
SHELLFIRE! A GERMAN STRIKE COLUMN!
AAGHH!
The German vehicles raced in fast and the airfield defenders saw there was no chance
THE AIRFIELD IS OURS – AND WITHOUT NEEDLESS BLOODSHED.
SO YOU ARE THE ONE WHO FOUGHT BRAVELY – BUT WHERE IS THE REST OF YOUR PARACHUTE UNIT?
LOOK – THE JUNKERS!
THEY'RE DROPPING ON US!
JA, BUT A LITTLE TOO LATE FOR ANY ACTION.
THE AIRFIELD – IT IS ALREADY IN OUR HANDS!
AT'S RIGHT, HUNG –
FALLMAN! YOU-YOU MADE IT!
YES, HUNG, I MADE IT. THANKS TO YOU I'VE HAD MY FIRST BATTLE JUMP. BUT NEXT TIME THE GREEN LIGHT GOES ON WE'LL ALL BE LEAPING FOR DEATH OR GLORY TOGETHER!
AND I'LL KEEP ON MAKING SURE THE NAME OF FALLMAN AND MY FAMILY IS ONE TO RESPECT.

THE S.S. SEND FALLMAN ON A MISSION OF CERTAIN DEATH NEXT WEEK !

JUMP INTO ACTION WITH PARATROOPER PAUL FALLMAN IN 'OPERATION YELLOW' !

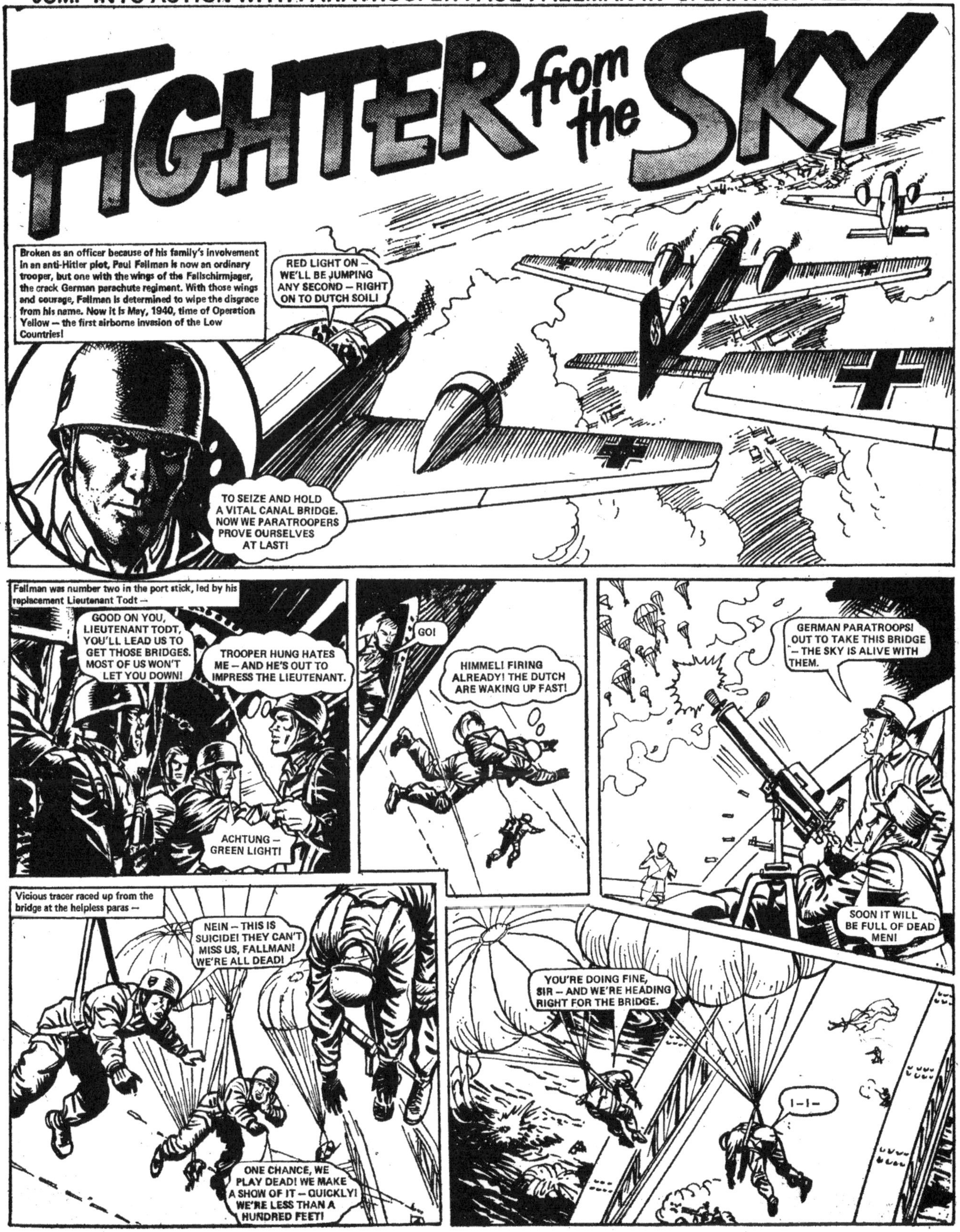
FIGHTER from the SKY
Broken as an officer because of his family's involvement in an anti-Hitler plot, Paul Fallman is now an ordinary trooper, but one with the wings of the Fallschirmjager, the crack German parachute regiment. With those wings and courage, Fallman is determined to wipe the disgrace from his name. Now it is May, 1940, time of Operation Yellow — the first airborne invasion of the Low Countries!
RED LIGHT ON — WE'LL BE JUMPING ANY SECOND — RIGHT ON TO DUTCH SOIL!
TO SEIZE AND HOLD A VITAL CANAL BRIDGE. NOW WE PARATROOPERS PROVE OURSELVES AT LAST!
Fallman was number two in the port stick, led by his replacement Lieutenant Todt —
GOOD ON YOU, LIEUTENANT TODT, YOU'LL LEAD US TO GET THOSE BRIDGES. MOST OF US WON'T LET YOU DOWN!
TROOPER HUNG HATES ME — AND HE'S OUT TO IMPRESS THE LIEUTENANT.
ACHTUNG — GREEN LIGHT!
GO!
HIMMEL! FIRING ALREADY! THE DUTCH ARE WAKING UP FAST!
GERMAN PARATROOPS! OUT TO TAKE THIS BRIDGE — THE SKY IS ALIVE WITH THEM.
SOON IT WILL BE FULL OF DEAD MEN!
Vicious tracer raced up from the bridge at the helpless paras —
NEIN — THIS IS SUICIDE! THEY CAN'T MISS US, FALLMAN! WE'RE ALL DEAD!
ONE CHANCE, WE PLAY DEAD! WE MAKE A SHOW OF IT — QUICKLY! WE'RE LESS THAN A HUNDRED FEET!
YOU'RE DOING FINE, SIR — AND WE'RE HEADING RIGHT FOR THE BRIDGE.
I — I —

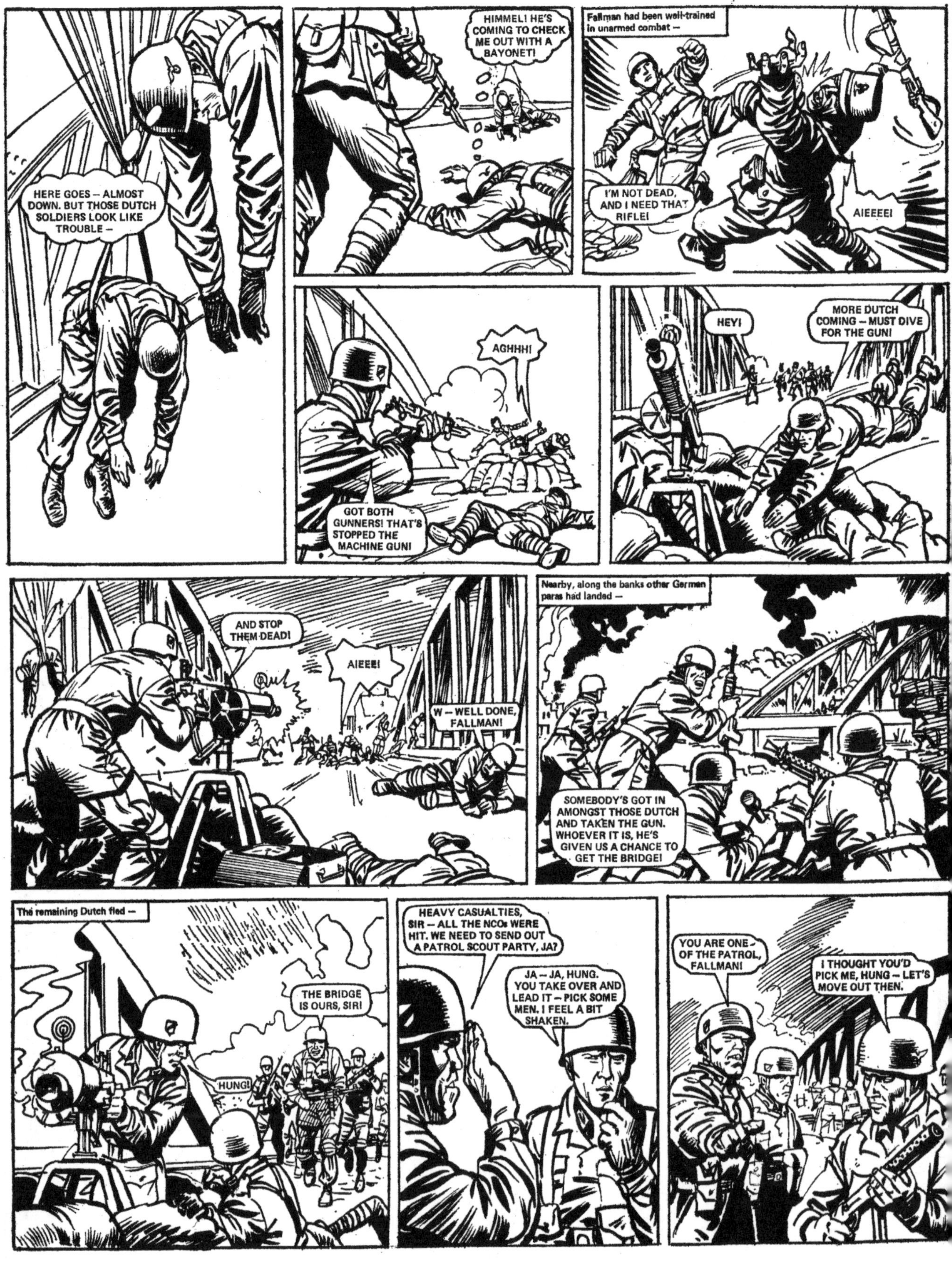
HERE GOES — ALMOST DOWN. BUT THOSE DUTCH SOLDIERS LOOK LIKE TROUBLE —
HIMMEL! HE'S COMING TO CHECK ME OUT WITH A BAYONET!
Fallman had been well-trained in unarmed combat —
I'M NOT DEAD, AND I NEED THAT RIFLE!
AIEEEE!
AGHHH!
GOT BOTH GUNNERS! THAT'S STOPPED THE MACHINE GUN!
HEY!
MORE DUTCH COMING — MUST DIVE FOR THE GUN!
AND STOP THEM DEAD!
AIEEE!
W — WELL DONE, FALLMAN!
Nearby, along the banks other German paras had landed —
SOMEBODY'S GOT IN AMONGST THOSE DUTCH AND TAKEN THE GUN. WHOEVER IT IS, HE'S GIVEN US A CHANCE TO GET THE BRIDGE!
The remaining Dutch fled —
THE BRIDGE IS OURS, SIR!
HUNG!
HEAVY CASUALTIES, SIR — ALL THE NCOs WERE HIT. WE NEED TO SEND OUT A PATROL SCOUT PARTY, JA?
JA — JA, HUNG. YOU TAKE OVER AND LEAD IT — PICK SOME MEN. I FEEL A BIT SHAKEN.
YOU ARE ONE OF THE PATROL, FALLMAN!
I THOUGHT YOU'D PICK ME, HUNG — LET'S MOVE OUT THEN.

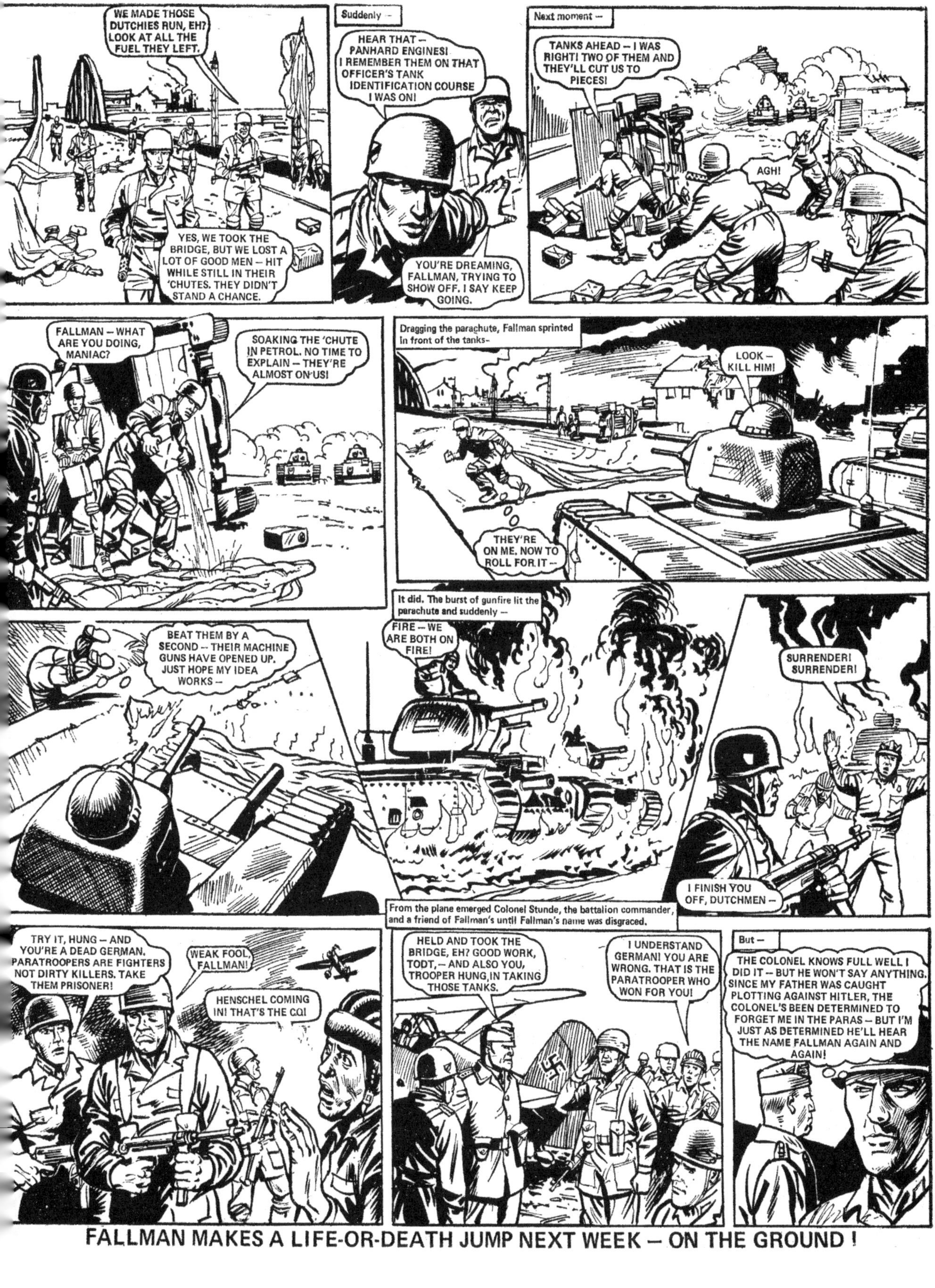

WE MADE THOSE DUTCHIES RUN, EH? LOOK AT ALL THE FUEL THEY LEFT.
YES, WE TOOK THE BRIDGE, BUT WE LOST A LOT OF GOOD MEN — HIT WHILE STILL IN THEIR 'CHUTES. THEY DIDN'T STAND A CHANCE.
Suddenly —
HEAR THAT — PANHARD ENGINES! I REMEMBER THEM ON THAT OFFICER'S TANK IDENTIFICATION COURSE I WAS ON!
YOU'RE DREAMING, FALLMAN, TRYING TO SHOW OFF. I SAY KEEP GOING.
Next moment —
TANKS AHEAD — I WAS RIGHT! TWO OF THEM AND THEY'LL CUT US TO PIECES!
AGH!
FALLMAN — WHAT ARE YOU DOING, MANIAC?
SOAKING THE 'CHUTE IN PETROL. NO TIME TO EXPLAIN — THEY'RE ALMOST ON US!
Dragging the parachute, Fallman sprinted in front of the tanks—
LOOK — KILL HIM!
THEY'RE ON ME. NOW TO ROLL FOR IT —
BEAT THEM BY A SECOND — THEIR MACHINE GUNS HAVE OPENED UP. JUST HOPE MY IDEA WORKS —
It did. The burst of gunfire lit the parachute and suddenly —
FIRE — WE ARE BOTH ON FIRE!
SURRENDER! SURRENDER!
I FINISH YOU OFF, DUTCHMEN —
TRY IT, HUNG — AND YOU'RE A DEAD GERMAN. PARATROOPERS ARE FIGHTERS NOT DIRTY KILLERS. TAKE THEM PRISONER!
WEAK FOOL, FALLMAN!
HENSCHEL COMING IN! THAT'S THE CO!
From the plane emerged Colonel Stunde, the battalion commander, and a friend of Fallman's until Fallman's name was disgraced.
HELD AND TOOK THE BRIDGE, EH? GOOD WORK, TODT, — AND ALSO YOU, TROOPER HUNG, IN TAKING THOSE TANKS.
I UNDERSTAND GERMAN! YOU ARE WRONG. THAT IS THE PARATROOPER WHO WON FOR YOU!
But —
THE COLONEL KNOWS FULL WELL I DID IT — BUT HE WON'T SAY ANYTHING. SINCE MY FATHER WAS CAUGHT PLOTTING AGAINST HITLER, THE COLONEL'S BEEN DETERMINED TO FORGET ME IN THE PARAS — BUT I'M JUST AS DETERMINED HE'LL HEAR THE NAME FALLMAN AGAIN AND AGAIN!

FALLMAN MAKES A LIFE-OR-DEATH JUMP NEXT WEEK — ON THE GROUND !

JUMP INTO FAST-MOVING ACTION WITH THE PARATROOPER FRAMED BY THE S.S.!

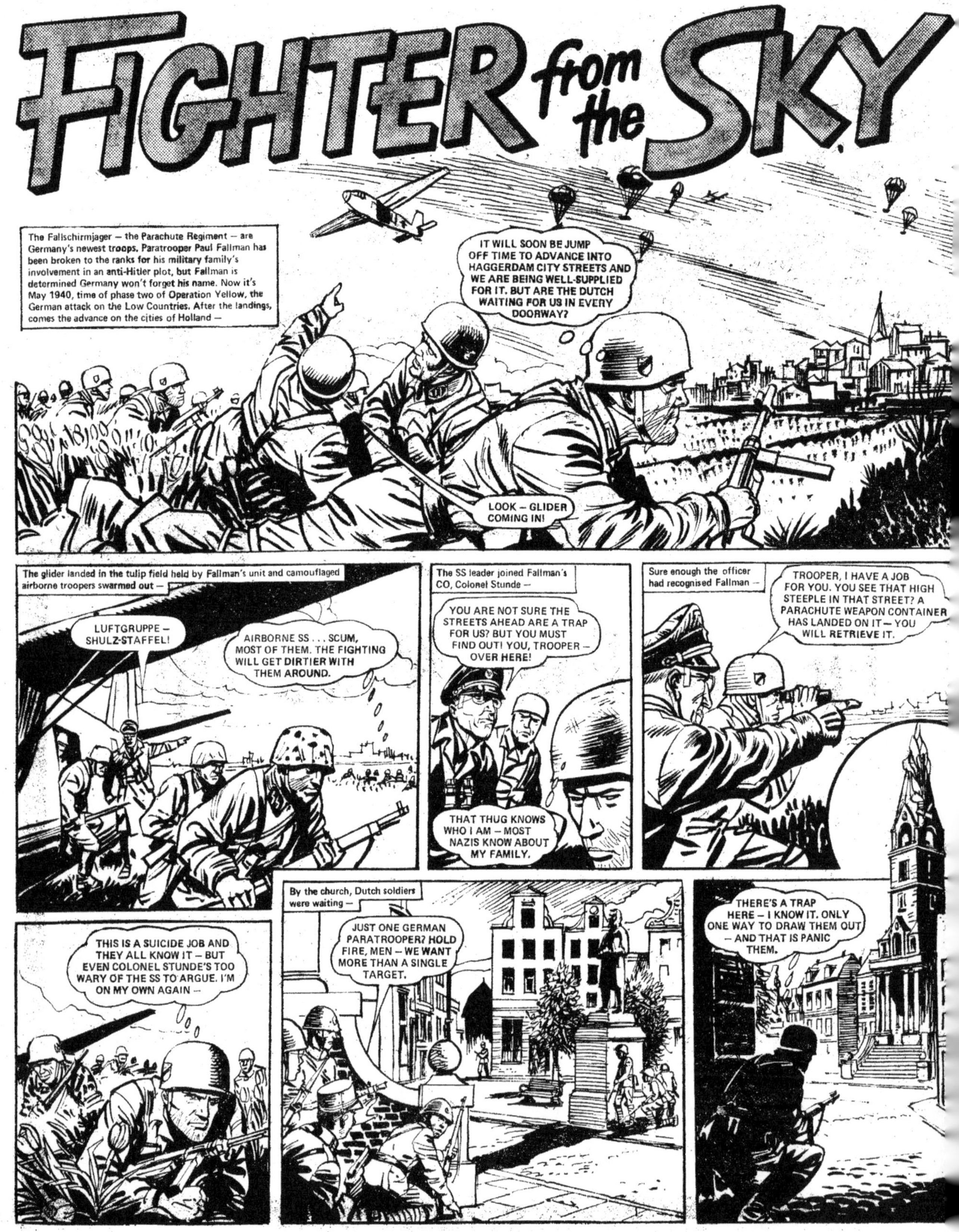
FIGHTER from the SKY
The Fallschirmjager — the Parachute Regiment — are Germany's newest troops. Paratrooper Paul Fallman has been broken to the ranks for his military family's involvement in an anti-Hitler plot, but Fallman is determined Germany won't forget his name. Now it's May 1940, time of phase two of Operation Yellow, the German attack on the Low Countries. After the landings, comes the advance on the cities of Holland —
IT WILL SOON BE JUMP OFF TIME TO ADVANCE INTO HAGGERDAM CITY STREETS AND WE ARE BEING WELL-SUPPLIED FOR IT. BUT ARE THE DUTCH WAITING FOR US IN EVERY DOORWAY?
LOOK — GLIDER COMING IN!
The glider landed in the tulip field held by Fallman's unit and camouflaged airborne troopers swarmed out —
LUFTGRUPPE — SHULZ-STAFFEL!
AIRBORNE SS . . . SCUM, MOST OF THEM. THE FIGHTING WILL GET DIRTIER WITH THEM AROUND.
The SS leader joined Fallman's CO, Colonel Stunde —
YOU ARE NOT SURE THE STREETS AHEAD ARE A TRAP FOR US? BUT YOU MUST FIND OUT! YOU, TROOPER — OVER HERE!
THAT THUG KNOWS WHO I AM — MOST NAZIS KNOW ABOUT MY FAMILY.
Sure enough the officer had recognised Fallman —
TROOPER, I HAVE A JOB FOR YOU. YOU SEE THAT HIGH STEEPLE IN THAT STREET? A PARACHUTE WEAPON CONTAINER HAS LANDED ON IT — YOU WILL RETRIEVE IT.
THIS IS A SUICIDE JOB AND THEY ALL KNOW IT — BUT EVEN COLONEL STUNDE'S TOO WARY OF THE SS TO ARGUE. I'M ON MY OWN AGAIN —
By the church, Dutch soldiers were waiting —
JUST ONE GERMAN PARATROOPER? HOLD FIRE, MEN — WE WANT MORE THAN A SINGLE TARGET.
THERE'S A TRAP HERE — I KNOW IT. ONLY ONE WAY TO DRAW THEM OUT — AND THAT IS PANIC THEM.

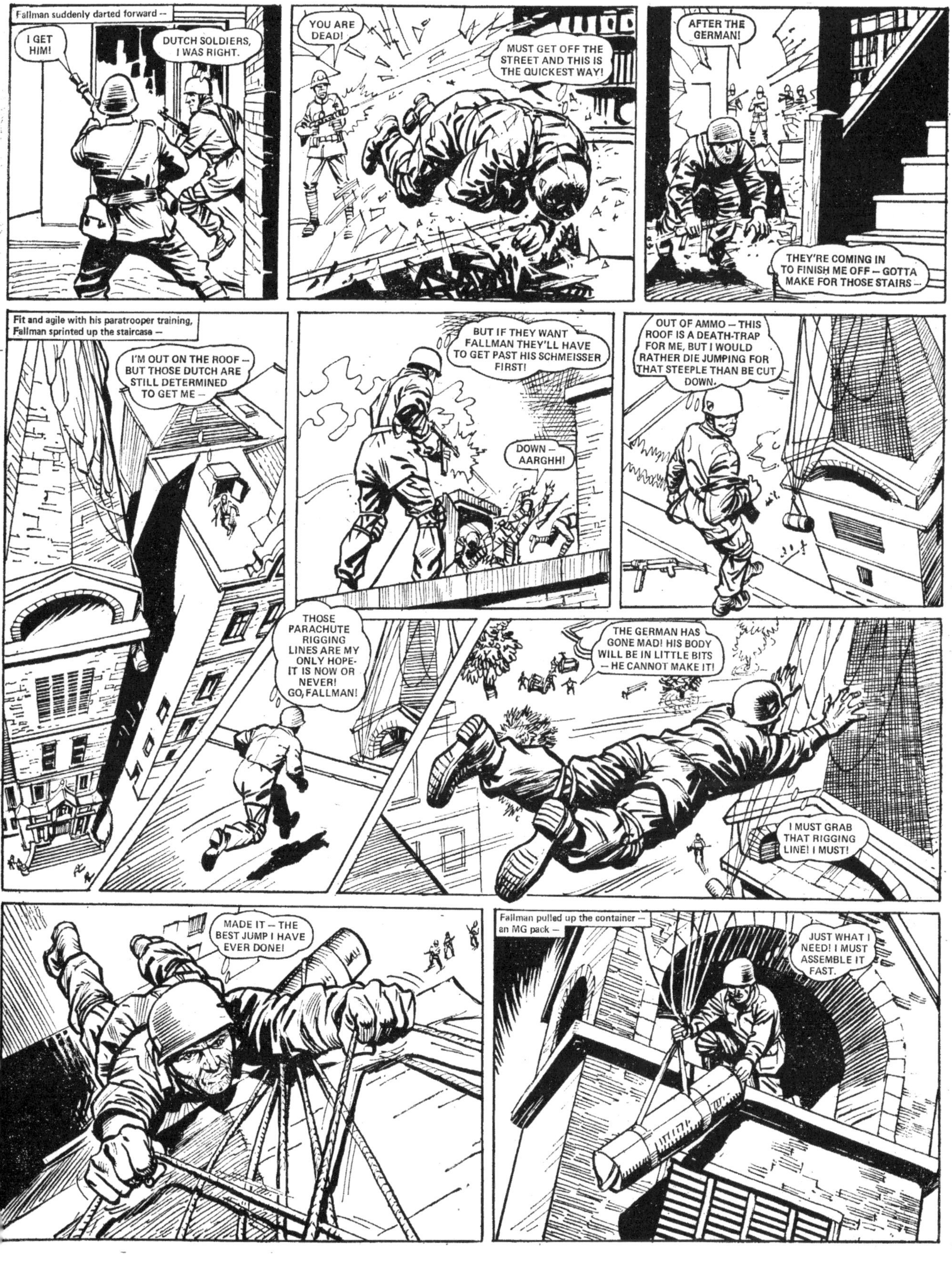

Fallman suddenly darted forward --
I GET HIM!
DUTCH SOLDIERS, I WAS RIGHT.
YOU ARE DEAD!
MUST GET OFF THE STREET AND THIS IS THE QUICKEST WAY!
AFTER THE GERMAN!
THEY'RE COMING IN TO FINISH ME OFF — GOTTA MAKE FOR THOSE STAIRS —
Fit and agile with his paratrooper training, Fallman sprinted up the staircase —
I'M OUT ON THE ROOF — BUT THOSE DUTCH ARE STILL DETERMINED TO GET ME —
BUT IF THEY WANT FALLMAN THEY'LL HAVE TO GET PAST HIS SCHMEISSER FIRST!
DOWN — AARGHH!
OUT OF AMMO — THIS ROOF IS A DEATH-TRAP FOR ME, BUT I WOULD RATHER DIE JUMPING FOR THAT STEEPLE THAN BE CUT DOWN.
THOSE PARACHUTE RIGGING LINES ARE MY ONLY HOPE-IT IS NOW OR NEVER! GO, FALLMAN!
THE GERMAN HAS GONE MAD! HIS BODY WILL BE IN LITTLE BITS — HE CANNOT MAKE IT!
I MUST GRAB THAT RIGGING LINE! I MUST!
MADE IT — THE BEST JUMP I HAVE EVER DONE!
Fallman pulled up the container — an MG pack —
JUST WHAT I NEED! I MUST ASSEMBLE IT FAST.

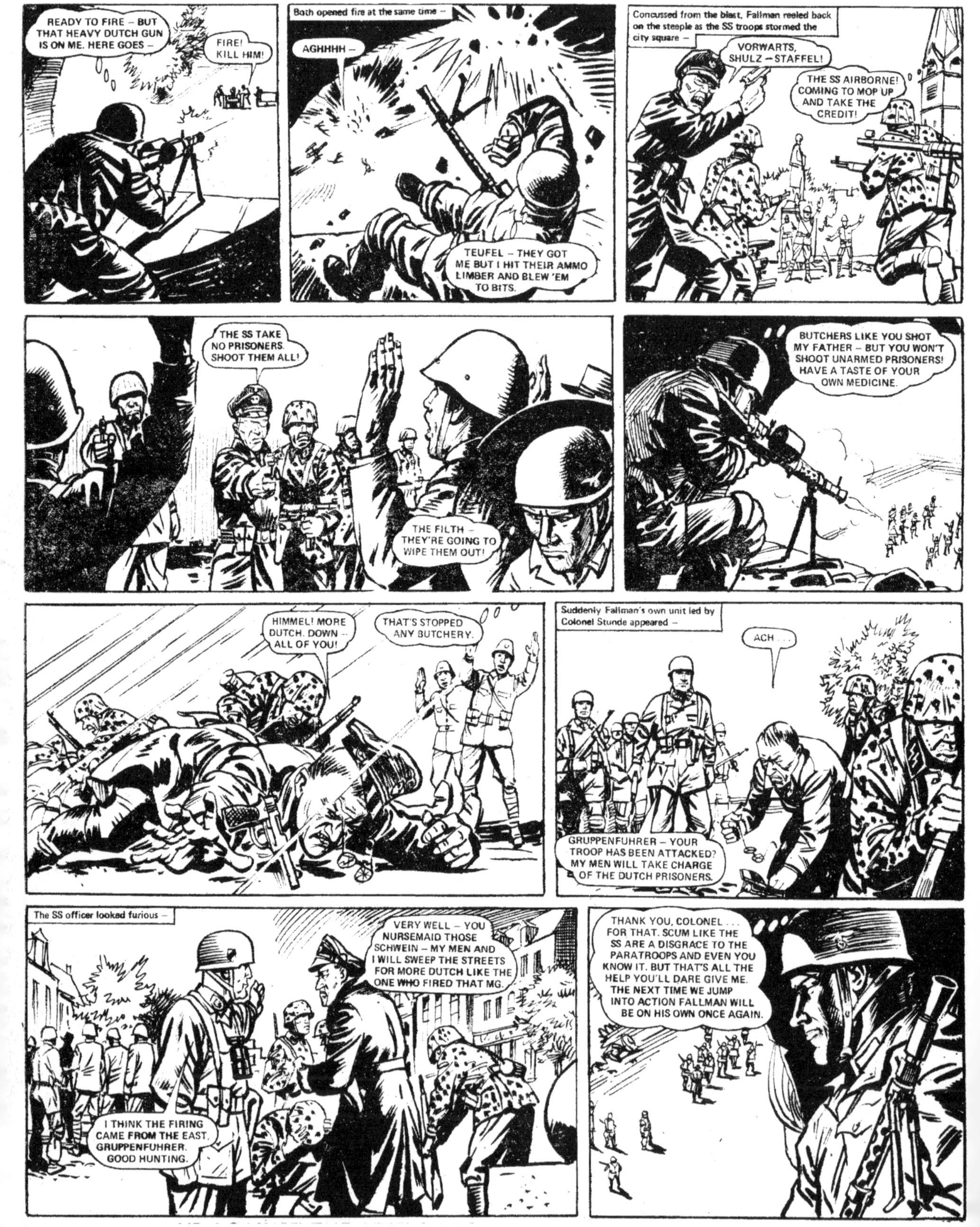
READY TO FIRE – BUT THAT HEAVY DUTCH GUN IS ON ME. HERE GOES –
FIRE! KILL HIM!
Both opened fire at the same time –
AGHHHH –
TEUFEL – THEY GOT ME BUT I HIT THEIR AMMO LIMBER AND BLEW 'EM TO BITS.
Concussed from the blast, Fallman reeled back on the steeple as the SS troops stormed the city square –
VORWARTS, SHULZ – STAFFEL!
THE SS AIRBORNE! COMING TO MOP UP AND TAKE THE CREDIT!
THE SS TAKE NO PRISONERS. SHOOT THEM ALL!
THE FILTH – THEY'RE GOING TO WIPE THEM OUT!
BUTCHERS LIKE YOU SHOT MY FATHER – BUT YOU WON'T SHOOT UNARMED PRISONERS! HAVE A TASTE OF YOUR OWN MEDICINE.
HIMMEL! MORE DUTCH. DOWN – ALL OF YOU!
THAT'S STOPPED ANY BUTCHERY.
Suddenly Fallman's own unit led by Colonel Stunde appeared –
ACH . . .
GRUPPENFUHRER – YOUR TROOP HAS BEEN ATTACKED? MY MEN WILL TAKE CHARGE OF THE DUTCH PRISONERS.
The SS officer looked furious –
VERY WELL – YOU NURSEMAID THOSE SCHWEIN – MY MEN AND I WILL SWEEP THE STREETS FOR MORE DUTCH LIKE THE ONE WHO FIRED THAT MG.
I THINK THE FIRING CAME FROM THE EAST, GRUPPENFUHRER. GOOD HUNTING.
THANK YOU, COLONEL . . . FOR THAT. SCUM LIKE THE SS ARE A DISGRACE TO THE PARATROOPS AND EVEN YOU KNOW IT. BUT THAT'S ALL THE HELP YOU'LL DARE GIVE ME. THE NEXT TIME WE JUMP INTO ACTION FALLMAN WILL BE ON HIS OWN ONCE AGAIN.
MISSION ENDS...MISSION ENDS...MISSION ENDS...MISSION ENDS...MISSION ENDS...MISSION ENI

HOLD HILL 109

"THIRTEEN MEN AND SIX DAYS TO HOLD THIS DAMN PLACE...."

In the burning heat of the North African desert, a platoon of men — whittled down to just thirteen battle-weary Eighth Army veterans — have been ordered to defend a vital pass from the might of Rommel's advancing Afrika Korps. It's up to Sgt Nick Armstrong and his twelve exhausted compatriots to hold Hill 109 for the next six days, until a relief column can reach them.

Using a technique that helped to create a real sense of tension, 'Hold Hill 109' was a complete story told across six weekly instalments. It was a technique that kept the reader hooked and the outcome unknown until the final episode.

NOTES FROM THE FRONTLINE:

"You could really believe in the character because of the gritty, realistic art. When I was editor, the way of storytelling wasn't the Fleetway approach — episodic with a cliffhanger. Everything was self-contained. 'Hold Hill 109' was one of those short, sharp stories — an experiment, if you will."
— Dave Hunt

WRITTEN BY Steve MacManus
DRAWN BY Jim Watson

ACTION WITH A BUNCH OF MEN TOLD TO HOLD ON OR DIE IN THE ATTEMPT !

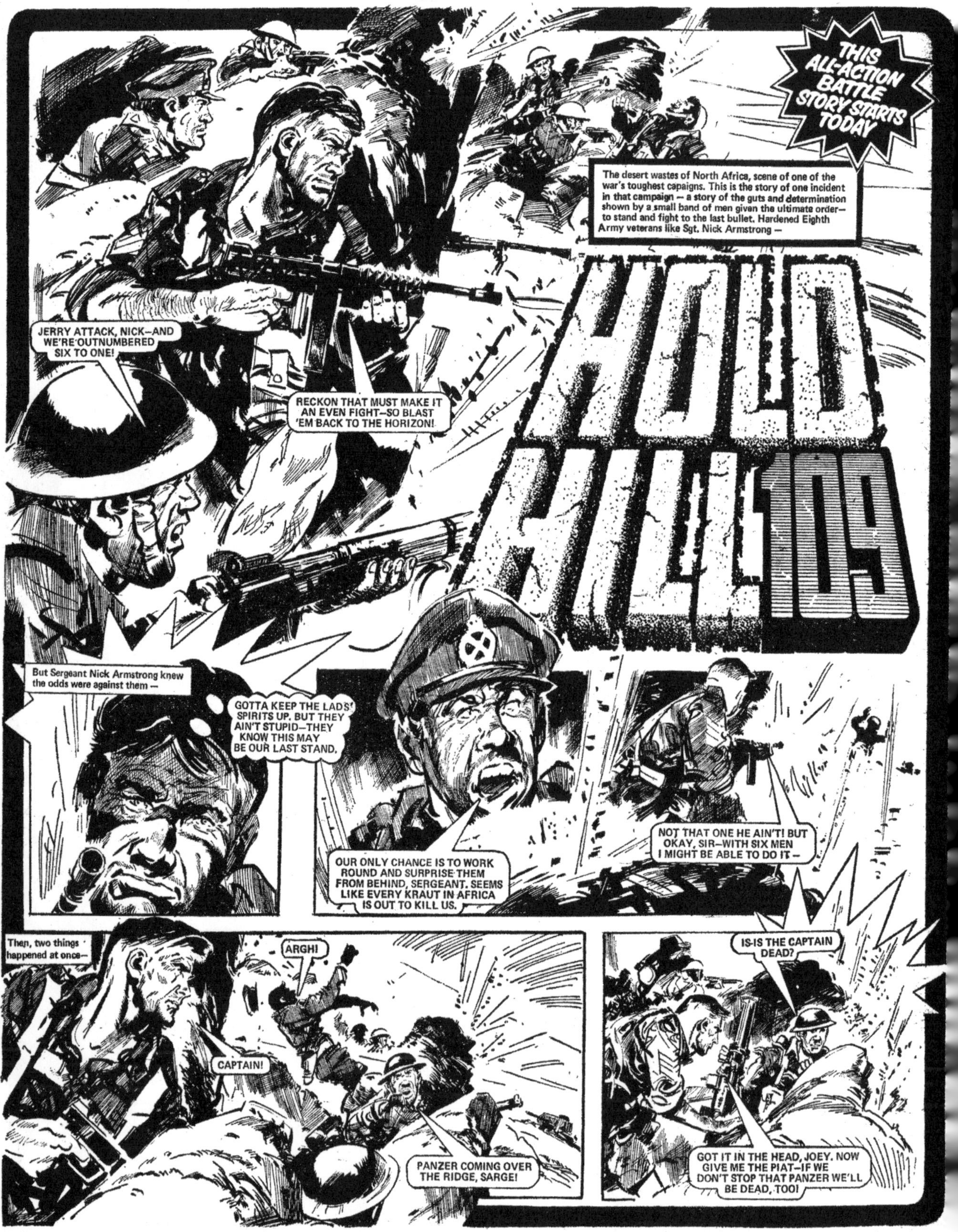

THIS ALL-ACTION BATTLE STORY STARTS TODAY
The desert wastes of North Africa, scene of one of the war's toughest capaigns. This is the story of one incident in that campaign — a story of the guts and determination shown by a small band of men given the ultimate order— to stand and fight to the last bullet. Hardened Eighth Army veterans like Sgt. Nick Armstrong —
HOLD HILL 109
JERRY ATTACK, NICK—AND WE'RE OUTNUMBERED SIX TO ONE!
RECKON THAT MUST MAKE IT AN EVEN FIGHT—SO BLAST 'EM BACK TO THE HORIZON!
But Sergeant Nick Armstrong knew the odds were against them —
GOTTA KEEP THE LADS' SPIRITS UP. BUT THEY AIN'T STUPID—THEY KNOW THIS MAY BE OUR LAST STAND.
OUR ONLY CHANCE IS TO WORK ROUND AND SURPRISE THEM FROM BEHIND, SERGEANT. SEEMS LIKE EVERY KRAUT IN AFRICA IS OUT TO KILL US.
NOT THAT ONE HE AIN'T! BUT OKAY, SIR—WITH SIX MEN I MIGHT BE ABLE TO DO IT —
Then, two things happened at once—
ARGH!
CAPTAIN!
PANZER COMING OVER THE RIDGE, SARGE!
IS-IS THE CAPTAIN DEAD?
GOT IT IN THE HEAD, JOEY. NOW GIVE ME THE PIAT—IF WE DON'T STOP THAT PANZER WE'LL BE DEAD, TOO!

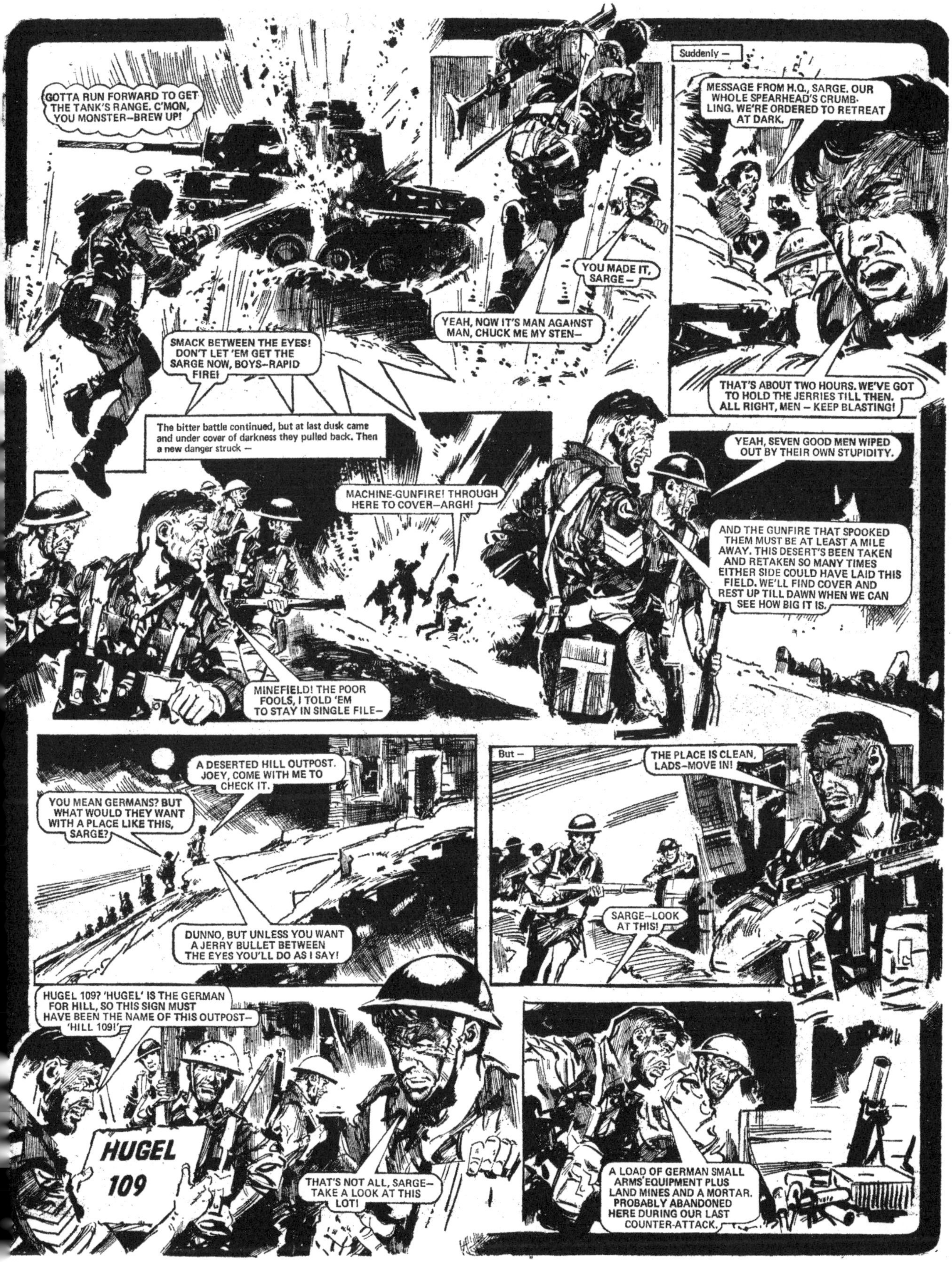

GOTTA RUN FORWARD TO GET THE TANK'S RANGE. C'MON, YOU MONSTER—BREW UP!
SMACK BETWEEN THE EYES! DON'T LET 'EM GET THE SARGE NOW, BOYS—RAPID FIRE!
YOU MADE IT, SARGE—
YEAH, NOW IT'S MAN AGAINST MAN, CHUCK ME MY STEN—
Suddenly —
MESSAGE FROM H.Q., SARGE. OUR WHOLE SPEARHEAD'S CRUMBLING. WE'RE ORDERED TO RETREAT AT DARK.
THAT'S ABOUT TWO HOURS. WE'VE GOT TO HOLD THE JERRIES TILL THEN. ALL RIGHT, MEN — KEEP BLASTING!
The bitter battle continued, but at last dusk came and under cover of darkness they pulled back. Then a new danger struck —
MACHINE-GUNFIRE! THROUGH HERE TO COVER—ARGH!
MINEFIELD! THE POOR FOOLS, I TOLD 'EM TO STAY IN SINGLE FILE—
YEAH, SEVEN GOOD MEN WIPED OUT BY THEIR OWN STUPIDITY.
AND THE GUNFIRE THAT SPOOKED THEM MUST BE AT LEAST A MILE AWAY. THIS DESERT'S BEEN TAKEN AND RETAKEN SO MANY TIMES EITHER SIDE COULD HAVE LAID THIS FIELD. WE'LL FIND COVER AND REST UP TILL DAWN WHEN WE CAN SEE HOW BIG IT IS.
A DESERTED HILL OUTPOST. JOEY, COME WITH ME TO CHECK IT.
YOU MEAN GERMANS? BUT WHAT WOULD THEY WANT WITH A PLACE LIKE THIS, SARGE?
DUNNO, BUT UNLESS YOU WANT A JERRY BULLET BETWEEN THE EYES YOU'LL DO AS I SAY!
But —
THE PLACE IS CLEAN, LADS—MOVE IN!
SARGE—LOOK AT THIS!
HUGEL 109? 'HUGEL' IS THE GERMAN FOR HILL, SO THIS SIGN MUST HAVE BEEN THE NAME OF THIS OUTPOST—'HILL 109!'
HUGEL 109
THAT'S NOT ALL, SARGE—TAKE A LOOK AT THIS LOT!
A LOAD OF GERMAN SMALL ARMS EQUIPMENT PLUS LAND MINES AND A MORTAR. PROBABLY ABANDONED HERE DURING OUR LAST COUNTER-ATTACK.

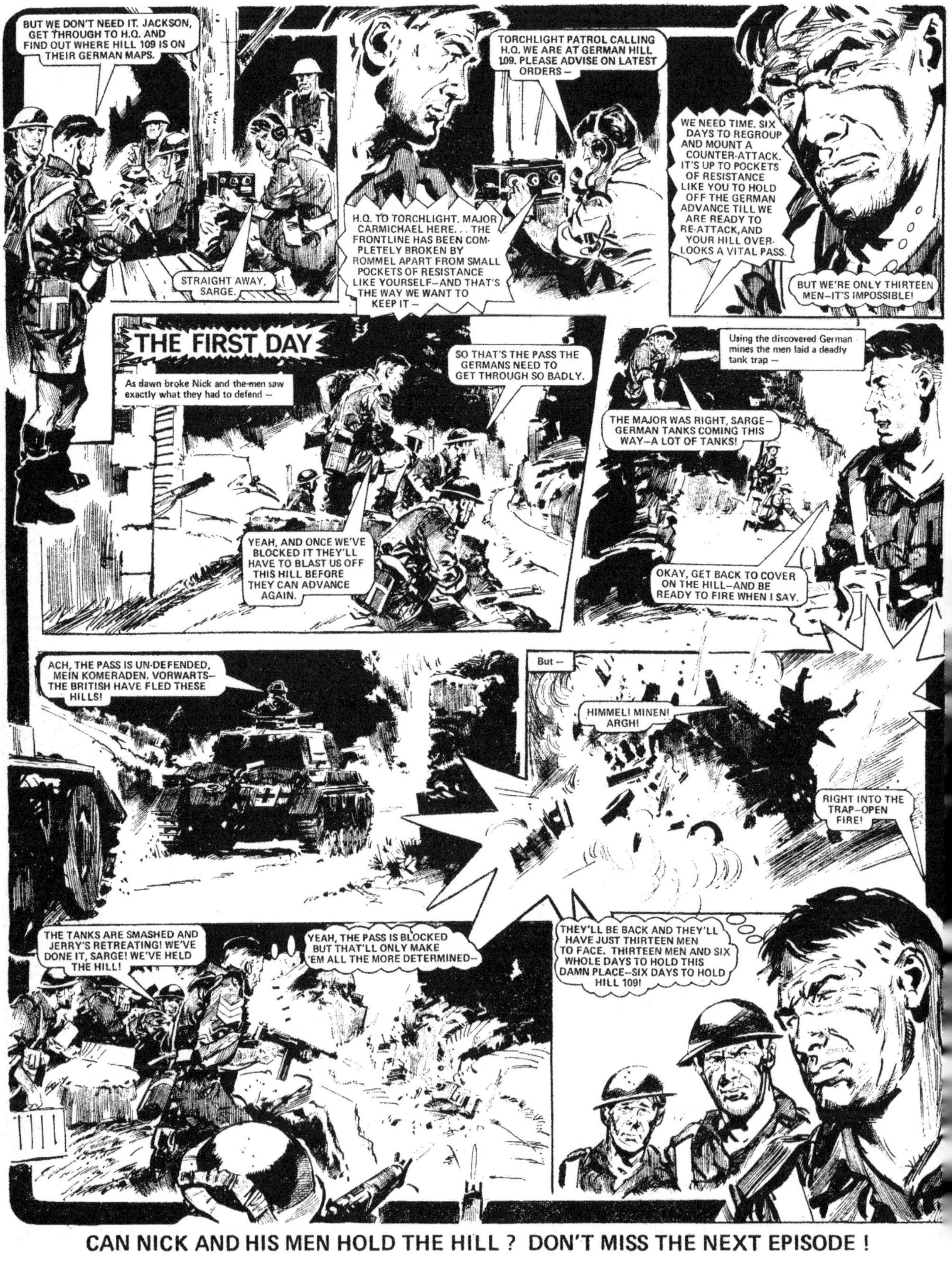

BUT WE DON'T NEED IT. JACKSON, GET THROUGH TO H.Q. AND FIND OUT WHERE HILL 109 IS ON THEIR GERMAN MAPS.
STRAIGHT AWAY, SARGE.
TORCHLIGHT PATROL CALLING H.Q. WE ARE AT GERMAN HILL 109. PLEASE ADVISE ON LATEST ORDERS –
H.Q. TO TORCHLIGHT. MAJOR CARMICHAEL HERE. . . THE FRONTLINE HAS BEEN COMPLETELY BROKEN BY ROMMEL APART FROM SMALL POCKETS OF RESISTANCE LIKE YOURSELF–AND THAT'S THE WAY WE WANT TO KEEP IT –
WE NEED TIME. SIX DAYS TO REGROUP AND MOUNT A COUNTER-ATTACK. IT'S UP TO POCKETS OF RESISTANCE LIKE YOU TO HOLD OFF THE GERMAN ADVANCE TILL WE ARE READY TO RE-ATTACK, AND YOUR HILL OVERLOOKS A VITAL PASS.
BUT WE'RE ONLY THIRTEEN MEN–IT'S IMPOSSIBLE!
THE FIRST DAY
As dawn broke Nick and the men saw exactly what they had to defend –
SO THAT'S THE PASS THE GERMANS NEED TO GET THROUGH SO BADLY.
YEAH, AND ONCE WE'VE BLOCKED IT THEY'LL HAVE TO BLAST US OFF THIS HILL BEFORE THEY CAN ADVANCE AGAIN.
Using the discovered German mines the men laid a deadly tank trap –
THE MAJOR WAS RIGHT, SARGE–GERMAN TANKS COMING THIS WAY–A LOT OF TANKS!
OKAY, GET BACK TO COVER ON THE HILL–AND BE READY TO FIRE WHEN I SAY.
ACH, THE PASS IS UN-DEFENDED, MEIN KOMERADEN. VORWARTS–THE BRITISH HAVE FLED THESE HILLS!
But –
HIMMEL! MINEN! ARGH!
RIGHT INTO THE TRAP–OPEN FIRE!
THE TANKS ARE SMASHED AND JERRY'S RETREATING! WE'VE DONE IT, SARGE! WE'VE HELD THE HILL!
YEAH, THE PASS IS BLOCKED BUT THAT'LL ONLY MAKE 'EM ALL THE MORE DETERMINED–
THEY'LL BE BACK AND THEY'LL HAVE JUST THIRTEEN MEN TO FACE. THIRTEEN MEN AND SIX WHOLE DAYS TO HOLD THIS DAMN PLACE–SIX DAYS TO HOLD HILL 109!

CAN NICK AND HIS MEN HOLD THE HILL ? DON'T MISS THE NEXT EPISODE !

THIRTEEN BRITISH TOMMIES WITH SIX DAYS TO FIGHT – OR DIE !

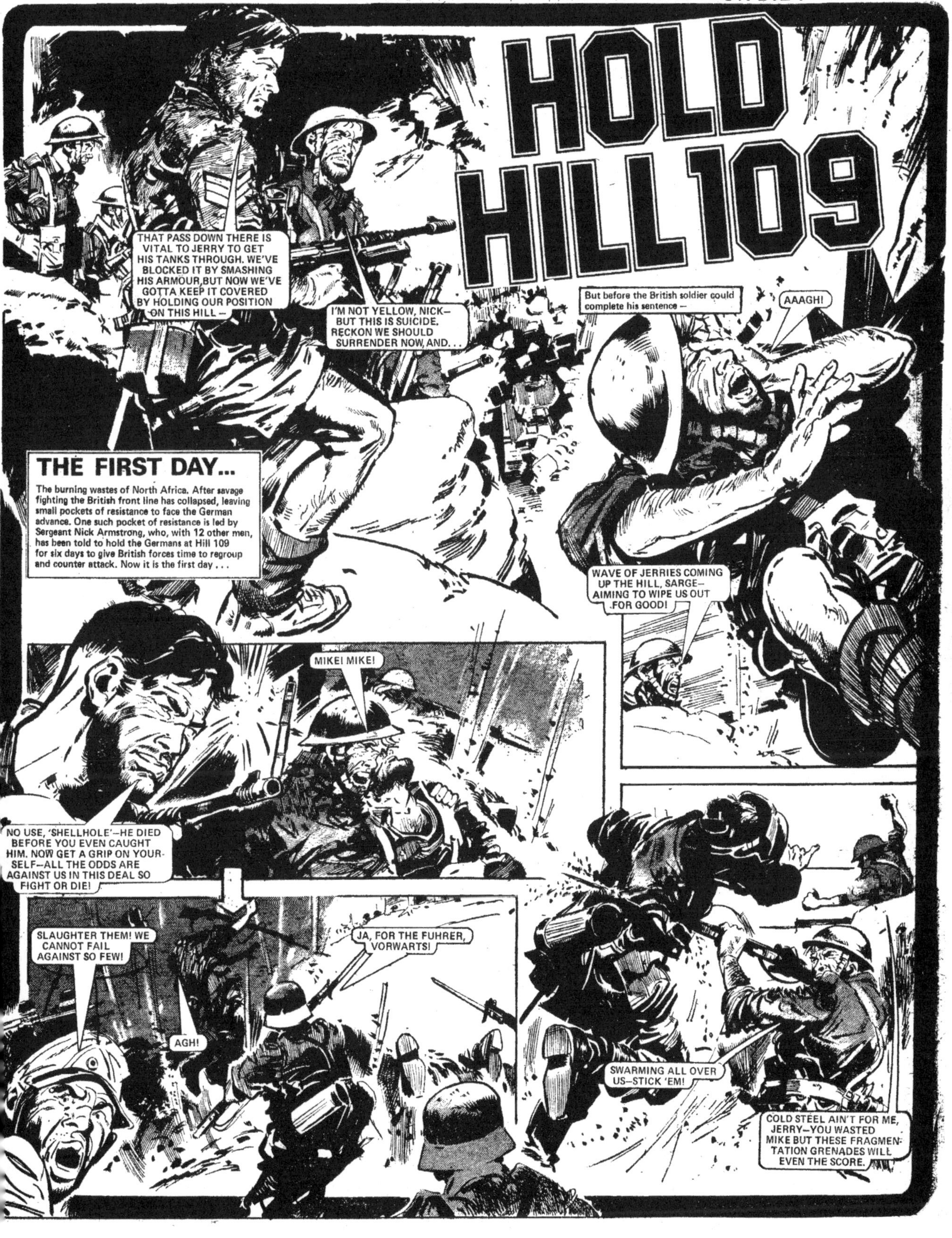

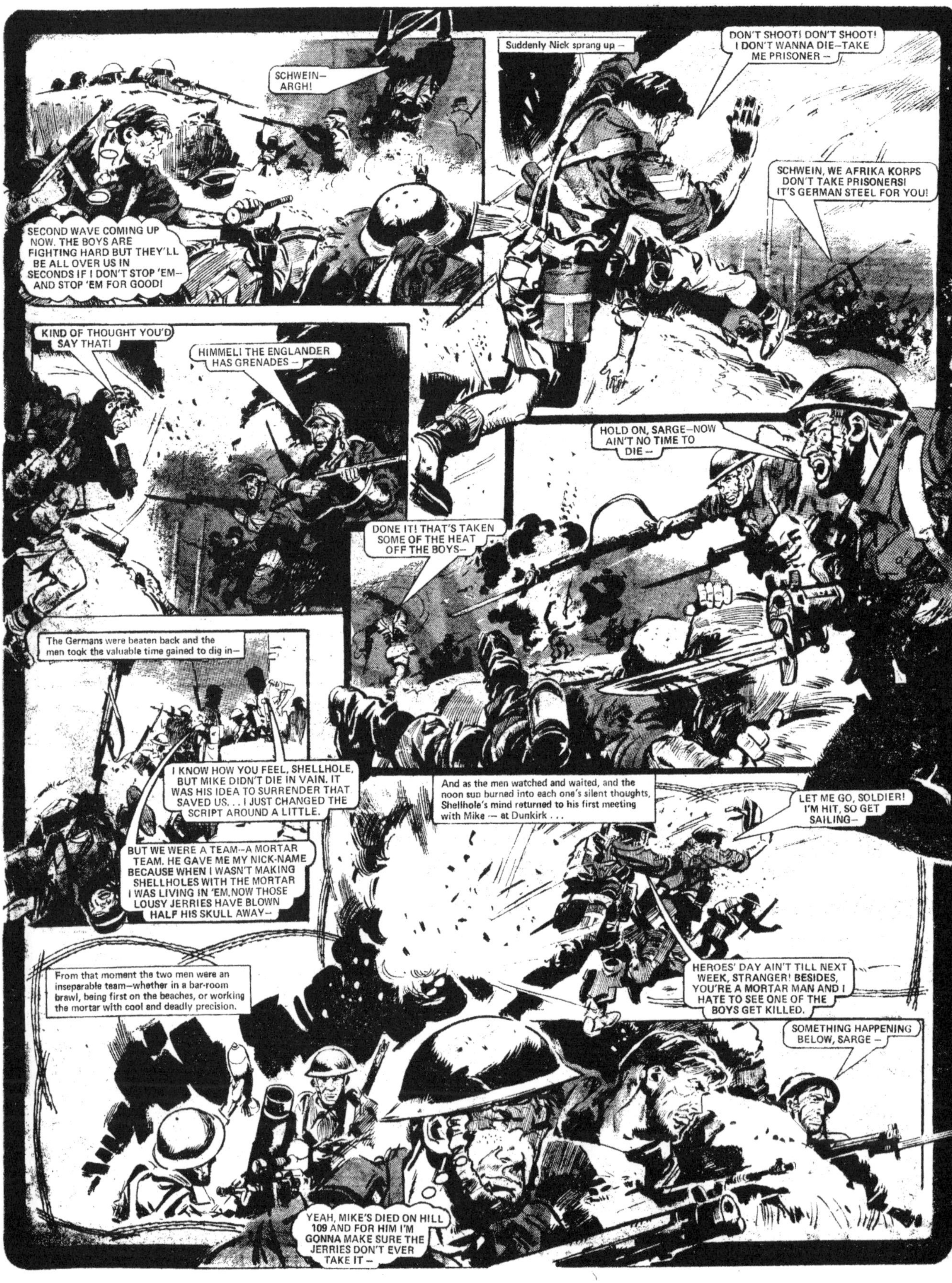
SCHWEIN-
ARGH!
SECOND WAVE COMING UP NOW. THE BOYS ARE FIGHTING HARD BUT THEY'LL BE ALL OVER US IN SECONDS IF I DON'T STOP 'EM-- AND STOP 'EM FOR GOOD!
Suddenly Nick sprang up --
DON'T SHOOT! DON'T SHOOT! I DON'T WANNA DIE-TAKE ME PRISONER --
SCHWEIN, WE AFRIKA KORPS DON'T TAKE PRISONERS! IT'S GERMAN STEEL FOR YOU!
KIND OF THOUGHT YOU'D SAY THAT!
HIMMEL! THE ENGLANDER HAS GRENADES --
HOLD ON, SARGE--NOW AIN'T NO TIME TO DIE --
DONE IT! THAT'S TAKEN SOME OF THE HEAT OFF THE BOYS--
The Germans were beaten back and the men took the valuable time gained to dig in--
I KNOW HOW YOU FEEL, SHELLHOLE, BUT MIKE DIDN'T DIE IN VAIN. IT WAS HIS IDEA TO SURRENDER THAT SAVED US. . . I JUST CHANGED THE SCRIPT AROUND A LITTLE.
BUT WE WERE A TEAM--A MORTAR TEAM. HE GAVE ME MY NICK-NAME BECAUSE WHEN I WASN'T MAKING SHELLHOLES WITH THE MORTAR I WAS LIVING IN 'EM. NOW THOSE LOUSY JERRIES HAVE BLOWN HALF HIS SKULL AWAY--
And as the men watched and waited, and the noon sun burned into each one's silent thoughts, Shellhole's mind returned to his first meeting with Mike -- at Dunkirk . . .
LET ME GO, SOLDIER! I'M HIT, SO GET SAILING--
HEROES' DAY AIN'T TILL NEXT WEEK, STRANGER! BESIDES, YOU'RE A MORTAR MAN AND I HATE TO SEE ONE OF THE BOYS GET KILLED.
From that moment the two men were an inseparable team--whether in a bar-room brawl, being first on the beaches, or working the mortar with cool and deadly precision.
SOMETHING HAPPENING BELOW, SARGE --
YEAH, MIKE'S DIED ON HILL 109 AND FOR HIM I'M GONNA MAKE SURE THE JERRIES DON'T EVER TAKE IT --

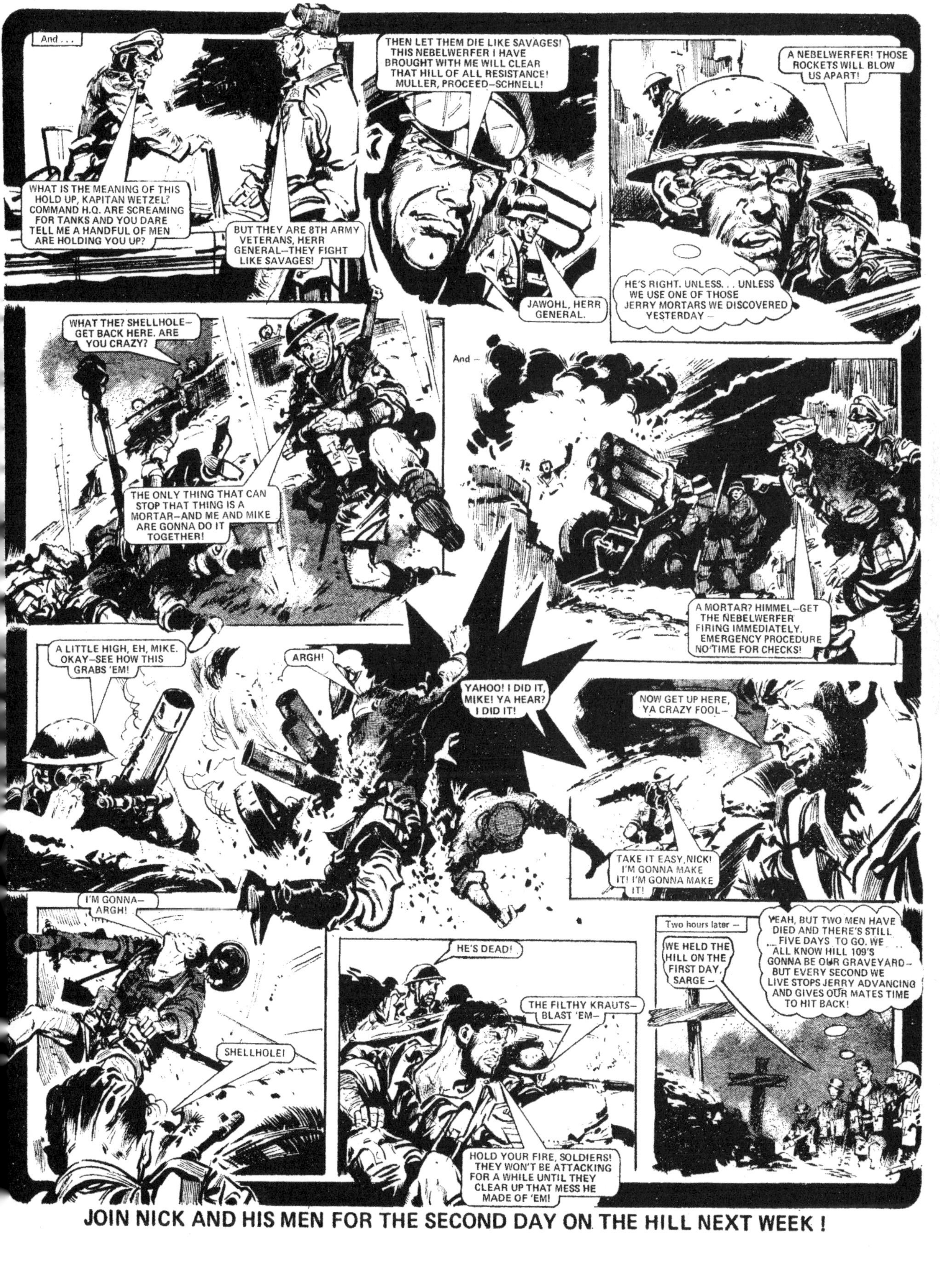
And . . .
WHAT IS THE MEANING OF THIS HOLD UP, KAPITAN WETZEL? COMMAND H.Q. ARE SCREAMING FOR TANKS AND YOU DARE TELL ME A HANDFUL OF MEN ARE HOLDING YOU UP?
BUT THEY ARE 8TH ARMY VETERANS, HERR GENERAL—THEY FIGHT LIKE SAVAGES!
THEN LET THEM DIE LIKE SAVAGES! THIS NEBELWERFER I HAVE BROUGHT WITH ME WILL CLEAR THAT HILL OF ALL RESISTANCE! MULLER, PROCEED—SCHNELL!
JAWOHL, HERR GENERAL.
A NEBELWERFER! THOSE ROCKETS WILL BLOW US APART!
HE'S RIGHT. UNLESS. . . UNLESS WE USE ONE OF THOSE JERRY MORTARS WE DISCOVERED YESTERDAY —
WHAT THE? SHELLHOLE—GET BACK HERE. ARE YOU CRAZY?
THE ONLY THING THAT CAN STOP THAT THING IS A MORTAR—AND ME AND MIKE ARE GONNA DO IT TOGETHER!
And —
A MORTAR? HIMMEL—GET THE NEBELWERFER FIRING IMMEDIATELY. EMERGENCY PROCEDURE NO TIME FOR CHECKS!
A LITTLE HIGH, EH, MIKE. OKAY—SEE HOW THIS GRABS 'EM!
ARGH!
YAHOO! I DID IT, MIKE! YA HEAR? I DID IT!
NOW GET UP HERE, YA CRAZY FOOL—
TAKE IT EASY, NICK! I'M GONNA MAKE IT! I'M GONNA MAKE IT!
I'M GONNA—ARGH!
SHELLHOLE!
HE'S DEAD!
THE FILTHY KRAUTS—BLAST 'EM—
HOLD YOUR FIRE, SOLDIERS! THEY WON'T BE ATTACKING FOR A WHILE UNTIL THEY CLEAR UP THAT MESS HE MADE OF 'EM!
Two hours later —
WE HELD THE HILL ON THE FIRST DAY, SARGE—
YEAH, BUT TWO MEN HAVE DIED AND THERE'S STILL FIVE DAYS TO GO. WE ALL KNOW HILL 109'S GONNA BE OUR GRAVEYARD—BUT EVERY SECOND WE LIVE STOPS JERRY ADVANCING AND GIVES OUR MATES TIME TO HIT BACK!

JOIN NICK AND HIS MEN FOR THE SECOND DAY ON THE HILL NEXT WEEK !

NICK HAS TO CHOOSE BETWEEN A MAN'S LIFE AND HIS ORDERS TO HOLD THE HILL !

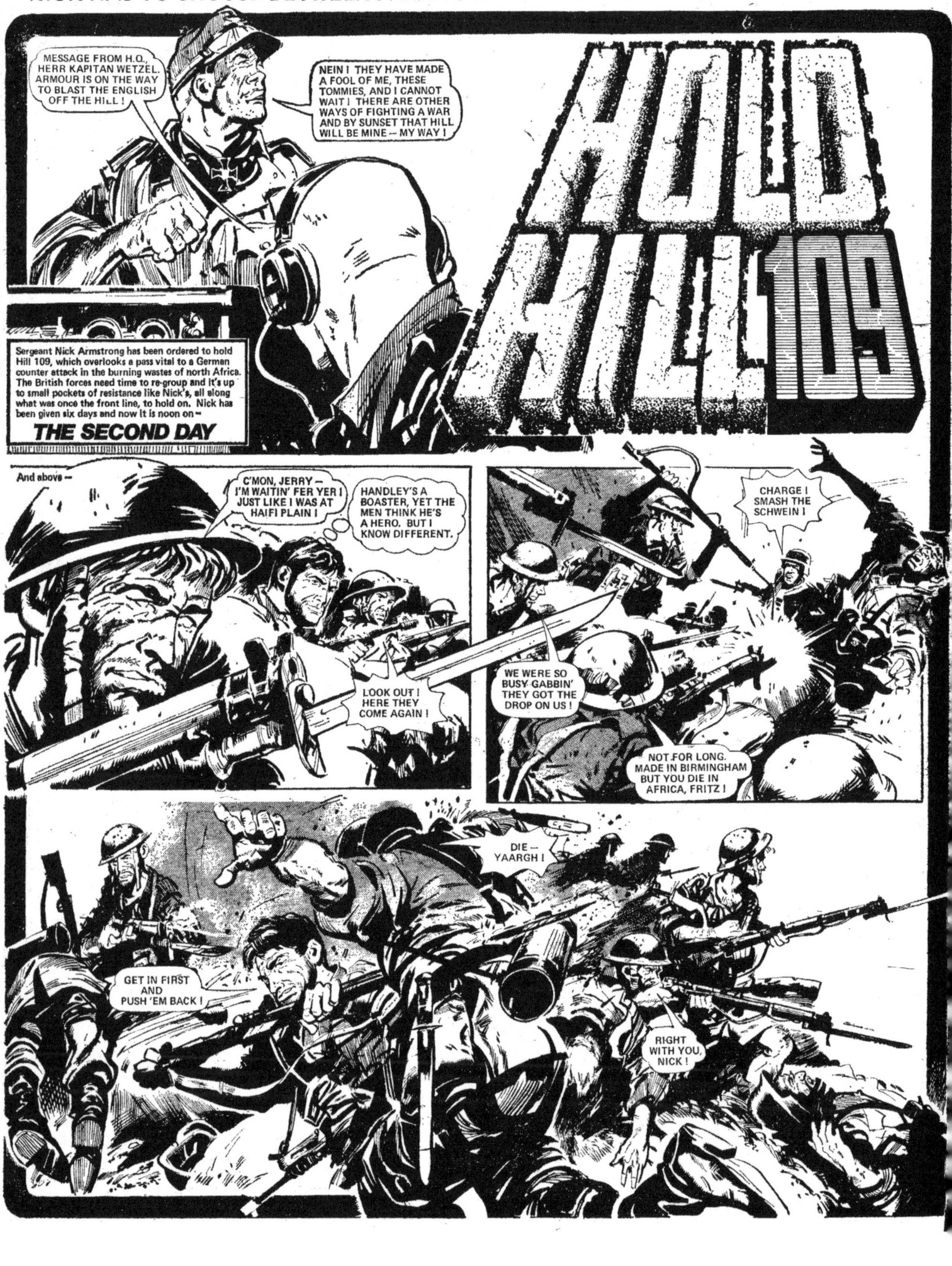

MESSAGE FROM H.Q., HERR KAPITAN WETZEL. ARMOUR IS ON THE WAY TO BLAST THE ENGLISH OFF THE HILL !
NEIN ! THEY HAVE MADE A FOOL OF ME, THESE TOMMIES, AND I CANNOT WAIT ! THERE ARE OTHER WAYS OF FIGHTING A WAR AND BY SUNSET THAT HILL WILL BE MINE — MY WAY !
HOLD HILL 109
Sergeant Nick Armstrong has been ordered to hold Hill 109, which overlooks a pass vital to a German counter attack in the burning wastes of north Africa. The British forces need time to re-group and it's up to small pockets of resistance like Nick's, all along what was once the front line, to hold on. Nick has been given six days and now it is noon on —
THE SECOND DAY
And above —
C'MON, JERRY — I'M WAITIN' FER YER ! JUST LIKE I WAS AT HAIFI PLAIN !
HANDLEY'S A BOASTER, YET THE MEN THINK HE'S A HERO. BUT I KNOW DIFFERENT.
LOOK OUT ! HERE THEY COME AGAIN !
CHARGE ! SMASH THE SCHWEIN !
WE WERE SO BUSY GABBIN' THEY GOT THE DROP ON US !
NOT FOR LONG. MADE IN BIRMINGHAM BUT YOU DIE IN AFRICA, FRITZ !
DIE — YAARGH !
GET IN FIRST AND PUSH 'EM BACK !
RIGHT WITH YOU, NICK !

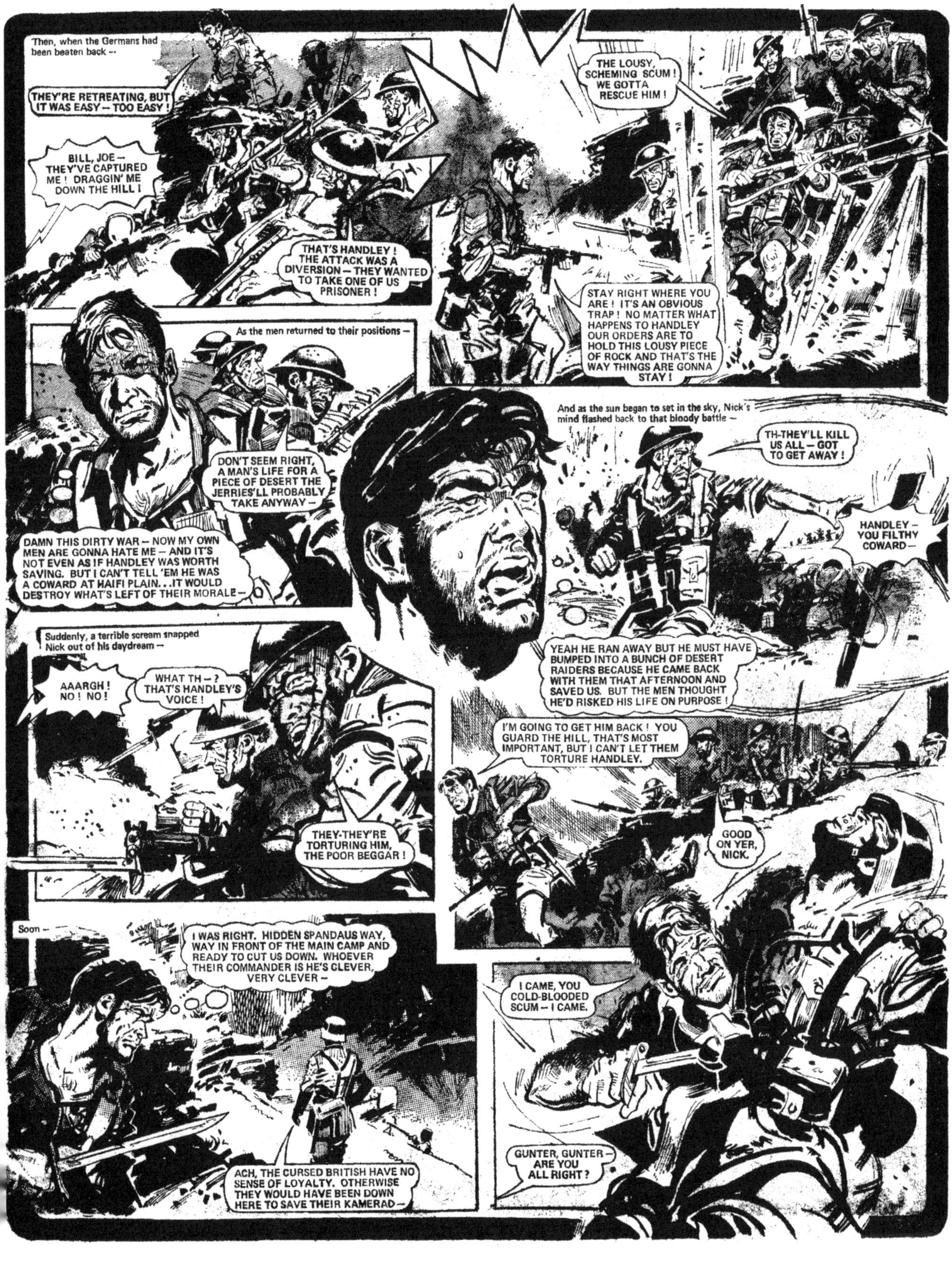

Then, when the Germans had been beaten back –
THEY'RE RETREATING, BUT IT WAS EASY – TOO EASY!
BILL, JOE – THEY'VE CAPTURED ME! DRAGGIN' ME DOWN THE HILL!
THAT'S HANDLEY! THE ATTACK WAS A DIVERSION – THEY WANTED TO TAKE ONE OF US PRISONER!
THE LOUSY, SCHEMING SCUM! WE GOTTA RESCUE HIM!
STAY RIGHT WHERE YOU ARE! IT'S AN OBVIOUS TRAP! NO MATTER WHAT HAPPENS TO HANDLEY OUR ORDERS ARE TO HOLD THIS LOUSY PIECE OF ROCK AND THAT'S THE WAY THINGS ARE GONNA STAY!
As the men returned to their positions –
DON'T SEEM RIGHT, A MAN'S LIFE FOR A PIECE OF DESERT THE JERRIES'LL PROBABLY TAKE ANYWAY –
DAMN THIS DIRTY WAR – NOW MY OWN MEN ARE GONNA HATE ME – AND IT'S NOT EVEN AS IF HANDLEY WAS WORTH SAVING. BUT I CAN'T TELL 'EM HE WAS A COWARD AT HAIFI PLAIN. . . IT WOULD DESTROY WHAT'S LEFT OF THEIR MORALE –
And as the sun began to set in the sky, Nick's mind flashed back to that bloody battle –
TH-THEY'LL KILL US ALL – GOT TO GET AWAY!
HANDLEY – YOU FILTHY COWARD –
YEAH HE RAN AWAY BUT HE MUST HAVE BUMPED INTO A BUNCH OF DESERT RAIDERS BECAUSE HE CAME BACK WITH THEM THAT AFTERNOON AND SAVED US. BUT THE MEN THOUGHT HE'D RISKED HIS LIFE ON PURPOSE!
Suddenly, a terrible scream snapped Nick out of his daydream –
AAARGH! NO! NO!
WHAT TH – ? THAT'S HANDLEY'S VOICE!
THEY-THEY'RE TORTURING HIM, THE POOR BEGGAR!
I'M GOING TO GET HIM BACK! YOU GUARD THE HILL, THAT'S MOST IMPORTANT, BUT I CAN'T LET THEM TORTURE HANDLEY.
GOOD ON YER, NICK.
Soon –
I WAS RIGHT. HIDDEN SPANDAUS WAY, WAY IN FRONT OF THE MAIN CAMP AND READY TO CUT US DOWN. WHOEVER THEIR COMMANDER IS HE'S CLEVER, VERY CLEVER –
ACH, THE CURSED BRITISH HAVE NO SENSE OF LOYALTY. OTHERWISE THEY WOULD HAVE BEEN DOWN HERE TO SAVE THEIR KAMERAD –
I CAME, YOU COLD-BLOODED SCUM – I CAME.
GUNTER, GUNTER – ARE YOU ALL RIGHT?

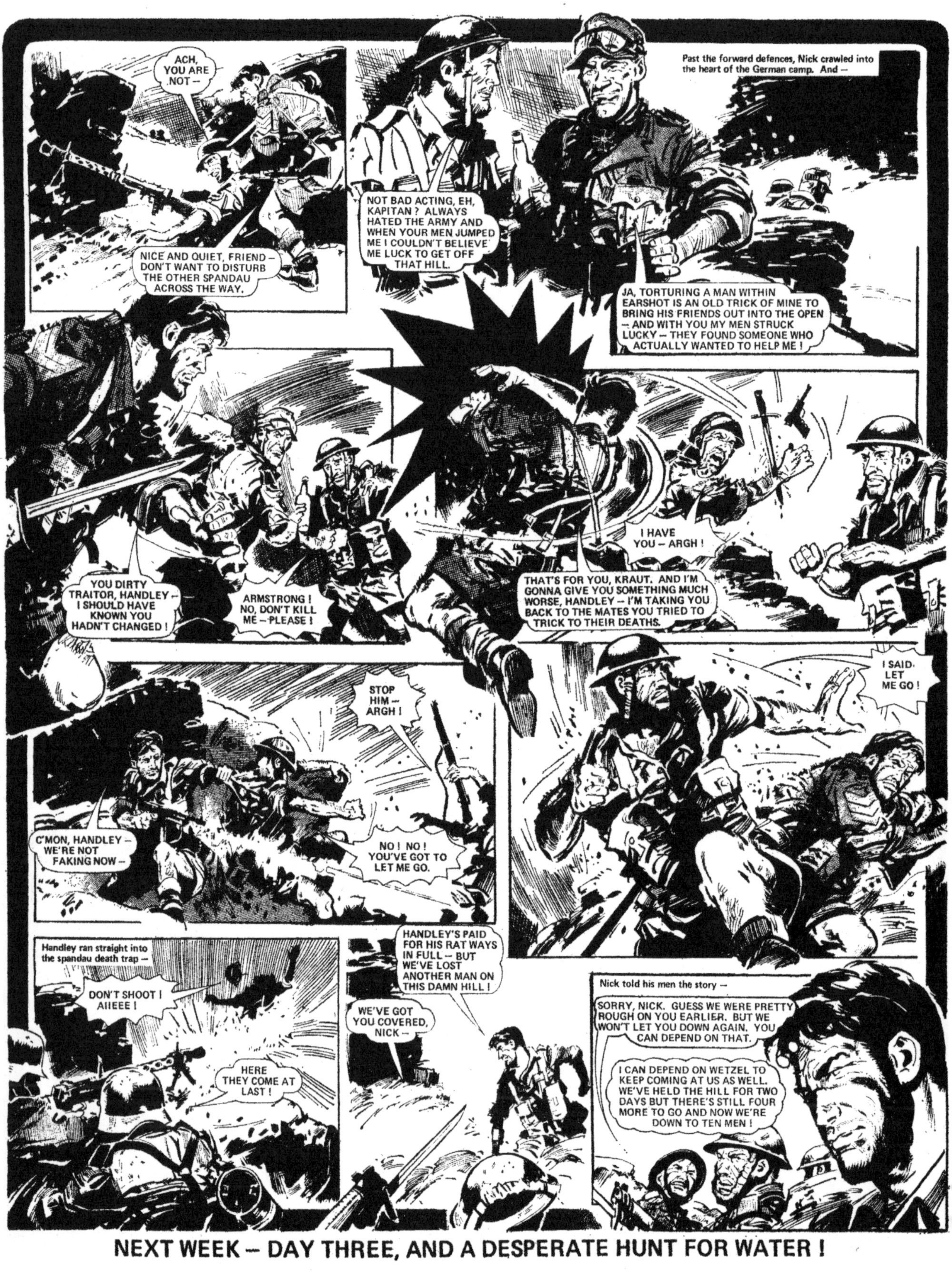

ACH, YOU ARE NOT –
NICE AND QUIET, FRIEND – DON'T WANT TO DISTURB THE OTHER SPANDAU ACROSS THE WAY.
Past the forward defences, Nick crawled into the heart of the German camp. And –
NOT BAD ACTING, EH, KAPITAN ? ALWAYS HATED THE ARMY AND WHEN YOUR MEN JUMPED ME I COULDN'T BELIEVE ME LUCK TO GET OFF THAT HILL.
JA, TORTURING A MAN WITHIN EARSHOT IS AN OLD TRICK OF MINE TO BRING HIS FRIENDS OUT INTO THE OPEN – AND WITH YOU MY MEN STRUCK LUCKY – THEY FOUND SOMEONE WHO ACTUALLY WANTED TO HELP ME !
YOU DIRTY TRAITOR, HANDLEY – I SHOULD HAVE KNOWN YOU HADN'T CHANGED !
ARMSTRONG ! NO, DON'T KILL ME – PLEASE !
I HAVE YOU – ARGH !
THAT'S FOR YOU, KRAUT. AND I'M GONNA GIVE YOU SOMETHING MUCH WORSE, HANDLEY – I'M TAKING YOU BACK TO THE MATES YOU TRIED TO TRICK TO THEIR DEATHS.
STOP HIM – ARGH !
C'MON, HANDLEY – WE'RE NOT FAKING NOW –
NO ! NO ! YOU'VE GOT TO LET ME GO.
I SAID, LET ME GO !
Handley ran straight into the spandau death trap –
DON'T SHOOT ! AIIEEE !
HERE THEY COME AT LAST !
WE'VE GOT YOU COVERED, NICK –
HANDLEY'S PAID FOR HIS RAT WAYS IN FULL – BUT WE'VE LOST ANOTHER MAN ON THIS DAMN HILL !
Nick told his men the story –
SORRY, NICK. GUESS WE WERE PRETTY ROUGH ON YOU EARLIER. BUT WE WON'T LET YOU DOWN AGAIN. YOU CAN DEPEND ON THAT.
I CAN DEPEND ON WETZEL TO KEEP COMING AT US AS WELL. WE'VE HELD THE HILL FOR TWO DAYS BUT THERE'S STILL FOUR MORE TO GO AND NOW WE'RE DOWN TO TEN MEN !

NEXT WEEK – DAY THREE, AND A DESPERATE HUNT FOR WATER !

A BULLET CAN KILL, BUT DEATH FROM THIRST IS AGONY !

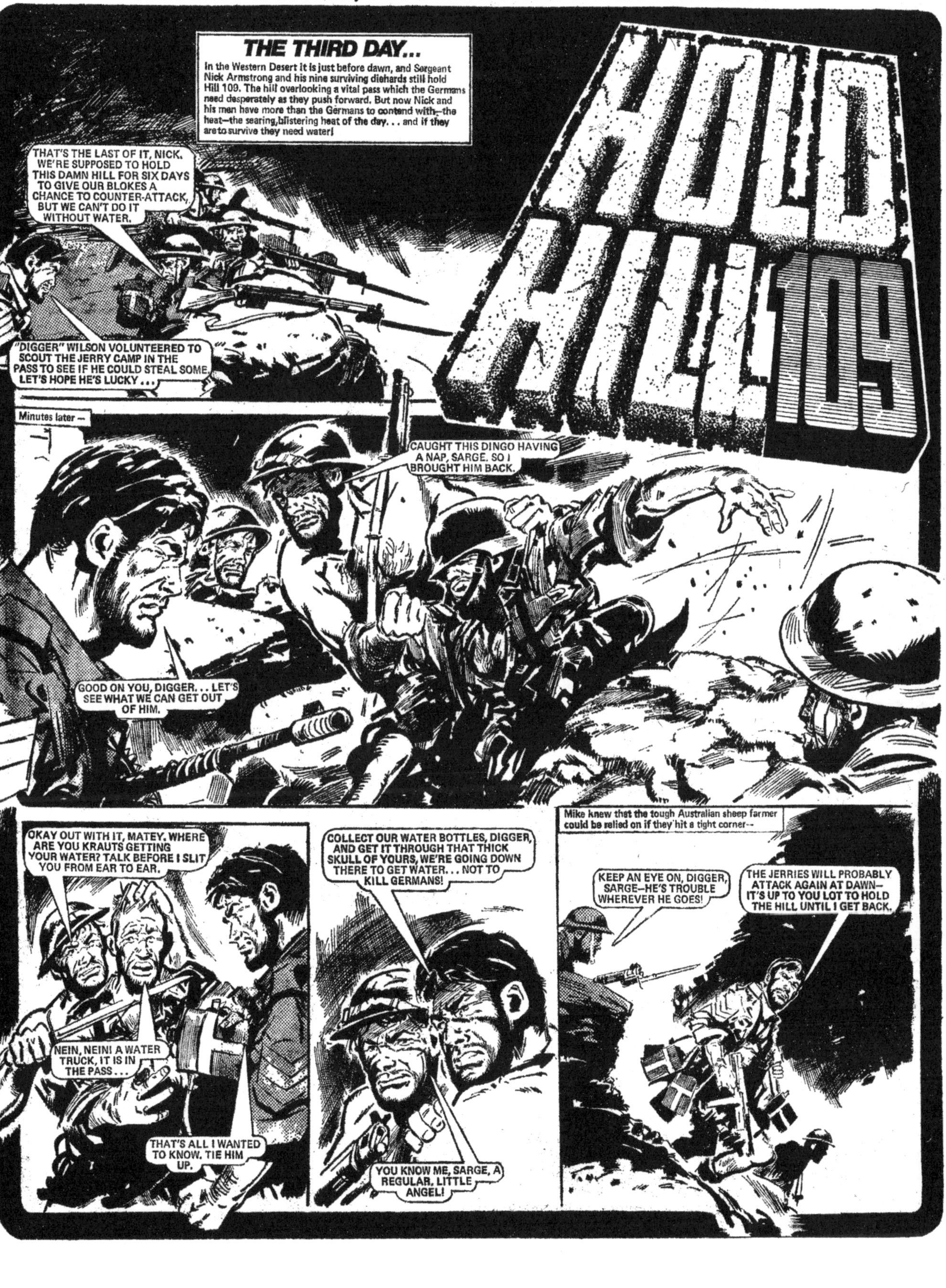
THE THIRD DAY...
In the Western Desert it is just before dawn, and Sergeant Nick Armstrong and his nine surviving diehards still hold Hill 109. The hill overlooking a vital pass which the Germans need desperately as they push forward. But now Nick and his men have more than the Germans to contend with,—the heat—the searing, blistering heat of the day. . . and if they are to survive they need water!
HOLD HILL 109
THAT'S THE LAST OF IT, NICK. WE'RE SUPPOSED TO HOLD THIS DAMN HILL FOR SIX DAYS TO GIVE OUR BLOKES A CHANCE TO COUNTER-ATTACK, BUT WE CAN'T DO IT WITHOUT WATER.
"DIGGER" WILSON VOLUNTEERED TO SCOUT THE JERRY CAMP IN THE PASS TO SEE IF HE COULD STEAL SOME. LET'S HOPE HE'S LUCKY . . .
Minutes later —
CAUGHT THIS DINGO HAVING A NAP, SARGE. SO I BROUGHT HIM BACK.
GOOD ON YOU, DIGGER. . . LET'S SEE WHAT WE CAN GET OUT OF HIM.
OKAY OUT WITH IT, MATEY. WHERE ARE YOU KRAUTS GETTING YOUR WATER? TALK BEFORE I SLIT YOU FROM EAR TO EAR.
NEIN, NEIN! A WATER TRUCK, IT IS IN THE PASS . . .
THAT'S ALL I WANTED TO KNOW. TIE HIM UP.
COLLECT OUR WATER BOTTLES, DIGGER, AND GET IT THROUGH THAT THICK SKULL OF YOURS, WE'RE GOING DOWN THERE TO GET WATER. . . NOT TO KILL GERMANS!
YOU KNOW ME, SARGE, A REGULAR, LITTLE ANGEL!
Mike knew that the tough Australian sheep farmer could be relied on if they hit a tight corner--
KEEP AN EYE ON, DIGGER, SARGE—HE'S TROUBLE WHEREVER HE GOES!
THE JERRIES WILL PROBABLY ATTACK AGAIN AT DAWN— IT'S UP TO YOU LOT TO HOLD THE HILL UNTIL I GET BACK.

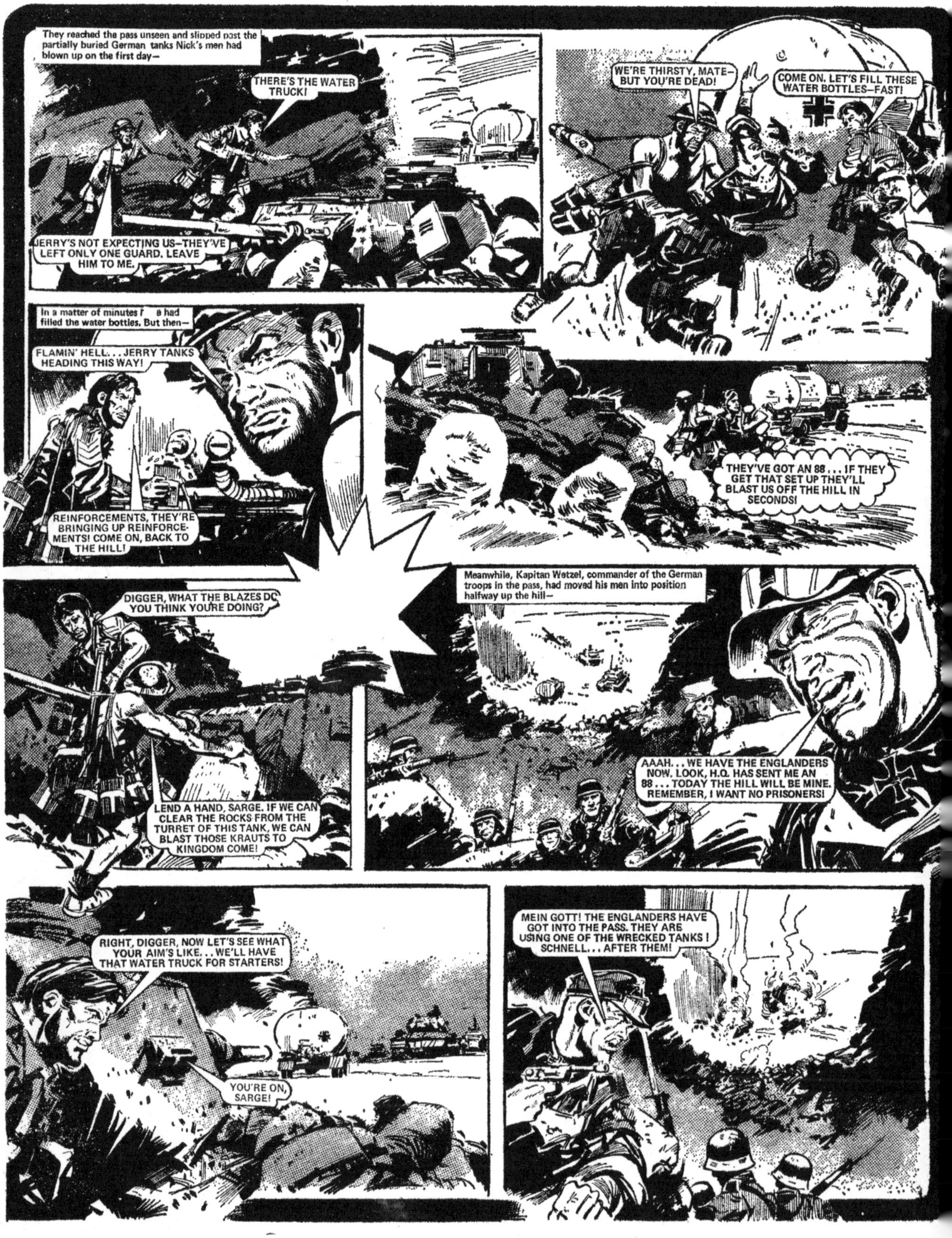
They reached the pass unseen and slipped past the partially buried German tanks Nick's men had blown up on the first day—
THERE'S THE WATER TRUCK!
JERRY'S NOT EXPECTING US—THEY'VE LEFT ONLY ONE GUARD. LEAVE HIM TO ME.
WE'RE THIRSTY, MATE— BUT YOU'RE DEAD!
COME ON. LET'S FILL THESE WATER BOTTLES—FAST!
In a matter of minutes t e had filled the water bottles. But then—
FLAMIN' HELL... JERRY TANKS HEADING THIS WAY!
REINFORCEMENTS, THEY'RE BRINGING UP REINFORCEMENTS! COME ON, BACK TO THE HILL!
THEY'VE GOT AN 88... IF THEY GET THAT SET UP THEY'LL BLAST US OFF THE HILL IN SECONDS!
DIGGER, WHAT THE BLAZES DC YOU THINK YOU'RE DOING?
LEND A HAND, SARGE. IF WE CAN CLEAR THE ROCKS FROM THE TURRET OF THIS TANK, WE CAN BLAST THOSE KRAUTS TO KINGDOM COME!
Meanwhile, Kapitan Wetzel, commander of the German troops in the pass, had moved his men into position halfway up the hill—
AAAH... WE HAVE THE ENGLANDERS NOW. LOOK, H.Q. HAS SENT ME AN 88... TODAY THE HILL WILL BE MINE. REMEMBER, I WANT NO PRISONERS!
RIGHT, DIGGER, NOW LET'S SEE WHAT YOUR AIM'S LIKE... WE'LL HAVE THAT WATER TRUCK FOR STARTERS!
YOU'RE ON, SARGE!
MEIN GOTT! THE ENGLANDERS HAVE GOT INTO THE PASS. THEY ARE USING ONE OF THE WRECKED TANKS! SCHNELL... AFTER THEM!

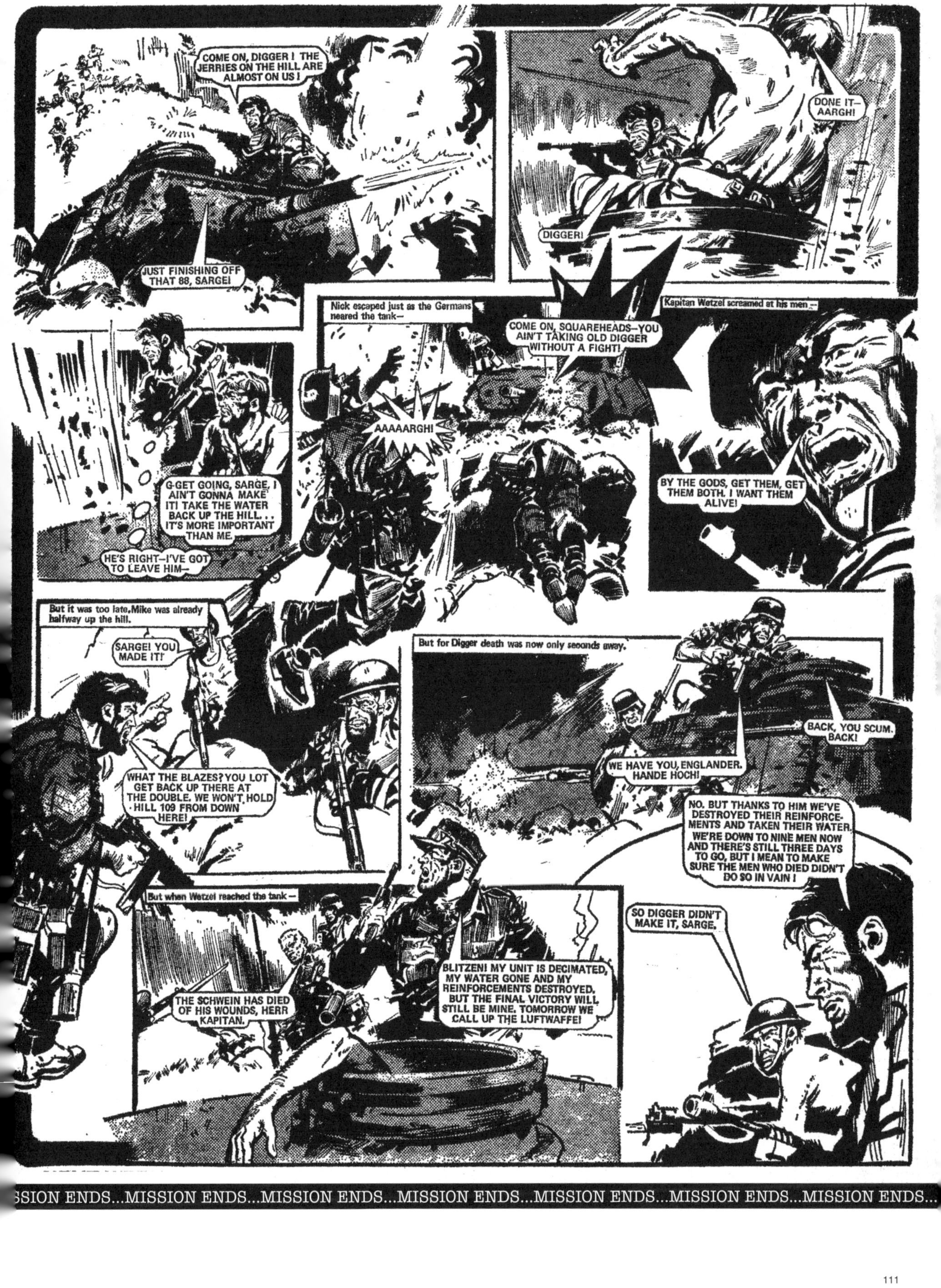
COME ON, DIGGER ! THE JERRIES ON THE HILL ARE ALMOST ON US !
JUST FINISHING OFF THAT 88, SARGE!
DONE IT— AARGH!
DIGGER!
G-GET GOING, SARGE, I AIN'T GONNA MAKE IT! TAKE THE WATER BACK UP THE HILL . . IT'S MORE IMPORTANT THAN ME.
HE'S RIGHT—I'VE GOT TO LEAVE HIM—
Nick escaped just as the Germans neared the tank—
COME ON, SQUAREHEADS—YOU AIN'T TAKING OLD DIGGER WITHOUT A FIGHT!
AAAAARGH!
Kapitan Wetzel screamed at his men —
BY THE GODS, GET THEM, GET THEM BOTH. I WANT THEM ALIVE!
But it was too late. Mike was already halfway up the hill.
SARGE! YOU MADE IT!
WHAT THE BLAZES? YOU LOT GET BACK UP THERE AT THE DOUBLE. WE WON'T HOLD HILL 109 FROM DOWN HERE!
But for Digger death was now only seconds away.
BACK, YOU SCUM. BACK!
WE HAVE YOU, ENGLANDER. HANDE HOCH!
But when Wetzel reached the tank —
THE SCHWEIN HAS DIED OF HIS WOUNDS, HERR KAPITAN.
BLITZEN! MY UNIT IS DECIMATED, MY WATER GONE AND MY REINFORCEMENTS DESTROYED, BUT THE FINAL VICTORY WILL STILL BE MINE. TOMORROW WE CALL UP THE LUFTWAFFE!
SO DIGGER DIDN'T MAKE IT, SARGE.
NO. BUT THANKS TO HIM WE'VE DESTROYED THEIR REINFORCEMENTS AND TAKEN THEIR WATER. WE'RE DOWN TO NINE MEN NOW AND THERE'S STILL THREE DAYS TO GO, BUT I MEAN TO MAKE SURE THE MEN WHO DIED DIDN'T DO SO IN VAIN !

SSION ENDS...MISSION ENDS...MISSION ENDS...MISSION ENDS...MISSION ENDS...MISSION ENDS...MISSION ENDS...

DARKIE'S MOB

"I'LL KILL THE FIRST MAN THAT TURNS COWARD!"

Brutal, unflinching, blood-soaked and notorious: this is the legend of Joe Darkie, as recounted in the journal of Private Richard 'Shorty' Shortland.

In the hot, humid Burmese jungle, Captain Joe Darkie forges a battle-fatigued platoon of men into the most savage fighting force the Japanese have ever known and leads them on a personal crusade against the entire Japanese army.

The portrayal of the Japanese in British war comics had never been good, but for 'Darkie's Mob', writer John Wagner and artist Mike Western brought a new level of brutality to the jungle. The readers of *Battle* had never seen anything as uncompromising before.

NOTES FROM THE FRONTLINE:

"This and 'Charley's War' were the only two stories where John Wagner and I sat down and said, 'Right, we're going to write something ourselves'. Bear in mind what we were doing a lot of the time was creating or facilitating stuff like 'Hellman', or moving on to new projects and editing. But in the case of 'Darkie's Mob', I think it was the first story where John had actually sat down and said, 'I'm going to put a bit of myself into this story', because Darkie does have elements of John's alter-ego about it.

There's a lot of John in Darkie. And I think 'Darkie's Mob' and 'Charley's War' were probably the only two stories for *Battle* that John and I have written in any major way." — **Pat Mills**

WRITTEN BY John Wagner
DRAWN BY Mike Western

NEW STORY! THEY FEARED THE JAPS – BUT THEY HATED DARKIE!

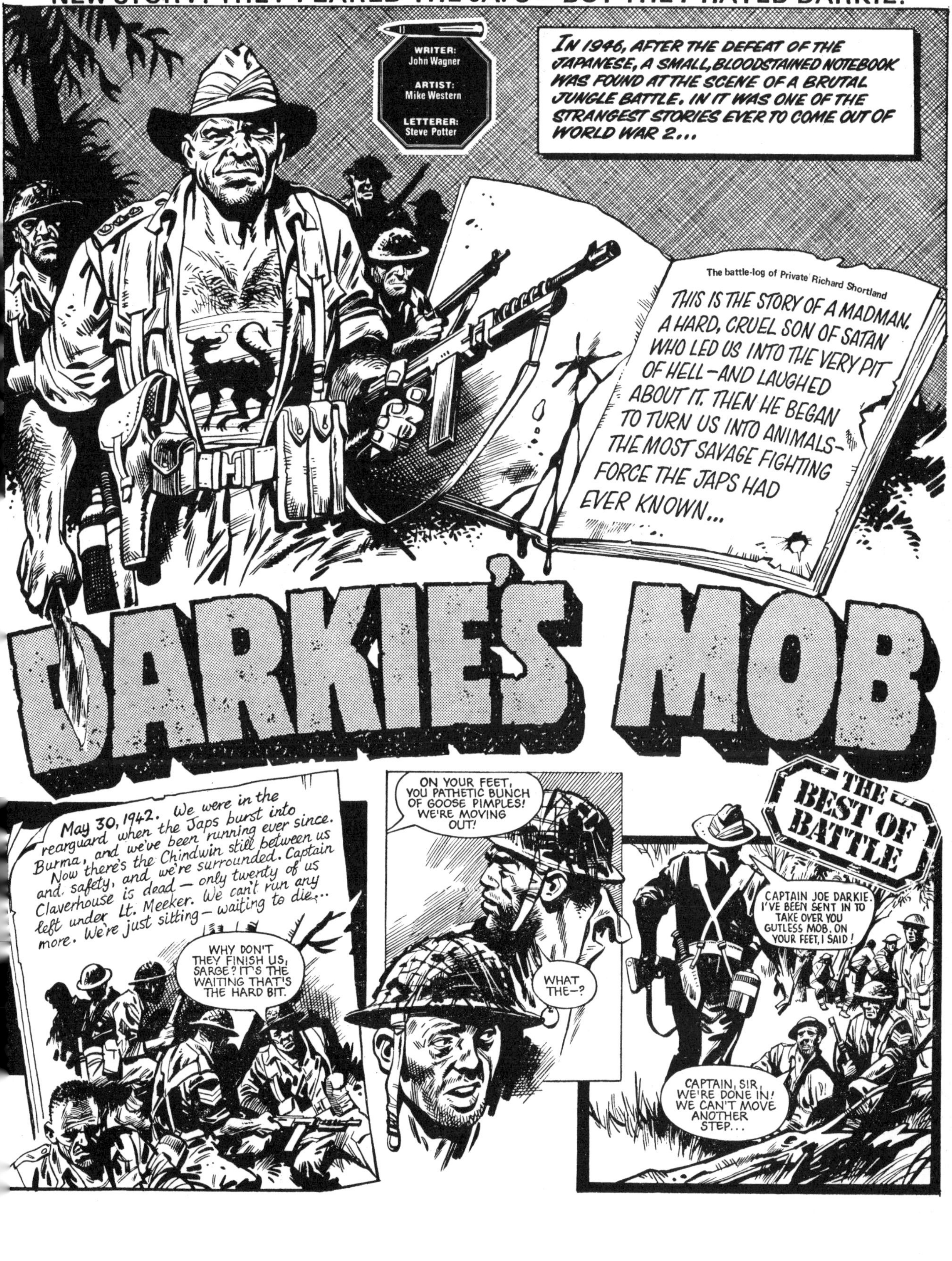

WRITER: John Wagner
ARTIST: Mike Western
LETTERER: Steve Potter
IN 1946, AFTER THE DEFEAT OF THE JAPANESE, A SMALL, BLOODSTAINED NOTEBOOK WAS FOUND AT THE SCENE OF A BRUTAL JUNGLE BATTLE. IN IT WAS ONE OF THE STRANGEST STORIES EVER TO COME OUT OF WORLD WAR 2...
The battle-log of Private Richard Shortland
THIS IS THE STORY OF A MADMAN. A HARD, CRUEL SON OF SATAN WHO LED US INTO THE VERY PIT OF HELL–AND LAUGHED ABOUT IT. THEN HE BEGAN TO TURN US INTO ANIMALS–THE MOST SAVAGE FIGHTING FORCE THE JAPS HAD EVER KNOWN...
DARKIE'S MOB
THE BEST OF BATTLE
May 30, 1942. We were in the rearguard when the Japs burst into Burma, and we've been running ever since. Now there's the Chindwin still between us and safety, and we're surrounded. Captain Claverhouse is dead – only twenty of us left under Lt. Meeker. We can't run any more. We're just sitting – waiting to die...
WHY DON'T THEY FINISH US, SARGE? IT'S THE WAITING THAT'S THE HARD BIT.
ON YOUR FEET, YOU PATHETIC BUNCH OF GOOSE PIMPLES! WE'RE MOVING OUT!
WHAT THE–?
CAPTAIN JOE DARKIE. I'VE BEEN SENT IN TO TAKE OVER YOU GUTLESS MOB. ON YOUR FEET, I SAID!
CAPTAIN, SIR, WE'RE DONE IN! WE CAN'T MOVE ANOTHER STEP...

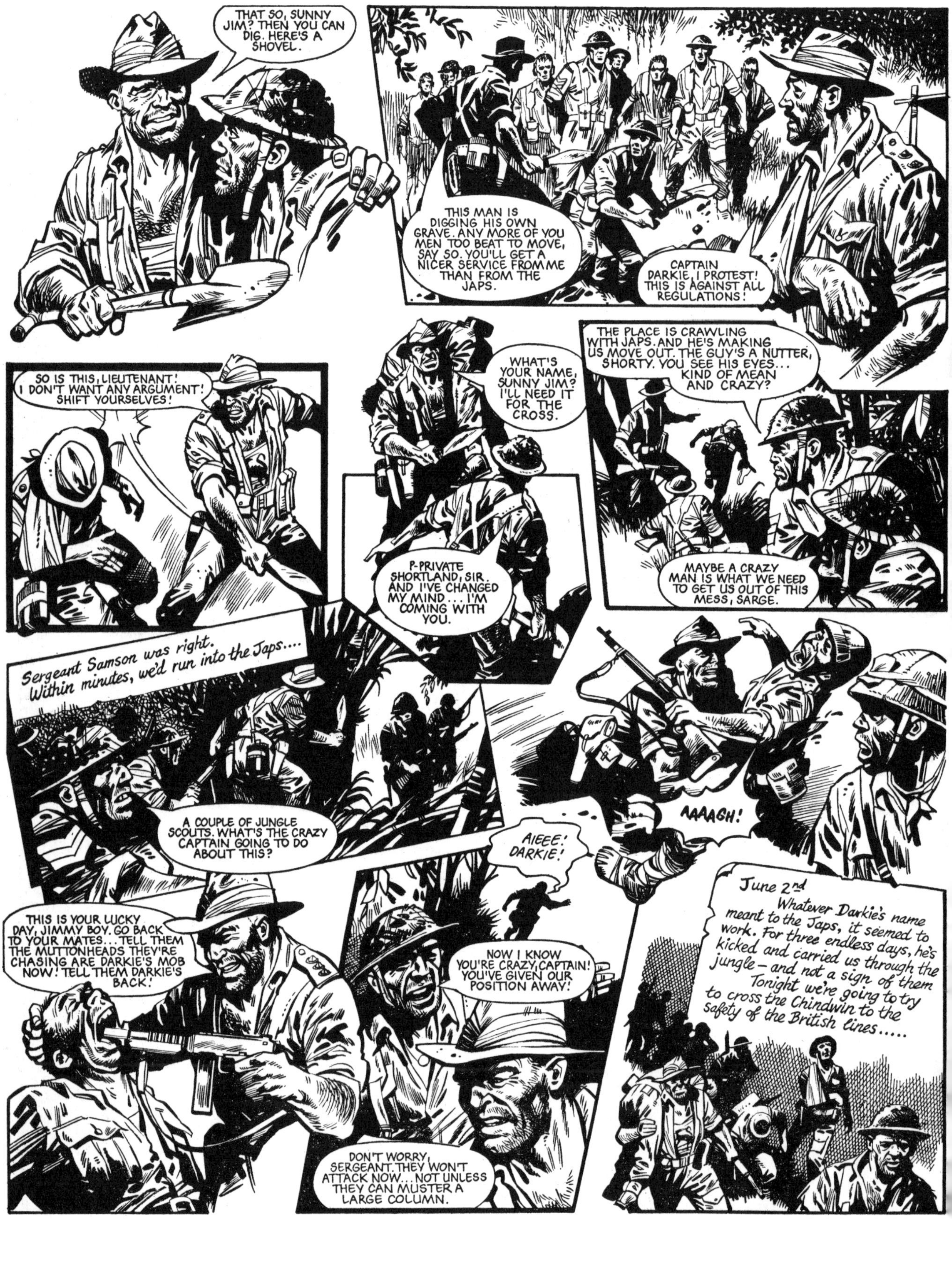

THAT SO, SUNNY JIM? THEN YOU CAN DIG. HERE'S A SHOVEL.
THIS MAN IS DIGGING HIS OWN GRAVE. ANY MORE OF YOU MEN TOO BEAT TO MOVE, SAY SO. YOU'LL GET A NICER SERVICE FROM ME THAN FROM THE JAPS.
CAPTAIN DARKIE, I PROTEST! THIS IS AGAINST ALL REGULATIONS!
SO IS THIS, LIEUTENANT! I DON'T WANT ANY ARGUMENT! SHIFT YOURSELVES!
WHAT'S YOUR NAME, SUNNY JIM? I'LL NEED IT FOR THE CROSS.
P-PRIVATE SHORTLAND, SIR. AND I'VE CHANGED MY MIND... I'M COMING WITH YOU.
THE PLACE IS CRAWLING WITH JAPS. AND HE'S MAKING US MOVE OUT. THE GUY'S A NUTTER, SHORTY. YOU SEE HIS EYES... KIND OF MEAN AND CRAZY?
MAYBE A CRAZY MAN IS WHAT WE NEED TO GET US OUT OF THIS MESS, SARGE.
Sergeant Samson was right. Within minutes, we'd run into the Japs....
A COUPLE OF JUNGLE SCOUTS. WHAT'S THE CRAZY CAPTAIN GOING TO DO ABOUT THIS?
AAAAGH!
AIEEE! DARKIE!
THIS IS YOUR LUCKY DAY, JIMMY BOY. GO BACK TO YOUR MATES... TELL THEM THE MUTTONHEADS THEY'RE CHASING ARE DARKIE'S MOB NOW! TELL THEM DARKIE'S BACK!
NOW I KNOW YOU'RE CRAZY, CAPTAIN! YOU'VE GIVEN OUR POSITION AWAY!
DON'T WORRY, SERGEANT. THEY WON'T ATTACK NOW... NOT UNLESS THEY CAN MUSTER A LARGE COLUMN.
June 2nd
Whatever Darkie's name meant to the Japs, it seemed to work. For three endless days, he's kicked and carried us through the jungle – and not a sign of them
Tonight we're going to try to cross the Chindwin to the safety of the British lines.....

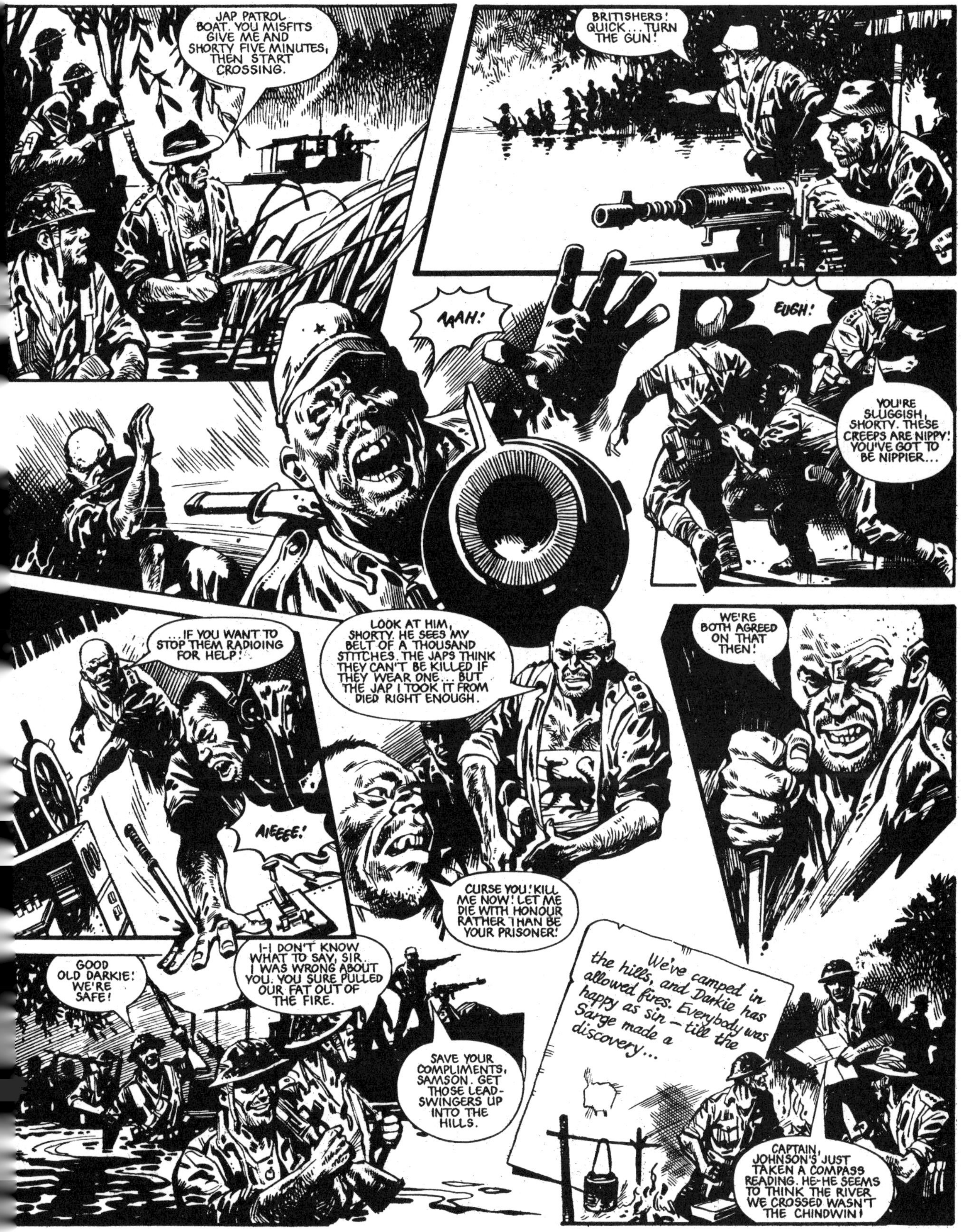
JAP PATROL BOAT. YOU MISFITS GIVE ME AND SHORTY FIVE MINUTES, THEN START CROSSING.
BRITISHERS! QUICK... TURN THE GUN!
AAAH!
EUGH!
YOU'RE SLUGGISH, SHORTY. THESE CREEPS ARE NIPPY! YOU'VE GOT TO BE NIPPIER...
...IF YOU WANT TO STOP THEM RADIOING FOR HELP!
AIEEEE!
LOOK AT HIM, SHORTY. HE SEES MY BELT OF A THOUSAND STITCHES. THE JAPS THINK THEY CAN'T BE KILLED IF THEY WEAR ONE... BUT THE JAP I TOOK IT FROM DIED RIGHT ENOUGH.
CURSE YOU! KILL ME NOW! LET ME DIE WITH HONOUR RATHER THAN BE YOUR PRISONER!
WE'RE BOTH AGREED ON THAT THEN!
GOOD OLD DARKIE! WE'RE SAFE!
I-I DON'T KNOW WHAT TO SAY, SIR. I WAS WRONG ABOUT YOU. YOU SURE PULLED OUR FAT OUT OF THE FIRE.
SAVE YOUR COMPLIMENTS, SAMSON. GET THOSE LEAD-SWINGERS UP INTO THE HILLS.
We've camped in the hills, and Darkie has allowed fires. Everybody was happy as sin — till the Sarge made a discovery...
CAPTAIN, JOHNSON'S JUST TAKEN A COMPASS READING. HE-HE SEEMS TO THINK THE RIVER WE CROSSED WASN'T THE CHINDWIN!

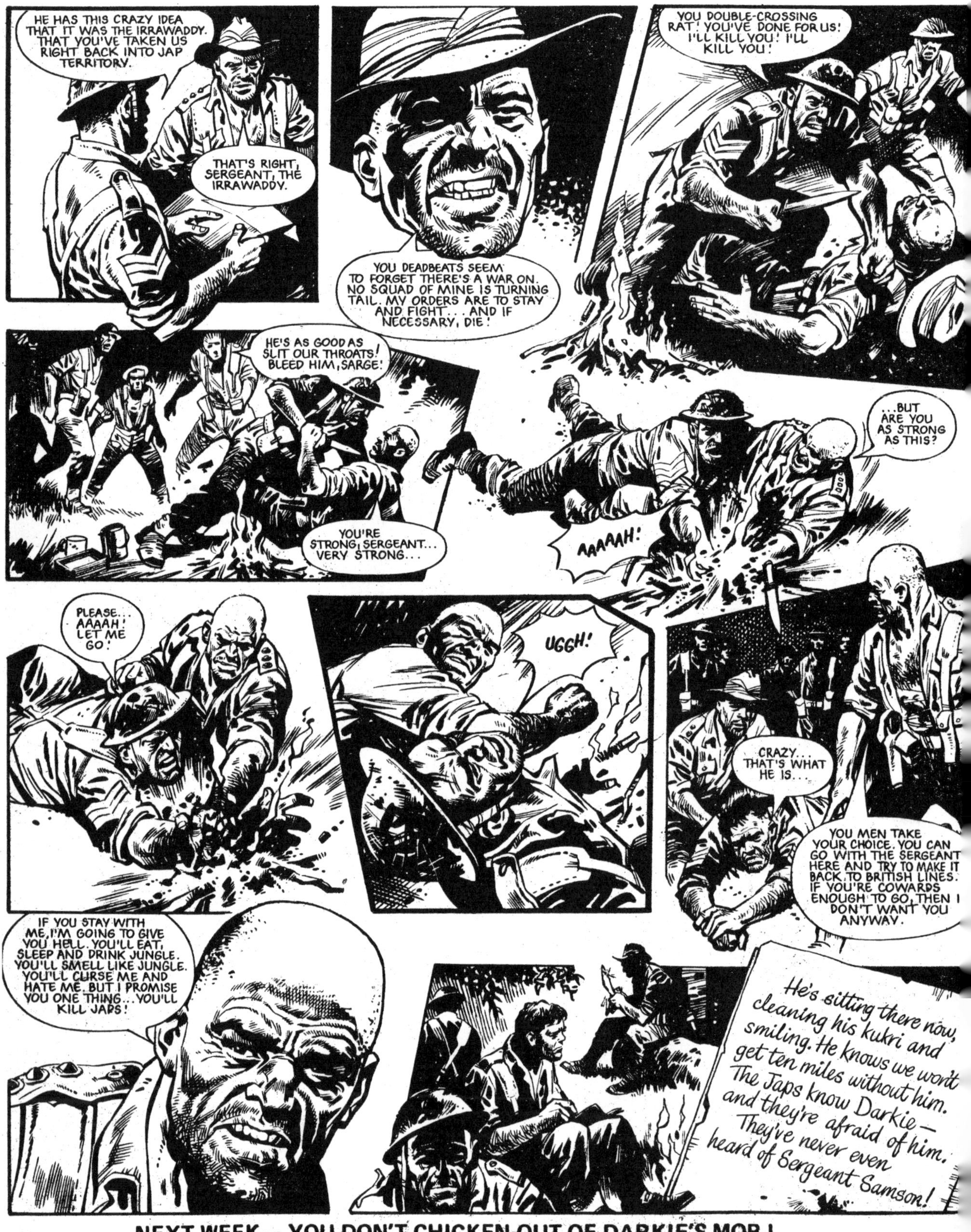
HE HAS THIS CRAZY IDEA THAT IT WAS THE IRRAWADDY. THAT YOU'VE TAKEN US RIGHT BACK INTO JAP TERRITORY.
THAT'S RIGHT, SERGEANT, THE IRRAWADDY.
YOU DEADBEATS SEEM TO FORGET THERE'S A WAR ON. NO SQUAD OF MINE IS TURNING TAIL. MY ORDERS ARE TO STAY AND FIGHT. . . AND IF NECESSARY, DIE!
YOU DOUBLE-CROSSING RAT! YOU'VE DONE FOR US! I'LL KILL YOU! I'LL KILL YOU!
HE'S AS GOOD AS SLIT OUR THROATS! BLEED HIM, SARGE!
YOU'RE STRONG, SERGEANT... VERY STRONG...
...BUT ARE YOU AS STRONG AS THIS?
AAAAAH!
PLEASE... AAAAH! LET ME GO!
UGGH!
CRAZY... THAT'S WHAT HE IS...
YOU MEN TAKE YOUR CHOICE. YOU CAN GO WITH THE SERGEANT HERE AND TRY TO MAKE IT BACK TO BRITISH LINES. IF YOU'RE COWARDS ENOUGH TO GO, THEN I DON'T WANT YOU ANYWAY.
IF YOU STAY WITH ME, I'M GOING TO GIVE YOU HELL. YOU'LL EAT, SLEEP AND DRINK JUNGLE. YOU'LL SMELL LIKE JUNGLE. YOU'LL CURSE ME AND HATE ME. BUT I PROMISE YOU ONE THING... YOU'LL KILL JAPS!
He's sitting there now, cleaning his kukri and smiling. He knows we won't get ten miles without him. The Japs know Darkie — and they're afraid of him. They've never even heard of Sergeant Samson!

NEXT WEEK – YOU DON'T CHICKEN OUT OF DARKIE'S MOB !

IN THE JUNGLE THERE WERE THE BRITISH, THE JAPS – AND DARKIE !

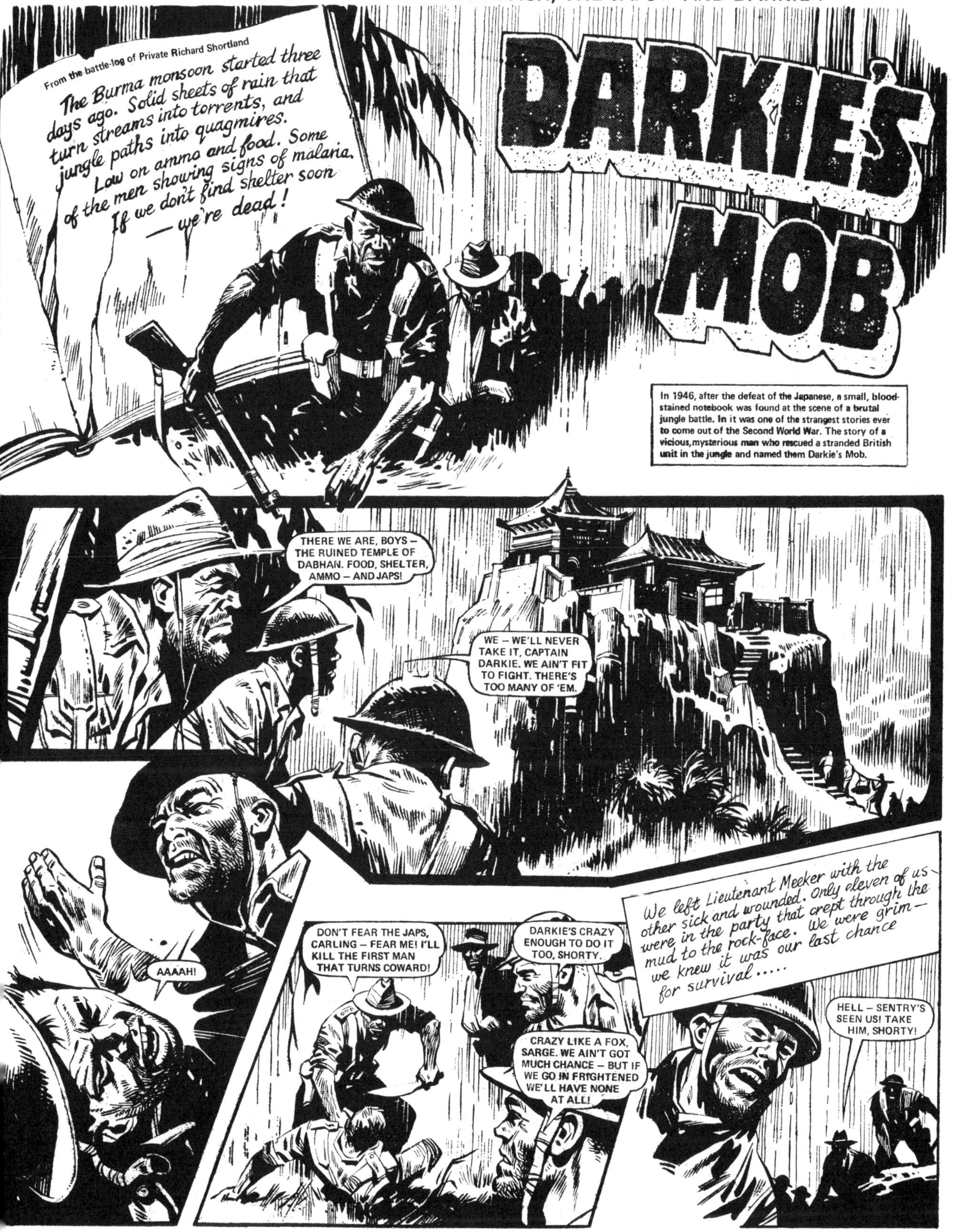

From the battle-log of Private Richard Shortland
The Burma monsoon started three days ago. Solid sheets of rain that turn streams into torrents, and jungle paths into quagmires. Low on ammo and food. Some of the men showing signs of malaria. If we don't find shelter soon — we're dead!
DARKIE'S MOB
In 1946, after the defeat of the Japanese, a small, blood-stained notebook was found at the scene of a brutal jungle battle. In it was one of the strangest stories ever to come out of the Second World War. The story of a vicious, mysterious man who rescued a stranded British unit in the jungle and named them Darkie's Mob.
THERE WE ARE, BOYS – THE RUINED TEMPLE OF DABHAN. FOOD, SHELTER, AMMO – AND JAPS!
WE – WE'LL NEVER TAKE IT, CAPTAIN DARKIE. WE AIN'T FIT TO FIGHT. THERE'S TOO MANY OF 'EM.
AAAAH!
DON'T FEAR THE JAPS, CARLING – FEAR ME! I'LL KILL THE FIRST MAN THAT TURNS COWARD!
DARKIE'S CRAZY ENOUGH TO DO IT TOO, SHORTY.
CRAZY LIKE A FOX, SARGE. WE AIN'T GOT MUCH CHANCE – BUT IF WE GO IN FRIGHTENED WE'LL HAVE NONE AT ALL!
We left Lieutenant Meeker with the other sick and wounded. Only eleven of us were in the party that crept through the mud to the rock-face. We were grim — we knew it was our last chance for survival.....
HELL – SENTRY'S SEEN US! TAKE HIM, SHORTY!

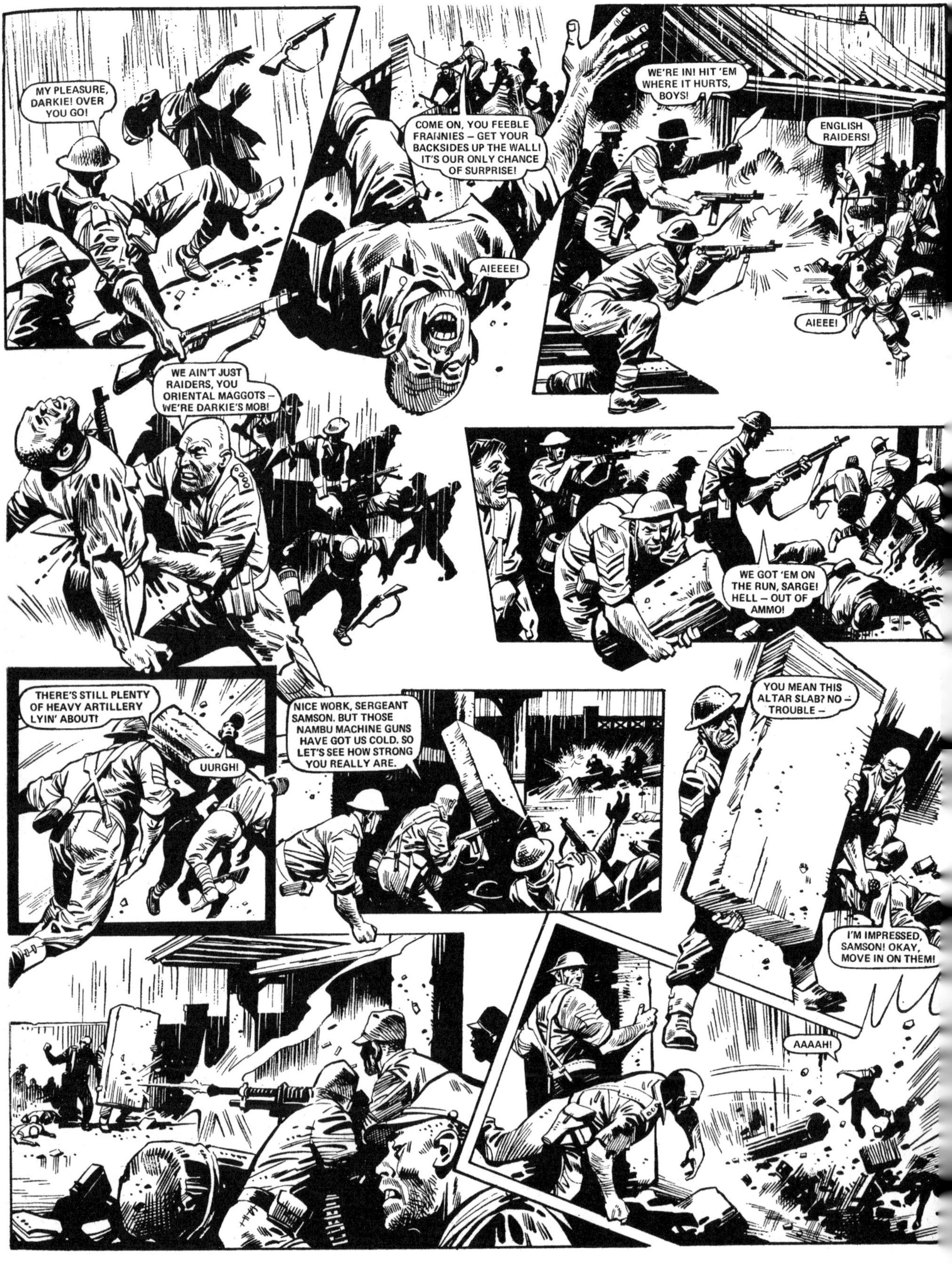
MY PLEASURE, DARKIE! OVER YOU GO!
COME ON, YOU FEEBLE FANNIES – GET YOUR BACKSIDES UP THE WALL! IT'S OUR ONLY CHANCE OF SURPRISE!
AIEEEE!
WE'RE IN! HIT 'EM WHERE IT HURTS, BOYS!
ENGLISH RAIDERS!
AIEEE!
WE AIN'T JUST RAIDERS, YOU ORIENTAL MAGGOTS – WE'RE DARKIE'S MOB!
WE GOT 'EM ON THE RUN, SARGE! HELL – OUT OF AMMO!
THERE'S STILL PLENTY OF HEAVY ARTILLERY LYIN' ABOUT!
UURGH!
NICE WORK, SERGEANT SAMSON. BUT THOSE NAMBU MACHINE GUNS HAVE GOT US COLD. SO LET'S SEE HOW STRONG YOU REALLY ARE.
YOU MEAN THIS ALTAR SLAB? NO – TROUBLE –
I'M IMPRESSED, SAMSON! OKAY, MOVE IN ON THEM!
AAAAH!

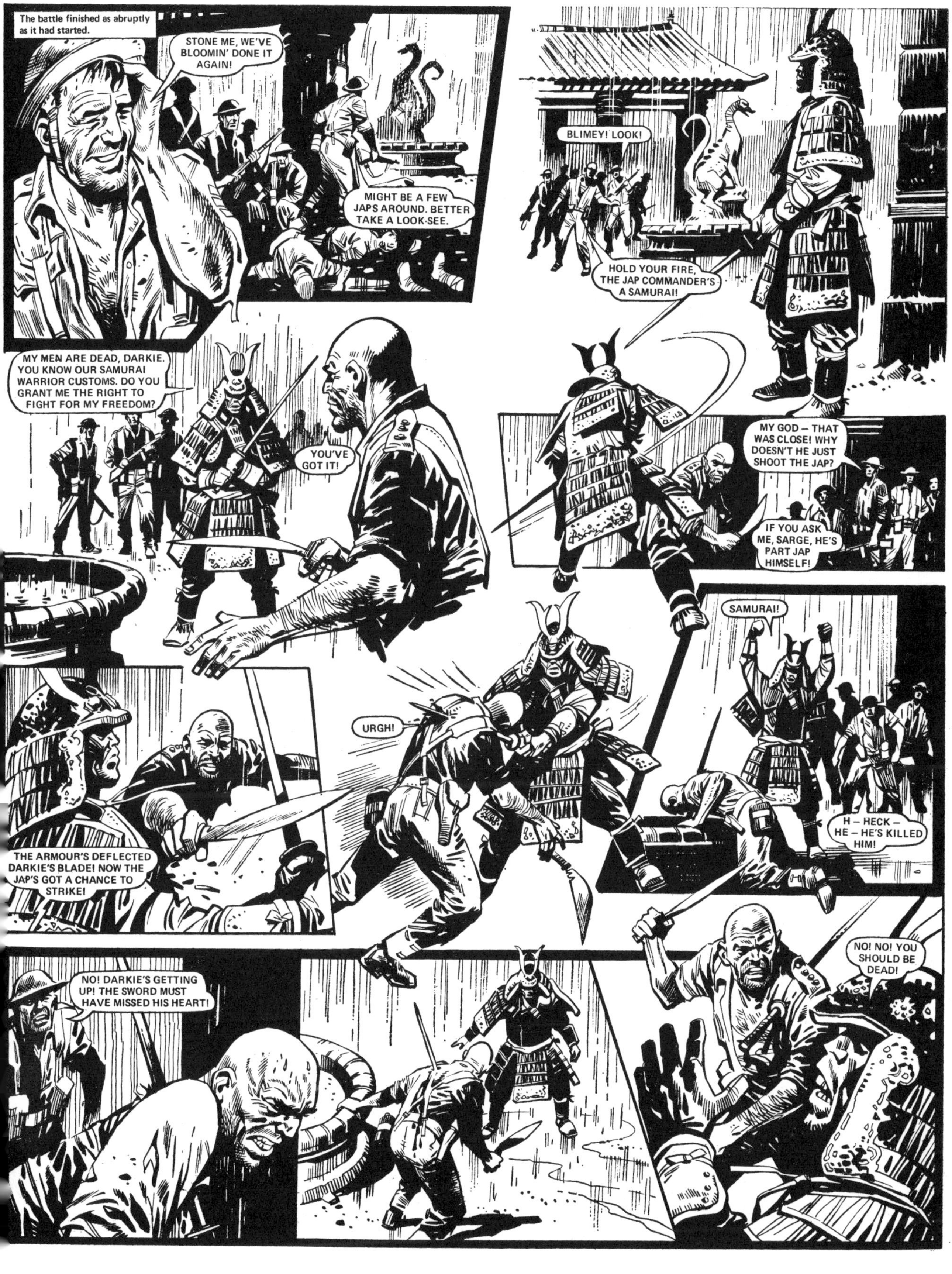

The battle finished as abruptly as it had started.
STONE ME, WE'VE BLOOMIN' DONE IT AGAIN!
MIGHT BE A FEW JAPS AROUND. BETTER TAKE A LOOK-SEE.
BLIMEY! LOOK!
HOLD YOUR FIRE, THE JAP COMMANDER'S A SAMURAI!
MY MEN ARE DEAD, DARKIE. YOU KNOW OUR SAMURAI WARRIOR CUSTOMS. DO YOU GRANT ME THE RIGHT TO FIGHT FOR MY FREEDOM?
YOU'VE GOT IT!
MY GOD — THAT WAS CLOSE! WHY DOESN'T HE JUST SHOOT THE JAP?
IF YOU ASK ME, SARGE, HE'S PART JAP HIMSELF!
THE ARMOUR'S DEFLECTED DARKIE'S BLADE! NOW THE JAP'S GOT A CHANCE TO STRIKE!
URGH!
SAMURAI!
H — HECK — HE — HE'S KILLED HIM!
NO! DARKIE'S GETTING UP! THE SWORD MUST HAVE MISSED HIS HEART!
NO! NO! YOU SHOULD BE DEAD!

DARKIE'S WON! I'VE NEVER SEEN ANYTHING LIKE IT! THE GUY'S HARDLY HUMAN.
Later, as Darkie's wound was attended to, and the men cooked their first hot meal for a long time –
REMEMBER THIS WELL, MEN . . . THE RABBIT IS SWIFTER THAN THE SNAKE – YET HE SITS IN FEAR AND WAITS FOR DEATH. FEAR IS THE KILLER. LEARN TO WELCOME DEATH, AND YOU'LL NEVER BE AFRAID.
Darkie disappeared. an hour passed and he didn't reappear. We were getting worried. In the end, Sarge Samson and me found him in the pagoda ......
I HAVE GIVEN MY SOUL TO YOU – BUT MY BLADE IS PLEDGED TO THE DEVIL. WHEN THE JAPANESE ARE BEATEN, THEN I WILL PAY. MY KUKRI WILL CLAIM MY OWN LIFE.
WELL, THAT BEATS IT ALL. OUR CAPTAIN DARKIE'S A FLIPPIN' BUDDHIST!
THE GUY'S A NUTTER WITH A CAPITAL "N"! BUT I'LL TELL YOU SOMETHING, SHORTY – I'M BEGINNIN' TO GET KINDA GLAD HE'S FIGHTIN' ON OUR SIDE!
I WONDER HOW YOU'D FEEL IF YOU KNEW HE WASN'T EVEN IN THE BRITISH ARMY? BUT WHOEVER HE IS, I'LL NEVER SAY A WORD. 'COS WITHOUT DARKIE, WE CAN START DIGGIN' OUR OWN GRAVES!

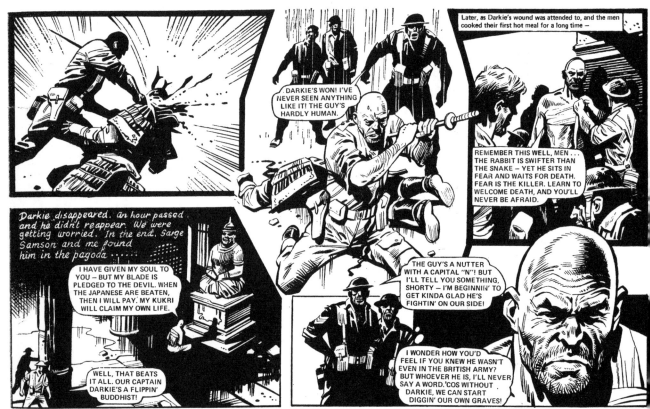

NEXT WEEK – A HIDDEN KILLER STRIKES AT DARKIE'S MOB !

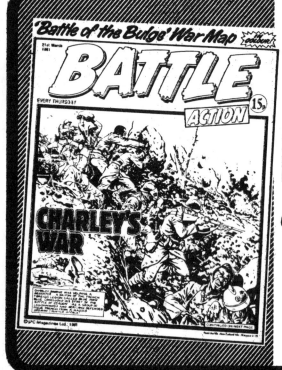

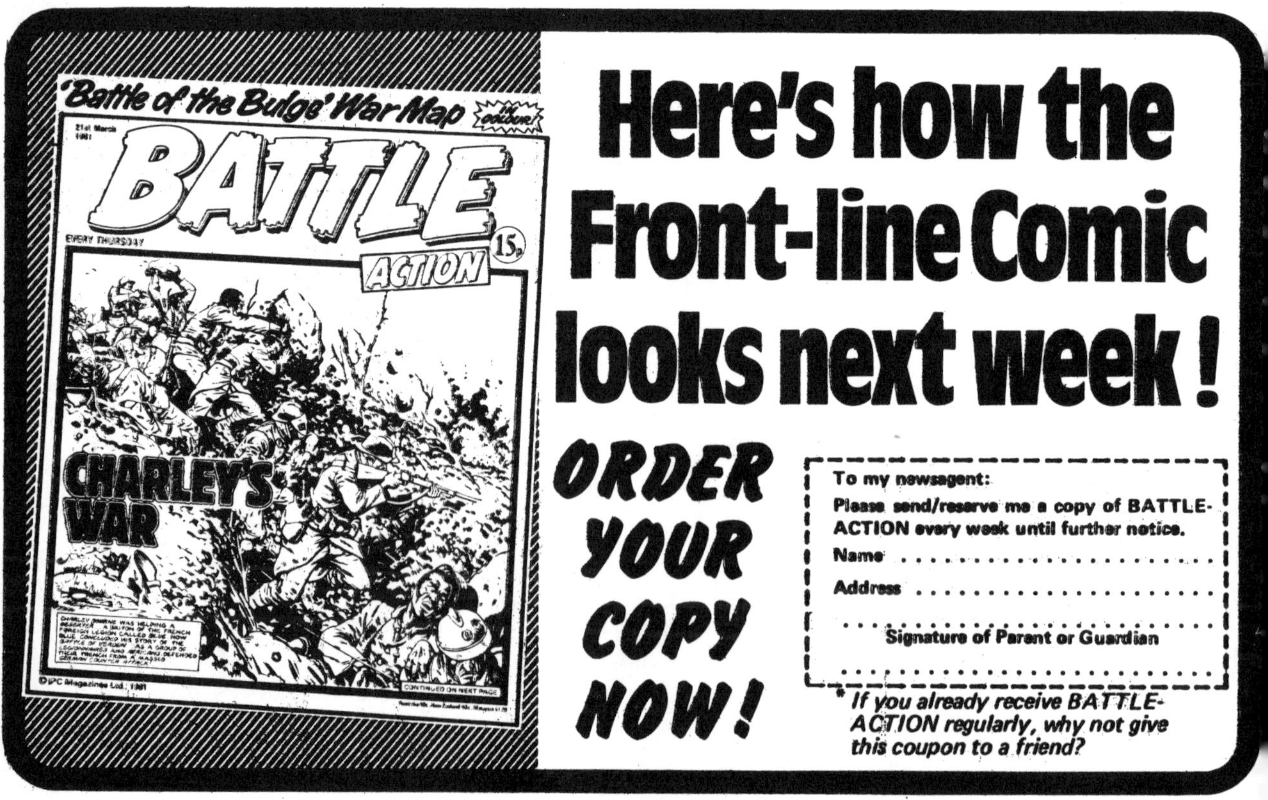

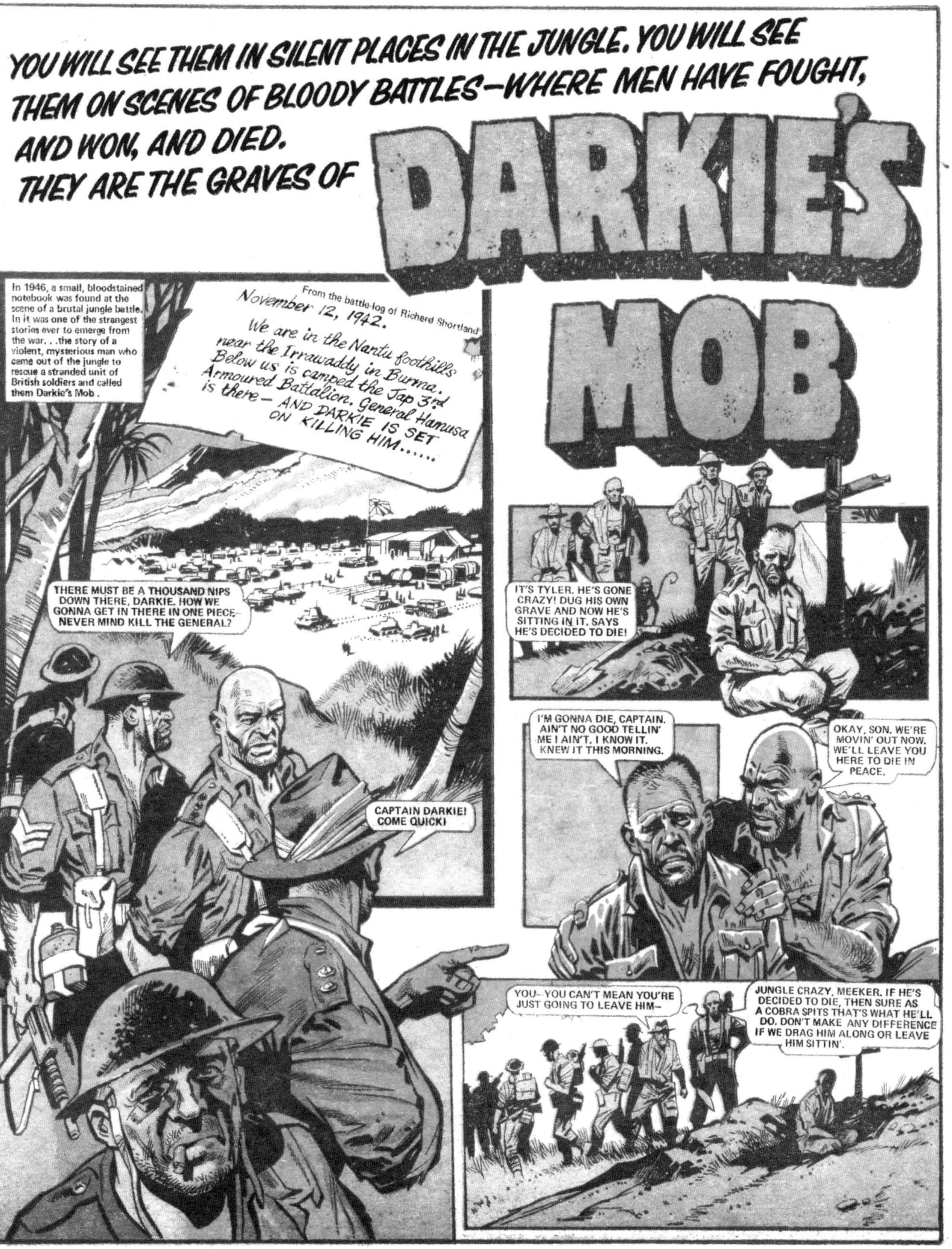
YOU WILL SEE THEM IN SILENT PLACES IN THE JUNGLE. YOU WILL SEE THEM ON SCENES OF BLOODY BATTLES—WHERE MEN HAVE FOUGHT, AND WON, AND DIED.
THEY ARE THE GRAVES OF
DARKIE'S MOB
In 1946, a small, bloodstained notebook was found at the scene of a brutal jungle battle. In it was one of the strangest stories ever to emerge from the war. . .the story of a violent, mysterious man who came out of the jungle to rescue a stranded unit of British soldiers and called them Darkie's Mob.
From the battle-log of Richard Shortland
November 12, 1942.
We are in the Nantu foothills near the Irrawaddy in Burma. Below us is camped the Jap 3rd Armoured Battalion. General Hamusa is there— AND DARKIE IS SET ON KILLING HIM......
THERE MUST BE A THOUSAND NIPS DOWN THERE, DARKIE. HOW WE GONNA GET IN THERE IN ONE PIECE— NEVER MIND KILL THE GENERAL?
CAPTAIN DARKIE! COME QUICK!
IT'S TYLER. HE'S GONE CRAZY! DUG HIS OWN GRAVE AND NOW HE'S SITTING IN IT. SAYS HE'S DECIDED TO DIE!
I'M GONNA DIE, CAPTAIN. AIN'T NO GOOD TELLIN' ME I AIN'T. I KNOW IT. KNEW IT THIS MORNING.
OKAY, SON. WE'RE MOVIN' OUT NOW. WE'LL LEAVE YOU HERE TO DIE IN PEACE.
YOU—YOU CAN'T MEAN YOU'RE JUST GOING TO LEAVE HIM—
JUNGLE CRAZY, MEEKER. IF HE'S DECIDED TO DIE, THEN SURE AS A COBRA SPITS THAT'S WHAT HE'LL DO. DON'T MAKE ANY DIFFERENCE IF WE DRAG HIM ALONG OR LEAVE HIM SITTIN'.

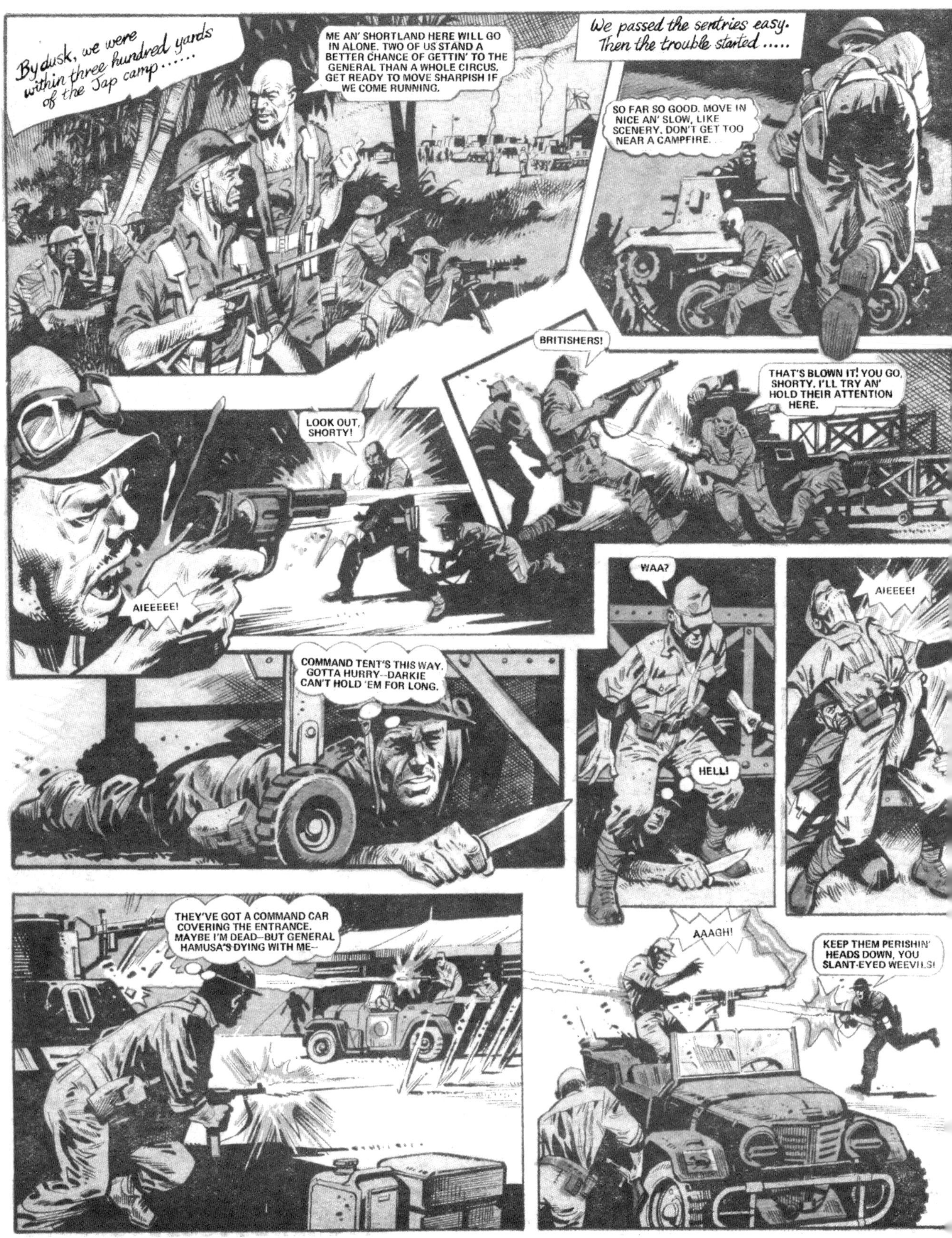
By dusk, we were within three hundred yards of the Jap camp......
ME AN' SHORTLAND HERE WILL GO IN ALONE. TWO OF US STAND A BETTER CHANCE OF GETTIN' TO THE GENERAL THAN A WHOLE CIRCUS. GET READY TO MOVE SHARPISH IF WE COME RUNNING.
We passed the sentries easy. Then the trouble started.....
SO FAR SO GOOD. MOVE IN NICE AN' SLOW, LIKE SCENERY. DON'T GET TOO NEAR A CAMPFIRE...
BRITISHERS!
THAT'S BLOWN IT! YOU GO, SHORTY. I'LL TRY AN' HOLD THEIR ATTENTION HERE.
LOOK OUT, SHORTY!
AIEEEEE!
WAA?
AIEEEE!
COMMAND TENT'S THIS WAY. GOTTA HURRY--DARKIE CAN'T HOLD 'EM FOR LONG.
HELL!
THEY'VE GOT A COMMAND CAR COVERING THE ENTRANCE. MAYBE I'M DEAD--BUT GENERAL HAMUSA'S DYING WITH ME--
AAAGH!
KEEP THEM PERISHIN' HEADS DOWN, YOU SLANT-EYED WEEVILS!

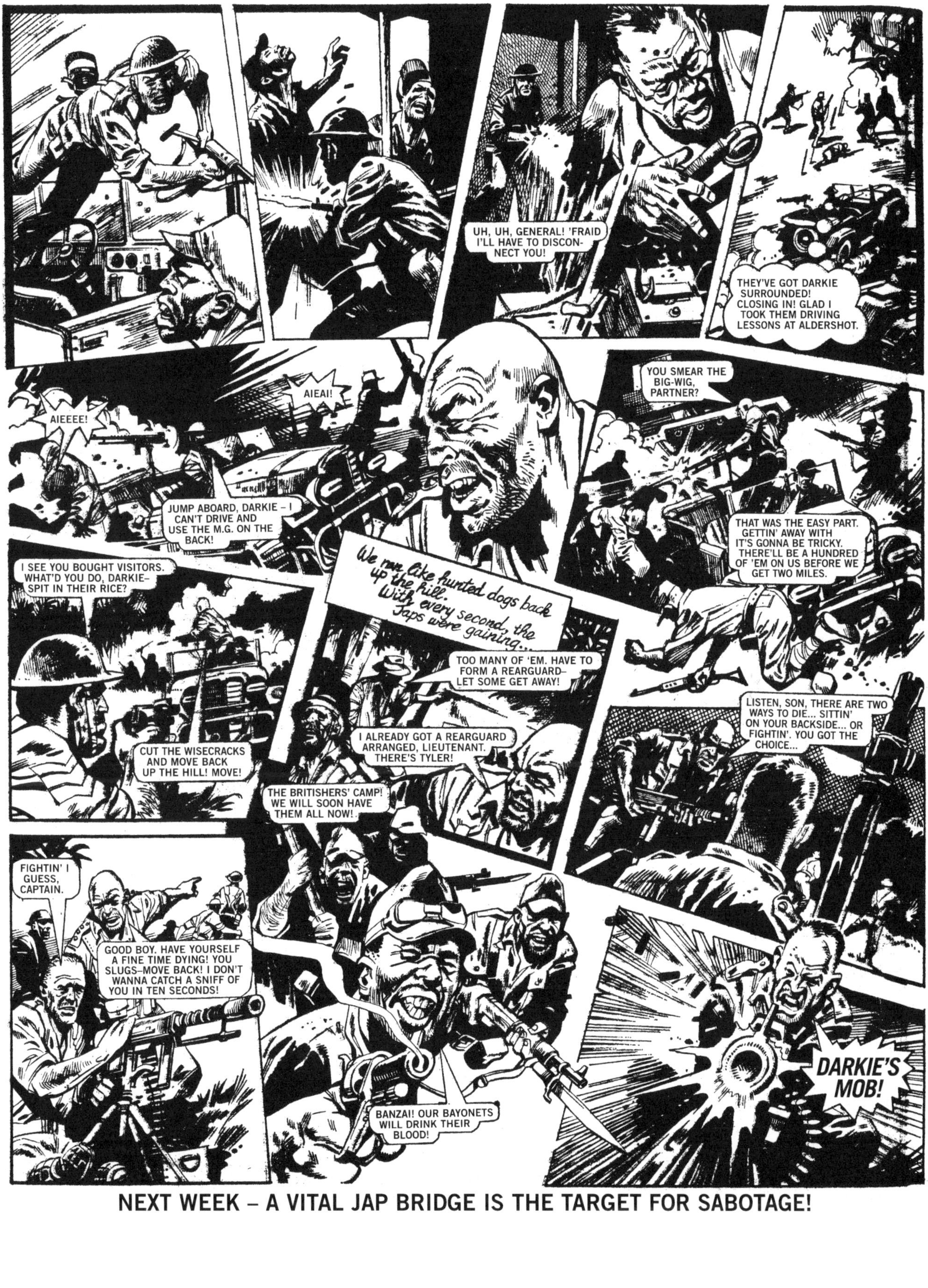

UH, UH, GENERAL! 'FRAID I'LL HAVE TO DISCON-NECT YOU!
THEY'VE GOT DARKIE SURROUNDED! CLOSING IN! GLAD I TOOK THEM DRIVING LESSONS AT ALDERSHOT.
AIEEEE!
AIEAI!
JUMP ABOARD, DARKIE – I CAN'T DRIVE AND USE THE M.G. ON THE BACK!
YOU SMEAR THE BIG-WIG, PARTNER?
THAT WAS THE EASY PART. GETTIN' AWAY WITH IT'S GONNA BE TRICKY. THERE'LL BE A HUNDRED OF 'EM ON US BEFORE WE GET TWO MILES.
I SEE YOU BOUGHT VISITORS. WHAT'D YOU DO, DARKIE–SPIT IN THEIR RICE?
CUT THE WISECRACKS AND MOVE BACK UP THE HILL! MOVE!
We ran like hunted dogs back up the hill. With every second, the Japs were gaining...
TOO MANY OF 'EM. HAVE TO FORM A REARGUARD–LET SOME GET AWAY!
I ALREADY GOT A REARGUARD ARRANGED, LIEUTENANT. THERE'S TYLER!
LISTEN, SON, THERE ARE TWO WAYS TO DIE... SITTIN' ON YOUR BACKSIDE... OR FIGHTIN'. YOU GOT THE CHOICE...
FIGHTIN' I GUESS, CAPTAIN.
GOOD BOY. HAVE YOURSELF A FINE TIME DYING! YOU SLUGS–MOVE BACK! I DON'T WANNA CATCH A SNIFF OF YOU IN TEN SECONDS!
THE BRITISHERS' CAMP! WE WILL SOON HAVE THEM ALL NOW!
BANZAI! OUR BAYONETS WILL DRINK THEIR BLOOD!
DARKIE'S MOB!

NEXT WEEK – A VITAL JAP BRIDGE IS THE TARGET FOR SABOTAGE!

CHRISTMAS DAY IS JUST LIKE ANY OTHER WHEN YOU FIGHT FOR DARKIE'S MOB !

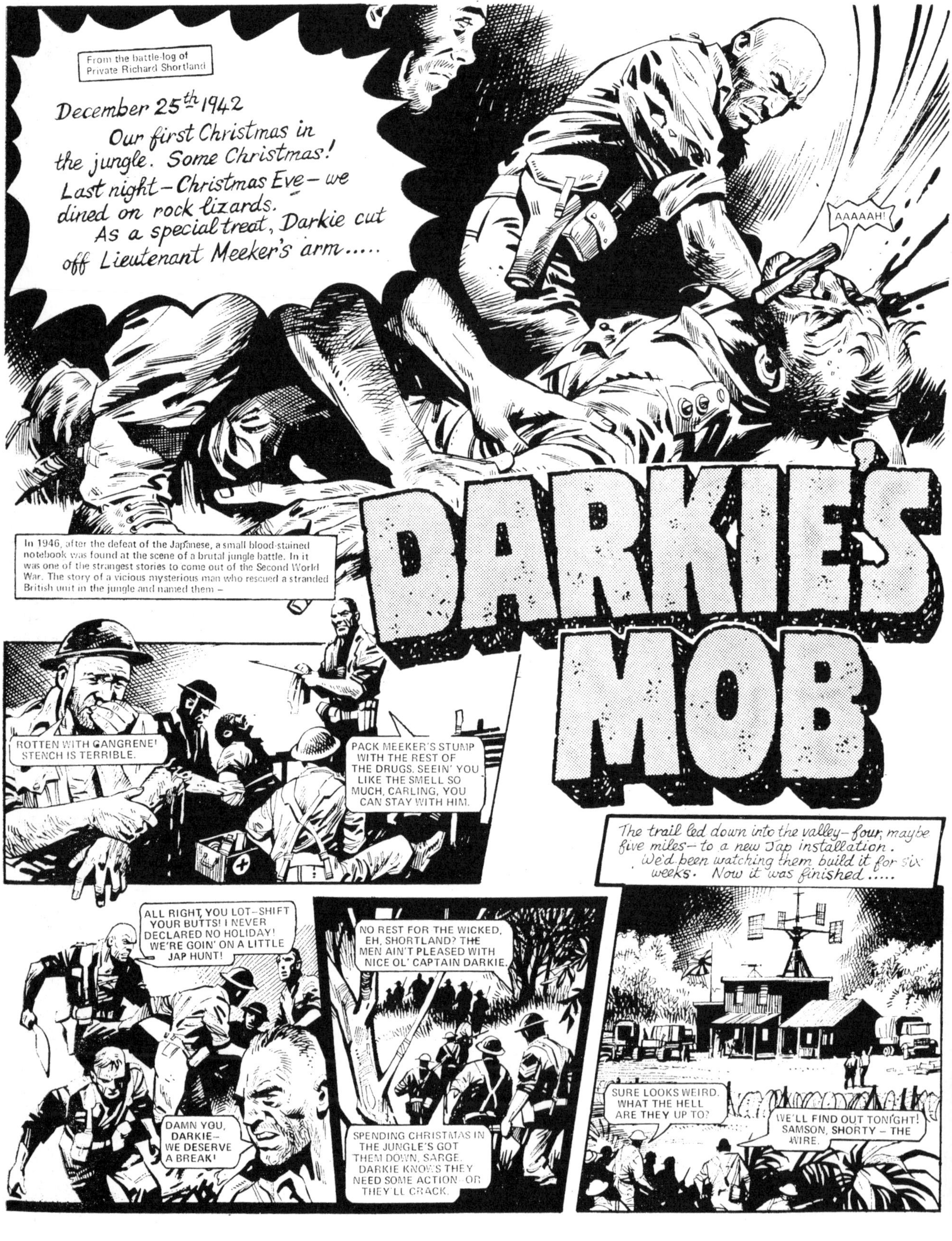

From the battle-log of Private Richard Shortland
December 25th 1942 Our first Christmas in the jungle. Some Christmas! Last night – Christmas Eve – we dined on rock lizards. As a special treat, Darkie cut off Lieutenant Meeker's arm.....
AAAAAH!
DARKIE'S MOB
In 1946, after the defeat of the Japanese, a small blood-stained notebook was found at the scene of a brutal jungle battle. In it was one of the strangest stories to come out of the Second World War. The story of a vicious mysterious man who rescued a stranded British unit in the jungle and named them –
ROTTEN WITH GANGRENE! STENCH IS TERRIBLE.
PACK MEEKER'S STUMP WITH THE REST OF THE DRUGS. SEEIN' YOU LIKE THE SMELL SO MUCH, CARLING, YOU CAN STAY WITH HIM.
The trail led down into the valley – four, maybe five miles – to a new Jap installation. We'd been watching them build it for six weeks. Now it was finished.....
ALL RIGHT, YOU LOT – SHIFT YOUR BUTTS! I NEVER DECLARED NO HOLIDAY! WE'RE GOIN' ON A LITTLE JAP HUNT!
DAMN YOU, DARKIE – WE DESERVE A BREAK!
NO REST FOR THE WICKED, EH, SHORTLAND? THE MEN AIN'T PLEASED WITH NICE OL' CAPTAIN DARKIE.
SPENDING CHRISTMAS IN THE JUNGLE'S GOT THEM DOWN, SARGE. DARKIE KNOWS THEY NEED SOME ACTION – OR THEY'LL CRACK.
SURE LOOKS WEIRD. WHAT THE HELL ARE THEY UP TO?
WE'LL FIND OUT TONIGHT! SAMSON, SHORTY – THE WIRE.

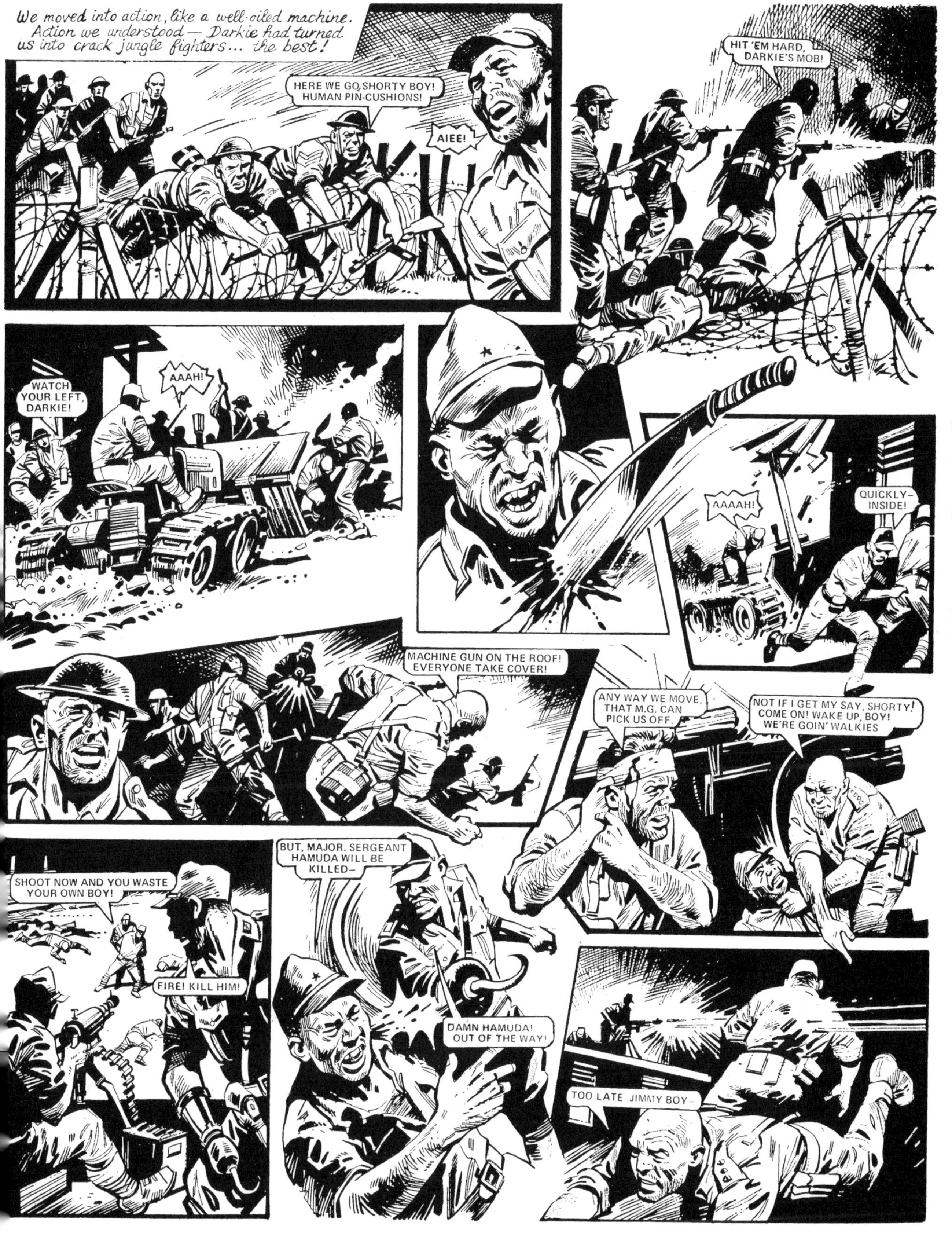

We moved into action, like a well-oiled machine. Action we understood — Darkie had turned us into crack jungle fighters... the best!
HERE WE GO, SHORTY BOY! HUMAN PIN-CUSHIONS!
AIEE!
HIT 'EM HARD, DARKIE'S MOB!
WATCH YOUR LEFT, DARKIE!
AAAH!
AAAAH!
QUICKLY– INSIDE!
MACHINE GUN ON THE ROOF! EVERYONE TAKE COVER!
ANY WAY WE MOVE, THAT M.G. CAN PICK US OFF.
NOT IF I GET MY SAY, SHORTY! COME ON! WAKE UP, BOY! WE'RE GOIN' WALKIES
SHOOT NOW AND YOU WASTE YOUR OWN BOY!
FIRE! KILL HIM!
BUT, MAJOR. SERGEANT HAMUDA WILL BE KILLED–
DAMN HAMUDA! OUT OF THE WAY!
TOO LATE JIMMY BOY–

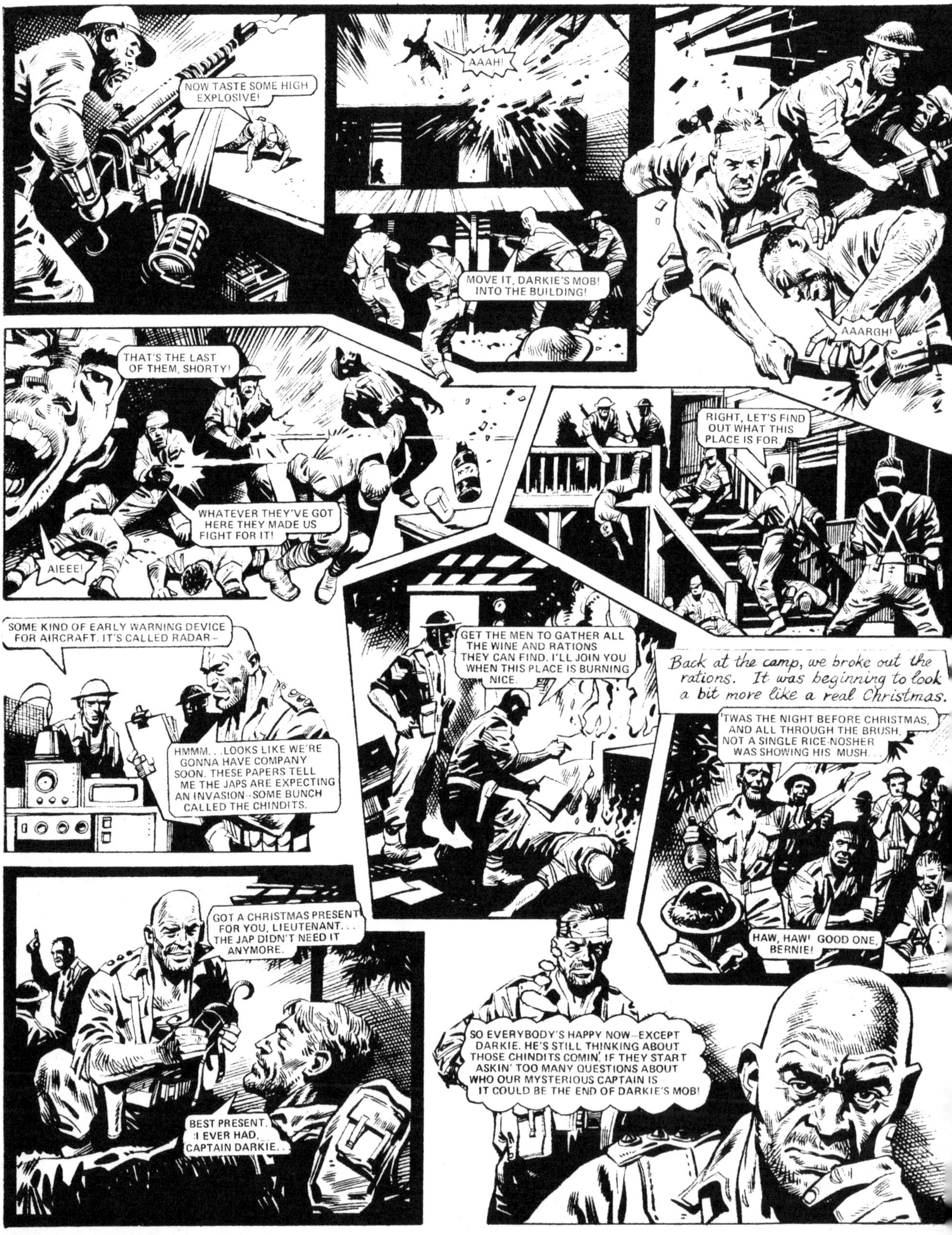
NOW TASTE SOME HIGH EXPLOSIVE!
AAAH!
MOVE IT, DARKIE'S MOB! INTO THE BUILDING!
AAARGH!
THAT'S THE LAST OF THEM, SHORTY!
WHATEVER THEY'VE GOT HERE THEY MADE US FIGHT FOR IT!
AIEEE!
RIGHT, LET'S FIND OUT WHAT THIS PLACE IS FOR.
SOME KIND OF EARLY WARNING DEVICE FOR AIRCRAFT. IT'S CALLED RADAR--
HMMM. . .LOOKS LIKE WE'RE GONNA HAVE COMPANY SOON. THESE PAPERS TELL ME THE JAPS ARE EXPECTING AN INVASION--SOME BUNCH CALLED THE CHINDITS.
GET THE MEN TO GATHER ALL THE WINE AND RATIONS THEY CAN FIND. I'LL JOIN YOU WHEN THIS PLACE IS BURNING NICE.
Back at the camp, we broke out the rations. It was beginning to look a bit more like a real Christmas.
'TWAS THE NIGHT BEFORE CHRISTMAS, AND ALL THROUGH THE BRUSH, NOT A SINGLE RICE-NOSHER WAS SHOWING HIS MUSH. . .
HAW, HAW! GOOD ONE, BERNIE!
GOT A CHRISTMAS PRESENT FOR YOU, LIEUTENANT. . . THE JAP DIDN'T NEED IT ANYMORE.
BEST PRESENT I EVER HAD, CAPTAIN DARKIE. .
SO EVERYBODY'S HAPPY NOW--EXCEPT DARKIE. HE'S STILL THINKING ABOUT THOSE CHINDITS COMIN'. IF THEY START ASKIN' TOO MANY QUESTIONS ABOUT WHO OUR MYSTERIOUS CAPTAIN IS-- IT COULD BE THE END OF DARKIE'S MOB!

MISSION ENDS...MISSION ENDS...MISSION ENDS...MISSION ENDS...MISSION ENDS...MISSION ENDS

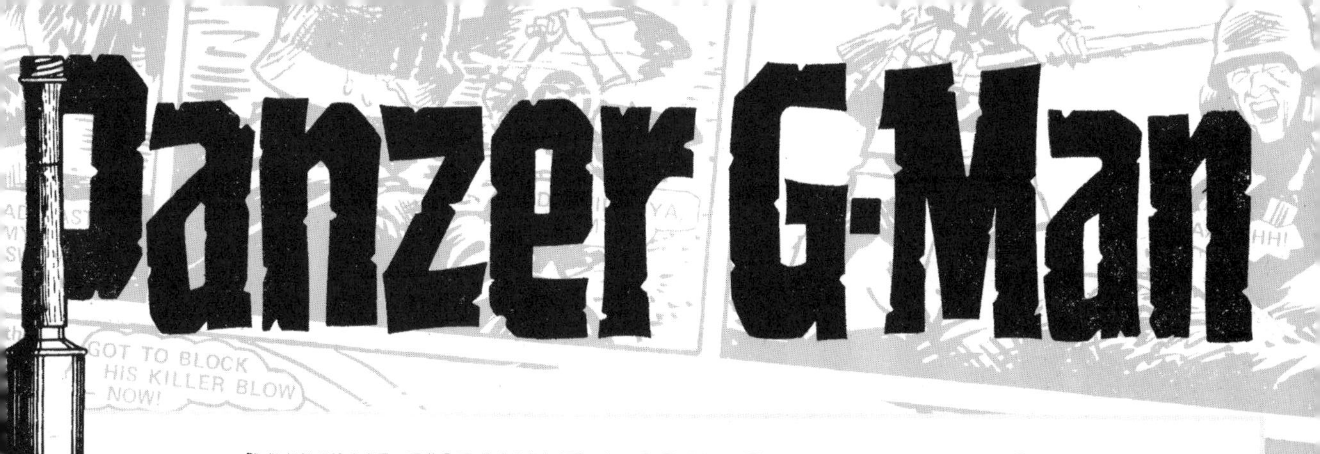
GOT TO BLOCK HIS KILLER BLOW NOW!

Panzer G-Man

"ANYONE ELSE WANT A GRENADE IN THE TEETH?"

Despite his bravery and valour, German tank gunner Kurt Slinger has been wrongly charged with cowardice and demoted to the rank of Panzergrenadier ("G-Man"), after surviving a Russian tank attack during Operation Barbarossa. Now armed with stick grenades and a machine gun, Slinger is forced to run alongside the mighty Panzers — fighting not only the Russians, but also his own men to clear his name.

"We have the courage to tell it from the Germans' viewpoint!" cried an early tagline from the cover of *Battle*, as it championed another of its unique German heroes. Once again, a man is wrongly accused and forced to clear his name — not an uncommon theme among *Battle*'s German characters.

NOTES FROM THE FRONTLINE:

"Another Gerry Finley-Day-scripted strip; he was very interested in those kind of German-themed stories.

This was the era of the Sven Hassel stories: we were all reading them and we all wanted to know what it was like from the other point of view. You can't just demonise an entire nation — you have to look: where was the heroism, where was the courage?

And the readers really liked the German heroes — they had no problem whatsoever. However, there were problems in editorial — to do with having anything that made the Germans look positive — but as far as the readers were concerned, they were very happy." **— Pat Mills**

WRITTEN BY Gerry Finley-Day
DRAWN BY Geoff Campion

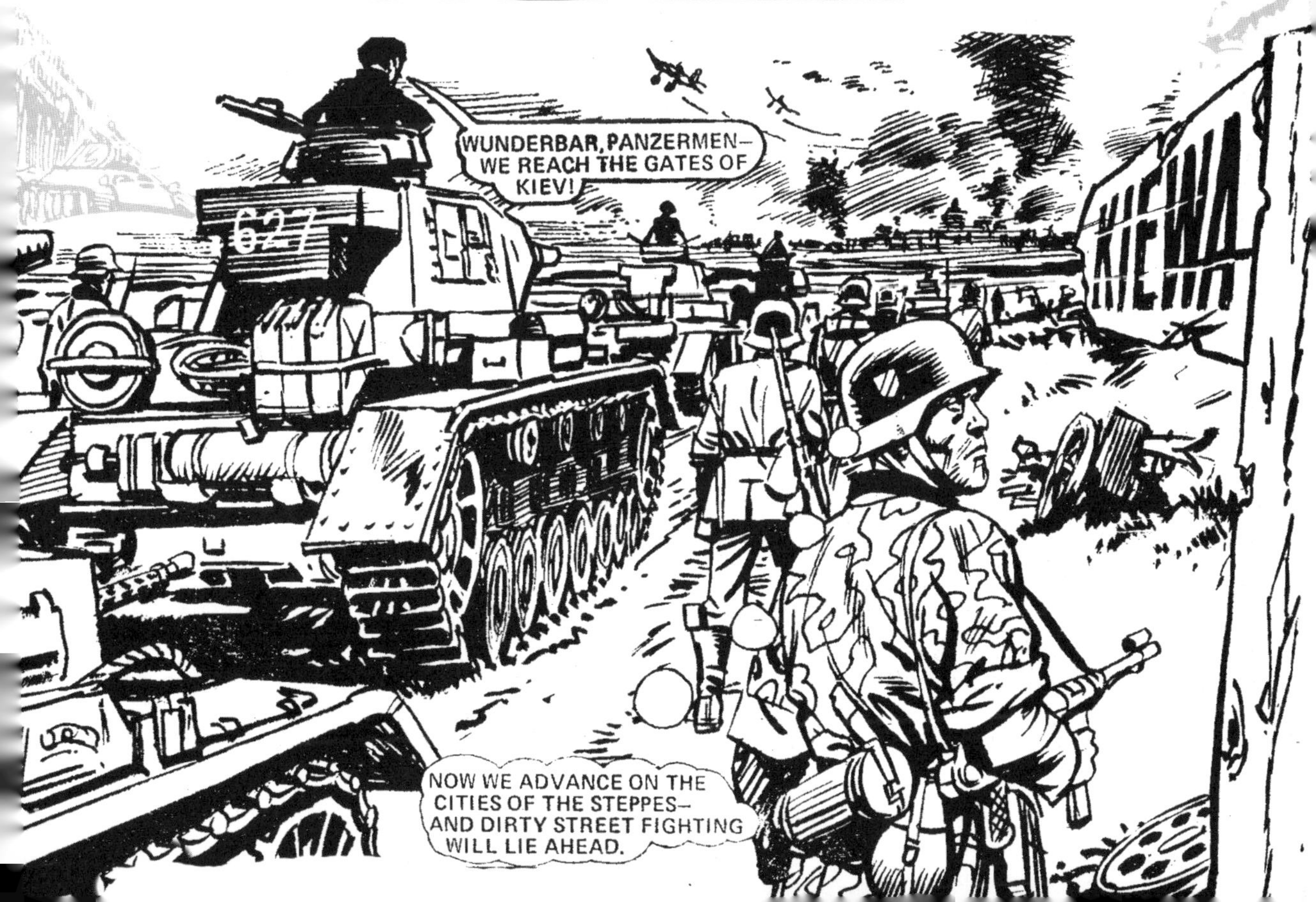
WUNDERBAR, PANZERMEN— WE REACH THE GATES OF KIEV!
627
NOW WE ADVANCE ON THE CITIES OF THE STEPPES— AND DIRTY STREET FIGHTING WILL LIE AHEAD.

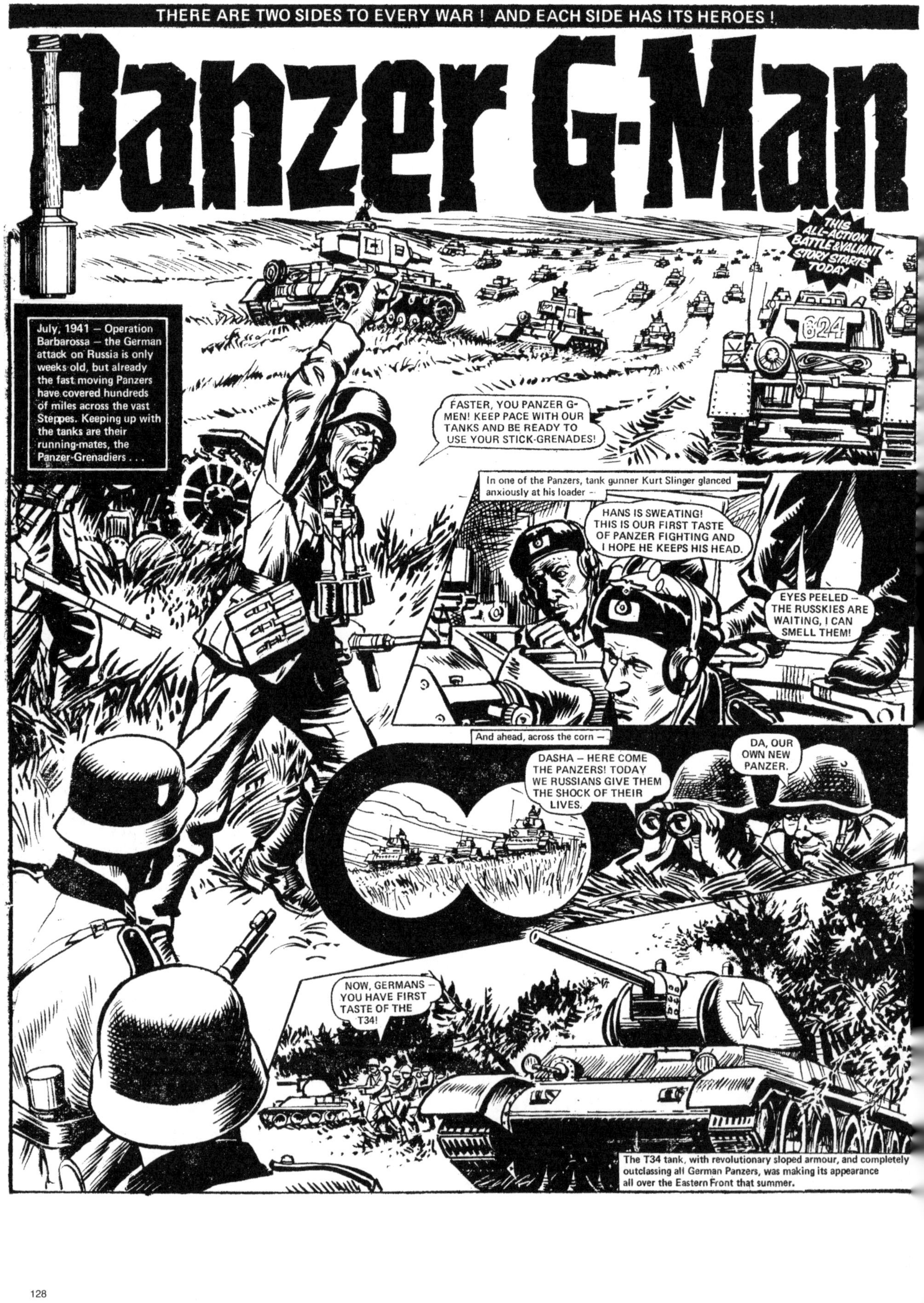
THERE ARE TWO SIDES TO EVERY WAR ! AND EACH SIDE HAS ITS HEROES !
Panzer G-Man
THIS ALL-ACTION BATTLE & VALIANT STORY STARTS TODAY
July, 1941 — Operation Barbarossa — the German attack on Russia is only weeks old, but already the fast moving Panzers have covered hundreds of miles across the vast Steppes. Keeping up with the tanks are their running-mates, the Panzer-Grenadiers . . .
624
FASTER, YOU PANZER G-MEN! KEEP PACE WITH OUR TANKS AND BE READY TO USE YOUR STICK-GRENADES!
In one of the Panzers, tank gunner Kurt Slinger glanced anxiously at his loader —
HANS IS SWEATING! THIS IS OUR FIRST TASTE OF PANZER FIGHTING AND I HOPE HE KEEPS HIS HEAD.
EYES PEELED — THE RUSSKIES ARE WAITING, I CAN SMELL THEM!
And ahead, across the corn —
DASHA — HERE COME THE PANZERS! TODAY WE RUSSIANS GIVE THEM THE SHOCK OF THEIR LIVES.
DA, OUR OWN NEW PANZER.
NOW, GERMANS — YOU HAVE FIRST TASTE OF THE T34!
The T34 tank, with revolutionary sloped armour, and completely outclassing all German Panzers, was making its appearance all over the Eastern Front that summer.

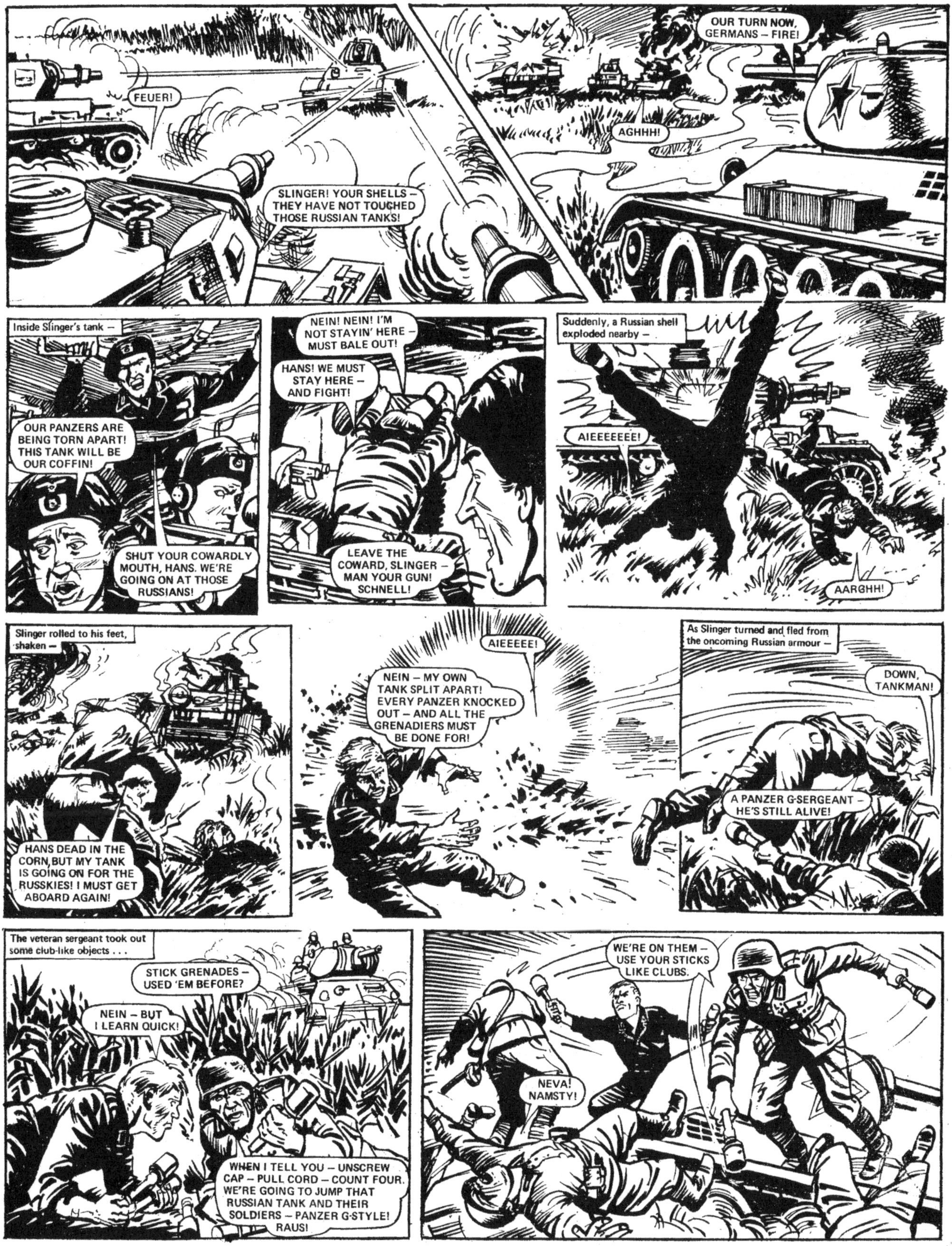

FEUER!
SLINGER! YOUR SHELLS – THEY HAVE NOT TOUCHED THOSE RUSSIAN TANKS!
OUR TURN NOW, GERMANS – FIRE!
AGHHH!
Inside Slinger's tank –
OUR PANZERS ARE BEING TORN APART! THIS TANK WILL BE OUR COFFIN!
SHUT YOUR COWARDLY MOUTH, HANS. WE'RE GOING ON AT THOSE RUSSIANS!
NEIN! NEIN! I'M NOT STAYIN' HERE – MUST BALE OUT!
HANS! WE MUST STAY HERE – AND FIGHT!
LEAVE THE COWARD, SLINGER – MAN YOUR GUN! SCHNELL!
Suddenly, a Russian shell exploded nearby –
AIEEEEEEE!
AARGHH!
Slinger rolled to his feet, shaken –
HANS DEAD IN THE CORN, BUT MY TANK IS GOING ON FOR THE RUSSKIES! I MUST GET ABOARD AGAIN!
AIEEEEE!
NEIN – MY OWN TANK SPLIT APART! EVERY PANZER KNOCKED OUT – AND ALL THE GRENADIERS MUST BE DONE FOR!
As Slinger turned and fled from the oncoming Russian armour –
DOWN, TANKMAN!
A PANZER G-SERGEANT – HE'S STILL ALIVE!
The veteran sergeant took out some club-like objects . . .
STICK GRENADES – USED 'EM BEFORE?
NEIN – BUT I LEARN QUICK!
WHEN I TELL YOU – UNSCREW CAP – PULL CORD – COUNT FOUR. WE'RE GOING TO JUMP THAT RUSSIAN TANK AND THEIR SOLDIERS – PANZER G-STYLE! RAUS!
WE'RE ON THEM – USE YOUR STICKS LIKE CLUBS.
NEVA! NAMSTY!

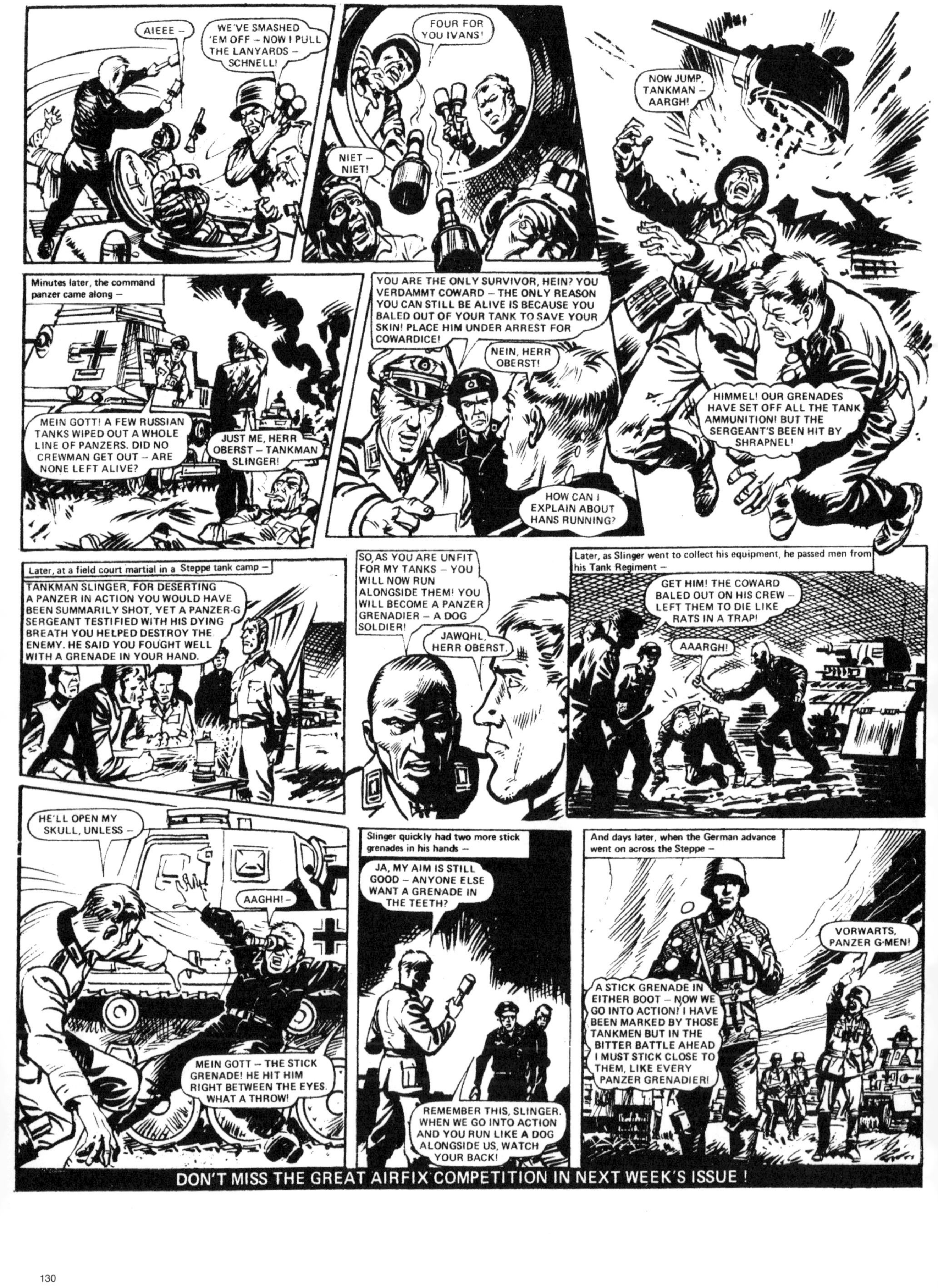

AIEEE –
WE'VE SMASHED 'EM OFF – NOW I PULL THE LANYARDS – SCHNELL!
FOUR FOR YOU IVANS!
NIET – NIET!
NOW JUMP, TANKMAN – AARGH!
Minutes later, the command panzer came along –
MEIN GOTT! A FEW RUSSIAN TANKS WIPED OUT A WHOLE LINE OF PANZERS. DID NO CREWMAN GET OUT – ARE NONE LEFT ALIVE?
JUST ME, HERR OBERST – TANKMAN SLINGER!
YOU ARE THE ONLY SURVIVOR, HEIN? YOU VERDAMMT COWARD – THE ONLY REASON YOU CAN STILL BE ALIVE IS BECAUSE YOU BALED OUT OF YOUR TANK TO SAVE YOUR SKIN! PLACE HIM UNDER ARREST FOR COWARDICE!
NEIN, HERR OBERST!
HOW CAN I EXPLAIN ABOUT HANS RUNNING?
HIMMEL! OUR GRENADES HAVE SET OFF ALL THE TANK AMMUNITION! BUT THE SERGEANT'S BEEN HIT BY SHRAPNEL!
Later, at a field court martial in a Steppe tank camp –
TANKMAN SLINGER, FOR DESERTING A PANZER IN ACTION YOU WOULD HAVE BEEN SUMMARILY SHOT, YET A PANZER-G SERGEANT TESTIFIED WITH HIS DYING BREATH YOU HELPED DESTROY THE ENEMY. HE SAID YOU FOUGHT WELL WITH A GRENADE IN YOUR HAND.
SO, AS YOU ARE UNFIT FOR MY TANKS – YOU WILL NOW RUN ALONGSIDE THEM! YOU WILL BECOME A PANZER GRENADIER – A DOG SOLDIER!
JAWOHL, HERR OBERST.
Later, as Slinger went to collect his equipment, he passed men from his Tank Regiment –
GET HIM! THE COWARD BALED OUT ON HIS CREW – LEFT THEM TO DIE LIKE RATS IN A TRAP!
AAARGH!
HE'LL OPEN MY SKULL, UNLESS –
AAGHH! –
MEIN GOTT – THE STICK GRENADE! HE HIT HIM RIGHT BETWEEN THE EYES. WHAT A THROW!
Slinger quickly had two more stick grenades in his hands –
JA, MY AIM IS STILL GOOD – ANYONE ELSE WANT A GRENADE IN THE TEETH?
REMEMBER THIS, SLINGER. WHEN WE GO INTO ACTION AND YOU RUN LIKE A DOG ALONGSIDE US, WATCH YOUR BACK!
And days later, when the German advance went on across the Steppe –
VORWARTS, PANZER G-MEN!
A STICK GRENADE IN EITHER BOOT – NOW WE GO INTO ACTION! I HAVE BEEN MARKED BY THOSE TANKMEN BUT IN THE BITTER BATTLE AHEAD I MUST STICK CLOSE TO THEM, LIKE EVERY PANZER GRENADIER!

DON'T MISS THE GREAT AIRFIX COMPETITION IN NEXT WEEK'S ISSUE !

TAKE A GRENADE, ADD A GOOD THROWING ARM, AND YOU'VE GOT A...

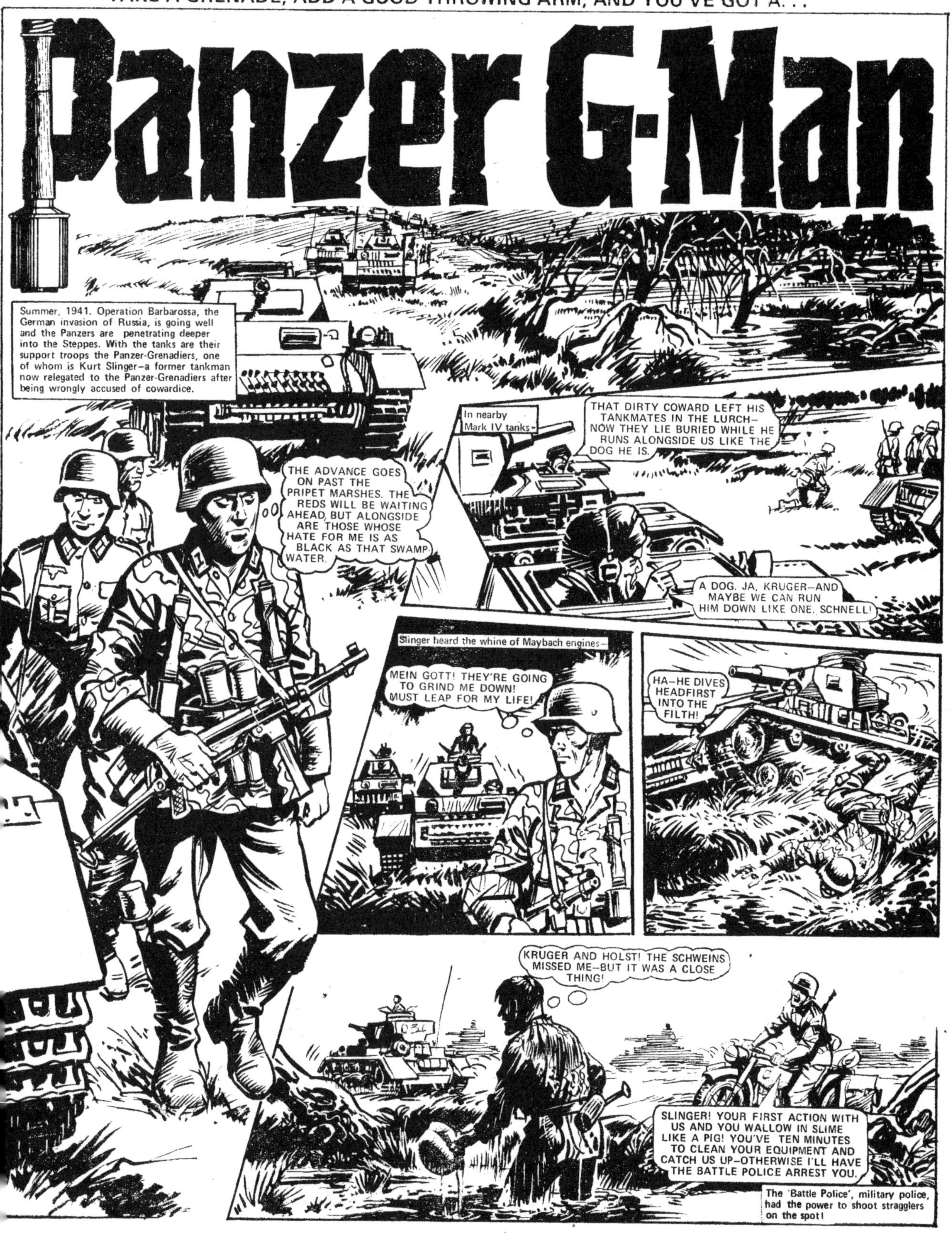
Panzer G-Man
Summer, 1941. Operation Barbarossa, the German invasion of Russia, is going well and the Panzers are penetrating deeper into the Steppes. With the tanks are their support troops the Panzer-Grenadiers, one of whom is Kurt Slinger—a former tankman now relegated to the Panzer-Grenadiers after being wrongly accused of cowardice.
THE ADVANCE GOES ON PAST THE PRIPET MARSHES. THE REDS WILL BE WAITING AHEAD, BUT ALONGSIDE ARE THOSE WHOSE HATE FOR ME IS AS BLACK AS THAT SWAMP-WATER.
In nearby Mark IV tanks—
THAT DIRTY COWARD LEFT HIS TANKMATES IN THE LURCH—NOW THEY LIE BURIED WHILE HE RUNS ALONGSIDE US LIKE THE DOG HE IS.
A DOG. JA, KRUGER—AND MAYBE WE CAN RUN HIM DOWN LIKE ONE. SCHNELL!
Slinger heard the whine of Maybach engines—
MEIN GOTT! THEY'RE GOING TO GRIND ME DOWN! MUST LEAP FOR MY LIFE!
HA—HE DIVES HEADFIRST INTO THE FILTH!
KRUGER AND HOLST! THE SCHWEINS MISSED ME--BUT IT WAS A CLOSE THING!
SLINGER! YOUR FIRST ACTION WITH US AND YOU WALLOW IN SLIME LIKE A PIG! YOU'VE TEN MINUTES TO CLEAN YOUR EQUIPMENT AND CATCH US UP—OTHERWISE I'LL HAVE THE BATTLE POLICE ARREST YOU.
The 'Battle Police', military police, had the power to shoot stragglers on the spot!

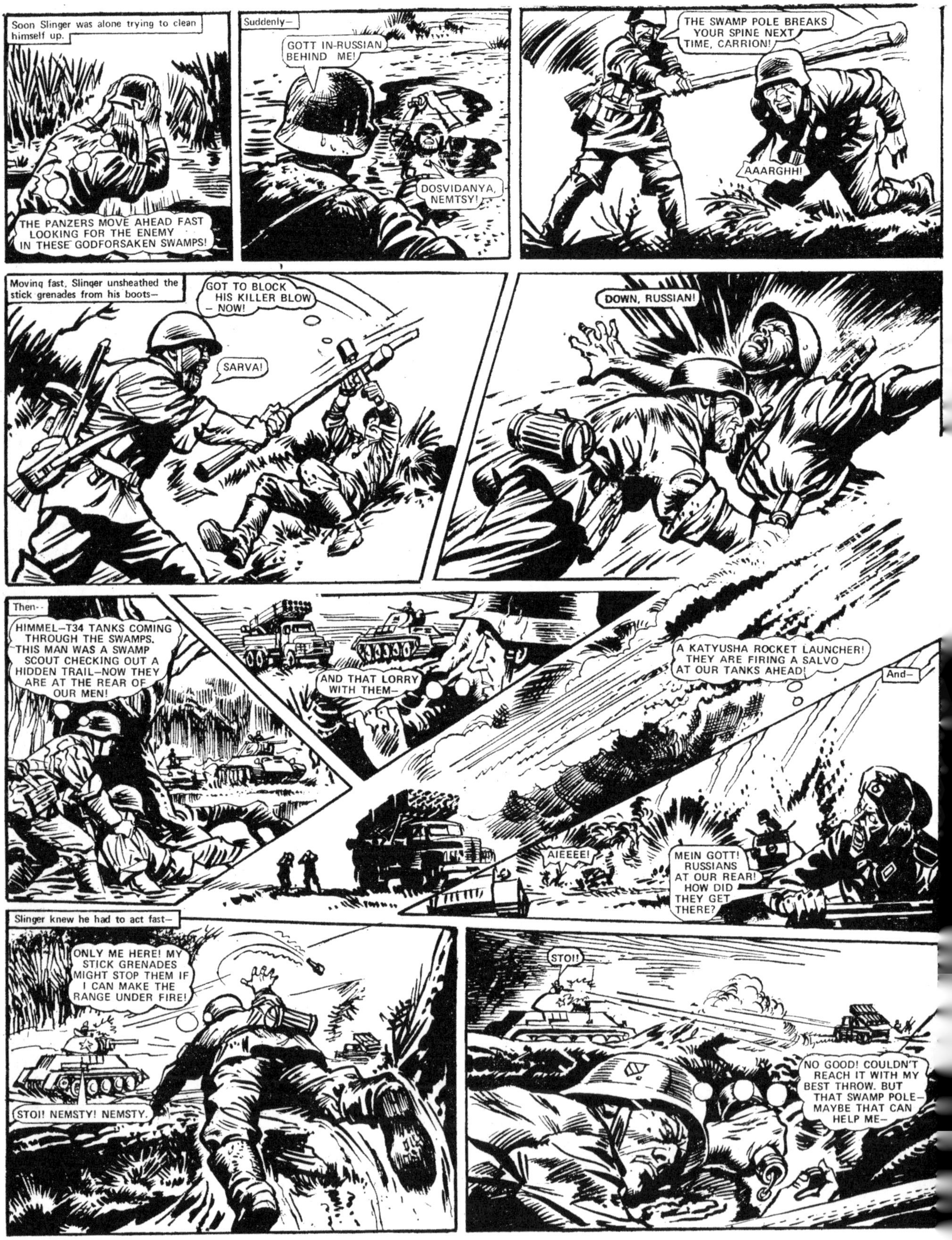

Soon Slinger was alone trying to clean himself up.
THE PANZERS MOVE AHEAD FAST LOOKING FOR THE ENEMY IN THESE GODFORSAKEN SWAMPS!
Suddenly—
GOTT IN-RUSSIAN BEHIND ME!
DOSVIDANYA, NEMTSY!
THE SWAMP POLE BREAKS YOUR SPINE NEXT TIME, CARRION!
AAARGHH!
Moving fast, Slinger unsheathed the stick grenades from his boots—
GOT TO BLOCK HIS KILLER BLOW —NOW!
SARVA!
DOWN, RUSSIAN!
Then--
HIMMEL—T34 TANKS COMING THROUGH THE SWAMPS. THIS MAN WAS A SWAMP SCOUT CHECKING OUT A HIDDEN TRAIL—NOW THEY ARE AT THE REAR OF OUR MEN!
AND THAT LORRY WITH THEM—
A KATYUSHA ROCKET LAUNCHER! THEY ARE FIRING A SALVO AT OUR TANKS AHEAD!
And—
AIEEEE!
MEIN GOTT! RUSSIANS AT OUR REAR! HOW DID THEY GET THERE?
Slinger knew he had to act fast—
ONLY ME HERE! MY STICK GRENADES MIGHT STOP THEM IF I CAN MAKE THE RANGE UNDER FIRE!
STOI! NEMSTY! NEMSTY.
STOI!
NO GOOD! COULDN'T REACH IT WITH MY BEST THROW. BUT THAT SWAMP POLE—MAYBE THAT CAN HELP ME—

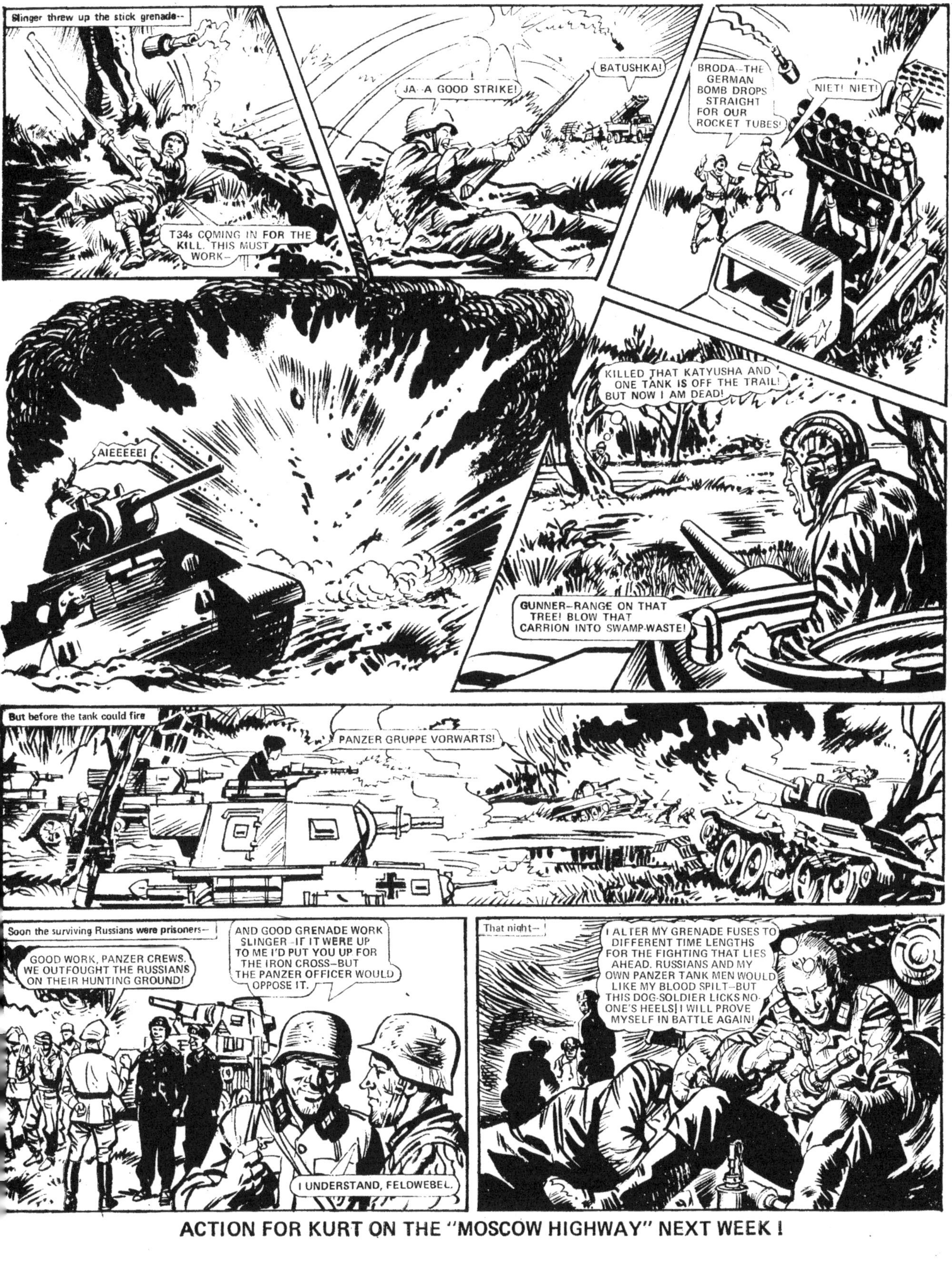
Slinger threw up the stick grenade--
T34s COMING IN FOR THE KILL. THIS MUST WORK--
JA--A GOOD STRIKE!
BATUSHKA!
BRODA--THE GERMAN BOMB DROPS STRAIGHT FOR OUR ROCKET TUBES!
NIET! NIET!
AIEEEEE!
KILLED THAT KATYUSHA AND ONE TANK IS OFF THE TRAIL! BUT NOW I AM DEAD!
GUNNER--RANGE ON THAT TREE! BLOW THAT CARRION INTO SWAMP-WASTE!
But before the tank could fire
PANZER GRUPPE VORWARTS!
Soon the surviving Russians were prisoners--
GOOD WORK, PANZER CREWS. WE OUTFOUGHT THE RUSSIANS ON THEIR HUNTING GROUND!
AND GOOD GRENADE WORK SLINGER--IF IT WERE UP TO ME I'D PUT YOU UP FOR THE IRON CROSS--BUT THE PANZER OFFICER WOULD OPPOSE IT.
I UNDERSTAND, FELDWEBEL.
That night--
I ALTER MY GRENADE FUSES TO DIFFERENT TIME LENGTHS FOR THE FIGHTING THAT LIES AHEAD. RUSSIANS AND MY OWN PANZER TANK MEN WOULD LIKE MY BLOOD SPILT--BUT THIS DOG-SOLDIER LICKS NO-ONE'S HEELS! I WILL PROVE MYSELF IN BATTLE AGAIN!

ACTION FOR KURT ON THE "MOSCOW HIGHWAY" NEXT WEEK !

ACTION ! ACTION ! ACTION ! KURT SLINGER STARS IN . . .

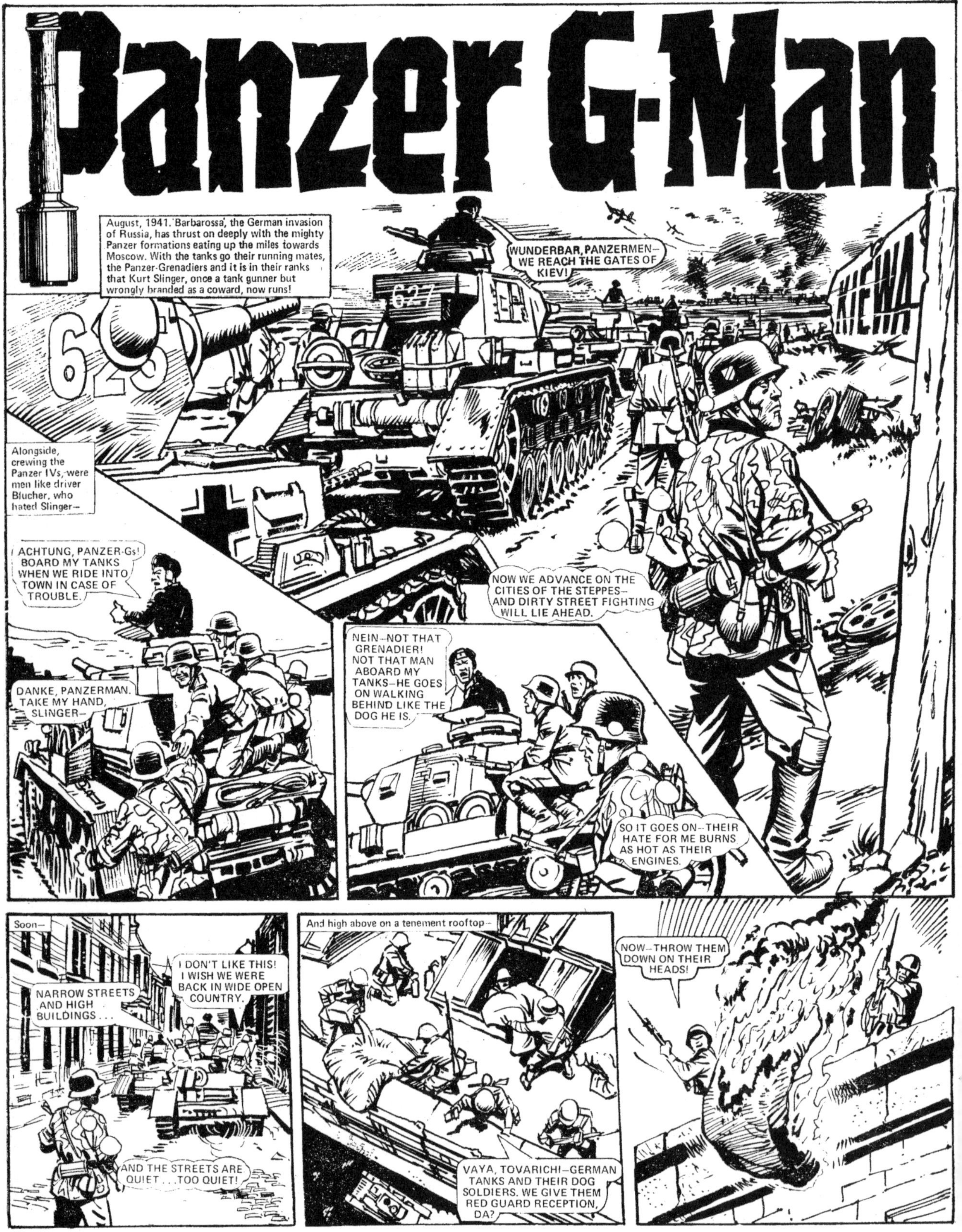

Panzer G-Man
August, 1941. 'Barbarossa', the German invasion of Russia, has thrust on deeply with the mighty Panzer formations eating up the miles towards Moscow. With the tanks go their running mates, the Panzer-Grenadiers and it is in their ranks that Kurt Slinger, once a tank gunner but wrongly branded as a coward, now runs!
WUNDERBAR, PANZERMEN–WE REACH THE GATES OF KIEV!
KIEWA
NOW WE ADVANCE ON THE CITIES OF THE STEPPES–AND DIRTY STREET FIGHTING WILL LIE AHEAD.
Alongside, crewing the Panzer IVs, were men like driver Blucher, who hated Slinger–
ACHTUNG, PANZER-Gs! BOARD MY TANKS WHEN WE RIDE INTO TOWN IN CASE OF TROUBLE.
DANKE, PANZERMAN. TAKE MY HAND, SLINGER–
NEIN–NOT THAT GRENADIER! NOT THAT MAN ABOARD MY TANKS–HE GOES ON WALKING BEHIND LIKE THE DOG HE IS.
SO IT GOES ON–THEIR HATE FOR ME BURNS AS HOT AS THEIR ENGINES.
Soon–
NARROW STREETS AND HIGH BUILDINGS . . .
I DON'T LIKE THIS! I WISH WE WERE BACK IN WIDE OPEN COUNTRY.
AND THE STREETS ARE QUIET . . . TOO QUIET!
And high above on a tenement rooftop–
VAYA, TOVARICH!–GERMAN TANKS AND THEIR DOG SOLDIERS. WE GIVE THEM RED GUARD RECEPTION, DA?
NOW–THROW THEM DOWN ON THEIR HEADS!

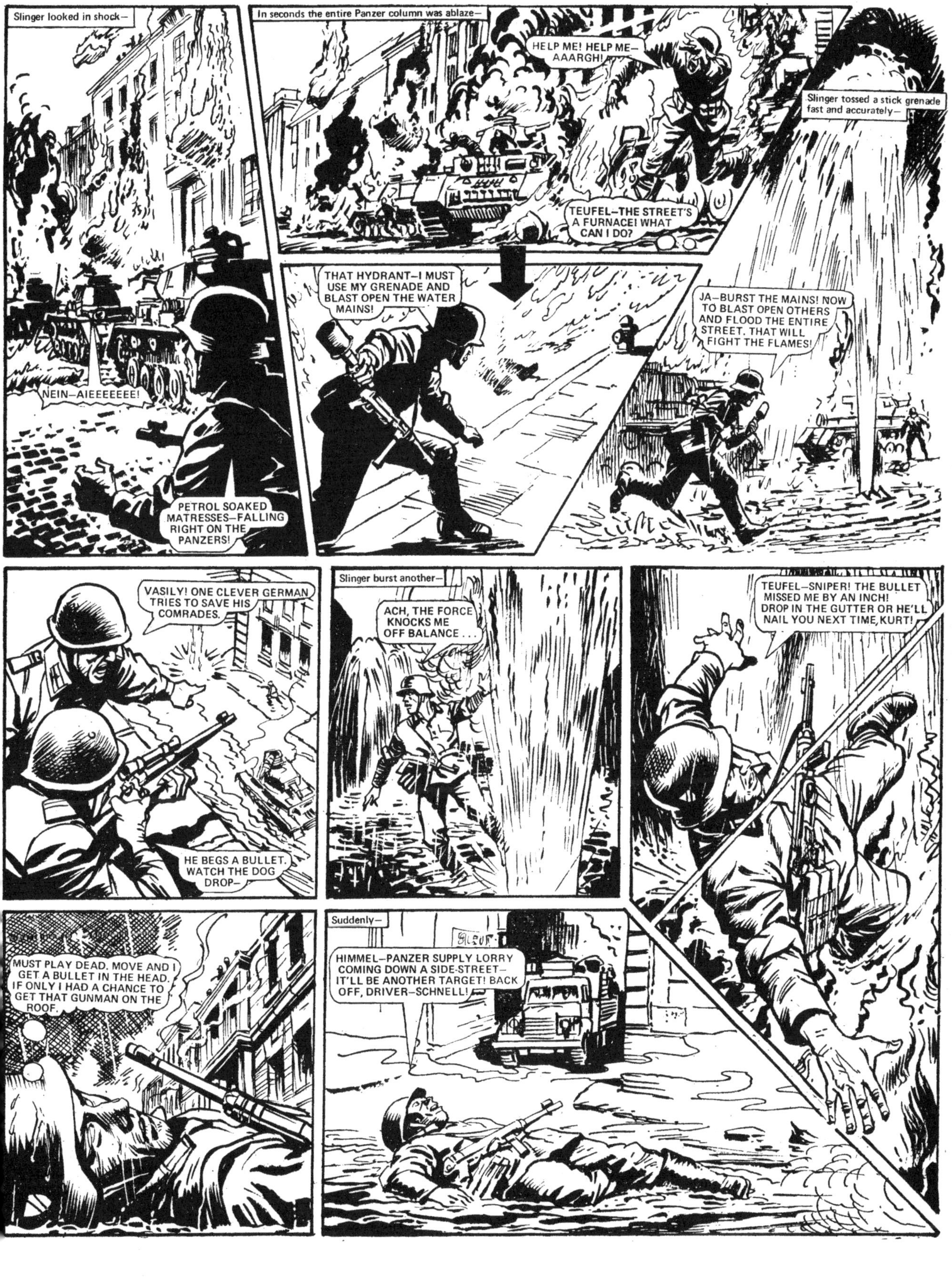

Slinger looked in shock—
NEIN—AIEEEEEEE!
PETROL SOAKED MATRESSES—FALLING RIGHT ON THE PANZERS!
In seconds the entire Panzer column was ablaze—
HELP ME! HELP ME—AAARGH!
TEUFEL—THE STREET'S A FURNACE! WHAT CAN I DO?
THAT HYDRANT—I MUST USE MY GRENADE AND BLAST OPEN THE WATER MAINS!
Slinger tossed a stick grenade fast and accurately—
JA—BURST THE MAINS! NOW TO BLAST OPEN OTHERS AND FLOOD THE ENTIRE STREET. THAT WILL FIGHT THE FLAMES!
VASILY! ONE CLEVER GERMAN TRIES TO SAVE HIS COMRADES.
HE BEGS A BULLET. WATCH THE DOG DROP—
Slinger burst another—
ACH, THE FORCE KNOCKS ME OFF BALANCE . . .
TEUFEL—SNIPER! THE BULLET MISSED ME BY AN INCH! DROP IN THE GUTTER OR HE'LL NAIL YOU NEXT TIME, KURT!
MUST PLAY DEAD. MOVE AND I GET A BULLET IN THE HEAD. IF ONLY I HAD A CHANCE TO GET THAT GUNMAN ON THE ROOF.
Suddenly—
HIMMEL—PANZER SUPPLY LORRY COMING DOWN A SIDE-STREET—IT'LL BE ANOTHER TARGET! BACK OFF, DRIVER—SCHNELL!

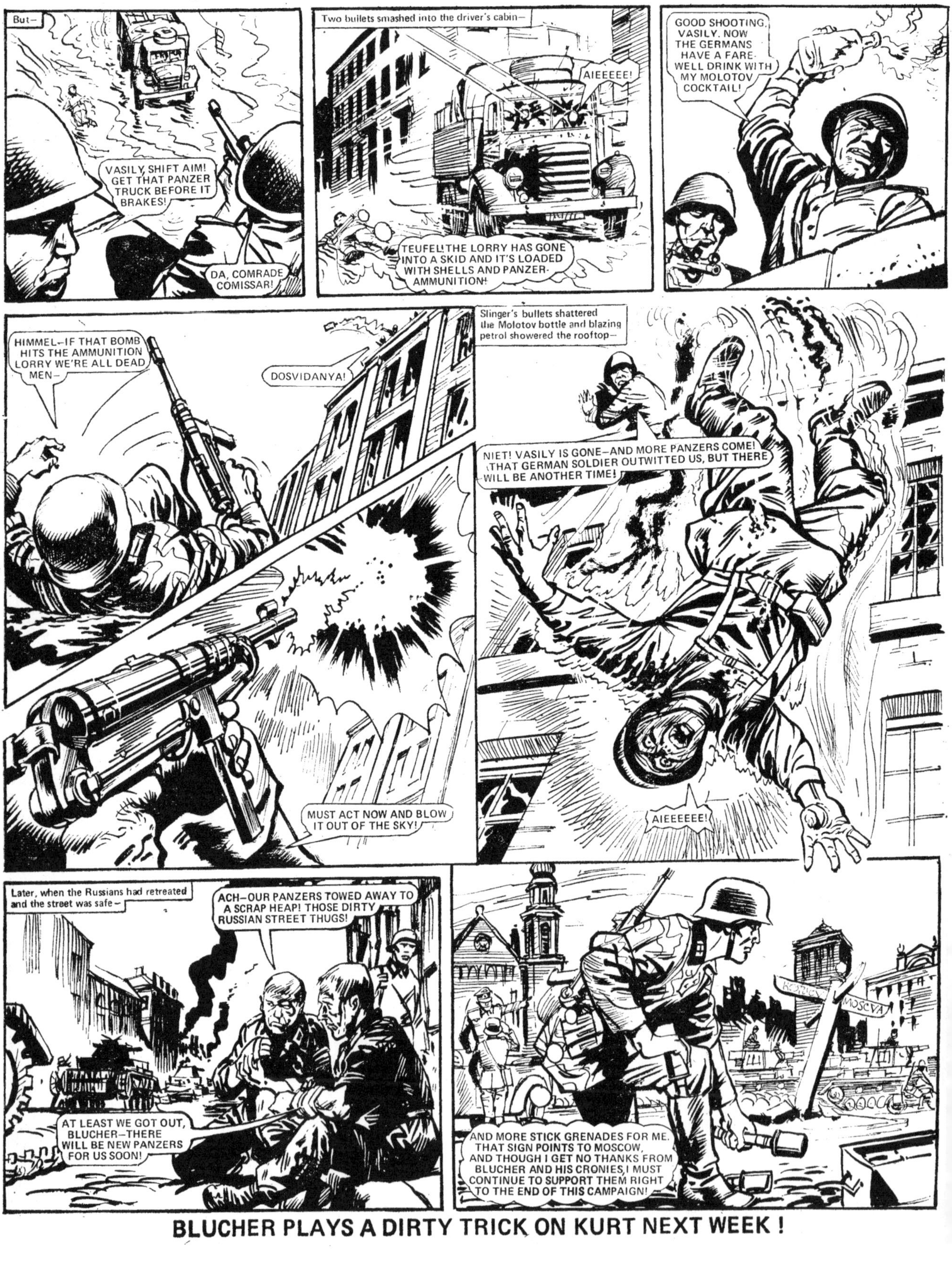
But–
VASILY, SHIFT AIM! GET THAT PANZER TRUCK BEFORE IT BRAKES!
DA, COMRADE COMISSAR!
Two bullets smashed into the driver's cabin–
AIEEEEE!
TEUFEL! THE LORRY HAS GONE INTO A SKID AND IT'S LOADED WITH SHELLS AND PANZER-AMMUNITION!
GOOD SHOOTING, VASILY. NOW THE GERMANS HAVE A FARE-WELL DRINK WITH MY MOLOTOV COCKTAIL!
HIMMEL–IF THAT BOMB HITS THE AMMUNITION LORRY WE'RE ALL DEAD MEN–
DOSVIDANYA!
MUST ACT NOW AND BLOW IT OUT OF THE SKY!
Slinger's bullets shattered the Molotov bottle and blazing petrol showered the rooftop–
NIET! VASILY IS GONE–AND MORE PANZERS COME! THAT GERMAN SOLDIER OUTWITTED US, BUT THERE WILL BE ANOTHER TIME!
AIEEEEEE!
Later, when the Russians had retreated and the street was safe–
ACH–OUR PANZERS TOWED AWAY TO A SCRAP HEAP! THOSE DIRTY RUSSIAN STREET THUGS!
AT LEAST WE GOT OUT, BLUCHER–THERE WILL BE NEW PANZERS FOR US SOON!
MOSCVA
AND MORE STICK GRENADES FOR ME. THAT SIGN POINTS TO MOSCOW, AND THOUGH I GET NO THANKS FROM BLUCHER AND HIS CRONIES, I MUST CONTINUE TO SUPPORT THEM RIGHT TO THE END OF THIS CAMPAIGN!

BLUCHER PLAYS A DIRTY TRICK ON KURT NEXT WEEK !

KURT SLINGER IS IN THE PANZER GRENADIERS. WE CALL HIM. . .

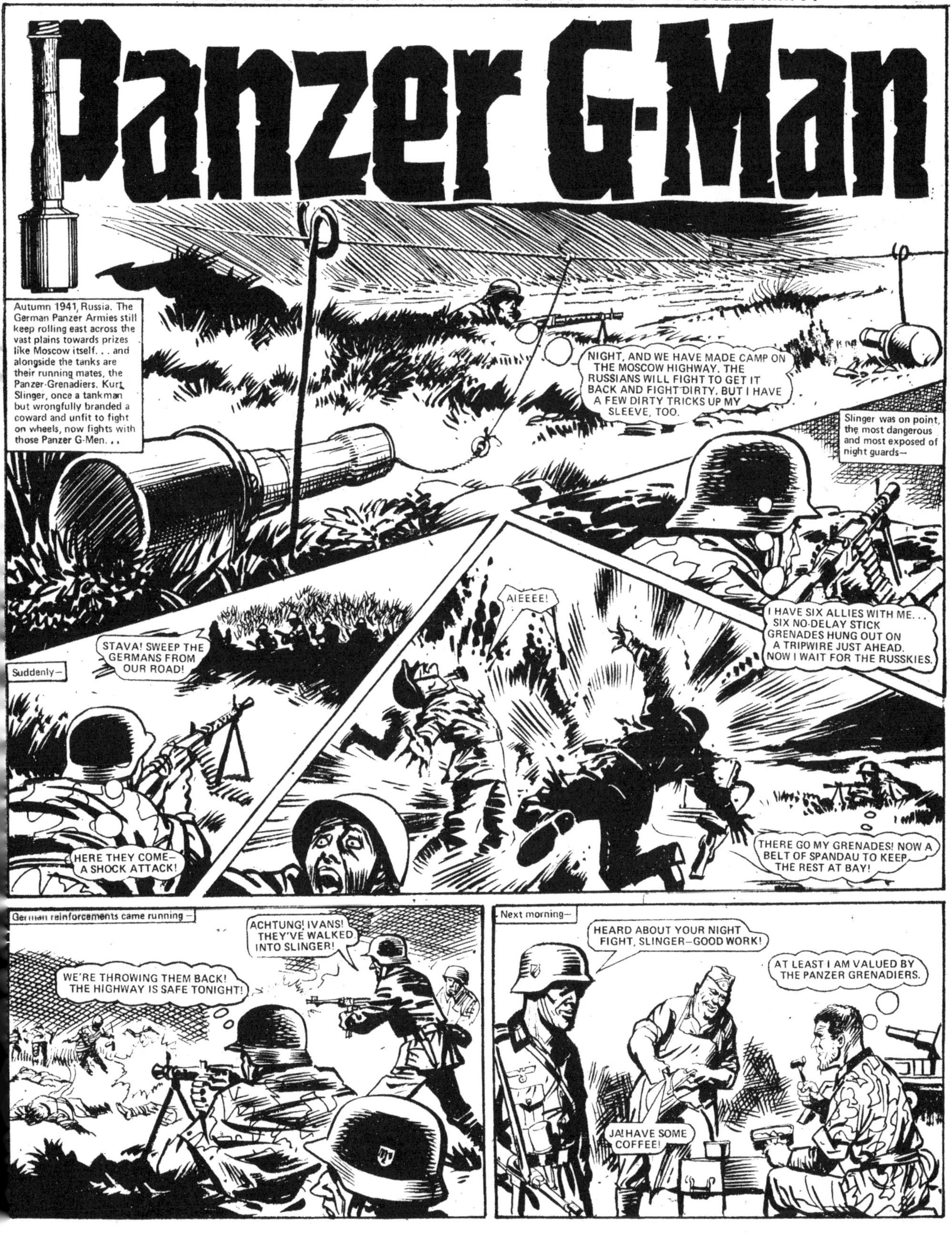

Panzer G-Man
Autumn 1941, Russia. The German Panzer Armies still keep rolling east across the vast plains towards prizes like Moscow itself. . . and alongside the tanks are their running mates, the Panzer-Grenadiers. Kurt Slinger, once a tankman but wrongfully branded a coward and unfit to fight on wheels, now fights with those Panzer G-Men. . .
NIGHT, AND WE HAVE MADE CAMP ON THE MOSCOW HIGHWAY. THE RUSSIANS WILL FIGHT TO GET IT BACK AND FIGHT DIRTY. BUT I HAVE A FEW DIRTY TRICKS UP MY SLEEVE, TOO.
Slinger was on point, the most dangerous and most exposed of night guards—
I HAVE SIX ALLIES WITH ME. . . SIX NO-DELAY STICK GRENADES HUNG OUT ON A TRIPWIRE JUST AHEAD. NOW I WAIT FOR THE RUSSKIES.
Suddenly—
STAVA! SWEEP THE GERMANS FROM OUR ROAD!
HERE THEY COME— A SHOCK ATTACK!
AIEEEE!
THERE GO MY GRENADES! NOW A BELT OF SPANDAU TO KEEP THE REST AT BAY!
German reinforcements came running—
ACHTUNG! IVANS! THEY'VE WALKED INTO SLINGER!
WE'RE THROWING THEM BACK! THE HIGHWAY IS SAFE TONIGHT!
Next morning—
HEARD ABOUT YOUR NIGHT FIGHT, SLINGER—GOOD WORK!
AT LEAST I AM VALUED BY THE PANZER GRENADIERS.
JA! HAVE SOME COFFEE!

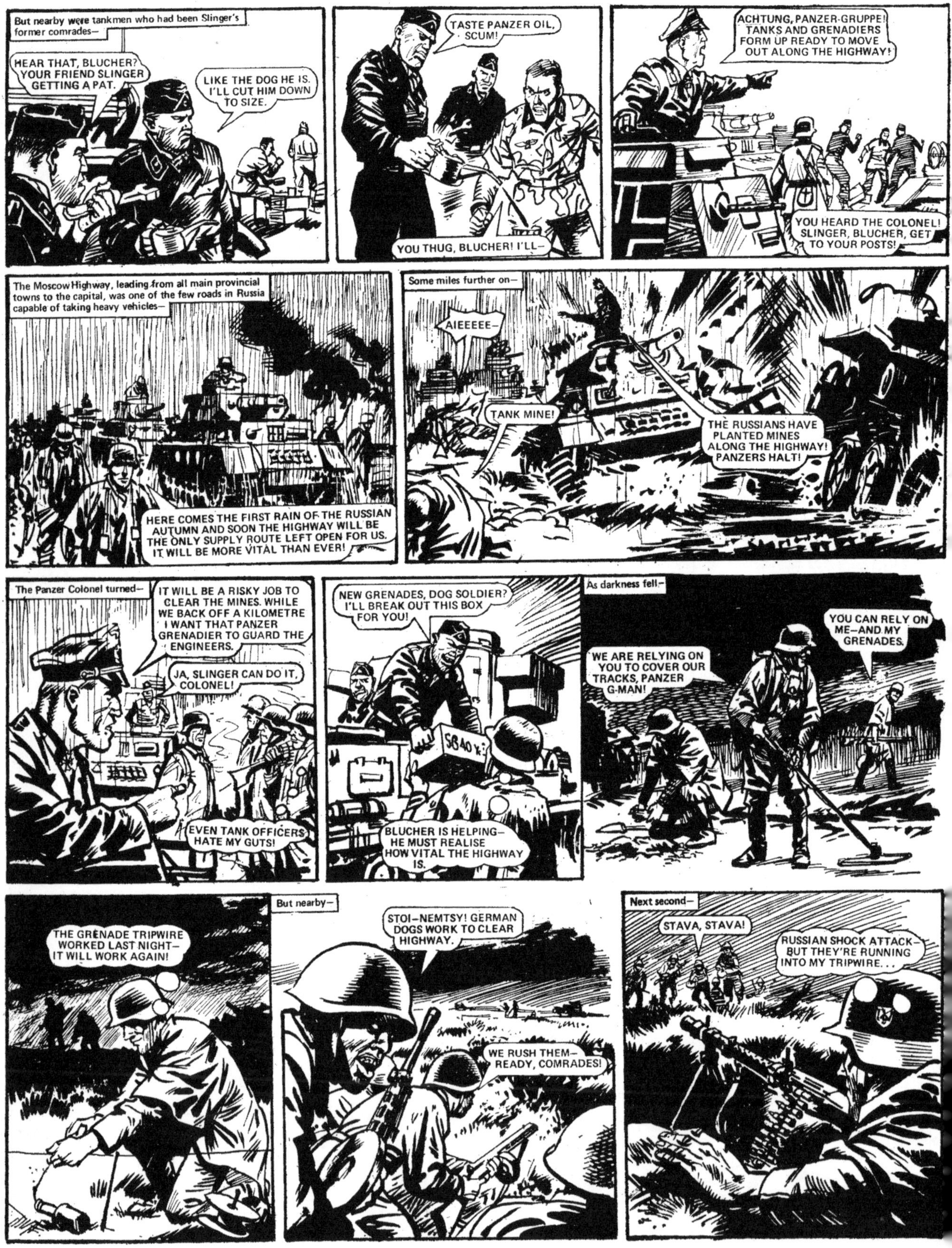

But nearby were tankmen who had been Slinger's former comrades—
HEAR THAT, BLUCHER? YOUR FRIEND SLINGER GETTING A PAT.
LIKE THE DOG HE IS. I'LL CUT HIM DOWN TO SIZE.
TASTE PANZER OIL, SCUM!
YOU THUG, BLUCHER! I'LL—
ACHTUNG, PANZER-GRUPPE! TANKS AND GRENADIERS FORM UP READY TO MOVE OUT ALONG THE HIGHWAY!
YOU HEARD THE COLONEL! SLINGER, BLUCHER, GET TO YOUR POSTS!
The Moscow Highway, leading from all main provincial towns to the capital, was one of the few roads in Russia capable of taking heavy vehicles—
HERE COMES THE FIRST RAIN OF THE RUSSIAN AUTUMN AND SOON THE HIGHWAY WILL BE THE ONLY SUPPLY ROUTE LEFT OPEN FOR US. IT WILL BE MORE VITAL THAN EVER!
Some miles further on—
AIEEEEE—
TANK MINE!
THE RUSSIANS HAVE PLANTED MINES ALONG THE HIGHWAY! PANZERS HALT!
The Panzer Colonel turned—
IT WILL BE A RISKY JOB TO CLEAR THE MINES. WHILE WE BACK OFF A KILOMETRE I WANT THAT PANZER GRENADIER TO GUARD THE ENGINEERS.
JA, SLINGER CAN DO IT, COLONEL!
EVEN TANK OFFICERS HATE MY GUTS!
NEW GRENADES, DOG SOLDIER? I'LL BREAK OUT THIS BOX FOR YOU!
BLUCHER IS HELPING—HE MUST REALISE HOW VITAL THE HIGHWAY IS.
As darkness fell—
YOU CAN RELY ON ME—AND MY GRENADES.
WE ARE RELYING ON YOU TO COVER OUR TRACKS, PANZER G-MAN!
THE GRENADE TRIPWIRE WORKED LAST NIGHT—IT WILL WORK AGAIN!
But nearby—
STOI—NEMTSY! GERMAN DOGS WORK TO CLEAR HIGHWAY.
WE RUSH THEM—READY, COMRADES!
Next second—
STAVA, STAVA!
RUSSIAN SHOCK ATTACK—BUT THEY'RE RUNNING INTO MY TRIPWIRE . . .

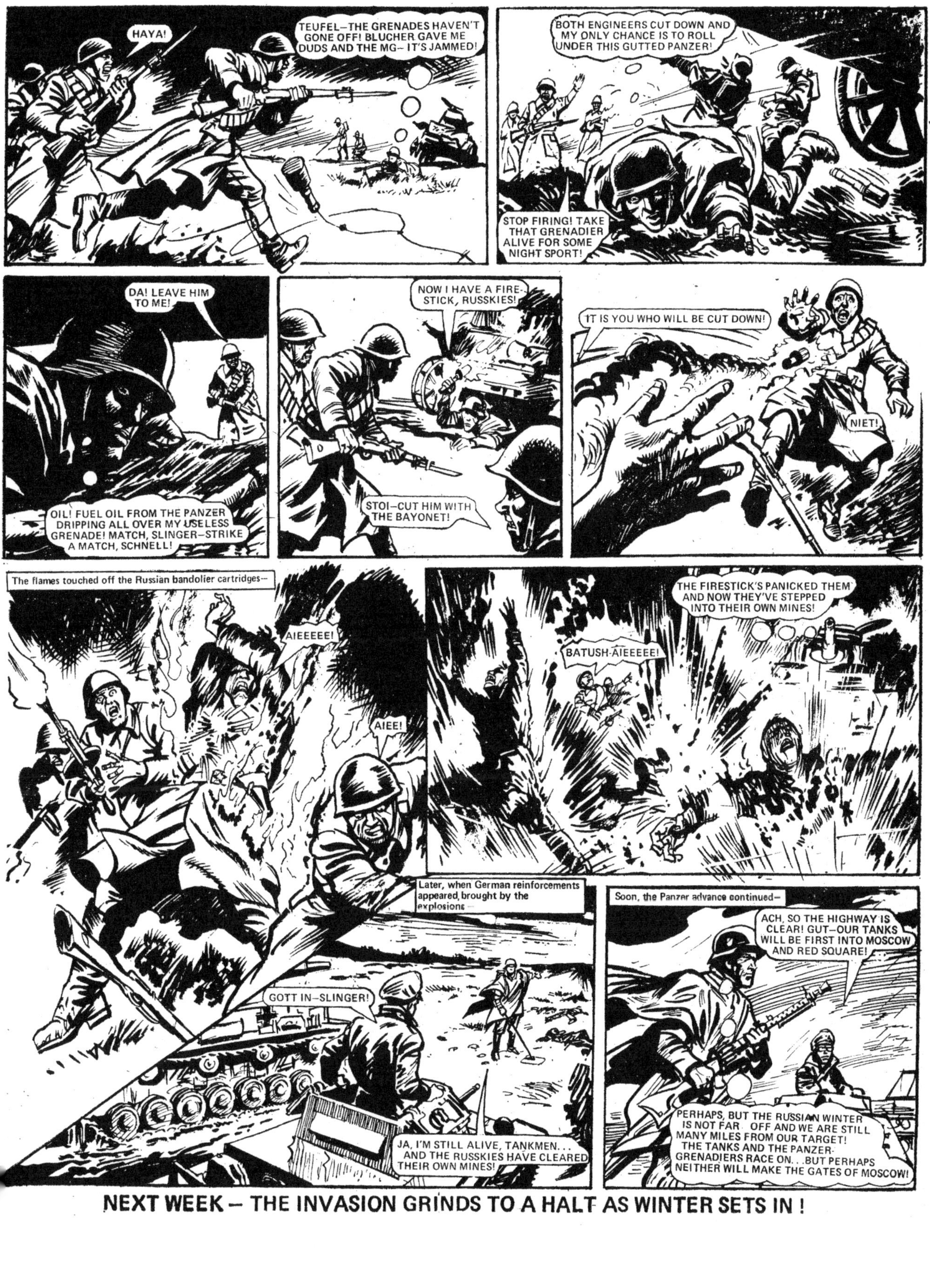

HAYA!
TEUFEL—THE GRENADES HAVEN'T GONE OFF! BLUCHER GAVE ME DUDS AND THE MG— IT'S JAMMED!
BOTH ENGINEERS CUT DOWN AND MY ONLY CHANCE IS TO ROLL UNDER THIS GUTTED PANZER!
STOP FIRING! TAKE THAT GRENADIER ALIVE FOR SOME NIGHT SPORT!
DA! LEAVE HIM TO ME!
OIL! FUEL OIL FROM THE PANZER DRIPPING ALL OVER MY USELESS GRENADE! MATCH, SLINGER—STRIKE A MATCH, SCHNELL!
NOW I HAVE A FIRE-STICK, RUSSKIES!
STOI—CUT HIM WITH THE BAYONET!
IT IS YOU WHO WILL BE CUT DOWN!
NIET!
The flames touched off the Russian bandolier cartridges—
AIEEEEE!
AIEE!
THE FIRESTICK'S PANICKED THEM AND NOW THEY'VE STEPPED INTO THEIR OWN MINES!
BATUSH-AIEEEEE!
Later, when German reinforcements appeared, brought by the explosions—
GOTT IN—SLINGER!
JA, I'M STILL ALIVE, TANKMEN... AND THE RUSSKIES HAVE CLEARED THEIR OWN MINES!
Soon, the Panzer advance continued—
ACH, SO THE HIGHWAY IS CLEAR! GUT—OUR TANKS WILL BE FIRST INTO MOSCOW AND RED SQUARE!
PERHAPS, BUT THE RUSSIAN WINTER IS NOT FAR OFF AND WE ARE STILL MANY MILES FROM OUR TARGET!
THE TANKS AND THE PANZER-GRENADIERS RACE ON...BUT PERHAPS NEITHER WILL MAKE THE GATES OF MOSCOW!

NEXT WEEK – THE INVASION GRINDS TO A HALT AS WINTER SETS IN !

WE HAVE THE COURAGE TO TELL IT FROM THE GERMANS' VIEWPOINT !

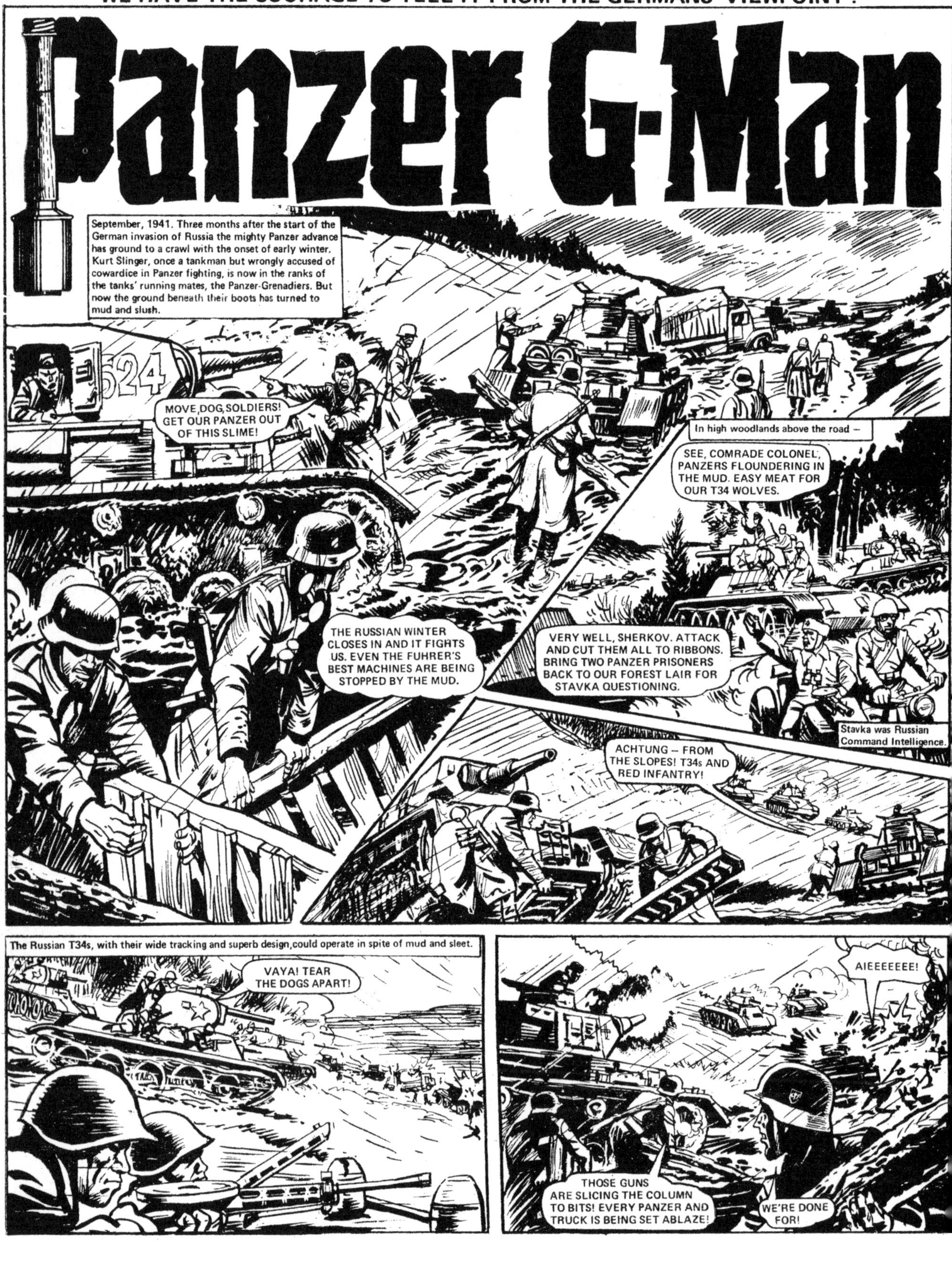
Panzer G-Man
September, 1941. Three months after the start of the German invasion of Russia the mighty Panzer advance has ground to a crawl with the onset of early winter. Kurt Slinger, once a tankman but wrongly accused of cowardice in Panzer fighting, is now in the ranks of the tanks' running mates, the Panzer-Grenadiers. But now the ground beneath their boots has turned to mud and slush.
624
MOVE, DOG, SOLDIERS! GET OUR PANZER OUT OF THIS SLIME!
THE RUSSIAN WINTER CLOSES IN AND IT FIGHTS US. EVEN THE FUHRER'S BEST MACHINES ARE BEING STOPPED BY THE MUD.
In high woodlands above the road –
SEE, COMRADE COLONEL, PANZERS FLOUNDERING IN THE MUD. EASY MEAT FOR OUR T34 WOLVES.
VERY WELL, SHERKOV. ATTACK AND CUT THEM ALL TO RIBBONS. BRING TWO PANZER PRISONERS BACK TO OUR FOREST LAIR FOR STAVKA QUESTIONING.
Stavka was Russian Command Intelligence.
ACHTUNG – FROM THE SLOPES! T34s AND RED INFANTRY!
The Russian T34s, with their wide tracking and superb design, could operate in spite of mud and sleet.
VAYA! TEAR THE DOGS APART!
AIEEEEEEE!
THOSE GUNS ARE SLICING THE COLUMN TO BITS! EVERY PANZER AND TRUCK IS BEING SET ABLAZE!
WE'RE DONE FOR!

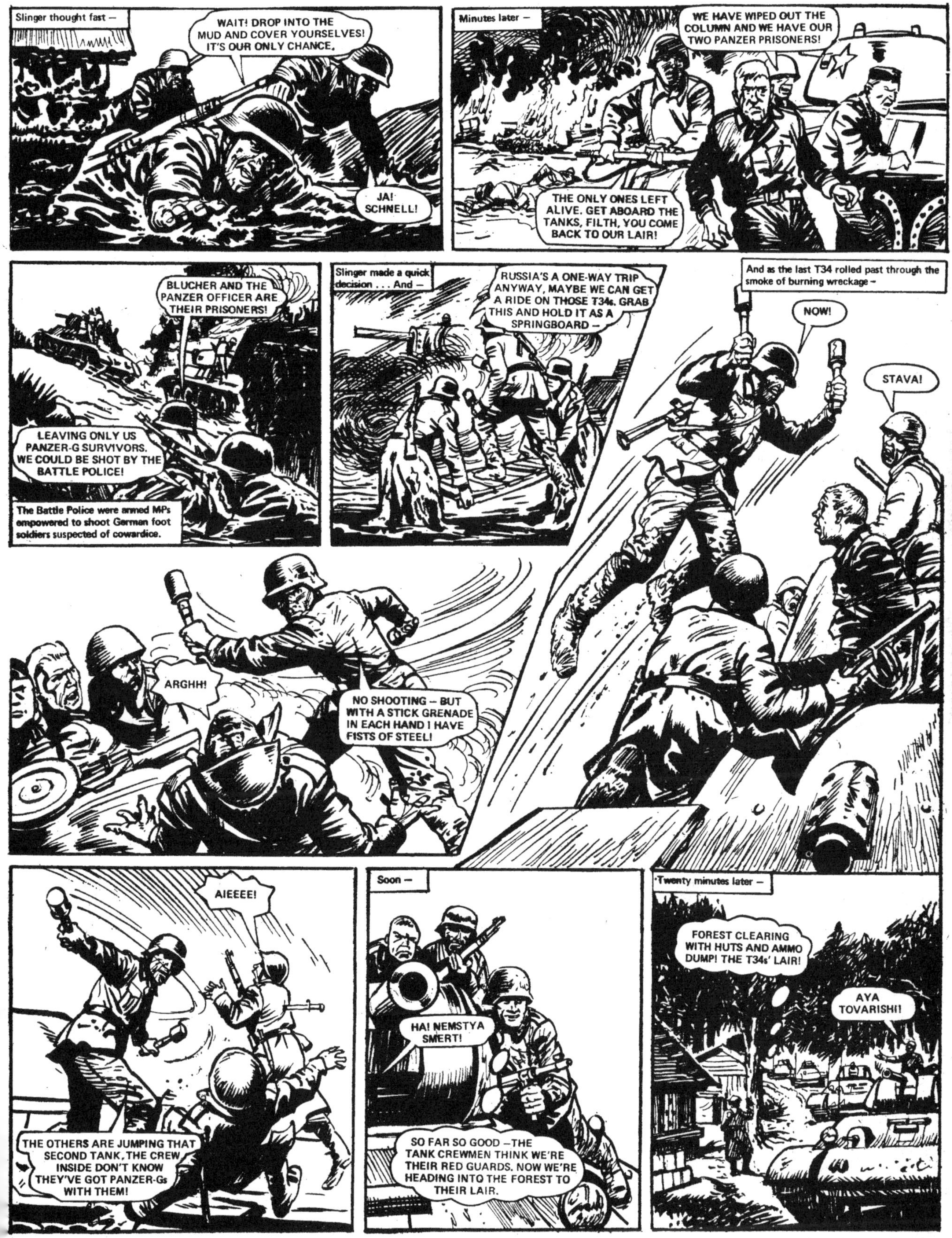
Slinger thought fast –
WAIT! DROP INTO THE MUD AND COVER YOURSELVES! IT'S OUR ONLY CHANCE.
JA! SCHNELL!
Minutes later –
WE HAVE WIPED OUT THE COLUMN AND WE HAVE OUR TWO PANZER PRISONERS!
THE ONLY ONES LEFT ALIVE. GET ABOARD THE TANKS, FILTH, YOU COME BACK TO OUR LAIR!
BLUCHER AND THE PANZER OFFICER ARE THEIR PRISONERS!
LEAVING ONLY US PANZER-G SURVIVORS. WE COULD BE SHOT BY THE BATTLE POLICE!
The Battle Police were armed MPs empowered to shoot German foot soldiers suspected of cowardice.
Slinger made a quick decision . . . And –
RUSSIA'S A ONE-WAY TRIP ANYWAY, MAYBE WE CAN GET A RIDE ON THOSE T34s. GRAB THIS AND HOLD IT AS A SPRINGBOARD –
And as the last T34 rolled past through the smoke of burning wreckage –
NOW!
STAVA!
ARGHH!
NO SHOOTING – BUT WITH A STICK GRENADE IN EACH HAND I HAVE FISTS OF STEEL!
AIEEEE!
THE OTHERS ARE JUMPING THAT SECOND TANK, THE CREW INSIDE DON'T KNOW THEY'VE GOT PANZER-Gs WITH THEM!
Soon –
HA! NEMSTYA SMERT!
SO FAR SO GOOD – THE TANK CREWMEN THINK WE'RE THEIR RED GUARDS. NOW WE'RE HEADING INTO THE FOREST TO THEIR LAIR.
Twenty minutes later –
FOREST CLEARING WITH HUTS AND AMMO DUMP! THE T34s' LAIR!
AYA TOVARISHI!

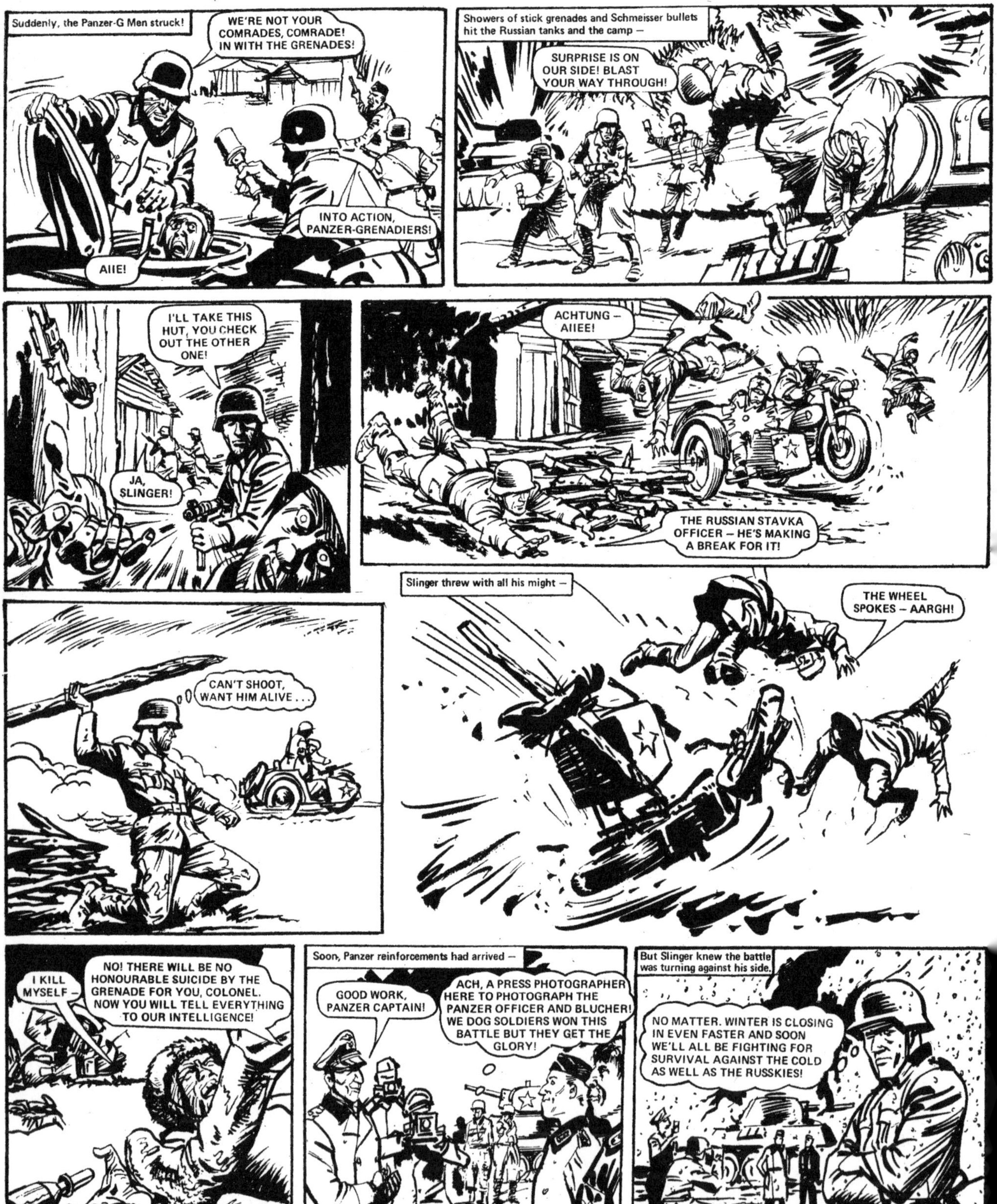

Suddenly, the Panzer-G Men struck!
WE'RE NOT YOUR COMRADES, COMRADE! IN WITH THE GRENADES!
INTO ACTION, PANZER-GRENADIERS!
AIIE!
Showers of stick grenades and Schmeisser bullets hit the Russian tanks and the camp –
SURPRISE IS ON OUR SIDE! BLAST YOUR WAY THROUGH!
I'LL TAKE THIS HUT, YOU CHECK OUT THE OTHER ONE!
JA, SLINGER!
ACHTUNG – AIIEE!
THE RUSSIAN STAVKA OFFICER – HE'S MAKING A BREAK FOR IT!
CAN'T SHOOT, WANT HIM ALIVE . . .
Slinger threw with all his might –
THE WHEEL SPOKES – AARGH!
I KILL MYSELF –
NO! THERE WILL BE NO HONOURABLE SUICIDE BY THE GRENADE FOR YOU, COLONEL. NOW YOU WILL TELL EVERYTHING TO OUR INTELLIGENCE!
Soon, Panzer reinforcements had arrived –
GOOD WORK, PANZER CAPTAIN!
ACH, A PRESS PHOTOGRAPHER HERE TO PHOTOGRAPH THE PANZER OFFICER AND BLUCHER! WE DOG SOLDIERS WON THIS BATTLE BUT THEY GET THE GLORY!
But Slinger knew the battle was turning against his side.
NO MATTER. WINTER IS CLOSING IN EVEN FASTER AND SOON WE'LL ALL BE FIGHTING FOR SURVIVAL AGAINST THE COLD AS WELL AS THE RUSSKIES!

MISSION ENDS...MISSION ENDS...MISSION ENDS...MISSION ENDS...MISSION ENDS...MISSION ENDS...MISSION END

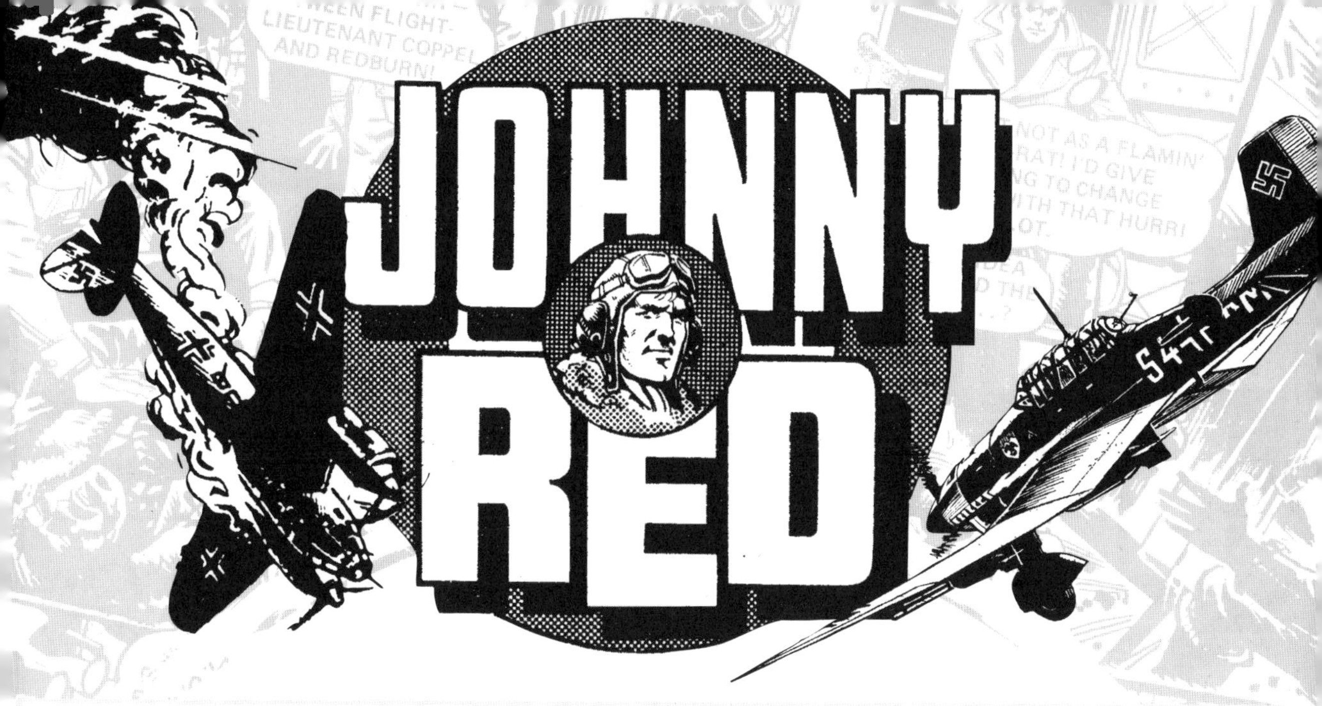
JOHNNY RED

"HAVE SOME LEAD FROM JOHNNY RED!"

On a cargo ship bound for Murmansk, hot-headed but brilliant flyer Johnny Redburn, dishonourably discharged from the R.A.F, thought his flying career was as good as dead until the day he hijacked a ship-launched Hurricane and single-handedly took on a squadron of Stukas and Junkers.

Now he's a signed-up member of the Soviet Union's 5th Air Brigade, "Falcon Squadron", and fighting a war on the bitter Russian front.

Lasting ten years and over 500 episodes, 'Johnny Red' was arguably *Battle*'s most popular strip. Created by writer Tom Tully and artist Joe Colquhoun (who drew the first 100 episodes) it ran from January 1977's issue #100 of *Battle* until January 1987, during which time Carlos Pino replaced the strip's longest-serving artist, John Cooper.

NOTES FROM THE FRONTLINE:

"'Johnny Red' was written by Tom Tully who despite being very marinated in old-style comic traditions still managed to adapt successfully to *Battle*'s new approach. He would take the time to research Leningrad, Stalingrad and so forth: prior to *Battle*, research was pretty much non-existent in British comics. I think that shows in some of the comics before *Battle*. 'Johnny Red' is actually very authentic — there were British pilots flying on the Russian front. It's one of the ironies of war comics that real life is often very similar in style." — **Pat Mills**

WRITTEN BY Tom Tully
DRAWN BY Joe Colquhoun

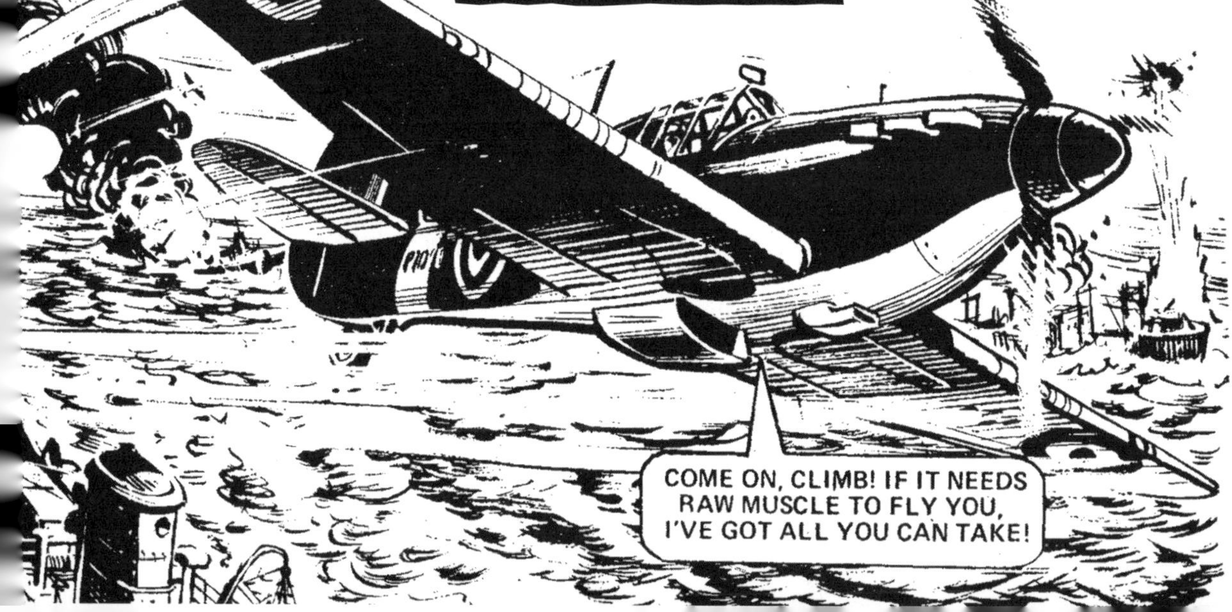
COME ON, CLIMB! IF IT NEEDS RAW MUSCLE TO FLY YOU, I'VE GOT ALL YOU CAN TAKE!

STARTS TODAY! AERIAL ACTION WITH THE LAD THEY CALL RED – JOHNNY RED!

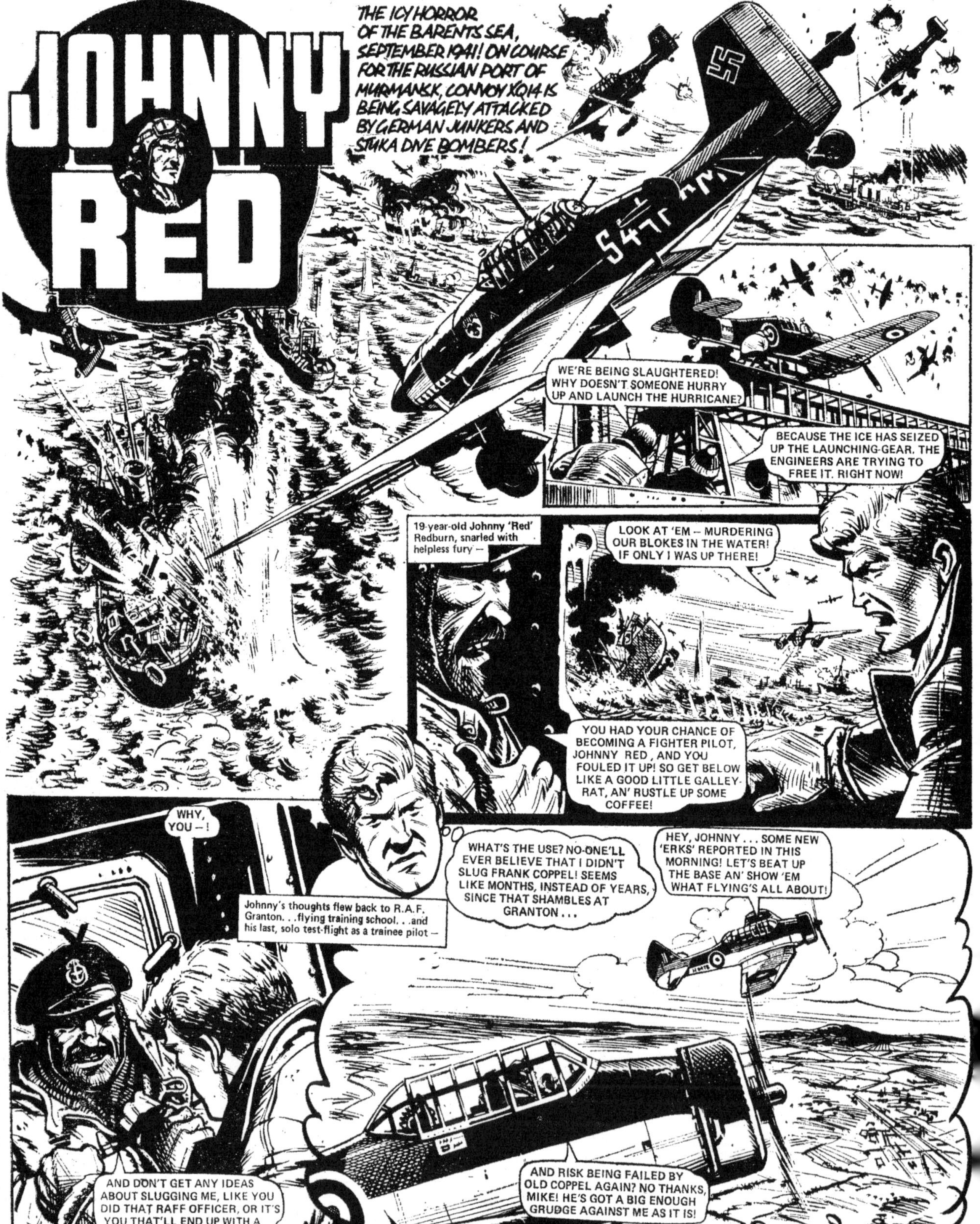
JOHNNY RED
THE ICY HORROR OF THE BARENTS SEA, SEPTEMBER 1941! ON COURSE FOR THE RUSSIAN PORT OF MURMANSK, CONVOY XQ14 IS BEING SAVAGELY ATTACKED BY GERMAN JUNKERS AND STUKA DIVE BOMBERS!
WE'RE BEING SLAUGHTERED! WHY DOESN'T SOMEONE HURRY UP AND LAUNCH THE HURRICANE?
BECAUSE THE ICE HAS SEIZED UP THE LAUNCHING-GEAR. THE ENGINEERS ARE TRYING TO FREE IT. RIGHT NOW!
19-year-old Johnny 'Red' Redburn, snarled with helpless fury –
LOOK AT 'EM – MURDERING OUR BLOKES IN THE WATER! IF ONLY I WAS UP THERE!
YOU HAD YOUR CHANCE OF BECOMING A FIGHTER PILOT, JOHNNY RED, AND YOU FOULED IT UP! SO GET BELOW LIKE A GOOD LITTLE GALLEY-RAT, AN' RUSTLE UP SOME COFFEE!
WHY, YOU –!
AND DON'T GET ANY IDEAS ABOUT SLUGGING ME, LIKE YOU DID THAT RAFF OFFICER, OR IT'S YOU THAT'LL END UP WITH A BROKEN SKULL!
WHAT'S THE USE? NO-ONE'LL EVER BELIEVE THAT I DIDN'T SLUG FRANK COPPEL! SEEMS LIKE MONTHS, INSTEAD OF YEARS, SINCE THAT SHAMBLES AT GRANTON...
Johnny's thoughts flew back to R.A.F. Granton... flying training school... and his last, solo test-flight as a trainee pilot –
HEY, JOHNNY... SOME NEW 'ERKS' REPORTED IN THIS MORNING! LET'S BEAT UP THE BASE AN' SHOW 'EM WHAT FLYING'S ALL ABOUT!
AND RISK BEING FAILED BY OLD COPPEL AGAIN? NO THANKS, MIKE! HE'S GOT A BIG ENOUGH GRUDGE AGAINST ME AS IT IS!

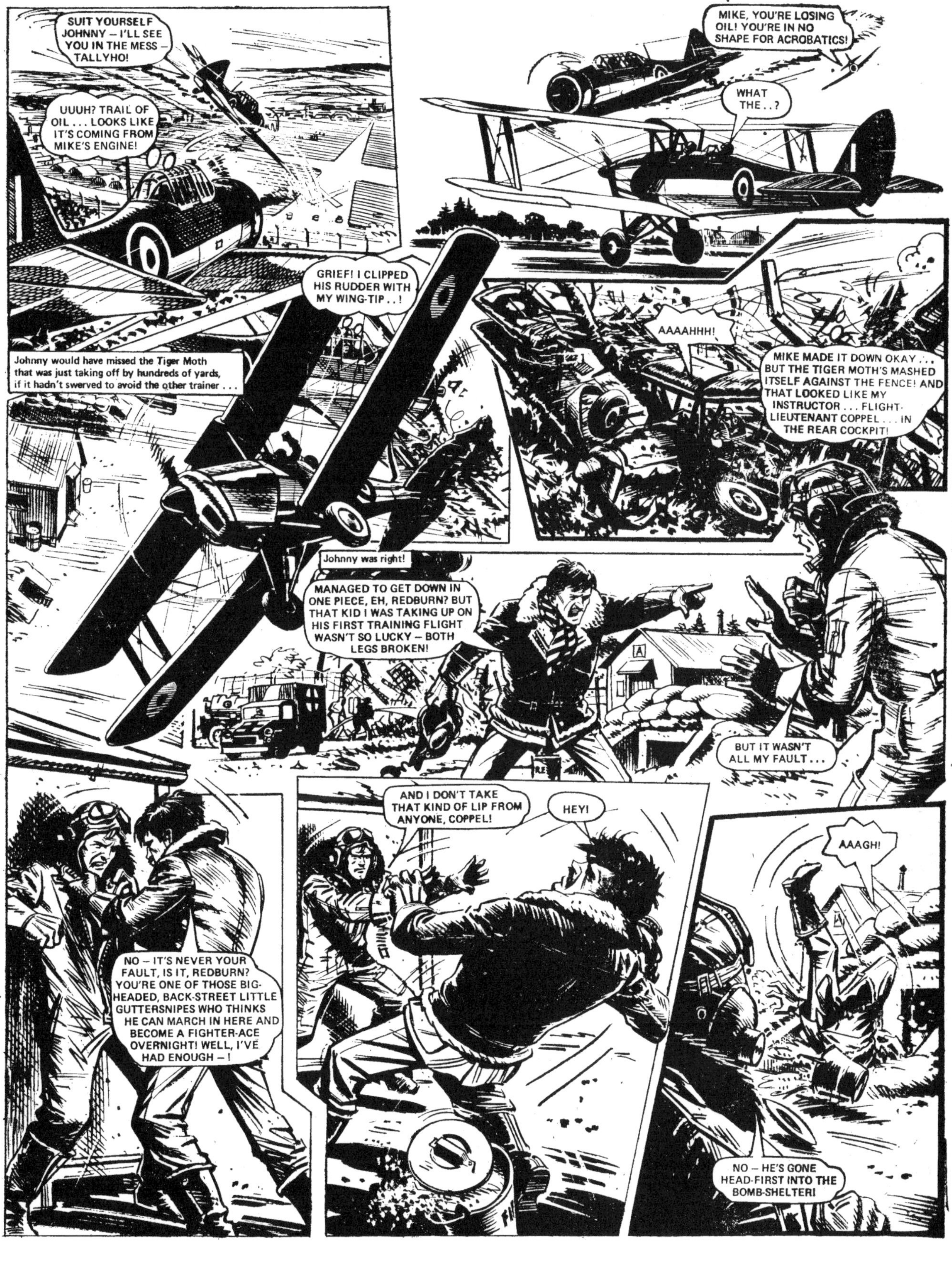

SUIT YOURSELF JOHNNY – I'LL SEE YOU IN THE MESS – TALLYHO!
UUUH? TRAIL OF OIL . . . LOOKS LIKE IT'S COMING FROM MIKE'S ENGINE!
MIKE, YOU'RE LOSING OIL! YOU'RE IN NO SHAPE FOR ACROBATICS!
WHAT THE . . ?
Johnny would have missed the Tiger Moth that was just taking off by hundreds of yards, if it hadn't swerved to avoid the other trainer . . .
GRIEF! I CLIPPED HIS RUDDER WITH MY WING-TIP . . !
AAAAHHH!
MIKE MADE IT DOWN OKAY . . . BUT THE TIGER MOTH'S MASHED ITSELF AGAINST THE FENCE! AND THAT LOOKED LIKE MY INSTRUCTOR . . . FLIGHT-LIEUTENANT COPPEL . . . IN THE REAR COCKPIT!
Johnny was right!
MANAGED TO GET DOWN IN ONE PIECE, EH, REDBURN? BUT THAT KID I WAS TAKING UP ON HIS FIRST TRAINING FLIGHT WASN'T SO LUCKY – BOTH LEGS BROKEN!
BUT IT WASN'T ALL MY FAULT . . .
NO – IT'S NEVER YOUR FAULT, IS IT, REDBURN? YOU'RE ONE OF THOSE BIG-HEADED, BACK-STREET LITTLE GUTTERSNIPES WHO THINKS HE CAN MARCH IN HERE AND BECOME A FIGHTER-ACE OVERNIGHT! WELL, I'VE HAD ENOUGH – !
AND I DON'T TAKE THAT KIND OF LIP FROM ANYONE, COPPEL!
HEY!
AAAGH!
NO – HE'S GONE HEAD-FIRST INTO THE BOMB-SHELTER!

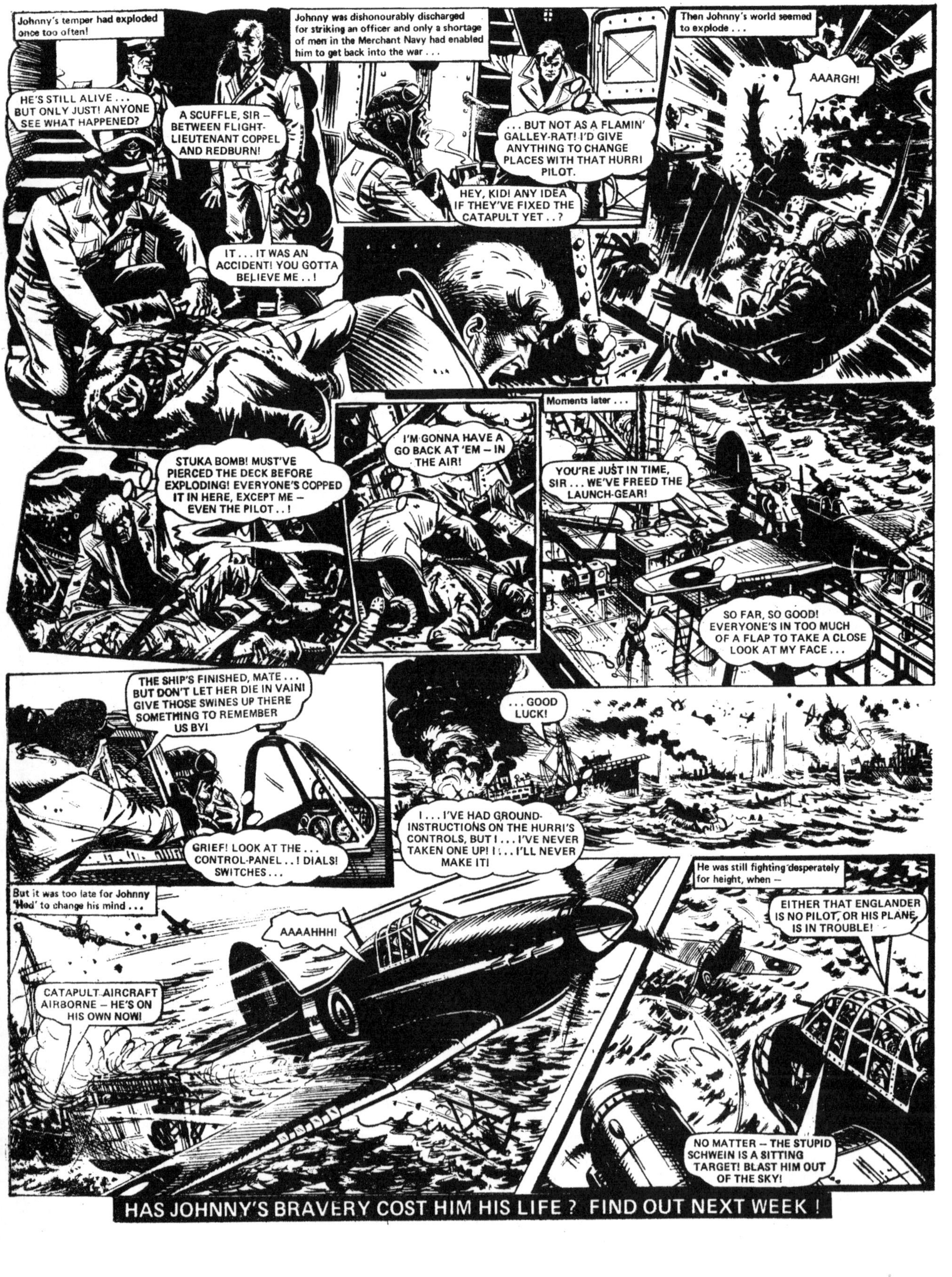

Johnny's temper had exploded once too often!
HE'S STILL ALIVE... BUT ONLY JUST! ANYONE SEE WHAT HAPPENED?
A SCUFFLE, SIR — BETWEEN FLIGHT-LIEUTENANT COPPEL AND REDBURN!
IT... IT WAS AN ACCIDENT! YOU GOTTA BELIEVE ME..!
Johnny was dishonourably discharged for striking an officer and only a shortage of men in the Merchant Navy had enabled him to get back into the war...
HEY, KID! ANY IDEA IF THEY'VE FIXED THE CATAPULT YET..?
...BUT NOT AS A FLAMIN' GALLEY-RAT! I'D GIVE ANYTHING TO CHANGE PLACES WITH THAT HURRI PILOT.
Then Johnny's world seemed to explode...
AAARGH!
STUKA BOMB! MUST'VE PIERCED THE DECK BEFORE EXPLODING! EVERYONE'S COPPED IT IN HERE, EXCEPT ME — EVEN THE PILOT..!
I'M GONNA HAVE A GO BACK AT 'EM — IN THE AIR!
Moments later...
YOU'RE JUST IN TIME, SIR... WE'VE FREED THE LAUNCH-GEAR!
SO FAR, SO GOOD! EVERYONE'S IN TOO MUCH OF A FLAP TO TAKE A CLOSE LOOK AT MY FACE...
THE SHIP'S FINISHED, MATE... BUT DON'T LET HER DIE IN VAIN! GIVE THOSE SWINES UP THERE SOMETHING TO REMEMBER US BY!
GRIEF! LOOK AT THE... CONTROL-PANEL..! DIALS! SWITCHES...
...GOOD LUCK!
I... I'VE HAD GROUND-INSTRUCTIONS ON THE HURRI'S CONTROLS, BUT I... I'VE NEVER TAKEN ONE UP! I... I'LL NEVER MAKE IT!
But it was too late for Johnny 'Red' to change his mind...
AAAAHHH!
CATAPULT AIRCRAFT AIRBORNE — HE'S ON HIS OWN NOW!
He was still fighting desperately for height, when —
EITHER THAT ENGLANDER IS NO PILOT, OR HIS PLANE IS IN TROUBLE!
NO MATTER — THE STUPID SCHWEIN IS A SITTING TARGET! BLAST HIM OUT OF THE SKY!
HAS JOHNNY'S BRAVERY COST HIM HIS LIFE? FIND OUT NEXT WEEK!

BLAZING AERIAL ACTION WITH THE BOY THEY CALL JOHNNY RED !

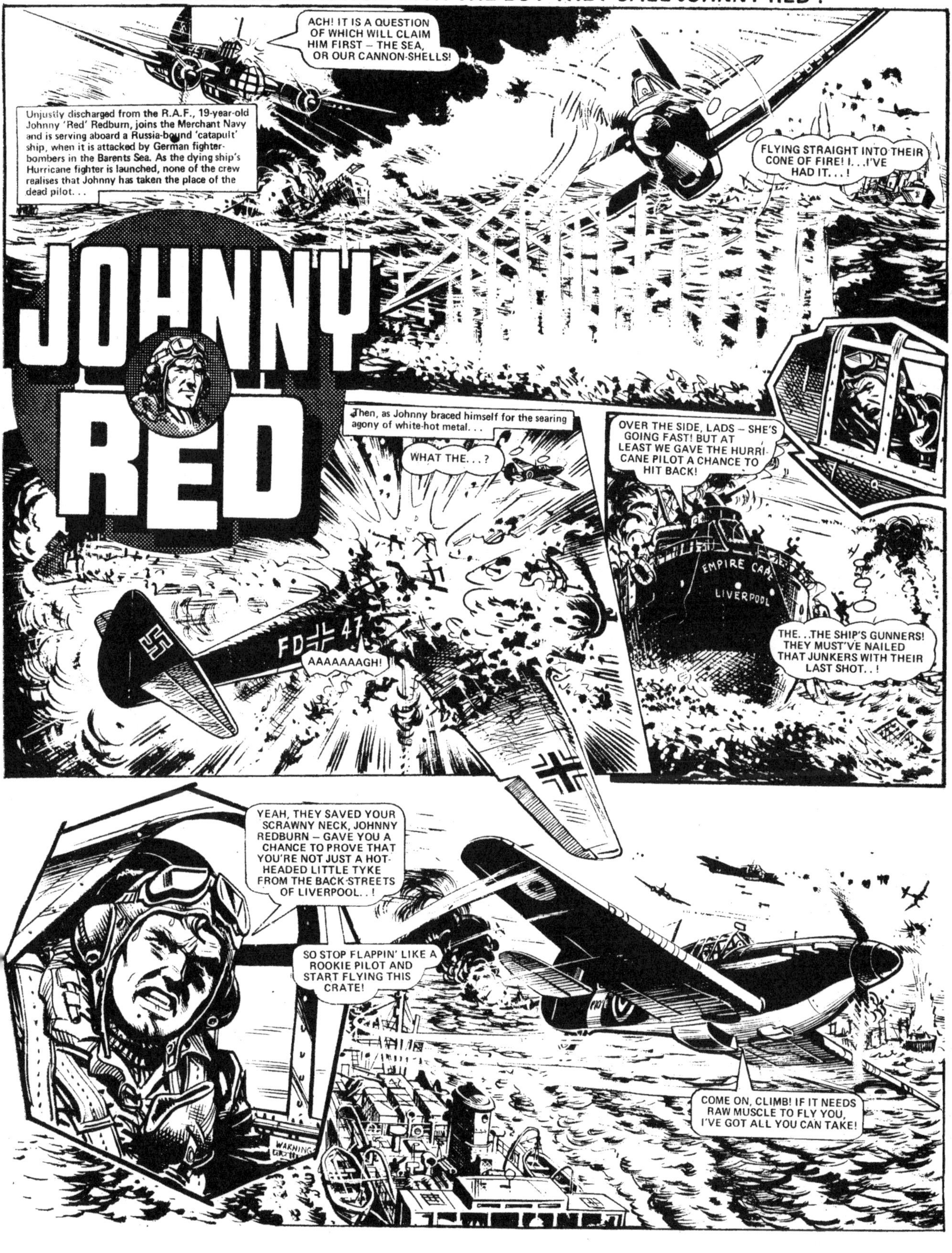

ACH! IT IS A QUESTION OF WHICH WILL CLAIM HIM FIRST – THE SEA, OR OUR CANNON-SHELLS!
Unjustly discharged from the R.A.F., 19-year-old Johnny 'Red' Redburn, joins the Merchant Navy and is serving aboard a Russia-bound 'catapult' ship, when it is attacked by German fighter-bombers in the Barents Sea. As the dying ship's Hurricane fighter is launched, none of the crew realises that Johnny has taken the place of the dead pilot. . .
FLYING STRAIGHT INTO THEIR CONE OF FIRE! I. . .I'VE HAD IT. . . !
JOHNNY RED
Then, as Johnny braced himself for the searing agony of white-hot metal. . .
WHAT THE. . .?
FD+47
AAAAAAAGH!
OVER THE SIDE, LADS – SHE'S GOING FAST! BUT AT LEAST WE GAVE THE HURRICANE PILOT A CHANCE TO HIT BACK!
EMPIRE CAPE
LIVERPOOL
THE. . .THE SHIP'S GUNNERS! THEY MUST'VE NAILED THAT JUNKERS WITH THEIR LAST SHOT. . !
YEAH, THEY SAVED YOUR SCRAWNY NECK, JOHNNY REDBURN – GAVE YOU A CHANCE TO PROVE THAT YOU'RE NOT JUST A HOT-HEADED LITTLE TYKE FROM THE BACK-STREETS OF LIVERPOOL. . !
SO STOP FLAPPIN' LIKE A ROOKIE PILOT AND START FLYING THIS CRATE!
COME ON, CLIMB! IF IT NEEDS RAW MUSCLE TO FLY YOU, I'VE GOT ALL YOU CAN TAKE!
WARNING

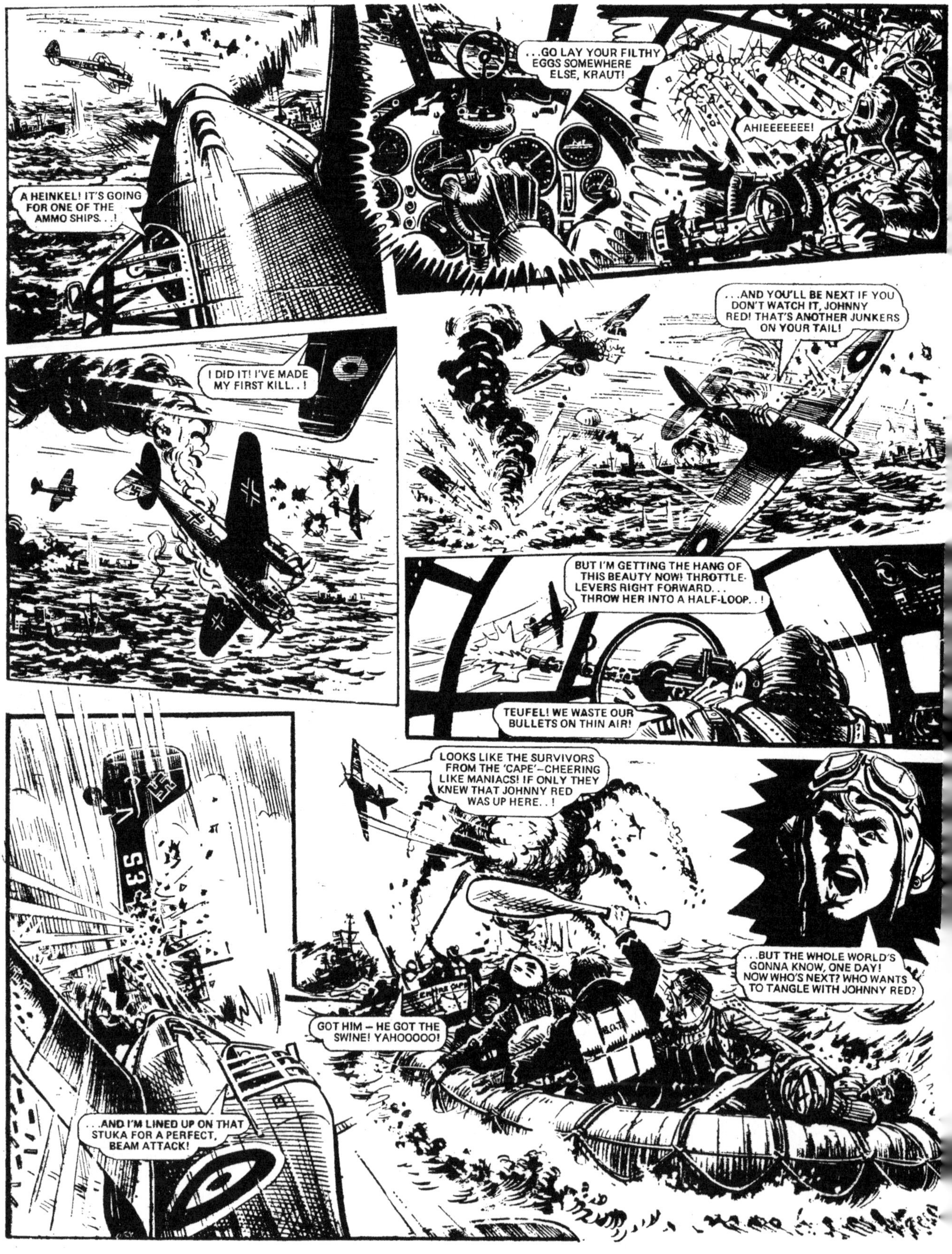

A HEINKEL! IT'S GOING FOR ONE OF THE AMMO SHIPS...!
...GO LAY YOUR FILTHY EGGS SOMEWHERE ELSE, KRAUT!
AHIEEEEEEE!
I DID IT! I'VE MADE MY FIRST KILL..!
...AND YOU'LL BE NEXT IF YOU DON'T WATCH IT, JOHNNY RED! THAT'S ANOTHER JUNKERS ON YOUR TAIL!
BUT I'M GETTING THE HANG OF THIS BEAUTY NOW! THROTTLE-LEVERS RIGHT FORWARD... THROW HER INTO A HALF-LOOP..!
TEUFEL! WE WASTE OUR BULLETS ON THIN AIR!
...AND I'M LINED UP ON THAT STUKA FOR A PERFECT, BEAM ATTACK!
LOOKS LIKE THE SURVIVORS FROM THE 'CAPE'–CHEERING LIKE MANIACS! IF ONLY THEY KNEW THAT JOHNNY RED WAS UP HERE..!
GOT HIM – HE GOT THE SWINE! YAHOOOOO!
...BUT THE WHOLE WORLD'S GONNA KNOW, ONE DAY! NOW WHO'S NEXT? WHO WANTS TO TANGLE WITH JOHNNY RED?

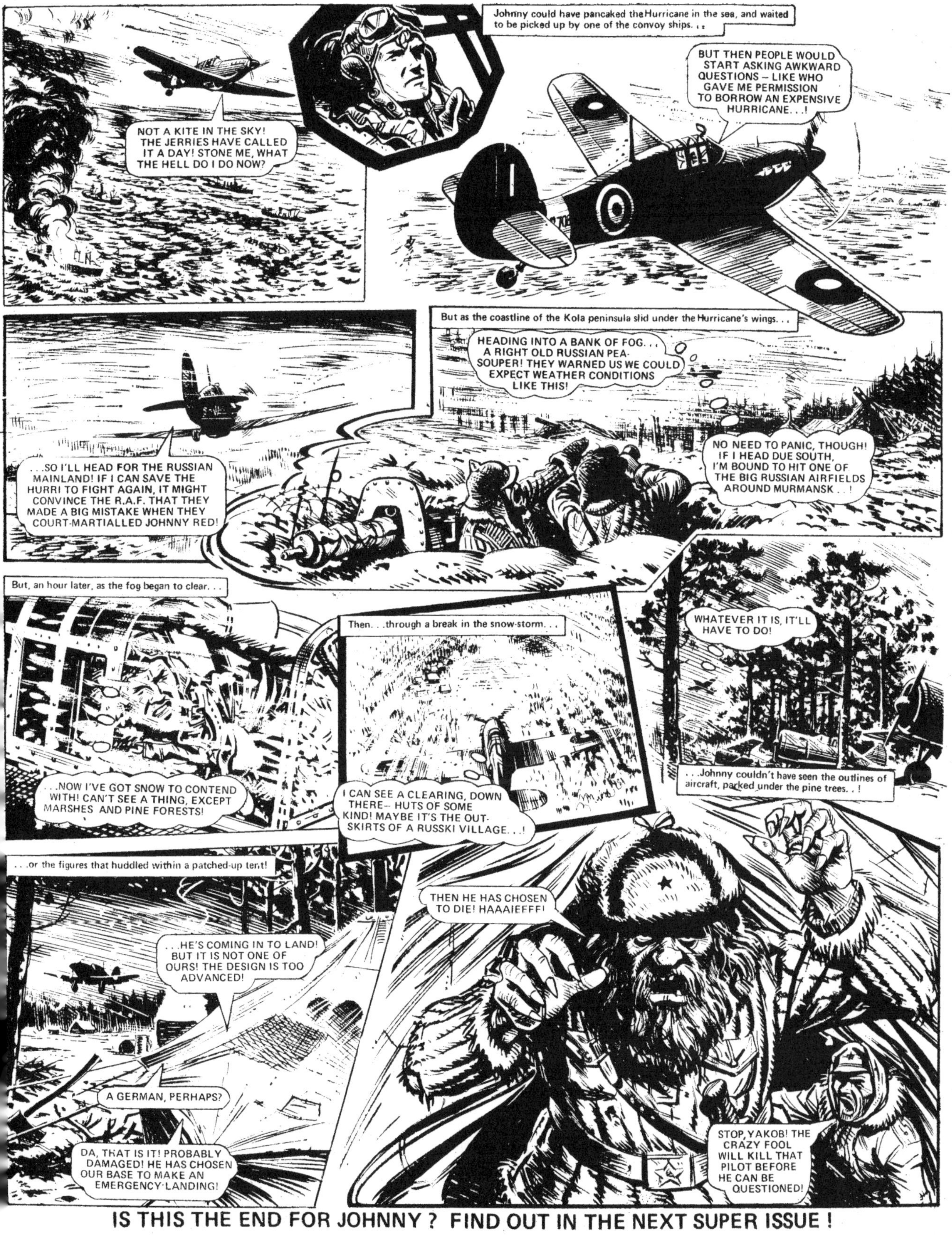

Johnny could have pancaked the Hurricane in the sea, and waited to be picked up by one of the convoy ships. . .
NOT A KITE IN THE SKY! THE JERRIES HAVE CALLED IT A DAY! STONE ME, WHAT THE HELL DO I DO NOW?
BUT THEN PEOPLE WOULD START ASKING AWKWARD QUESTIONS – LIKE WHO GAVE ME PERMISSION TO BORROW AN EXPENSIVE HURRICANE. . .!
. . .SO I'LL HEAD FOR THE RUSSIAN MAINLAND! IF I CAN SAVE THE HURRI TO FIGHT AGAIN, IT MIGHT CONVINCE THE R.A.F. THAT THEY MADE A BIG MISTAKE WHEN THEY COURT-MARTIALLED JOHNNY RED!
But as the coastline of the Kola peninsula slid under the Hurricane's wings. . .
HEADING INTO A BANK OF FOG. . . A RIGHT OLD RUSSIAN PEA-SOUPER! THEY WARNED US WE COULD EXPECT WEATHER CONDITIONS LIKE THIS!
NO NEED TO PANIC, THOUGH! IF I HEAD DUE SOUTH, I'M BOUND TO HIT ONE OF THE BIG RUSSIAN AIRFIELDS AROUND MURMANSK. . !
But, an hour later, as the fog began to clear. . .
. . .NOW I'VE GOT SNOW TO CONTEND WITH! CAN'T SEE A THING, EXCEPT MARSHES AND PINE FORESTS!
Then. . .through a break in the snow-storm. . .
I CAN SEE A CLEARING, DOWN THERE– HUTS OF SOME KIND! MAYBE IT'S THE OUT-SKIRTS OF A RUSSKI VILLAGE. . .!
WHATEVER IT IS, IT'LL HAVE TO DO!
. . .Johnny couldn't have seen the outlines of aircraft, parked under the pine trees. . !
. . .or the figures that huddled within a patched-up tent!
. . .HE'S COMING IN TO LAND! BUT IT IS NOT ONE OF OURS! THE DESIGN IS TOO ADVANCED!
A GERMAN, PERHAPS?
DA, THAT IS IT! PROBABLY DAMAGED! HE HAS CHOSEN OUR BASE TO MAKE AN EMERGENCY LANDING!
THEN HE HAS CHOSEN TO DIE! HAAAIEFFF!
STOP, YAKOB! THE CRAZY FOOL WILL KILL THAT PILOT BEFORE HE CAN BE QUESTIONED!

IS THIS THE END FOR JOHNNY ? FIND OUT IN THE NEXT SUPER ISSUE !

"HAVE SOME LEAD FROM JOHNNY RED !" FIGHTING TALK FROM A FIGHTING FLIER !

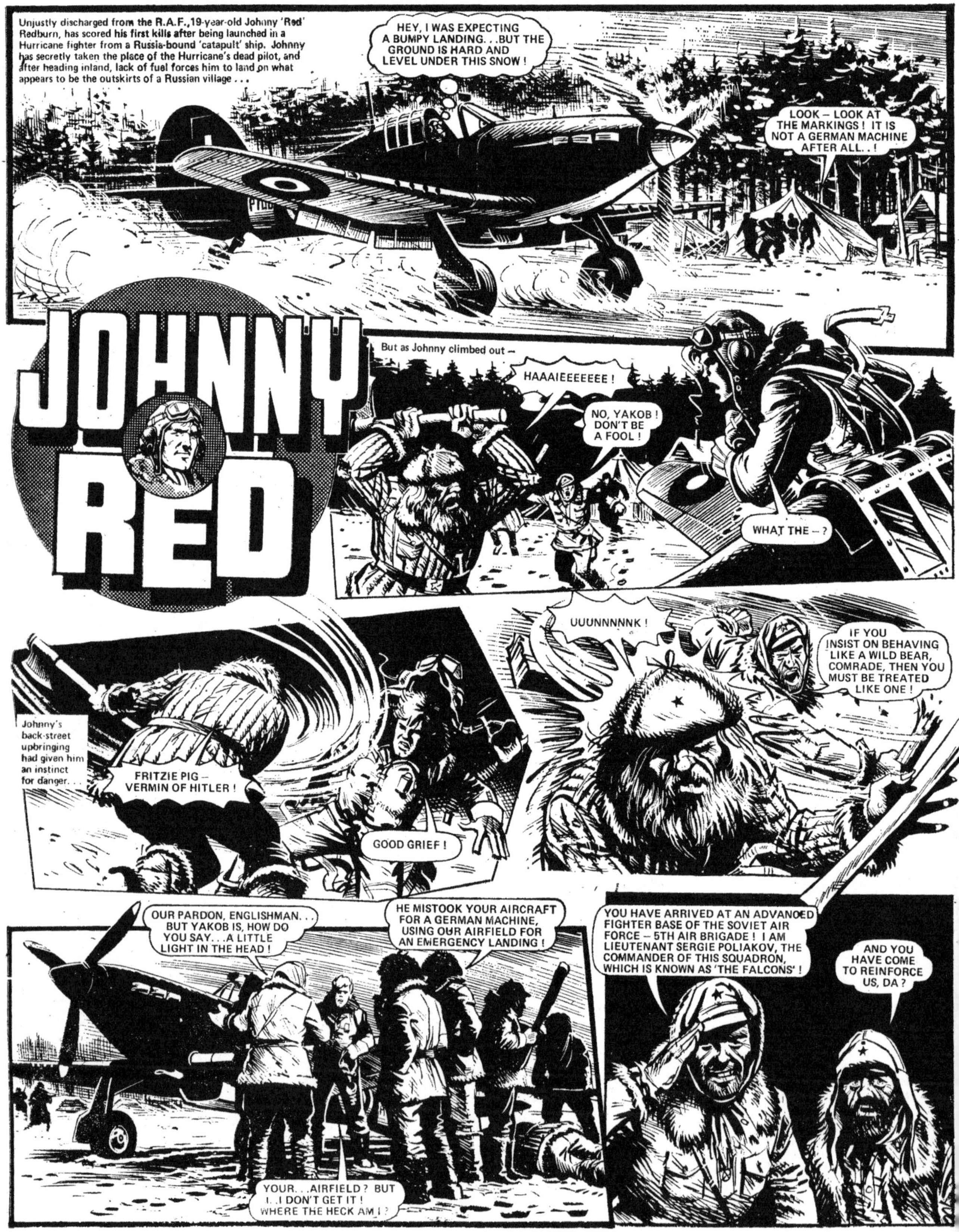
Unjustly discharged from the R.A.F., 19-year-old Johnny 'Red' Redburn, has scored his first kills after being launched in a Hurricane fighter from a Russia-bound 'catapult' ship. Johnny has secretly taken the place of the Hurricane's dead pilot, and after heading inland, lack of fuel forces him to land on what appears to be the outskirts of a Russian village . . .
HEY, I WAS EXPECTING A BUMPY LANDING. . .BUT THE GROUND IS HARD AND LEVEL UNDER THIS SNOW !
LOOK – LOOK AT THE MARKINGS ! IT IS NOT A GERMAN MACHINE AFTER ALL. . !
JOHNNY RED
But as Johnny climbed out –
HAAAIEEEEEEE !
NO, YAKOB ! DON'T BE A FOOL !
WHAT THE – ?
Johnny's back-street upbringing had given him an instinct for danger. . .
FRITZIE PIG – VERMIN OF HITLER !
GOOD GRIEF !
UUUNNNNNK !
IF YOU INSIST ON BEHAVING LIKE A WILD BEAR, COMRADE, THEN YOU MUST BE TREATED LIKE ONE !
OUR PARDON, ENGLISHMAN. . . BUT YAKOB IS, HOW DO YOU SAY. . .A LITTLE LIGHT IN THE HEAD !
HE MISTOOK YOUR AIRCRAFT FOR A GERMAN MACHINE, USING OUR AIRFIELD FOR AN EMERGENCY LANDING !
YOUR. . .AIRFIELD? BUT I. . .I DON'T GET IT ! WHERE THE HECK AM I ?
YOU HAVE ARRIVED AT AN ADVANCED FIGHTER BASE OF THE SOVIET AIR FORCE – 5TH AIR BRIGADE ! I AM LIEUTENANT SERGIE POLIAKOV, THE COMMANDER OF THIS SQUADRON, WHICH IS KNOWN AS 'THE FALCONS' !
AND YOU HAVE COME TO REINFORCE US, DA ?

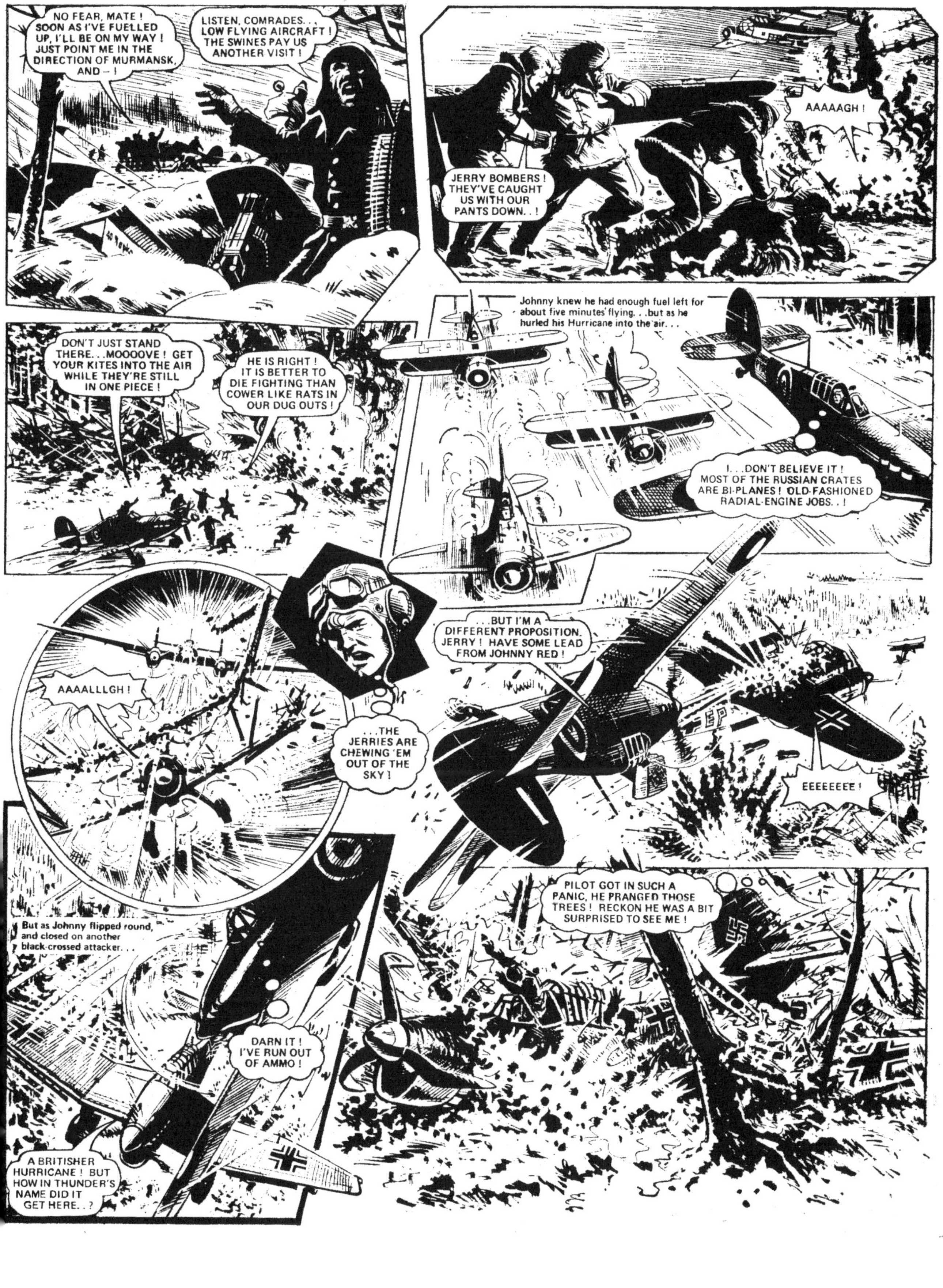
NO FEAR, MATE ! SOON AS I'VE FUELLED UP, I'LL BE ON MY WAY ! JUST POINT ME IN THE DIRECTION OF MURMANSK, AND – !
LISTEN, COMRADES. . . LOW FLYING AIRCRAFT ! THE SWINES PAY US ANOTHER VISIT !
JERRY BOMBERS ! THEY'VE CAUGHT US WITH OUR PANTS DOWN. . !
AAAAAGH !
DON'T JUST STAND THERE. . . MOOOOVE ! GET YOUR KITES INTO THE AIR WHILE THEY'RE STILL IN ONE PIECE !
HE IS RIGHT ! IT IS BETTER TO DIE FIGHTING THAN COWER LIKE RATS IN OUR DUG OUTS !
Johnny knew he had enough fuel left for about five minutes' flying. . . but as he hurled his Hurricane into the air. . .
I. . . DON'T BELIEVE IT ! MOST OF THE RUSSIAN CRATES ARE BI-PLANES ! OLD-FASHIONED RADIAL-ENGINE JOBS. . !
AAAALLLGH !
. . . THE JERRIES ARE CHEWING 'EM OUT OF THE SKY !
. . . BUT I'M A DIFFERENT PROPOSITION, JERRY ! HAVE SOME LEAD FROM JOHNNY RED !
EEEEEEEE !
But as Johnny flipped round, and closed on another black-crossed attacker. . .
DARN IT ! I'VE RUN OUT OF AMMO !
A BRITISHER HURRICANE ! BUT HOW IN THUNDER'S NAME DID IT GET HERE. . ?
PILOT GOT IN SUCH A PANIC, HE PRANGED THOSE TREES ! RECKON HE WAS A BIT SURPRISED TO SEE ME !

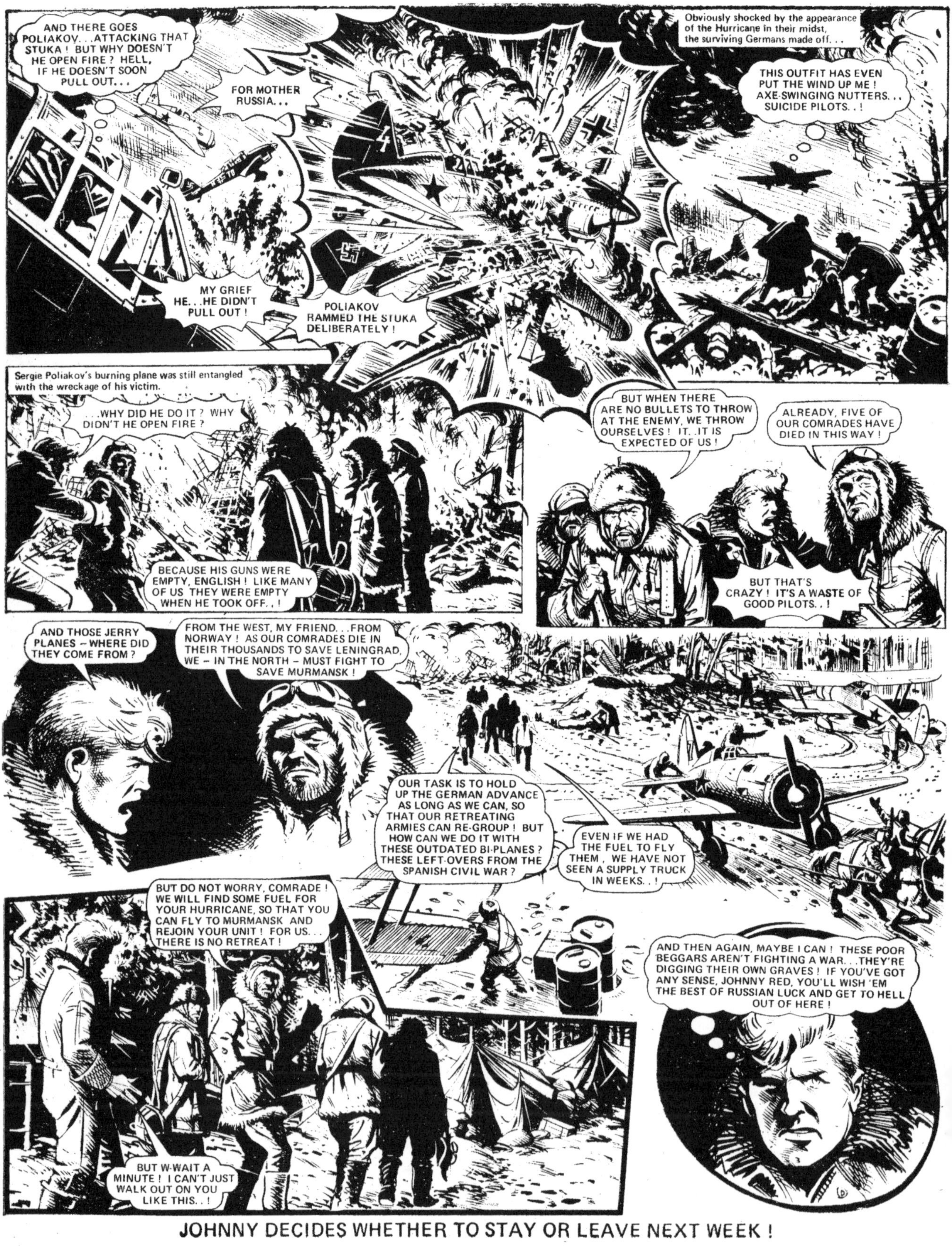
AND THERE GOES POLIAKOV. . .ATTACKING THAT STUKA ! BUT WHY DOESN'T HE OPEN FIRE ? HELL, IF HE DOESN'T SOON PULL OUT. . .
FOR MOTHER RUSSIA. . .
MY GRIEF HE. . .HE DIDN'T PULL OUT !
POLIAKOV RAMMED THE STUKA DELIBERATELY !
Obviously shocked by the appearance of the Hurricane in their midst, the surviving Germans made off. . .
THIS OUTFIT HAS EVEN PUT THE WIND UP ME ! AXE-SWINGING NUTTERS. . . SUICIDE PILOTS. . !
Sergie Poliakov's burning plane was still entangled with the wreckage of his victim.
. . .WHY DID HE DO IT ? WHY DIDN'T HE OPEN FIRE ?
BECAUSE HIS GUNS WERE EMPTY, ENGLISH ! LIKE MANY OF US THEY WERE EMPTY WHEN HE TOOK OFF. . !
BUT WHEN THERE ARE NO BULLETS TO THROW AT THE ENEMY, WE THROW OURSELVES ! IT. .IT IS EXPECTED OF US !
ALREADY, FIVE OF OUR COMRADES HAVE DIED IN THIS WAY !
BUT THAT'S CRAZY ! IT'S A WASTE OF GOOD PILOTS. . !
AND THOSE JERRY PLANES – WHERE DID THEY COME FROM ?
FROM THE WEST, MY FRIEND. . .FROM NORWAY ! AS OUR COMRADES DIE IN THEIR THOUSANDS TO SAVE LENINGRAD, WE – IN THE NORTH – MUST FIGHT TO SAVE MURMANSK !
OUR TASK IS TO HOLD UP THE GERMAN ADVANCE AS LONG AS WE CAN, SO THAT OUR RETREATING ARMIES CAN RE-GROUP ! BUT HOW CAN WE DO IT WITH THESE OUTDATED BI-PLANES ? THESE LEFT-OVERS FROM THE SPANISH CIVIL WAR ?
EVEN IF WE HAD THE FUEL TO FLY THEM, WE HAVE NOT SEEN A SUPPLY TRUCK IN WEEKS. . !
BUT DO NOT WORRY, COMRADE ! WE WILL FIND SOME FUEL FOR YOUR HURRICANE, SO THAT YOU CAN FLY TO MURMANSK AND REJOIN YOUR UNIT ! FOR US. . . THERE IS NO RETREAT !
BUT W-WAIT A MINUTE ! I CAN'T JUST WALK OUT ON YOU LIKE THIS. . !
AND THEN AGAIN, MAYBE I CAN ! THESE POOR BEGGARS AREN'T FIGHTING A WAR. . .THEY'RE DIGGING THEIR OWN GRAVES ! IF YOU'VE GOT ANY SENSE, JOHNNY RED, YOU'LL WISH 'EM THE BEST OF RUSSIAN LUCK AND GET TO HELL OUT OF HERE !

JOHNNY DECIDES WHETHER TO STAY OR LEAVE NEXT WEEK !

JOHNNY MASTERMINDS AN ATTACK ON A RUSSIAN CONVOY. . .HELPED BY RUSSIANS !

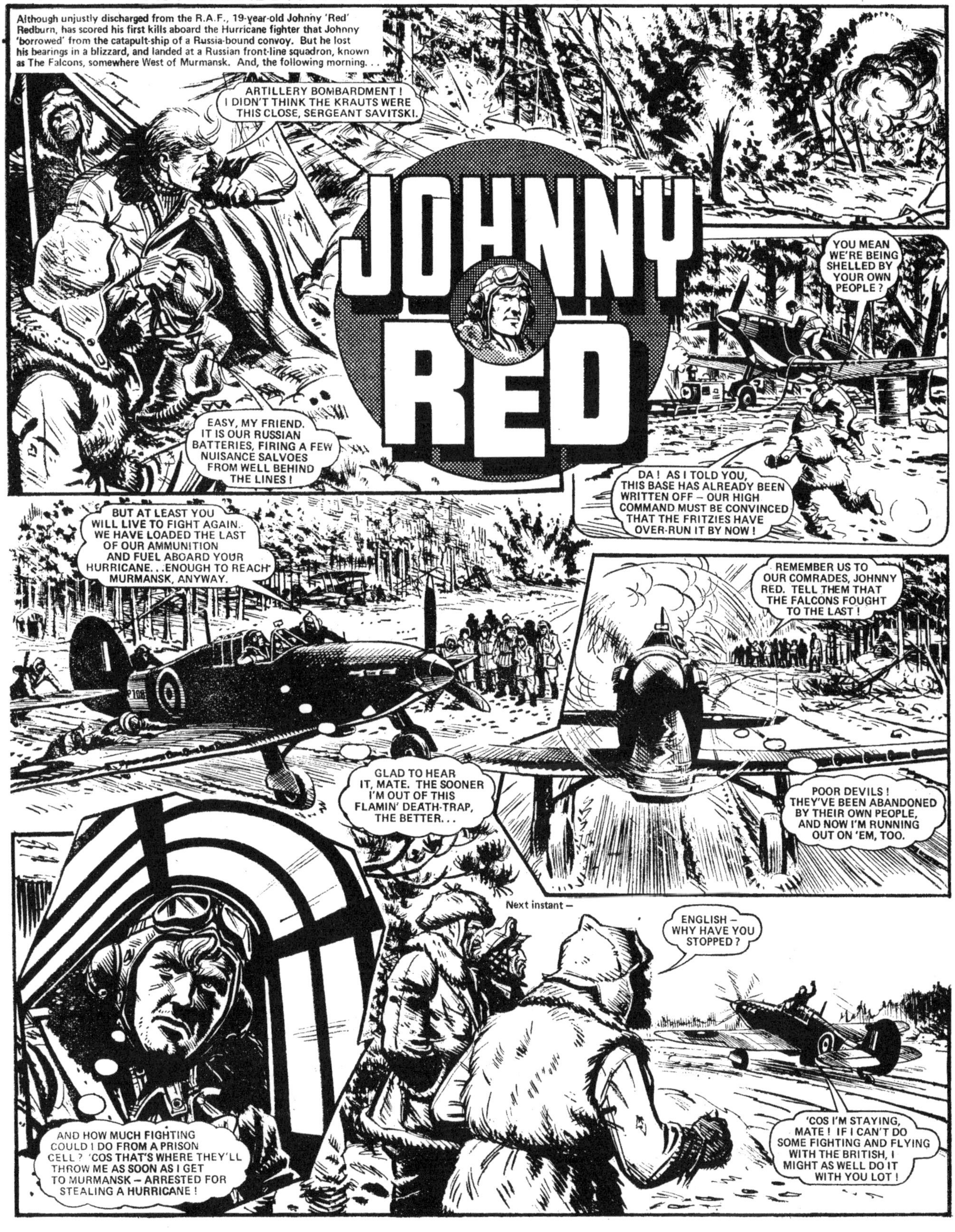
Although unjustly discharged from the R.A.F., 19-year-old Johnny 'Red' Redburn, has scored his first kills aboard the Hurricane fighter that Johnny 'borrowed' from the catapult-ship of a Russia-bound convoy. But he lost his bearings in a blizzard, and landed at a Russian front-line squadron, known as The Falcons, somewhere West of Murmansk. And, the following morning. . .
ARTILLERY BOMBARDMENT ! I DIDN'T THINK THE KRAUTS WERE THIS CLOSE, SERGEANT SAVITSKI.
JOHNNY RED
EASY, MY FRIEND. IT IS OUR RUSSIAN BATTERIES, FIRING A FEW NUISANCE SALVOES FROM WELL BEHIND THE LINES !
YOU MEAN WE'RE BEING SHELLED BY YOUR OWN PEOPLE ?
DA ! AS I TOLD YOU, THIS BASE HAS ALREADY BEEN WRITTEN OFF – OUR HIGH COMMAND MUST BE CONVINCED THAT THE FRITZIES HAVE OVER-RUN IT BY NOW !
BUT AT LEAST YOU WILL LIVE TO FIGHT AGAIN. WE HAVE LOADED THE LAST OF OUR AMMUNITION AND FUEL ABOARD YOUR HURRICANE. . .ENOUGH TO REACH MURMANSK, ANYWAY.
GLAD TO HEAR IT, MATE. THE SOONER I'M OUT OF THIS FLAMIN' DEATH-TRAP, THE BETTER. . .
REMEMBER US TO OUR COMRADES, JOHNNY RED. TELL THEM THAT THE FALCONS FOUGHT TO THE LAST !
POOR DEVILS ! THEY'VE BEEN ABANDONED BY THEIR OWN PEOPLE, AND NOW I'M RUNNING OUT ON 'EM, TOO.
AND HOW MUCH FIGHTING COULD I DO FROM A PRISON CELL ? 'COS THAT'S WHERE THEY'LL THROW ME AS SOON AS I GET TO MURMANSK – ARRESTED FOR STEALING A HURRICANE !
Next instant –
ENGLISH – WHY HAVE YOU STOPPED ?
'COS I'M STAYING, MATE ! IF I CAN'T DO SOME FIGHTING AND FLYING WITH THE BRITISH, I MIGHT AS WELL DO IT WITH YOU LOT !

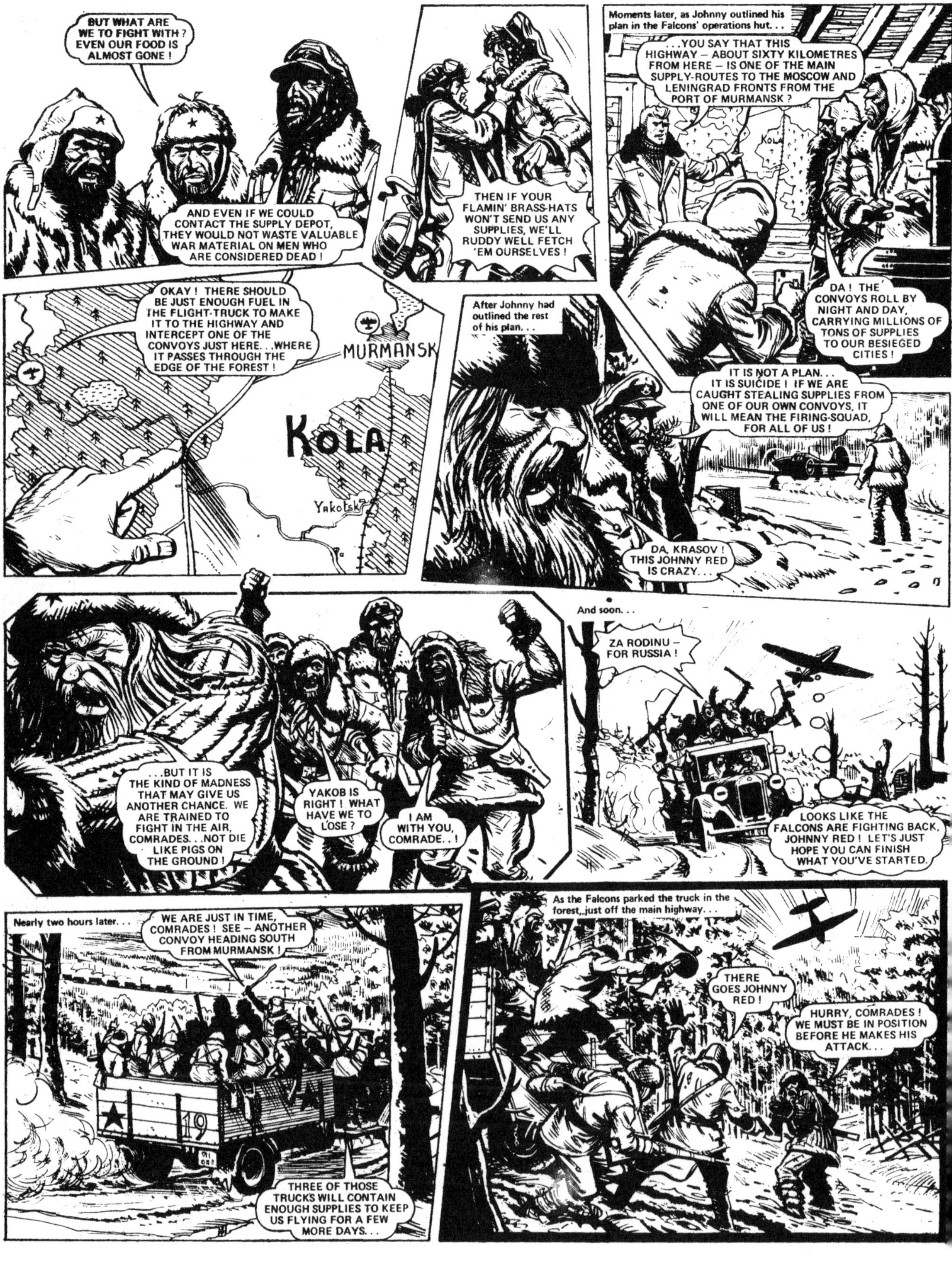

BUT WHAT ARE WE TO FIGHT WITH? EVEN OUR FOOD IS ALMOST GONE!
AND EVEN IF WE COULD CONTACT THE SUPPLY DEPOT, THEY WOULD NOT WASTE VALUABLE WAR MATERIAL ON MEN WHO ARE CONSIDERED DEAD!
THEN IF YOUR FLAMIN' BRASS-HATS WON'T SEND US ANY SUPPLIES, WE'LL RUDDY WELL FETCH 'EM OURSELVES!
Moments later, as Johnny outlined his plan in the Falcons' operations hut...
...YOU SAY THAT THIS HIGHWAY – ABOUT SIXTY KILOMETRES FROM HERE – IS ONE OF THE MAIN SUPPLY-ROUTES TO THE MOSCOW AND LENINGRAD FRONTS FROM THE PORT OF MURMANSK?
DA! THE CONVOYS ROLL BY NIGHT AND DAY, CARRYING MILLIONS OF TONS OF SUPPLIES TO OUR BESIEGED CITIES!
OKAY! THERE SHOULD BE JUST ENOUGH FUEL IN THE FLIGHT-TRUCK TO MAKE IT TO THE HIGHWAY AND INTERCEPT ONE OF THE CONVOYS JUST HERE...WHERE IT PASSES THROUGH THE EDGE OF THE FOREST!
MURMANSK
KOLA
Yakotsk
After Johnny had outlined the rest of his plan...
IT IS NOT A PLAN... IT IS SUICIDE! IF WE ARE CAUGHT STEALING SUPPLIES FROM ONE OF OUR OWN CONVOYS, IT WILL MEAN THE FIRING-SQUAD, FOR ALL OF US!
DA, KRASOV! THIS JOHNNY RED IS CRAZY...
...BUT IT IS THE KIND OF MADNESS THAT MAY GIVE US ANOTHER CHANCE. WE ARE TRAINED TO FIGHT IN THE AIR, COMRADES...NOT DIE LIKE PIGS ON THE GROUND!
YAKOB IS RIGHT! WHAT HAVE WE TO LOSE?
I AM WITH YOU, COMRADE..!
And soon...
ZA RODINU – FOR RUSSIA!
LOOKS LIKE THE FALCONS ARE FIGHTING BACK, JOHNNY RED! LET'S JUST HOPE YOU CAN FINISH WHAT YOU'VE STARTED.
Nearly two hours later...
WE ARE JUST IN TIME, COMRADES! SEE – ANOTHER CONVOY HEADING SOUTH FROM MURMANSK!
19
THREE OF THOSE TRUCKS WILL CONTAIN ENOUGH SUPPLIES TO KEEP US FLYING FOR A FEW MORE DAYS...
As the Falcons parked the truck in the forest, just off the main highway...
THERE GOES JOHNNY RED!
HURRY, COMRADES! WE MUST BE IN POSITION BEFORE HE MAKES HIS ATTACK...

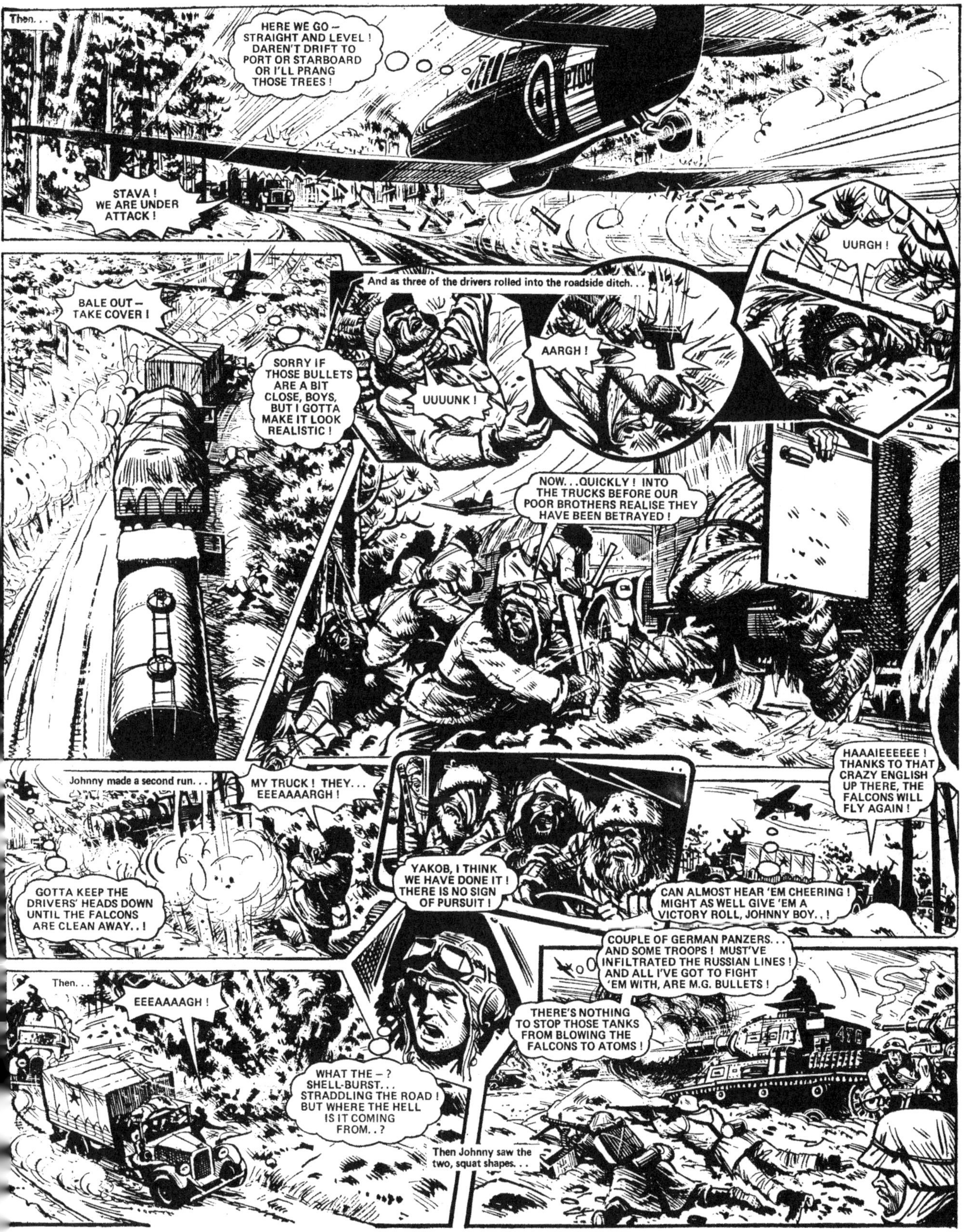
Then. . .
HERE WE GO – STRAIGHT AND LEVEL ! DAREN'T DRIFT TO PORT OR STARBOARD OR I'LL PRANG THOSE TREES !
STAVA ! WE ARE UNDER ATTACK !
BALE OUT – TAKE COVER !
SORRY IF THOSE BULLETS ARE A BIT CLOSE, BOYS, BUT I GOTTA MAKE IT LOOK REALISTIC !
And as three of the drivers rolled into the roadside ditch. . .
UUUUNK !
AARGH !
UURGH !
NOW. . .QUICKLY ! INTO THE TRUCKS BEFORE OUR POOR BROTHERS REALISE THEY HAVE BEEN BETRAYED !
Johnny made a second run. . .
MY TRUCK ! THEY. . . EEEAAAARGH !
GOTTA KEEP THE DRIVERS' HEADS DOWN UNTIL THE FALCONS ARE CLEAN AWAY. . !
YAKOB, I THINK WE HAVE DONE IT ! THERE IS NO SIGN OF PURSUIT !
HAAAIEEEEEE ! THANKS TO THAT CRAZY ENGLISH UP THERE, THE FALCONS WILL FLY AGAIN !
CAN ALMOST HEAR 'EM CHEERING ! MIGHT AS WELL GIVE 'EM A VICTORY ROLL, JOHNNY BOY. . !
Then. . .
EEEAAAAGH !
WHAT THE – ? SHELL-BURST. . . STRADDLING THE ROAD ! BUT WHERE THE HELL IS IT COMING FROM. . ?
COUPLE OF GERMAN PANZERS. . . AND SOME TROOPS ! MUST'VE INFILTRATED THE RUSSIAN LINES ! AND ALL I'VE GOT TO FIGHT 'EM WITH, ARE M.G. BULLETS !
THERE'S NOTHING TO STOP THOSE TANKS FROM BLOWING THE FALCONS TO ATOMS !
Then Johnny saw the two, squat shapes. . .

HURRICANE VERSUS TANKS – IT'S A BATTLE YOU DARE NOT MISS !

HURRICANE VERSUS TANK – JOHNNY RED VERSUS DEATH !

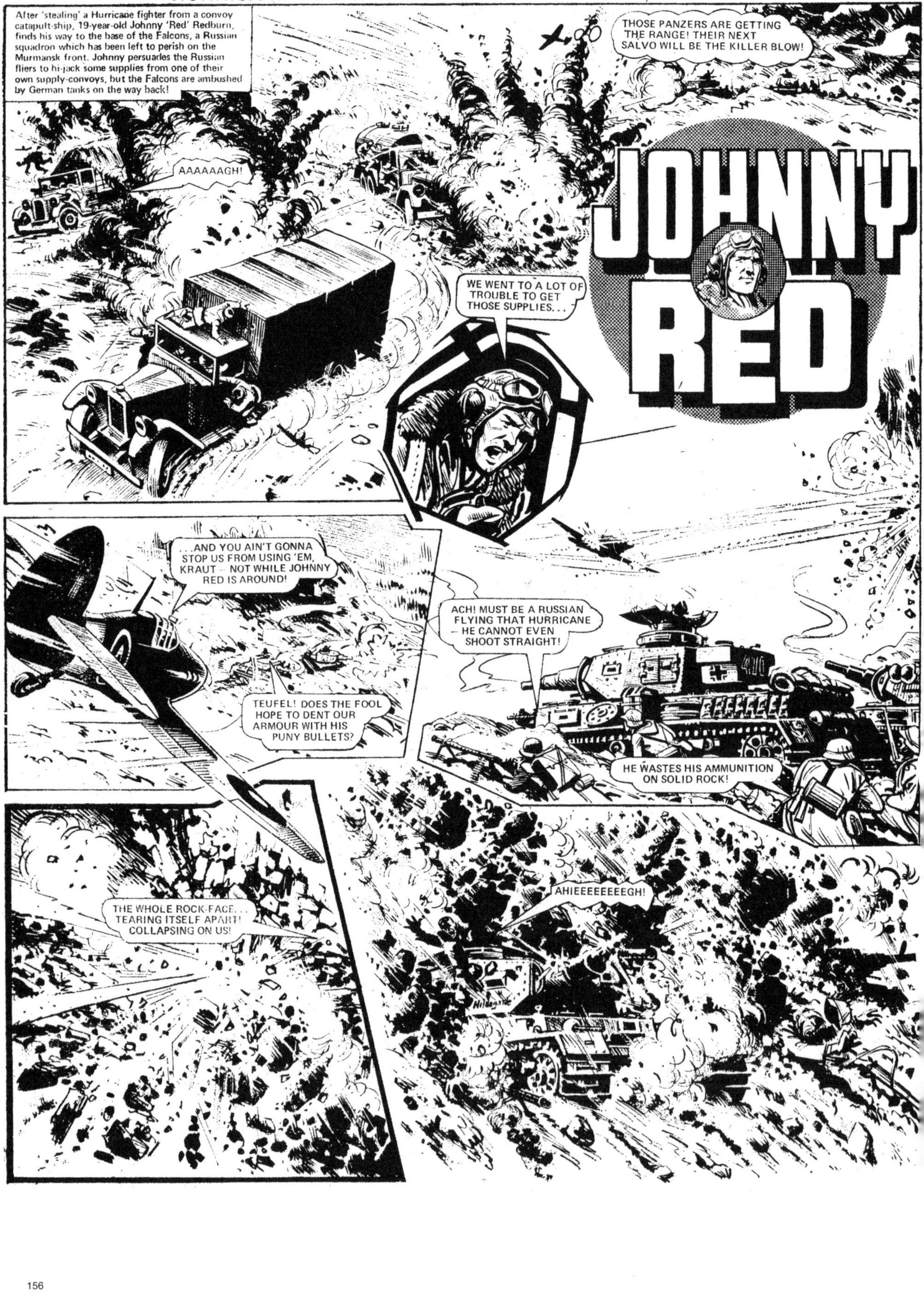

After 'stealing' a Hurricane fighter from a convoy catapult-ship, 19-year-old Johnny 'Red' Redburn, finds his way to the base of the Falcons, a Russian squadron which has been left to perish on the Murmansk front. Johnny persuades the Russian fliers to hi-jack some supplies from one of their own supply-convoys, but the Falcons are ambushed by German tanks on the way back!
AAAAAAGH!
THOSE PANZERS ARE GETTING THE RANGE! THEIR NEXT SALVO WILL BE THE KILLER BLOW!
JOHNNY RED
WE WENT TO A LOT OF TROUBLE TO GET THOSE SUPPLIES...
...AND YOU AIN'T GONNA STOP US FROM USING 'EM, KRAUT – NOT WHILE JOHNNY RED IS AROUND!
TEUFEL! DOES THE FOOL HOPE TO DENT OUR ARMOUR WITH HIS PUNY BULLETS?
ACH! MUST BE A RUSSIAN FLYING THAT HURRICANE – HE CANNOT EVEN SHOOT STRAIGHT!
HE WASTES HIS AMMUNITION ON SOLID ROCK!
THE WHOLE ROCK-FACE... TEARING ITSELF APART! COLLAPSING ON US!
AHIEEEEEEEEGH!

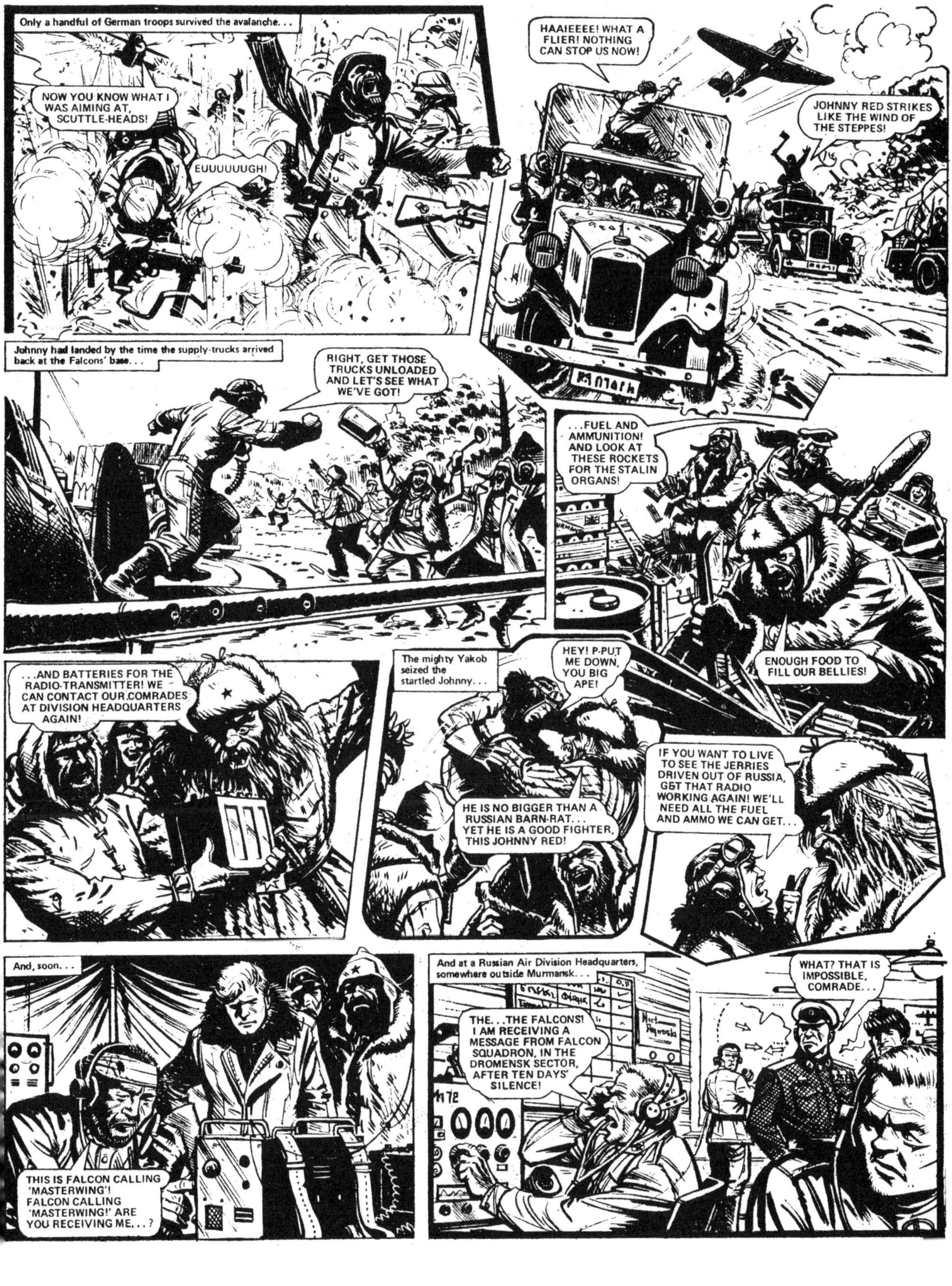

Only a handful of German troops survived the avalanche...
NOW YOU KNOW WHAT I WAS AIMING AT, SCUTTLE-HEADS!
EUUUUUUGH!
HAAIEEEE! WHAT A FLIER! NOTHING CAN STOP US NOW!
JOHNNY RED STRIKES LIKE THE WIND OF THE STEPPES!
Johnny had landed by the time the supply-trucks arrived back at the Falcons' base...
RIGHT, GET THOSE TRUCKS UNLOADED AND LET'S SEE WHAT WE'VE GOT!
...FUEL AND AMMUNITION! AND LOOK AT THESE ROCKETS FOR THE STALIN ORGANS!
ENOUGH FOOD TO FILL OUR BELLIES!
...AND BATTERIES FOR THE RADIO-TRANSMITTER! WE CAN CONTACT OUR COMRADES AT DIVISION HEADQUARTERS AGAIN!
The mighty Yakob seized the startled Johnny...
HEY! P-PUT ME DOWN, YOU BIG APE!
HE IS NO BIGGER THAN A RUSSIAN BARN-RAT... YET HE IS A GOOD FIGHTER, THIS JOHNNY RED!
IF YOU WANT TO LIVE TO SEE THE JERRIES DRIVEN OUT OF RUSSIA, GET THAT RADIO WORKING AGAIN! WE'LL NEED ALL THE FUEL AND AMMO WE CAN GET...
And, soon...
THIS IS FALCON CALLING 'MASTERWING'! FALCON CALLING 'MASTERWING!' ARE YOU RECEIVING ME...?
And at a Russian Air Division Headquarters, somewhere outside Murmansk...
THE...THE FALCONS! I AM RECEIVING A MESSAGE FROM FALCON SQUADRON, IN THE DROMENSK SECTOR, AFTER TEN DAYS' SILENCE!
WHAT? THAT IS IMPOSSIBLE, COMRADE...

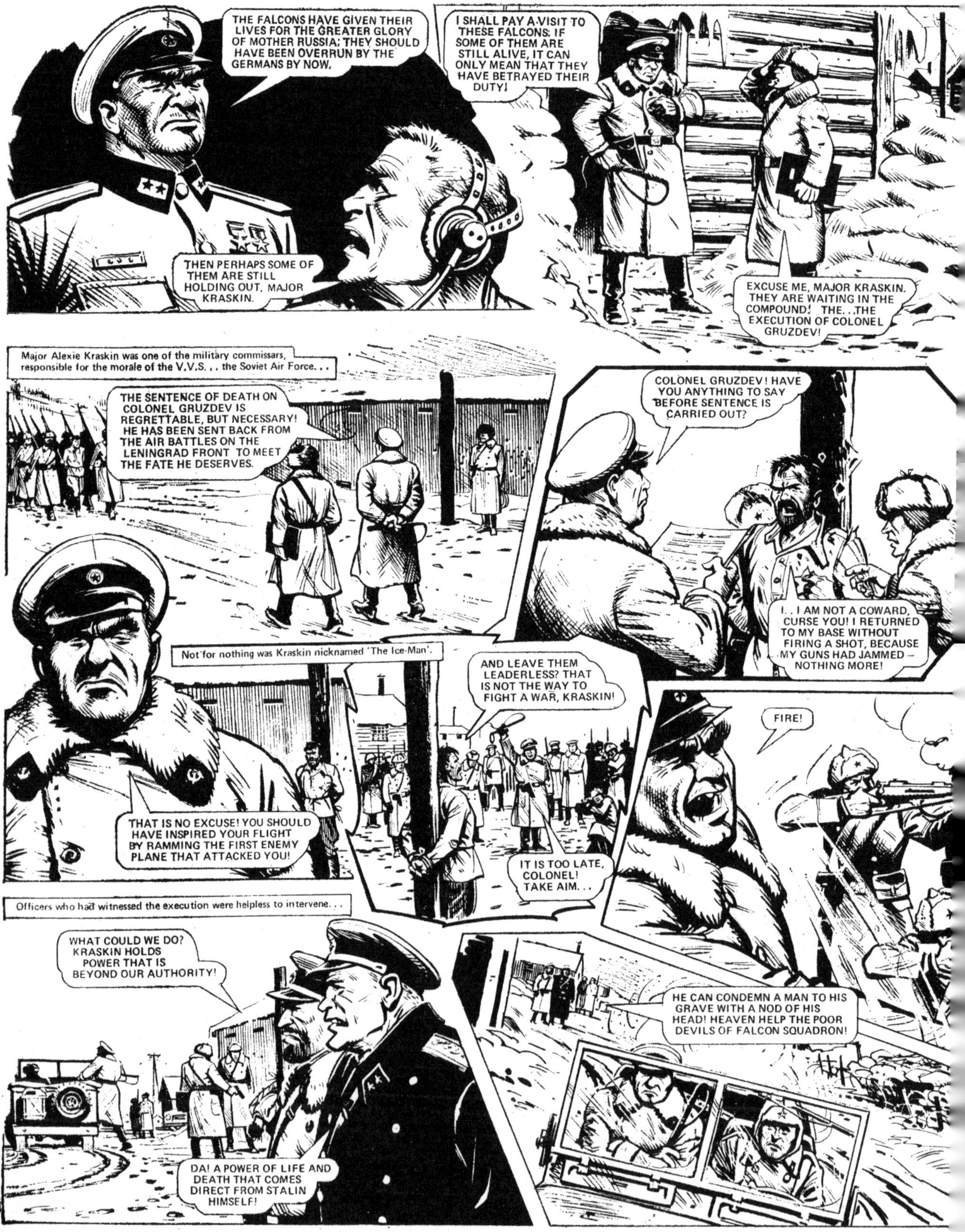
THE FALCONS HAVE GIVEN THEIR LIVES FOR THE GREATER GLORY OF MOTHER RUSSIA; THEY SHOULD HAVE BEEN OVERRUN BY THE GERMANS BY NOW.
THEN PERHAPS SOME OF THEM ARE STILL HOLDING OUT, MAJOR KRASKIN.
I SHALL PAY A VISIT TO THESE FALCONS; IF SOME OF THEM ARE STILL ALIVE, IT CAN ONLY MEAN THAT THEY HAVE BETRAYED THEIR DUTY!
EXCUSE ME, MAJOR KRASKIN. THEY ARE WAITING IN THE COMPOUND. THE. . .THE EXECUTION OF COLONEL GRUZDEV!
Major Alexie Kraskin was one of the military commissars, responsible for the morale of the V.V.S. . . the Soviet Air Force. . .
THE SENTENCE OF DEATH ON COLONEL GRUZDEV IS REGRETTABLE, BUT NECESSARY! HE HAS BEEN SENT BACK FROM THE AIR BATTLES ON THE LENINGRAD FRONT TO MEET THE FATE HE DESERVES.
COLONEL GRUZDEV! HAVE YOU ANYTHING TO SAY BEFORE SENTENCE IS CARRIED OUT?
I. . I AM NOT A COWARD, CURSE YOU! I RETURNED TO MY BASE WITHOUT FIRING A SHOT, BECAUSE MY GUNS HAD JAMMED – NOTHING MORE!
Not for nothing was Kraskin nicknamed 'The Ice-Man'.
THAT IS NO EXCUSE! YOU SHOULD HAVE INSPIRED YOUR FLIGHT BY RAMMING THE FIRST ENEMY PLANE THAT ATTACKED YOU!
AND LEAVE THEM LEADERLESS? THAT IS NOT THE WAY TO FIGHT A WAR, KRASKIN!
IT IS TOO LATE, COLONEL! TAKE AIM. . .
FIRE!
Officers who had witnessed the execution were helpless to intervene. . .
WHAT COULD WE DO? KRASKIN HOLDS POWER THAT IS BEYOND OUR AUTHORITY!
DA! A POWER OF LIFE AND DEATH THAT COMES DIRECT FROM STALIN HIMSELF!
HE CAN CONDEMN A MAN TO HIS GRAVE WITH A NOD OF HIS HEAD! HEAVEN HELP THE POOR DEVILS OF FALCON SQUADRON!

..MISSION ENDS...MISSION ENDS...MISSION ENDS...MISSION ENDS...MISSION ENDS...MISSION ENDS...MISSION EN

JOE TWO BEANS

"I DON'T BELIEVE IT! LOOK AT THAT CRAZY INDIAN!"

Forcibly recruited into the "White Man's War", six foot nine man-mountain Joe Two Beans is a silent but deadly Blackfoot Indian, a man trained to be as lethal and stealthy as a panther. But Joe only decides to fight for the US after his fellow Marine Sawdust Smith saves his life — and Joe sees the cruelty of the Japanese first-hand. Together, these two unlikely brothers in arms will fight the bloodiest conflicts of their lives, across the entire Pacific theatre of war.

Running from January 1977 until April 1978, 'Joe Two Beans' was a valiant attempt by *Battle* to experiment with its standard hero template and was obviously inspired by the success of *One Flew Over the Cuckoo's Nest*.

NOTES FROM THE FRONTLINE:

"There was, I suppose, a little take on *One Flew Over the Cuckoo's Nest*, the hero being this intense Red Indian character, very moralistic, but who never spoke. John did his damnedest to create script after script with the main hero not talking, but eventually he had to admit defeat, he had to have him talking. But I think the whole concept initially would have been to have a guy who never spoke from start to finish which would have been quite an achievement in a comic book. That was typical of John, he was good to work with and a good laugh."
— **Dave Hunt**

WRITTEN BY John Wagner
DRAWN BY Eric Bradbury

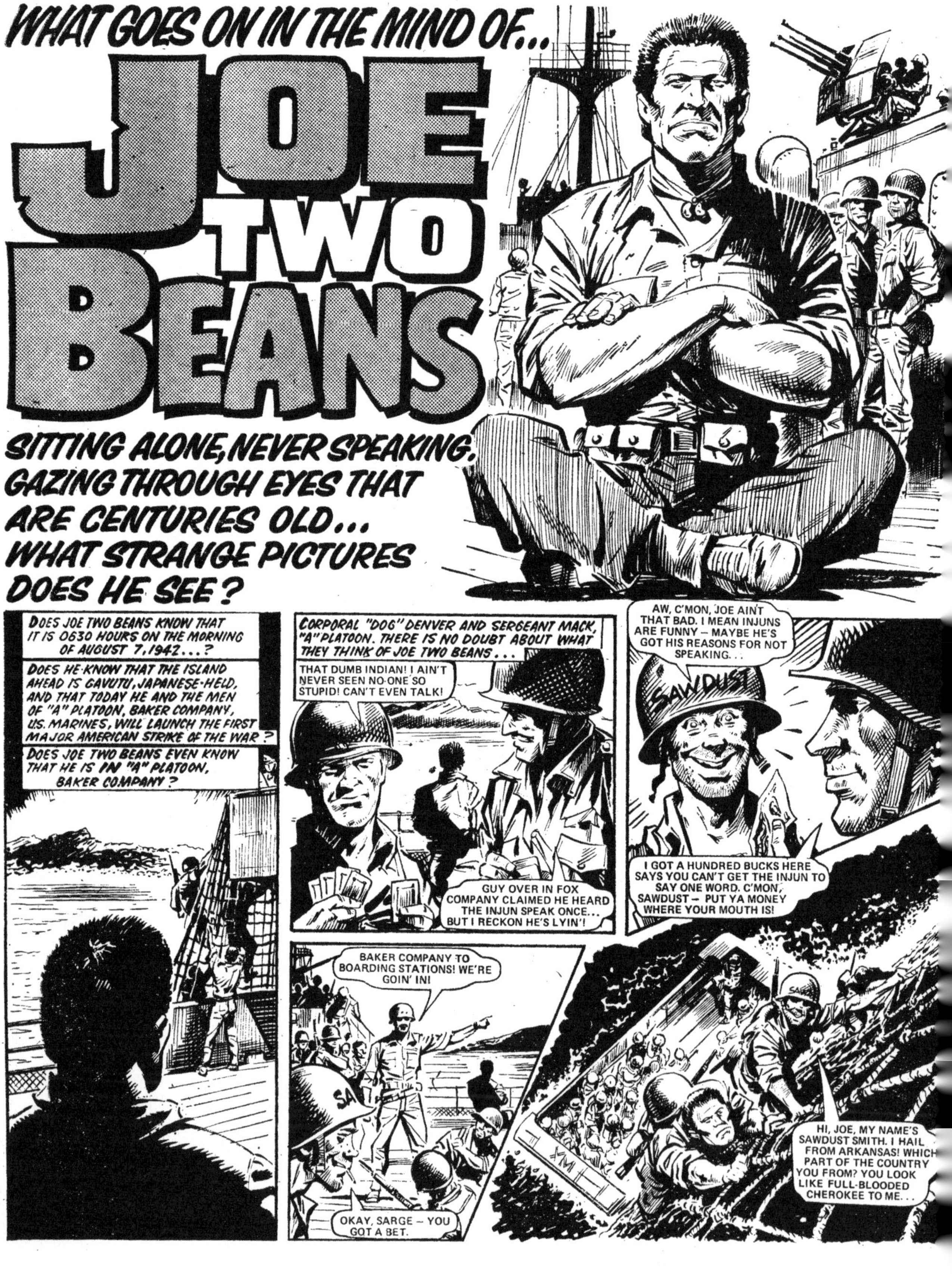
WHAT GOES ON IN THE MIND OF...
JOE TWO BEANS
SITTING ALONE, NEVER SPEAKING, GAZING THROUGH EYES THAT ARE CENTURIES OLD... WHAT STRANGE PICTURES DOES HE SEE?
DOES JOE TWO BEANS KNOW THAT IT IS 0630 HOURS ON THE MORNING OF AUGUST 7, 1942...?
DOES HE KNOW THAT THE ISLAND AHEAD IS GAVUTU, JAPANESE-HELD, AND THAT TODAY HE AND THE MEN OF "A" PLATOON, BAKER COMPANY, U.S. MARINES, WILL LAUNCH THE FIRST MAJOR AMERICAN STRIKE OF THE WAR?
DOES JOE TWO BEANS EVEN KNOW THAT HE IS IN "A" PLATOON, BAKER COMPANY?
CORPORAL "DOG" DENVER AND SERGEANT MACK, "A" PLATOON. THERE IS NO DOUBT ABOUT WHAT THEY THINK OF JOE TWO BEANS...
THAT DUMB INDIAN! I AIN'T NEVER SEEN NO-ONE SO STUPID! CAN'T EVEN TALK!
GUY OVER IN FOX COMPANY CLAIMED HE HEARD THE INJUN SPEAK ONCE... BUT I RECKON HE'S LYIN'!
AW, C'MON, JOE AIN'T THAT BAD. I MEAN INJUNS ARE FUNNY – MAYBE HE'S GOT HIS REASONS FOR NOT SPEAKING...
SAWDUST
I GOT A HUNDRED BUCKS HERE SAYS YOU CAN'T GET THE INJUN TO SAY ONE WORD. C'MON, SAWDUST – PUT YA MONEY WHERE YOUR MOUTH IS!
BAKER COMPANY TO BOARDING STATIONS! WE'RE GOIN' IN!
OKAY, SARGE – YOU GOT A BET.
HI, JOE, MY NAME'S SAWDUST SMITH. I HAIL FROM ARKANSAS! WHICH PART OF THE COUNTRY YOU FROM? YOU LOOK LIKE FULL-BLOODED CHEROKEE TO ME...

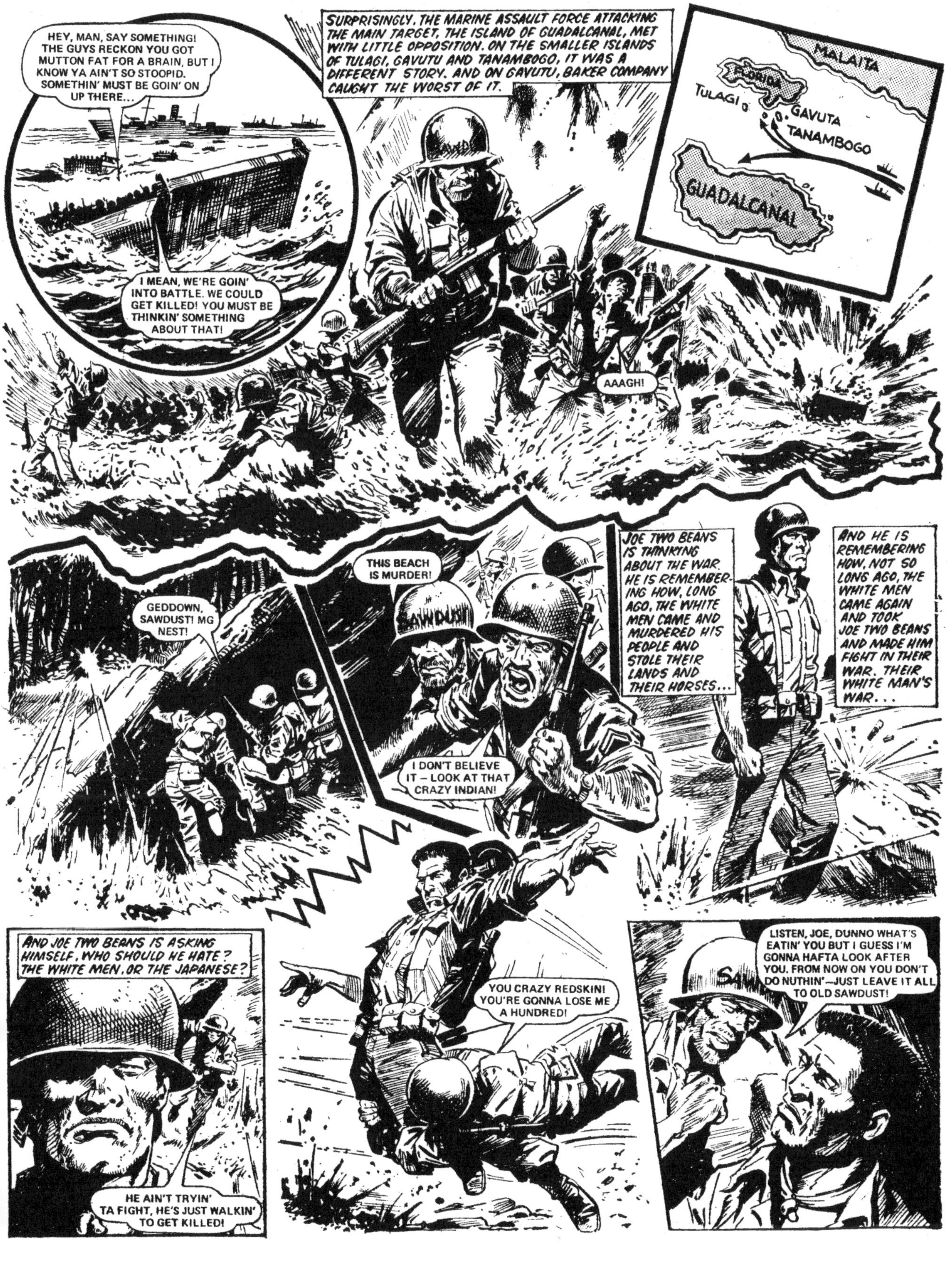
SURPRISINGLY, THE MARINE ASSAULT FORCE ATTACKING THE MAIN TARGET, THE ISLAND OF GUADALCANAL, MET WITH LITTLE OPPOSITION. ON THE SMALLER ISLANDS OF TULAGI, GAVUTU AND TANAMBOGO, IT WAS A DIFFERENT STORY. AND ON GAVUTU, BAKER COMPANY CAUGHT THE WORST OF IT.
MALAITA
FLORIDA
TULAGI
GAVUTA
TANAMBOGO
GUADALCANAL
HEY, MAN, SAY SOMETHING! THE GUYS RECKON YOU GOT MUTTON FAT FOR A BRAIN, BUT I KNOW YA AIN'T SO STOOPID. SOMETHIN' MUST BE GOIN' ON UP THERE...
I MEAN, WE'RE GOIN' INTO BATTLE. WE COULD GET KILLED! YOU MUST BE THINKIN' SOMETHING ABOUT THAT!
AAAGH!
GEDDOWN, SAWDUST! MG NEST!
THIS BEACH IS MURDER!
SAWDUST
I DON'T BELIEVE IT – LOOK AT THAT CRAZY INDIAN!
JOE TWO BEANS IS THINKING ABOUT THE WAR. HE IS REMEMBERING HOW, LONG AGO, THE WHITE MEN CAME AND MURDERED HIS PEOPLE AND STOLE THEIR LANDS AND THEIR HORSES...
AND HE IS REMEMBERING HOW, NOT SO LONG AGO, THE WHITE MEN CAME AGAIN AND TOOK JOE TWO BEANS AND MADE HIM FIGHT IN THEIR WAR. THEIR WHITE MAN'S WAR...
AND JOE TWO BEANS IS ASKING HIMSELF, WHO SHOULD HE HATE? THE WHITE MEN, OR THE JAPANESE?
HE AIN'T TRYIN' TA FIGHT, HE'S JUST WALKIN' TO GET KILLED!
YOU CRAZY REDSKIN! YOU'RE GONNA LOSE ME A HUNDRED!
LISTEN, JOE, DUNNO WHAT'S EATIN' YOU BUT I GUESS I'M GONNA HAFTA LOOK AFTER YOU. FROM NOW ON YOU DON'T DO NUTHIN'—JUST LEAVE IT ALL TO OLD SAWDUST!

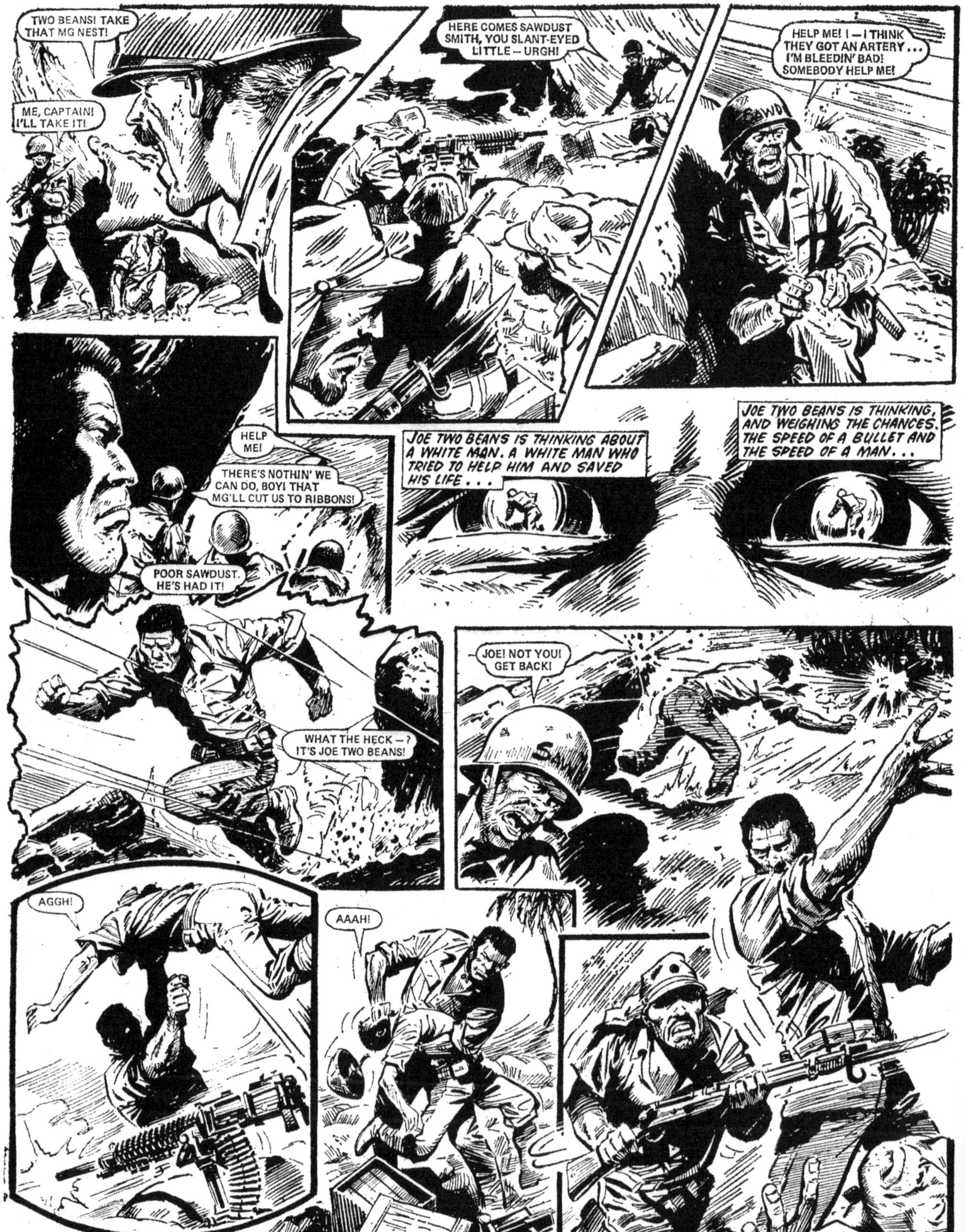
TWO BEANS! TAKE THAT MG NEST!
ME, CAPTAIN! I'LL TAKE IT!
HERE COMES SAWDUST SMITH, YOU SLANT-EYED LITTLE -- URGH!
HELP ME! I -- I THINK THEY GOT AN ARTERY... I'M BLEEDIN' BAD! SOMEBODY HELP ME!
HELP ME!
THERE'S NOTHIN' WE CAN DO, BOY! THAT MG'LL CUT US TO RIBBONS!
POOR SAWDUST. HE'S HAD IT!
JOE TWO BEANS IS THINKING ABOUT A WHITE MAN. A WHITE MAN WHO TRIED TO HELP HIM AND SAVED HIS LIFE...
JOE TWO BEANS IS THINKING, AND WEIGHING THE CHANCES. THE SPEED OF A BULLET AND THE SPEED OF A MAN...
WHAT THE HECK --? IT'S JOE TWO BEANS!
JOE! NOT YOU! GET BACK!
AGGH!
AAAH!

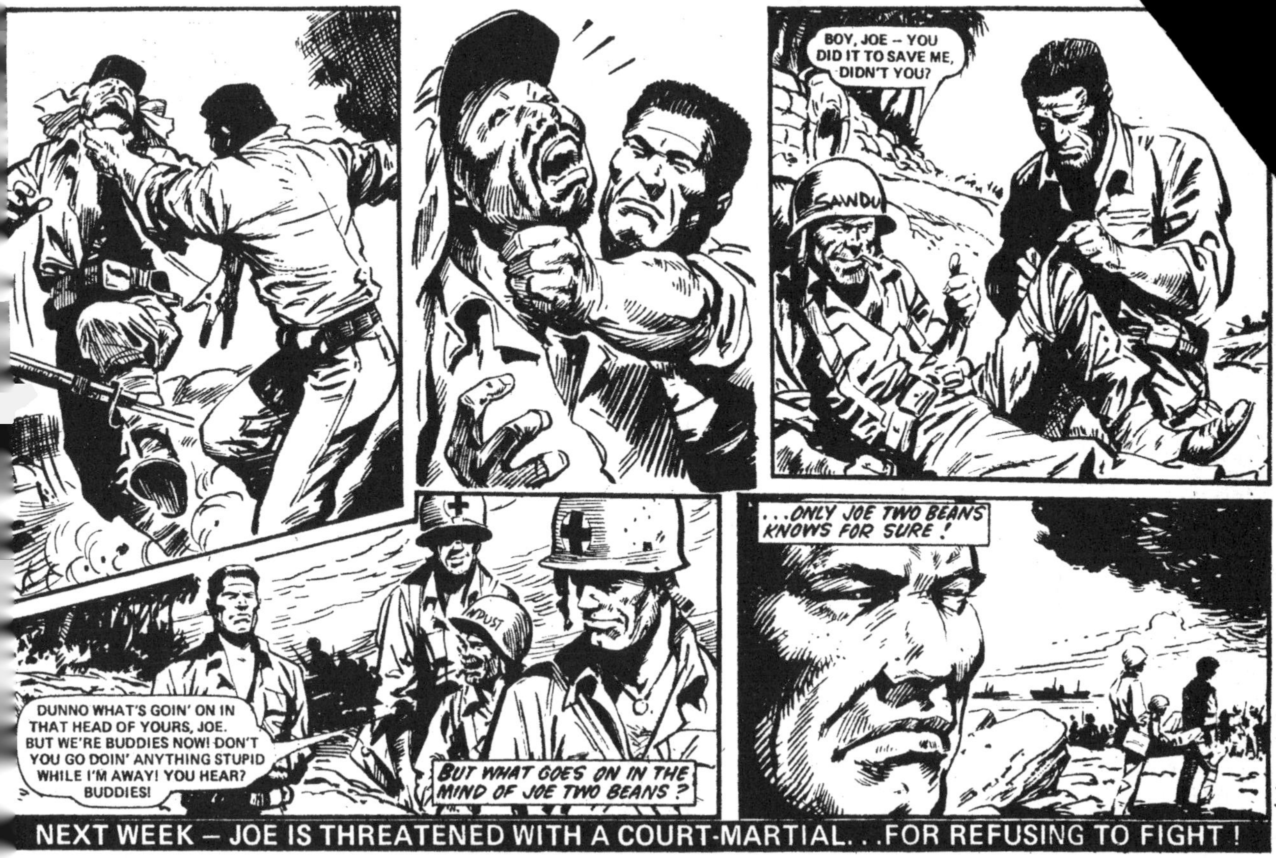
BOY, JOE -- YOU DID IT TO SAVE ME, DIDN'T YOU?
DUNNO WHAT'S GOIN' ON IN THAT HEAD OF YOURS, JOE. BUT WE'RE BUDDIES NOW! DON'T YOU GO DOIN' ANYTHING STUPID WHILE I'M AWAY! YOU HEAR? BUDDIES!
BUT WHAT GOES ON IN THE MIND OF JOE TWO BEANS?
...ONLY JOE TWO BEANS KNOWS FOR SURE!
NEXT WEEK – JOE IS THREATENED WITH A COURT-MARTIAL...FOR REFUSING TO FIGHT!

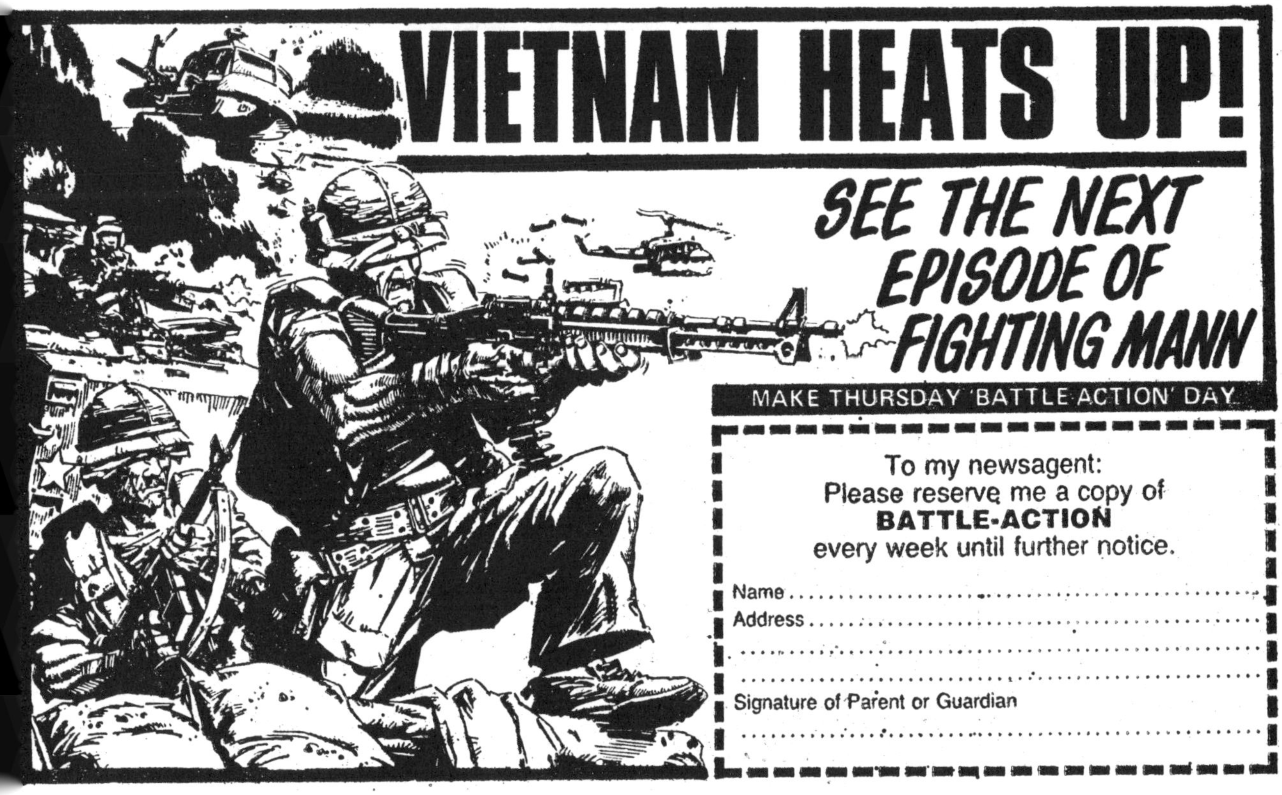
VIETNAM HEATS UP!
SEE THE NEXT EPISODE OF FIGHTING MANN
MAKE THURSDAY 'BATTLE-ACTION' DAY
To my newsagent:
Please reserve me a copy of
BATTLE-ACTION
every week until further notice.
Name ....
Address ....
Signature of Parent or Guardian

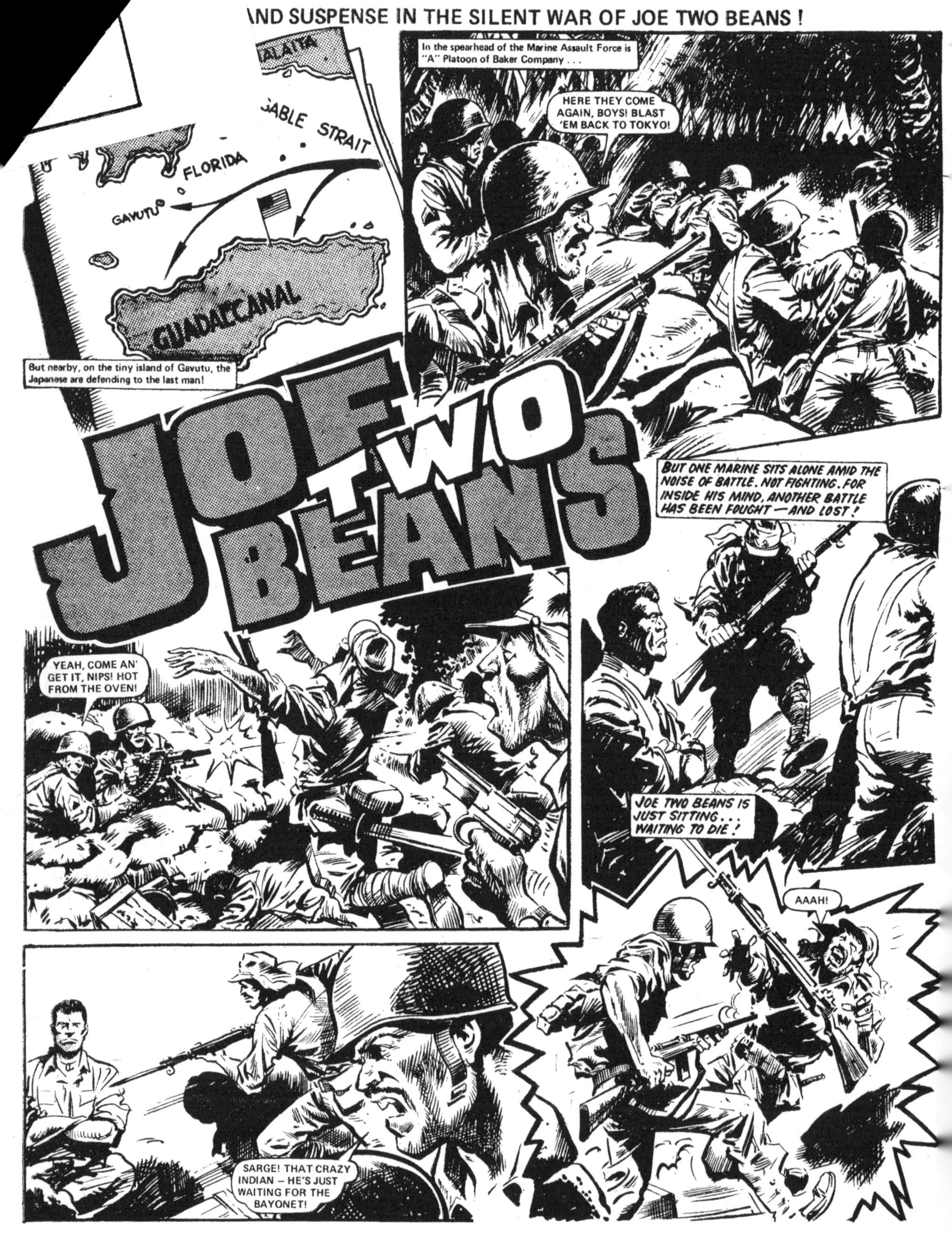
AND SUSPENSE IN THE SILENT WAR OF JOE TWO BEANS !
MALAITA
SABLE STRAIT
FLORIDA
GAVUTU
GUADALCANAL
But nearby, on the tiny island of Gavutu, the Japanese are defending to the last man!
In the spearhead of the Marine Assault Force is "A" Platoon of Baker Company . . .
HERE THEY COME AGAIN, BOYS! BLAST 'EM BACK TO TOKYO!
JOE TWO BEANS
YEAH, COME AN' GET IT, NIPS! HOT FROM THE OVEN!
BUT ONE MARINE SITS ALONE AMID THE NOISE OF BATTLE. NOT FIGHTING. FOR INSIDE HIS MIND, ANOTHER BATTLE HAS BEEN FOUGHT — AND LOST !
JOE TWO BEANS IS JUST SITTING . . . WAITING TO DIE !
SARGE! THAT CRAZY INDIAN – HE'S JUST WAITING FOR THE BAYONET!
AAAH!

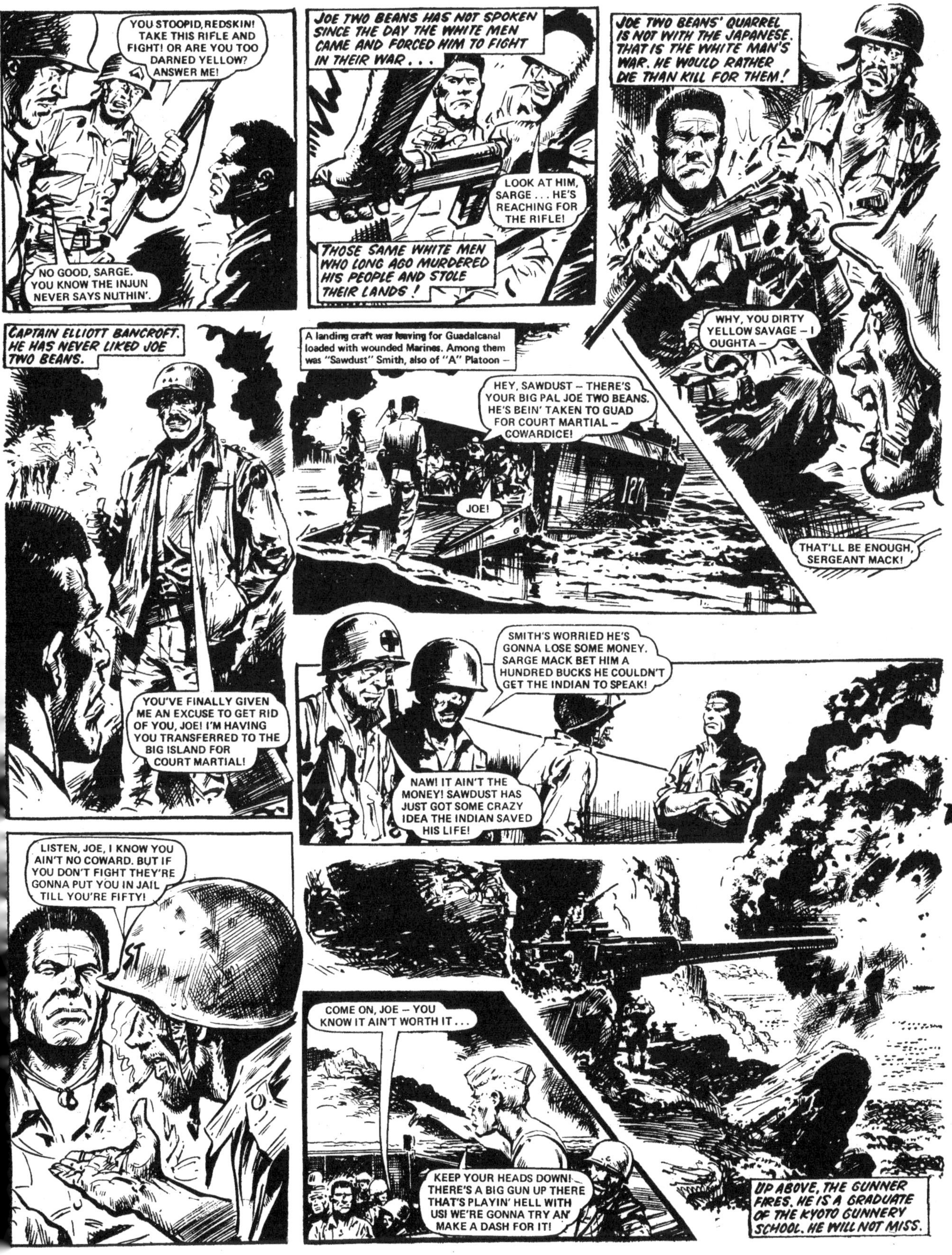
YOU STOOPID, REDSKIN! TAKE THIS RIFLE AND FIGHT! OR ARE YOU TOO DARNED YELLOW? ANSWER ME!
NO GOOD, SARGE. YOU KNOW THE INJUN NEVER SAYS NUTHIN'.
JOE TWO BEANS HAS NOT SPOKEN SINCE THE DAY THE WHITE MEN CAME AND FORCED HIM TO FIGHT IN THEIR WAR . . .
LOOK AT HIM, SARGE . . . HE'S REACHING FOR THE RIFLE!
THOSE SAME WHITE MEN WHO LONG AGO MURDERED HIS PEOPLE AND STOLE THEIR LANDS!
JOE TWO BEANS' QUARREL IS NOT WITH THE JAPANESE. THAT IS THE WHITE MAN'S WAR. HE WOULD RATHER DIE THAN KILL FOR THEM!
WHY, YOU DIRTY YELLOW SAVAGE – I OUGHTA –
THAT'LL BE ENOUGH, SERGEANT MACK!
CAPTAIN ELLIOTT BANCROFT. HE HAS NEVER LIKED JOE TWO BEANS.
YOU'VE FINALLY GIVEN ME AN EXCUSE TO GET RID OF YOU, JOE! I'M HAVING YOU TRANSFERRED TO THE BIG ISLAND FOR COURT MARTIAL!
A landing craft was leaving for Guadalcanal loaded with wounded Marines. Among them was "Sawdust" Smith, also of "A" Platoon –
HEY, SAWDUST – THERE'S YOUR BIG PAL JOE TWO BEANS. HE'S BEIN' TAKEN TO GUAD FOR COURT MARTIAL – COWARDICE!
JOE!
SMITH'S WORRIED HE'S GONNA LOSE SOME MONEY. SARGE MACK BET HIM A HUNDRED BUCKS HE COULDN'T GET THE INDIAN TO SPEAK!
NAW! IT AIN'T THE MONEY! SAWDUST HAS JUST GOT SOME CRAZY IDEA THE INDIAN SAVED HIS LIFE!
LISTEN, JOE, I KNOW YOU AIN'T NO COWARD. BUT IF YOU DON'T FIGHT THEY'RE GONNA PUT YOU IN JAIL TILL YOU'RE FIFTY!
COME ON, JOE – YOU KNOW IT AIN'T WORTH IT . . .
KEEP YOUR HEADS DOWN! THERE'S A BIG GUN UP THERE THAT'S PLAYIN' HELL WITH US! WE'RE GONNA TRY AN' MAKE A DASH FOR IT!
UP ABOVE, THE GUNNER FIRES. HE IS A GRADUATE OF THE KYOTO GUNNERY SCHOOL. HE WILL NOT MISS.

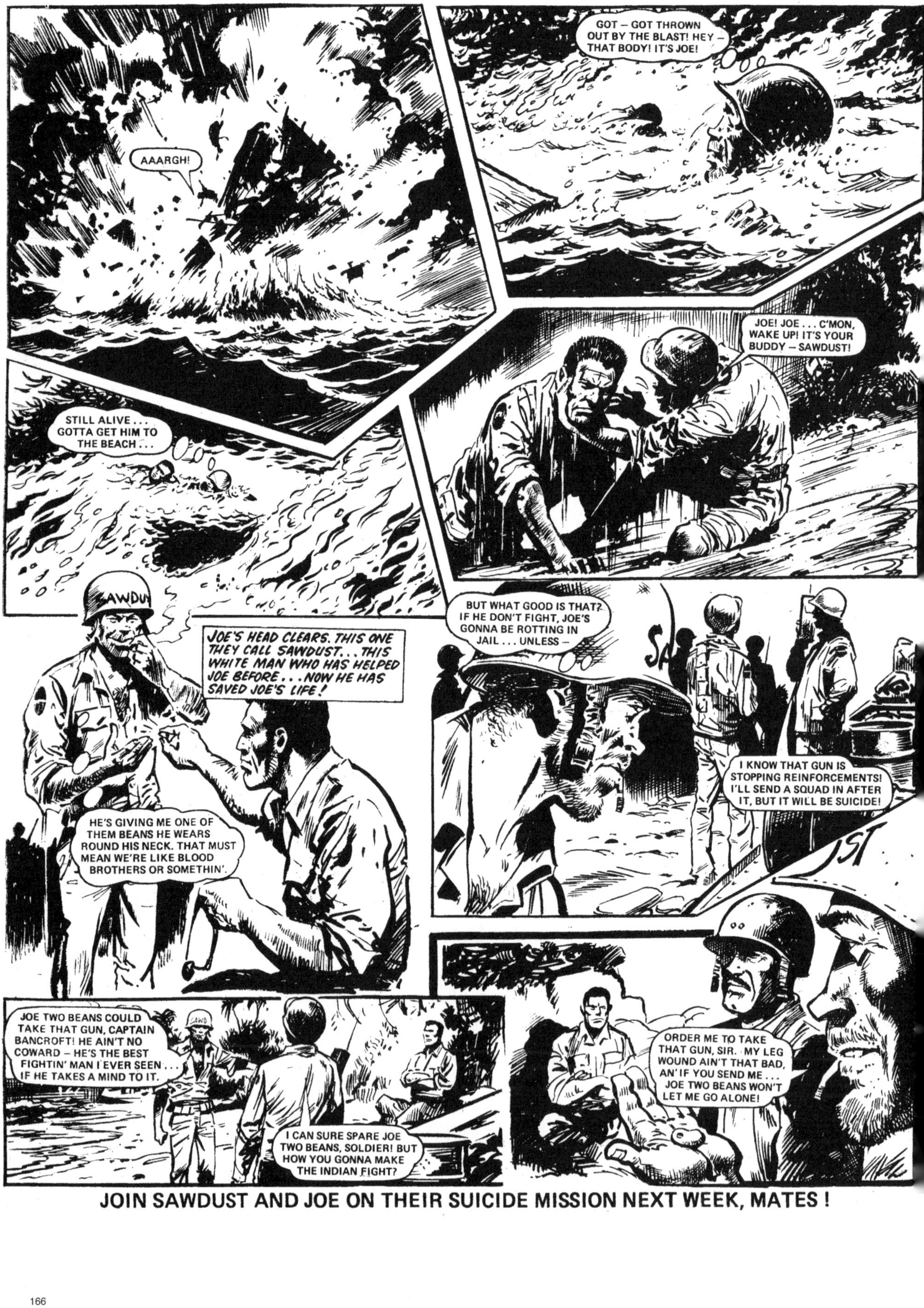
AAARGH!
GOT – GOT THROWN OUT BY THE BLAST! HEY – THAT BODY! IT'S JOE!
STILL ALIVE . . . GOTTA GET HIM TO THE BEACH . . .
JOE! JOE . . . C'MON, WAKE UP! IT'S YOUR BUDDY – SAWDUST!
JOE'S HEAD CLEARS. THIS ONE THEY CALL SAWDUST . . . THIS WHITE MAN WHO HAS HELPED JOE BEFORE . . . NOW HE HAS SAVED JOE'S LIFE!
HE'S GIVING ME ONE OF THEM BEANS HE WEARS ROUND HIS NECK. THAT MUST MEAN WE'RE LIKE BLOOD BROTHERS OR SOMETHIN'.
BUT WHAT GOOD IS THAT? IF HE DON'T FIGHT, JOE'S GONNA BE ROTTING IN JAIL . . . UNLESS –
I KNOW THAT GUN IS STOPPING REINFORCEMENTS! I'LL SEND A SQUAD IN AFTER IT, BUT IT WILL BE SUICIDE!
JOE TWO BEANS COULD TAKE THAT GUN, CAPTAIN BANCROFT! HE AIN'T NO COWARD – HE'S THE BEST FIGHTIN' MAN I EVER SEEN . . . IF HE TAKES A MIND TO IT.
I CAN SURE SPARE JOE TWO BEANS, SOLDIER! BUT HOW YOU GONNA MAKE THE INDIAN FIGHT?
ORDER ME TO TAKE THAT GUN, SIR. MY LEG WOUND AIN'T THAT BAD, AN' IF YOU SEND ME . . . JOE TWO BEANS WON'T LET ME GO ALONE!

JOIN SAWDUST AND JOE ON THEIR SUICIDE MISSION NEXT WEEK, MATES !

1 MARINE + 1 INDIAN = A WHOLE LOT OF TROUBLE FOR THE JAPS !

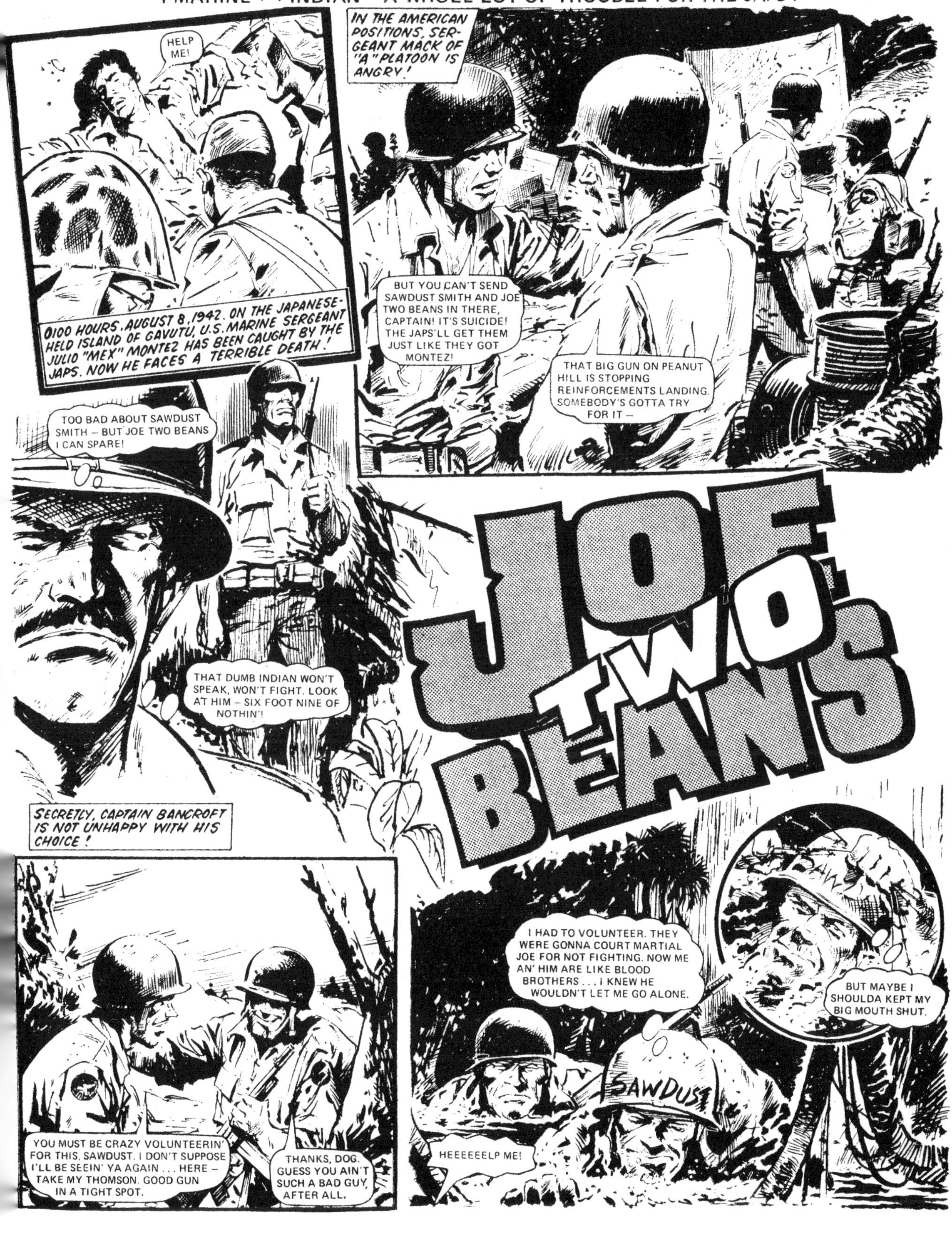
HELP ME!
0100 HOURS, AUGUST 8, 1942. ON THE JAPANESE-HELD ISLAND OF GAVUTU, U.S. MARINE SERGEANT JULIO "MEX" MONTEZ HAS BEEN CAUGHT BY THE JAPS. NOW HE FACES A TERRIBLE DEATH!
IN THE AMERICAN POSITIONS, SERGEANT MACK OF "A" PLATOON IS ANGRY!
BUT YOU CAN'T SEND SAWDUST SMITH AND JOE TWO BEANS IN THERE, CAPTAIN! IT'S SUICIDE! THE JAPS'LL GET THEM JUST LIKE THEY GOT MONTEZ!
THAT BIG GUN ON PEANUT HILL IS STOPPING REINFORCEMENTS LANDING. SOMEBODY'S GOTTA TRY FOR IT –
TOO BAD ABOUT SAWDUST SMITH – BUT JOE TWO BEANS I CAN SPARE!
THAT DUMB INDIAN WON'T SPEAK, WON'T FIGHT. LOOK AT HIM – SIX FOOT NINE OF NOTHIN'!
JOE TWO BEANS
SECRETLY, CAPTAIN BANCROFT IS NOT UNHAPPY WITH HIS CHOICE!
YOU MUST BE CRAZY VOLUNTEERIN' FOR THIS, SAWDUST. I DON'T SUPPOSE I'LL BE SEEIN' YA AGAIN . . . HERE – TAKE MY THOMSON. GOOD GUN IN A TIGHT SPOT.
THANKS, DOG. GUESS YOU AIN'T SUCH A BAD GUY, AFTER ALL.
I HAD TO VOLUNTEER. THEY WERE GONNA COURT MARTIAL JOE FOR NOT FIGHTING. NOW ME AN' HIM ARE LIKE BLOOD BROTHERS . . . I KNEW HE WOULDN'T LET ME GO ALONE.
BUT MAYBE I SHOULDA KEPT MY BIG MOUTH SHUT.
HEEEEEELP ME!
SAWDUST

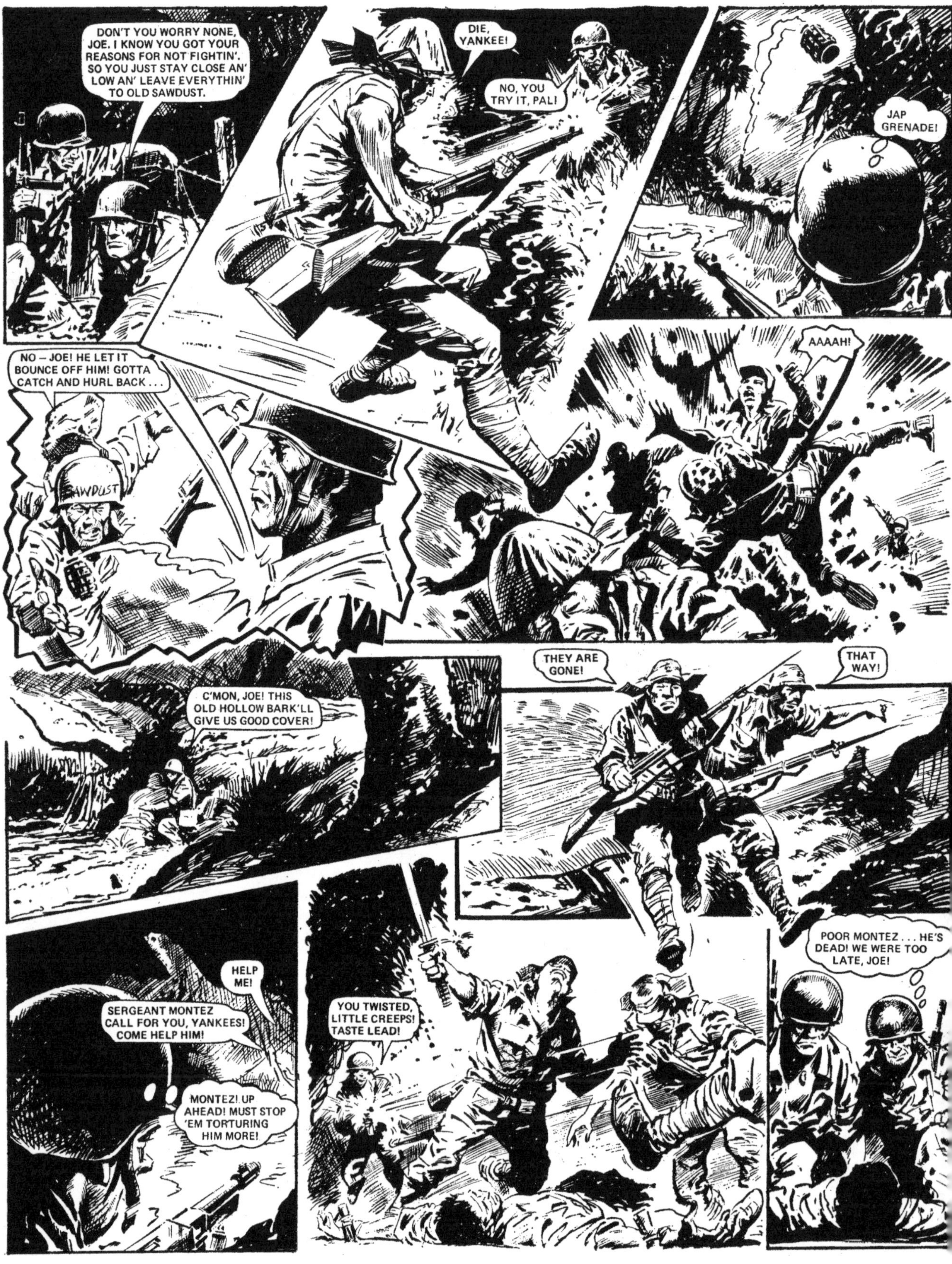

DON'T YOU WORRY NONE, JOE. I KNOW YOU GOT YOUR REASONS FOR NOT FIGHTIN'. SO YOU JUST STAY CLOSE AN' LOW AN' LEAVE EVERYTHIN' TO OLD SAWDUST.
DIE, YANKEE!
NO, YOU TRY IT, PAL!
JAP GRENADE!
NO – JOE! HE LET IT BOUNCE OFF HIM! GOTTA CATCH AND HURL BACK . . .
SAWDUST
AAAAH!
C'MON, JOE! THIS OLD HOLLOW BARK'LL GIVE US GOOD COVER!
THEY ARE GONE!
THAT WAY!
HELP ME!
SERGEANT MONTEZ CALL FOR YOU, YANKEES! COME HELP HIM!
MONTEZ! UP AHEAD! MUST STOP 'EM TORTURING HIM MORE!
YOU TWISTED, LITTLE CREEPS! TASTE LEAD!
POOR MONTEZ . . . HE'S DEAD! WE WERE TOO LATE, JOE!

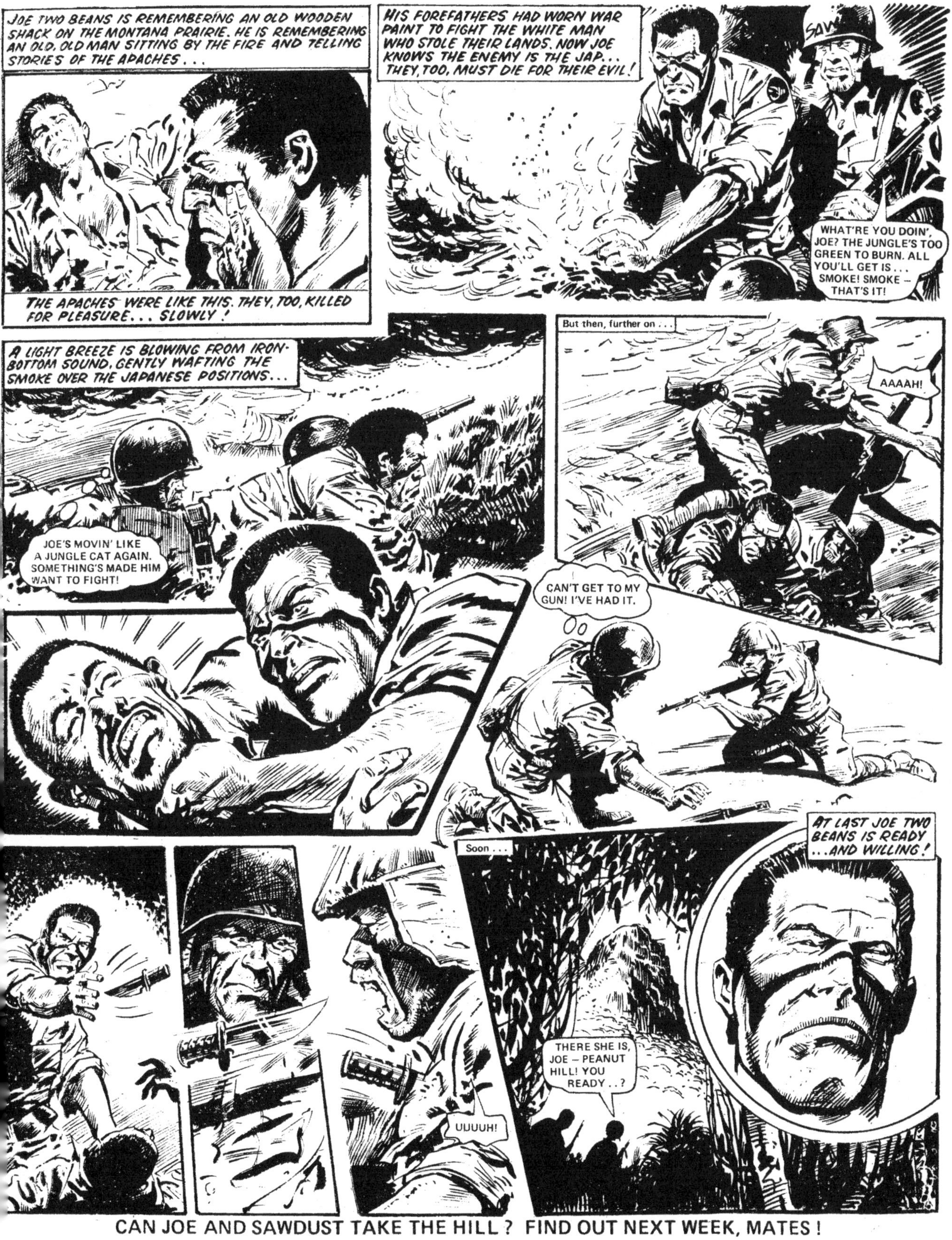
JOE TWO BEANS IS REMEMBERING AN OLD WOODEN SHACK ON THE MONTANA PRAIRIE. HE IS REMEMBERING AN OLD, OLD MAN SITTING BY THE FIRE AND TELLING STORIES OF THE APACHES . . .
THE APACHES WERE LIKE THIS. THEY, TOO, KILLED FOR PLEASURE... SLOWLY!
HIS FOREFATHERS HAD WORN WAR PAINT TO FIGHT THE WHITE MAN WHO STOLE THEIR LANDS. NOW JOE KNOWS THE ENEMY IS THE JAP... THEY, TOO, MUST DIE FOR THEIR EVIL!
WHAT'RE YOU DOIN', JOE? THE JUNGLE'S TOO GREEN TO BURN. ALL YOU'LL GET IS . . . SMOKE! SMOKE – THAT'S IT!
A LIGHT BREEZE IS BLOWING FROM IRON-BOTTOM SOUND, GENTLY WAFTING THE SMOKE OVER THE JAPANESE POSITIONS...
JOE'S MOVIN' LIKE A JUNGLE CAT AGAIN. SOMETHING'S MADE HIM WANT TO FIGHT!
But then, further on . . .
AAAAH!
CAN'T GET TO MY GUN! I'VE HAD IT.
UUUUH!
Soon . . .
THERE SHE IS, JOE – PEANUT HILL! YOU READY . . ?
AT LAST JOE TWO BEANS IS READY ...AND WILLING!

CAN JOE AND SAWDUST TAKE THE HILL ? FIND OUT NEXT WEEK, MATES !

ACTIONS SPEAK LOUDER THAN WORDS FOR BLACKFOOT INDIAN JOE TWO BEANS !

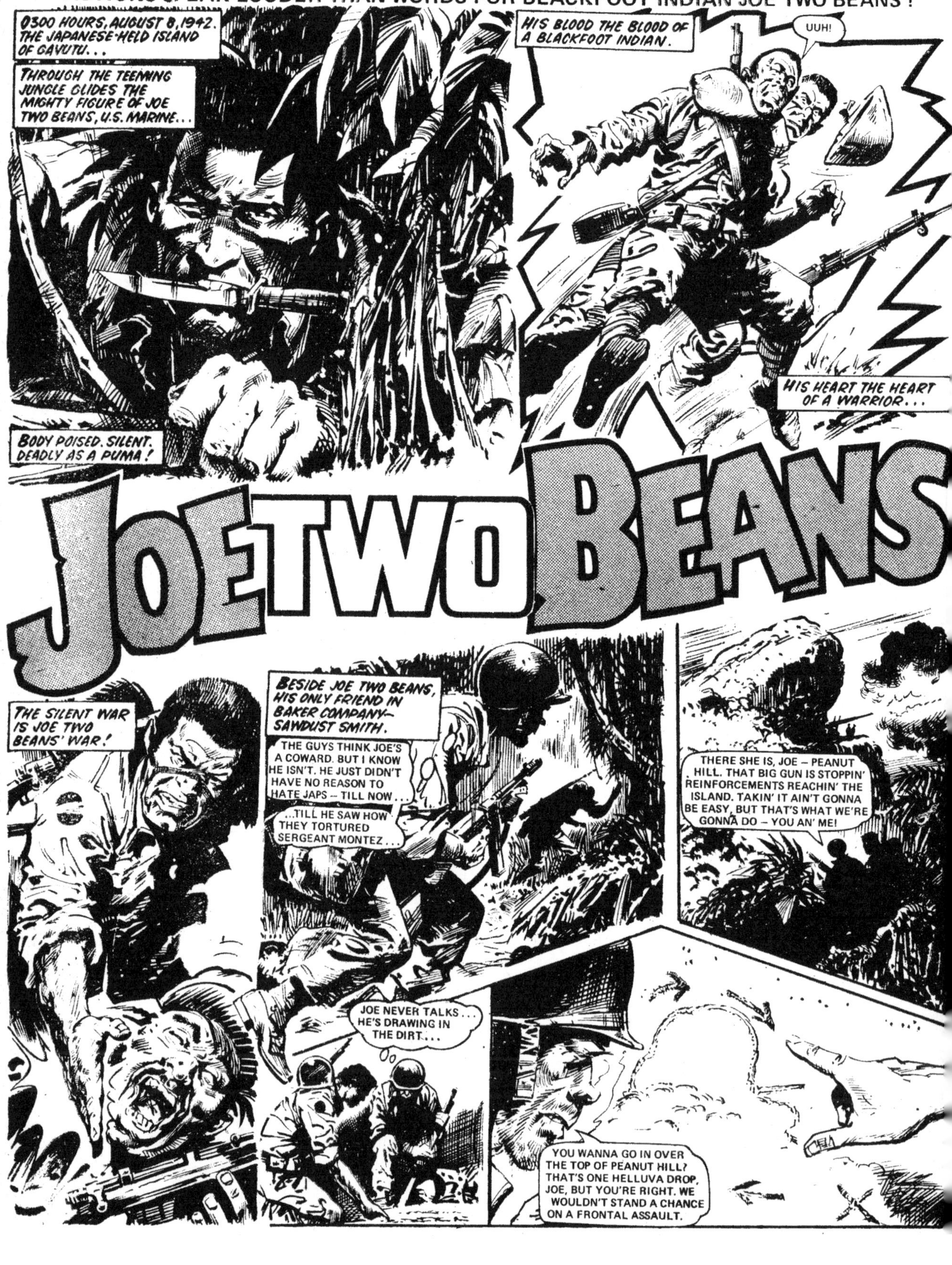

0300 HOURS, AUGUST 8, 1942. THE JAPANESE-HELD ISLAND OF GAVUTU...
THROUGH THE TEEMING JUNGLE GLIDES THE MIGHTY FIGURE OF JOE TWO BEANS, U.S. MARINE...
BODY POISED. SILENT. DEADLY AS A PUMA!
HIS BLOOD THE BLOOD OF A BLACKFOOT INDIAN.
UUH!
HIS HEART THE HEART OF A WARRIOR...
JOE TWO BEANS
THE SILENT WAR IS JOE TWO BEANS' WAR!
BESIDE JOE TWO BEANS, HIS ONLY FRIEND IN BAKER COMPANY— SAWDUST SMITH.
THE GUYS THINK JOE'S A COWARD. BUT I KNOW HE ISN'T. HE JUST DIDN'T HAVE NO REASON TO HATE JAPS -- TILL NOW...
...TILL HE SAW HOW THEY TORTURED SERGEANT MONTEZ...
THERE SHE IS, JOE – PEANUT HILL. THAT BIG GUN IS STOPPIN' REINFORCEMENTS REACHIN' THE ISLAND. TAKIN' IT AIN'T GONNA BE EASY, BUT THAT'S WHAT WE'RE GONNA DO – YOU AN' ME!
JOE NEVER TALKS... HE'S DRAWING IN THE DIRT...
YOU WANNA GO IN OVER THE TOP OF PEANUT HILL? THAT'S ONE HELLUVA DROP, JOE, BUT YOU'RE RIGHT. WE WOULDN'T STAND A CHANCE ON A FRONTAL ASSAULT.

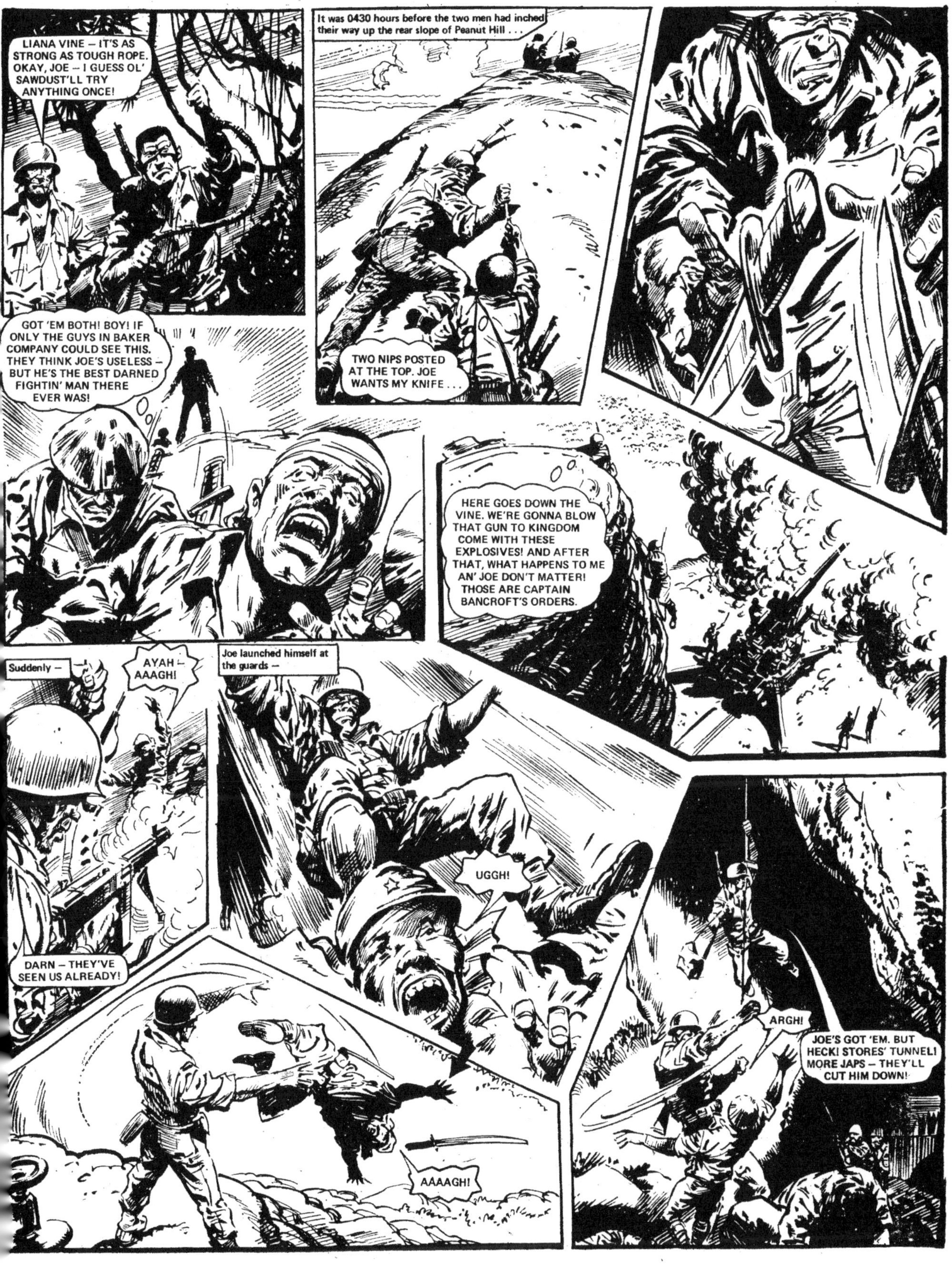
LIANA VINE – IT'S AS STRONG AS TOUGH ROPE. OKAY, JOE – I GUESS OL' SAWDUST'LL TRY ANYTHING ONCE!
It was 0430 hours before the two men had inched their way up the rear slope of Peanut Hill . . .
TWO NIPS POSTED AT THE TOP. JOE WANTS MY KNIFE . . .
GOT 'EM BOTH! BOY! IF ONLY THE GUYS IN BAKER COMPANY COULD SEE THIS. THEY THINK JOE'S USELESS – BUT HE'S THE BEST DARNED FIGHTIN' MAN THERE EVER WAS!
HERE GOES DOWN THE VINE. WE'RE GONNA BLOW THAT GUN TO KINGDOM COME WITH THESE EXPLOSIVES! AND AFTER THAT, WHAT HAPPENS TO ME AN' JOE DON'T MATTER! THOSE ARE CAPTAIN BANCROFT'S ORDERS.
Suddenly –
AYAH – AAAGH!
DARN – THEY'VE SEEN US ALREADY!
Joe launched himself at the guards –
UGGH!
AAAAGH!
ARGH!
JOE'S GOT 'EM. BUT HECK! STORES' TUNNEL! MORE JAPS – THEY'LL CUT HIM DOWN!

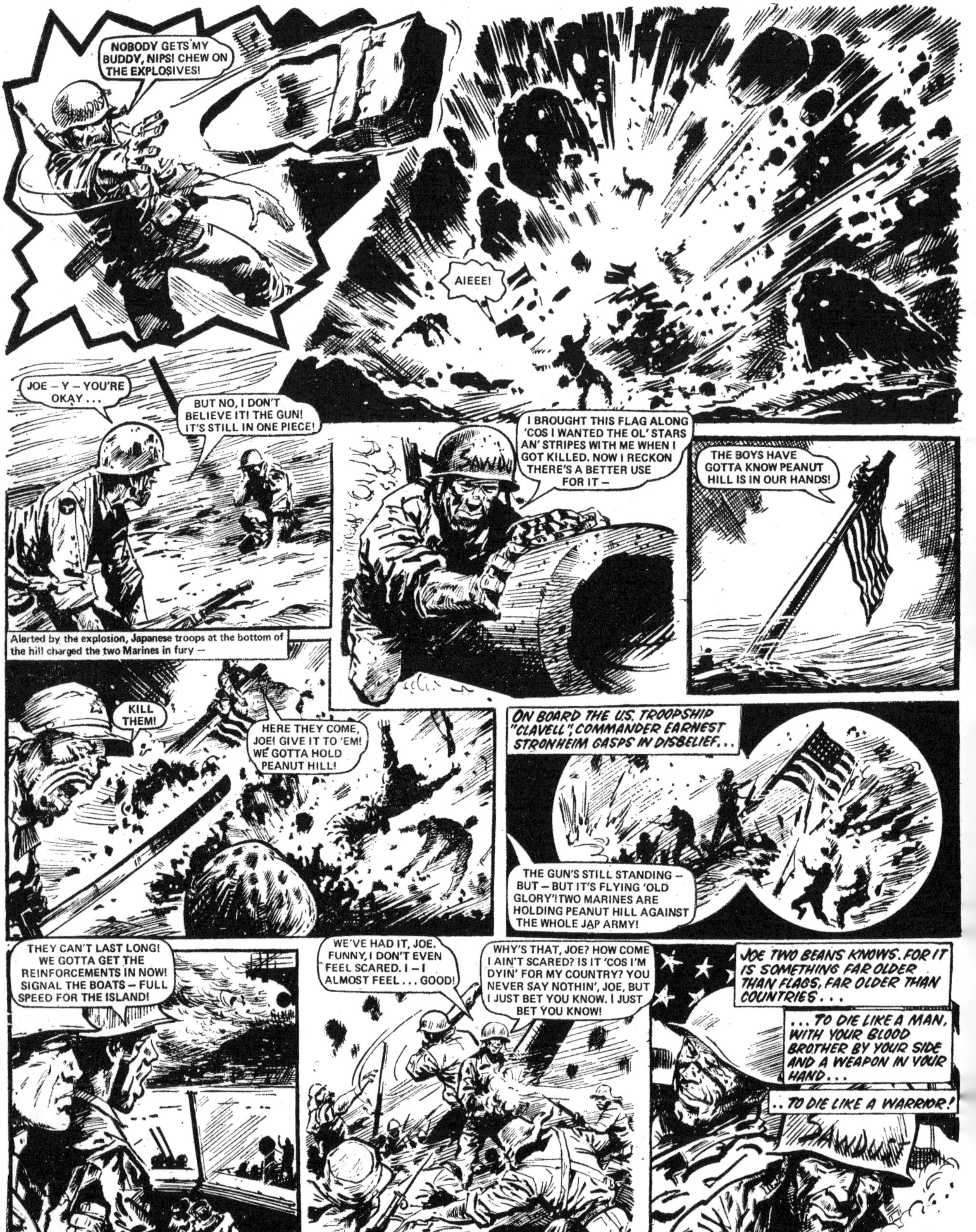
NOBODY GETS MY BUDDY, NIPS! CHEW ON THE EXPLOSIVES!
AIEEE!
JOE – Y – YOU'RE OKAY . . .
BUT NO, I DON'T BELIEVE IT! THE GUN! IT'S STILL IN ONE PIECE!
I BROUGHT THIS FLAG ALONG 'COS I WANTED THE OL' STARS AN' STRIPES WITH ME WHEN I GOT KILLED. NOW I RECKON THERE'S A BETTER USE FOR IT –
THE BOYS HAVE GOTTA KNOW PEANUT HILL IS IN OUR HANDS!
Alerted by the explosion, Japanese troops at the bottom of the hill charged the two Marines in fury –
KILL THEM!
HERE THEY COME, JOE! GIVE IT TO 'EM! WE GOTTA HOLD PEANUT HILL!
ON BOARD THE U.S. TROOPSHIP "CLAVELL", COMMANDER EARNEST STRONHEIM GASPS IN DISBELIEF...
THE GUN'S STILL STANDING – BUT – BUT IT'S FLYING 'OLD GLORY'! TWO MARINES ARE HOLDING PEANUT HILL AGAINST THE WHOLE JAP ARMY!
THEY CAN'T LAST LONG! WE GOTTA GET THE REINFORCEMENTS IN NOW! SIGNAL THE BOATS – FULL SPEED FOR THE ISLAND!
WE'VE HAD IT, JOE. FUNNY, I DON'T EVEN FEEL SCARED. I – I ALMOST FEEL . . . GOOD!
WHY'S THAT, JOE? HOW COME I AIN'T SCARED? IS IT 'COS I'M DYIN' FOR MY COUNTRY? YOU NEVER SAY NOTHIN', JOE, BUT I JUST BET YOU KNOW. I JUST BET YOU KNOW!
JOE TWO BEANS KNOWS. FOR IT IS SOMETHING FAR OLDER THAN FLAGS, FAR OLDER THAN COUNTRIES . . .
. . . TO DIE LIKE A MAN, WITH YOUR BLOOD BROTHER BY YOUR SIDE AND A WEAPON IN YOUR HAND . . .
. . TO DIE LIKE A WARRIOR!

ENDS...MISSION ENDS...MISSION ENDS...MISSION ENDS...MISSION ENDS...MISSION ENDS...MISSION ENDS...MISS

THE SARGE

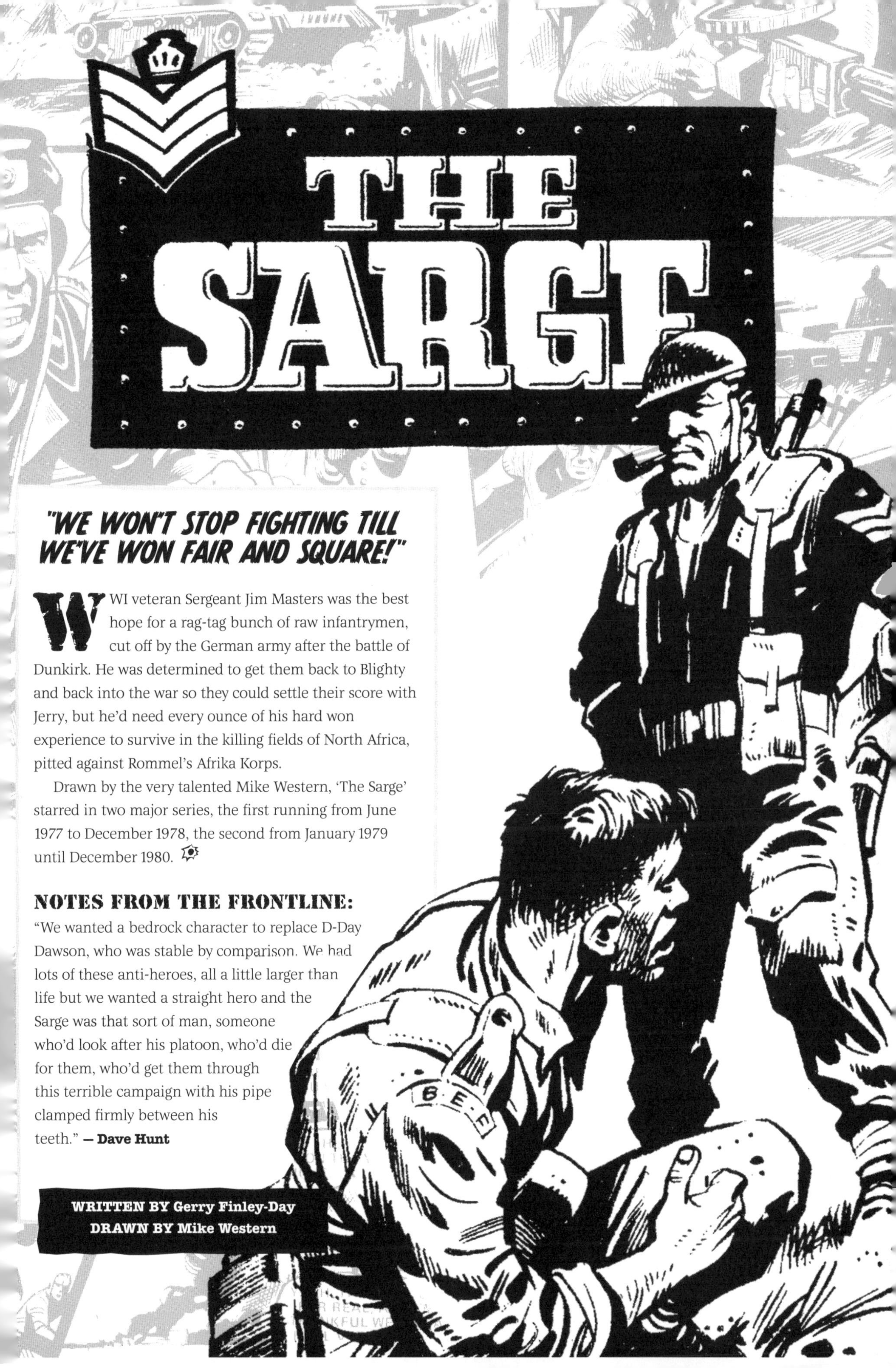
B.E.F.

"WE WON'T STOP FIGHTING TILL WE'VE WON FAIR AND SQUARE!"

WWI veteran Sergeant Jim Masters was the best hope for a rag-tag bunch of raw infantrymen, cut off by the German army after the battle of Dunkirk. He was determined to get them back to Blighty and back into the war so they could settle their score with Jerry, but he'd need every ounce of his hard won experience to survive in the killing fields of North Africa, pitted against Rommel's Afrika Korps.

Drawn by the very talented Mike Western, 'The Sarge' starred in two major series, the first running from June 1977 to December 1978, the second from January 1979 until December 1980.

NOTES FROM THE FRONTLINE:

"We wanted a bedrock character to replace D-Day Dawson, who was stable by comparison. We had lots of these anti-heroes, all a little larger than life but we wanted a straight hero and the Sarge was that sort of man, someone who'd look after his platoon, who'd die for them, who'd get them through this terrible campaign with his pipe clamped firmly between his teeth." **— Dave Hunt**

WRITTEN BY Gerry Finley-Day
DRAWN BY Mike Western

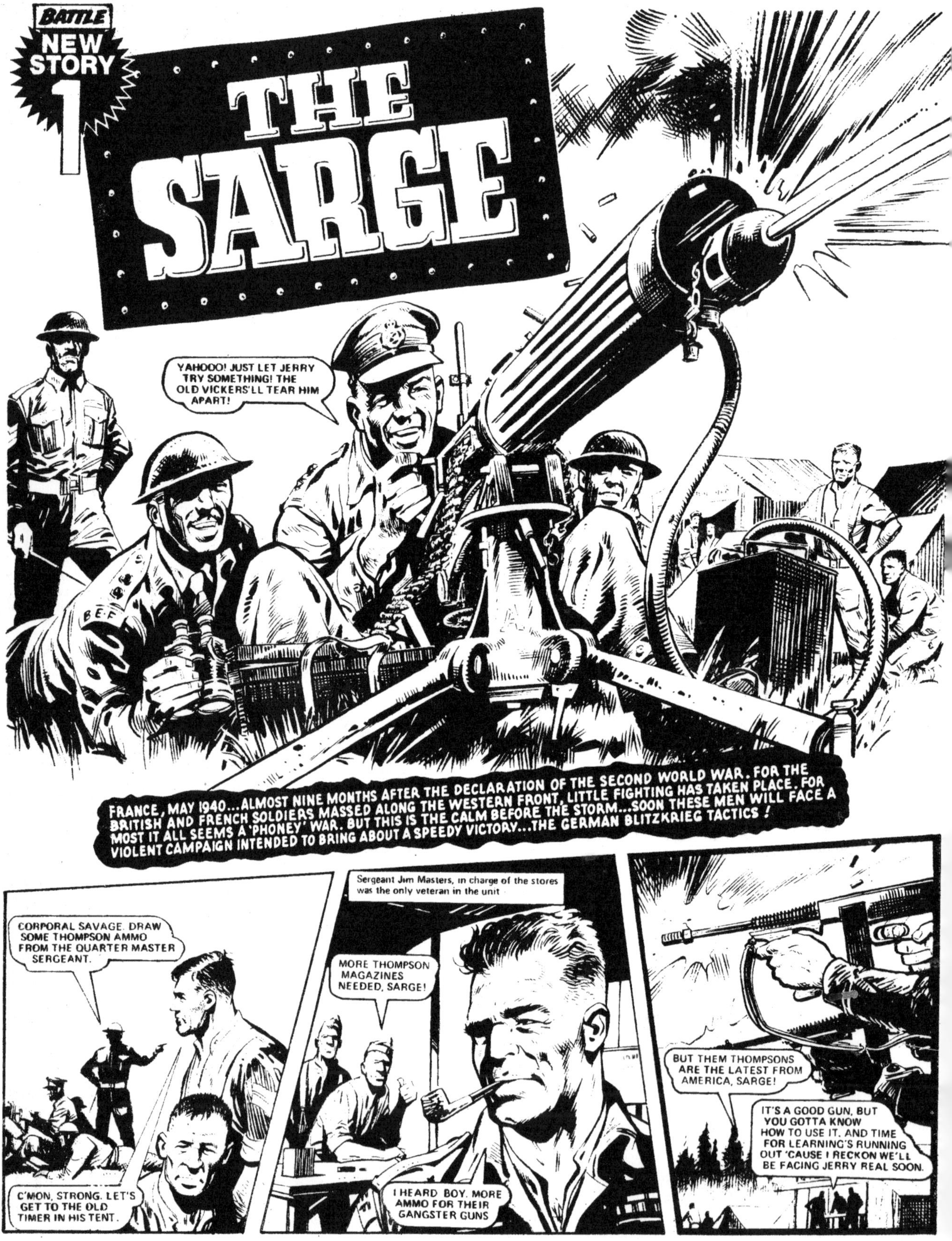
BATTLE
NEW STORY
1
THE SARGE
YAHOOO! JUST LET JERRY TRY SOMETHING! THE OLD VICKERS'LL TEAR HIM APART!
B.E.F
FRANCE, MAY 1940...ALMOST NINE MONTHS AFTER THE DECLARATION OF THE SECOND WORLD WAR. FOR THE BRITISH AND FRENCH SOLDIERS MASSED ALONG THE WESTERN FRONT, LITTLE FIGHTING HAS TAKEN PLACE. FOR MOST IT ALL SEEMS A 'PHONEY' WAR. BUT THIS IS THE CALM BEFORE THE STORM...SOON THESE MEN WILL FACE A VIOLENT CAMPAIGN INTENDED TO BRING ABOUT A SPEEDY VICTORY...THE GERMAN BLITZKRIEG TACTICS!
CORPORAL SAVAGE. DRAW SOME THOMPSON AMMO FROM THE QUARTER MASTER SERGEANT.
C'MON, STRONG. LET'S GET TO THE OLD TIMER IN HIS TENT.
Sergeant Jim Masters, in charge of the stores was the only veteran in the unit
MORE THOMPSON MAGAZINES NEEDED, SARGE!
I HEARD BOY. MORE AMMO FOR THEIR GANGSTER GUNS
BUT THEM THOMPSONS ARE THE LATEST FROM AMERICA, SARGE!
IT'S A GOOD GUN, BUT YOU GOTTA KNOW HOW TO USE IT. AND TIME FOR LEARNING'S RUNNING OUT 'CAUSE I RECKON WE'LL BE FACING JERRY REAL SOON.

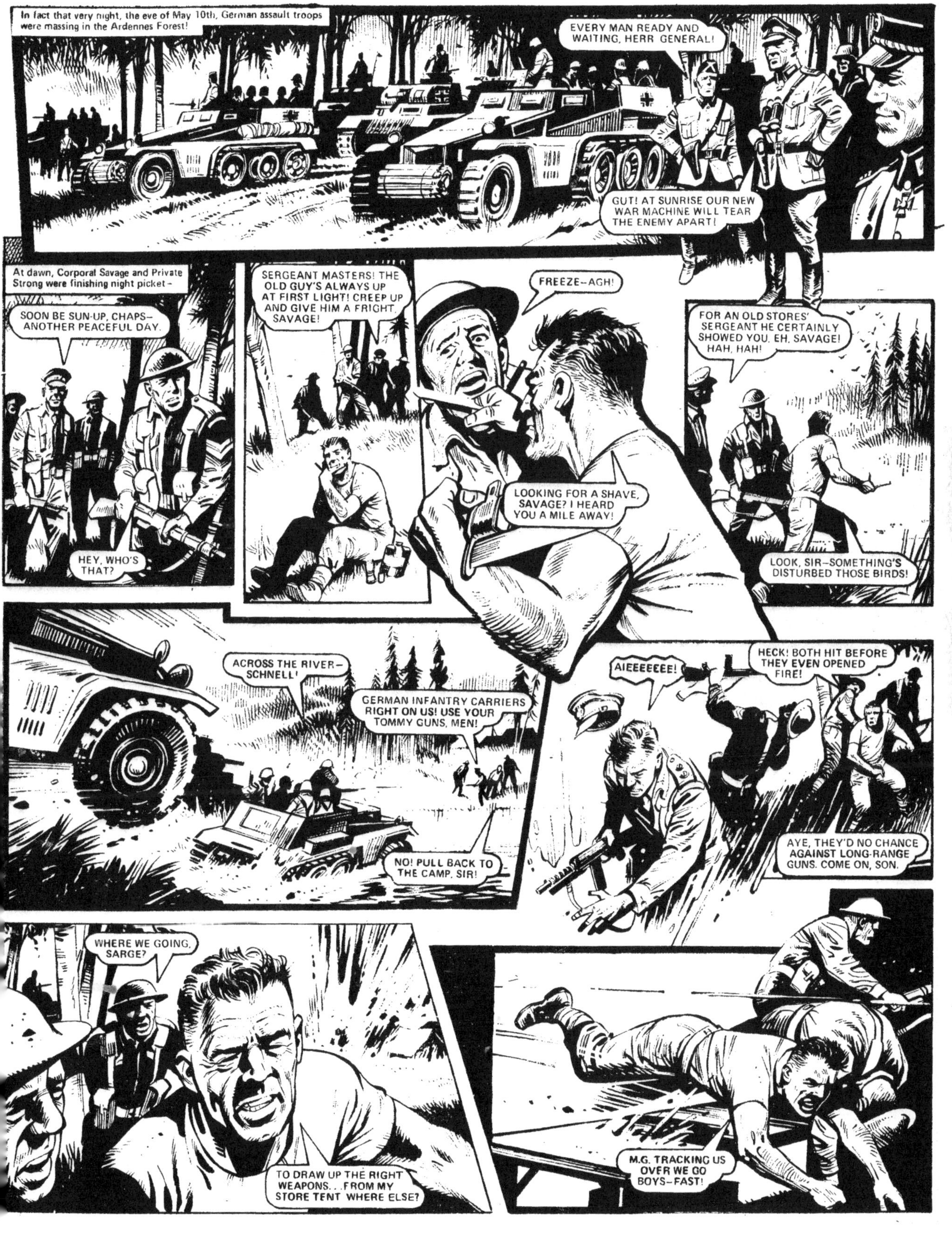

In fact that very night, the eve of May 10th, German assault troops were massing in the Ardennes Forest!
EVERY MAN READY AND WAITING, HERR GENERAL!
GUT! AT SUNRISE OUR NEW WAR MACHINE WILL TEAR THE ENEMY APART!
At dawn, Corporal Savage and Private Strong were finishing night picket –
SOON BE SUN-UP, CHAPS– ANOTHER PEACEFUL DAY.
HEY, WHO'S THAT?
SERGEANT MASTERS! THE OLD GUY'S ALWAYS UP AT FIRST LIGHT! CREEP UP AND GIVE HIM A FRIGHT, SAVAGE!
FREEZE–AGH!
LOOKING FOR A SHAVE, SAVAGE? I HEARD YOU A MILE AWAY!
FOR AN OLD STORES' SERGEANT HE CERTAINLY SHOWED YOU, EH, SAVAGE! HAH, HAH!
LOOK, SIR–SOMETHING'S DISTURBED THOSE BIRDS!
ACROSS THE RIVER– SCHNELL!
GERMAN INFANTRY CARRIERS RIGHT ON US! USE YOUR TOMMY GUNS, MEN!
NO! PULL BACK TO THE CAMP, SIR!
AIEEEEEEE!
HECK! BOTH HIT BEFORE THEY EVEN OPENED FIRE!
AYE, THEY'D NO CHANCE AGAINST LONG-RANGE GUNS. COME ON, SON.
WHERE WE GOING, SARGE?
TO DRAW UP THE RIGHT WEAPONS. . .FROM MY STORE TENT WHERE ELSE?
M.G. TRACKING US OVER WE GO BOYS–FAST!

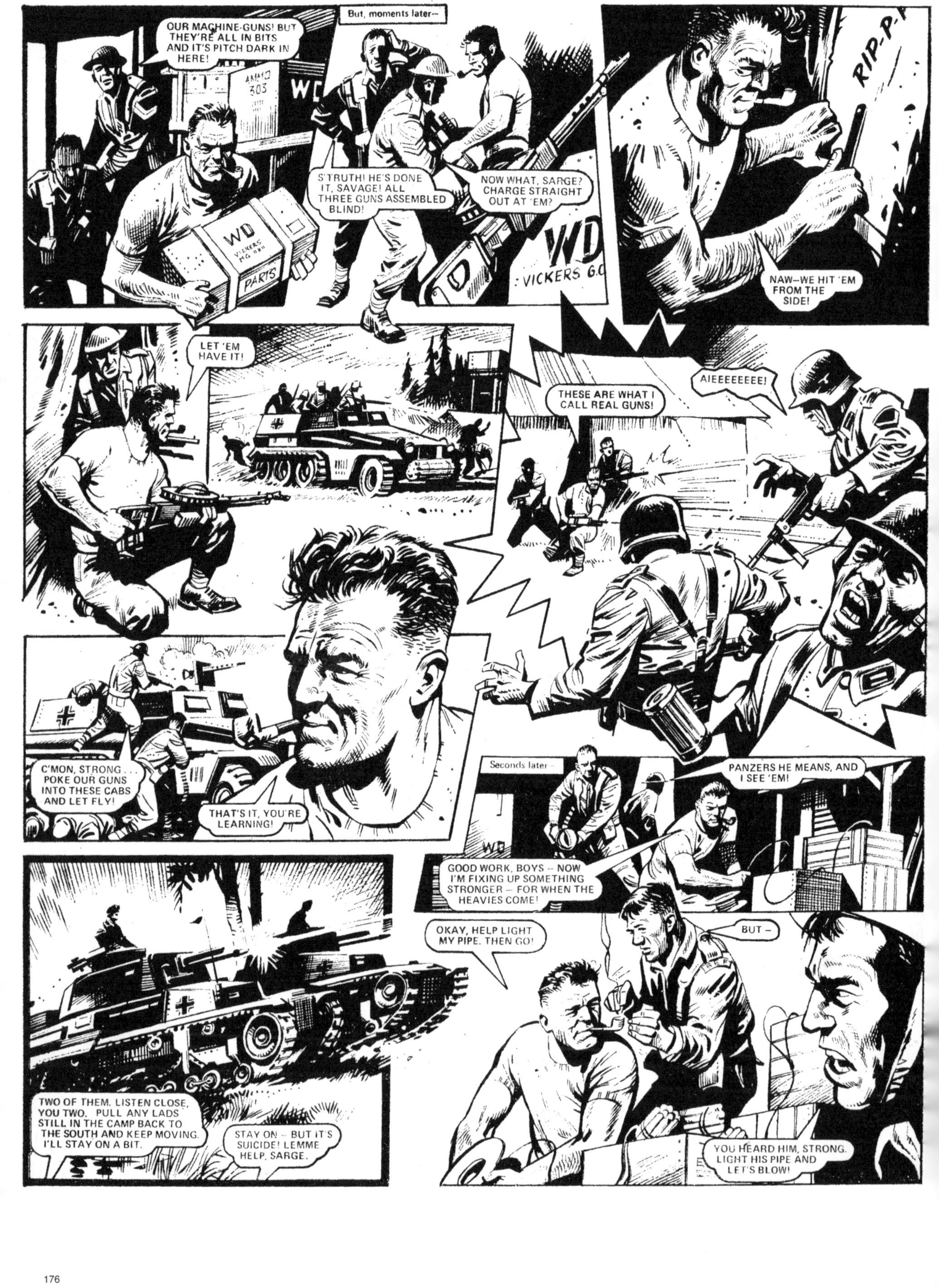
OUR MACHINE-GUNS! BUT THEY'RE ALL IN BITS AND IT'S PITCH DARK IN HERE!
AMMO 303
WD
WD VICKERS PARTS
But, moments later—
S'TRUTH! HE'S DONE IT, SAVAGE! ALL THREE GUNS ASSEMBLED BLIND!
NOW WHAT, SARGE? CHARGE STRAIGHT OUT AT 'EM?
WD VICKERS G.C
RIP-P-P
NAW—WE HIT 'EM FROM THE SIDE!
LET 'EM HAVE IT!
THESE ARE WHAT I CALL REAL GUNS!
AIEEEEEEEE!
C'MON, STRONG . . . POKE OUR GUNS INTO THESE CABS AND LET FLY!
THAT'S IT, YOU'RE LEARNING!
Seconds later—
PANZERS HE MEANS, AND I SEE 'EM!
GOOD WORK, BOYS — NOW I'M FIXING UP SOMETHING STRONGER — FOR WHEN THE HEAVIES COME!
TWO OF THEM. LISTEN CLOSE, YOU TWO. PULL ANY LADS STILL IN THE CAMP BACK TO THE SOUTH AND KEEP MOVING. I'LL STAY ON A BIT.
STAY ON — BUT IT'S SUICIDE! LEMME HELP, SARGE.
OKAY, HELP LIGHT MY PIPE. THEN GO!
BUT —
YOU HEARD HIM, STRONG. LIGHT HIS PIPE AND LET'S BLOW!

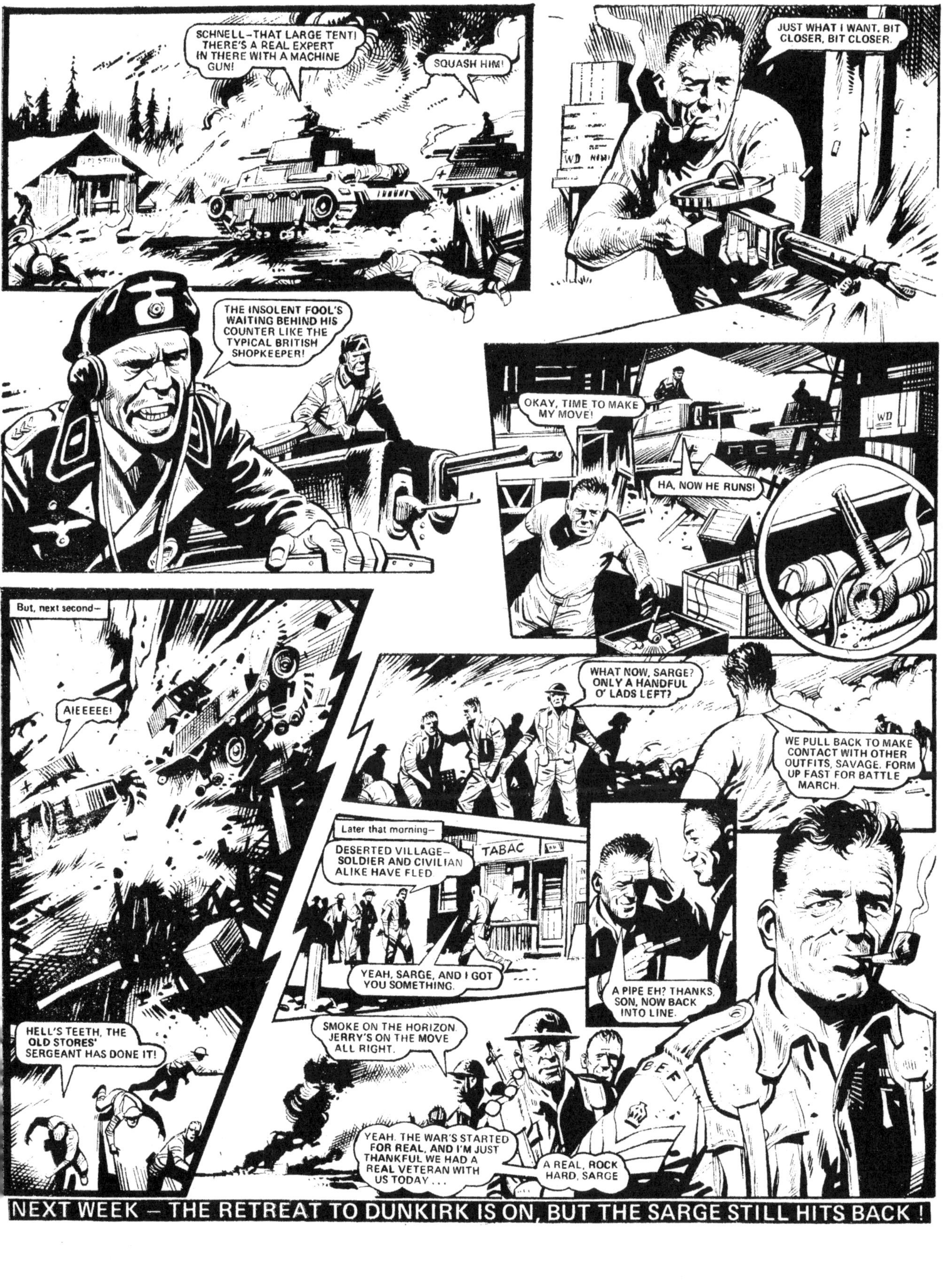
SCHNELL–THAT LARGE TENT! THERE'S A REAL EXPERT IN THERE WITH A MACHINE GUN!
SQUASH HIM!
JUST WHAT I WANT. BIT CLOSER, BIT CLOSER.
THE INSOLENT FOOL'S WAITING BEHIND HIS COUNTER LIKE THE TYPICAL BRITISH SHOPKEEPER!
OKAY, TIME TO MAKE MY MOVE!
HA, NOW HE RUNS!
WD
But, next second–
AIEEEEE!
HELL'S TEETH, THE OLD STORES' SERGEANT HAS DONE IT!
WHAT NOW, SARGE? ONLY A HANDFUL O' LADS LEFT?
WE PULL BACK TO MAKE CONTACT WITH OTHER OUTFITS, SAVAGE. FORM UP FAST FOR BATTLE MARCH.
Later that morning–
DESERTED VILLAGE– SOLDIER AND CIVILIAN ALIKE HAVE FLED.
TABAC
YEAH, SARGE, AND I GOT YOU SOMETHING.
A PIPE EH? THANKS, SON, NOW BACK INTO LINE.
SMOKE ON THE HORIZON. JERRY'S ON THE MOVE ALL RIGHT.
YEAH. THE WAR'S STARTED FOR REAL, AND I'M JUST THANKFUL WE HAD A REAL VETERAN WITH US TODAY . . .
A REAL, ROCK HARD, SARGE
B.E.F.
NEXT WEEK – THE RETREAT TO DUNKIRK IS ON, BUT THE SARGE STILL HITS BACK !

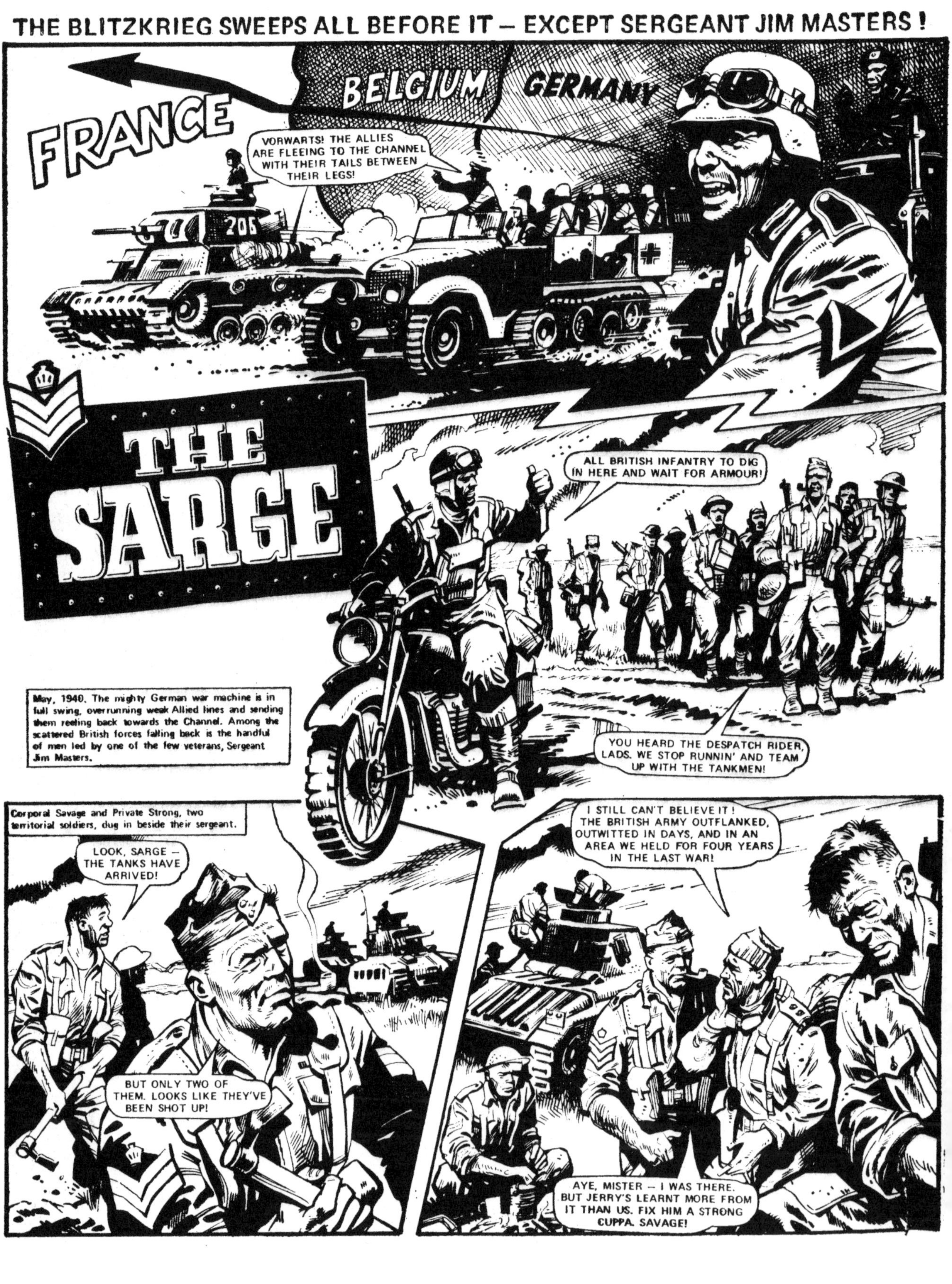
THE BLITZKRIEG SWEEPS ALL BEFORE IT – EXCEPT SERGEANT JIM MASTERS !
FRANCE
BELGIUM
GERMANY
VORWARTS! THE ALLIES ARE FLEEING TO THE CHANNEL WITH THEIR TAILS BETWEEN THEIR LEGS!
206
THE SARGE
ALL BRITISH INFANTRY TO DIG IN HERE AND WAIT FOR ARMOUR!
May, 1940. The mighty German war machine is in full swing, overrunning weak Allied lines and sending them reeling back towards the Channel. Among the scattered British forces falling back is the handful of men led by one of the few veterans, Sergeant Jim Masters.
YOU HEARD THE DESPATCH RIDER, LADS. WE STOP RUNNIN' AND TEAM UP WITH THE TANKMEN!
Corporal Savage and Private Strong, two territorial soldiers, dug in beside their sergeant.
LOOK, SARGE – THE TANKS HAVE ARRIVED!
BUT ONLY TWO OF THEM. LOOKS LIKE THEY'VE BEEN SHOT UP!
I STILL CAN'T BELIEVE IT! THE BRITISH ARMY OUTFLANKED, OUTWITTED IN DAYS, AND IN AN AREA WE HELD FOR FOUR YEARS IN THE LAST WAR!
AYE, MISTER – I WAS THERE. BUT JERRY'S LEARNT MORE FROM IT THAN US. FIX HIM A STRONG CUPPA, SAVAGE!

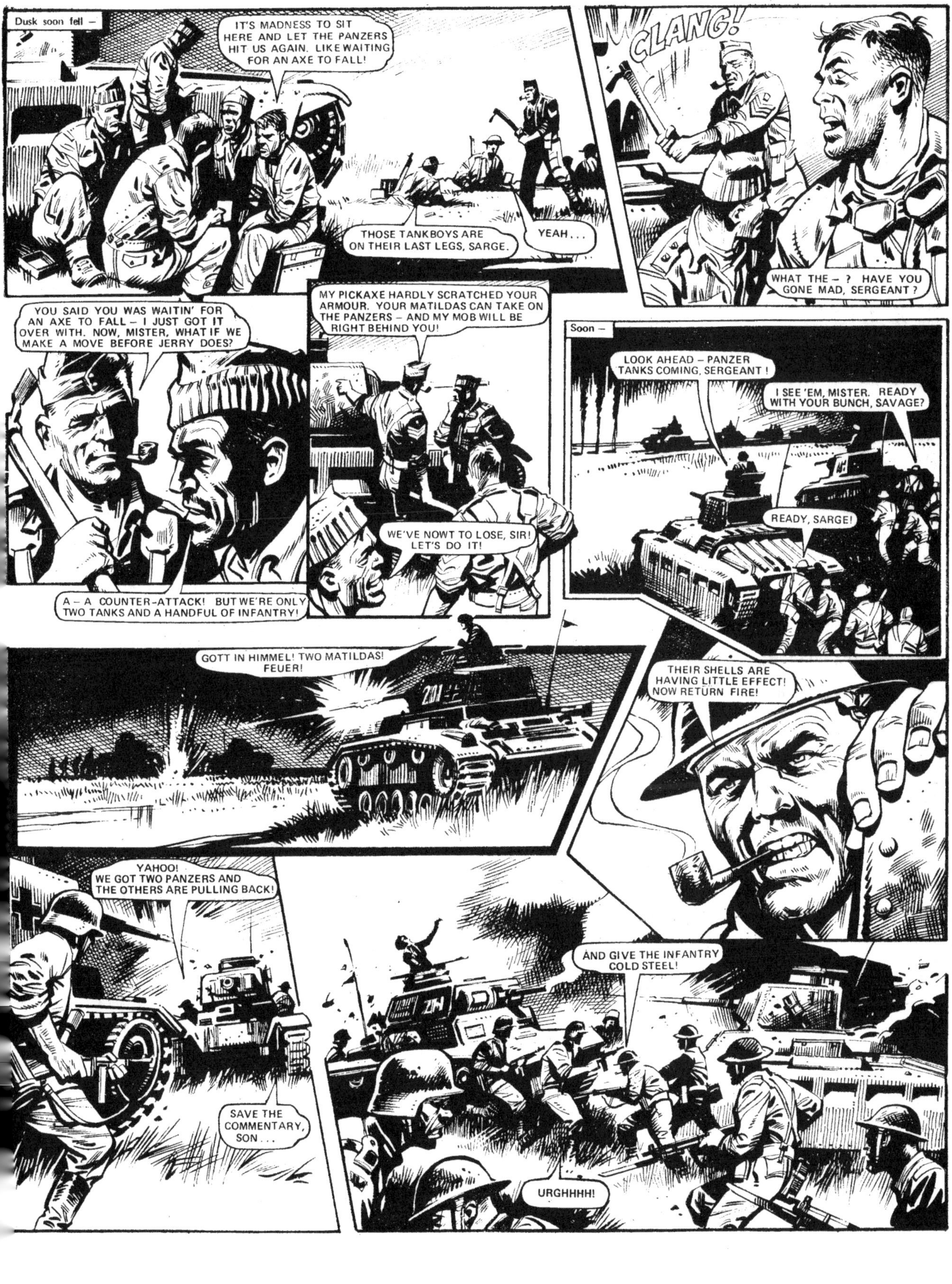

Dusk soon fell –
IT'S MADNESS TO SIT HERE AND LET THE PANZERS HIT US AGAIN. LIKE WAITING FOR AN AXE TO FALL!
THOSE TANKBOYS ARE ON THEIR LAST LEGS, SARGE.
YEAH . . .
CLANG!
WHAT THE – ? HAVE YOU GONE MAD, SERGEANT ?
YOU SAID YOU WAS WAITIN' FOR AN AXE TO FALL – I JUST GOT IT OVER WITH. NOW, MISTER, WHAT IF WE MAKE A MOVE BEFORE JERRY DOES?
A – A COUNTER-ATTACK! BUT WE'RE ONLY TWO TANKS AND A HANDFUL OF INFANTRY!
MY PICKAXE HARDLY SCRATCHED YOUR ARMOUR. YOUR MATILDAS CAN TAKE ON THE PANZERS – AND MY MOB WILL BE RIGHT BEHIND YOU!
WE'VE NOWT TO LOSE, SIR! LET'S DO IT!
Soon –
LOOK AHEAD – PANZER TANKS COMING, SERGEANT !
I SEE 'EM, MISTER. READY WITH YOUR BUNCH, SAVAGE?
READY, SARGE!
GOTT IN HIMMEL! TWO MATILDAS! FEUER!
THEIR SHELLS ARE HAVING LITTLE EFFECT! NOW RETURN FIRE!
YAHOO! WE GOT TWO PANZERS AND THE OTHERS ARE PULLING BACK!
SAVE THE COMMENTARY, SON . . .
AND GIVE THE INFANTRY COLD STEEL!
URGHHHH!

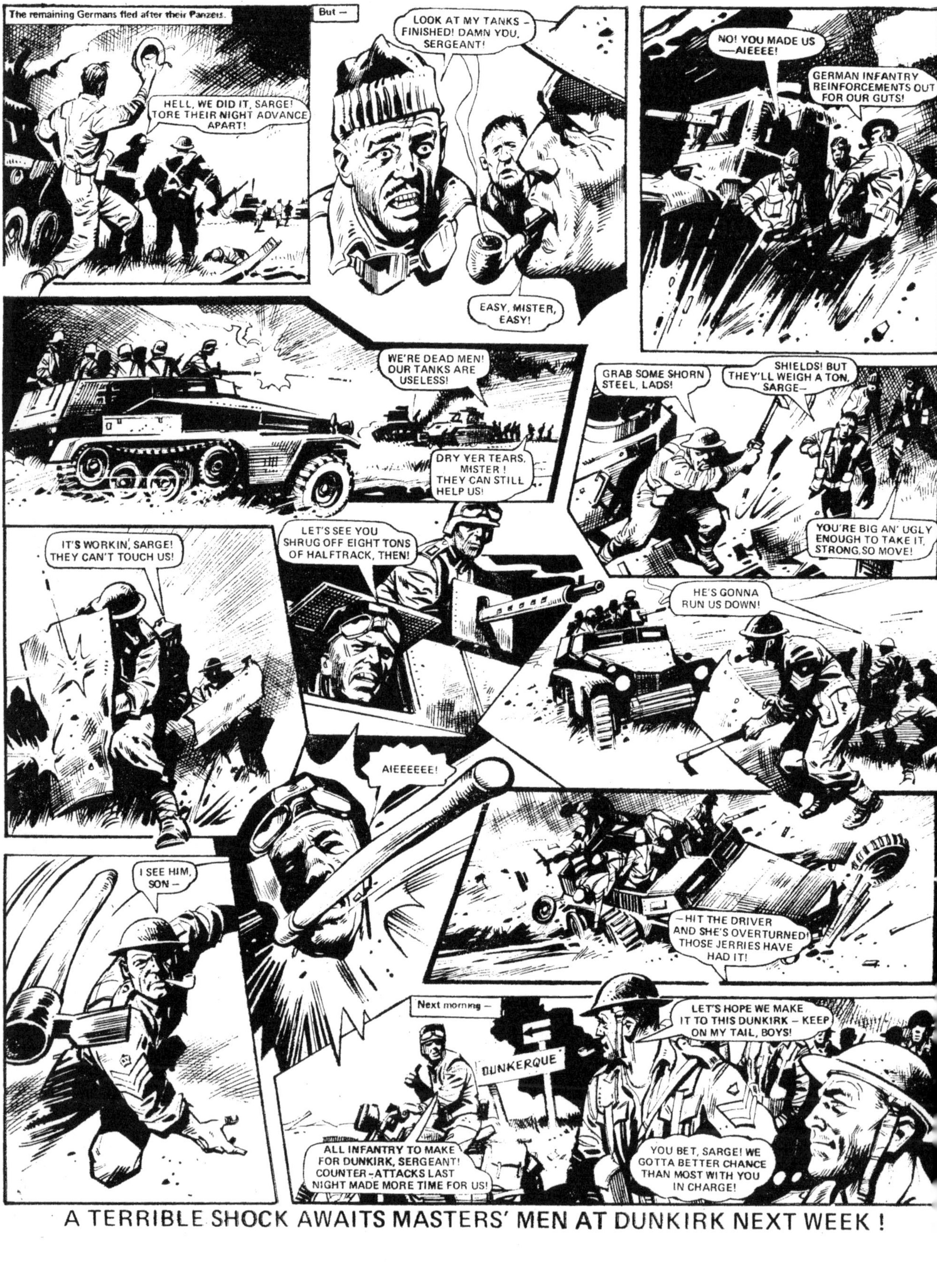

The remaining Germans fled after their Panzers.
HELL, WE DID IT, SARGE! TORE THEIR NIGHT ADVANCE APART!
But –
LOOK AT MY TANKS – FINISHED! DAMN YOU, SERGEANT!
EASY, MISTER, EASY!
NO! YOU MADE US —AIEEEE!
GERMAN INFANTRY REINFORCEMENTS OUT FOR OUR GUTS!
WE'RE DEAD MEN! OUR TANKS ARE USELESS!
DRY YER TEARS, MISTER ! THEY CAN STILL HELP US!
GRAB SOME SHORN STEEL, LADS!
SHIELDS! BUT THEY'LL WEIGH A TON, SARGE–
YOU'RE BIG AN' UGLY ENOUGH TO TAKE IT, STRONG, SO MOVE!
IT'S WORKIN', SARGE! THEY CAN'T TOUCH US!
LET'S SEE YOU SHRUG OFF EIGHT TONS OF HALFTRACK, THEN!
HE'S GONNA RUN US DOWN!
AIEEEEEE!
I SEE HIM, SON –
–HIT THE DRIVER AND SHE'S OVERTURNED! THOSE JERRIES HAVE HAD IT!
Next morning –
DUNKERQUE
LET'S HOPE WE MAKE IT TO THIS DUNKIRK – KEEP ON MY TAIL, BOYS!
ALL INFANTRY TO MAKE FOR DUNKIRK, SERGEANT! COUNTER-ATTACKS LAST NIGHT MADE MORE TIME FOR US!
YOU BET, SARGE! WE GOTTA BETTER CHANCE THAN MOST WITH YOU IN CHARGE!

A TERRIBLE SHOCK AWAITS MASTERS' MEN AT DUNKIRK NEXT WEEK !

BATTLE-ACTION WITH A BATTLE-HARDENED VETERAN !

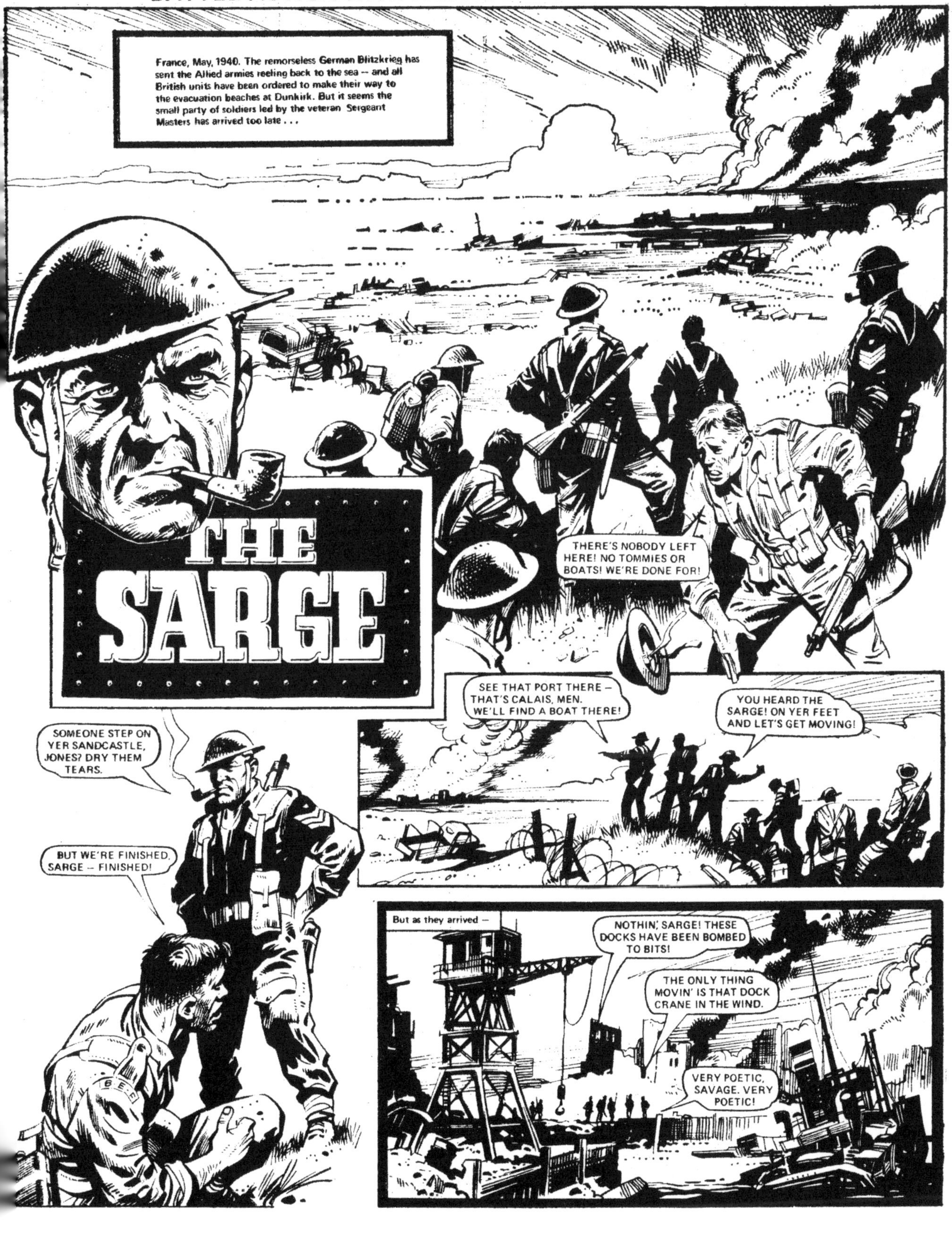

France, May, 1940. The remorseless German Blitzkrieg has sent the Allied armies reeling back to the sea -- and all British units have been ordered to make their way to the evacuation beaches at Dunkirk. But it seems the small party of soldiers led by the veteran Sergeant Masters has arrived too late . . .
THE SARGE
THERE'S NOBODY LEFT HERE! NO TOMMIES OR BOATS! WE'RE DONE FOR!
SOMEONE STEP ON YER SANDCASTLE, JONES? DRY THEM TEARS.
BUT WE'RE FINISHED, SARGE -- FINISHED!
SEE THAT PORT THERE -- THAT'S CALAIS, MEN. WE'LL FIND A BOAT THERE!
YOU HEARD THE SARGE! ON YER FEET AND LET'S GET MOVING!
But as they arrived --
NOTHIN', SARGE! THESE DOCKS HAVE BEEN BOMBED TO BITS!
THE ONLY THING MOVIN' IS THAT DOCK CRANE IN THE WIND.
VERY POETIC, SAVAGE. VERY POETIC!

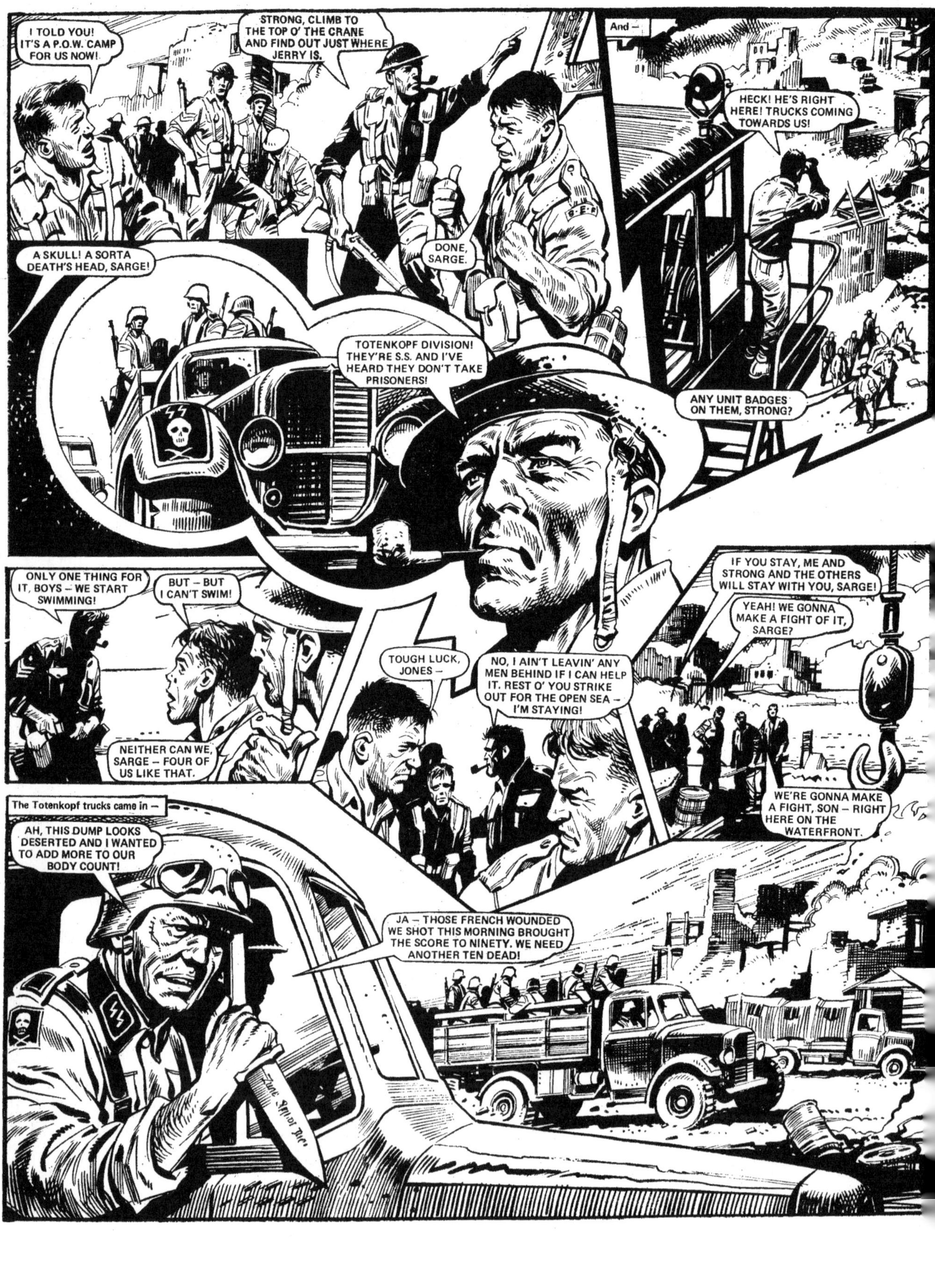

I TOLD YOU! IT'S A P.O.W. CAMP FOR US NOW!
STRONG, CLIMB TO THE TOP O' THE CRANE AND FIND OUT JUST WHERE JERRY IS.
DONE, SARGE.
And –
HECK! HE'S RIGHT HERE! TRUCKS COMING TOWARDS US!
ANY UNIT BADGES ON THEM, STRONG?
A SKULL! A SORTA DEATH'S HEAD, SARGE!
TOTENKOPF DIVISION! THEY'RE S.S. AND I'VE HEARD THEY DON'T TAKE PRISONERS!
ONLY ONE THING FOR IT, BOYS – WE START SWIMMING!
BUT – BUT I CAN'T SWIM!
NEITHER CAN WE, SARGE – FOUR OF US LIKE THAT.
TOUGH LUCK, JONES –
NO, I AIN'T LEAVIN' ANY MEN BEHIND IF I CAN HELP IT. REST O' YOU STRIKE OUT FOR THE OPEN SEA – I'M STAYING!
IF YOU STAY, ME AND STRONG AND THE OTHERS WILL STAY WITH YOU, SARGE!
YEAH! WE GONNA MAKE A FIGHT OF IT, SARGE?
WE'RE GONNA MAKE A FIGHT, SON – RIGHT HERE ON THE WATERFRONT.
The Totenkopf trucks came in –
AH, THIS DUMP LOOKS DESERTED AND I WANTED TO ADD MORE TO OUR BODY COUNT!
JA – THOSE FRENCH WOUNDED WE SHOT THIS MORNING BROUGHT THE SCORE TO NINETY. WE NEED ANOTHER TEN DEAD!

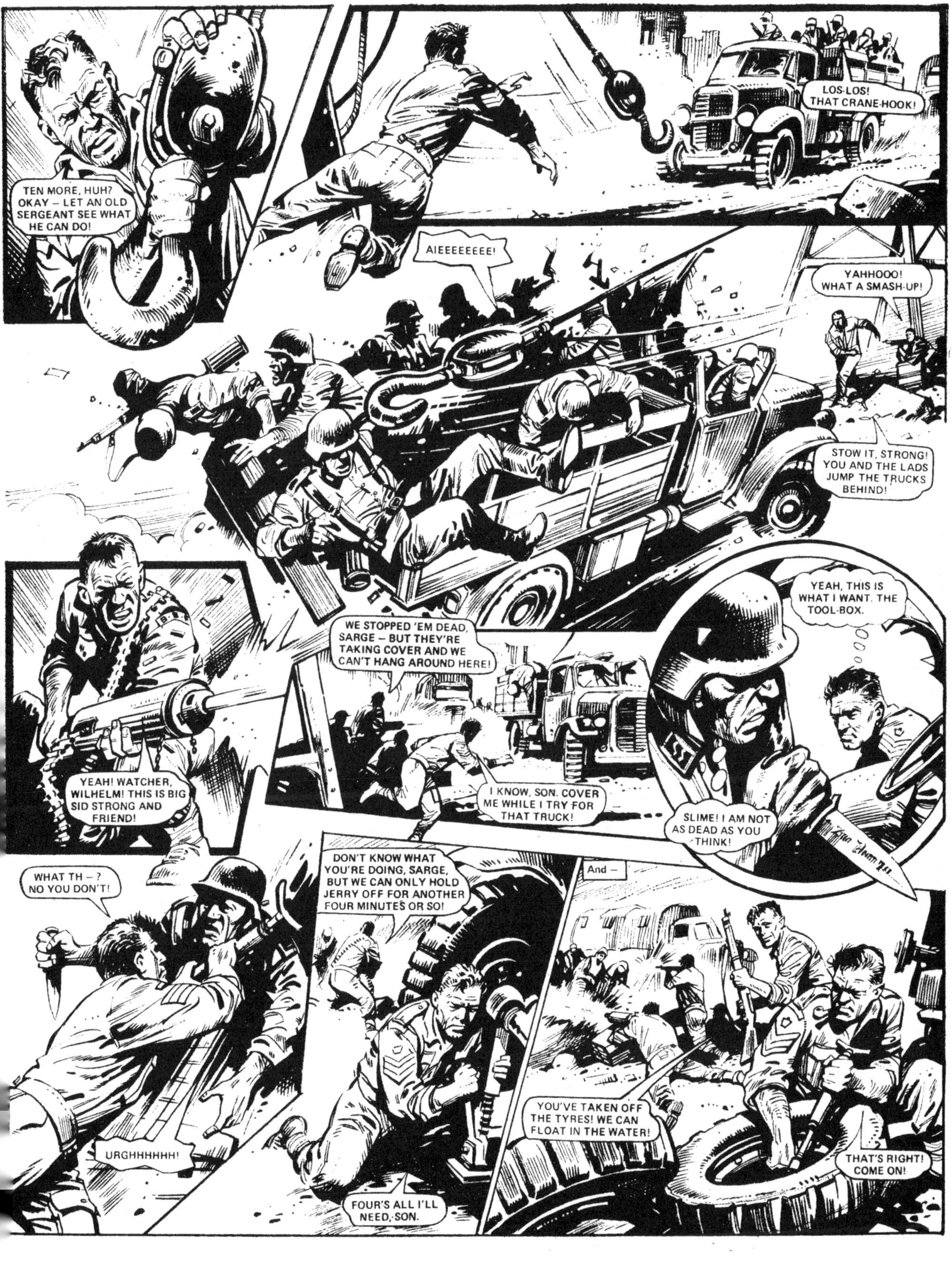

TEN MORE, HUH? OKAY – LET AN OLD SERGEANT SEE WHAT HE CAN DO!
LOS-LOS! THAT CRANE-HOOK!
AIEEEEEEEE!
YAHHOOO! WHAT A SMASH-UP!
STOW IT, STRONG! YOU AND THE LADS JUMP THE TRUCKS BEHIND!
YEAH! WATCHER, WILHELM! THIS IS BIG SID STRONG AND FRIEND!
WE STOPPED 'EM DEAD, SARGE – BUT THEY'RE TAKING COVER AND WE CAN'T HANG AROUND HERE!
I KNOW, SON. COVER ME WHILE I TRY FOR THAT TRUCK!
YEAH, THIS IS WHAT I WANT. THE TOOL-BOX.
SLIME! I AM NOT AS DEAD AS YOU THINK!
WHAT TH – ? NO YOU DON'T!
URGHHHHHH!
DON'T KNOW WHAT YOU'RE DOING, SARGE, BUT WE CAN ONLY HOLD JERRY OFF FOR ANOTHER FOUR MINUTES OR SO!
FOUR'S ALL I'LL NEED, SON.
And –
YOU'VE TAKEN OFF THE TYRES! WE CAN FLOAT IN THE WATER!
THAT'S RIGHT! COME ON!

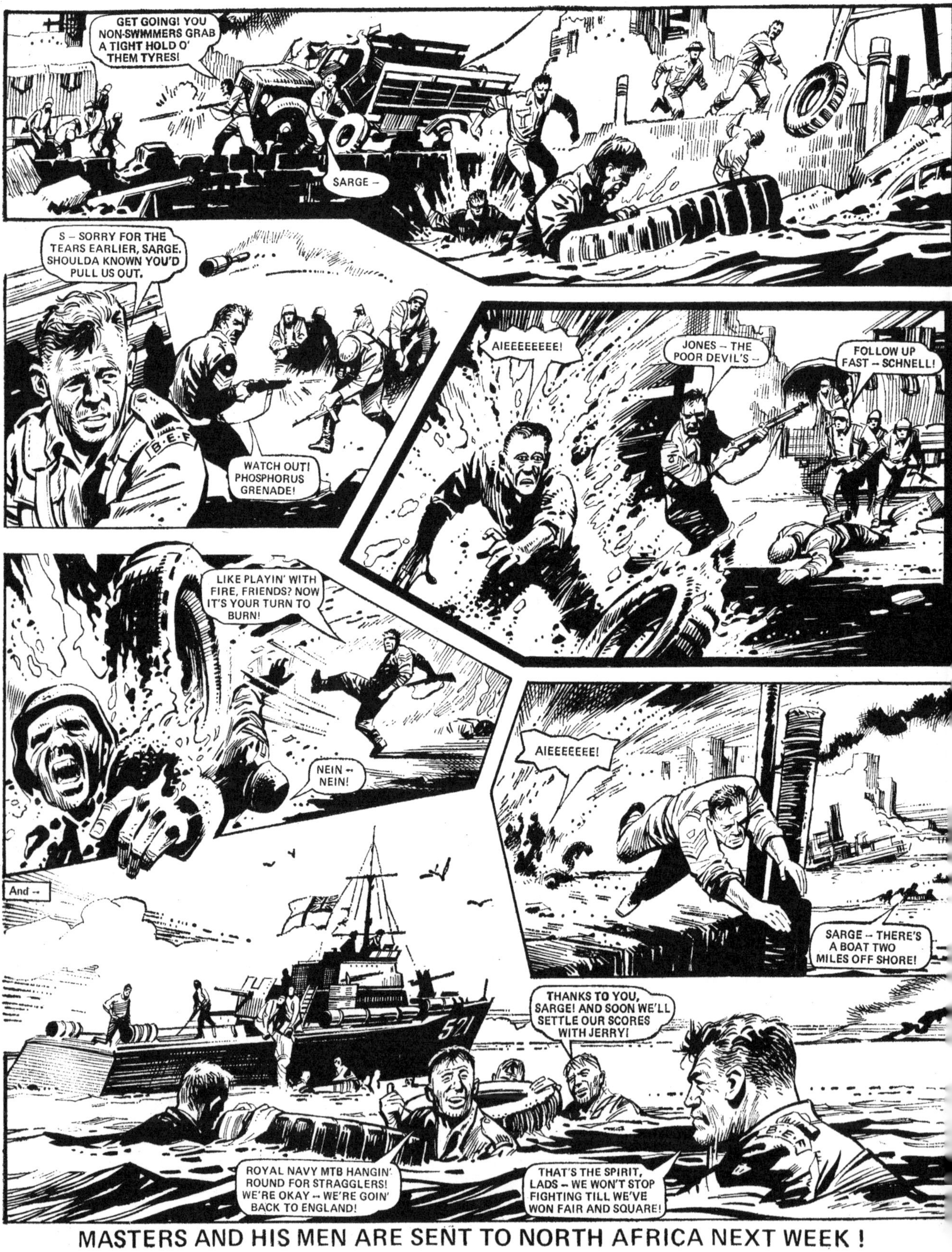

GET GOING! YOU NON-SWIMMERS GRAB A TIGHT HOLD O' THEM TYRES!
SARGE –
S – SORRY FOR THE TEARS EARLIER, SARGE. SHOULDA KNOWN YOU'D PULL US OUT.
WATCH OUT! PHOSPHORUS GRENADE!
AIEEEEEEEE!
JONES – THE POOR DEVIL'S –
FOLLOW UP FAST – SCHNELL!
LIKE PLAYIN' WITH FIRE, FRIENDS? NOW IT'S YOUR TURN TO BURN!
NEIN – NEIN!
AIEEEEEEE!
SARGE – THERE'S A BOAT TWO MILES OFF SHORE!
And –
THANKS TO YOU, SARGE! AND SOON WE'LL SETTLE OUR SCORES WITH JERRY!
ROYAL NAVY MTB HANGIN' ROUND FOR STRAGGLERS! WE'RE OKAY – WE'RE GOIN' BACK TO ENGLAND!
THAT'S THE SPIRIT, LADS – WE WON'T STOP FIGHTING TILL WE'VE WON FAIR AND SQUARE!

MASTERS AND HIS MEN ARE SENT TO NORTH AFRICA NEXT WEEK !

ACTION WITH JIM MASTERS – – A TOUGH SERGEANT WHO REALLY CAN SMELL TROUBLE !

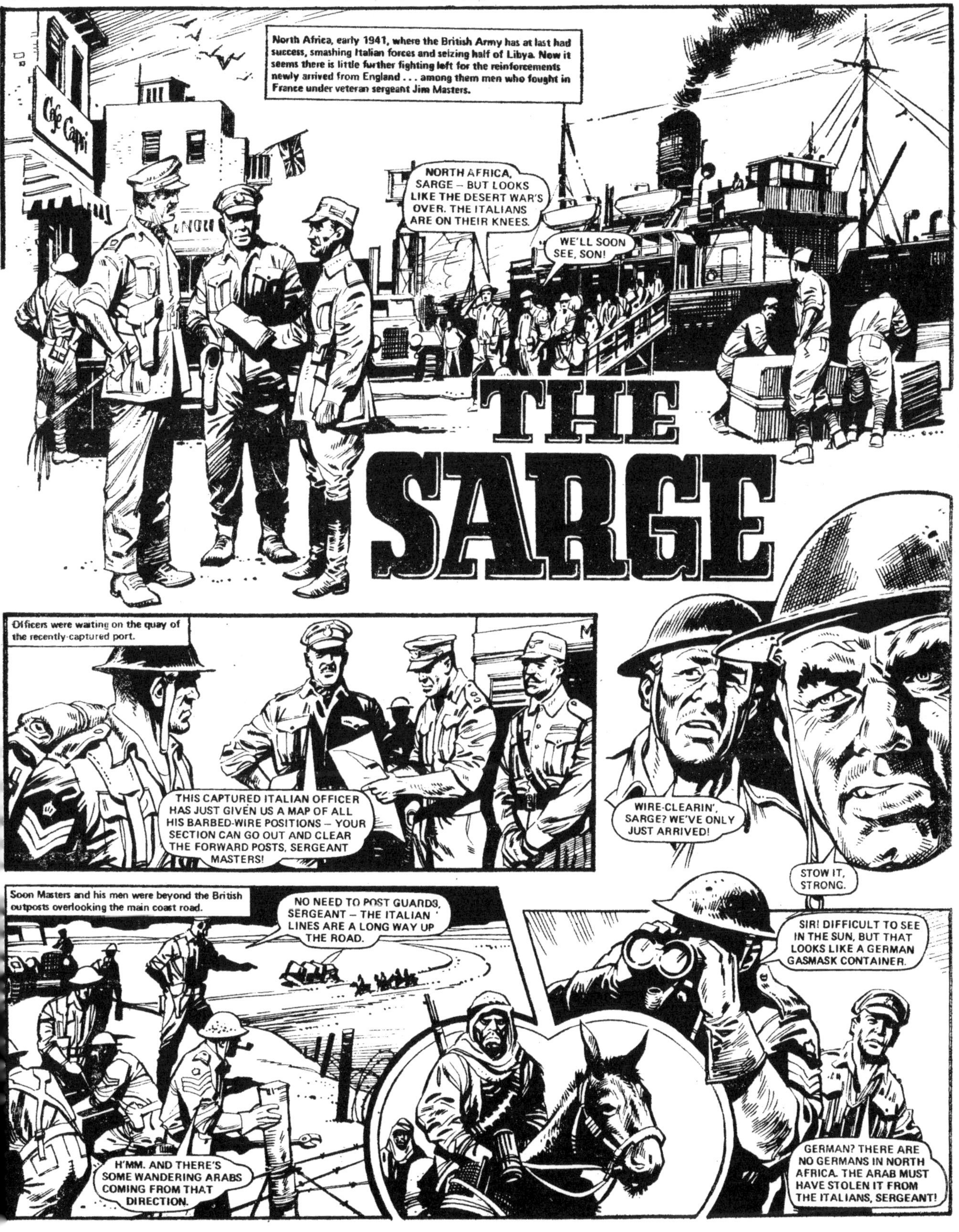
North Africa, early 1941, where the British Army has at last had success, smashing Italian forces and seizing half of Libya. Now it seems there is little further fighting left for the reinforcements newly arrived from England . . . among them men who fought in France under veteran sergeant Jim Masters.
Cafe Capri
NORTH AFRICA, SARGE – BUT LOOKS LIKE THE DESERT WAR'S OVER. THE ITALIANS ARE ON THEIR KNEES.
WE'LL SOON SEE, SON!
THE SARGE
Officers were waiting on the quay of the recently-captured port.
THIS CAPTURED ITALIAN OFFICER HAS JUST GIVEN US A MAP OF ALL HIS BARBED-WIRE POSITIONS – YOUR SECTION CAN GO OUT AND CLEAR THE FORWARD POSTS, SERGEANT MASTERS!
WIRE-CLEARIN', SARGE? WE'VE ONLY JUST ARRIVED!
STOW IT, STRONG.
Soon Masters and his men were beyond the British outposts overlooking the main coast road.
NO NEED TO POST GUARDS, SERGEANT – THE ITALIAN LINES ARE A LONG WAY UP THE ROAD.
H'MM. AND THERE'S SOME WANDERING ARABS COMING FROM THAT DIRECTION.
SIR! DIFFICULT TO SEE IN THE SUN, BUT THAT LOOKS LIKE A GERMAN GASMASK CONTAINER.
GERMAN? THERE ARE NO GERMANS IN NORTH AFRICA. THE ARAB MUST HAVE STOLEN IT FROM THE ITALIANS, SERGEANT!

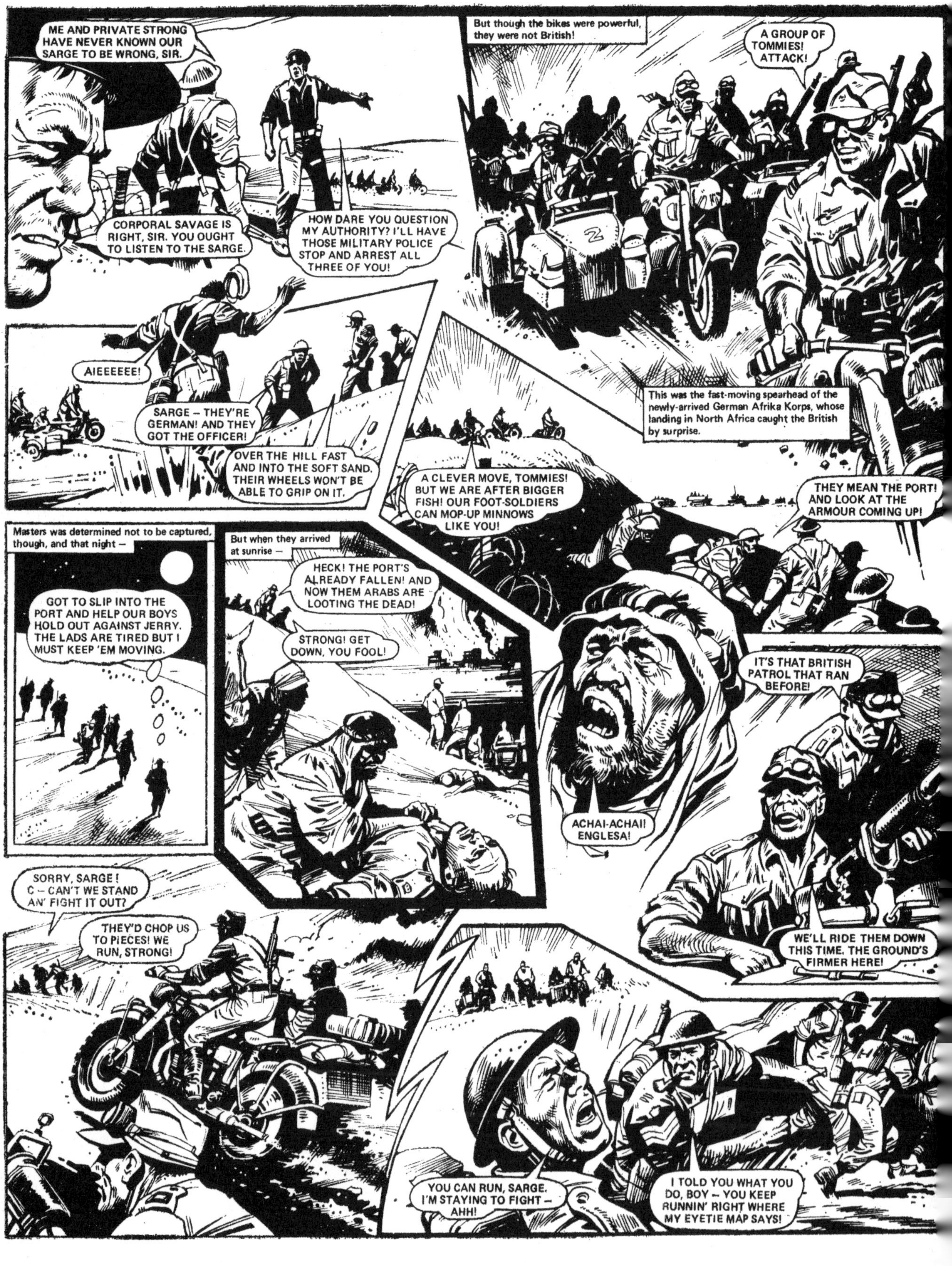
ME AND PRIVATE STRONG HAVE NEVER KNOWN OUR SARGE TO BE WRONG, SIR.
CORPORAL SAVAGE IS RIGHT, SIR. YOU OUGHT TO LISTEN TO THE SARGE.
HOW DARE YOU QUESTION MY AUTHORITY? I'LL HAVE THOSE MILITARY POLICE STOP AND ARREST ALL THREE OF YOU!
But though the bikes were powerful, they were not British!
A GROUP OF TOMMIES! ATTACK!
This was the fast-moving spearhead of the newly-arrived German Afrika Korps, whose landing in North Africa caught the British by surprise.
AIEEEEEE!
SARGE – THEY'RE GERMAN! AND THEY GOT THE OFFICER!
OVER THE HILL FAST AND INTO THE SOFT SAND. THEIR WHEELS WON'T BE ABLE TO GRIP ON IT.
A CLEVER MOVE, TOMMIES! BUT WE ARE AFTER BIGGER FISH! OUR FOOT-SOLDIERS CAN MOP-UP MINNOWS LIKE YOU!
THEY MEAN THE PORT! AND LOOK AT THE ARMOUR COMING UP!
Masters was determined not to be captured, though, and that night –
GOT TO SLIP INTO THE PORT AND HELP OUR BOYS HOLD OUT AGAINST JERRY. THE LADS ARE TIRED BUT I MUST KEEP 'EM MOVING.
But when they arrived at sunrise –
HECK! THE PORT'S ALREADY FALLEN! AND NOW THEM ARABS ARE LOOTING THE DEAD!
STRONG! GET DOWN, YOU FOOL!
ACHAI-ACHAI! ENGLESA!
IT'S THAT BRITISH PATROL THAT RAN BEFORE!
WE'LL RIDE THEM DOWN THIS TIME. THE GROUND'S FIRMER HERE!
SORRY, SARGE! C – CAN'T WE STAND AN' FIGHT IT OUT?
THEY'D CHOP US TO PIECES! WE RUN, STRONG!
YOU CAN RUN, SARGE. I'M STAYING TO FIGHT – AHH!
I TOLD YOU WHAT YOU DO, BOY – YOU KEEP RUNNIN' RIGHT WHERE MY EYETIE MAP SAYS!

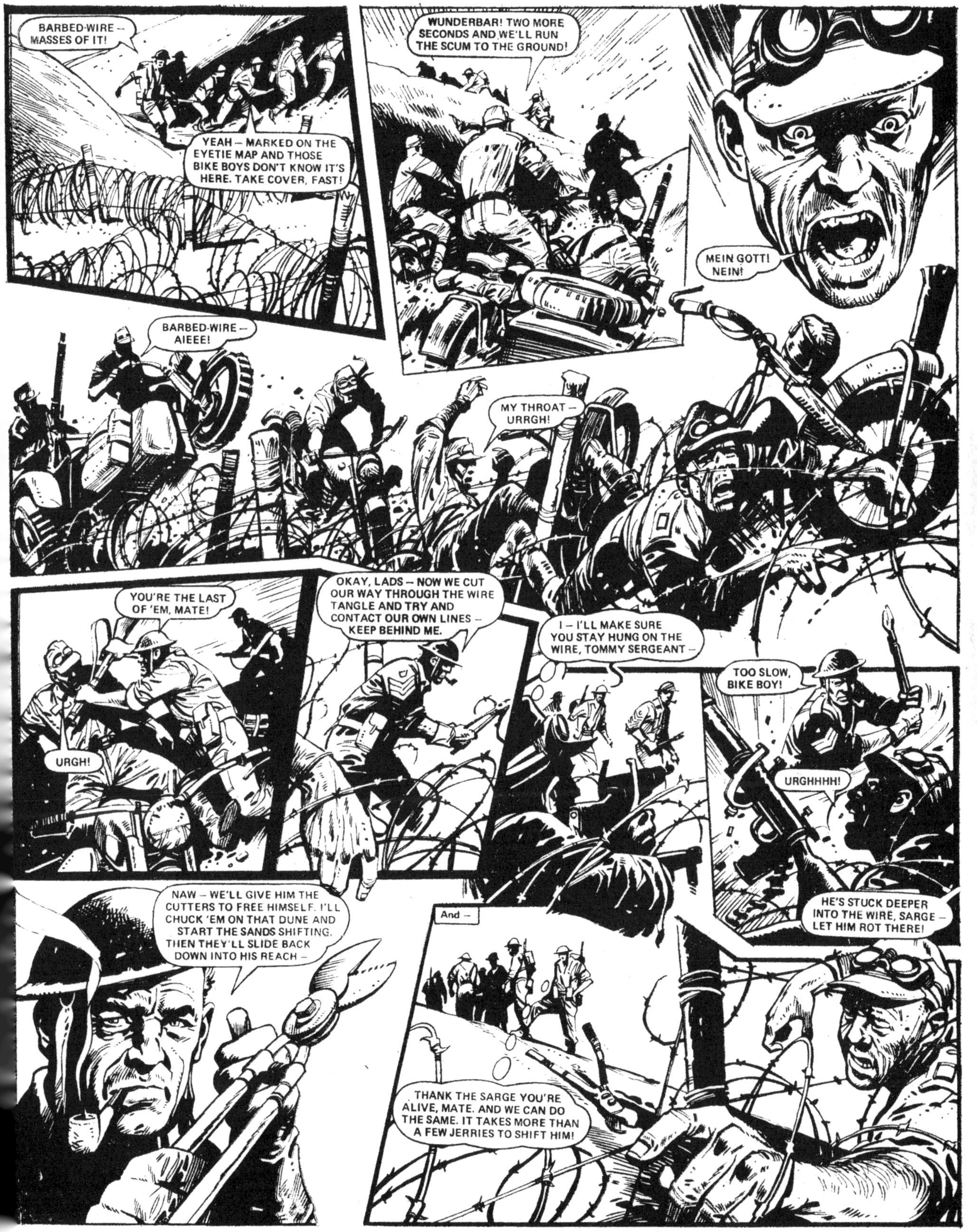

BARBED-WIRE – MASSES OF IT!
YEAH – MARKED ON THE EYETIE MAP AND THOSE BIKE BOYS DON'T KNOW IT'S HERE. TAKE COVER, FAST!
WUNDERBAR! TWO MORE SECONDS AND WE'LL RUN THE SCUM TO THE GROUND!
MEIN GOTT! NEIN!
BARBED-WIRE – AIEEE!
MY THROAT – URRGH!
YOU'RE THE LAST OF 'EM, MATE!
URGH!
OKAY, LADS – NOW WE CUT OUR WAY THROUGH THE WIRE TANGLE AND TRY AND CONTACT OUR OWN LINES – KEEP BEHIND ME.
I – I'LL MAKE SURE YOU STAY HUNG ON THE WIRE, TOMMY SERGEANT –
TOO SLOW, BIKE BOY!
URGHHHH!
HE'S STUCK DEEPER INTO THE WIRE, SARGE – LET HIM ROT THERE!
NAW – WE'LL GIVE HIM THE CUTTERS TO FREE HIMSELF. I'LL CHUCK 'EM ON THAT DUNE AND START THE SANDS SHIFTING. THEN THEY'LL SLIDE BACK DOWN INTO HIS REACH –
And –
THANK THE SARGE YOU'RE ALIVE, MATE. AND WE CAN DO THE SAME. IT TAKES MORE THAN A FEW JERRIES TO SHIFT HIM!

SSION ENDS...MISSION ENDS...MISSION ENDS...MISSION ENDS...MISSION ENDS...MISSION ENDS...MISSION ENDS...

THE EARLY ADVENTURES OF... HELLMAN OF HAMMER FORCE

"NOW TO DRIVE LIKE A BAT OUT OF HELL!"

A man of swift and decisive action, Panzer Commander Major Kurt Hellman has lived his life by the warrior's code, refusing to kill civilians or the unarmed. Blonde, blue-eyed and Teutonic, he is an exceptional battlefield tactician and everything a good Nazi shouldn't be — courageous, honourable and decent. Now he's leading his loyal tank division, "Hammer Force", against not only the combined might of the Allied forces but also the creeping evil of the Waffen SS.

When *Battle* merged with *Action* in November 1977 only three of the latter's strips survived, one of which was 'Hellman'. Written by Gerry Finley-Day and drawn by Mike Dorey, this revised Hellman lacked the impact of the earlier *Action* incarnation and the strip finally concluded in February 1978.

NOTES FROM THE FRONTLINE:

"The look of 'Hellman' was based on Robert Shaw from *The Battle of the Bulge*, mixed with a little bit of *From Russia with Love*'s Red Grant. While on *Action*, I really started to choreograph the characters and their looks — and that's why you'll find *Action* is often a bit more visual than *Battle* was in the same era. I can remember that for the end of the first episode I said, 'I want a big image of this guy, Hellman. I want him standing there, I want him unshaven and I want a fag hanging out of the end of his mouth.' And he just looked the business and I said, 'Yeah, that's what I want. That's perfect, he's great!'"

— Pat Mills

WRITTEN BY Gerry Finley-Day
DRAWN BY Mike Western, Mike Dorey & Jim Watson

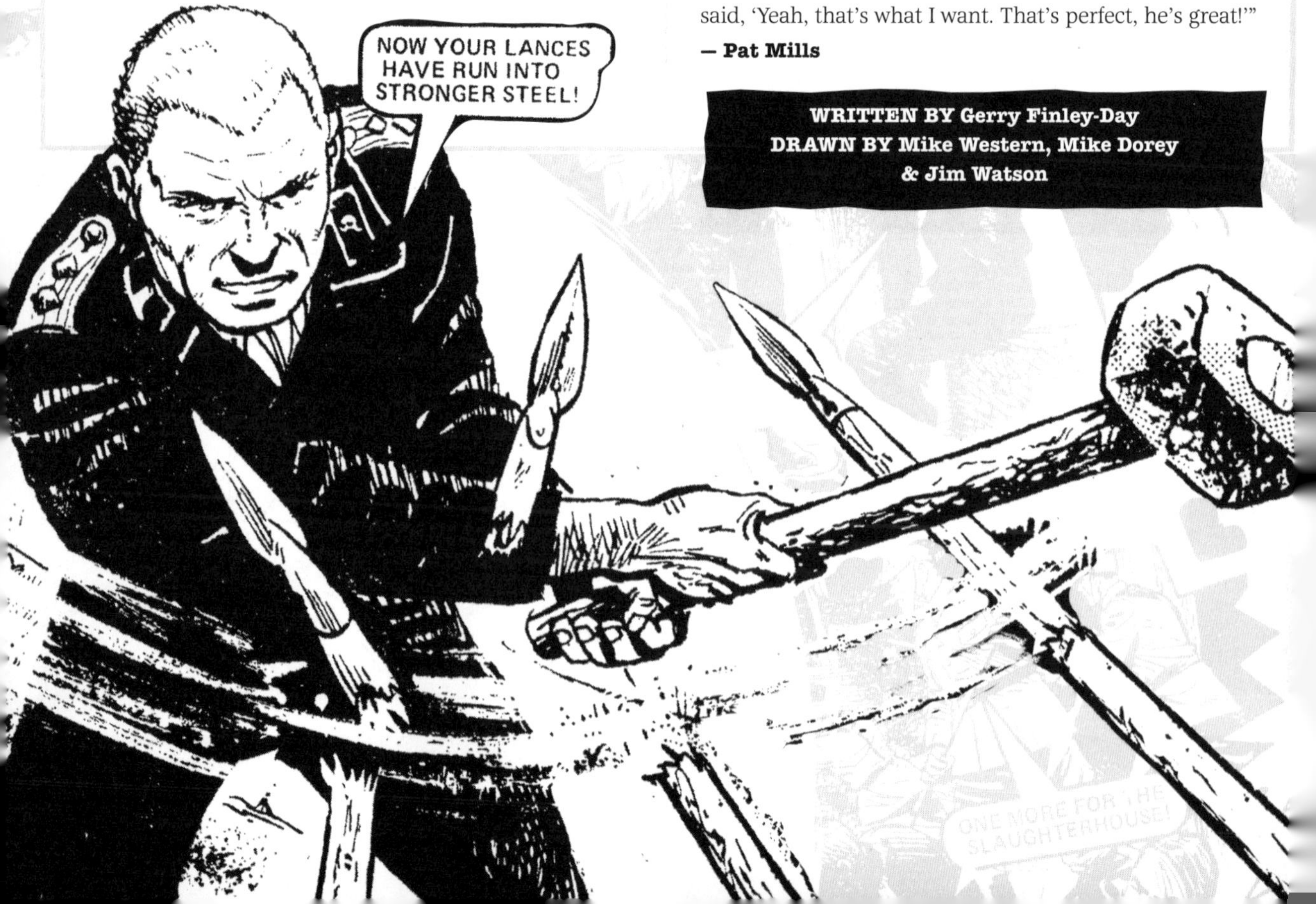
NOW YOUR LANCES HAVE RUN INTO STRONGER STEEL!

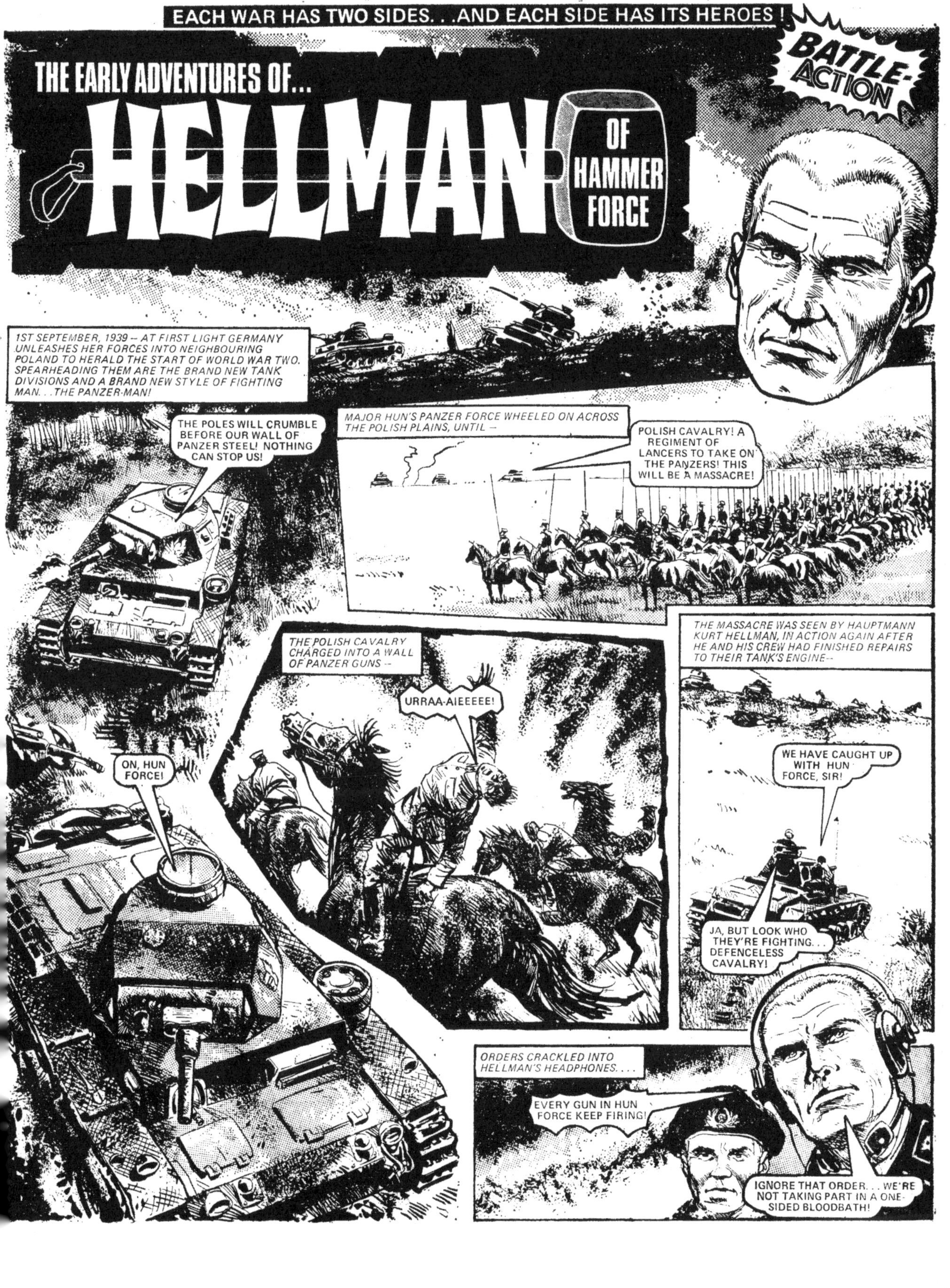
EACH WAR HAS TWO SIDES. . .AND EACH SIDE HAS ITS HEROES!
BATTLE-ACTION
THE EARLY ADVENTURES OF...
HELLMAN OF HAMMER FORCE
1ST SEPTEMBER, 1939 – AT FIRST LIGHT GERMANY UNLEASHES HER FORCES INTO NEIGHBOURING POLAND TO HERALD THE START OF WORLD WAR TWO. SPEARHEADING THEM ARE THE BRAND NEW TANK DIVISIONS AND A BRAND NEW STYLE OF FIGHTING MAN. . .THE PANZER-MAN!
THE POLES WILL CRUMBLE BEFORE OUR WALL OF PANZER STEEL! NOTHING CAN STOP US!
MAJOR HUN'S PANZER FORCE WHEELED ON ACROSS THE POLISH PLAINS, UNTIL –
POLISH CAVALRY! A REGIMENT OF LANCERS TO TAKE ON THE PANZERS! THIS WILL BE A MASSACRE!
ON, HUN FORCE!
THE POLISH CAVALRY CHARGED INTO A WALL OF PANZER GUNS --
URRAA-AIEEEEE!
THE MASSACRE WAS SEEN BY HAUPTMANN KURT HELLMAN, IN ACTION AGAIN AFTER HE AND HIS CREW HAD FINISHED REPAIRS TO THEIR TANK'S ENGINE--
WE HAVE CAUGHT UP WITH HUN FORCE, SIR!
JA, BUT LOOK WHO THEY'RE FIGHTING. . . DEFENCELESS CAVALRY!
ORDERS CRACKLED INTO HELLMAN'S HEADPHONES. . . .
EVERY GUN IN HUN FORCE KEEP FIRING!
IGNORE THAT ORDER. . . WE'RE NOT TAKING PART IN A ONE-SIDED BLOODBATH!

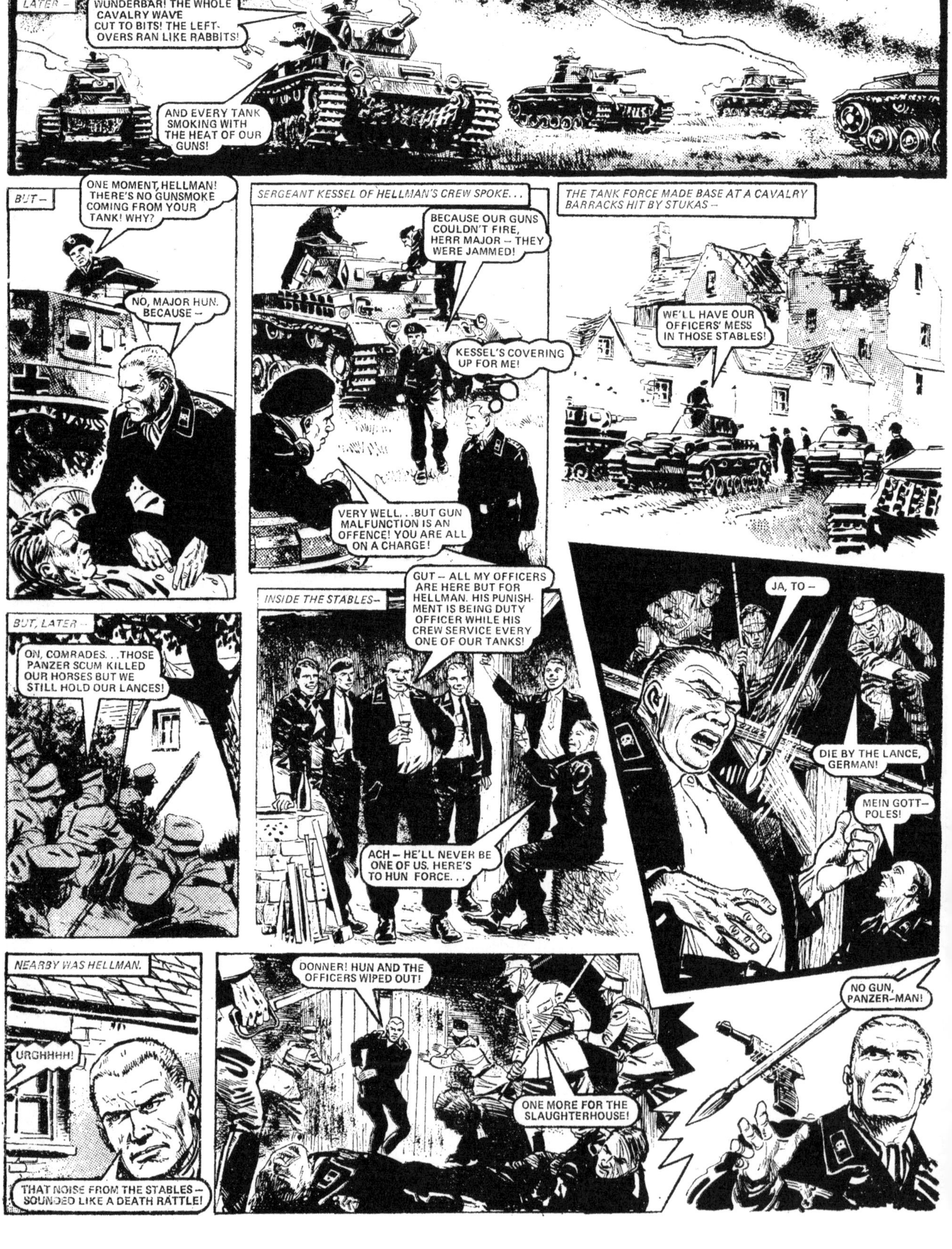
LATER –
WUNDERBAR! THE WHOLE CAVALRY WAVE CUT TO BITS! THE LEFT-OVERS RAN LIKE RABBITS!
AND EVERY TANK SMOKING WITH THE HEAT OF OUR GUNS!
BUT –
ONE MOMENT, HELLMAN! THERE'S NO GUNSMOKE COMING FROM YOUR TANK! WHY?
NO, MAJOR HUN. BECAUSE –
SERGEANT KESSEL OF HELLMAN'S CREW SPOKE...
BECAUSE OUR GUNS COULDN'T FIRE, HERR MAJOR – THEY WERE JAMMED!
KESSEL'S COVERING UP FOR ME!
VERY WELL...BUT GUN MALFUNCTION IS AN OFFENCE! YOU ARE ALL ON A CHARGE!
THE TANK FORCE MADE BASE AT A CAVALRY BARRACKS HIT BY STUKAS –
WE'LL HAVE OUR OFFICERS' MESS IN THOSE STABLES!
BUT, LATER –
ON, COMRADES...THOSE PANZER SCUM KILLED OUR HORSES BUT WE STILL HOLD OUR LANCES!
INSIDE THE STABLES –
GUT – ALL MY OFFICERS ARE HERE BUT FOR HELLMAN. HIS PUNISHMENT IS BEING DUTY OFFICER WHILE HIS CREW SERVICE EVERY ONE OF OUR TANKS!
ACH – HE'LL NEVER BE ONE OF US. HERE'S TO HUN FORCE...
JA, TO –
DIE BY THE LANCE, GERMAN!
MEIN GOTT – POLES!
NEARBY WAS HELLMAN.
URGHHHH!
THAT NOISE FROM THE STABLES – SOUNDED LIKE A DEATH RATTLE!
DONNER! HUN AND THE OFFICERS WIPED OUT!
ONE MORE FOR THE SLAUGHTERHOUSE!
NO GUN, PANZER-MAN!

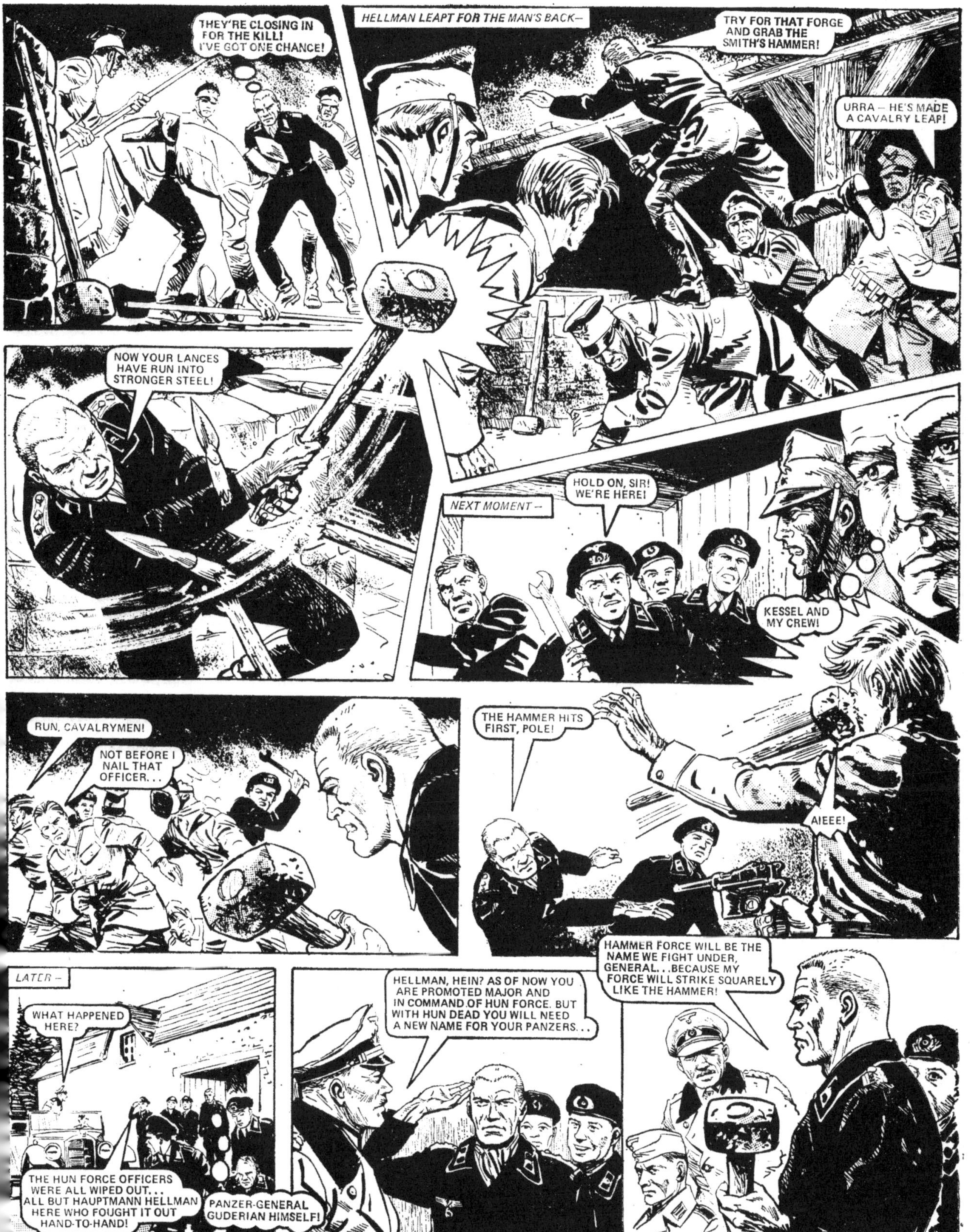
THEY'RE CLOSING IN FOR THE KILL! I'VE GOT ONE CHANCE!
HELLMAN LEAPT FOR THE MAN'S BACK—
TRY FOR THAT FORGE AND GRAB THE SMITH'S HAMMER!
URRA – HE'S MADE A CAVALRY LEAP!
NOW YOUR LANCES HAVE RUN INTO STRONGER STEEL!
NEXT MOMENT —
HOLD ON, SIR! WE'RE HERE!
KESSEL AND MY CREW!
RUN, CAVALRYMEN!
NOT BEFORE I NAIL THAT OFFICER...
THE HAMMER HITS FIRST, POLE!
AIEEE!
LATER —
WHAT HAPPENED HERE?
THE HUN FORCE OFFICERS WERE ALL WIPED OUT... ALL BUT HAUPTMANN HELLMAN HERE WHO FOUGHT IT OUT HAND-TO-HAND!
PANZER-GENERAL GUDERIAN HIMSELF!
HELLMAN, HEIN? AS OF NOW YOU ARE PROMOTED MAJOR AND IN COMMAND OF HUN FORCE. BUT WITH HUN DEAD YOU WILL NEED A NEW NAME FOR YOUR PANZERS...
HAMMER FORCE WILL BE THE NAME WE FIGHT UNDER, GENERAL... BECAUSE MY FORCE WILL STRIKE SQUARELY LIKE THE HAMMER!

HAMMER INTO BATTLE WITH HELLMAN EVERY WEEK IN BATTLE-ACTION !

TANK ACTION WITH MAJOR KURT HELLMAN !

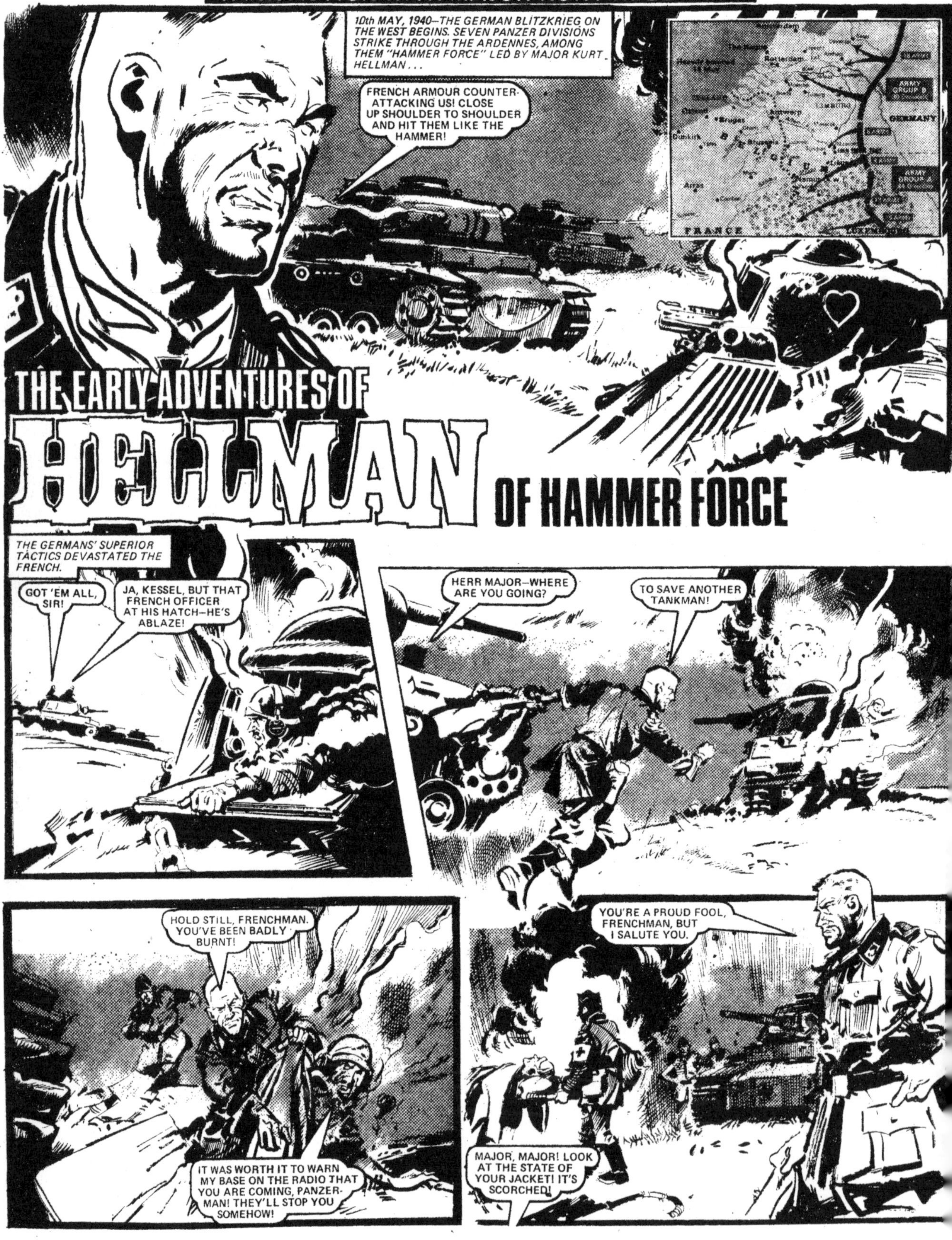

10th MAY, 1940–THE GERMAN BLITZKRIEG ON THE WEST BEGINS. SEVEN PANZER DIVISIONS STRIKE THROUGH THE ARDENNES, AMONG THEM "HAMMER FORCE" LED BY MAJOR KURT HELLMAN . . .
FRENCH ARMOUR COUNTER-ATTACKING US! CLOSE UP SHOULDER TO SHOULDER AND HIT THEM LIKE THE HAMMER!
GERMANY
FRANCE
THE EARLY ADVENTURES OF
HELLMAN
OF HAMMER FORCE
THE GERMANS' SUPERIOR TACTICS DEVASTATED THE FRENCH.
GOT 'EM ALL, SIR!
JA, KESSEL, BUT THAT FRENCH OFFICER AT HIS HATCH–HE'S ABLAZE!
HERR MAJOR–WHERE ARE YOU GOING?
TO SAVE ANOTHER TANKMAN!
HOLD STILL, FRENCHMAN. YOU'VE BEEN BADLY BURNT!
IT WAS WORTH IT TO WARN MY BASE ON THE RADIO THAT YOU ARE COMING, PANZER-MAN! THEY'LL STOP YOU SOMEHOW!
YOU'RE A PROUD FOOL, FRENCHMAN, BUT I SALUTE YOU.
MAJOR, MAJOR! LOOK AT THE STATE OF YOUR JACKET! IT'S SCORCHED!

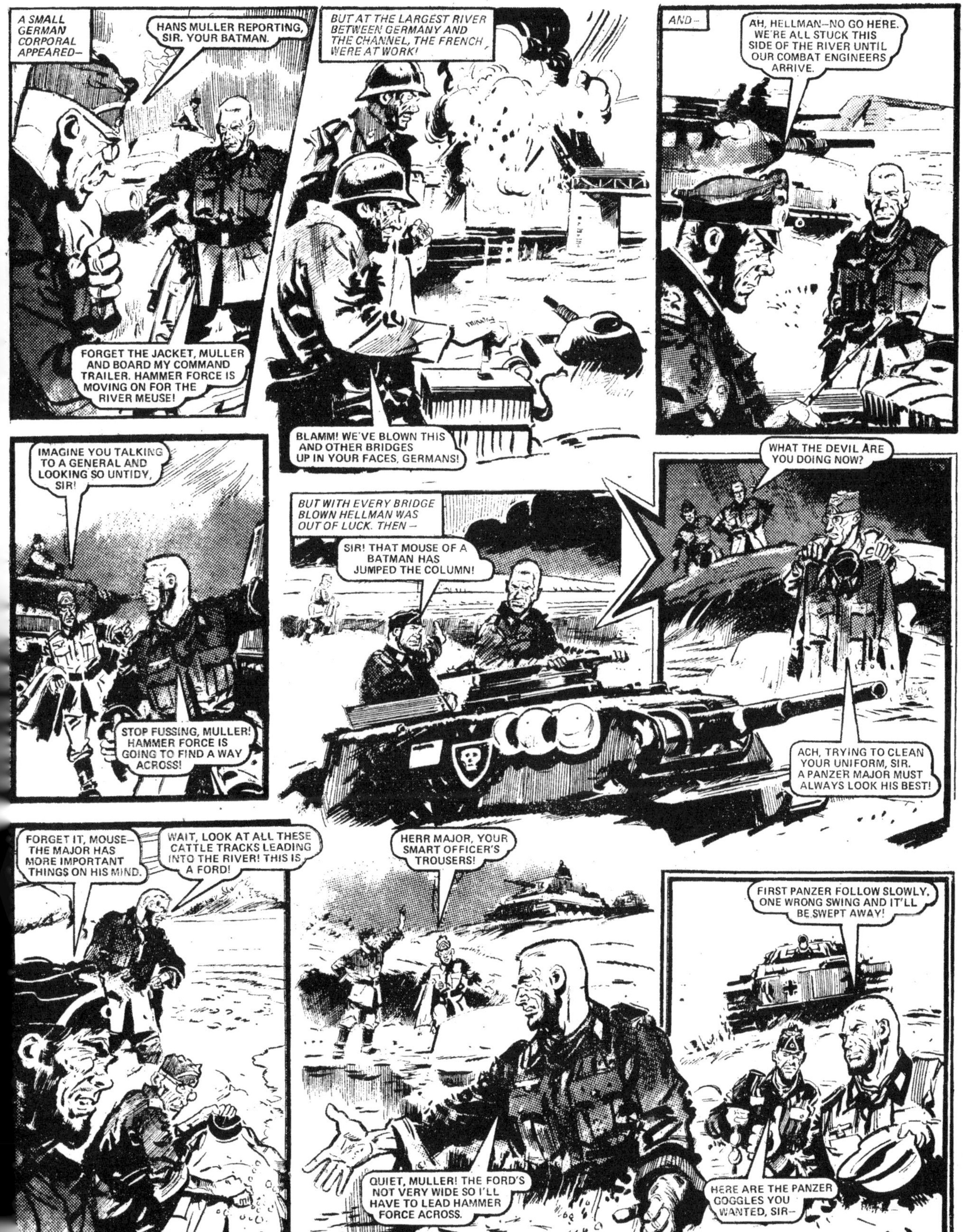

A SMALL GERMAN CORPORAL APPEARED—
HANS MULLER REPORTING, SIR. YOUR BATMAN.
FORGET THE JACKET, MULLER AND BOARD MY COMMAND TRAILER. HAMMER FORCE IS MOVING ON FOR THE RIVER MEUSE!
BUT AT THE LARGEST RIVER BETWEEN GERMANY AND THE CHANNEL, THE FRENCH WERE AT WORK!
BLAMM! WE'VE BLOWN THIS AND OTHER BRIDGES UP IN YOUR FACES, GERMANS!
AND—
AH, HELLMAN—NO GO HERE. WE'RE ALL STUCK THIS SIDE OF THE RIVER UNTIL OUR COMBAT ENGINEERS ARRIVE.
IMAGINE YOU TALKING TO A GENERAL AND LOOKING SO UNTIDY, SIR!
STOP FUSSING, MULLER! HAMMER FORCE IS GOING TO FIND A WAY ACROSS!
BUT WITH EVERY BRIDGE BLOWN HELLMAN WAS OUT OF LUCK. THEN—
SIR! THAT MOUSE OF A BATMAN HAS JUMPED THE COLUMN!
WHAT THE DEVIL ARE YOU DOING NOW?
ACH, TRYING TO CLEAN YOUR UNIFORM, SIR. A PANZER MAJOR MUST ALWAYS LOOK HIS BEST!
FORGET IT, MOUSE—THE MAJOR HAS MORE IMPORTANT THINGS ON HIS MIND.
WAIT, LOOK AT ALL THESE CATTLE TRACKS LEADING INTO THE RIVER! THIS IS A FORD!
HERR MAJOR, YOUR SMART OFFICER'S TROUSERS!
QUIET, MULLER! THE FORD'S NOT VERY WIDE SO I'LL HAVE TO LEAD HAMMER FORCE ACROSS.
FIRST PANZER FOLLOW SLOWLY. ONE WRONG SWING AND IT'LL BE SWEPT AWAY!
HERE ARE THE PANZER GOGGLES YOU WANTED, SIR—

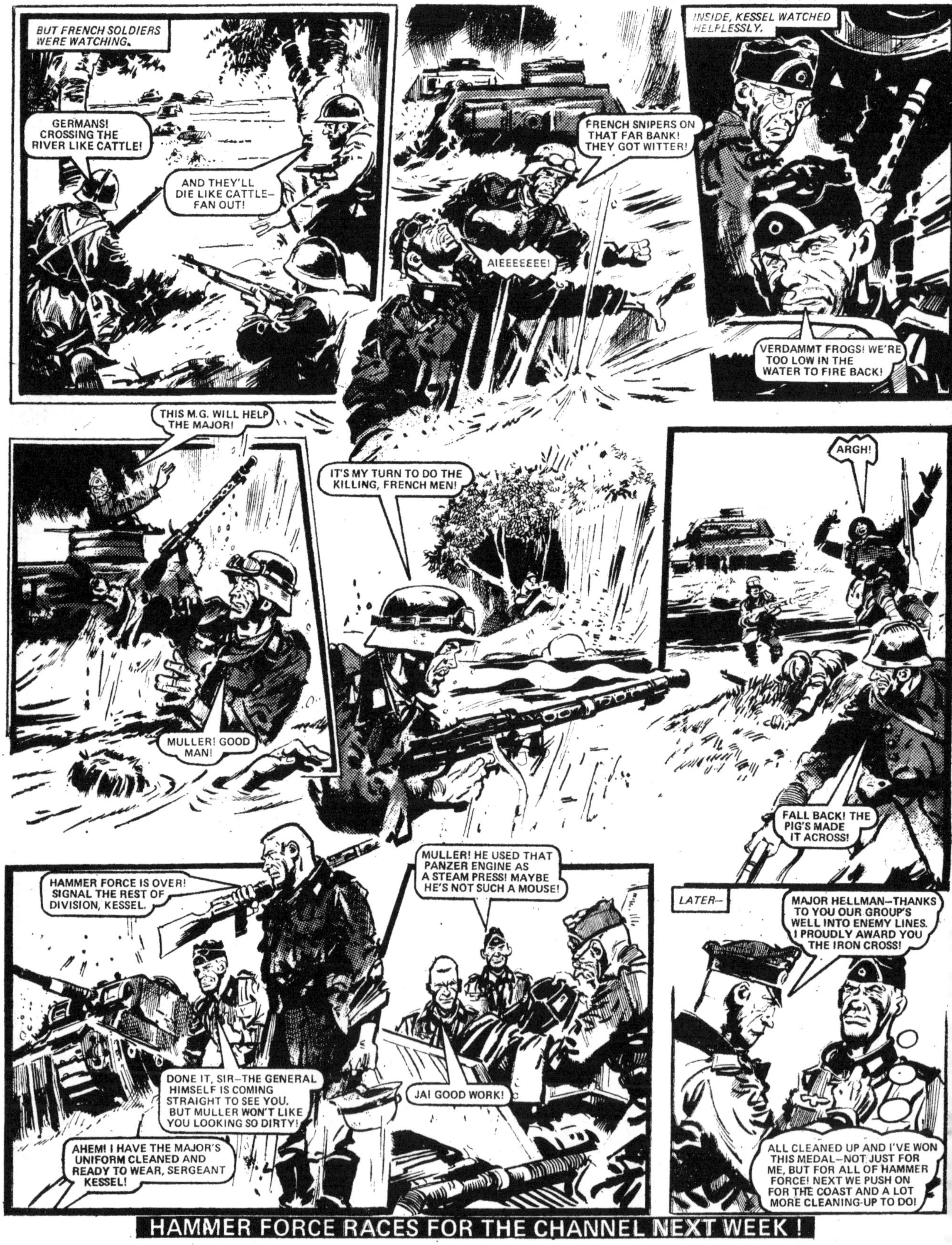
BUT FRENCH SOLDIERS WERE WATCHING.
GERMANS! CROSSING THE RIVER LIKE CATTLE!
AND THEY'LL DIE LIKE CATTLE– FAN OUT!
FRENCH SNIPERS ON THAT FAR BANK! THEY GOT WITTER!
AIEEEEEEE!
INSIDE, KESSEL WATCHED HELPLESSLY.
VERDAMMT FROGS! WE'RE TOO LOW IN THE WATER TO FIRE BACK!
THIS M.G. WILL HELP THE MAJOR!
MULLER! GOOD MAN!
IT'S MY TURN TO DO THE KILLING, FRENCH MEN!
ARGH!
FALL BACK! THE PIG'S MADE IT ACROSS!
HAMMER FORCE IS OVER! SIGNAL THE REST OF DIVISION, KESSEL.
DONE IT, SIR–THE GENERAL HIMSELF IS COMING STRAIGHT TO SEE YOU, BUT MULLER WON'T LIKE YOU LOOKING SO DIRTY!
AHEM! I HAVE THE MAJOR'S UNIFORM CLEANED AND READY TO WEAR, SERGEANT KESSEL!
MULLER! HE USED THAT PANZER ENGINE AS A STEAM PRESS! MAYBE HE'S NOT SUCH A MOUSE!
JA! GOOD WORK!
LATER–
MAJOR HELLMAN–THANKS TO YOU OUR GROUP'S WELL INTO ENEMY LINES. I PROUDLY AWARD YOU THE IRON CROSS!
ALL CLEANED UP AND I'VE WON THIS MEDAL–NOT JUST FOR ME, BUT FOR ALL OF HAMMER FORCE! NEXT WE PUSH ON FOR THE COAST AND A LOT MORE CLEANING-UP TO DO!

HAMMER FORCE RACES FOR THE CHANNEL NEXT WEEK !

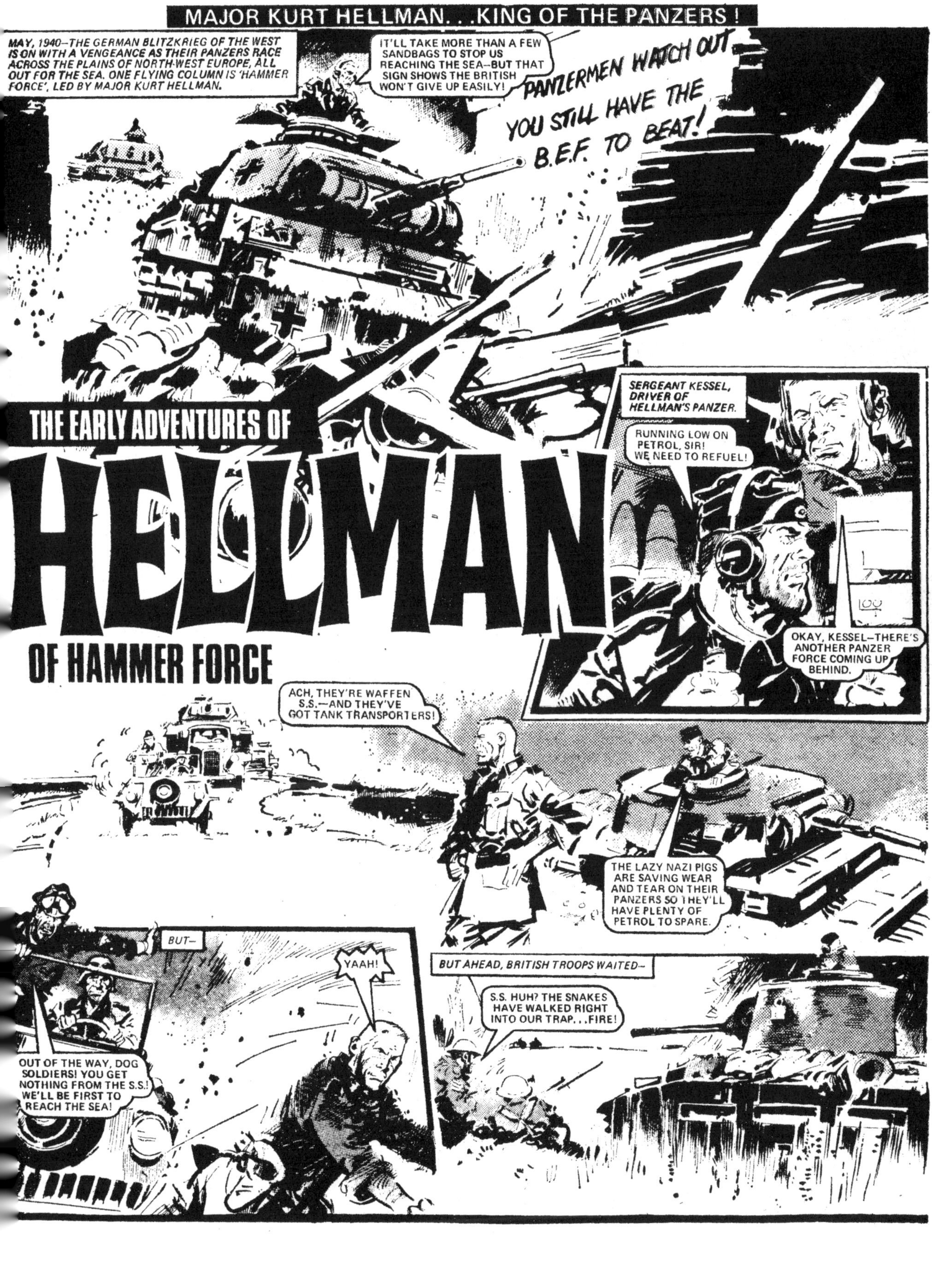
MAJOR KURT HELLMAN. . .KING OF THE PANZERS!
MAY, 1940—THE GERMAN BLITZKRIEG OF THE WEST IS ON WITH A VENGEANCE AS THEIR PANZERS RACE ACROSS THE PLAINS OF NORTH-WEST EUROPE, ALL OUT FOR THE SEA. ONE FLYING COLUMN IS 'HAMMER FORCE', LED BY MAJOR KURT HELLMAN.
IT'LL TAKE MORE THAN A FEW SANDBAGS TO STOP US REACHING THE SEA—BUT THAT SIGN SHOWS THE BRITISH WON'T GIVE UP EASILY!
PANZERMEN WATCH OUT YOU STILL HAVE THE B.E.F. TO BEAT!
THE EARLY ADVENTURES OF
HELLMAN
OF HAMMER FORCE
SERGEANT KESSEL, DRIVER OF HELLMAN'S PANZER.
RUNNING LOW ON PETROL, SIR! WE NEED TO REFUEL!
OKAY, KESSEL—THERE'S ANOTHER PANZER FORCE COMING UP BEHIND.
ACH, THEY'RE WAFFEN S.S.—AND THEY'VE GOT TANK TRANSPORTERS!
THE LAZY NAZI PIGS ARE SAVING WEAR AND TEAR ON THEIR PANZERS SO THEY'LL HAVE PLENTY OF PETROL TO SPARE.
BUT—
YAAH!
OUT OF THE WAY, DOG SOLDIERS! YOU GET NOTHING FROM THE S.S.! WE'LL BE FIRST TO REACH THE SEA!
BUT AHEAD, BRITISH TROOPS WAITED—
S.S. HUH? THE SNAKES HAVE WALKED RIGHT INTO OUR TRAP. . .FIRE!

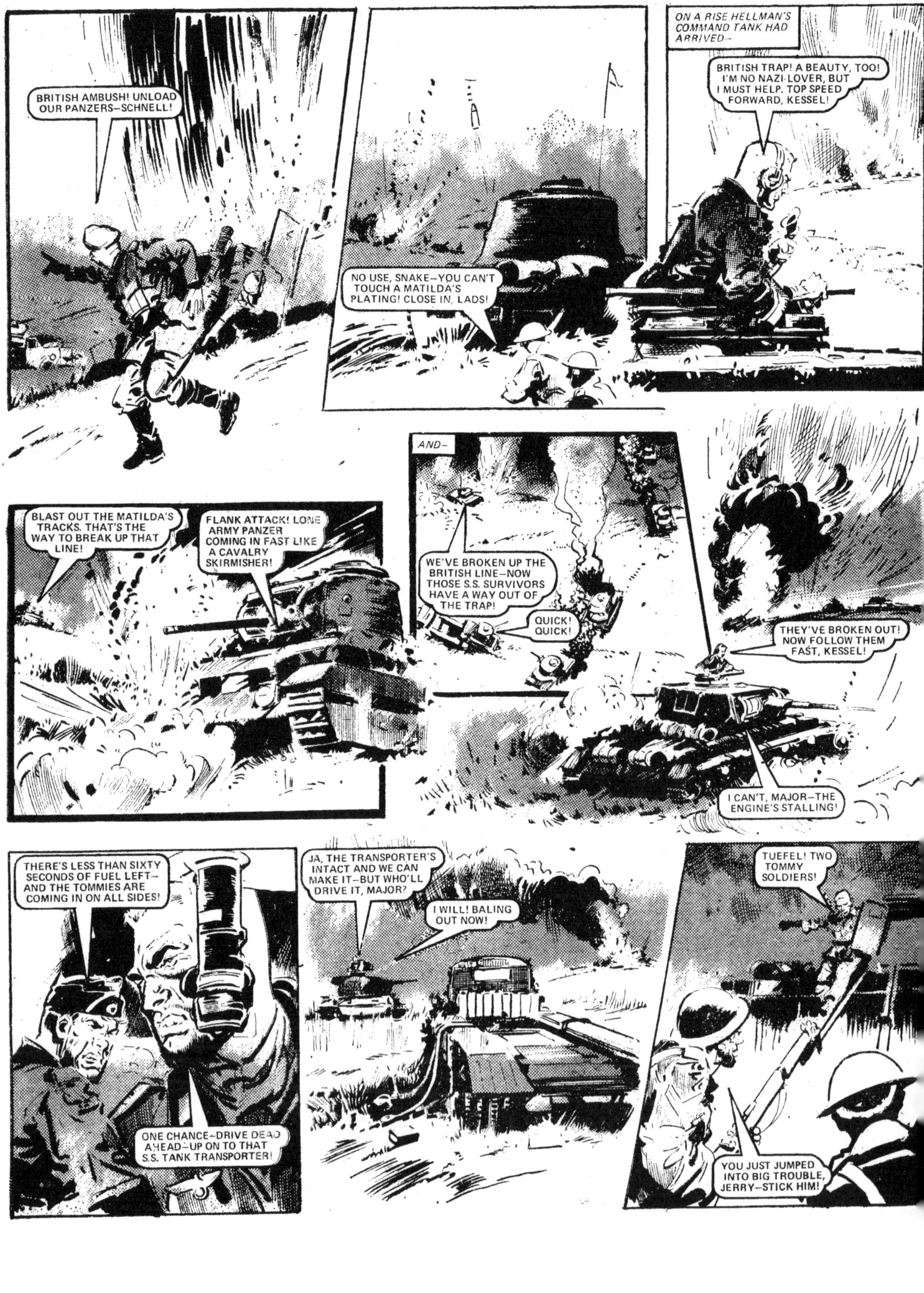

BRITISH AMBUSH! UNLOAD OUR PANZERS–SCHNELL!
NO USE, SNAKE–YOU CAN'T TOUCH A MATILDA'S PLATING! CLOSE IN, LADS!
ON A RISE HELLMAN'S COMMAND TANK HAD ARRIVED–
BRITISH TRAP! A BEAUTY, TOO! I'M NO NAZI-LOVER, BUT I MUST HELP. TOP SPEED FORWARD, KESSEL!
BLAST OUT THE MATILDA'S TRACKS. THAT'S THE WAY TO BREAK UP THAT LINE!
FLANK ATTACK! LONE ARMY PANZER COMING IN FAST LIKE A CAVALRY SKIRMISHER!
AND–
WE'VE BROKEN UP THE BRITISH LINE–NOW THOSE S.S. SURVIVORS HAVE A WAY OUT OF THE TRAP!
QUICK! QUICK!
THEY'VE BROKEN OUT! NOW FOLLOW THEM FAST, KESSEL!
I CAN'T, MAJOR–THE ENGINE'S STALLING!
THERE'S LESS THAN SIXTY SECONDS OF FUEL LEFT–AND THE TOMMIES ARE COMING IN ON ALL SIDES!
ONE CHANCE–DRIVE DEAD AHEAD–UP ON TO THAT S.S. TANK TRANSPORTER!
JA, THE TRANSPORTER'S INTACT AND WE CAN MAKE IT–BUT WHO'LL DRIVE IT, MAJOR?
I WILL! BALING OUT NOW!
TUEFEL! TWO TOMMY SOLDIERS!
YOU JUST JUMPED INTO BIG TROUBLE, JERRY–STICK HIM!

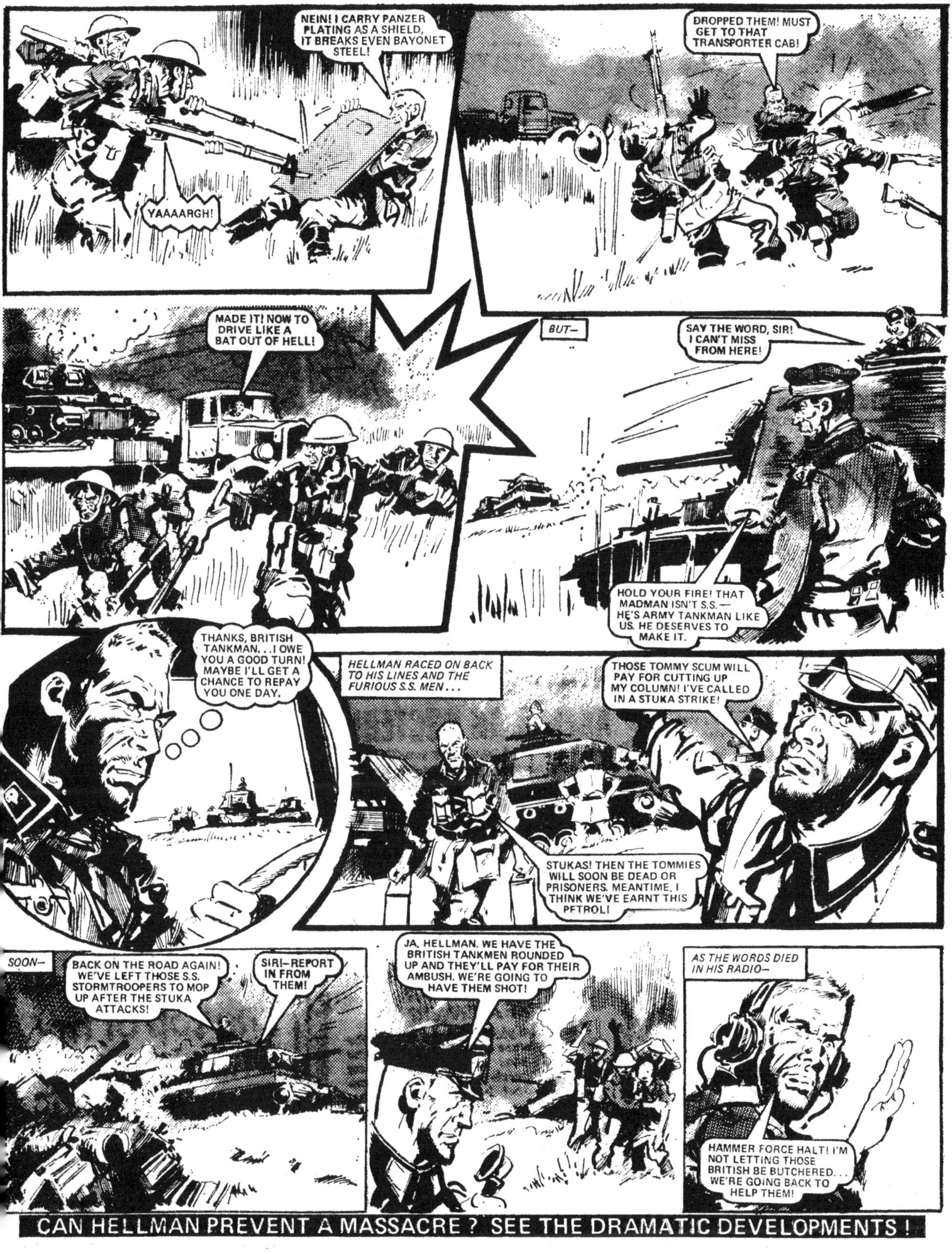
NEIN! I CARRY PANZER PLATING AS A SHIELD, IT BREAKS EVEN BAYONET STEEL!
YAAAARGH!
DROPPED THEM! MUST GET TO THAT TRANSPORTER CAB!
MADE IT! NOW TO DRIVE LIKE A BAT OUT OF HELL!
BUT—
SAY THE WORD, SIR! I CAN'T MISS FROM HERE!
HOLD YOUR FIRE! THAT MADMAN ISN'T S.S.— HE'S ARMY TANKMAN LIKE US. HE DESERVES TO MAKE IT.
THANKS, BRITISH TANKMAN. . . I OWE YOU A GOOD TURN! MAYBE I'LL GET A CHANCE TO REPAY YOU ONE DAY.
HELLMAN RACED ON BACK TO HIS LINES AND THE FURIOUS S.S. MEN . . .
THOSE TOMMY SCUM WILL PAY FOR CUTTING UP MY COLUMN! I'VE CALLED IN A STUKA STRIKE!
STUKAS! THEN THE TOMMIES WILL SOON BE DEAD OR PRISONERS. MEANTIME, I THINK WE'VE EARNT THIS PETROL!
SOON—
BACK ON THE ROAD AGAIN! WE'VE LEFT THOSE S.S. STORMTROOPERS TO MOP UP AFTER THE STUKA ATTACKS!
SIR!—REPORT IN FROM THEM!
JA, HELLMAN. WE HAVE THE BRITISH TANKMEN ROUNDED UP AND THEY'LL PAY FOR THEIR AMBUSH. WE'RE GOING TO HAVE THEM SHOT!
AS THE WORDS DIED IN HIS RADIO—
HAMMER FORCE HALT! I'M NOT LETTING THOSE BRITISH BE BUTCHERED. . . WE'RE GOING BACK TO HELP THEM!
CAN HELLMAN PREVENT A MASSACRE ? SEE THE DRAMATIC DEVELOPMENTS !

HELLMAN MAKES A BRAVE DECISION... BUT IT COULD COST HIM HIS LIFE !

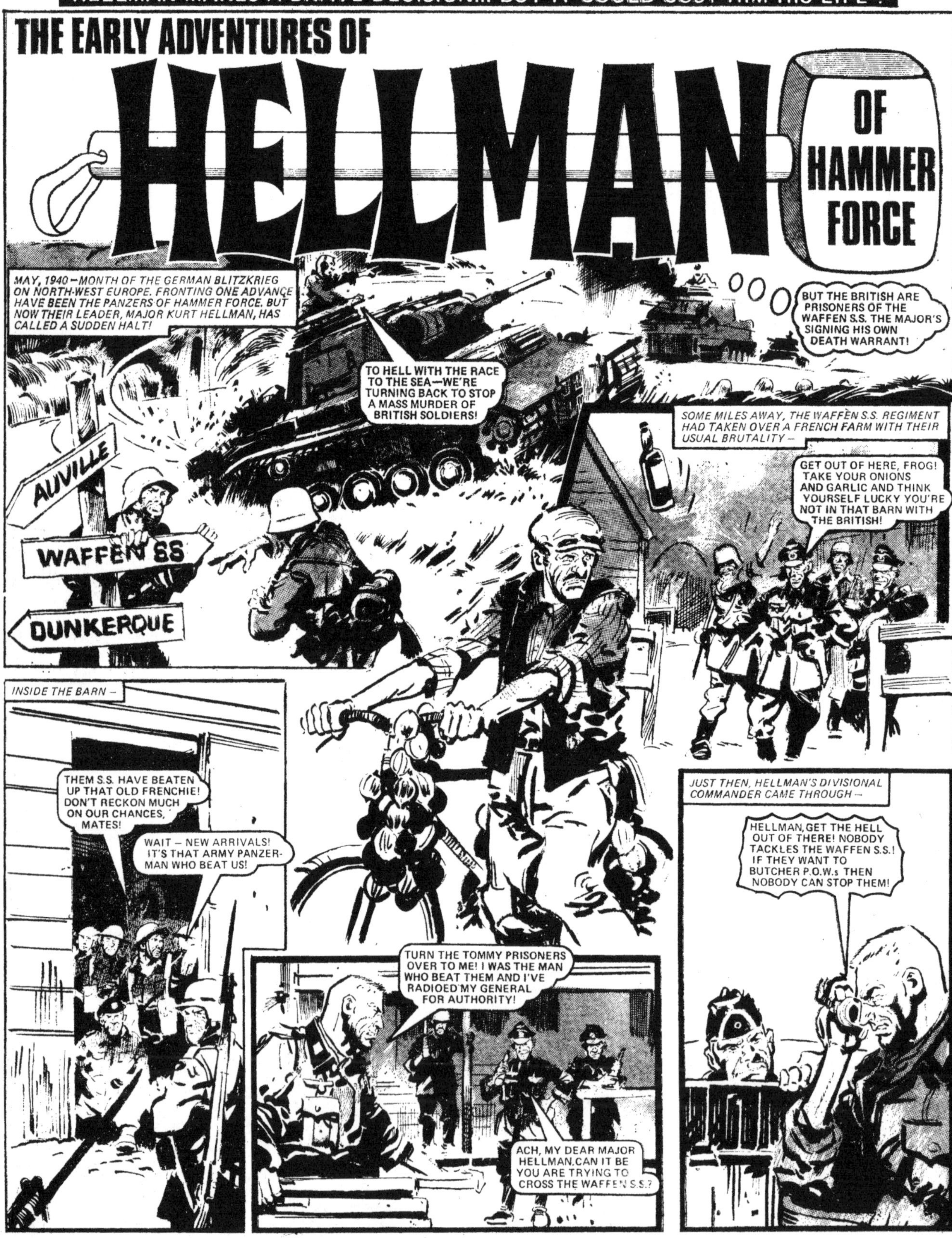

THE EARLY ADVENTURES OF
HELLMAN
OF HAMMER FORCE
MAY, 1940—MONTH OF THE GERMAN BLITZKRIEG ON NORTH-WEST EUROPE. FRONTING ONE ADVANCE HAVE BEEN THE PANZERS OF HAMMER FORCE. BUT NOW THEIR LEADER, MAJOR KURT HELLMAN, HAS CALLED A SUDDEN HALT!
TO HELL WITH THE RACE TO THE SEA—WE'RE TURNING BACK TO STOP A MASS MURDER OF BRITISH SOLDIERS!
BUT THE BRITISH ARE PRISONERS OF THE WAFFEN S.S. THE MAJOR'S SIGNING HIS OWN DEATH WARRANT!
AUVILLE
WAFFEN SS
DUNKERQUE
SOME MILES AWAY, THE WAFFEN S.S. REGIMENT HAD TAKEN OVER A FRENCH FARM WITH THEIR USUAL BRUTALITY—
GET OUT OF HERE, FROG! TAKE YOUR ONIONS AND GARLIC AND THINK YOURSELF LUCKY YOU'RE NOT IN THAT BARN WITH THE BRITISH!
INSIDE THE BARN—
THEM S.S. HAVE BEATEN UP THAT OLD FRENCHIE! DON'T RECKON MUCH ON OUR CHANCES, MATES!
WAIT — NEW ARRIVALS! IT'S THAT ARMY PANZER-MAN WHO BEAT US!
TURN THE TOMMY PRISONERS OVER TO ME! I WAS THE MAN WHO BEAT THEM AND I'VE RADIOED MY GENERAL FOR AUTHORITY!
ACH, MY DEAR MAJOR HELLMAN, CAN IT BE YOU ARE TRYING TO CROSS THE WAFFEN S.S.?
JUST THEN, HELLMAN'S DIVISIONAL COMMANDER CAME THROUGH—
HELLMAN, GET THE HELL OUT OF THERE! NOBODY TACKLES THE WAFFEN S.S.! IF THEY WANT TO BUTCHER P.O.W.s THEN NOBODY CAN STOP THEM!

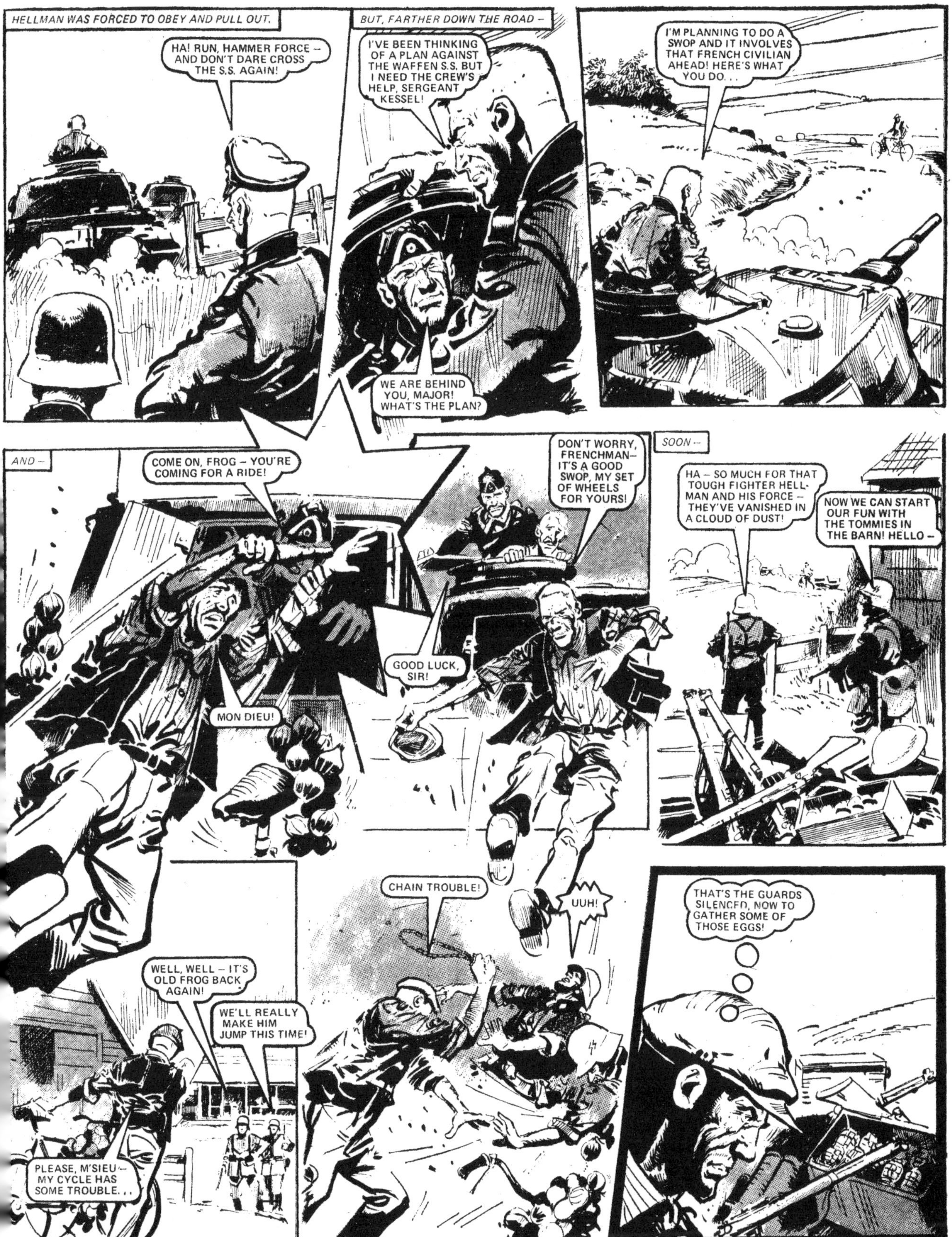
HELLMAN WAS FORCED TO OBEY AND PULL OUT.
HA! RUN, HAMMER FORCE – AND DON'T DARE CROSS THE S.S. AGAIN!
BUT, FARTHER DOWN THE ROAD –
I'VE BEEN THINKING OF A PLAN AGAINST THE WAFFEN S.S. BUT I NEED THE CREW'S HELP, SERGEANT KESSEL!
WE ARE BEHIND YOU, MAJOR! WHAT'S THE PLAN?
I'M PLANNING TO DO A SWOP AND IT INVOLVES THAT FRENCH CIVILIAN AHEAD! HERE'S WHAT YOU DO. . .
AND –
COME ON, FROG – YOU'RE COMING FOR A RIDE!
MON DIEU!
DON'T WORRY, FRENCHMAN – IT'S A GOOD SWOP, MY SET OF WHEELS FOR YOURS!
GOOD LUCK, SIR!
SOON –
HA – SO MUCH FOR THAT TOUGH FIGHTER HELLMAN AND HIS FORCE – THEY'VE VANISHED IN A CLOUD OF DUST!
NOW WE CAN START OUR FUN WITH THE TOMMIES IN THE BARN! HELLO –
WELL, WELL – IT'S OLD FROG BACK AGAIN!
WE'LL REALLY MAKE HIM JUMP THIS TIME!
PLEASE, M'SIEU – MY CYCLE HAS SOME TROUBLE. . .
CHAIN TROUBLE!
UUH!
THAT'S THE GUARDS SILENCED, NOW TO GATHER SOME OF THOSE EGGS!

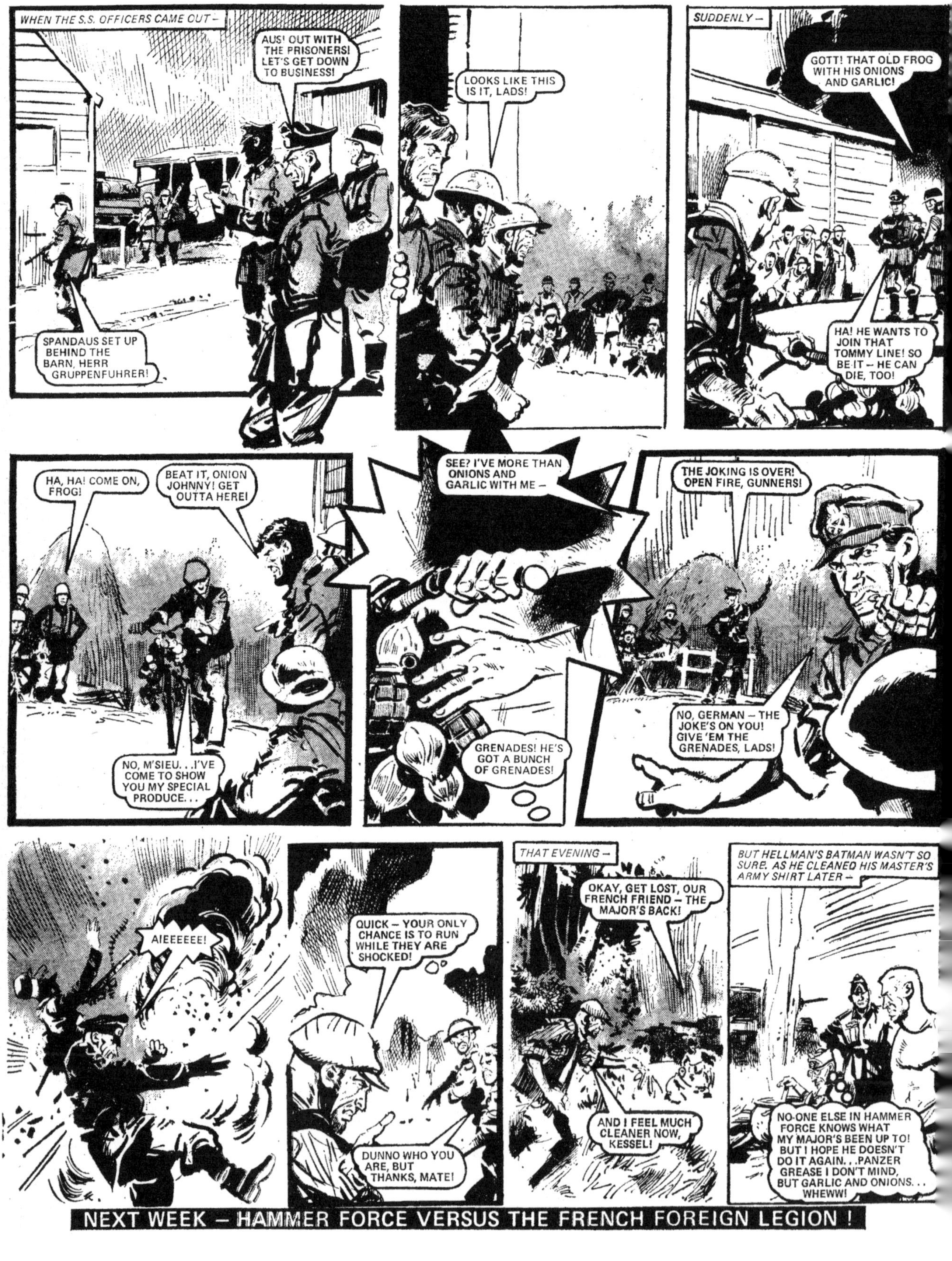
WHEN THE S.S. OFFICERS CAME OUT –
AUS! OUT WITH THE PRISONERS! LET'S GET DOWN TO BUSINESS!
SPANDAUS SET UP BEHIND THE BARN, HERR GRUPPENFUHRER!
LOOKS LIKE THIS IS IT, LADS!
SUDDENLY –
GOTT! THAT OLD FROG WITH HIS ONIONS AND GARLIC!
HA! HE WANTS TO JOIN THAT TOMMY LINE! SO BE IT – HE CAN DIE, TOO!
HA, HA! COME ON, FROG!
BEAT IT, ONION JOHNNY! GET OUTTA HERE!
NO, M'SIEU. . .I'VE COME TO SHOW YOU MY SPECIAL PRODUCE. . .
SEE? I'VE MORE THAN ONIONS AND GARLIC WITH ME –
GRENADES! HE'S GOT A BUNCH OF GRENADES!
THE JOKING IS OVER! OPEN FIRE, GUNNERS!
NO, GERMAN – THE JOKE'S ON YOU! GIVE 'EM THE GRENADES, LADS!
AIEEEEEE!
QUICK – YOUR ONLY CHANCE IS TO RUN WHILE THEY ARE SHOCKED!
DUNNO WHO YOU ARE, BUT THANKS, MATE!
THAT EVENING –
OKAY, GET LOST, OUR FRENCH FRIEND – THE MAJOR'S BACK!
AND I FEEL MUCH CLEANER NOW, KESSEL!
BUT HELLMAN'S BATMAN WASN'T SO SURE, AS HE CLEANED HIS MASTER'S ARMY SHIRT LATER –
NO-ONE ELSE IN HAMMER FORCE KNOWS WHAT MY MAJOR'S BEEN UP TO! BUT I HOPE HE DOESN'T DO IT AGAIN. . .PANZER GREASE I DON'T MIND, BUT GARLIC AND ONIONS. . . WHEWW!
NEXT WEEK – HAMMER FORCE VERSUS THE FRENCH FOREIGN LEGION!

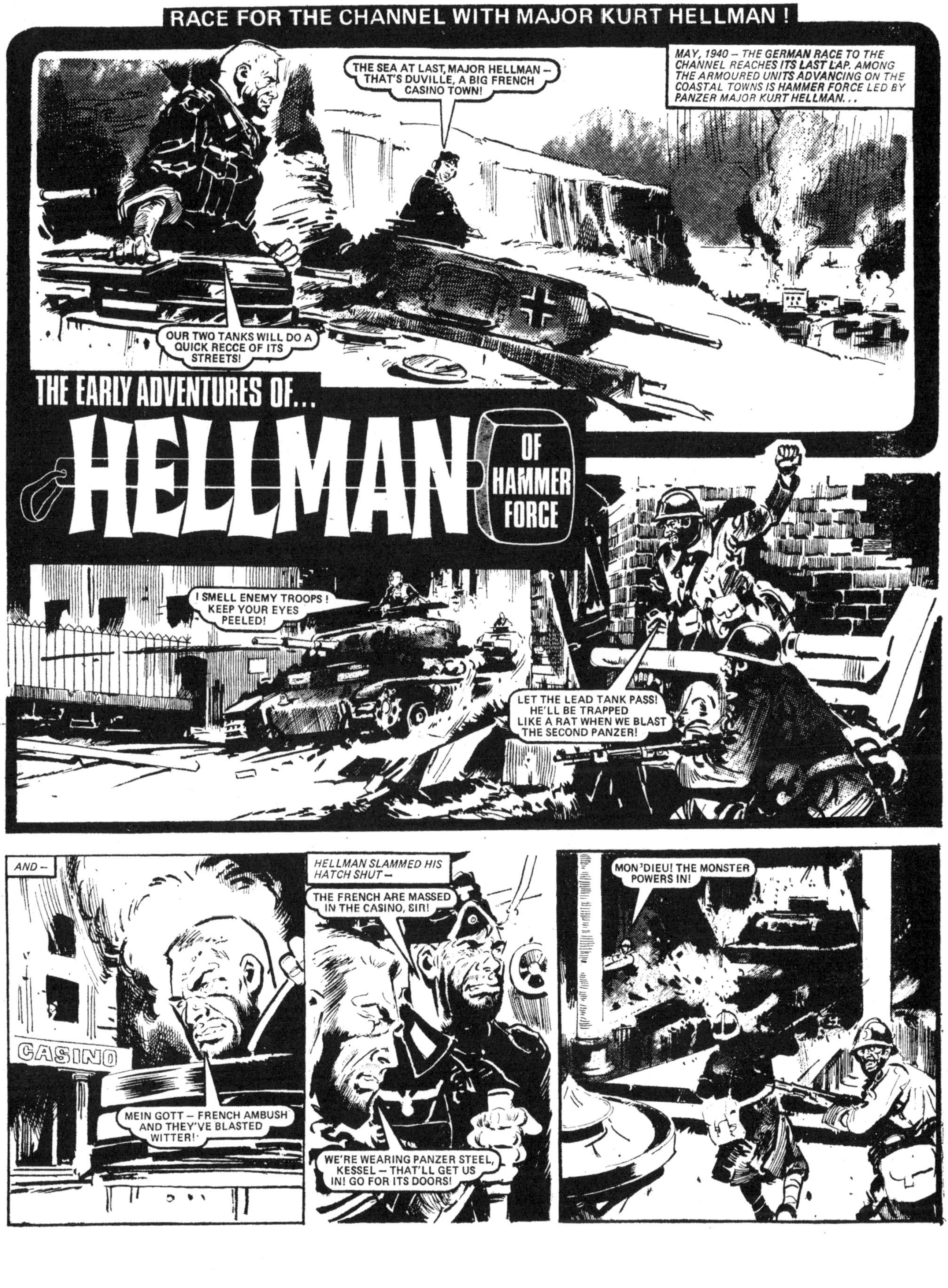

RACE FOR THE CHANNEL WITH MAJOR KURT HELLMAN !
MAY, 1940 – THE GERMAN RACE TO THE CHANNEL REACHES ITS LAST LAP. AMONG THE ARMOURED UNITS ADVANCING ON THE COASTAL TOWNS IS HAMMER FORCE LED BY PANZER MAJOR KURT HELLMAN. . .
THE SEA AT LAST, MAJOR HELLMAN – THAT'S DUVILLE, A BIG FRENCH CASINO TOWN!
OUR TWO TANKS WILL DO A QUICK RECCE OF ITS STREETS!
THE EARLY ADVENTURES OF...
HELLMAN
OF HAMMER FORCE
I SMELL ENEMY TROOPS ! KEEP YOUR EYES PEELED!
LET THE LEAD TANK PASS! HE'LL BE TRAPPED LIKE A RAT WHEN WE BLAST THE SECOND PANZER!
AND –
CASINO
MEIN GOTT – FRENCH AMBUSH AND THEY'VE BLASTED WITTER!
HELLMAN SLAMMED HIS HATCH SHUT –
THE FRENCH ARE MASSED IN THE CASINO, SIR!
WE'RE WEARING PANZER STEEL, KESSEL – THAT'LL GET US IN! GO FOR ITS DOORS!
MON DIEU! THE MONSTER POWERS IN!

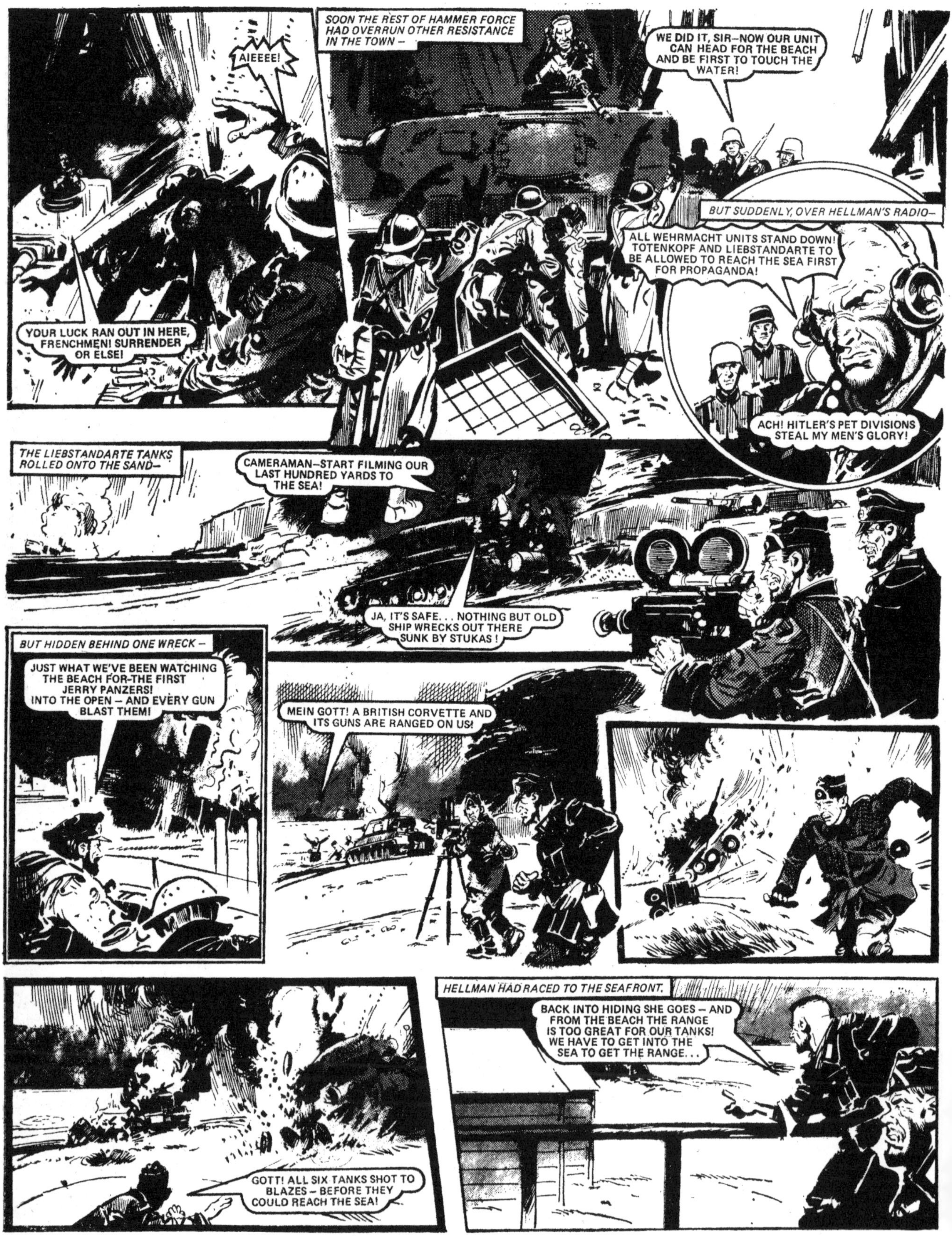
AIEEEE!
YOUR LUCK RAN OUT IN HERE, FRENCHMEN! SURRENDER OR ELSE!
SOON THE REST OF HAMMER FORCE HAD OVERRUN OTHER RESISTANCE IN THE TOWN –
WE DID IT, SIR–NOW OUR UNIT CAN HEAD FOR THE BEACH AND BE FIRST TO TOUCH THE WATER!
BUT SUDDENLY, OVER HELLMAN'S RADIO–
ALL WEHRMACHT UNITS STAND DOWN! TOTENKOPF AND LIEBSTANDARTE TO BE ALLOWED TO REACH THE SEA FIRST FOR PROPAGANDA!
ACH! HITLER'S PET DIVISIONS STEAL MY MEN'S GLORY!
THE LIEBSTANDARTE TANKS ROLLED ONTO THE SAND–
CAMERAMAN–START FILMING OUR LAST HUNDRED YARDS TO THE SEA!
JA, IT'S SAFE. . . NOTHING BUT OLD SHIP WRECKS OUT THERE SUNK BY STUKAS!
BUT HIDDEN BEHIND ONE WRECK –
JUST WHAT WE'VE BEEN WATCHING THE BEACH FOR–THE FIRST JERRY PANZERS! INTO THE OPEN – AND EVERY GUN BLAST THEM!
MEIN GOTT! A BRITISH CORVETTE AND ITS GUNS ARE RANGED ON US!
GOTT! ALL SIX TANKS SHOT TO BLAZES – BEFORE THEY COULD REACH THE SEA!
HELLMAN HAD RACED TO THE SEAFRONT.
BACK INTO HIDING SHE GOES – AND FROM THE BEACH THE RANGE IS TOO GREAT FOR OUR TANKS! WE HAVE TO GET INTO THE SEA TO GET THE RANGE. . .

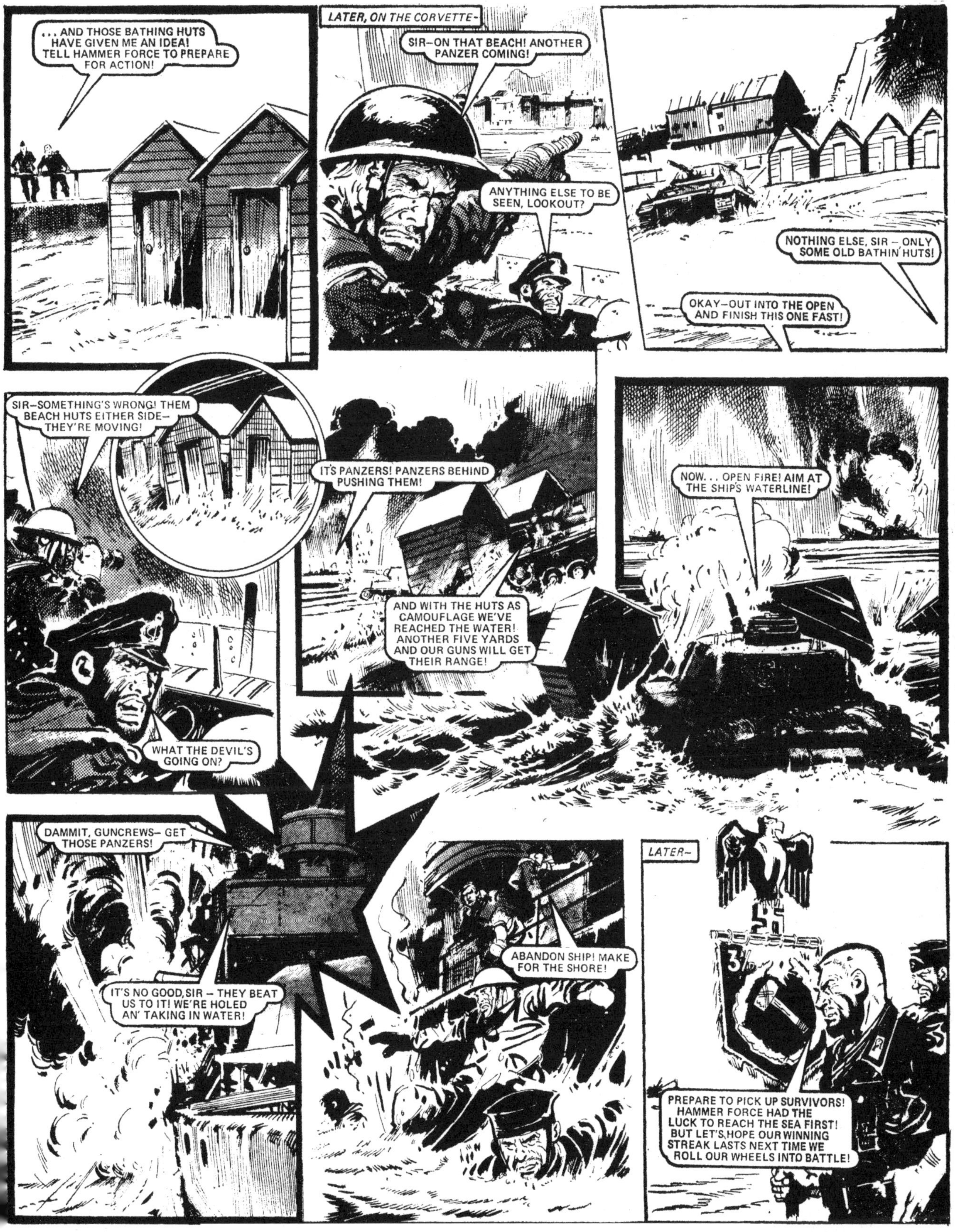

. . . AND THOSE BATHING HUTS HAVE GIVEN ME AN IDEA! TELL HAMMER FORCE TO PREPARE FOR ACTION!
LATER, ON THE CORVETTE-
SIR—ON THAT BEACH! ANOTHER PANZER COMING!
ANYTHING ELSE TO BE SEEN, LOOKOUT?
NOTHING ELSE, SIR – ONLY SOME OLD BATHIN' HUTS!
OKAY—OUT INTO THE OPEN AND FINISH THIS ONE FAST!
SIR—SOMETHING'S WRONG! THEM BEACH HUTS EITHER SIDE— THEY'RE MOVING!
WHAT THE DEVIL'S GOING ON?
IT'S PANZERS! PANZERS BEHIND PUSHING THEM!
AND WITH THE HUTS AS CAMOUFLAGE WE'VE REACHED THE WATER! ANOTHER FIVE YARDS AND OUR GUNS WILL GET THEIR RANGE!
NOW. . . OPEN FIRE! AIM AT THE SHIP'S WATERLINE!
DAMMIT, GUNCREWS– GET THOSE PANZERS!
IT'S NO GOOD, SIR – THEY BEAT US TO IT! WE'RE HOLED AN' TAKING IN WATER!
ABANDON SHIP! MAKE FOR THE SHORE!
LATER-
PREPARE TO PICK UP SURVIVORS! HAMMER FORCE HAD THE LUCK TO REACH THE SEA FIRST! BUT LET'S HOPE OUR WINNING STREAK LASTS NEXT TIME WE ROLL OUR WHEELS INTO BATTLE!
SSION ENDS...MISSION ENDS...MISSION ENDS...MISSION ENDS...MISSION ENDS...MISSION ENDS...MISSION ENDS...

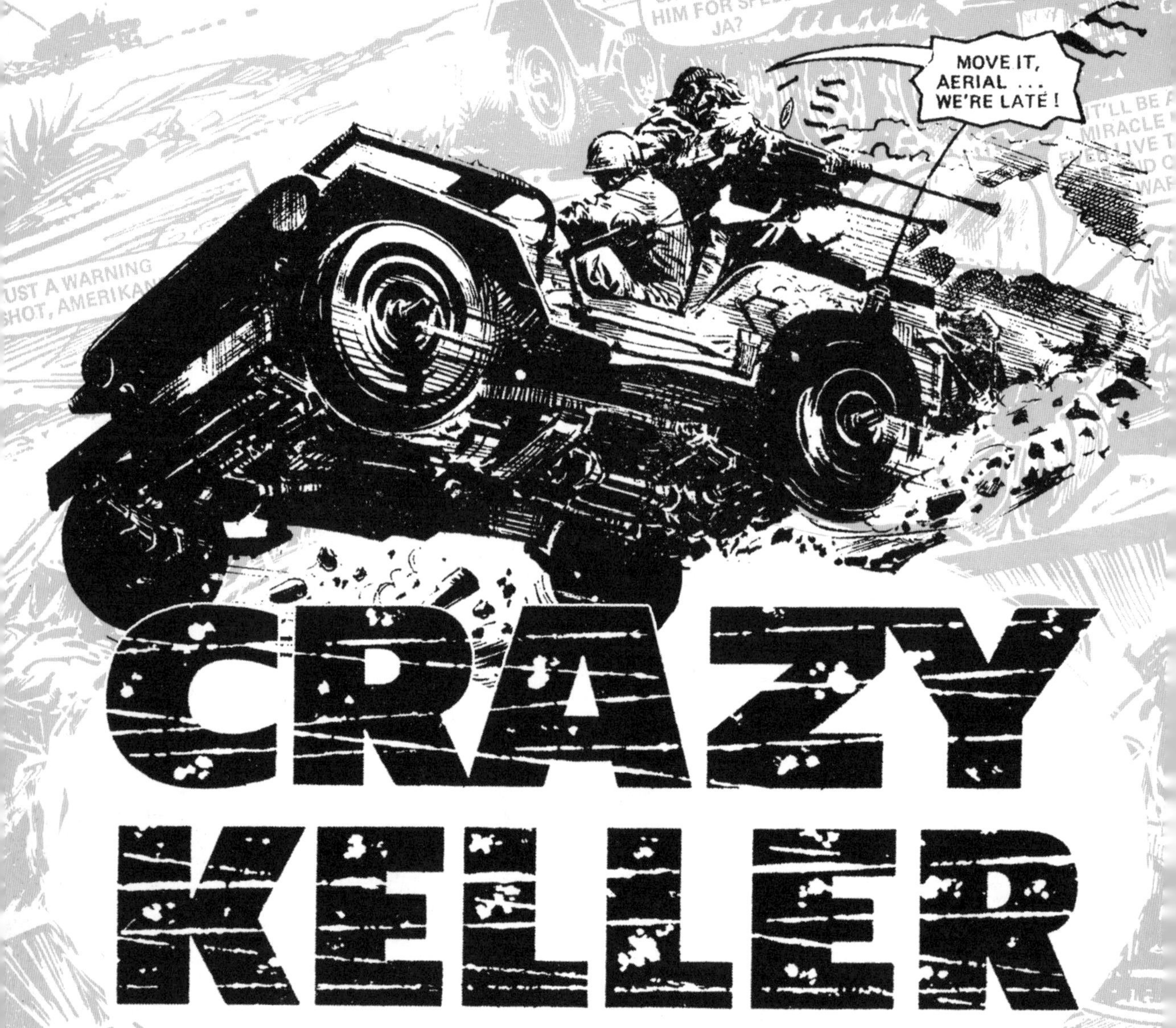
MOVE IT, AERIAL . . . WE'RE LATE !

CRAZY KELLER

"MOVE THAT TANK BEFORE I PUT YOUR FAT, STUPID HEAD INTO ORBIT!"

Freewheeling, shifty Kermit Keller was the fastest driver in the US Army Signal Corps, a scrounger and a war profiteer to boot — although almost always for a good cause. Aided by his long-suffering assistant, Corporal "Aerial" Arkin, Keller was determined to leave the war rich and God help any man that got in his way — Allies or Axis!

Now he races around the Italian countryside in "Scoot 3", his souped-up jeep, blasting the enemy with his mounted anti-aircraft guns while he tries to protect his ill-gotten gains.

A wholly irreverent war story, reminiscent in tone of the classic war movies *Kelly's Heroes* and *M*A*S*H*, 'Crazy Keller' crashed into *Battle* on July 1978 and lasted for fourteen months before going out with a bang.

NOTES FROM THE FRONTLINE:

"The title never sat easily with me, it felt contrived. And truth be told he wasn't one of my favourite characters. We were always trying to replace Major Eazy and wanted another rebellious character but I don't think we got it quite right. We needed a moral twist, so despite the fact he was a war profiteer, the story would have to end with Keller's actions being for the good of the war. Maybe he would have been a better character if he'd been an out-and-out villain? We were always treading dangerous ground with *Battle*. In one way we thought let's make it tough and gritty, but we had a lot of people on our backs — not just the management and parents but MPs too! I had to be careful otherwise some of my contributors would have gone really over board." — **Dave Hunt**

WRITTEN BY Alan Hebden
DRAWN BY Eric Bradbury

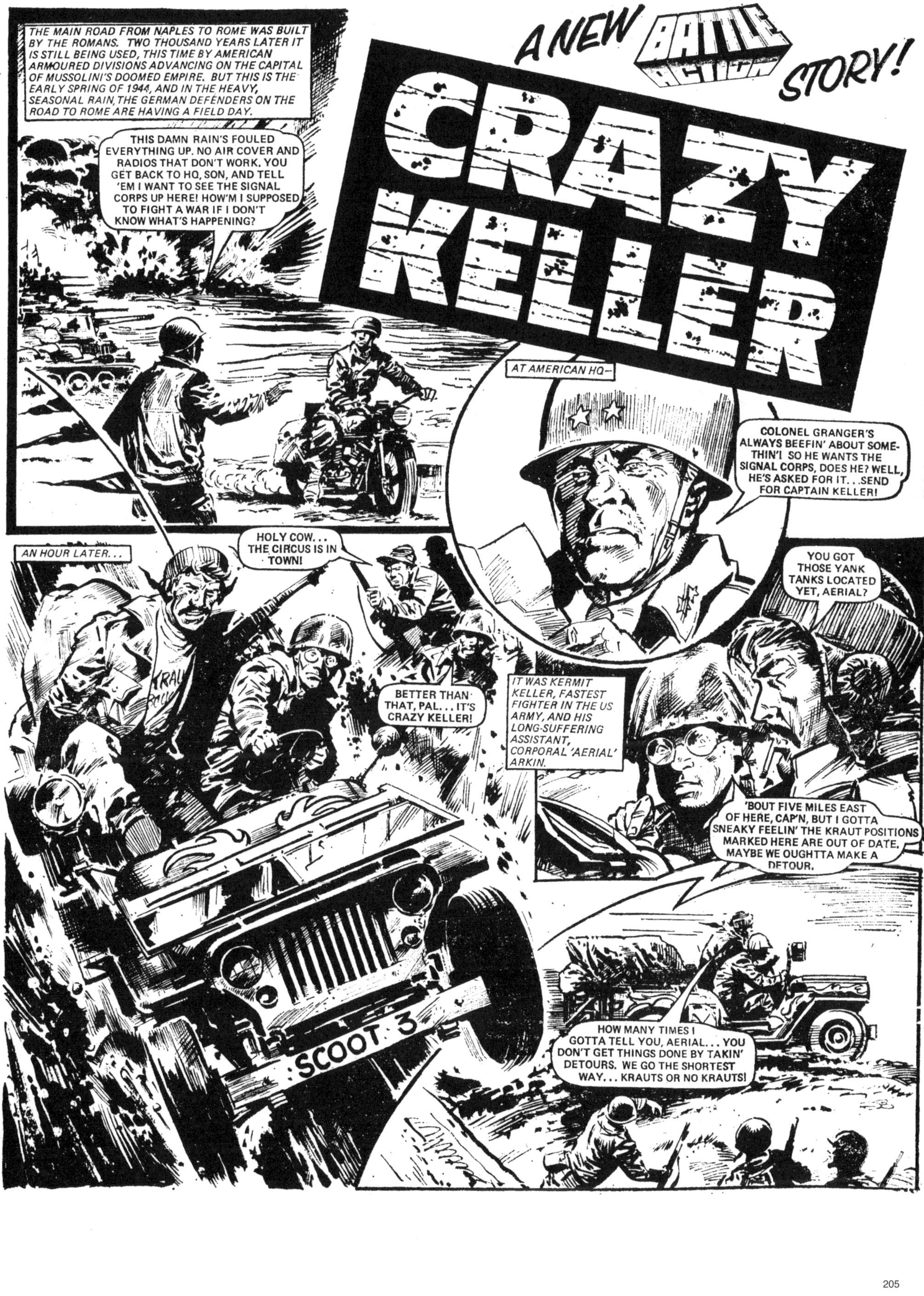
A NEW BATTLE ACTION STORY!
CRAZY KELLER
THE MAIN ROAD FROM NAPLES TO ROME WAS BUILT BY THE ROMANS. TWO THOUSAND YEARS LATER IT IS STILL BEING USED, THIS TIME BY AMERICAN ARMOURED DIVISIONS ADVANCING ON THE CAPITAL OF MUSSOLINI'S DOOMED EMPIRE. BUT THIS IS THE EARLY SPRING OF 1944, AND IN THE HEAVY, SEASONAL RAIN, THE GERMAN DEFENDERS ON THE ROAD TO ROME ARE HAVING A FIELD DAY.
THIS DAMN RAIN'S FOULED EVERYTHING UP. NO AIR COVER AND RADIOS THAT DON'T WORK. YOU GET BACK TO HQ, SON, AND TELL 'EM I WANT TO SEE THE SIGNAL CORPS UP HERE! HOW'M I SUPPOSED TO FIGHT A WAR IF I DON'T KNOW WHAT'S HAPPENING?
AT AMERICAN HQ—
COLONEL GRANGER'S ALWAYS BEEFIN' ABOUT SOMETHIN'! SO HE WANTS THE SIGNAL CORPS, DOES HE? WELL, HE'S ASKED FOR IT...SEND FOR CAPTAIN KELLER!
AN HOUR LATER...
HOLY COW... THE CIRCUS IS IN TOWN!
BETTER THAN THAT, PAL... IT'S CRAZY KELLER!
SCOOT 3
IT WAS KERMIT KELLER, FASTEST FIGHTER IN THE US ARMY, AND HIS LONG-SUFFERING ASSISTANT, CORPORAL 'AERIAL' ARKIN.
YOU GOT THOSE YANK TANKS LOCATED YET, AERIAL?
'BOUT FIVE MILES EAST OF HERE, CAP'N, BUT I GOTTA SNEAKY FEELIN' THE KRAUT POSITIONS MARKED HERE ARE OUT OF DATE. MAYBE WE OUGHTTA MAKE A DETOUR.
HOW MANY TIMES I GOTTA TELL YOU, AERIAL... YOU DON'T GET THINGS DONE BY TAKIN' DETOURS. WE GO THE SHORTEST WAY... KRAUTS OR NO KRAUTS!

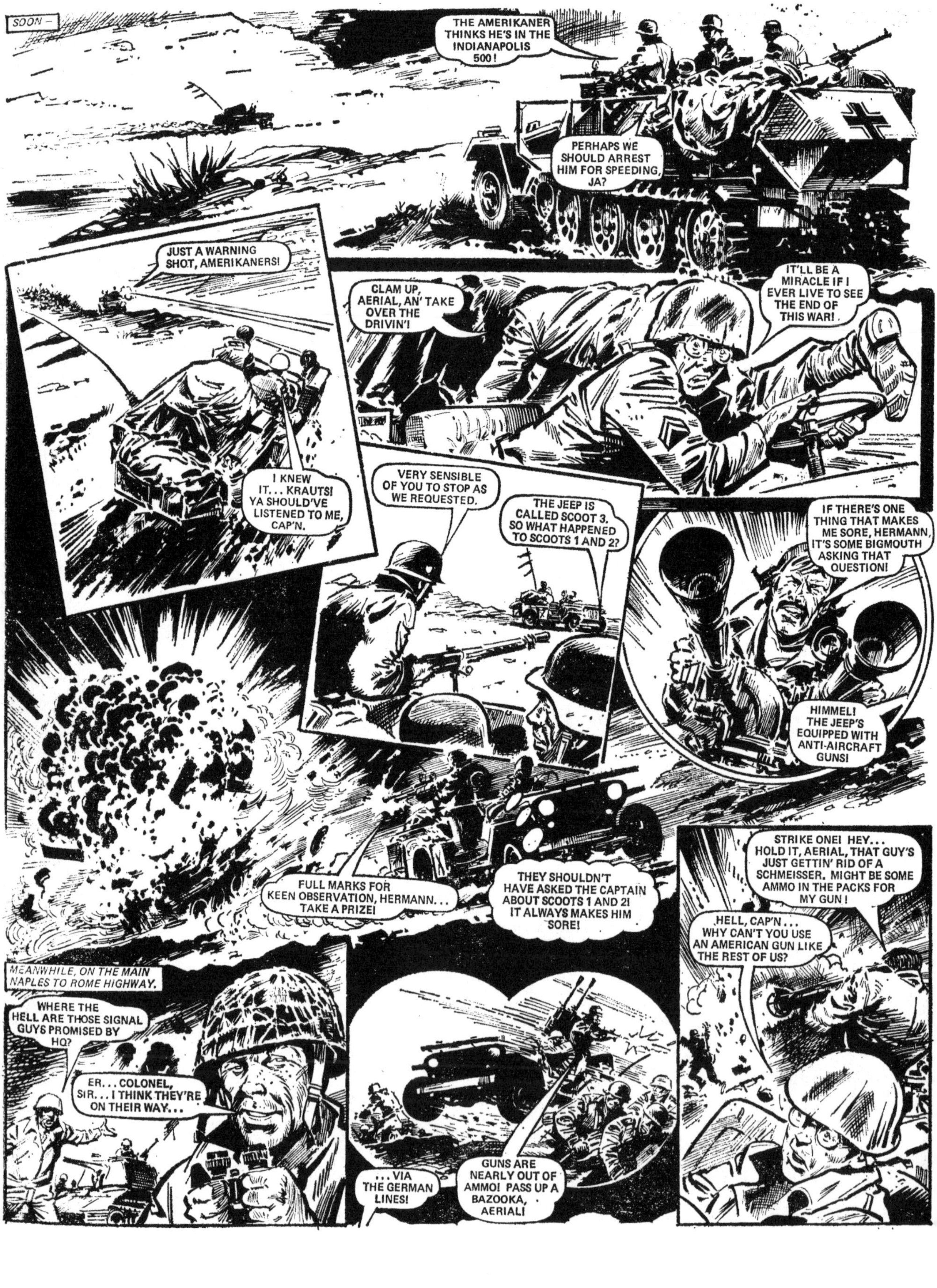
SOON —
THE AMERIKANER THINKS HE'S IN THE INDIANAPOLIS 500!
PERHAPS WE SHOULD ARREST HIM FOR SPEEDING, JA?
JUST A WARNING SHOT, AMERIKANERS!
I KNEW IT... KRAUTS! YA SHOULD'VE LISTENED TO ME, CAP'N.
CLAM UP, AERIAL, AN' TAKE OVER THE DRIVIN'!
IT'LL BE A MIRACLE IF I EVER LIVE TO SEE THE END OF THIS WAR!
VERY SENSIBLE OF YOU TO STOP AS WE REQUESTED.
THE JEEP IS CALLED SCOOT 3. SO WHAT HAPPENED TO SCOOTS 1 AND 2?
IF THERE'S ONE THING THAT MAKES ME SORE, HERMANN, IT'S SOME BIGMOUTH ASKING THAT QUESTION!
HIMMEL! THE JEEP'S EQUIPPED WITH ANTI-AIRCRAFT GUNS!
FULL MARKS FOR KEEN OBSERVATION, HERMANN... TAKE A PRIZE!
THEY SHOULDN'T HAVE ASKED THE CAPTAIN ABOUT SCOOTS 1 AND 2! IT ALWAYS MAKES HIM SORE!
STRIKE ONE! HEY... HOLD IT, AERIAL, THAT GUY'S JUST GETTIN' RID OF A SCHMEISSER. MIGHT BE SOME AMMO IN THE PACKS FOR MY GUN!
HELL, CAP'N... WHY CAN'T YOU USE AN AMERICAN GUN LIKE THE REST OF US?
MEANWHILE, ON THE MAIN NAPLES TO ROME HIGHWAY.
WHERE THE HELL ARE THOSE SIGNAL GUYS PROMISED BY HQ?
ER... COLONEL, SIR... I THINK THEY'RE ON THEIR WAY...
... VIA THE GERMAN LINES!
GUNS ARE NEARLY OUT OF AMMO! PASS UP A BAZOOKA, AERIAL!

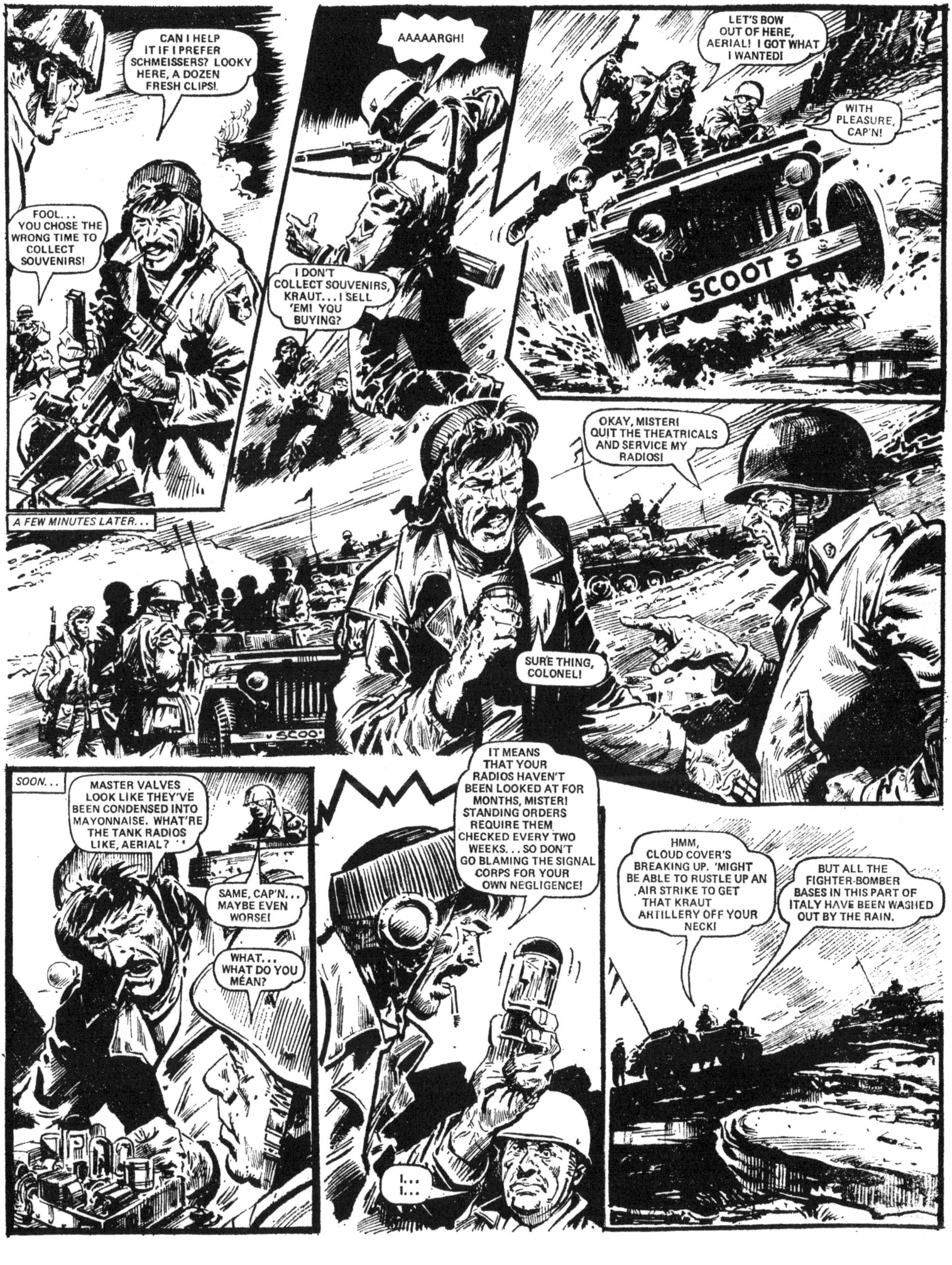
CAN I HELP IT IF I PREFER SCHMEISSERS? LOOKY HERE, A DOZEN FRESH CLIPS!.
FOOL... YOU CHOSE THE WRONG TIME TO COLLECT SOUVENIRS!
AAAAARGH!
I DON'T COLLECT SOUVENIRS, KRAUT... I SELL 'EM! YOU BUYING?
LET'S BOW OUT OF HERE, AERIAL! I GOT WHAT I WANTED!
WITH PLEASURE, CAP'N!
SCOOT 3
A FEW MINUTES LATER...
OKAY, MISTER! QUIT THE THEATRICALS AND SERVICE MY RADIOS!
SURE THING, COLONEL!
SCOO
SOON...
MASTER VALVES LOOK LIKE THEY'VE BEEN CONDENSED INTO MAYONNAISE. WHAT'RE THE TANK RADIOS LIKE, AERIAL?
SAME, CAP'N... MAYBE EVEN WORSE!
WHAT... WHAT DO YOU MEAN?
IT MEANS THAT YOUR RADIOS HAVEN'T BEEN LOOKED AT FOR MONTHS, MISTER! STANDING ORDERS REQUIRE THEM CHECKED EVERY TWO WEEKS... SO DON'T GO BLAMING THE SIGNAL CORPS FOR YOUR OWN NEGLIGENCE!
I... I...
HMM, CLOUD COVER'S BREAKING UP. 'MIGHT BE ABLE TO RUSTLE UP AN AIR STRIKE TO GET THAT KRAUT ARTILLERY OFF YOUR NECK!
BUT ALL THE FIGHTER-BOMBER BASES IN THIS PART OF ITALY HAVE BEEN WASHED OUT BY THE RAIN.

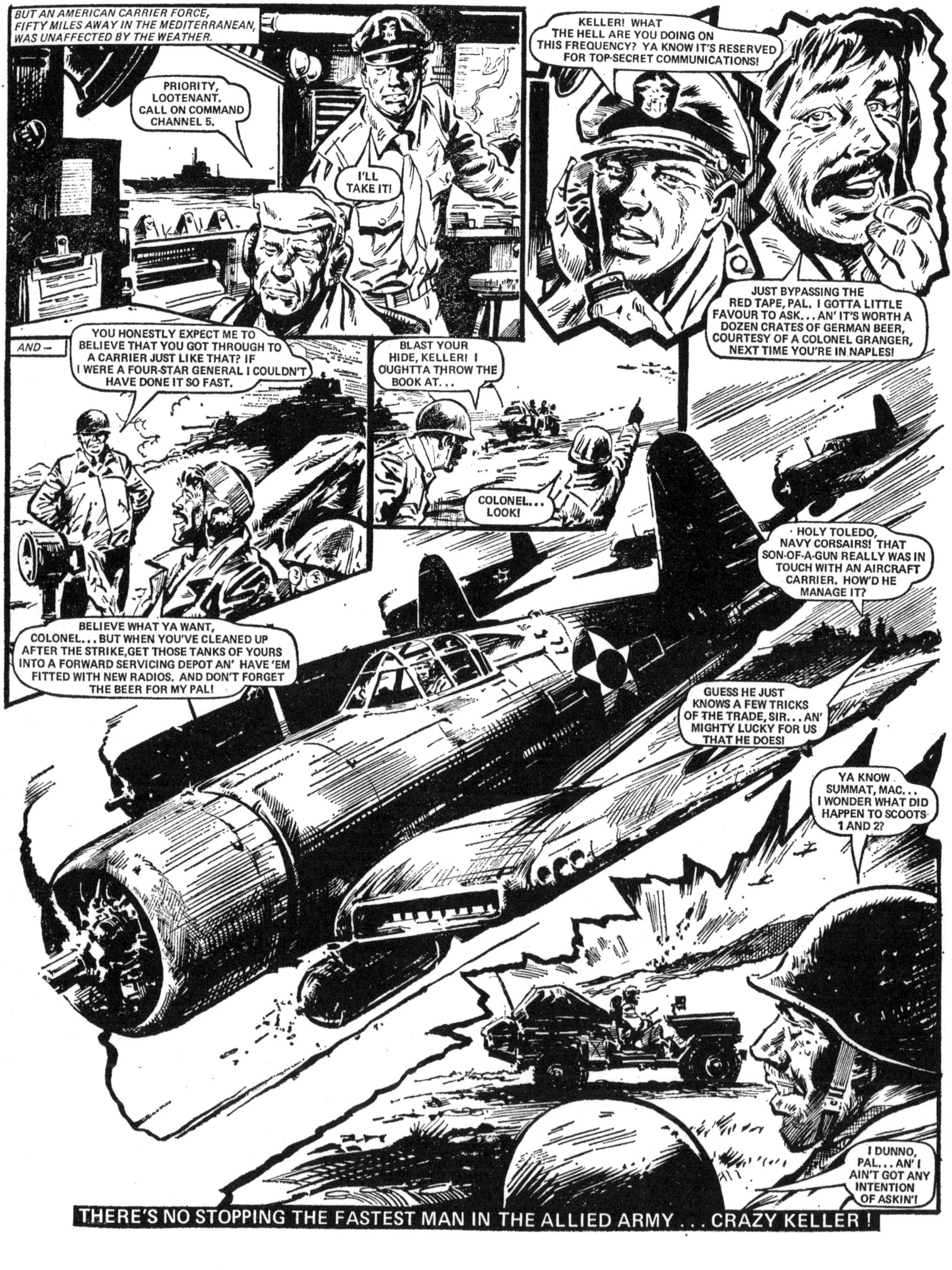
BUT AN AMERICAN CARRIER FORCE, FIFTY MILES AWAY IN THE MEDITERRANEAN, WAS UNAFFECTED BY THE WEATHER.
PRIORITY, LOOTENANT. CALL ON COMMAND CHANNEL 5.
I'LL TAKE IT!
KELLER! WHAT THE HELL ARE YOU DOING ON THIS FREQUENCY? YA KNOW IT'S RESERVED FOR TOP-SECRET COMMUNICATIONS!
JUST BYPASSING THE RED TAPE, PAL. I GOTTA LITTLE FAVOUR TO ASK... AN' IT'S WORTH A DOZEN CRATES OF GERMAN BEER, COURTESY OF A COLONEL GRANGER, NEXT TIME YOU'RE IN NAPLES!
AND –
YOU HONESTLY EXPECT ME TO BELIEVE THAT YOU GOT THROUGH TO A CARRIER JUST LIKE THAT? IF I WERE A FOUR-STAR GENERAL I COULDN'T HAVE DONE IT SO FAST.
BLAST YOUR HIDE, KELLER! I OUGHTTA THROW THE BOOK AT...
COLONEL... LOOK!
BELIEVE WHAT YA WANT, COLONEL... BUT WHEN YOU'VE CLEANED UP AFTER THE STRIKE, GET THOSE TANKS OF YOURS INTO A FORWARD SERVICING DEPOT AN' HAVE 'EM FITTED WITH NEW RADIOS. AND DON'T FORGET THE BEER FOR MY PAL!
HOLY TOLEDO, NAVY CORSAIRS! THAT SON-OF-A-GUN REALLY WAS IN TOUCH WITH AN AIRCRAFT CARRIER. HOW'D HE MANAGE IT?
GUESS HE JUST KNOWS A FEW TRICKS OF THE TRADE, SIR... AN' MIGHTY LUCKY FOR US THAT HE DOES!
YA KNOW SUMMAT, MAC... I WONDER WHAT DID HAPPEN TO SCOOTS 1 AND 2?
I DUNNO, PAL... AN' I AIN'T GOT ANY INTENTION OF ASKIN'!
THERE'S NO STOPPING THE FASTEST MAN IN THE ALLIED ARMY.... CRAZY KELLER!

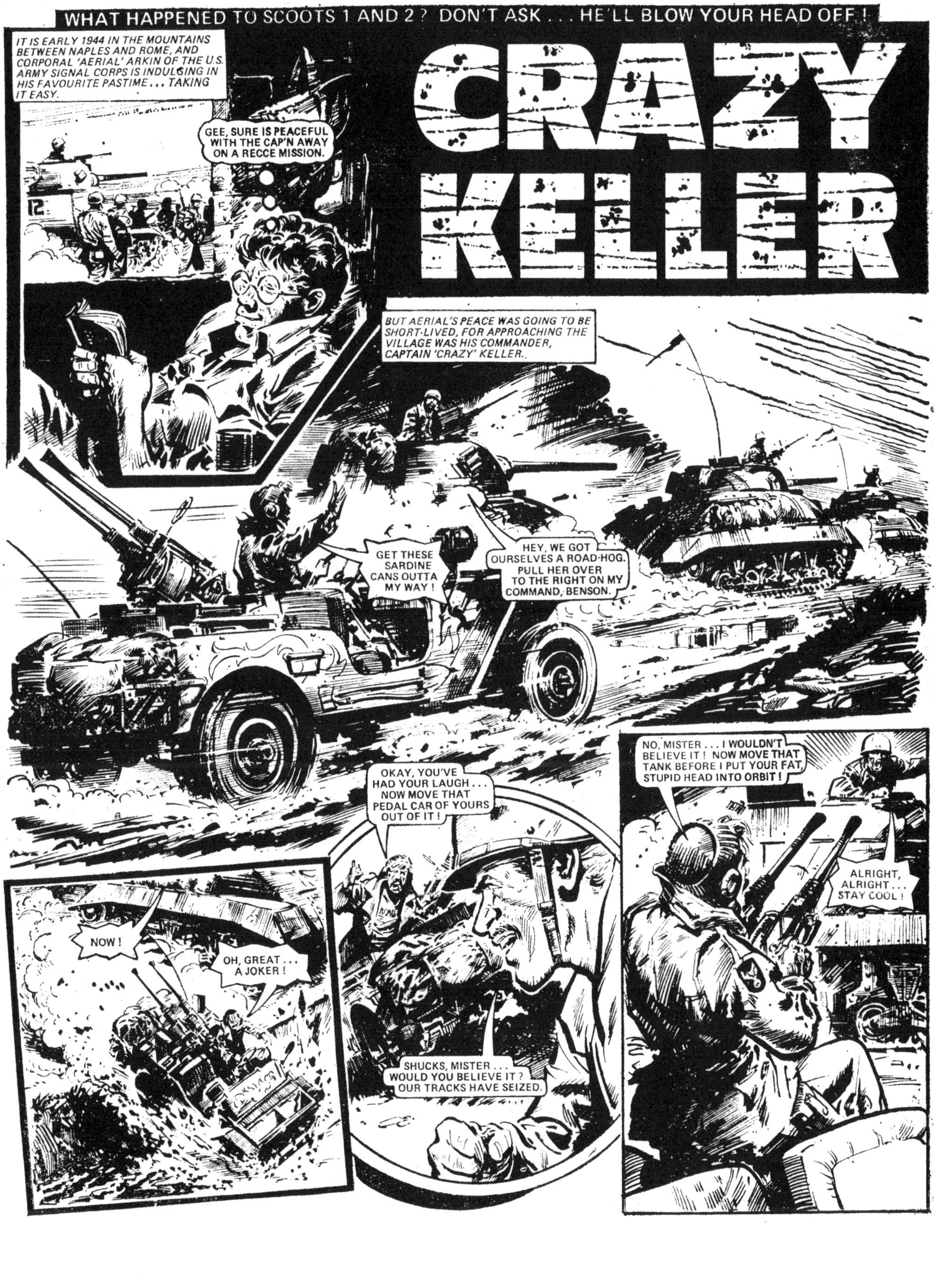
WHAT HAPPENED TO SCOOTS 1 AND 2? DON'T ASK . . . HE'LL BLOW YOUR HEAD OFF!
CRAZY KELLER
IT IS EARLY 1944 IN THE MOUNTAINS BETWEEN NAPLES AND ROME, AND CORPORAL 'AERIAL' ARKIN OF THE U.S. ARMY SIGNAL CORPS IS INDULGING IN HIS FAVOURITE PASTIME . . . TAKING IT EASY.
GEE, SURE IS PEACEFUL WITH THE CAP'N AWAY ON A RECCE MISSION.
BUT AERIAL'S PEACE WAS GOING TO BE SHORT-LIVED, FOR APPROACHING THE VILLAGE WAS HIS COMMANDER, CAPTAIN 'CRAZY' KELLER..
HEY, WE GOT OURSELVES A ROAD-HOG. PULL HER OVER TO THE RIGHT ON MY COMMAND, BENSON.
GET THESE SARDINE CANS OUTTA MY WAY!
NOW!
OH, GREAT . . . A JOKER!
OKAY, YOU'VE HAD YOUR LAUGH . . . NOW MOVE THAT PEDAL CAR OF YOURS OUT OF IT!
SHUCKS, MISTER . . . WOULD YOU BELIEVE IT? OUR TRACKS HAVE SEIZED.
NO, MISTER . . . I WOULDN'T BELIEVE IT! NOW MOVE THAT TANK BEFORE I PUT YOUR FAT, STUPID HEAD INTO ORBIT!
ALRIGHT, ALRIGHT . . . STAY COOL!

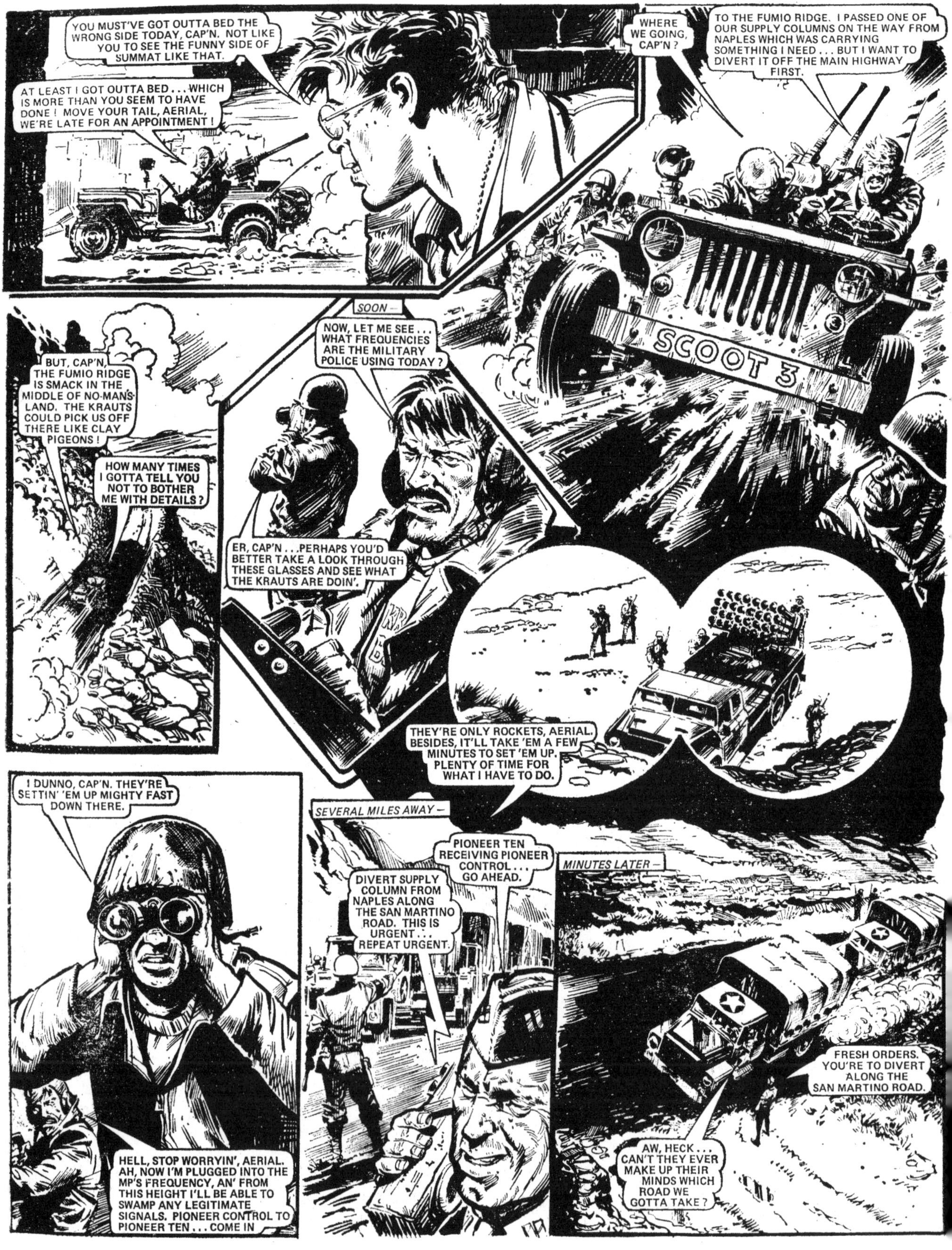
YOU MUST'VE GOT OUTTA BED THE WRONG SIDE TODAY, CAP'N. NOT LIKE YOU TO SEE THE FUNNY SIDE OF SUMMAT LIKE THAT.
AT LEAST I GOT OUTTA BED . . . WHICH IS MORE THAN YOU SEEM TO HAVE DONE ! MOVE YOUR TAIL, AERIAL, WE'RE LATE FOR AN APPOINTMENT !
WHERE WE GOING, CAP'N ?
TO THE FUMIO RIDGE. I PASSED ONE OF OUR SUPPLY COLUMNS ON THE WAY FROM NAPLES WHICH WAS CARRYING SOMETHING I NEED . . . BUT I WANT TO DIVERT IT OFF THE MAIN HIGHWAY FIRST.
SCOOT 3
BUT, CAP'N, THE FUMIO RIDGE IS SMACK IN THE MIDDLE OF NO-MANS-LAND. THE KRAUTS COULD PICK US OFF THERE LIKE CLAY PIGEONS !
HOW MANY TIMES I GOTTA TELL YOU NOT TO BOTHER ME WITH DETAILS ?
SOON —
NOW, LET ME SEE . . . WHAT FREQUENCIES ARE THE MILITARY POLICE USING TODAY ?
ER, CAP'N . . . PERHAPS YOU'D BETTER TAKE A LOOK THROUGH THESE GLASSES AND SEE WHAT THE KRAUTS ARE DOIN'.
THEY'RE ONLY ROCKETS, AERIAL. BESIDES, IT'LL TAKE 'EM A FEW MINUTES TO SET 'EM UP. PLENTY OF TIME FOR WHAT I HAVE TO DO.
I DUNNO, CAP'N. THEY'RE SETTIN' 'EM UP MIGHTY FAST DOWN THERE.
HELL, STOP WORRYIN', AERIAL. AH, NOW I'M PLUGGED INTO THE MP'S FREQUENCY, AN' FROM THIS HEIGHT I'LL BE ABLE TO SWAMP ANY LEGITIMATE SIGNALS. PIONEER CONTROL TO PIONEER TEN . . . COME IN
SEVERAL MILES AWAY —
PIONEER TEN RECEIVING PIONEER CONTROL . . . GO AHEAD.
DIVERT SUPPLY COLUMN FROM NAPLES ALONG THE SAN MARTINO ROAD. THIS IS URGENT . . . REPEAT URGENT.
MINUTES LATER —
FRESH ORDERS. YOU'RE TO DIVERT ALONG THE SAN MARTINO ROAD.
AW, HECK . . . CAN'T THEY EVER MAKE UP THEIR MINDS WHICH ROAD WE GOTTA TAKE ?

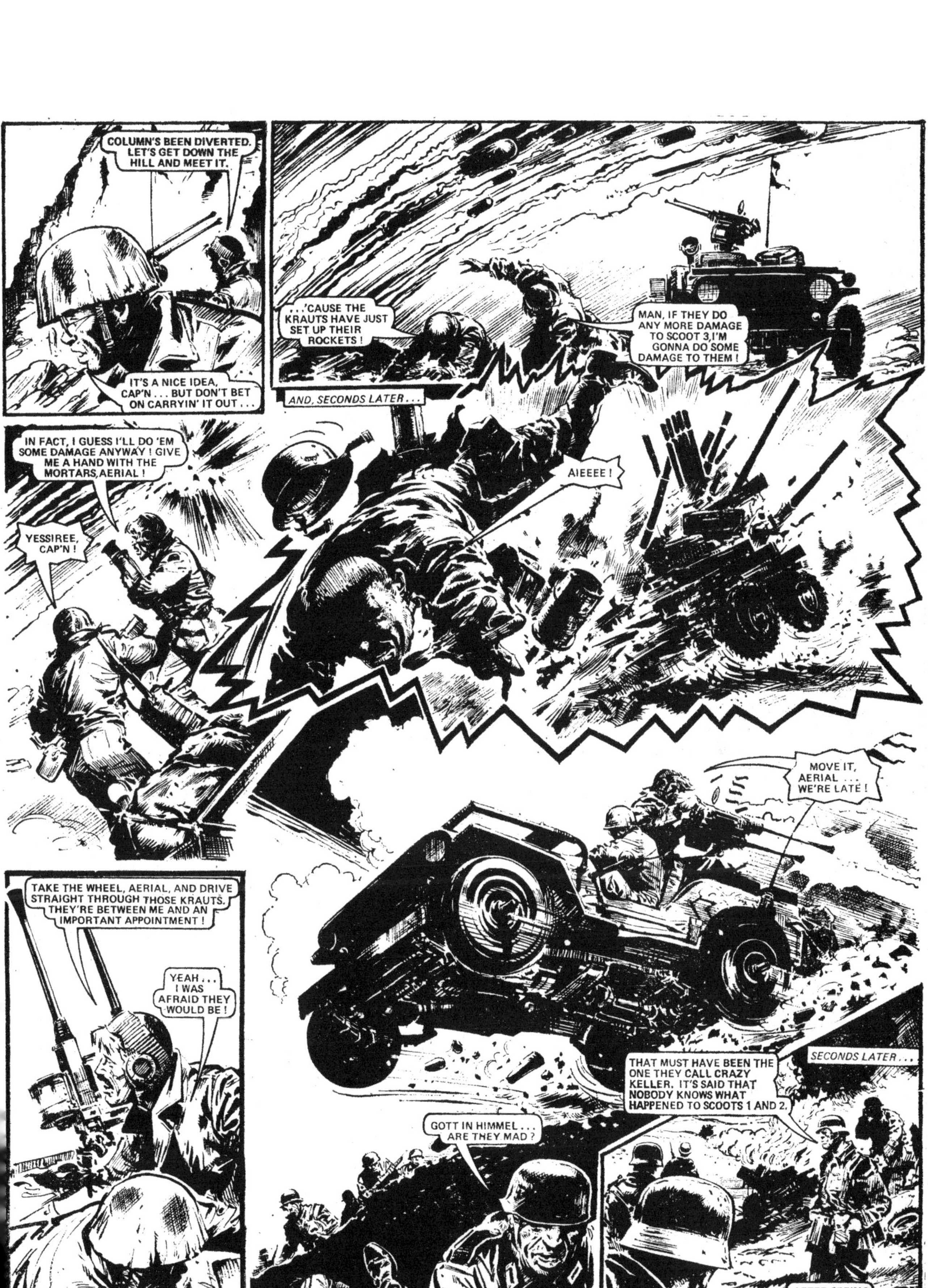
COLUMN'S BEEN DIVERTED. LET'S GET DOWN THE HILL AND MEET IT.
IT'S A NICE IDEA, CAP'N . . . BUT DON'T BET ON CARRYIN' IT OUT . . .
. . .'CAUSE THE KRAUTS HAVE JUST SET UP THEIR ROCKETS !
MAN, IF THEY DO ANY MORE DAMAGE TO SCOOT 3, I'M GONNA DO SOME DAMAGE TO THEM !
AND, SECONDS LATER . . .
IN FACT, I GUESS I'LL DO 'EM SOME DAMAGE ANYWAY ! GIVE ME A HAND WITH THE MORTARS, AERIAL !
YESSIREE, CAP'N !
AIEEEE !
TAKE THE WHEEL, AERIAL, AND DRIVE STRAIGHT THROUGH THOSE KRAUTS. THEY'RE BETWEEN ME AND AN IMPORTANT APPOINTMENT !
YEAH . . . I WAS AFRAID THEY WOULD BE !
MOVE IT, AERIAL . . . WE'RE LATE !
GOTT IN HIMMEL . . . ARE THEY MAD ?
SECONDS LATER . . .
THAT MUST HAVE BEEN THE ONE THEY CALL CRAZY KELLER. IT'S SAID THAT NOBODY KNOWS WHAT HAPPENED TO SCOOTS 1 AND 2.
AFTER SEEING THIS I HATE TO THINK !

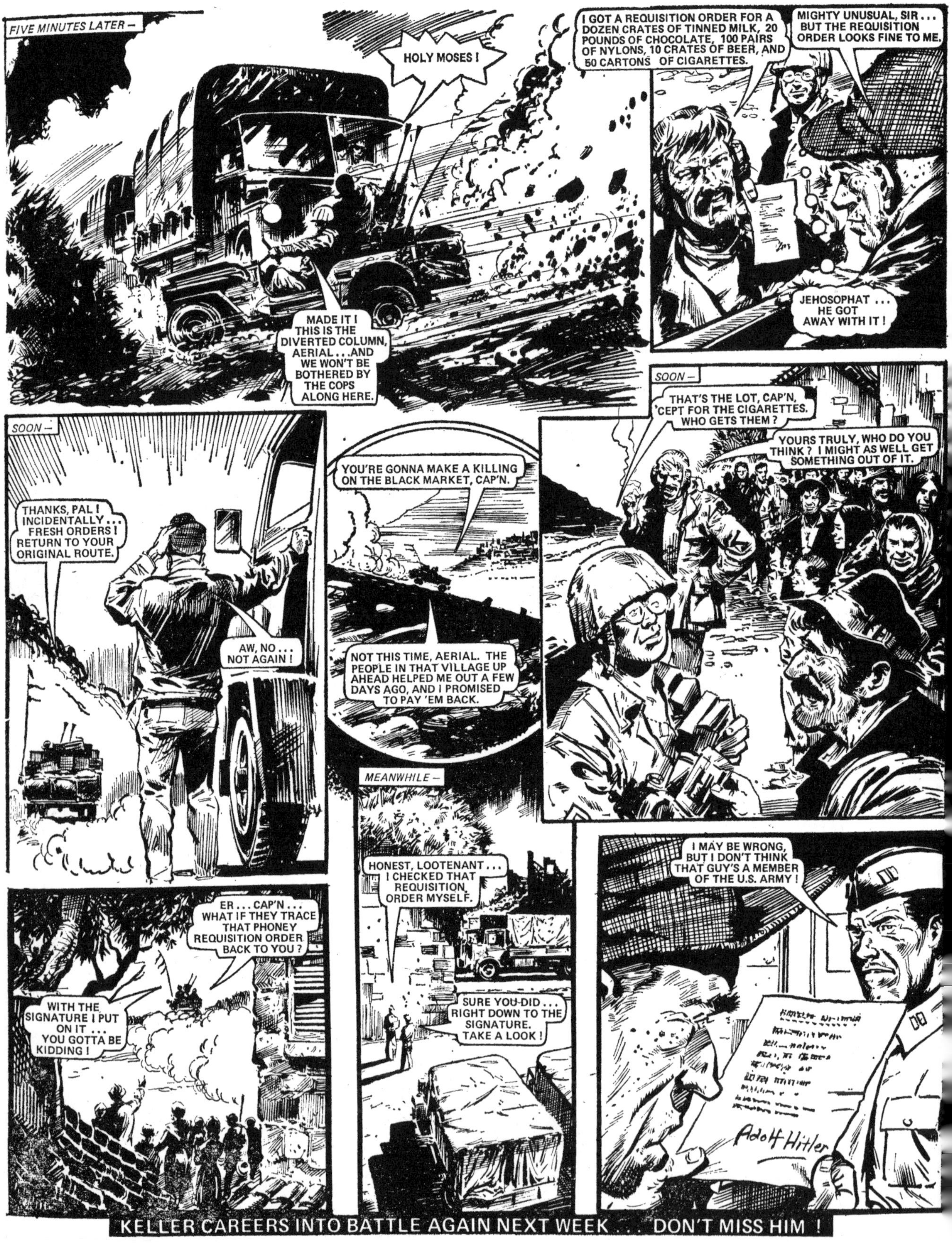
FIVE MINUTES LATER –
HOLY MOSES !
MADE IT ! THIS IS THE DIVERTED COLUMN, AERIAL . . . AND WE WON'T BE BOTHERED BY THE COPS ALONG HERE.
I GOT A REQUISITION ORDER FOR A DOZEN CRATES OF TINNED MILK, 20 POUNDS OF CHOCOLATE, 100 PAIRS OF NYLONS, 10 CRATES OF BEER, AND 50 CARTONS OF CIGARETTES.
MIGHTY UNUSUAL, SIR . . . BUT THE REQUISITION ORDER LOOKS FINE TO ME.
JEHOSOPHAT . . . HE GOT AWAY WITH IT !
SOON –
THANKS, PAL ! INCIDENTALLY . . . FRESH ORDERS ! RETURN TO YOUR ORIGINAL ROUTE.
AW, NO . . . NOT AGAIN !
YOU'RE GONNA MAKE A KILLING ON THE BLACK MARKET, CAP'N.
NOT THIS TIME, AERIAL. THE PEOPLE IN THAT VILLAGE UP AHEAD HELPED ME OUT A FEW DAYS AGO, AND I PROMISED TO PAY 'EM BACK.
SOON –
THAT'S THE LOT, CAP'N, 'CEPT FOR THE CIGARETTES. WHO GETS THEM ?
YOURS TRULY, WHO DO YOU THINK ? I MIGHT AS WELL GET SOMETHING OUT OF IT.
ER . . . CAP'N . . . WHAT IF THEY TRACE THAT PHONEY REQUISITION ORDER BACK TO YOU ?
WITH THE SIGNATURE I PUT ON IT . . . YOU GOTTA BE KIDDING !
MEANWHILE –
HONEST, LOOTENANT . . . I CHECKED THAT REQUISITION ORDER MYSELF.
SURE YOU DID . . . RIGHT DOWN TO THE SIGNATURE. TAKE A LOOK !
I MAY BE WRONG, BUT I DON'T THINK THAT GUY'S A MEMBER OF THE U.S. ARMY !
Adolf Hitler
KELLER CAREERS INTO BATTLE AGAIN NEXT WEEK . . . DON'T MISS HIM !

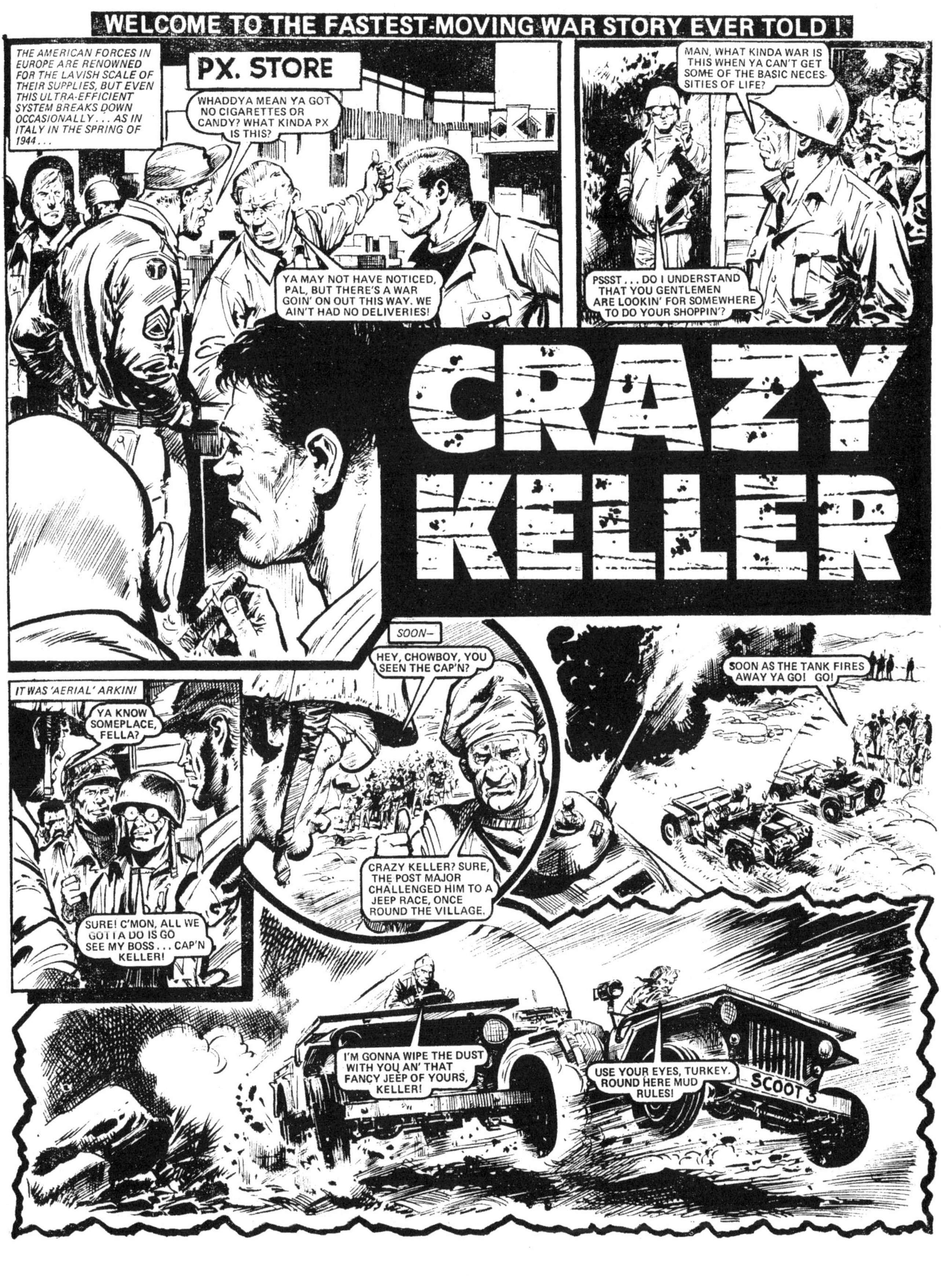
WELCOME TO THE FASTEST-MOVING WAR STORY EVER TOLD !
THE AMERICAN FORCES IN EUROPE ARE RENOWNED FOR THE LAVISH SCALE OF THEIR SUPPLIES, BUT EVEN THIS ULTRA-EFFICIENT SYSTEM BREAKS DOWN OCCASIONALLY . . . AS IN ITALY IN THE SPRING OF 1944 . . .
PX. STORE
WHADDYA MEAN YA GOT NO CIGARETTES OR CANDY? WHAT KINDA PX IS THIS?
YA MAY NOT HAVE NOTICED, PAL, BUT THERE'S A WAR GOIN' ON OUT THIS WAY. WE AIN'T HAD NO DELIVERIES!
MAN, WHAT KINDA WAR IS THIS WHEN YA CAN'T GET SOME OF THE BASIC NECES-SITIES OF LIFE?
PSSST . . . DO I UNDERSTAND THAT YOU GENTLEMEN ARE LOOKIN' FOR SOMEWHERE TO DO YOUR SHOPPIN'?
CRAZY KELLER
IT WAS 'AERIAL' ARKIN!
YA KNOW SOMEPLACE, FELLA?
SURE! C'MON, ALL WE GOTTA DO IS GO SEE MY BOSS . . . CAP'N KELLER!
SOON–
HEY, CHOWBOY, YOU SEEN THE CAP'N?
CRAZY KELLER? SURE, THE POST MAJOR CHALLENGED HIM TO A JEEP RACE, ONCE ROUND THE VILLAGE.
SOON AS THE TANK FIRES AWAY YA GO! GO!
I'M GONNA WIPE THE DUST WITH YOU AN' THAT FANCY JEEP OF YOURS, KELLER!
USE YOUR EYES, TURKEY. ROUND HERE MUD RULES!
SCOOT 3

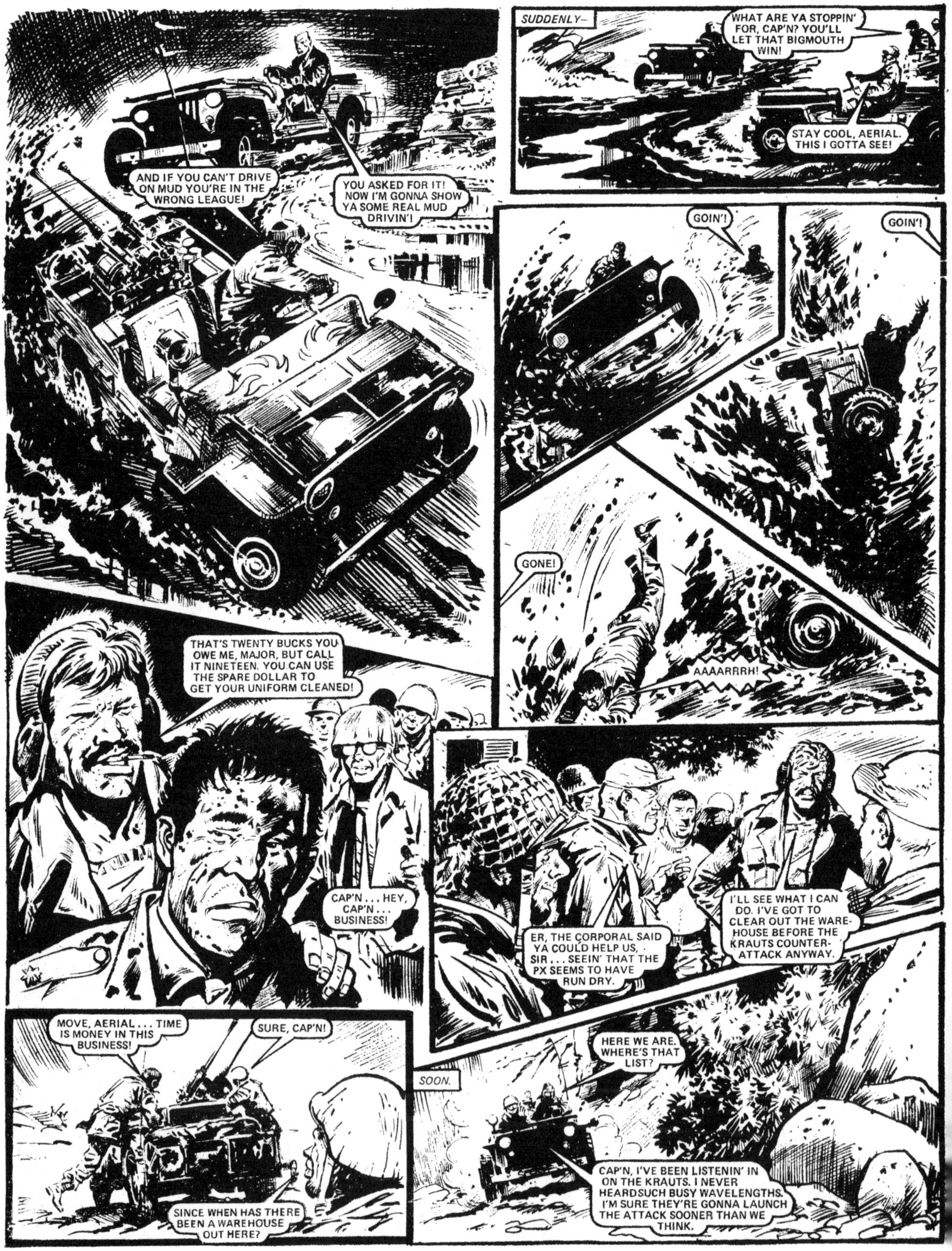

AND IF YOU CAN'T DRIVE ON MUD YOU'RE IN THE WRONG LEAGUE!
YOU ASKED FOR IT! NOW I'M GONNA SHOW YA SOME REAL MUD DRIVIN'!
SUDDENLY—
WHAT ARE YA STOPPIN' FOR, CAP'N? YOU'LL LET THAT BIGMOUTH WIN!
STAY COOL, AERIAL. THIS I GOTTA SEE!
GOIN'!
GOIN'!
GONE!
AAAARRRH!
THAT'S TWENTY BUCKS YOU OWE ME, MAJOR, BUT CALL IT NINETEEN. YOU CAN USE THE SPARE DOLLAR TO GET YOUR UNIFORM CLEANED!
CAP'N . . . HEY, CAP'N . . . BUSINESS!
ER, THE CORPORAL SAID YA COULD HELP US, SIR . . . SEEIN' THAT THE PX SEEMS TO HAVE RUN DRY.
I'LL SEE WHAT I CAN DO. I'VE GOT TO CLEAR OUT THE WAREHOUSE BEFORE THE KRAUTS COUNTER-ATTACK ANYWAY.
MOVE, AERIAL . . . TIME IS MONEY IN THIS BUSINESS!
SURE, CAP'N!
SINCE WHEN HAS THERE BEEN A WAREHOUSE OUT HERE?
SOON.
HERE WE ARE. WHERE'S THAT LIST?
CAP'N, I'VE BEEN LISTENIN' IN ON THE KRAUTS. I NEVER HEARDSUCH BUSY WAVELENGTHS. I'M SURE THEY'RE GONNA LAUNCH THE ATTACK SOONER THAN WE THINK.

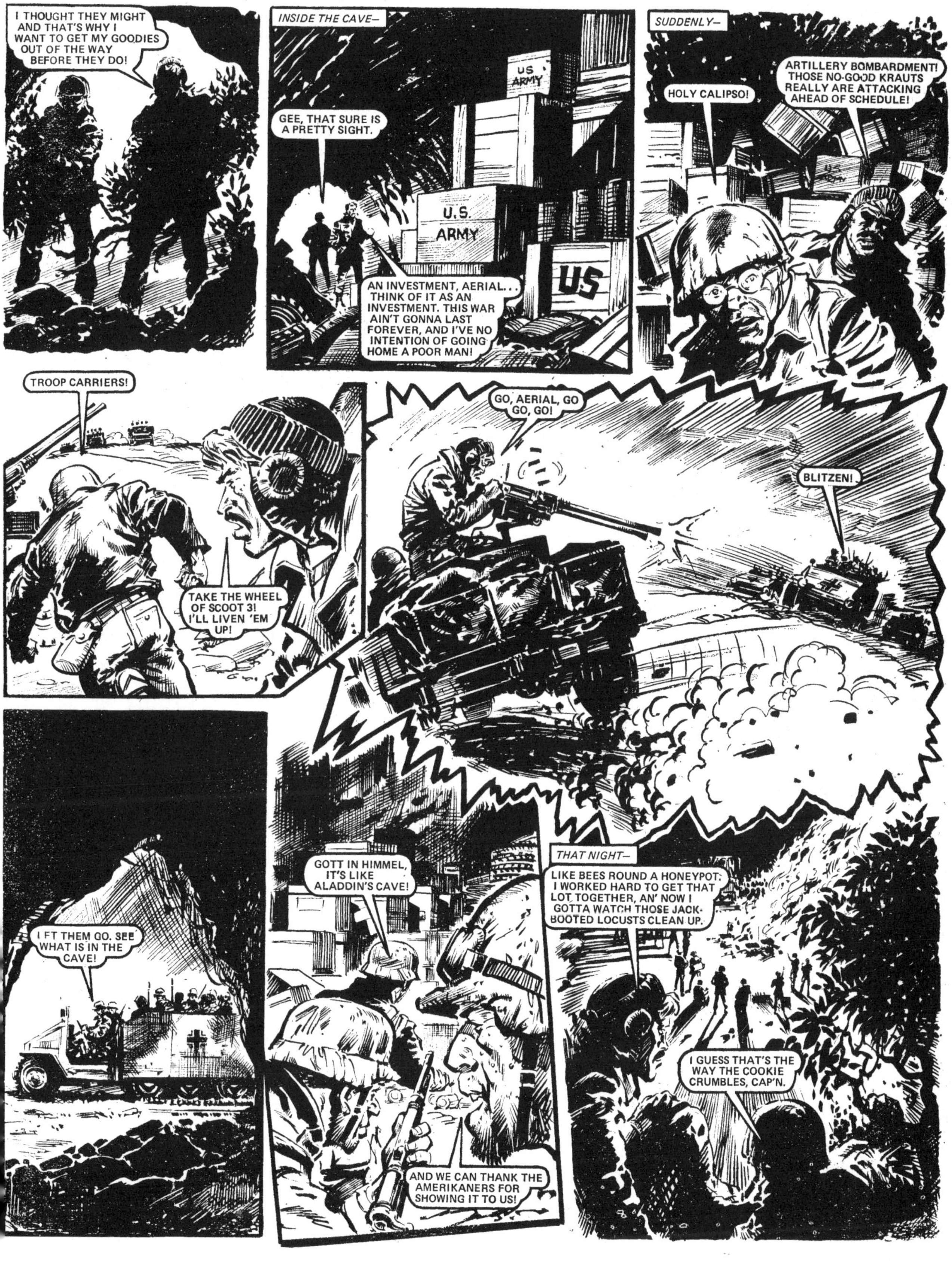

I THOUGHT THEY MIGHT AND THAT'S WHY I WANT TO GET MY GOODIES OUT OF THE WAY BEFORE THEY DO!
INSIDE THE CAVE—
GEE, THAT SURE IS A PRETTY SIGHT.
US ARMY
U.S. ARMY
US
AN INVESTMENT, AERIAL... THINK OF IT AS AN INVESTMENT. THIS WAR AIN'T GONNA LAST FOREVER, AND I'VE NO INTENTION OF GOING HOME A POOR MAN!
SUDDENLY—
HOLY CALIPSO!
ARTILLERY BOMBARDMENT! THOSE NO-GOOD KRAUTS REALLY ARE ATTACKING AHEAD OF SCHEDULE!
TROOP CARRIERS!
TAKE THE WHEEL OF SCOOT 3! I'LL LIVEN 'EM UP!
GO, AERIAL, GO GO, GO!
BLITZEN!
LET THEM GO. SEE WHAT IS IN THE CAVE!
GOTT IN HIMMEL, IT'S LIKE ALADDIN'S CAVE!
AND WE CAN THANK THE AMERIKANERS FOR SHOWING IT TO US!
THAT NIGHT—
LIKE BEES ROUND A HONEYPOT; I WORKED HARD TO GET THAT LOT TOGETHER, AN' NOW I GOTTA WATCH THOSE JACK-BOOTED LOCUSTS CLEAN UP.
I GUESS THAT'S THE WAY THE COOKIE CRUMBLES, CAP'N.

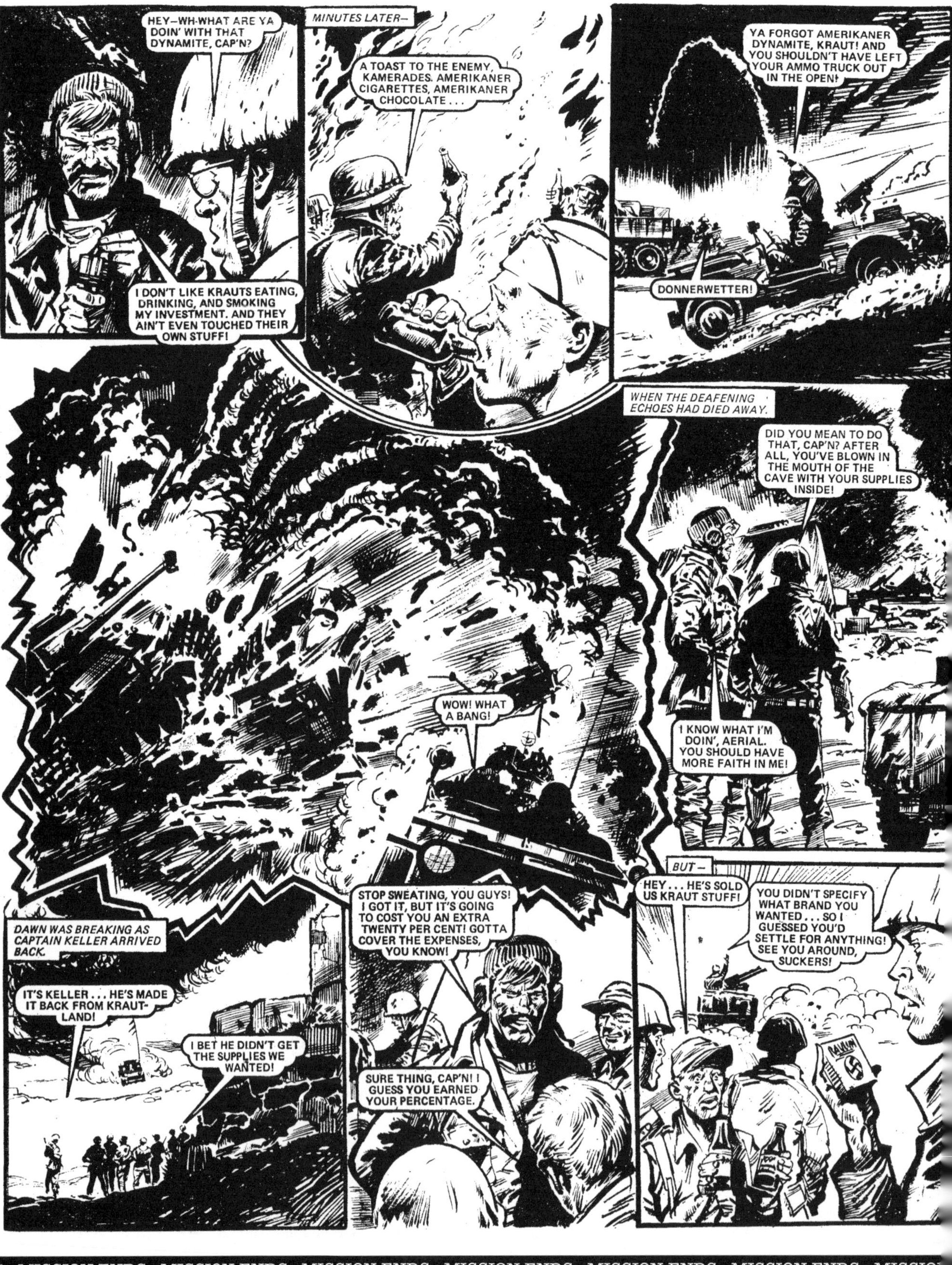

HEY–WH-WHAT ARE YA DOIN' WITH THAT DYNAMITE, CAP'N?
I DON'T LIKE KRAUTS EATING, DRINKING, AND SMOKING MY INVESTMENT. AND THEY AIN'T EVEN TOUCHED THEIR OWN STUFF!
MINUTES LATER–
A TOAST TO THE ENEMY, KAMERADES. AMERIKANER CIGARETTES, AMERIKANER CHOCOLATE . . .
YA FORGOT AMERIKANER DYNAMITE, KRAUT! AND YOU SHOULDN'T HAVE LEFT YOUR AMMO TRUCK OUT IN THE OPEN!
DONNERWETTER!
WOW! WHAT A BANG!
WHEN THE DEAFENING ECHOES HAD DIED AWAY.
DID YOU MEAN TO DO THAT, CAP'N? AFTER ALL, YOU'VE BLOWN IN THE MOUTH OF THE CAVE WITH YOUR SUPPLIES INSIDE!
I KNOW WHAT I'M DOIN', AERIAL. YOU SHOULD HAVE MORE FAITH IN ME!
DAWN WAS BREAKING AS CAPTAIN KELLER ARRIVED BACK.
IT'S KELLER . . . HE'S MADE IT BACK FROM KRAUT-LAND!
I BET HE DIDN'T GET THE SUPPLIES WE WANTED!
STOP SWEATING, YOU GUYS! I GOT IT, BUT IT'S GOING TO COST YOU AN EXTRA TWENTY PER CENT! GOTTA COVER THE EXPENSES, YOU KNOW!
SURE THING, CAP'N! I GUESS YOU EARNED YOUR PERCENTAGE.
BUT–
HEY . . . HE'S SOLD US KRAUT STUFF!
YOU DIDN'T SPECIFY WHAT BRAND YOU WANTED . . . SO I GUESSED YOU'D SETTLE FOR ANYTHING! SEE YOU AROUND, SUCKERS!

NDS...MISSION ENDS...MISSION ENDS...MISSION ENDS...MISSION ENDS...MISSION ENDS...MISSION ENDS...MISSIO

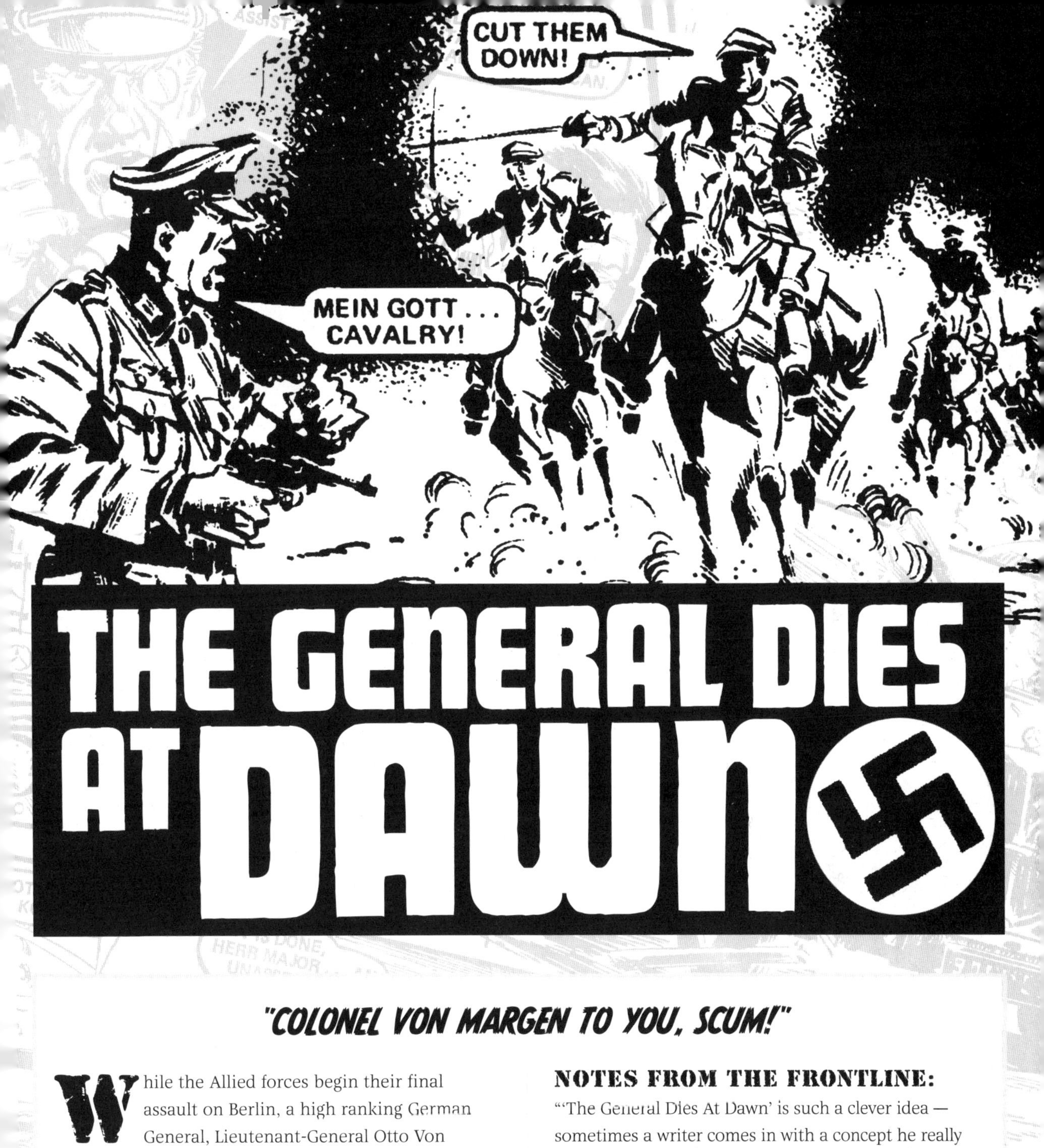
CUT THEM DOWN!
MEIN GOTT . . . CAVALRY!

THE GENERAL DIES AT DAWN

"COLONEL VON MARGEN TO YOU, SCUM!"

While the Allied forces begin their final assault on Berlin, a high ranking German General, Lieutenant-General Otto Von Margen — the "Wolf of Kiev" — has been found guilty of cowardice, disobedience and high treason, stripped of his rank and sentenced to die in front of a firing squad at dawn. With just eleven hours to go, Otto Von Margen spends his final hours recounting the story behind his death sentence to his jailor, describing the incidents and battles that led to his court-martial.

Using a similar plot device to 'Hold Hill 109', 'The General Dies at Dawn' was written by Gerry Finley-Day in eleven parts; each part counting down another hour before General Margen faces the firing squad, the last episode culminating in *Battle*'s 200th issue.

NOTES FROM THE FRONTLINE:

"'The General Dies At Dawn' is such a clever idea — sometimes a writer comes in with a concept he really believes in, and just runs with it. You may find another writer who has a stronger sense of realism but Gerry had a fundamental understanding of his subject matter at the end of the day. He had a background of spending time in the Territorial Army and he actually knew what he was talking about — you could see this in his scripts; they were ripe with little details that brought the characters to life. And with someone with that sort of certain talent, you've got to bring it out of them and that's what we did during our time working together on *Battle*." **— Pat Mills**

WRITTEN BY Gerry Finley-Day • **DRAWN BY** John Cooper

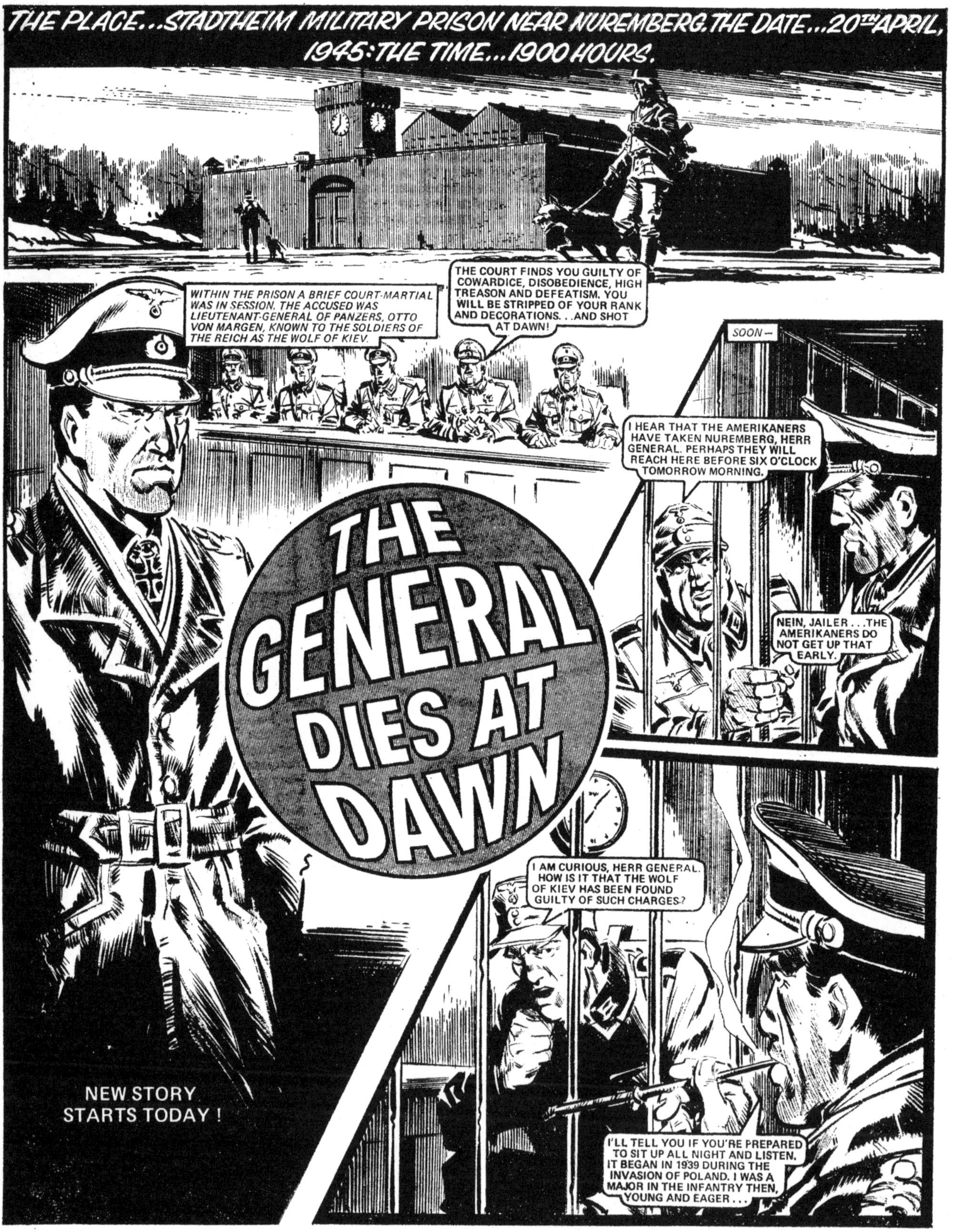
THE PLACE...STADTHEIM MILITARY PRISON NEAR NUREMBERG. THE DATE...20TH APRIL, 1945: THE TIME...1900 HOURS.
WITHIN THE PRISON A BRIEF COURT-MARTIAL WAS IN SESSION. THE ACCUSED WAS LIEUTENANT-GENERAL OF PANZERS, OTTO VON MARGEN, KNOWN TO THE SOLDIERS OF THE REICH AS THE WOLF OF KIEV.
THE COURT FINDS YOU GUILTY OF COWARDICE, DISOBEDIENCE, HIGH TREASON AND DEFEATISM. YOU WILL BE STRIPPED OF YOUR RANK AND DECORATIONS. . .AND SHOT AT DAWN!
THE GENERAL DIES AT DAWN
SOON—
I HEAR THAT THE AMERIKANERS HAVE TAKEN NUREMBERG, HERR GENERAL. PERHAPS THEY WILL REACH HERE BEFORE SIX O'CLOCK TOMORROW MORNING.
NEIN, JAILER . . . THE AMERIKANERS DO NOT GET UP THAT EARLY.
I AM CURIOUS, HERR GENERAL. HOW IS IT THAT THE WOLF OF KIEV HAS BEEN FOUND GUILTY OF SUCH CHARGES?
I'LL TELL YOU IF YOU'RE PREPARED TO SIT UP ALL NIGHT AND LISTEN. IT BEGAN IN 1939 DURING THE INVASION OF POLAND. I WAS A MAJOR IN THE INFANTRY THEN, YOUNG AND EAGER . . .
NEW STORY STARTS TODAY !

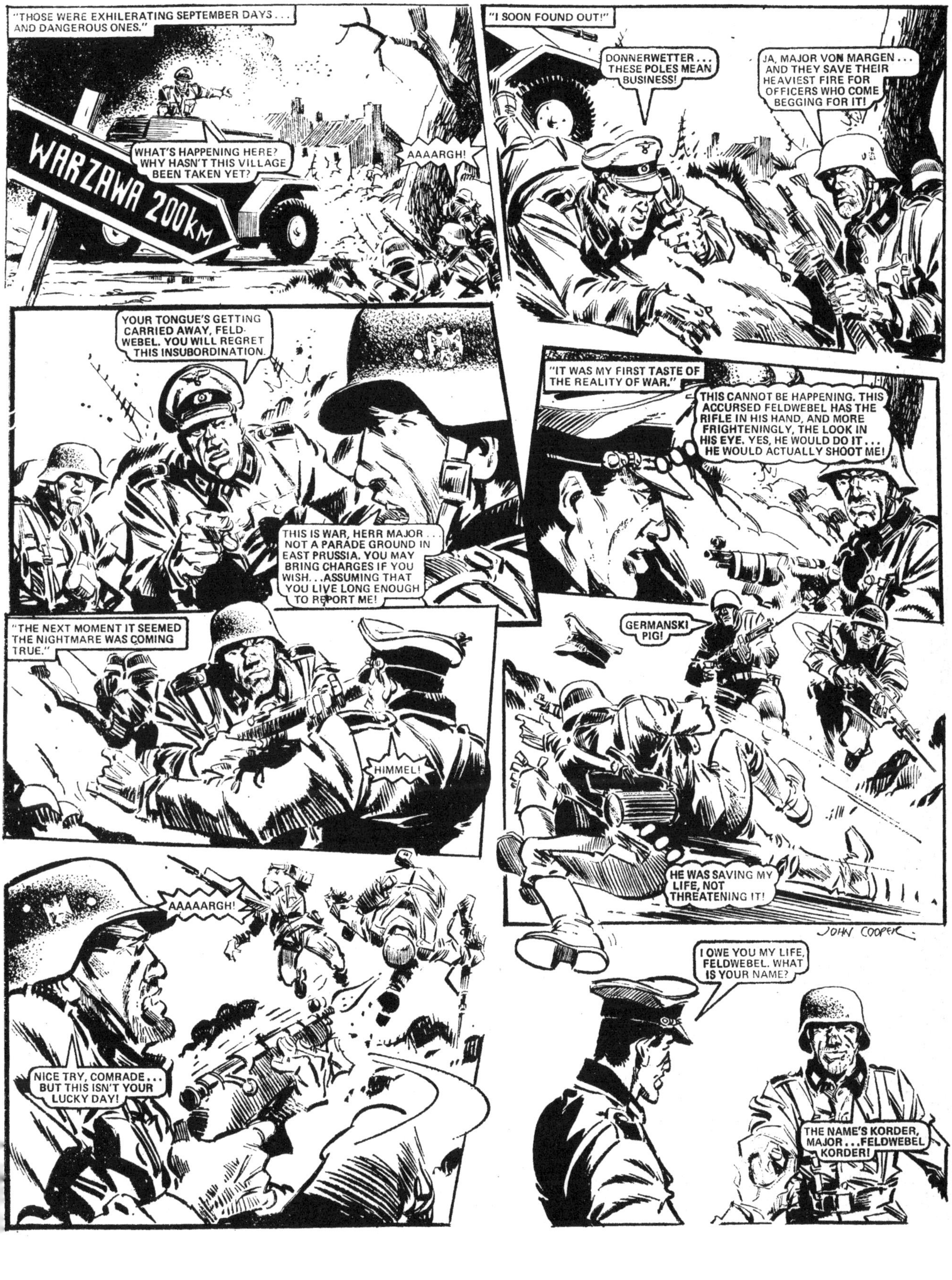
"THOSE WERE EXHILERATING SEPTEMBER DAYS . . . AND DANGEROUS ONES."
WARZAWA 200KM
WHAT'S HAPPENING HERE? WHY HASN'T THIS VILLAGE BEEN TAKEN YET?
AAAARGH!
"I SOON FOUND OUT!"
DONNERWETTER . . . THESE POLES MEAN BUSINESS!
JA, MAJOR VON MARGEN . . . AND THEY SAVE THEIR HEAVIEST FIRE FOR OFFICERS WHO COME BEGGING FOR IT!
YOUR TONGUE'S GETTING CARRIED AWAY, FELDWEBEL. YOU WILL REGRET THIS INSUBORDINATION.
THIS IS WAR, HERR MAJOR . . . NOT A PARADE GROUND IN EAST PRUSSIA. YOU MAY BRING CHARGES IF YOU WISH. . . ASSUMING THAT YOU LIVE LONG ENOUGH TO REPORT ME!
"IT WAS MY FIRST TASTE OF THE REALITY OF WAR."
THIS CANNOT BE HAPPENING. THIS ACCURSED FELDWEBEL HAS THE RIFLE IN HIS HAND, AND MORE FRIGHTENINGLY, THE LOOK IN HIS EYE. YES, HE WOULD DO IT . . . HE WOULD ACTUALLY SHOOT ME!
"THE NEXT MOMENT IT SEEMED THE NIGHTMARE WAS COMING TRUE."
HIMMEL!
GERMANSKI PIG!
HE WAS SAVING MY LIFE, NOT THREATENING IT!
JOHN COOPER
AAAAARGH!
NICE TRY, COMRADE . . . BUT THIS ISN'T YOUR LUCKY DAY!
I OWE YOU MY LIFE, FELDWEBEL. WHAT IS YOUR NAME?
THE NAME'S KORDER, MAJOR . . . FELDWEBEL KORDER!

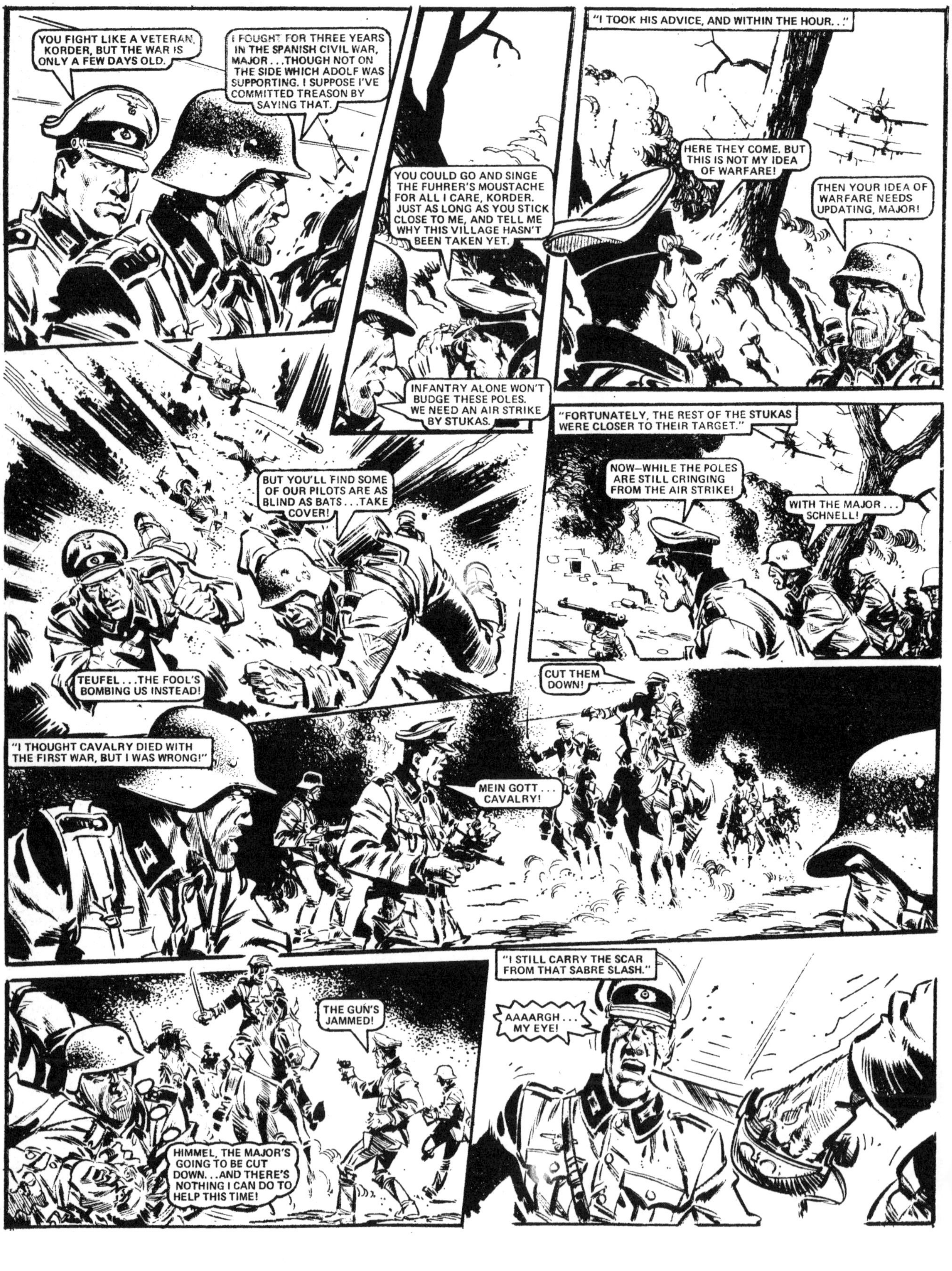

YOU FIGHT LIKE A VETERAN, KORDER, BUT THE WAR IS ONLY A FEW DAYS OLD.
I FOUGHT FOR THREE YEARS IN THE SPANISH CIVIL WAR, MAJOR . . . THOUGH NOT ON THE SIDE WHICH ADOLF WAS SUPPORTING. I SUPPOSE I'VE COMMITTED TREASON BY SAYING THAT.
YOU COULD GO AND SINGE THE FUHRER'S MOUSTACHE FOR ALL I CARE, KORDER. JUST AS LONG AS YOU STICK CLOSE TO ME, AND TELL ME WHY THIS VILLAGE HASN'T BEEN TAKEN YET.
INFANTRY ALONE WON'T BUDGE THESE POLES. WE NEED AN AIR STRIKE BY STUKAS.
"I TOOK HIS ADVICE, AND WITHIN THE HOUR. . ."
HERE THEY COME. BUT THIS IS NOT MY IDEA OF WARFARE!
THEN YOUR IDEA OF WARFARE NEEDS UPDATING, MAJOR!
BUT YOU'LL FIND SOME OF OUR PILOTS ARE AS BLIND AS BATS . . . TAKE COVER!
TEUFEL . . . THE FOOL'S BOMBING US INSTEAD!
"FORTUNATELY, THE REST OF THE STUKAS WERE CLOSER TO THEIR TARGET."
NOW–WHILE THE POLES ARE STILL CRINGING FROM THE AIR STRIKE!
WITH THE MAJOR . . . SCHNELL!
"I THOUGHT CAVALRY DIED WITH THE FIRST WAR, BUT I WAS WRONG!"
MEIN GOTT . . . CAVALRY!
CUT THEM DOWN!
THE GUN'S JAMMED!
HIMMEL, THE MAJOR'S GOING TO BE CUT DOWN. . . AND THERE'S NOTHING I CAN DO TO HELP THIS TIME!
"I STILL CARRY THE SCAR FROM THAT SABRE SLASH."
AAAARGH . . . MY EYE!

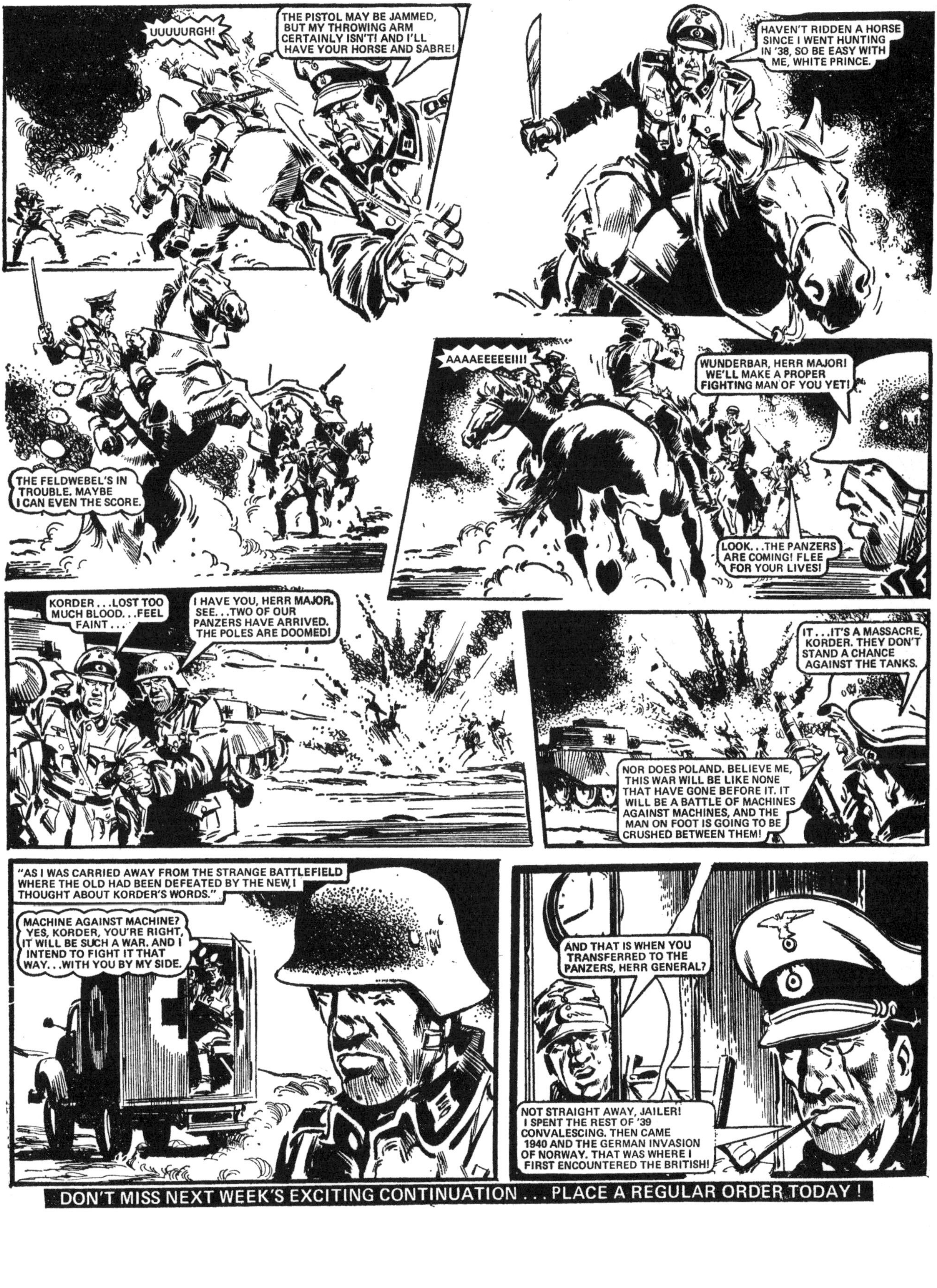
UUUUURGH!
THE PISTOL MAY BE JAMMED, BUT MY THROWING ARM CERTAINLY ISN'T! AND I'LL HAVE YOUR HORSE AND SABRE!
HAVEN'T RIDDEN A HORSE SINCE I WENT HUNTING IN '38, SO BE EASY WITH ME, WHITE PRINCE.
THE FELDWEBEL'S IN TROUBLE. MAYBE I CAN EVEN THE SCORE.
AAAAEEEEIII!
WUNDERBAR, HERR MAJOR! WE'LL MAKE A PROPER FIGHTING MAN OF YOU YET!
LOOK. . .THE PANZERS ARE COMING! FLEE FOR YOUR LIVES!
KORDER . . .LOST TOO MUCH BLOOD. . .FEEL FAINT . . .
I HAVE YOU, HERR MAJOR. SEE. . .TWO OF OUR PANZERS HAVE ARRIVED. THE POLES ARE DOOMED!
IT . . .IT'S A MASSACRE, KORDER. THEY DON'T STAND A CHANCE AGAINST THE TANKS.
NOR DOES POLAND. BELIEVE ME, THIS WAR WILL BE LIKE NONE THAT HAVE GONE BEFORE IT. IT WILL BE A BATTLE OF MACHINES AGAINST MACHINES, AND THE MAN ON FOOT IS GOING TO BE CRUSHED BETWEEN THEM!
"AS I WAS CARRIED AWAY FROM THE STRANGE BATTLEFIELD WHERE THE OLD HAD BEEN DEFEATED BY THE NEW, I THOUGHT ABOUT KORDER'S WORDS."
MACHINE AGAINST MACHINE? YES, KORDER, YOU'RE RIGHT, IT WILL BE SUCH A WAR. AND I INTEND TO FIGHT IT THAT WAY. . .WITH YOU BY MY SIDE.
AND THAT IS WHEN YOU TRANSFERRED TO THE PANZERS, HERR GENERAL?
NOT STRAIGHT AWAY, JAILER! I SPENT THE REST OF '39 CONVALESCING. THEN CAME 1940 AND THE GERMAN INVASION OF NORWAY. THAT WAS WHERE I FIRST ENCOUNTERED THE BRITISH!

DON'T MISS NEXT WEEK'S EXCITING CONTINUATION . . . PLACE A REGULAR ORDER TODAY !

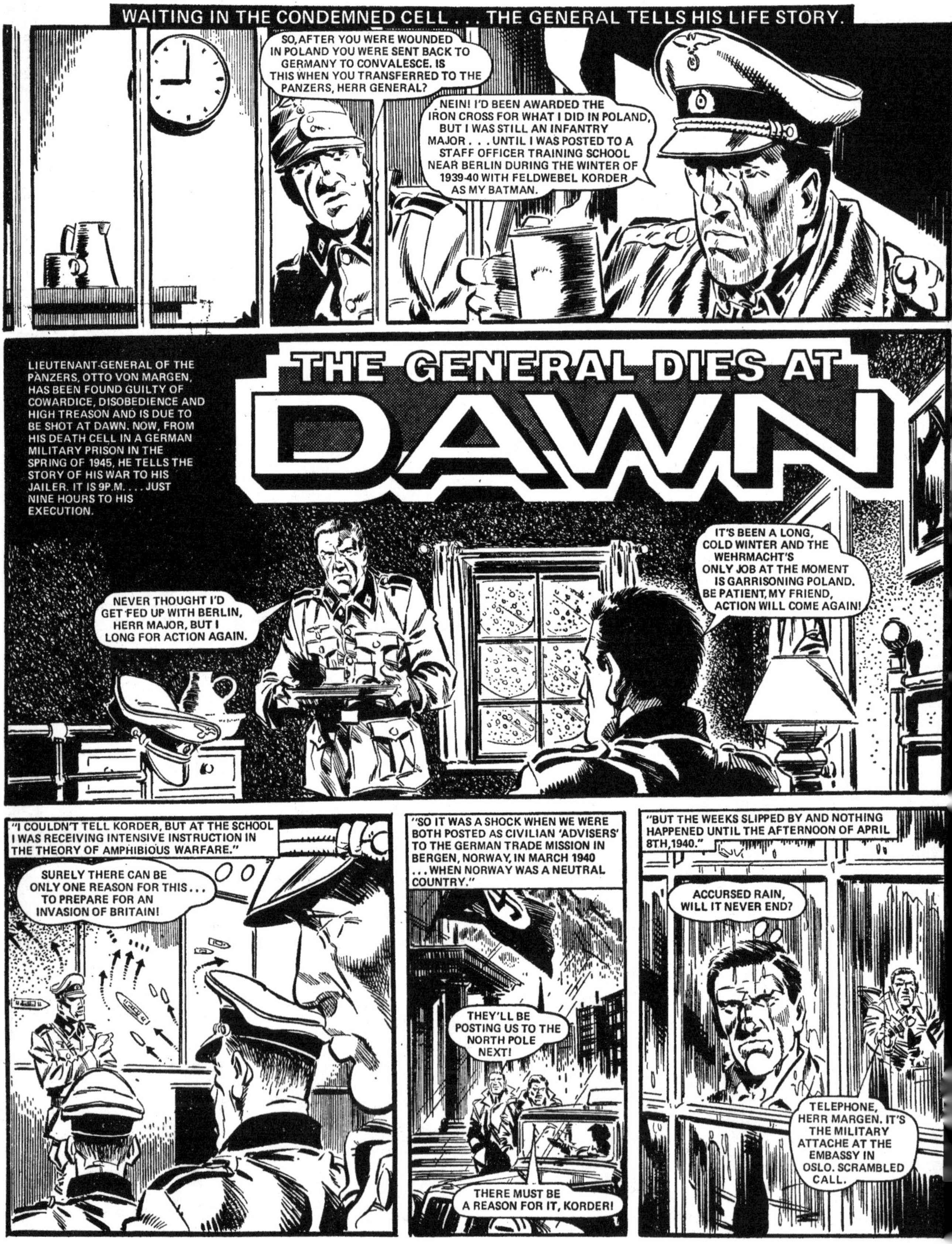

WAITING IN THE CONDEMNED CELL . . . THE GENERAL TELLS HIS LIFE STORY.
SO, AFTER YOU WERE WOUNDED IN POLAND YOU WERE SENT BACK TO GERMANY TO CONVALESCE. IS THIS WHEN YOU TRANSFERRED TO THE PANZERS, HERR GENERAL?
NEIN! I'D BEEN AWARDED THE IRON CROSS FOR WHAT I DID IN POLAND, BUT I WAS STILL AN INFANTRY MAJOR . . . UNTIL I WAS POSTED TO A STAFF OFFICER TRAINING SCHOOL NEAR BERLIN DURING THE WINTER OF 1939-40 WITH FELDWEBEL KORDER AS MY BATMAN.
THE GENERAL DIES AT DAWN
LIEUTENANT-GENERAL OF THE PANZERS, OTTO VON MARGEN, HAS BEEN FOUND GUILTY OF COWARDICE, DISOBEDIENCE AND HIGH TREASON AND IS DUE TO BE SHOT AT DAWN. NOW, FROM HIS DEATH CELL IN A GERMAN MILITARY PRISON IN THE SPRING OF 1945, HE TELLS THE STORY OF HIS WAR TO HIS JAILER. IT IS 9P.M. . . . JUST NINE HOURS TO HIS EXECUTION.
NEVER THOUGHT I'D GET FED UP WITH BERLIN, HERR MAJOR, BUT I LONG FOR ACTION AGAIN.
IT'S BEEN A LONG, COLD WINTER AND THE WEHRMACHT'S ONLY JOB AT THE MOMENT IS GARRISONING POLAND. BE PATIENT, MY FRIEND, ACTION WILL COME AGAIN!
"I COULDN'T TELL KORDER, BUT AT THE SCHOOL I WAS RECEIVING INTENSIVE INSTRUCTION IN THE THEORY OF AMPHIBIOUS WARFARE."
SURELY THERE CAN BE ONLY ONE REASON FOR THIS . . . TO PREPARE FOR AN INVASION OF BRITAIN!
"SO IT WAS A SHOCK WHEN WE WERE BOTH POSTED AS CIVILIAN 'ADVISERS' TO THE GERMAN TRADE MISSION IN BERGEN, NORWAY, IN MARCH 1940 . . . WHEN NORWAY WAS A NEUTRAL COUNTRY."
THEY'LL BE POSTING US TO THE NORTH POLE NEXT!
THERE MUST BE A REASON FOR IT, KORDER!
"BUT THE WEEKS SLIPPED BY AND NOTHING HAPPENED UNTIL THE AFTERNOON OF APRIL 8TH, 1940."
ACCURSED RAIN, WILL IT NEVER END?
TELEPHONE, HERR MARGEN. IT'S THE MILITARY ATTACHE AT THE EMBASSY IN OSLO. SCRAMBLED CALL.

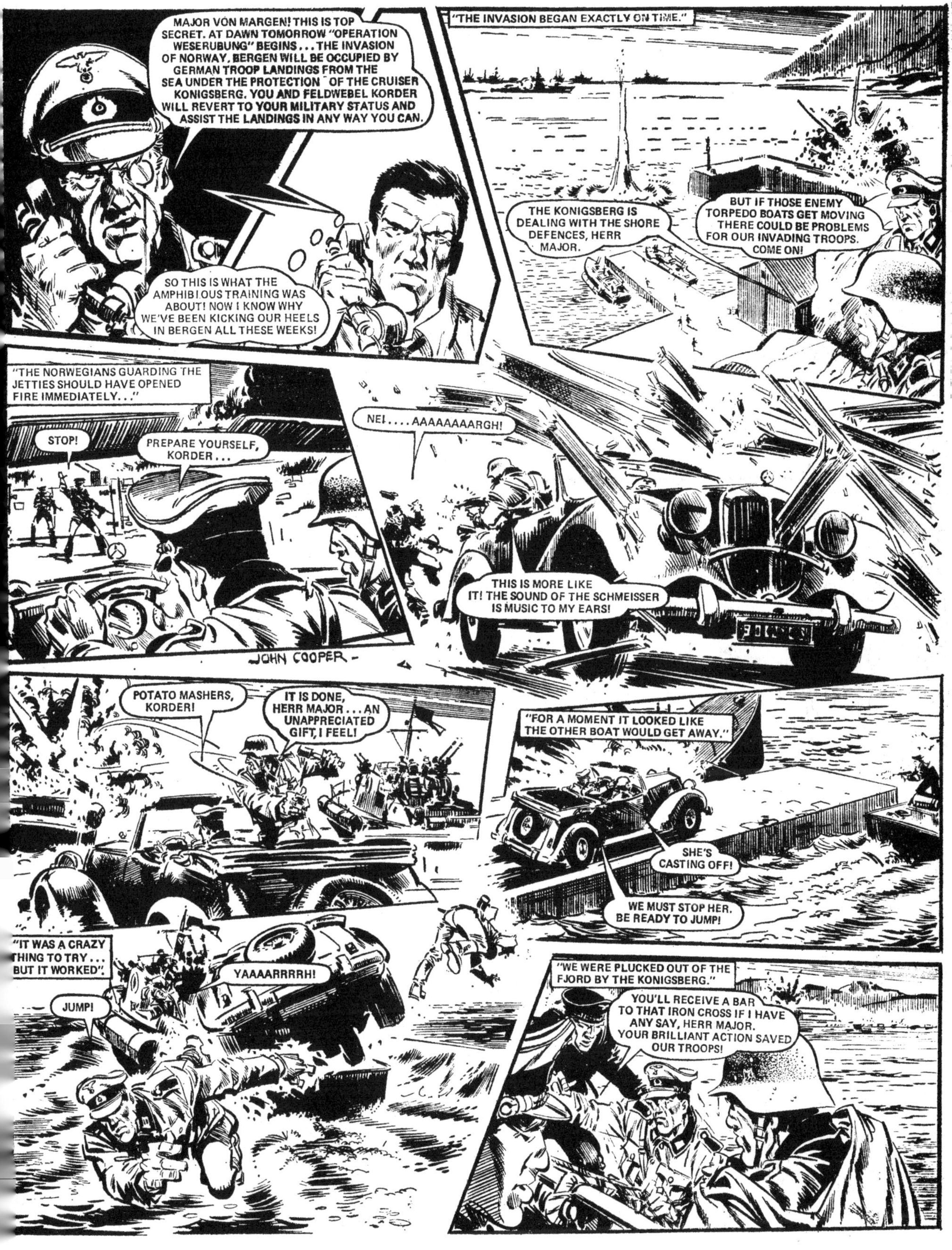
MAJOR VON MARGEN! THIS IS TOP SECRET. AT DAWN TOMORROW "OPERATION WESERUBUNG" BEGINS . . . THE INVASION OF NORWAY. BERGEN WILL BE OCCUPIED BY GERMAN TROOP LANDINGS FROM THE SEA UNDER THE PROTECTION OF THE CRUISER KONIGSBERG. YOU AND FELDWEBEL KORDER WILL REVERT TO YOUR MILITARY STATUS AND ASSIST THE LANDINGS IN ANY WAY YOU CAN.
SO THIS IS WHAT THE AMPHIBIOUS TRAINING WAS ABOUT! NOW I KNOW WHY WE'VE BEEN KICKING OUR HEELS IN BERGEN ALL THESE WEEKS!
"THE INVASION BEGAN EXACTLY ON TIME."
THE KONIGSBERG IS DEALING WITH THE SHORE DEFENCES, HERR MAJOR.
BUT IF THOSE ENEMY TORPEDO BOATS GET MOVING THERE COULD BE PROBLEMS FOR OUR INVADING TROOPS. COME ON!
"THE NORWEGIANS GUARDING THE JETTIES SHOULD HAVE OPENED FIRE IMMEDIATELY . . ."
STOP!
PREPARE YOURSELF, KORDER . . .
JOHN COOPER
NEI . . . . AAAAAAAARGH!
THIS IS MORE LIKE IT! THE SOUND OF THE SCHMEISSER IS MUSIC TO MY EARS!
POTATO MASHERS, KORDER!
IT IS DONE, HERR MAJOR . . . AN UNAPPRECIATED GIFT, I FEEL!
"FOR A MOMENT IT LOOKED LIKE THE OTHER BOAT WOULD GET AWAY."
SHE'S CASTING OFF!
WE MUST STOP HER. BE READY TO JUMP!
"IT WAS A CRAZY THING TO TRY . . . BUT IT WORKED".
YAAAARRRRH!
JUMP!
"WE WERE PLUCKED OUT OF THE FJORD BY THE KONIGSBERG."
YOU'LL RECEIVE A BAR TO THAT IRON CROSS IF I HAVE ANY SAY, HERR MAJOR. YOUR BRILLIANT ACTION SAVED OUR TROOPS!

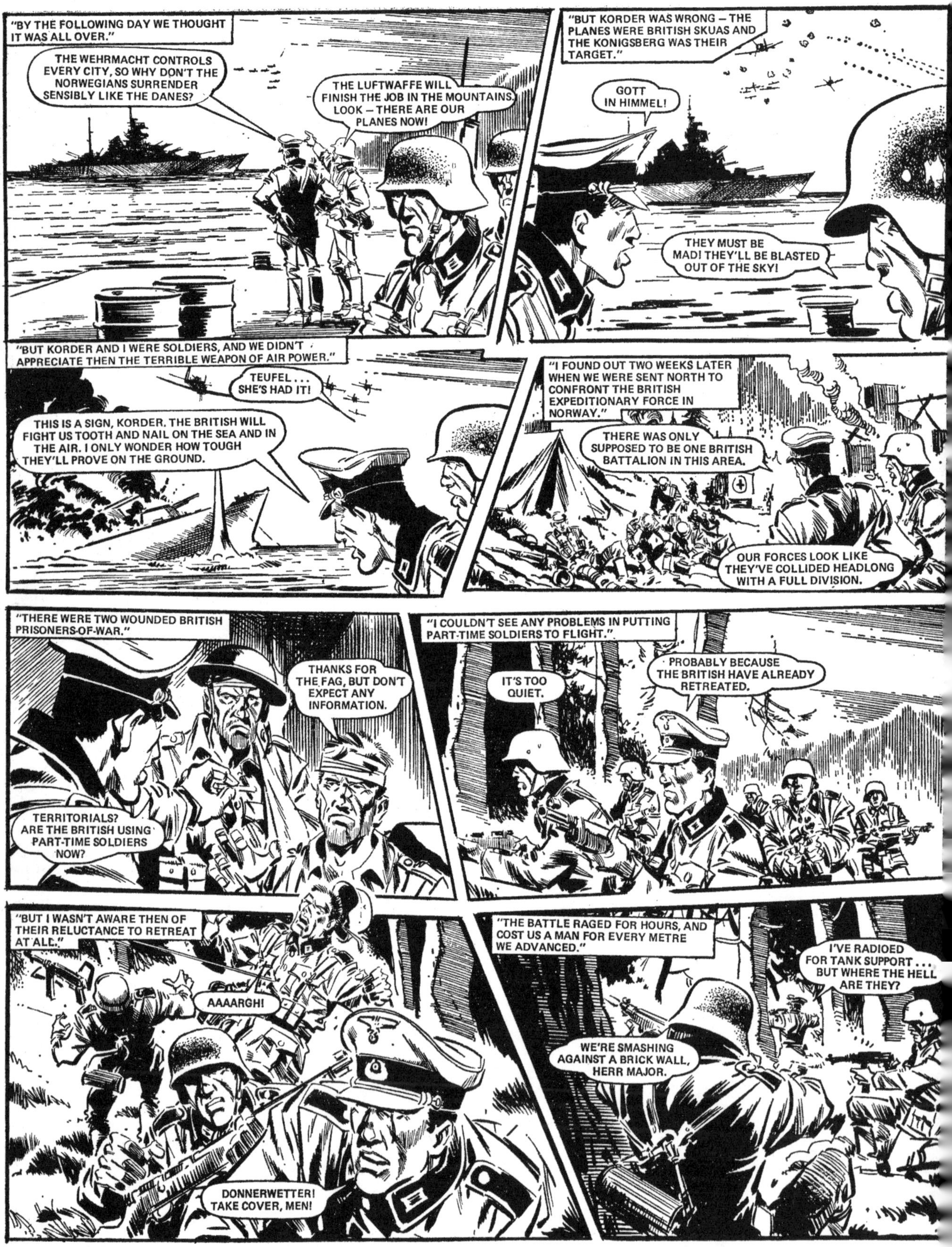
"BY THE FOLLOWING DAY WE THOUGHT IT WAS ALL OVER."
THE WEHRMACHT CONTROLS EVERY CITY, SO WHY DON'T THE NORWEGIANS SURRENDER SENSIBLY LIKE THE DANES?
THE LUFTWAFFE WILL FINISH THE JOB IN THE MOUNTAINS. LOOK – THERE ARE OUR PLANES NOW!
"BUT KORDER WAS WRONG – THE PLANES WERE BRITISH SKUAS AND THE KONIGSBERG WAS THEIR TARGET."
GOTT IN HIMMEL!
THEY MUST BE MAD! THEY'LL BE BLASTED OUT OF THE SKY!
"BUT KORDER AND I WERE SOLDIERS, AND WE DIDN'T APPRECIATE THEN THE TERRIBLE WEAPON OF AIR POWER."
TEUFEL . . . SHE'S HAD IT!
THIS IS A SIGN, KORDER. THE BRITISH WILL FIGHT US TOOTH AND NAIL ON THE SEA AND IN THE AIR. I ONLY WONDER HOW TOUGH THEY'LL PROVE ON THE GROUND.
"I FOUND OUT TWO WEEKS LATER WHEN WE WERE SENT NORTH TO CONFRONT THE BRITISH EXPEDITIONARY FORCE IN NORWAY."
THERE WAS ONLY SUPPOSED TO BE ONE BRITISH BATTALION IN THIS AREA.
OUR FORCES LOOK LIKE THEY'VE COLLIDED HEADLONG WITH A FULL DIVISION.
"THERE WERE TWO WOUNDED BRITISH PRISONERS-OF-WAR."
THANKS FOR THE FAG, BUT DON'T EXPECT ANY INFORMATION.
TERRITORIALS? ARE THE BRITISH USING PART-TIME SOLDIERS NOW?
"I COULDN'T SEE ANY PROBLEMS IN PUTTING PART-TIME SOLDIERS TO FLIGHT."
IT'S TOO QUIET.
PROBABLY BECAUSE THE BRITISH HAVE ALREADY RETREATED.
"BUT I WASN'T AWARE THEN OF THEIR RELUCTANCE TO RETREAT AT ALL."
AAAARGH!
DONNERWETTER! TAKE COVER, MEN!
"THE BATTLE RAGED FOR HOURS, AND COST US A MAN FOR EVERY METRE WE ADVANCED."
I'VE RADIOED FOR TANK SUPPORT . . . BUT WHERE THE HELL ARE THEY?
WE'RE SMASHING AGAINST A BRICK WALL, HERR MAJOR.

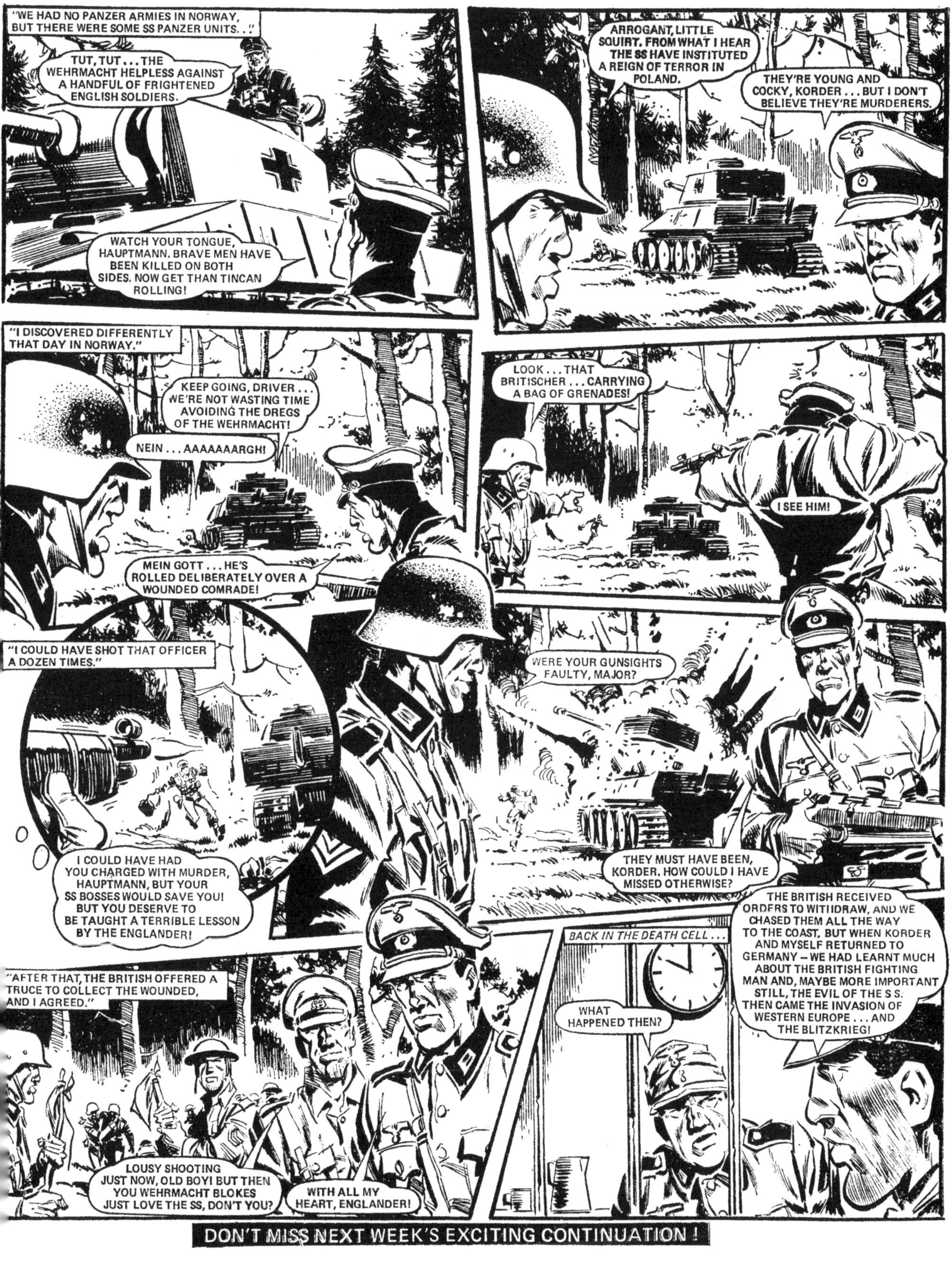
"WE HAD NO PANZER ARMIES IN NORWAY, BUT THERE WERE SOME SS PANZER UNITS. ."
TUT, TUT . . . THE WEHRMACHT HELPLESS AGAINST A HANDFUL OF FRIGHTENED ENGLISH SOLDIERS.
WATCH YOUR TONGUE, HAUPTMANN. BRAVE MEN HAVE BEEN KILLED ON BOTH SIDES. NOW GET THAN TINCAN ROLLING!
ARROGANT, LITTLE SQUIRT. FROM WHAT I HEAR THE SS HAVE INSTITUTED A REIGN OF TERROR IN POLAND.
THEY'RE YOUNG AND COCKY, KORDER . . . BUT I DON'T BELIEVE THEY'RE MURDERERS.
"I DISCOVERED DIFFERENTLY THAT DAY IN NORWAY."
KEEP GOING, DRIVER . . . WE'RE NOT WASTING TIME AVOIDING THE DREGS OF THE WEHRMACHT!
NEIN . . . AAAAAAARGH!
MEIN GOTT . . . HE'S ROLLED DELIBERATELY OVER A WOUNDED COMRADE!
LOOK . . . THAT BRITISCHER . . . CARRYING A BAG OF GRENADES!
I SEE HIM!
"I COULD HAVE SHOT THAT OFFICER A DOZEN TIMES."
WERE YOUR GUNSIGHTS FAULTY, MAJOR?
THEY MUST HAVE BEEN, KORDER. HOW COULD I HAVE MISSED OTHERWISE?
I COULD HAVE HAD YOU CHARGED WITH MURDER, HAUPTMANN, BUT YOUR SS BOSSES WOULD SAVE YOU! BUT YOU DESERVE TO BE TAUGHT A TERRIBLE LESSON BY THE ENGLANDER!
"AFTER THAT, THE BRITISH OFFERED A TRUCE TO COLLECT THE WOUNDED, AND I AGREED."
LOUSY SHOOTING JUST NOW, OLD BOY! BUT THEN YOU WEHRMACHT BLOKES JUST LOVE THE SS, DON'T YOU?
WITH ALL MY HEART, ENGLANDER!
BACK IN THE DEATH CELL . . .
WHAT HAPPENED THEN?
THE BRITISH RECEIVED ORDERS TO WITHDRAW, AND WE CHASED THEM ALL THE WAY TO THE COAST. BUT WHEN KORDER AND MYSELF RETURNED TO GERMANY – WE HAD LEARNT MUCH ABOUT THE BRITISH FIGHTING MAN AND, MAYBE MORE IMPORTANT STILL, THE EVIL OF THE S S. THEN CAME THE INVASION OF WESTERN EUROPE . . . AND THE BLITZKRIEG!

DON'T MISS NEXT WEEK'S EXCITING CONTINUATION !

FROM THE DEATH CELL A MAN REMEMBERS THE HELL OF WAR!

10 PM . . . AND LIEUTENANT-GENERAL OTTO VON MARGEN IS ONLY EIGHT HOURS AWAY FROM A FIRING SQUAD AT THE GERMAN MILITARY PRISON OF STADTHEIM IN APRIL, 1945. NOW, FROM THE CONDEMNED CELL, HE TELLS THE STORY OF HIS WAR TO HIS JAILER.

THE GENERAL DIES AT DAWN

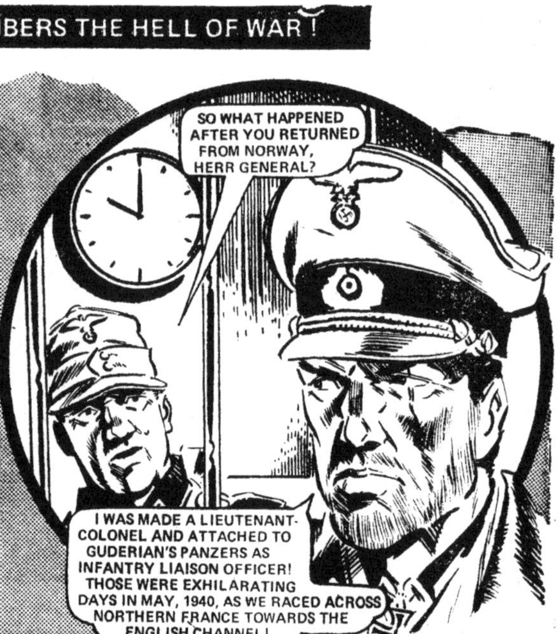
SO WHAT HAPPENED AFTER YOU RETURNED FROM NORWAY, HERR GENERAL?
I WAS MADE A LIEUTENANT-COLONEL AND ATTACHED TO GUDERIAN'S PANZERS AS INFANTRY LIAISON OFFICER! THOSE WERE EXHILARATING DAYS IN MAY, 1940, AS WE RACED ACROSS NORTHERN FRANCE TOWARDS THE ENGLISH CHANNEL!

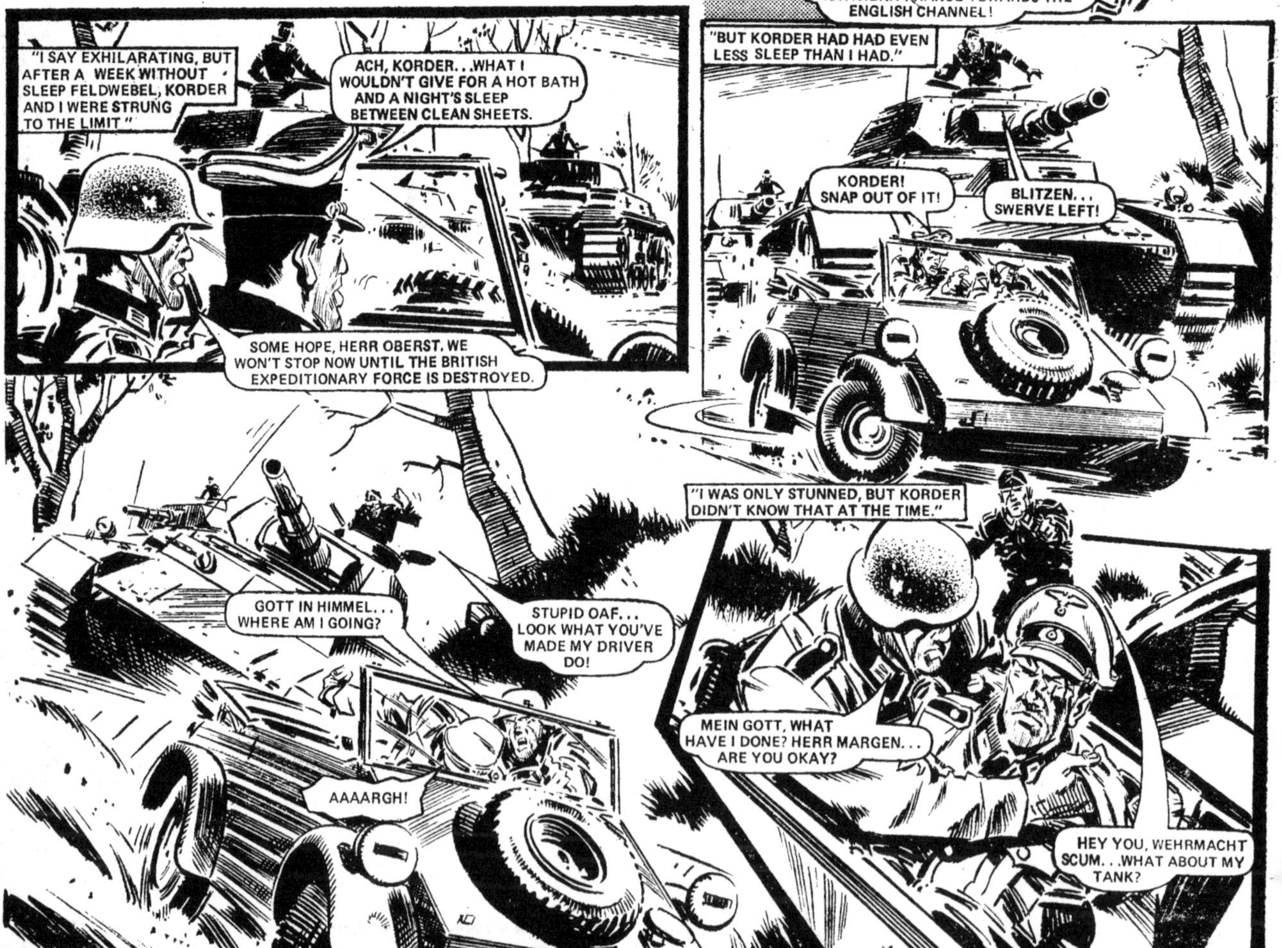
"I SAY EXHILARATING, BUT AFTER A WEEK WITHOUT SLEEP FELDWEBEL, KORDER AND I WERE STRUNG TO THE LIMIT."
ACH, KORDER...WHAT I WOULDN'T GIVE FOR A HOT BATH AND A NIGHT'S SLEEP BETWEEN CLEAN SHEETS.
SOME HOPE, HERR OBERST. WE WON'T STOP NOW UNTIL THE BRITISH EXPEDITIONARY FORCE IS DESTROYED.
"BUT KORDER HAD HAD EVEN LESS SLEEP THAN I HAD."
KORDER! SNAP OUT OF IT!
BLITZEN... SWERVE LEFT!
GOTT IN HIMMEL... WHERE AM I GOING?
STUPID OAF... LOOK WHAT YOU'VE MADE MY DRIVER DO!
AAAARGH!
"I WAS ONLY STUNNED, BUT KORDER DIDN'T KNOW THAT AT THE TIME."
MEIN GOTT, WHAT HAVE I DONE? HERR MARGEN... ARE YOU OKAY?
HEY YOU, WEHRMACHT SCUM...WHAT ABOUT MY TANK?

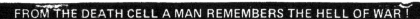

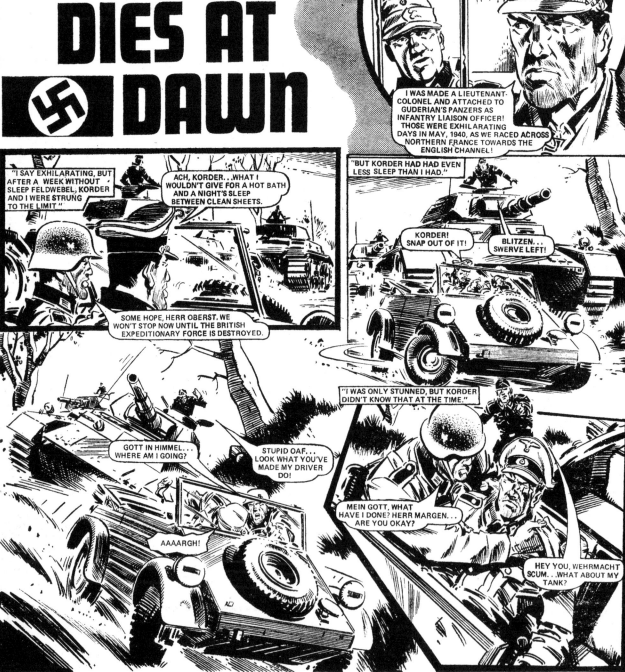

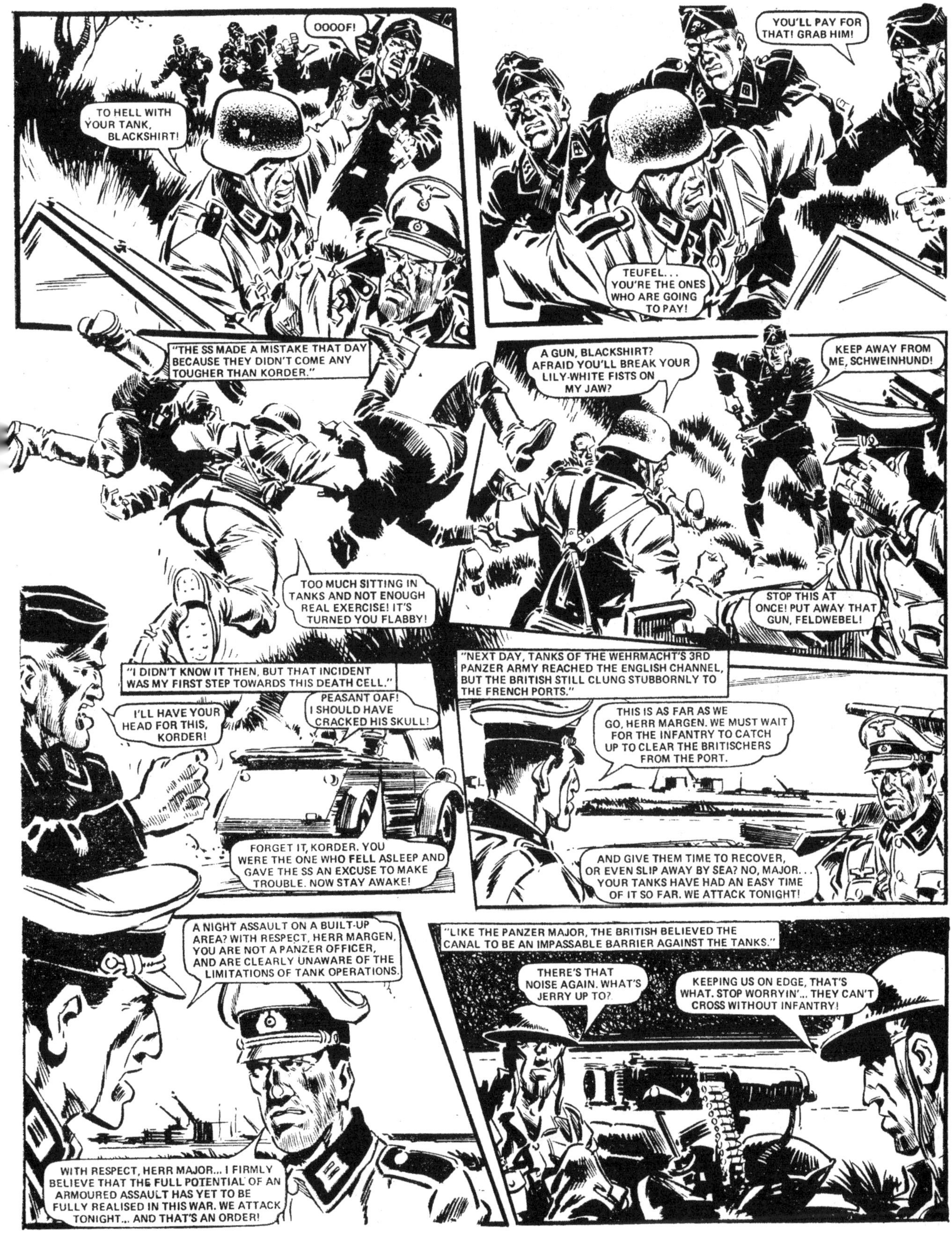
OOOOF!
TO HELL WITH YOUR TANK, BLACKSHIRT!
YOU'LL PAY FOR THAT! GRAB HIM!
TEUFEL... YOU'RE THE ONES WHO ARE GOING TO PAY!
"THE SS MADE A MISTAKE THAT DAY BECAUSE THEY DIDN'T COME ANY TOUGHER THAN KORDER."
TOO MUCH SITTING IN TANKS AND NOT ENOUGH REAL EXERCISE! IT'S TURNED YOU FLABBY!
A GUN, BLACKSHIRT? AFRAID YOU'LL BREAK YOUR LILY-WHITE FISTS ON MY JAW?
KEEP AWAY FROM ME, SCHWEINHUND!
STOP THIS AT ONCE! PUT AWAY THAT GUN, FELDWEBEL!
"I DIDN'T KNOW IT THEN, BUT THAT INCIDENT WAS MY FIRST STEP TOWARDS THIS DEATH CELL."
I'LL HAVE YOUR HEAD FOR THIS, KORDER!
PEASANT OAF! I SHOULD HAVE CRACKED HIS SKULL!
FORGET IT, KORDER. YOU WERE THE ONE WHO FELL ASLEEP AND GAVE THE SS AN EXCUSE TO MAKE TROUBLE. NOW STAY AWAKE!
"NEXT DAY, TANKS OF THE WEHRMACHT'S 3RD PANZER ARMY REACHED THE ENGLISH CHANNEL, BUT THE BRITISH STILL CLUNG STUBBORNLY TO THE FRENCH PORTS."
THIS IS AS FAR AS WE GO, HERR MARGEN. WE MUST WAIT FOR THE INFANTRY TO CATCH UP TO CLEAR THE BRITISCHERS FROM THE PORT.
AND GIVE THEM TIME TO RECOVER, OR EVEN SLIP AWAY BY SEA? NO, MAJOR... YOUR TANKS HAVE HAD AN EASY TIME OF IT SO FAR. WE ATTACK TONIGHT!
A NIGHT ASSAULT ON A BUILT-UP AREA? WITH RESPECT, HERR MARGEN, YOU ARE NOT A PANZER OFFICER, AND ARE CLEARLY UNAWARE OF THE LIMITATIONS OF TANK OPERATIONS.
WITH RESPECT, HERR MAJOR... I FIRMLY BELIEVE THAT THE FULL POTENTIAL OF AN ARMOURED ASSAULT HAS YET TO BE FULLY REALISED IN THIS WAR. WE ATTACK TONIGHT... AND THAT'S AN ORDER!
"LIKE THE PANZER MAJOR, THE BRITISH BELIEVED THE CANAL TO BE AN IMPASSABLE BARRIER AGAINST THE TANKS."
THERE'S THAT NOISE AGAIN. WHAT'S JERRY UP TO?
KEEPING US ON EDGE, THAT'S WHAT. STOP WORRYIN'... THEY CAN'T CROSS WITHOUT INFANTRY!

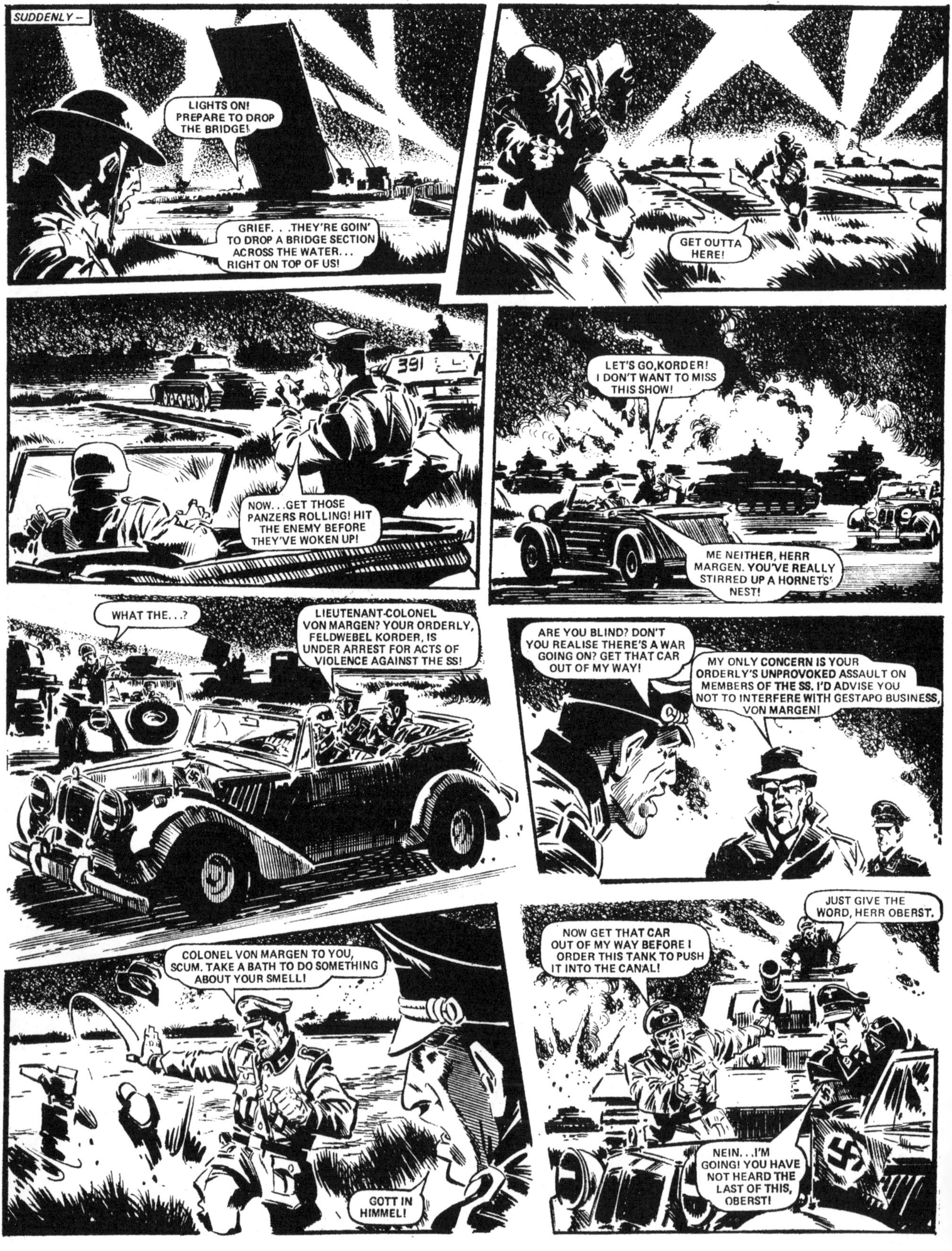
SUDDENLY —
LIGHTS ON! PREPARE TO DROP THE BRIDGE!
GRIEF. . .THEY'RE GOIN' TO DROP A BRIDGE SECTION ACROSS THE WATER. . . RIGHT ON TOP OF US!
GET OUTTA HERE!
391
NOW. . .GET THOSE PANZERS ROLLING! HIT THE ENEMY BEFORE THEY'VE WOKEN UP!
LET'S GO, KORDER! I DON'T WANT TO MISS THIS SHOW!
ME NEITHER, HERR MARGEN. YOU'VE REALLY STIRRED UP A HORNETS' NEST!
WHAT THE. . .?
LIEUTENANT-COLONEL VON MARGEN? YOUR ORDERLY, FELDWEBEL KORDER, IS UNDER ARREST FOR ACTS OF VIOLENCE AGAINST THE SS!
ARE YOU BLIND? DON'T YOU REALISE THERE'S A WAR GOING ON? GET THAT CAR OUT OF MY WAY!
MY ONLY CONCERN IS YOUR ORDERLY'S UNPROVOKED ASSAULT ON MEMBERS OF THE SS. I'D ADVISE YOU NOT TO INTERFERE WITH GESTAPO BUSINESS, VON MARGEN!
COLONEL VON MARGEN TO YOU, SCUM. TAKE A BATH TO DO SOMETHING ABOUT YOUR SMELL!
GOTT IN HIMMEL!
NOW GET THAT CAR OUT OF MY WAY BEFORE I ORDER THIS TANK TO PUSH IT INTO THE CANAL!
JUST GIVE THE WORD, HERR OBERST.
NEIN. . .I'M GOING! YOU HAVE NOT HEARD THE LAST OF THIS, OBERST!

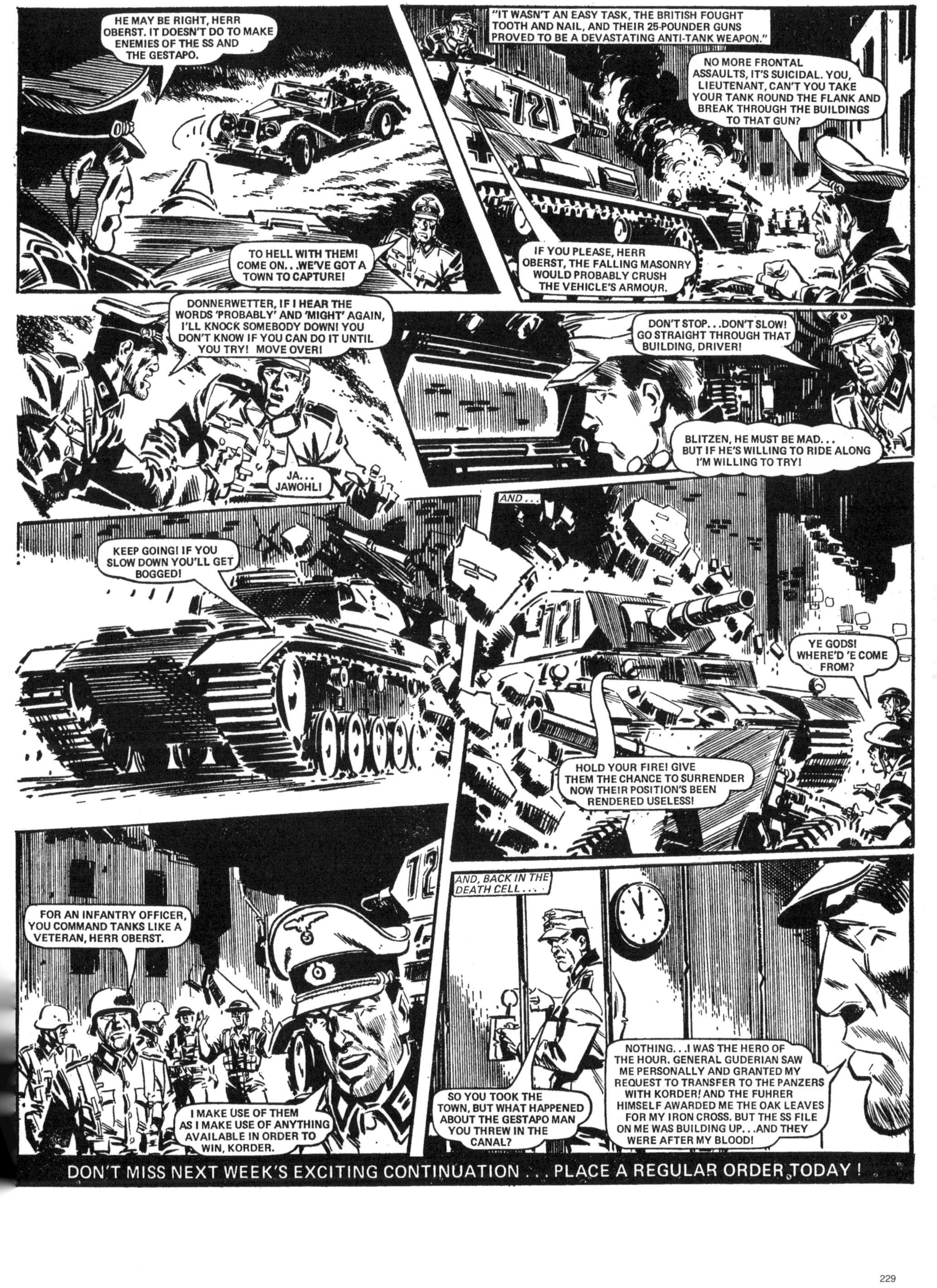
HE MAY BE RIGHT, HERR OBERST. IT DOESN'T DO TO MAKE ENEMIES OF THE SS AND THE GESTAPO.
TO HELL WITH THEM! COME ON. . .WE'VE GOT A TOWN TO CAPTURE!
"IT WASN'T AN EASY TASK, THE BRITISH FOUGHT TOOTH AND NAIL, AND THEIR 25-POUNDER GUNS PROVED TO BE A DEVASTATING ANTI-TANK WEAPON."
721
NO MORE FRONTAL ASSAULTS, IT'S SUICIDAL. YOU, LIEUTENANT, CAN'T YOU TAKE YOUR TANK ROUND THE FLANK AND BREAK THROUGH THE BUILDINGS TO THAT GUN?
IF YOU PLEASE, HERR OBERST, THE FALLING MASONRY WOULD PROBABLY CRUSH THE VEHICLE'S ARMOUR.
DONNERWETTER, IF I HEAR THE WORDS 'PROBABLY' AND 'MIGHT' AGAIN, I'LL KNOCK SOMEBODY DOWN! YOU DON'T KNOW IF YOU CAN DO IT UNTIL YOU TRY! MOVE OVER!
JA. . . JAWOHL!
DON'T STOP. . .DON'T SLOW! GO STRAIGHT THROUGH THAT BUILDING, DRIVER!
BLITZEN, HE MUST BE MAD. . . BUT IF HE'S WILLING TO RIDE ALONG I'M WILLING TO TRY!
KEEP GOING! IF YOU SLOW DOWN YOU'LL GET BOGGED!
AND. . .
721
YE GODS! WHERE'D 'E COME FROM?
HOLD YOUR FIRE! GIVE THEM THE CHANCE TO SURRENDER NOW THEIR POSITION'S BEEN RENDERED USELESS!
FOR AN INFANTRY OFFICER, YOU COMMAND TANKS LIKE A VETERAN, HERR OBERST.
I MAKE USE OF THEM AS I MAKE USE OF ANYTHING AVAILABLE IN ORDER TO WIN, KORDER.
AND, BACK IN THE DEATH CELL. . .
SO YOU TOOK THE TOWN, BUT WHAT HAPPENED ABOUT THE GESTAPO MAN YOU THREW IN THE CANAL?
NOTHING. . .I WAS THE HERO OF THE HOUR. GENERAL GUDERIAN SAW ME PERSONALLY AND GRANTED MY REQUEST TO TRANSFER TO THE PANZERS WITH KORDER! AND THE FUHRER HIMSELF AWARDED ME THE OAK LEAVES FOR MY IRON CROSS. BUT THE SS FILE ON ME WAS BUILDING UP. . .AND THEY WERE AFTER MY BLOOD!

DON'T MISS NEXT WEEK'S EXCITING CONTINUATION . . . PLACE A REGULAR ORDER TODAY !

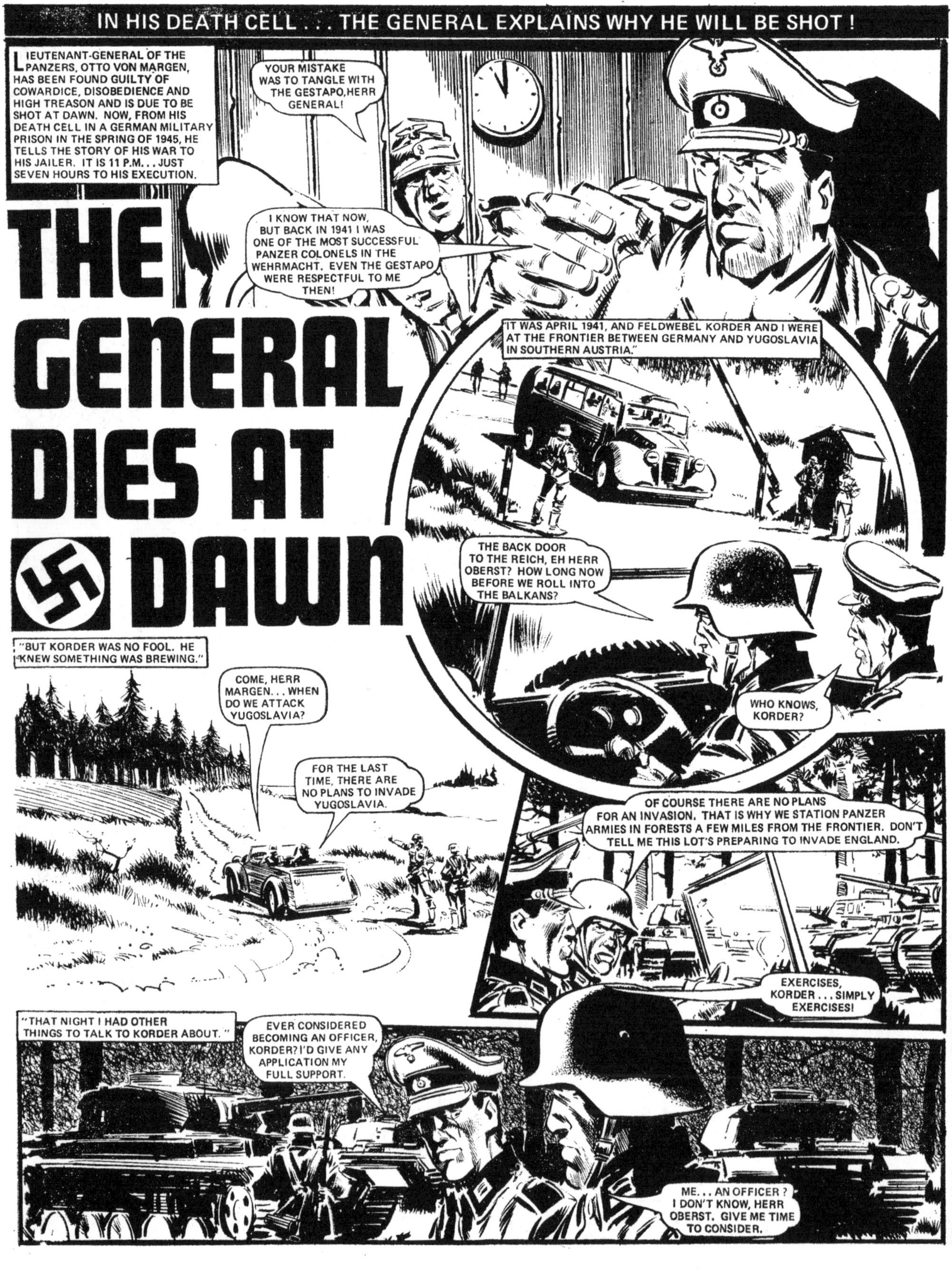

IN HIS DEATH CELL . . . THE GENERAL EXPLAINS WHY HE WILL BE SHOT !
LIEUTENANT-GENERAL OF THE PANZERS, OTTO VON MARGEN, HAS BEEN FOUND GUILTY OF COWARDICE, DISOBEDIENCE AND HIGH TREASON AND IS DUE TO BE SHOT AT DAWN. NOW, FROM HIS DEATH CELL IN A GERMAN MILITARY PRISON IN THE SPRING OF 1945, HE TELLS THE STORY OF HIS WAR TO HIS JAILER. IT IS 11 P.M. . . JUST SEVEN HOURS TO HIS EXECUTION.
YOUR MISTAKE WAS TO TANGLE WITH THE GESTAPO, HERR GENERAL!
I KNOW THAT NOW, BUT BACK IN 1941 I WAS ONE OF THE MOST SUCCESSFUL PANZER COLONELS IN THE WEHRMACHT. EVEN THE GESTAPO WERE RESPECTFUL TO ME THEN!
THE GENERAL DIES AT DAWN
"IT WAS APRIL 1941, AND FELDWEBEL KORDER AND I WERE AT THE FRONTIER BETWEEN GERMANY AND YUGOSLAVIA IN SOUTHERN AUSTRIA."
THE BACK DOOR TO THE REICH, EH HERR OBERST? HOW LONG NOW BEFORE WE ROLL INTO THE BALKANS?
WHO KNOWS, KORDER?
"BUT KORDER WAS NO FOOL. HE KNEW SOMETHING WAS BREWING."
COME, HERR MARGEN. . . WHEN DO WE ATTACK YUGOSLAVIA?
FOR THE LAST TIME, THERE ARE NO PLANS TO INVADE YUGOSLAVIA.
OF COURSE THERE ARE NO PLANS FOR AN INVASION. THAT IS WHY WE STATION PANZER ARMIES IN FORESTS A FEW MILES FROM THE FRONTIER. DON'T TELL ME THIS LOT'S PREPARING TO INVADE ENGLAND.
EXERCISES, KORDER . . . SIMPLY EXERCISES!
"THAT NIGHT I HAD OTHER THINGS TO TALK TO KORDER ABOUT."
EVER CONSIDERED BECOMING AN OFFICER, KORDER? I'D GIVE ANY APPLICATION MY FULL SUPPORT.
ME. . . AN OFFICER ? I DON'T KNOW, HERR OBERST. GIVE ME TIME TO CONSIDER.

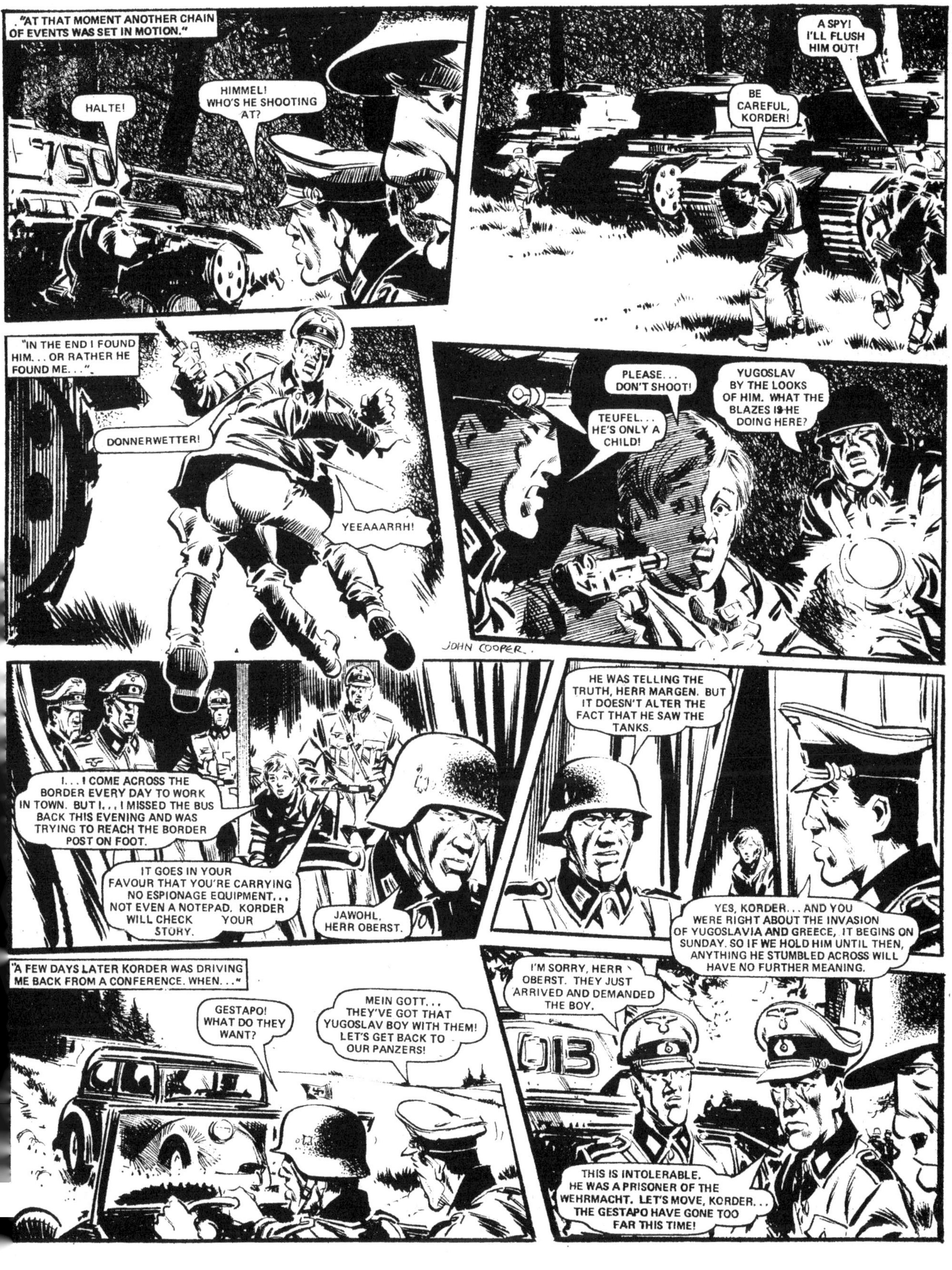
"AT THAT MOMENT ANOTHER CHAIN OF EVENTS WAS SET IN MOTION."
HALTE!
HIMMEL! WHO'S HE SHOOTING AT?
A SPY! I'LL FLUSH HIM OUT!
BE CAREFUL, KORDER!
"IN THE END I FOUND HIM. . . OR RATHER HE FOUND ME. . ."
DONNERWETTER!
YEEAAARRH!
PLEASE. . . DON'T SHOOT!
TEUFEL. . . HE'S ONLY A CHILD!
YUGOSLAV BY THE LOOKS OF HIM. WHAT THE BLAZES IS HE DOING HERE?
JOHN COOPER
I. . . I COME ACROSS THE BORDER EVERY DAY TO WORK IN TOWN. BUT I. . . I MISSED THE BUS BACK THIS EVENING AND WAS TRYING TO REACH THE BORDER POST ON FOOT.
IT GOES IN YOUR FAVOUR THAT YOU'RE CARRYING NO ESPIONAGE EQUIPMENT. . . NOT EVEN A NOTEPAD. KORDER WILL CHECK YOUR STORY.
JAWOHL, HERR OBERST.
HE WAS TELLING THE TRUTH, HERR MARGEN. BUT IT DOESN'T ALTER THE FACT THAT HE SAW THE TANKS.
YES, KORDER. . . AND YOU WERE RIGHT ABOUT THE INVASION OF YUGOSLAVIA AND GREECE, IT BEGINS ON SUNDAY. SO IF WE HOLD HIM UNTIL THEN, ANYTHING HE STUMBLED ACROSS WILL HAVE NO FURTHER MEANING.
"A FEW DAYS LATER KORDER WAS DRIVING ME BACK FROM A CONFERENCE. WHEN. . ."
GESTAPO! WHAT DO THEY WANT?
MEIN GOTT. . . THEY'VE GOT THAT YUGOSLAV BOY WITH THEM! LET'S GET BACK TO OUR PANZERS!
I'M SORRY, HERR OBERST. THEY JUST ARRIVED AND DEMANDED THE BOY.
THIS IS INTOLERABLE. HE WAS A PRISONER OF THE WEHRMACHT. LET'S MOVE, KORDER. . . THE GESTAPO HAVE GONE TOO FAR THIS TIME!

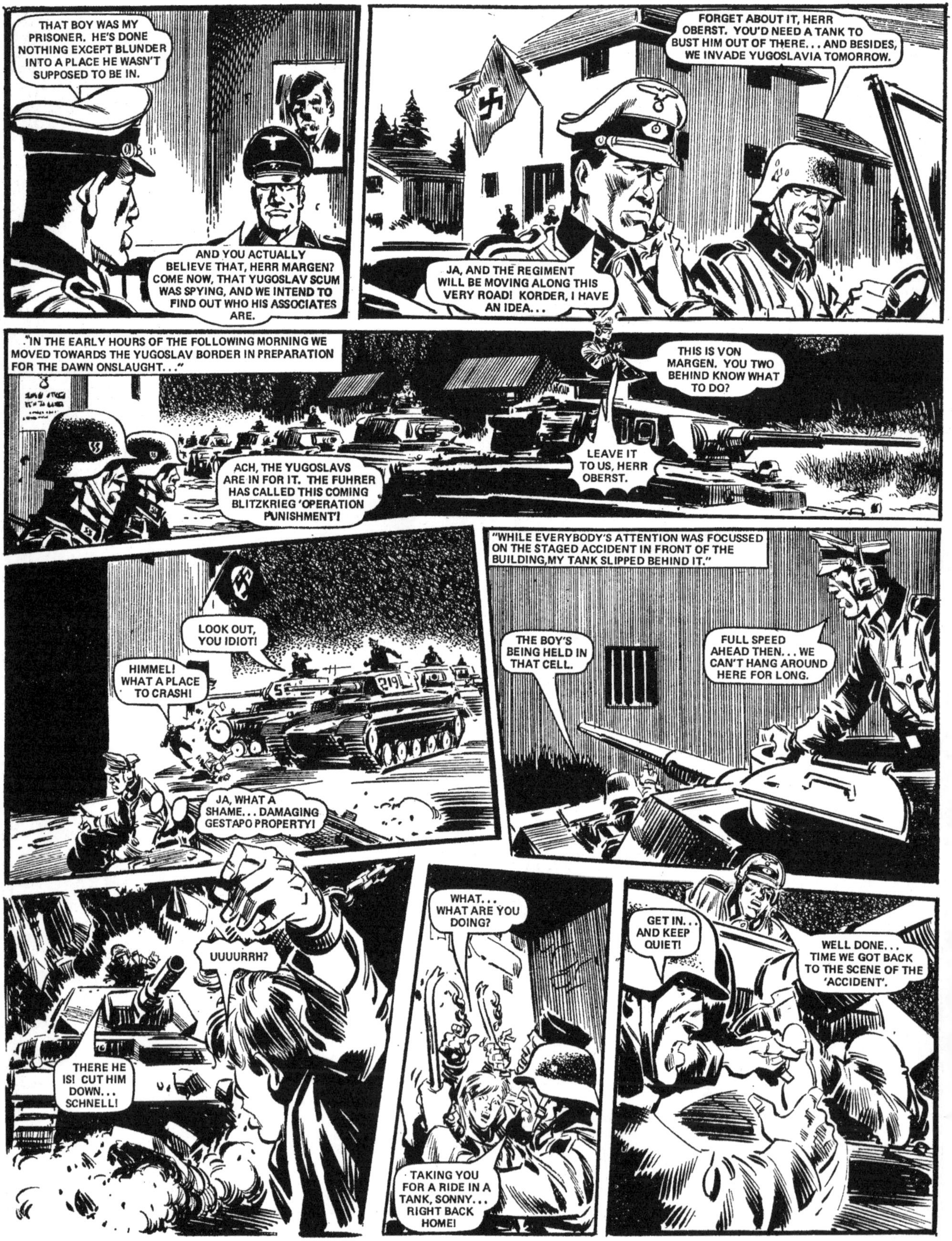
THAT BOY WAS MY PRISONER. HE'S DONE NOTHING EXCEPT BLUNDER INTO A PLACE HE WASN'T SUPPOSED TO BE IN.
AND YOU ACTUALLY BELIEVE THAT, HERR MARGEN? COME NOW, THAT YUGOSLAV SCUM WAS SPYING, AND WE INTEND TO FIND OUT WHO HIS ASSOCIATES ARE.
FORGET ABOUT IT, HERR OBERST. YOU'D NEED A TANK TO BUST HIM OUT OF THERE... AND BESIDES, WE INVADE YUGOSLAVIA TOMORROW.
JA, AND THE REGIMENT WILL BE MOVING ALONG THIS VERY ROAD! KORDER, I HAVE AN IDEA...
"IN THE EARLY HOURS OF THE FOLLOWING MORNING WE MOVED TOWARDS THE YUGOSLAV BORDER IN PREPARATION FOR THE DAWN ONSLAUGHT..."
ACH, THE YUGOSLAVS ARE IN FOR IT. THE FUHRER HAS CALLED THIS COMING BLITZKRIEG 'OPERATION PUNISHMENT'!
THIS IS VON MARGEN. YOU TWO BEHIND KNOW WHAT TO DO?
LEAVE IT TO US, HERR OBERST.
LOOK OUT, YOU IDIOT!
HIMMEL! WHAT A PLACE TO CRASH!
JA, WHAT A SHAME... DAMAGING GESTAPO PROPERTY!
"WHILE EVERYBODY'S ATTENTION WAS FOCUSSED ON THE STAGED ACCIDENT IN FRONT OF THE BUILDING,MY TANK SLIPPED BEHIND IT."
THE BOY'S BEING HELD IN THAT CELL.
FULL SPEED AHEAD THEN... WE CAN'T HANG AROUND HERE FOR LONG.
UUUURRH?
THERE HE IS! CUT HIM DOWN... SCHNELL!
WHAT... WHAT ARE YOU DOING?
TAKING YOU FOR A RIDE IN A TANK, SONNY... RIGHT BACK HOME!
GET IN... AND KEEP QUIET!
WELL DONE... TIME WE GOT BACK TO THE SCENE OF THE 'ACCIDENT'.

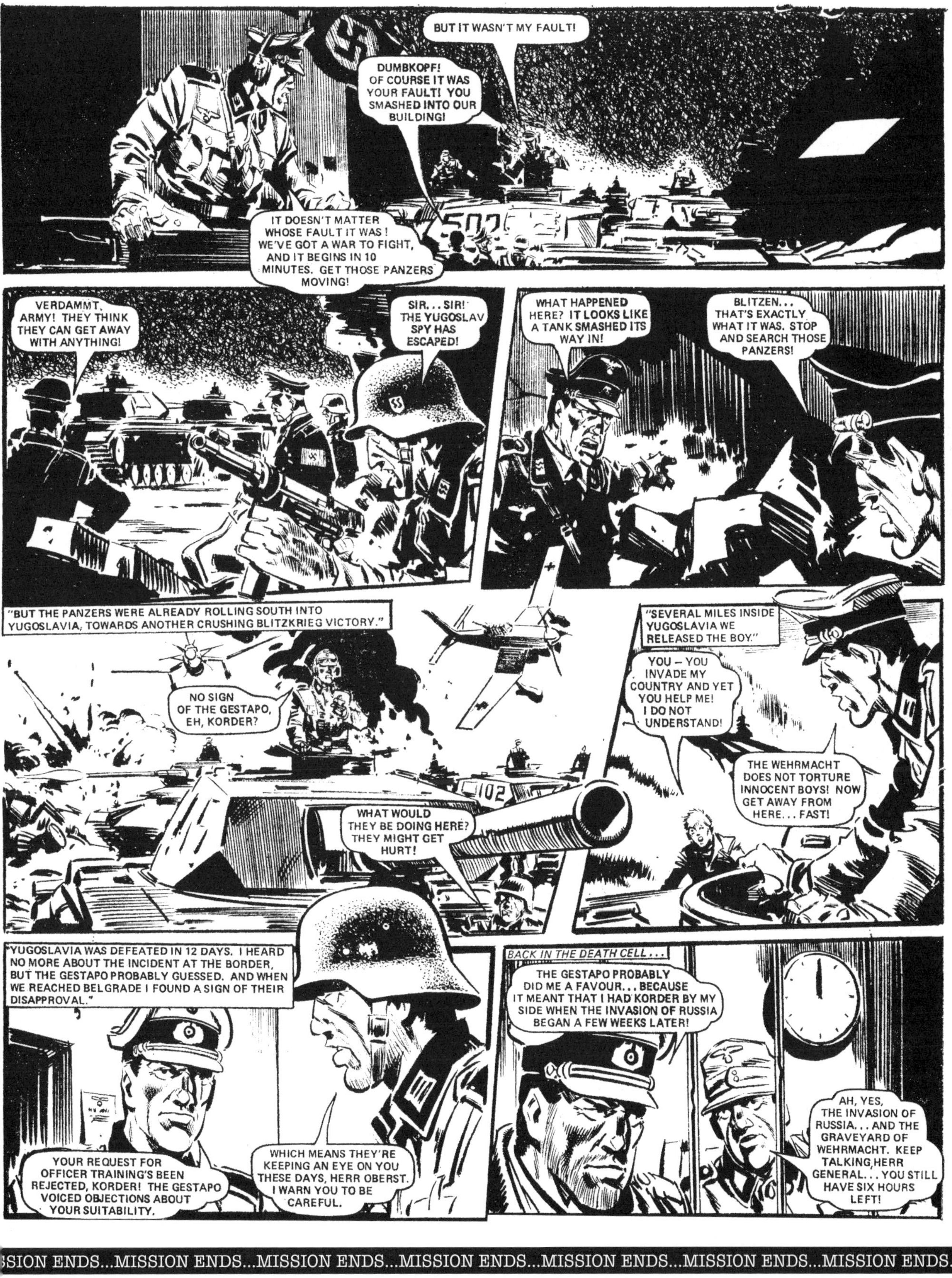
BUT IT WASN'T MY FAULT!
DUMBKOPF! OF COURSE IT WAS YOUR FAULT! YOU SMASHED INTO OUR BUILDING!
IT DOESN'T MATTER WHOSE FAULT IT WAS! WE'VE GOT A WAR TO FIGHT, AND IT BEGINS IN 10 MINUTES. GET THOSE PANZERS MOVING!
VERDAMMT ARMY! THEY THINK THEY CAN GET AWAY WITH ANYTHING!
SIR... SIR! THE YUGOSLAV SPY HAS ESCAPED!
WHAT HAPPENED HERE? IT LOOKS LIKE A TANK SMASHED ITS WAY IN!
BLITZEN... THAT'S EXACTLY WHAT IT WAS. STOP AND SEARCH THOSE PANZERS!
"BUT THE PANZERS WERE ALREADY ROLLING SOUTH INTO YUGOSLAVIA, TOWARDS ANOTHER CRUSHING BLITZKRIEG VICTORY."
NO SIGN OF THE GESTAPO, EH, KORDER?
WHAT WOULD THEY BE DOING HERE? THEY MIGHT GET HURT!
"SEVERAL MILES INSIDE YUGOSLAVIA WE RELEASED THE BOY."
YOU – YOU INVADE MY COUNTRY AND YET YOU HELP ME! I DO NOT UNDERSTAND!
THE WEHRMACHT DOES NOT TORTURE INNOCENT BOYS! NOW GET AWAY FROM HERE... FAST!
"YUGOSLAVIA WAS DEFEATED IN 12 DAYS. I HEARD NO MORE ABOUT THE INCIDENT AT THE BORDER, BUT THE GESTAPO PROBABLY GUESSED. AND WHEN WE REACHED BELGRADE I FOUND A SIGN OF THEIR DISAPPROVAL."
YOUR REQUEST FOR OFFICER TRAINING'S BEEN REJECTED, KORDER! THE GESTAPO VOICED OBJECTIONS ABOUT YOUR SUITABILITY.
WHICH MEANS THEY'RE KEEPING AN EYE ON YOU THESE DAYS, HERR OBERST. I WARN YOU TO BE CAREFUL.
BACK IN THE DEATH CELL...
THE GESTAPO PROBABLY DID ME A FAVOUR... BECAUSE IT MEANT THAT I HAD KORDER BY MY SIDE WHEN THE INVASION OF RUSSIA BEGAN A FEW WEEKS LATER!
AH, YES, THE INVASION OF RUSSIA... AND THE GRAVEYARD OF WEHRMACHT. KEEP TALKING, HERR GENERAL... YOU STILL HAVE SIX HOURS LEFT!

SSION ENDS...MISSION ENDS...MISSION ENDS...MISSION ENDS...MISSION ENDS...MISSION ENDS...MISSION ENDS...

CHARLEY'S WAR

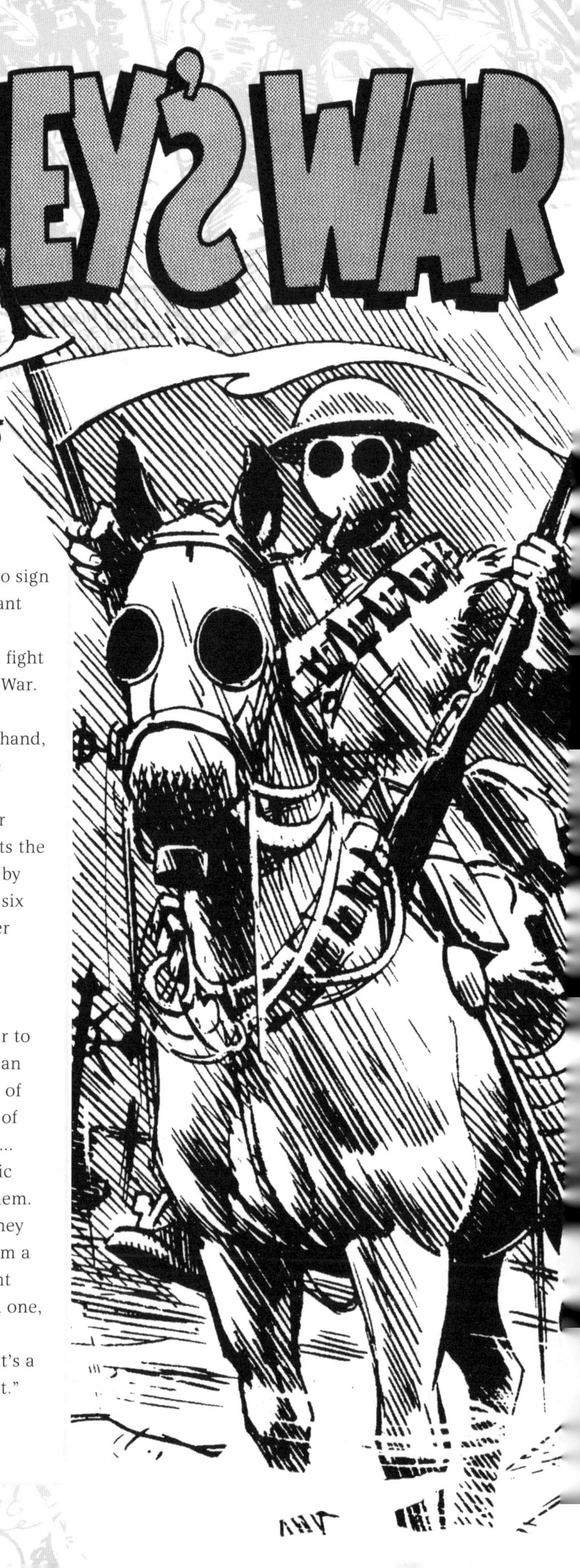

"ONCE THEY GET THE "ORRORS – THEY DON'T LAST LONG..."

Determined to do his bit, fourteen-year-old Charley Bourne was just an ordinary British lad who couldn't wait to sign up and fight for King and Country, even if it meant lying about his age.

Now he's volunteered to join the infantry and fight in the trenches of France during the First World War. But nothing could have prepared him for the harrowing adventures he would experience first hand, experiences that would change him from a naïve young boy into a battle-hardened man.

Described by many as "the greatest British war comic strip ever created", 'Charley's War' presents the pinnacle of war stories, meticulously researched by Mills and Colquhoun. The original series ran for six extraordinary years, from January 1979 to October 1985.

NOTES FROM THE FRONTLINE:

"My scripts tend to be pretty detailed, but it's fair to say that despite the detail, Joe would always add an extra layer himself. So the paintings on the walls of the homecoming scenes, the adverts on the side of buses and indeed a lot of the graphology of WWI... that would be Joe's. I think he had a photographic brain: he could remember things and recreate them. It's meant to be a gift that certain artists have; they see things from one angle and can imagine it from a completely different angle. Its particularly evident with tanks — where photos only show them from one, fairly bog-standard view, Joe's drawing of them showed them from every imaginable angle — that's a gift, and that's why I think Joe was a special artist."

— Pat Mills

WRITTEN BY Pat Mills
DRAWN BY Joe Colquhoun

CHARLEY'S WAR

THE STORY OF A SOLDIER IN WORLD WAR ONE

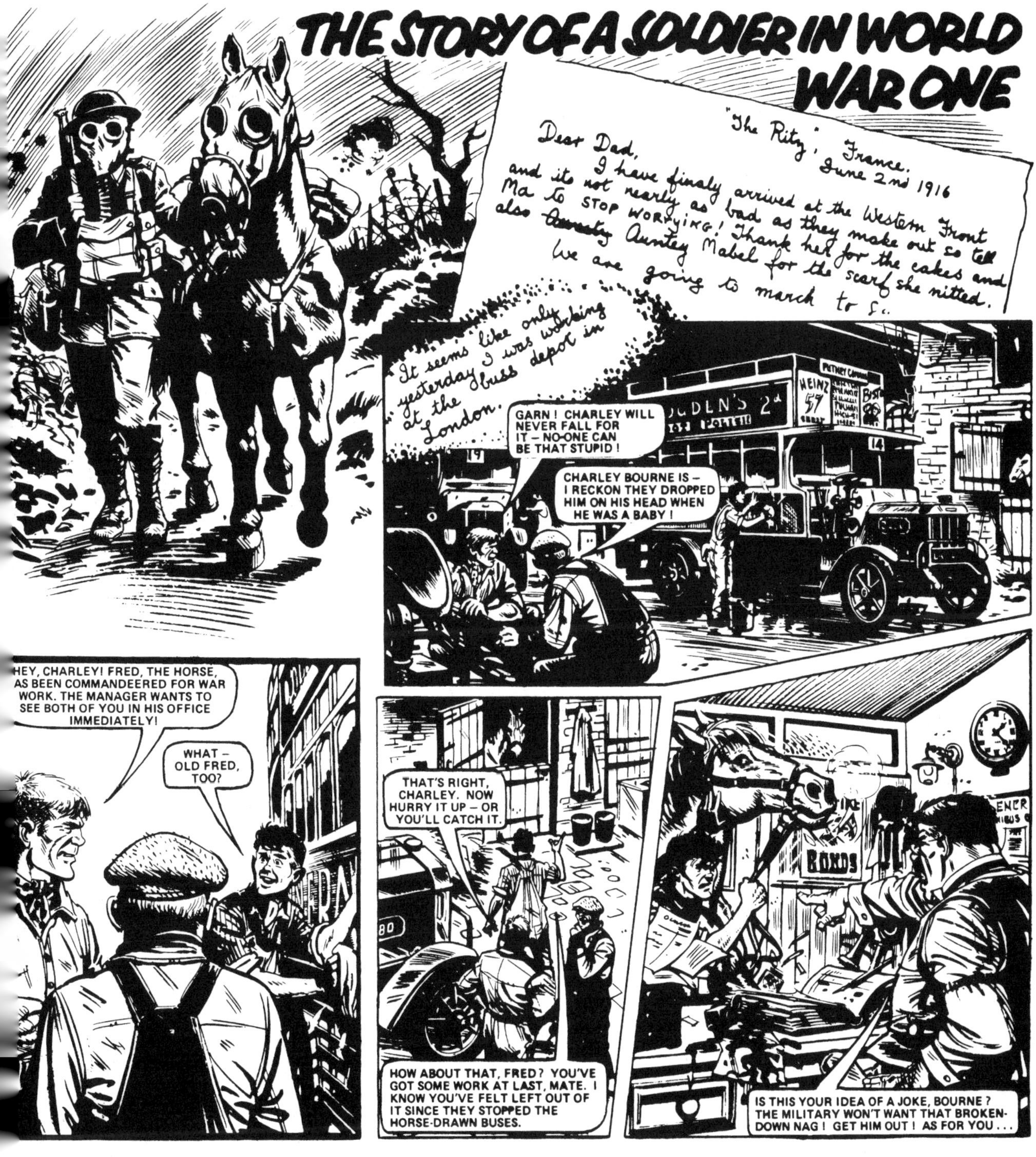

"The Ritz", France. June 2nd 1916
Dear Dad,
I have finaly arrived at the Western Front and its not nearly as bad as they make out so tell Ma to STOP WORRYING! Thank her for the cakes and also Auntey Mabel for the scarf she nitted.
We are going to march to S...
It seems like only yesterday I was working at the buss depot in London.
GARN! CHARLEY WILL NEVER FALL FOR IT – NO-ONE CAN BE THAT STUPID!
CHARLEY BOURNE IS – I RECKON THEY DROPPED HIM ON HIS HEAD WHEN HE WAS A BABY!
HEINZ 57
HEY, CHARLEY! FRED, THE HORSE, HAS BEEN COMMANDEERED FOR WAR WORK. THE MANAGER WANTS TO SEE BOTH OF YOU IN HIS OFFICE IMMEDIATELY!
WHAT – OLD FRED, TOO?
THAT'S RIGHT, CHARLEY. NOW HURRY IT UP – OR YOU'LL CATCH IT.
HOW ABOUT THAT, FRED? YOU'VE GOT SOME WORK AT LAST, MATE. I KNOW YOU'VE FELT LEFT OUT OF IT SINCE THEY STOPPED THE HORSE-DRAWN BUSES.
BONDS
IS THIS YOUR IDEA OF A JOKE, BOURNE? THE MILITARY WON'T WANT THAT BROKEN-DOWN NAG! GET HIM OUT! AS FOR YOU . . .

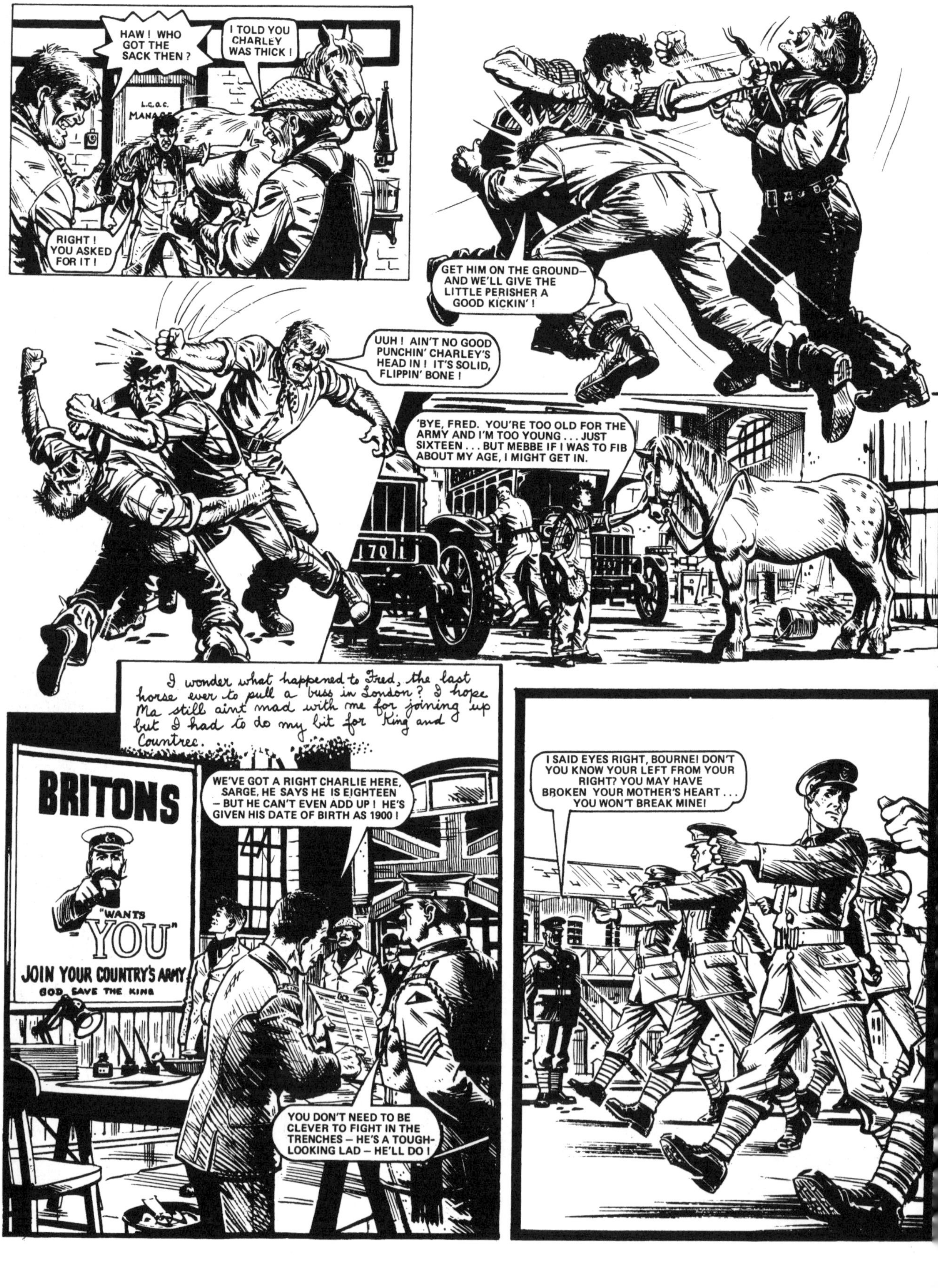
HAW ! WHO GOT THE SACK THEN ?
I TOLD YOU CHARLEY WAS THICK !
RIGHT ! YOU ASKED FOR IT !
GET HIM ON THE GROUND– AND WE'LL GIVE THE LITTLE PERISHER A GOOD KICKIN' !
UUH ! AIN'T NO GOOD PUNCHIN' CHARLEY'S HEAD IN ! IT'S SOLID, FLIPPIN' BONE !
'BYE, FRED. YOU'RE TOO OLD FOR THE ARMY AND I'M TOO YOUNG . . . JUST SIXTEEN . . . BUT MEBBE IF I WAS TO FIB ABOUT MY AGE, I MIGHT GET IN.
I wonder what happened to Fred, the last horse ever to pull a buss in London? I hope Ma still aint mad with me for joining up but I had to do my bit for King and Countree.
BRITONS
"WANTS YOU"
JOIN YOUR COUNTRY'S ARMY
GOD SAVE THE KING
WE'VE GOT A RIGHT CHARLIE HERE, SARGE, HE SAYS HE IS EIGHTEEN – BUT HE CAN'T EVEN ADD UP ! HE'S GIVEN HIS DATE OF BIRTH AS 1900 !
YOU DON'T NEED TO BE CLEVER TO FIGHT IN THE TRENCHES – HE'S A TOUGH-LOOKING LAD – HE'LL DO !
I SAID EYES RIGHT, BOURNE! DON'T YOU KNOW YOUR LEFT FROM YOUR RIGHT? YOU MAY HAVE BROKEN YOUR MOTHER'S HEART . . . YOU WON'T BREAK MINE!

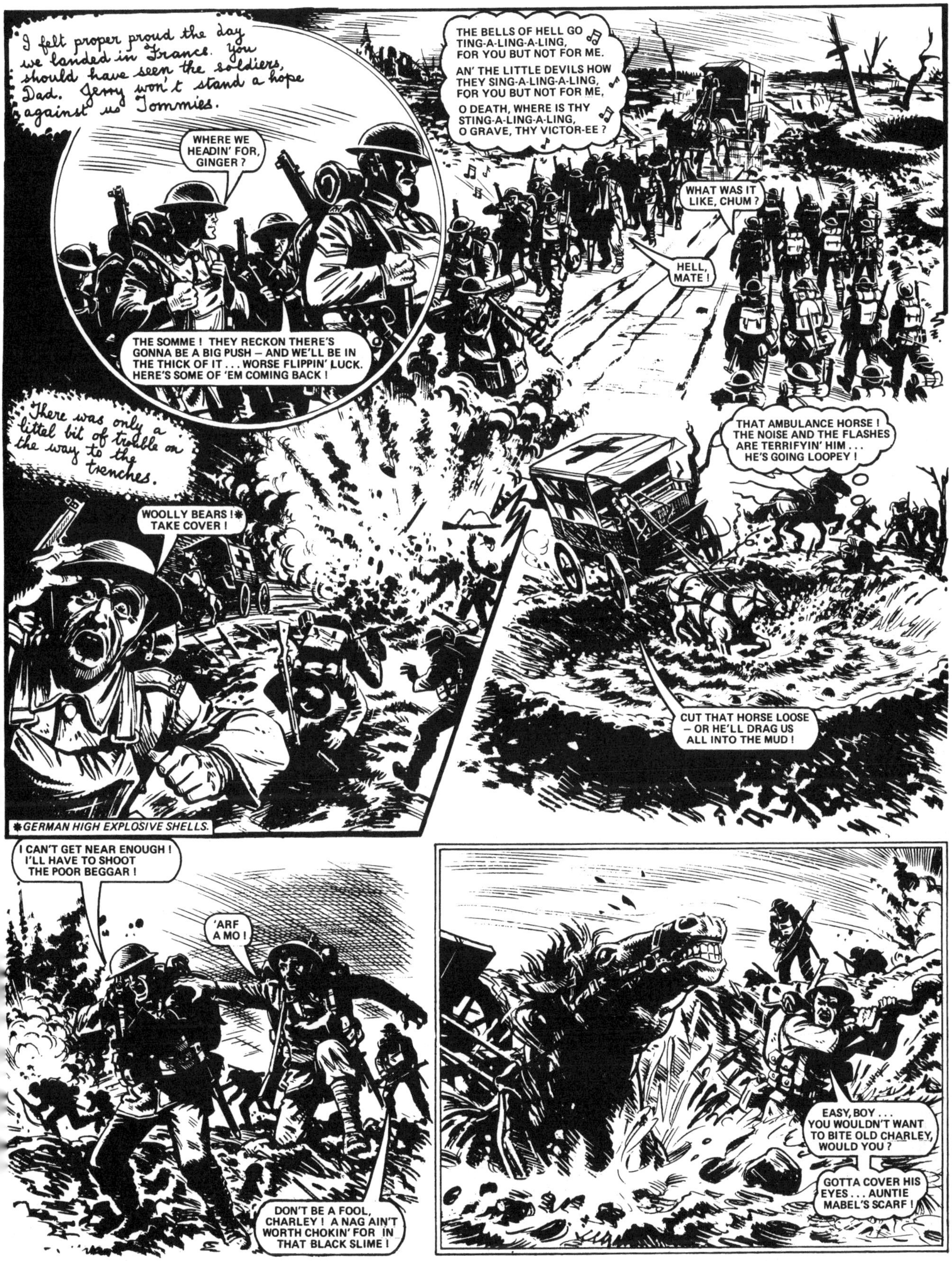

I felt proper proud the day we landed in France. You should have seen the soldiers, Dad. Jerry won't stand a hope against us Tommies.
WHERE WE HEADIN' FOR, GINGER?
THE SOMME! THEY RECKON THERE'S GONNA BE A BIG PUSH – AND WE'LL BE IN THE THICK OF IT . . . WORSE FLIPPIN' LUCK. HERE'S SOME OF 'EM COMING BACK!
THE BELLS OF HELL GO TING-A-LING-A-LING, FOR YOU BUT NOT FOR ME.
AN' THE LITTLE DEVILS HOW THEY SING-A-LING-A-LING, FOR YOU BUT NOT FOR ME,
O DEATH, WHERE IS THY STING-A-LING-A-LING, O GRAVE, THY VICTOR-EE?
WHAT WAS IT LIKE, CHUM?
HELL, MATE!
There was only a littel bit of trouble on the way to the trenches.
WOOLLY BEARS!* TAKE COVER!
*GERMAN HIGH EXPLOSIVE SHELLS.
THAT AMBULANCE HORSE! THE NOISE AND THE FLASHES ARE TERRIFYIN' HIM . . . HE'S GOING LOOPEY!
CUT THAT HORSE LOOSE – OR HE'LL DRAG US ALL INTO THE MUD!
I CAN'T GET NEAR ENOUGH! I'LL HAVE TO SHOOT THE POOR BEGGAR!
'ARF A MO!
DON'T BE A FOOL, CHARLEY! A NAG AIN'T WORTH CHOKIN' FOR IN THAT BLACK SLIME!
EASY, BOY . . . YOU WOULDN'T WANT TO BITE OLD CHARLEY, WOULD YOU?
GOTTA COVER HIS EYES . . . AUNTIE MABEL'S SCARF!

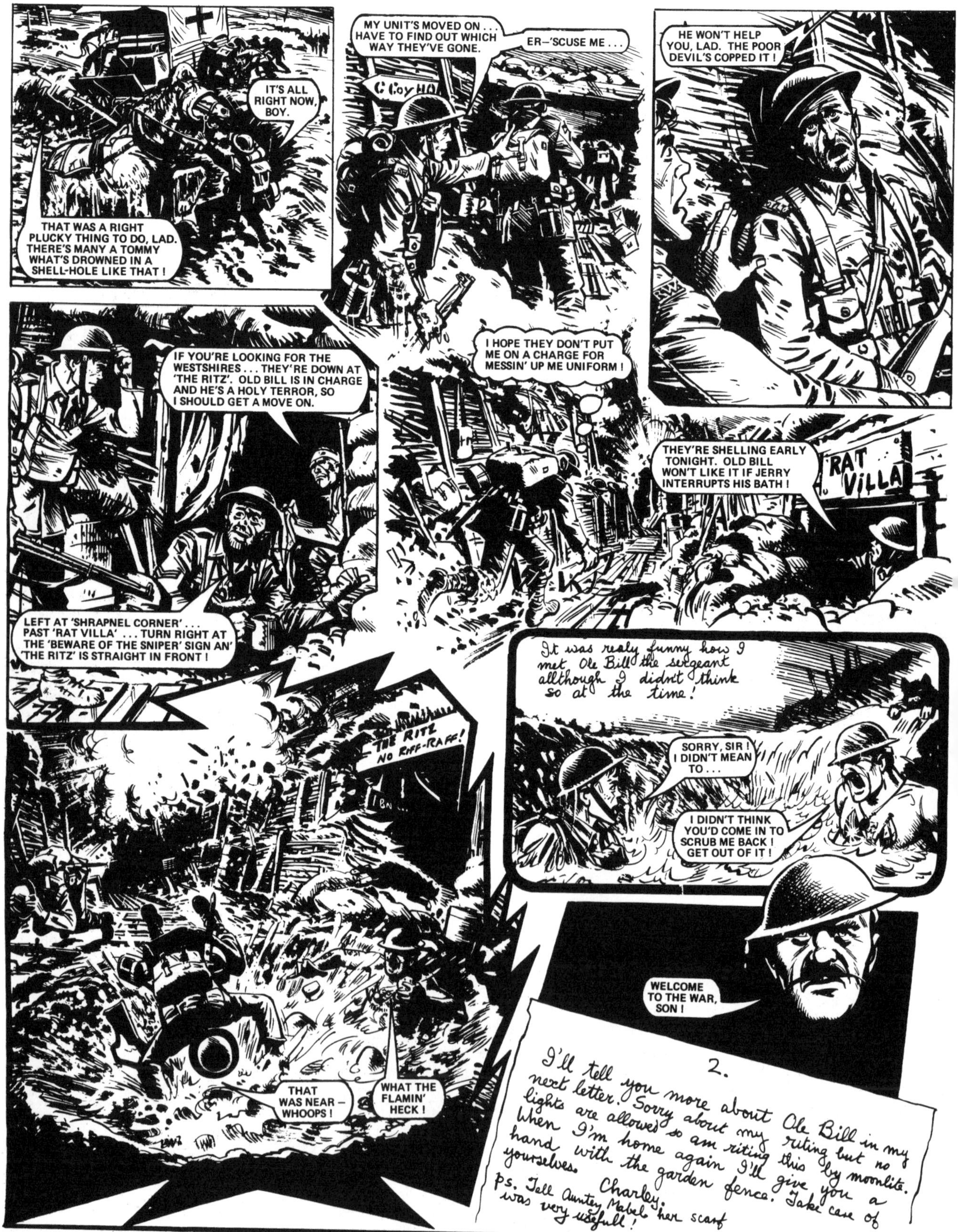
IT'S ALL RIGHT NOW, BOY.
THAT WAS A RIGHT PLUCKY THING TO DO, LAD. THERE'S MANY A TOMMY WHAT'S DROWNED IN A SHELL-HOLE LIKE THAT !
MY UNIT'S MOVED ON . . HAVE TO FIND OUT WHICH WAY THEY'VE GONE.
G Coy HQ
ER–'SCUSE ME . . .
HE WON'T HELP YOU, LAD. THE POOR DEVIL'S COPPED IT !
IF YOU'RE LOOKING FOR THE WESTSHIRES . . . THEY'RE DOWN AT 'THE RITZ'. OLD BILL IS IN CHARGE AND HE'S A HOLY TERROR, SO I SHOULD GET A MOVE ON.
LEFT AT 'SHRAPNEL CORNER' . . . PAST 'RAT VILLA' . . . TURN RIGHT AT THE 'BEWARE OF THE SNIPER' SIGN AN' 'THE RITZ' IS STRAIGHT IN FRONT !
I HOPE THEY DON'T PUT ME ON A CHARGE FOR MESSIN' UP ME UNIFORM !
THEY'RE SHELLING EARLY TONIGHT. OLD BILL WON'T LIKE IT IF JERRY INTERRUPTS HIS BATH !
RAT VILLA
THE RITZ NO RIFF-RAFF!
THAT WAS NEAR – WHOOPS !
WHAT THE FLAMIN' HECK !
It was realy funny how I met Ole Bill the sergeant allthough I didn't think so at the time!
SORRY, SIR ! I DIDN'T MEAN TO . . .
I DIDN'T THINK YOU'D COME IN TO SCRUB ME BACK ! GET OUT OF IT !
WELCOME TO THE WAR, SON !
2.
I'll tell you more about Ole Bill in my next letter. Sorry about my riting but no lights are allowed so am riting this by moonlite. When I'm home again I'll give you a hand with the garden fence. Take care of yourselves.
Charley.
Ps. Tell Auntey Mabel her scarf was very usefull!

CHARLEY'S WAR

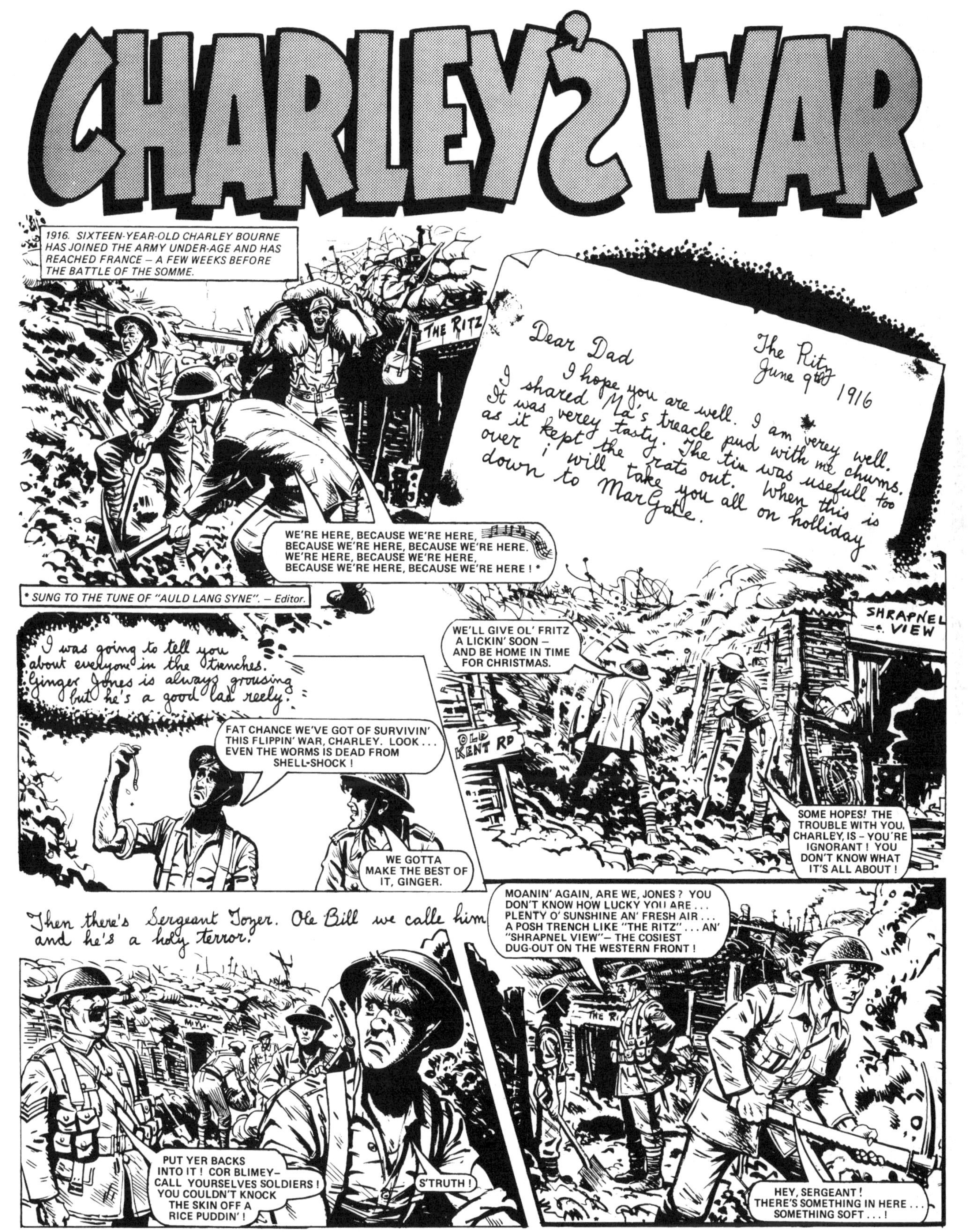

1916. SIXTEEN-YEAR-OLD CHARLEY BOURNE HAS JOINED THE ARMY UNDER-AGE AND HAS REACHED FRANCE – A FEW WEEKS BEFORE THE BATTLE OF THE SOMME.
THE RITZ
Dear Dad The Ritz June 9th 1916
I hope you are well. I am verey well. I shared Ma's treacle pud with me chums. It was verey tasty. The tin was usefull too as it kept the rats out. When this is over i will take you all on holliday down to MarGate.
WE'RE HERE, BECAUSE WE'RE HERE, BECAUSE WE'RE HERE, BECAUSE WE'RE HERE. WE'RE HERE, BECAUSE WE'RE HERE, BECAUSE WE'RE HERE, BECAUSE WE'RE HERE ! *
* SUNG TO THE TUNE OF "AULD LANG SYNE". – Editor.
I was going to tell you about everyone in the trenches. Ginger Jones is always grousing but he's a good lad reely.
FAT CHANCE WE'VE GOT OF SURVIVIN' THIS FLIPPIN' WAR, CHARLEY. LOOK . . . EVEN THE WORMS IS DEAD FROM SHELL-SHOCK !
WE GOTTA MAKE THE BEST OF IT, GINGER.
WE'LL GIVE OL' FRITZ A LICKIN' SOON – AND BE HOME IN TIME FOR CHRISTMAS.
SHRAPNEL VIEW
OLD KENT RD
SOME HOPES! THE TROUBLE WITH YOU, CHARLEY, IS – YOU'RE IGNORANT ! YOU DON'T KNOW WHAT IT'S ALL ABOUT !
Then there's Sergeant Tozer. Ole Bill we calle him and he's a holy terror.
PUT YER BACKS INTO IT ! COR BLIMEY– CALL YOURSELVES SOLDIERS ! YOU COULDN'T KNOCK THE SKIN OFF A RICE PUDDIN' !
S'TRUTH !
MOANIN' AGAIN, ARE WE, JONES ? YOU DON'T KNOW HOW LUCKY YOU ARE . . . PLENTY O' SUNSHINE AN' FRESH AIR . . . A POSH TRENCH LIKE "THE RITZ" . . . AN' "SHRAPNEL VIEW"– THE COSIEST DUG-OUT ON THE WESTERN FRONT !
HEY, SERGEANT ! THERE'S SOMETHING IN HERE . . . SOMETHING SOFT . . . !

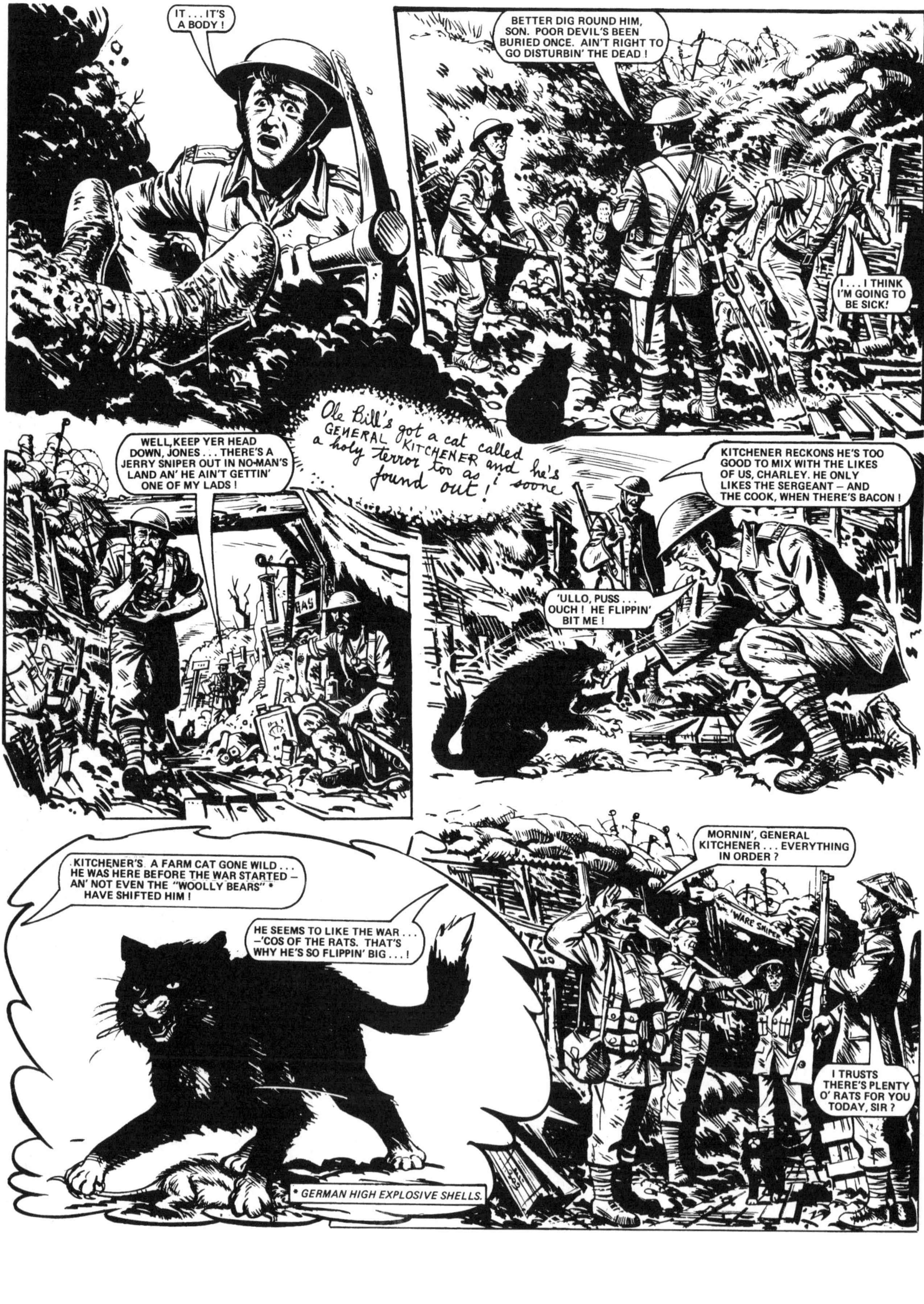

IT . . . IT'S A BODY !
BETTER DIG ROUND HIM, SON. POOR DEVIL'S BEEN BURIED ONCE. AIN'T RIGHT TO GO DISTURBIN' THE DEAD !
I . . . I THINK I'M GOING TO BE SICK!
Ole Bill's got a cat called GENERAL KITCHENER and he's a holy terror too as i soone found out!
WELL, KEEP YER HEAD DOWN, JONES . . . THERE'S A JERRY SNIPER OUT IN NO-MAN'S LAND AN' HE AIN'T GETTIN' ONE OF MY LADS !
GAS
KITCHENER RECKONS HE'S TOO GOOD TO MIX WITH THE LIKES OF US, CHARLEY. HE ONLY LIKES THE SERGEANT – AND THE COOK, WHEN THERE'S BACON !
'ULLO, PUSS . . . OUCH ! HE FLIPPIN' BIT ME !
KITCHENER'S A FARM CAT GONE WILD . . . HE WAS HERE BEFORE THE WAR STARTED – AN' NOT EVEN THE "WOOLLY BEARS" * HAVE SHIFTED HIM !
HE SEEMS TO LIKE THE WAR . . . –'COS OF THE RATS. THAT'S WHY HE'S SO FLIPPIN' BIG . . . !
* GERMAN HIGH EXPLOSIVE SHELLS.
MORNIN', GENERAL KITCHENER . . . EVERYTHING IN ORDER ?
'WARE SNIPER
I TRUSTS THERE'S PLENTY O' RATS FOR YOU TODAY, SIR ?

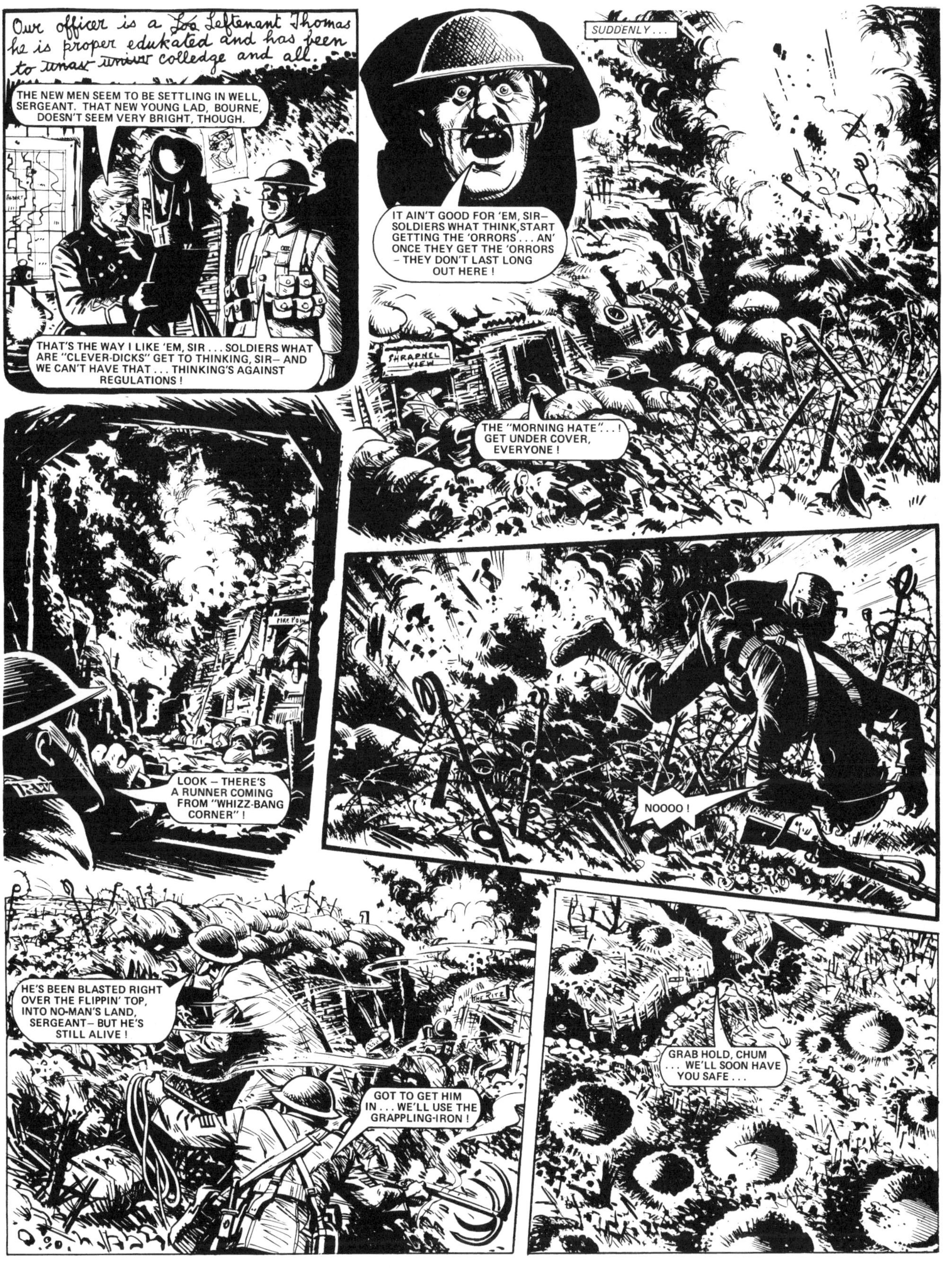
Our officer is a ~~Loo~~ Leftenant Thomas he is proper edukated and has been to colledge and all.
THE NEW MEN SEEM TO BE SETTLING IN WELL, SERGEANT. THAT NEW YOUNG LAD, BOURNE, DOESN'T SEEM VERY BRIGHT, THOUGH.
THAT'S THE WAY I LIKE 'EM, SIR . . . SOLDIERS WHAT ARE "CLEVER-DICKS" GET TO THINKING, SIR– AND WE CAN'T HAVE THAT . . . THINKING'S AGAINST REGULATIONS !
IT AIN'T GOOD FOR 'EM, SIR– SOLDIERS WHAT THINK, START GETTING THE 'ORRORS' . . . AN' ONCE THEY GET THE 'ORRORS – THEY DON'T LAST LONG OUT HERE !
SUDDENLY . . .
SHRAPNEL VIEW
THE "MORNING HATE" . . ! GET UNDER COVER, EVERYONE !
LOOK – THERE'S A RUNNER COMING FROM "WHIZZ-BANG CORNER" !
NOOOO !
HE'S BEEN BLASTED RIGHT OVER THE FLIPPIN' TOP, INTO NO-MAN'S LAND, SERGEANT– BUT HE'S STILL ALIVE !
THE RITZ
GOT TO GET HIM IN . . . WE'LL USE THE GRAPPLING-IRON !
GRAB HOLD, CHUM . . . WE'LL SOON HAVE YOU SAFE . . .

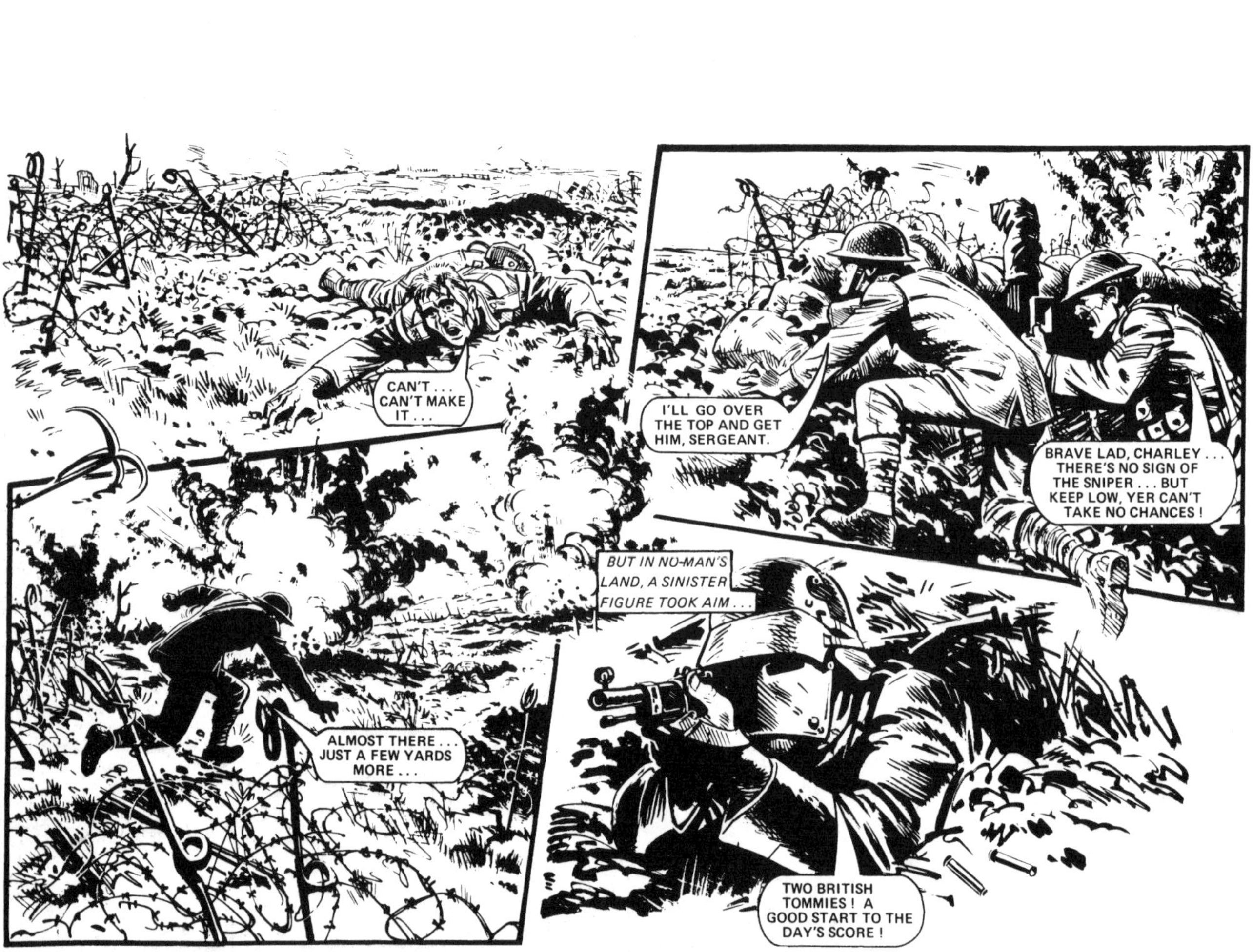
CAN'T . . . CAN'T MAKE IT . . .
I'LL GO OVER THE TOP AND GET HIM, SERGEANT.
BRAVE LAD, CHARLEY . . . THERE'S NO SIGN OF THE SNIPER . . . BUT KEEP LOW, YER CAN'T TAKE NO CHANCES !
ALMOST THERE . . . JUST A FEW YARDS MORE . . .
BUT IN NO-MAN'S LAND, A SINISTER FIGURE TOOK AIM . . .
TWO BRITISH TOMMIES ! A GOOD START TO THE DAY'S SCORE !

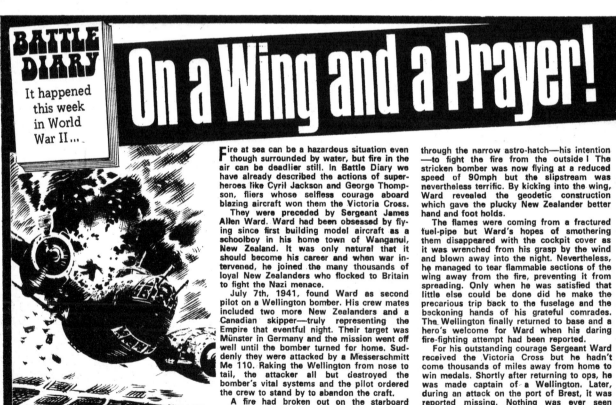

BATTLE DIARY

It happened this week in World War II...

On a Wing and a Prayer!

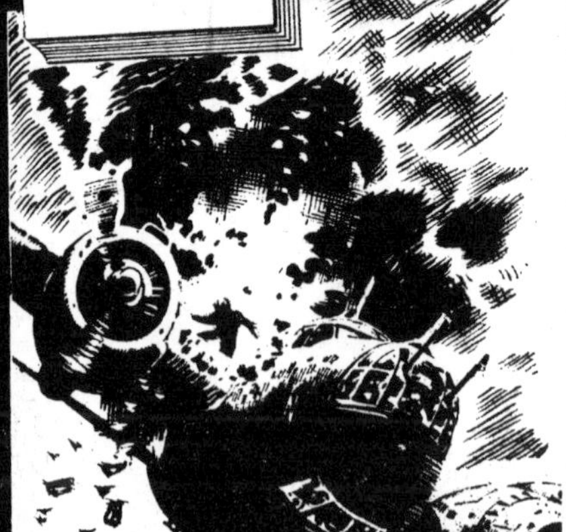

Fire at sea can be a hazardous situation even though surrounded by water, but fire in the air can be deadlier still. In Battle Diary we have already described the actions of super-heroes like Cyril Jackson and George Thompson, fliers whose selfless courage aboard blazing aircraft won them the Victoria Cross.

They were preceded by Sergeant James Allen Ward. Ward had been obsessed by flying since first building model aircraft as a schoolboy in his home town of Wanganui, New Zealand. It was only natural that it should become his career and when war intervened, he joined the many thousands of loyal New Zealanders who flocked to Britain to fight the Nazi menace.

July 7th, 1941, found Ward as second pilot on a Wellington bomber. His crew mates included two more New Zealanders and a Canadian skipper—truly representing the Empire that eventful night. Their target was Münster in Germany and the mission went off well until the bomber turned for home. Suddenly they were attacked by a Messerschmitt Me 110. Raking the Wellington from nose to tail, the attacker all but destroyed the bomber's vital systems and the pilot ordered the crew to stand by to abandon the craft.

A fire had broken out on the starboard wing which threatened the whole plane. Grabbing a spare cockpit cover Ward clambered through the narrow astro-hatch—his intention—to fight the fire from the outside! The stricken bomber was now flying at a reduced speed of 90mph but the slipstream was nevertheless terrific. By kicking into the wing, Ward revealed the geodetic construction which gave the plucky New Zealander better hand and foot holds.

The flames were coming from a fractured fuel-pipe but Ward's hopes of smothering them disappeared with the cockpit cover as it was wrenched from his grasp by the wind and blown away into the night. Nevertheless, he managed to tear flammable sections of the wing away from the fire, preventing it from spreading. Only when he was satisfied that little else could be done did he make the precarious trip back to the fuselage and the beckoning hands of his grateful comrades. The Wellington finally returned to base and a hero's welcome for Ward when his daring fire-fighting attempt had been reported.

For his outstanding courage Sergeant Ward received the Victoria Cross but he hadn't come thousands of miles away from home to win medals. Shortly after returning to ops, he was made captain of a Wellington. Later, during an attack on the port of Brest, it was reported missing. Nothing was ever seen again of the flier who had braved a blazing wing 2½ miles up.

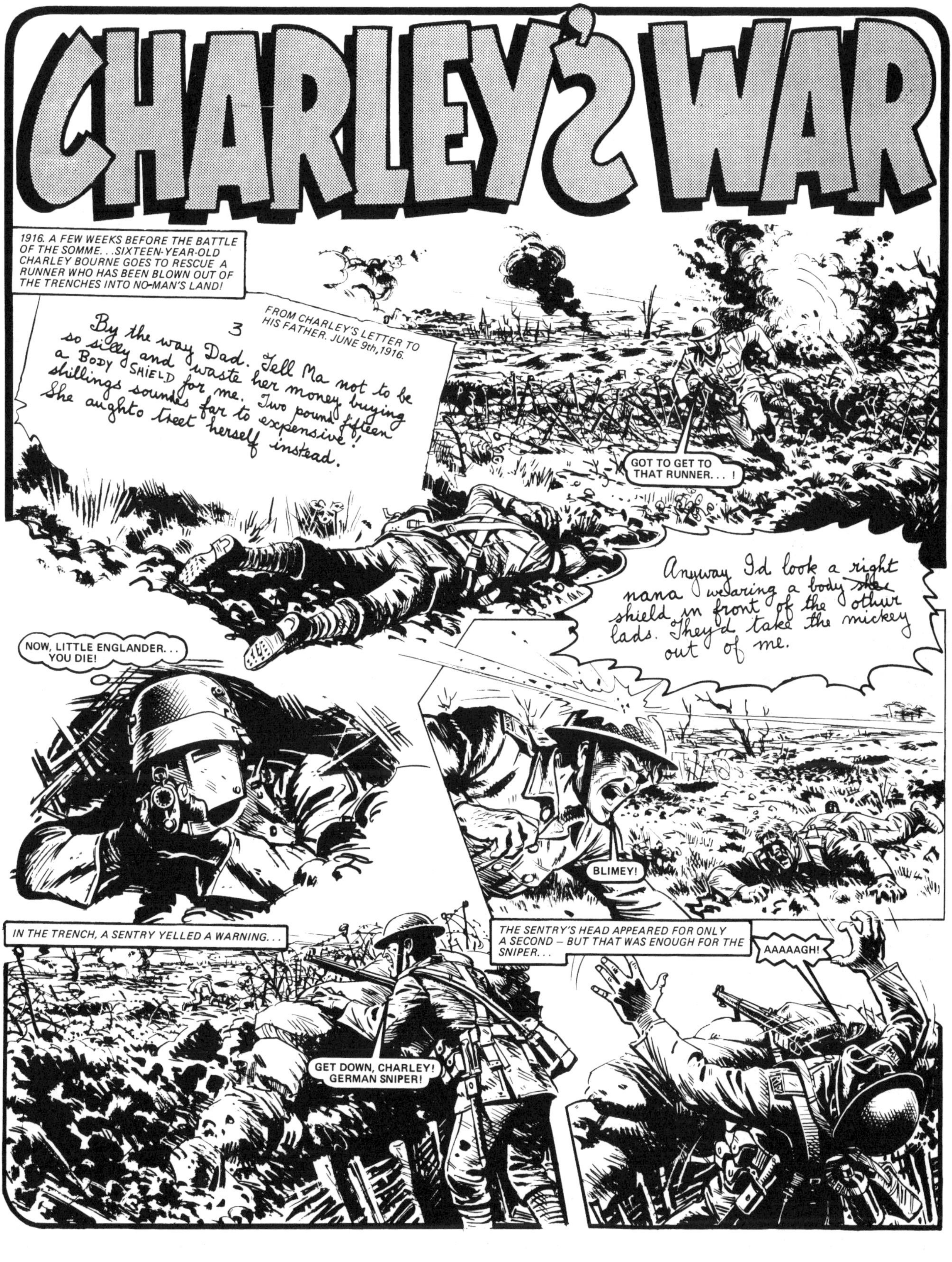

CHARLEY'S WAR
1916. A FEW WEEKS BEFORE THE BATTLE OF THE SOMME. . .SIXTEEN-YEAR-OLD CHARLEY BOURNE GOES TO RESCUE A RUNNER WHO HAS BEEN BLOWN OUT OF THE TRENCHES INTO NO-MAN'S LAND!
FROM CHARLEY'S LETTER TO HIS FATHER. JUNE 9th, 1916.
3
By the way Dad. Tell Ma not to be so silly and waste her money buying a BODY SHIELD for me. Two pound fifteen shillings sounds far to expensive! She aughto treet herself instead.
GOT TO GET TO THAT RUNNER. . . !
Anyway I'd look a right nana wearing a body shield in front of the othur lads. They'd take the mickey out of me.
NOW, LITTLE ENGLANDER. . . YOU DIE!
BLIMEY!
IN THE TRENCH, A SENTRY YELLED A WARNING. . .
GET DOWN, CHARLEY! GERMAN SNIPER!
THE SENTRY'S HEAD APPEARED FOR ONLY A SECOND – BUT THAT WAS ENOUGH FOR THE SNIPER. . .
AAAAAGH!

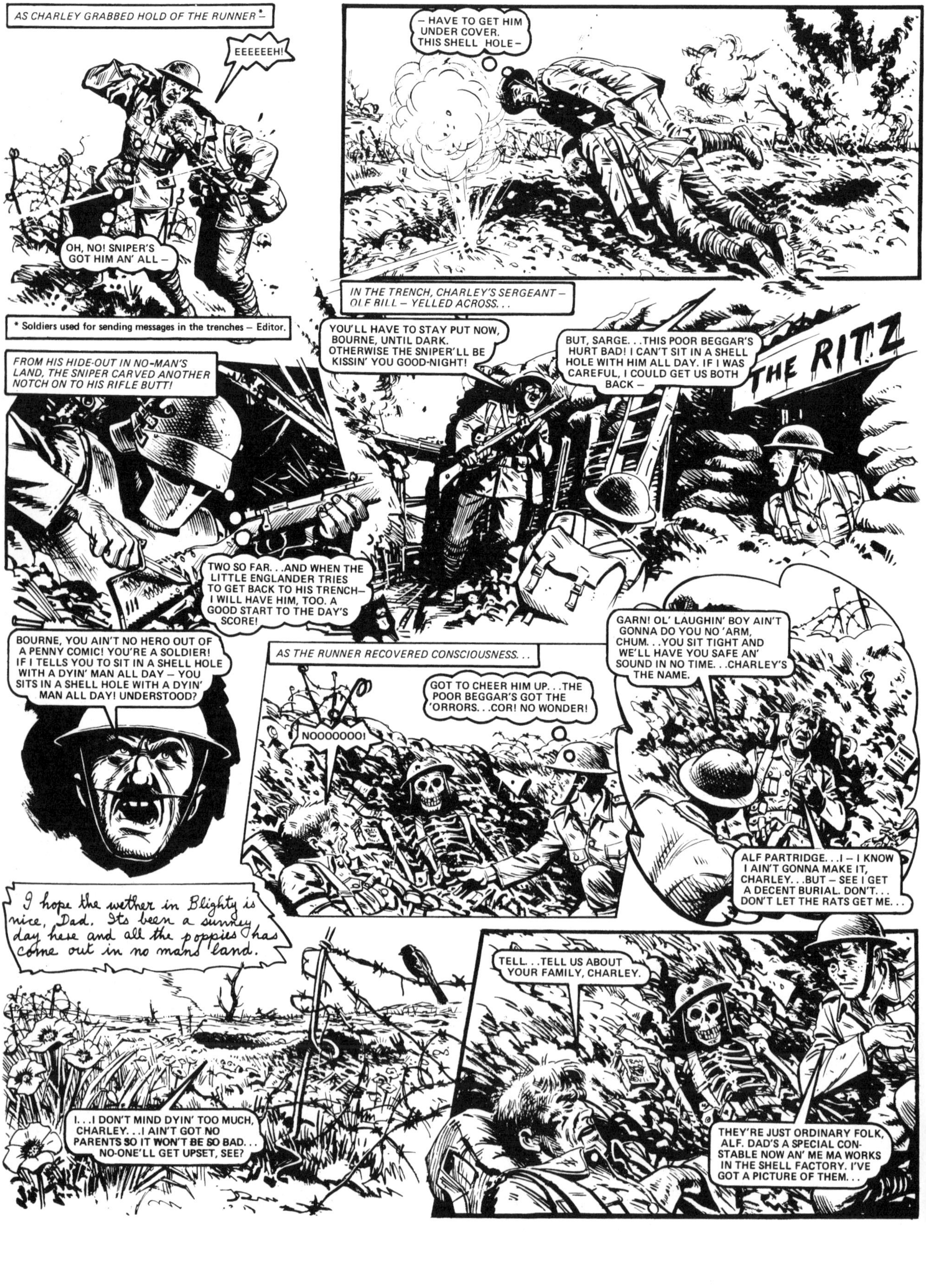
AS CHARLEY GRABBED HOLD OF THE RUNNER* –
EEEEEEH!
OH, NO! SNIPER'S GOT HIM AN' ALL –
* Soldiers used for sending messages in the trenches – Editor.
– HAVE TO GET HIM UNDER COVER. THIS SHELL HOLE –
FROM HIS HIDE-OUT IN NO-MAN'S LAND, THE SNIPER CARVED ANOTHER NOTCH ON TO HIS RIFLE BUTT!
TWO SO FAR...AND WHEN THE LITTLE ENGLANDER TRIES TO GET BACK TO HIS TRENCH– I WILL HAVE HIM, TOO. A GOOD START TO THE DAY'S SCORE!
IN THE TRENCH, CHARLEY'S SERGEANT – OLE BILL – YELLED ACROSS...
YOU'LL HAVE TO STAY PUT NOW, BOURNE, UNTIL DARK. OTHERWISE THE SNIPER'LL BE KISSIN' YOU GOOD-NIGHT!
BUT, SARGE...THIS POOR BEGGAR'S HURT BAD! I CAN'T SIT IN A SHELL HOLE WITH HIM ALL DAY. IF I WAS CAREFUL, I COULD GET US BOTH BACK –
THE RITZ
BOURNE, YOU AIN'T NO HERO OUT OF A PENNY COMIC! YOU'RE A SOLDIER! IF I TELLS YOU TO SIT IN A SHELL HOLE WITH A DYIN' MAN ALL DAY – YOU SITS IN A SHELL HOLE WITH A DYIN' MAN ALL DAY! UNDERSTOOD?
AS THE RUNNER RECOVERED CONSCIOUSNESS...
GOT TO CHEER HIM UP...THE POOR BEGGAR'S GOT THE 'ORRORS...COR! NO WONDER!
NOOOOOOO!
GARN! OL' LAUGHIN' BOY AIN'T GONNA DO YOU NO 'ARM, CHUM...YOU SIT TIGHT AND WE'LL HAVE YOU SAFE AN' SOUND IN NO TIME...CHARLEY'S THE NAME.
ALF PARTRIDGE...I – I KNOW I AIN'T GONNA MAKE IT, CHARLEY...BUT – SEE I GET A DECENT BURIAL. DON'T... DON'T LET THE RATS GET ME...
I hope the wether in Blighty is nice, Dad. Its been a sunney day here and all the poppies has come out in no mans land.
I...I DON'T MIND DYIN' TOO MUCH, CHARLEY...I AIN'T GOT NO PARENTS SO IT WON'T BE SO BAD... NO-ONE'LL GET UPSET, SEE?
TELL...TELL US ABOUT YOUR FAMILY, CHARLEY.
THEY'RE JUST ORDINARY FOLK, ALF. DAD'S A SPECIAL CONSTABLE NOW AN' ME MA WORKS IN THE SHELL FACTORY. I'VE GOT A PICTURE OF THEM...

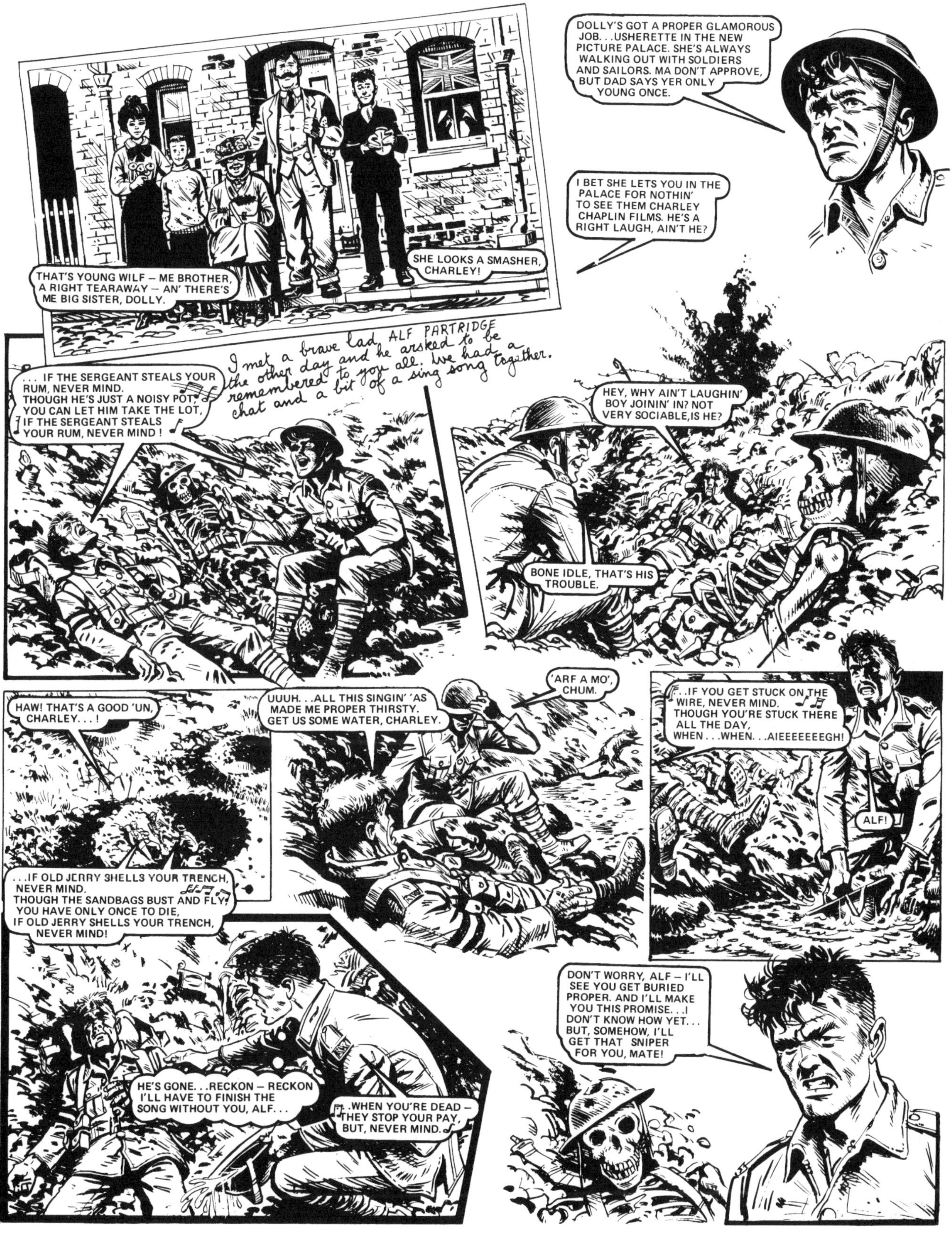
THAT'S YOUNG WILF – ME BROTHER, A RIGHT TEARAWAY – AN' THERE'S ME BIG SISTER, DOLLY.
SHE LOOKS A SMASHER, CHARLEY!
DOLLY'S GOT A PROPER GLAMOROUS JOB. . .USHERETTE IN THE NEW PICTURE PALACE. SHE'S ALWAYS WALKING OUT WITH SOLDIERS AND SAILORS. MA DON'T APPROVE, BUT DAD SAYS YER ONLY YOUNG ONCE.
I BET SHE LETS YOU IN THE PALACE FOR NOTHIN' TO SEE THEM CHARLEY CHAPLIN FILMS. HE'S A RIGHT LAUGH, AIN'T HE?
I met a brave lad, ALF PARTRIDGE the other day and he arsked to be remembered to you all. We had a chat and a bit of a sing song together.
. . . IF THE SERGEANT STEALS YOUR RUM, NEVER MIND. THOUGH HE'S JUST A NOISY POT, YOU CAN LET HIM TAKE THE LOT, IF THE SERGEANT STEALS YOUR RUM, NEVER MIND !
HEY, WHY AIN'T LAUGHIN' BOY JOININ' IN? NOT VERY SOCIABLE,IS HE?
BONE IDLE, THAT'S HIS TROUBLE.
HAW! THAT'S A GOOD 'UN, CHARLEY. . . !
. . .IF OLD JERRY SHELLS YOUR TRENCH, NEVER MIND. THOUGH THE SANDBAGS BUST AND FLY, YOU HAVE ONLY ONCE TO DIE, IF OLD JERRY SHELLS YOUR TRENCH, NEVER MIND!
UUUH. . .ALL THIS SINGIN' 'AS MADE ME PROPER THIRSTY. GET US SOME WATER, CHARLEY.
'ARF A MO', CHUM.
. . IF YOU GET STUCK ON THE WIRE, NEVER MIND. THOUGH YOU'RE STUCK THERE ALL THE DAY, WHEN. . .WHEN. . .AIEEEEEEEGH!
ALF!
HE'S GONE. . .RECKON – RECKON I'LL HAVE TO FINISH THE SONG WITHOUT YOU, ALF. . .
. .WHEN YOU'RE DEAD – THEY STOP YOUR PAY, BUT, NEVER MIND.
DON'T WORRY, ALF – I'LL SEE YOU GET BURIED PROPER. AND I'LL MAKE YOU THIS PROMISE. . .I DON'T KNOW HOW YET. . . BUT, SOMEHOW, I'LL GET THAT SNIPER FOR YOU, MATE!

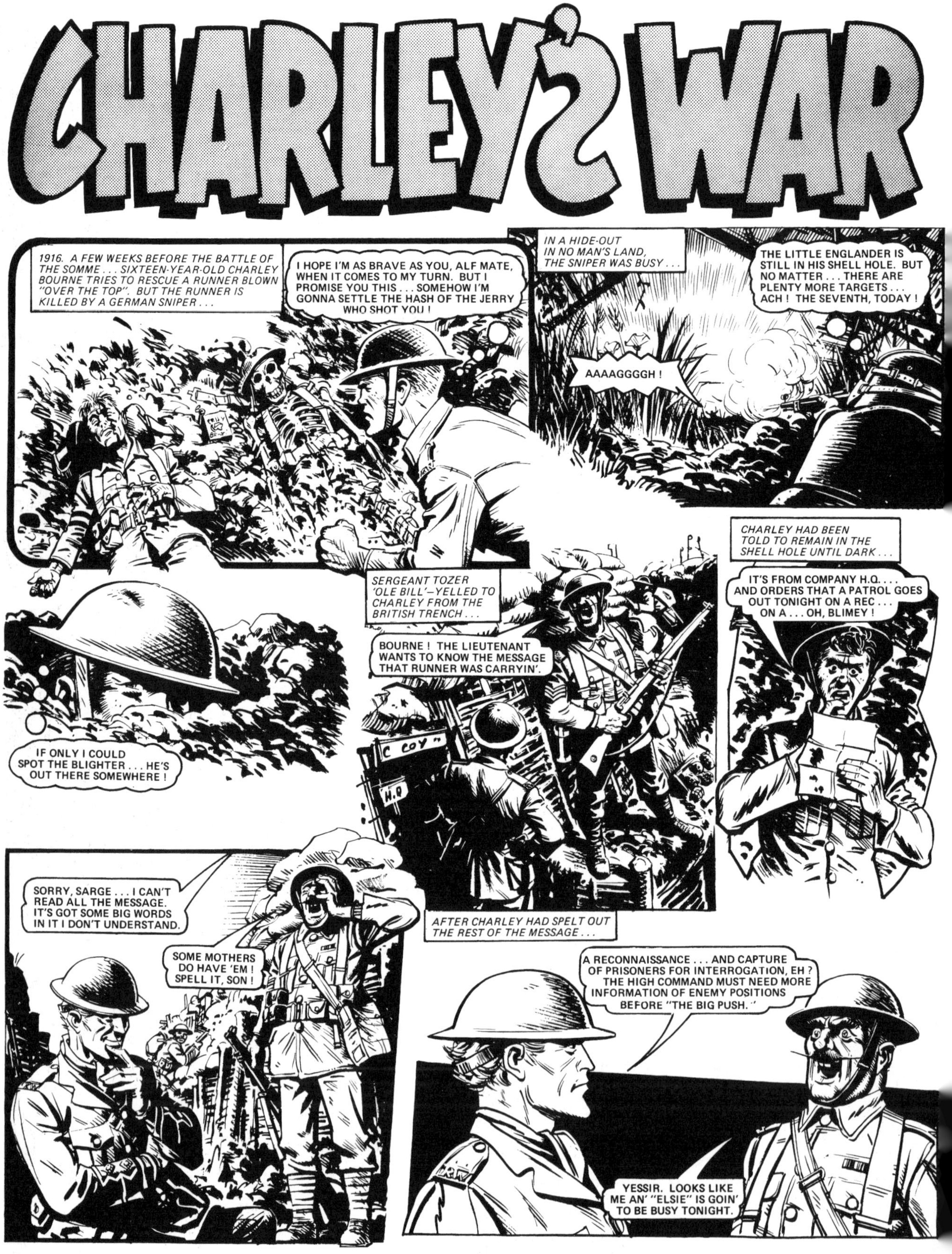
CHARLEY'S WAR
1916. A FEW WEEKS BEFORE THE BATTLE OF THE SOMME . . . SIXTEEN-YEAR-OLD CHARLEY BOURNE TRIES TO RESCUE A RUNNER BLOWN "OVER THE TOP". BUT THE RUNNER IS KILLED BY A GERMAN SNIPER . . .
I HOPE I'M AS BRAVE AS YOU, ALF MATE, WHEN IT COMES TO MY TURN. BUT I PROMISE YOU THIS . . . SOMEHOW I'M GONNA SETTLE THE HASH OF THE JERRY WHO SHOT YOU !
IN A HIDE-OUT IN NO MAN'S LAND, THE SNIPER WAS BUSY . . .
THE LITTLE ENGLANDER IS STILL IN HIS SHELL HOLE. BUT NO MATTER . . . THERE ARE PLENTY MORE TARGETS . . . ACH ! THE SEVENTH, TODAY !
AAAAGGGGH !
IF ONLY I COULD SPOT THE BLIGHTER . . . HE'S OUT THERE SOMEWHERE !
SERGEANT TOZER 'OLE BILL'—YELLED TO CHARLEY FROM THE BRITISH TRENCH . . .
BOURNE ! THE LIEUTENANT WANTS TO KNOW THE MESSAGE THAT RUNNER WAS CARRYIN'.
C COY
H.Q
CHARLEY HAD BEEN TOLD TO REMAIN IN THE SHELL HOLE UNTIL DARK . . .
IT'S FROM COMPANY H.Q. . . . AND ORDERS THAT A PATROL GOES OUT TONIGHT ON A REC . . . ON A . . . OH, BLIMEY !
SORRY, SARGE . . . I CAN'T READ ALL THE MESSAGE. IT'S GOT SOME BIG WORDS IN IT I DON'T UNDERSTAND.
SOME MOTHERS DO HAVE 'EM ! SPELL IT, SON !
AFTER CHARLEY HAD SPELT OUT THE REST OF THE MESSAGE . . .
A RECONNAISSANCE . . . AND CAPTURE OF PRISONERS FOR INTERROGATION, EH ? THE HIGH COMMAND MUST NEED MORE INFORMATION OF ENEMY POSITIONS BEFORE "THE BIG PUSH."
YESSIR. LOOKS LIKE ME AN' "ELSIE" IS GOIN' TO BE BUSY TONIGHT.

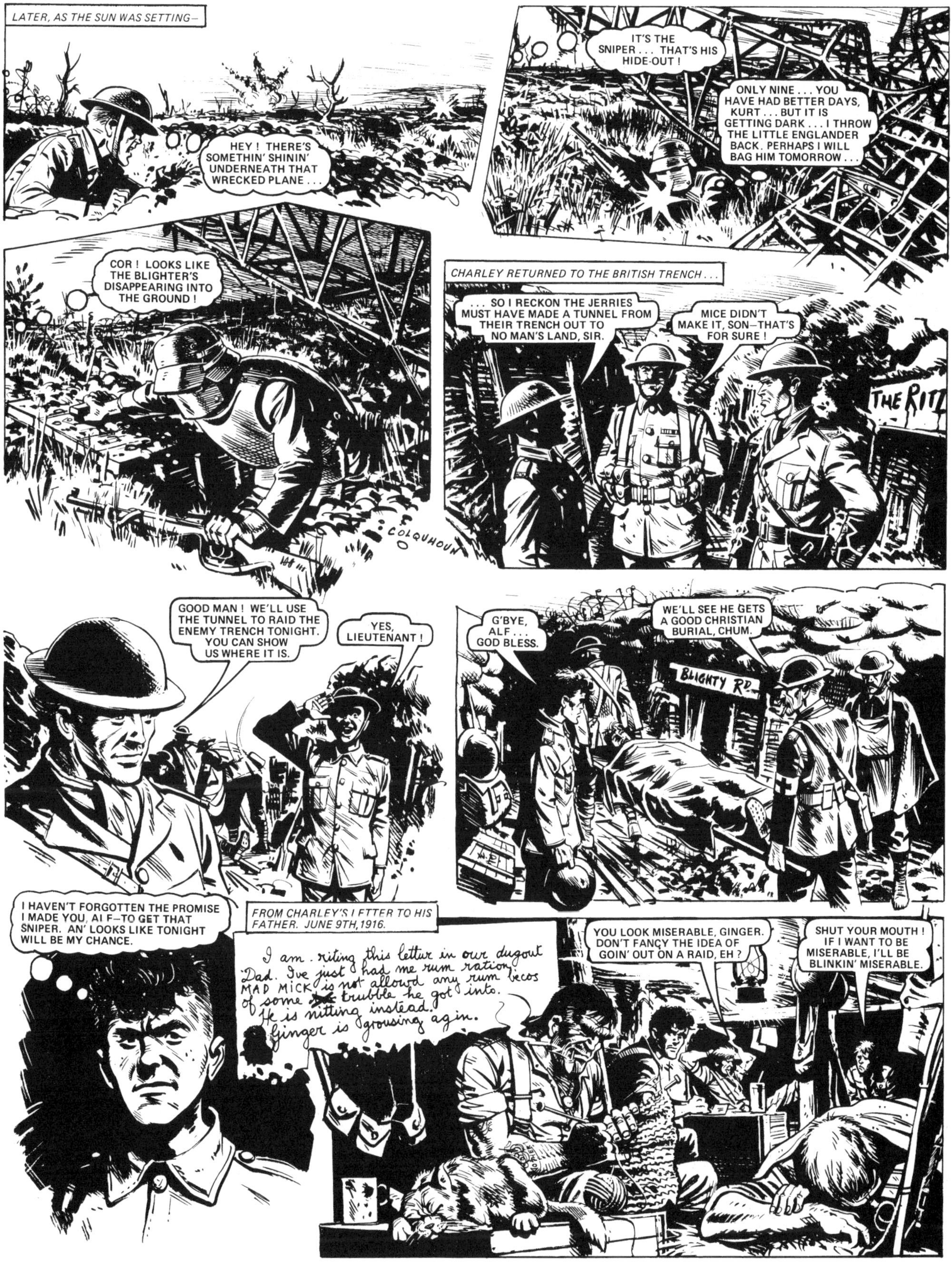

LATER, AS THE SUN WAS SETTING—
HEY ! THERE'S SOMETHIN' SHININ' UNDERNEATH THAT WRECKED PLANE . . .
IT'S THE SNIPER . . . THAT'S HIS HIDE-OUT !
ONLY NINE . . . YOU HAVE HAD BETTER DAYS, KURT . . . BUT IT IS GETTING DARK . . . I THROW THE LITTLE ENGLANDER BACK. PERHAPS I WILL BAG HIM TOMORROW . . .
COR ! LOOKS LIKE THE BLIGHTER'S DISAPPEARING INTO THE GROUND !
COLQUHOUN
CHARLEY RETURNED TO THE BRITISH TRENCH . . .
. . . SO I RECKON THE JERRIES MUST HAVE MADE A TUNNEL FROM THEIR TRENCH OUT TO NO MAN'S LAND, SIR.
MICE DIDN'T MAKE IT, SON—THAT'S FOR SURE !
THE RITZ
GOOD MAN ! WE'LL USE THE TUNNEL TO RAID THE ENEMY TRENCH TONIGHT. YOU CAN SHOW US WHERE IT IS.
YES, LIEUTENANT !
G'BYE, ALF . . . GOD BLESS.
WE'LL SEE HE GETS A GOOD CHRISTIAN BURIAL, CHUM.
BLIGHTY RD.
I HAVEN'T FORGOTTEN THE PROMISE I MADE YOU, ALF—TO GET THAT SNIPER. AN' LOOKS LIKE TONIGHT WILL BE MY CHANCE.
FROM CHARLEY'S LETTER TO HIS FATHER. JUNE 9TH, 1916.
I am riting this letter in our dugout Dad. Ive just had me rum ration. MAD MICK is not allowd any rum becos of some trubble he got into. He is nitting instead. Ginger is grousing agin.
YOU LOOK MISERABLE, GINGER. DON'T FANCY THE IDEA OF GOIN' OUT ON A RAID, EH ?
SHUT YOUR MOUTH ! IF I WANT TO BE MISERABLE, I'LL BE BLINKIN' MISERABLE.

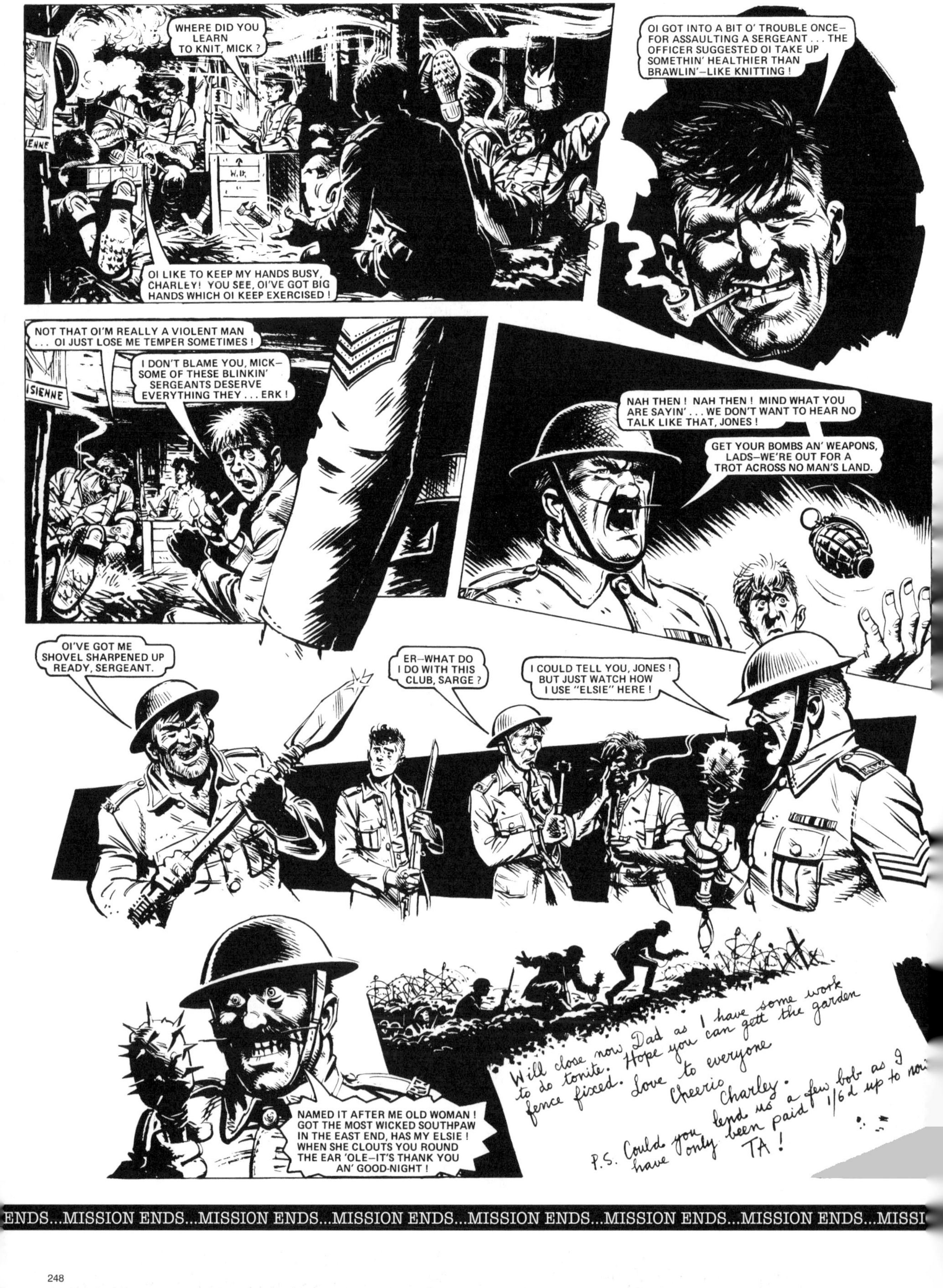
WHERE DID YOU LEARN TO KNIT, MICK ?
OI LIKE TO KEEP MY HANDS BUSY, CHARLEY! YOU SEE, OI'VE GOT BIG HANDS WHICH OI KEEP EXERCISED !
OI GOT INTO A BIT O' TROUBLE ONCE— FOR ASSAULTING A SERGEANT . . . THE OFFICER SUGGESTED OI TAKE UP SOMETHIN' HEALTHIER THAN BRAWLIN'—LIKE KNITTING !
NOT THAT OI'M REALLY A VIOLENT MAN . . . OI JUST LOSE ME TEMPER SOMETIMES !
I DON'T BLAME YOU, MICK— SOME OF THESE BLINKIN' SERGEANTS DESERVE EVERYTHING THEY . . . ERK !
NAH THEN ! NAH THEN ! MIND WHAT YOU ARE SAYIN' . . . WE DON'T WANT TO HEAR NO TALK LIKE THAT, JONES !
GET YOUR BOMBS AN' WEAPONS, LADS—WE'RE OUT FOR A TROT ACROSS NO MAN'S LAND.
OI'VE GOT ME SHOVEL SHARPENED UP READY, SERGEANT.
ER—WHAT DO I DO WITH THIS CLUB, SARGE ?
I COULD TELL YOU, JONES ! BUT JUST WATCH HOW I USE "ELSIE" HERE !
NAMED IT AFTER ME OLD WOMAN ! GOT THE MOST WICKED SOUTHPAW IN THE EAST END, HAS MY ELSIE ! WHEN SHE CLOUTS YOU ROUND THE EAR 'OLE—IT'S THANK YOU AN' GOOD-NIGHT !
Will close now Dad as I have some work to do tonite. Hope you can gett the garden fence fixed. Love to everyone
Cheerio
Charley.
P.S. Could you lend us a few bob as I have only been paid 1/6d up to no
TA !

ENDS...MISSION ENDS...MISSION ENDS...MISSION ENDS...MISSION ENDS...MISSION ENDS...MISSION ENDS...MISSI

FIGHTING MANN

"I UNDERSTAND YOUR INSTRUCTIONS... BUT I'M NOT GOING TO TAKE ANY NOTICE OF THEM!"

Vietnam, 1967 — the ex-military advisor to South Vietnam, a retired US Marine Colonel named Walter Mann, is back in action and demanding answers. A month ago his son, a Navy pilot, mysteriously disappeared whilst on a routine mission and has now been officially listed as "missing — believed deserted". Walter doesn't believe this is true for a second.

Now Mann's teaming up with two old friends — Korean soldier-turned-bartender Chol Chong and his old war buddy Air Cavalry Colonel Lance "Lunatic" Pepper — to find his boy.

'Fighting Mann' was the very first British war comic set during the Vietnam War. Debuting in July 1980, the strip ran until September 1981 and showcased the artwork of Cam Kennedy, whose unique drawing style was perfect for the setting.

NOTES FROM THE FRONTLINE:

"Cam Kennedy's artwork is great. He'd been working for DC Thomson but had some sort of falling out with them and sent us some samples... and crikey was I glad to get that guy on board! We tried to play to his strengths and use him as best as possible. We were running some one-off stories at the time — which we called "completes" — and I was sending him as many scripts as I could because I didn't want to lose him, at which time 'Fighting Mann' came up. He was a great guy to have working with us and the strip proved very popular with the readers." **— Dave Hunt**

WRITTEN BY Alan Hebden • DRAWN BY Cam Kennedy

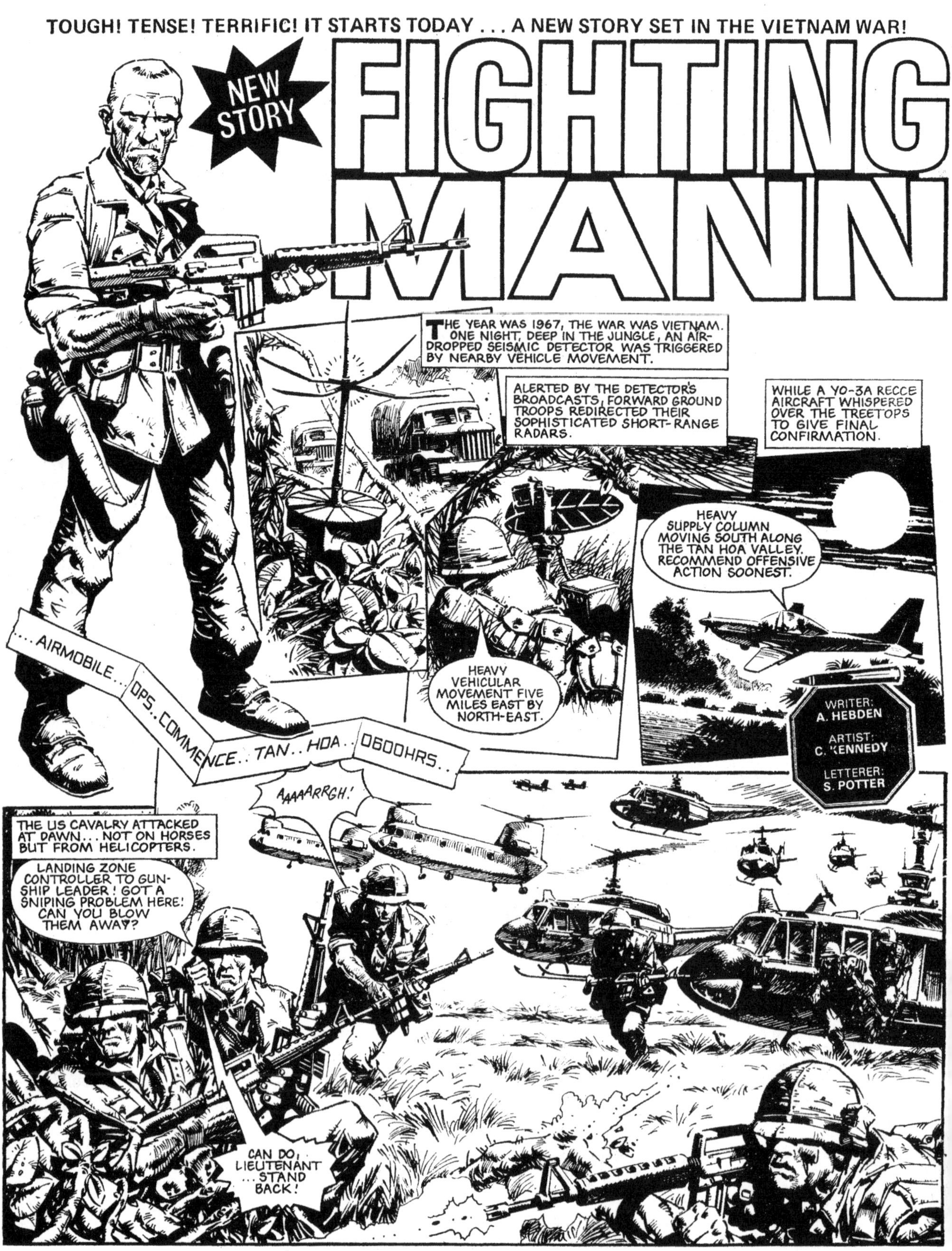

TOUGH! TENSE! TERRIFIC! IT STARTS TODAY . . . A NEW STORY SET IN THE VIETNAM WAR!
NEW STORY
FIGHTING MANN
THE YEAR WAS 1967, THE WAR WAS VIETNAM. ONE NIGHT, DEEP IN THE JUNGLE, AN AIR-DROPPED SEISMIC DETECTOR WAS TRIGGERED BY NEARBY VEHICLE MOVEMENT.
ALERTED BY THE DETECTOR'S BROADCASTS, FORWARD GROUND TROOPS REDIRECTED THEIR SOPHISTICATED SHORT-RANGE RADARS.
HEAVY VEHICULAR MOVEMENT FIVE MILES EAST BY NORTH-EAST.
WHILE A YO-3A RECCE AIRCRAFT WHISPERED OVER THE TREETOPS TO GIVE FINAL CONFIRMATION.
HEAVY SUPPLY COLUMN MOVING SOUTH ALONG THE TAN HOA VALLEY. RECOMMEND OFFENSIVE ACTION SOONEST.
...AIRMOBILE...OPS..COMMENCE..TAN..HOA..0600HRS..
WRITER: A. HEBDEN
ARTIST: C. KENNEDY
LETTERER: S. POTTER
THE US CAVALRY ATTACKED AT DAWN... NOT ON HORSES BUT FROM HELICOPTERS.
LANDING ZONE CONTROLLER TO GUN-SHIP LEADER! GOT A SNIPING PROBLEM HERE! CAN YOU BLOW THEM AWAY?
AAAAARRGH!
CAN DO, LIEUTENANT ...STAND BACK!

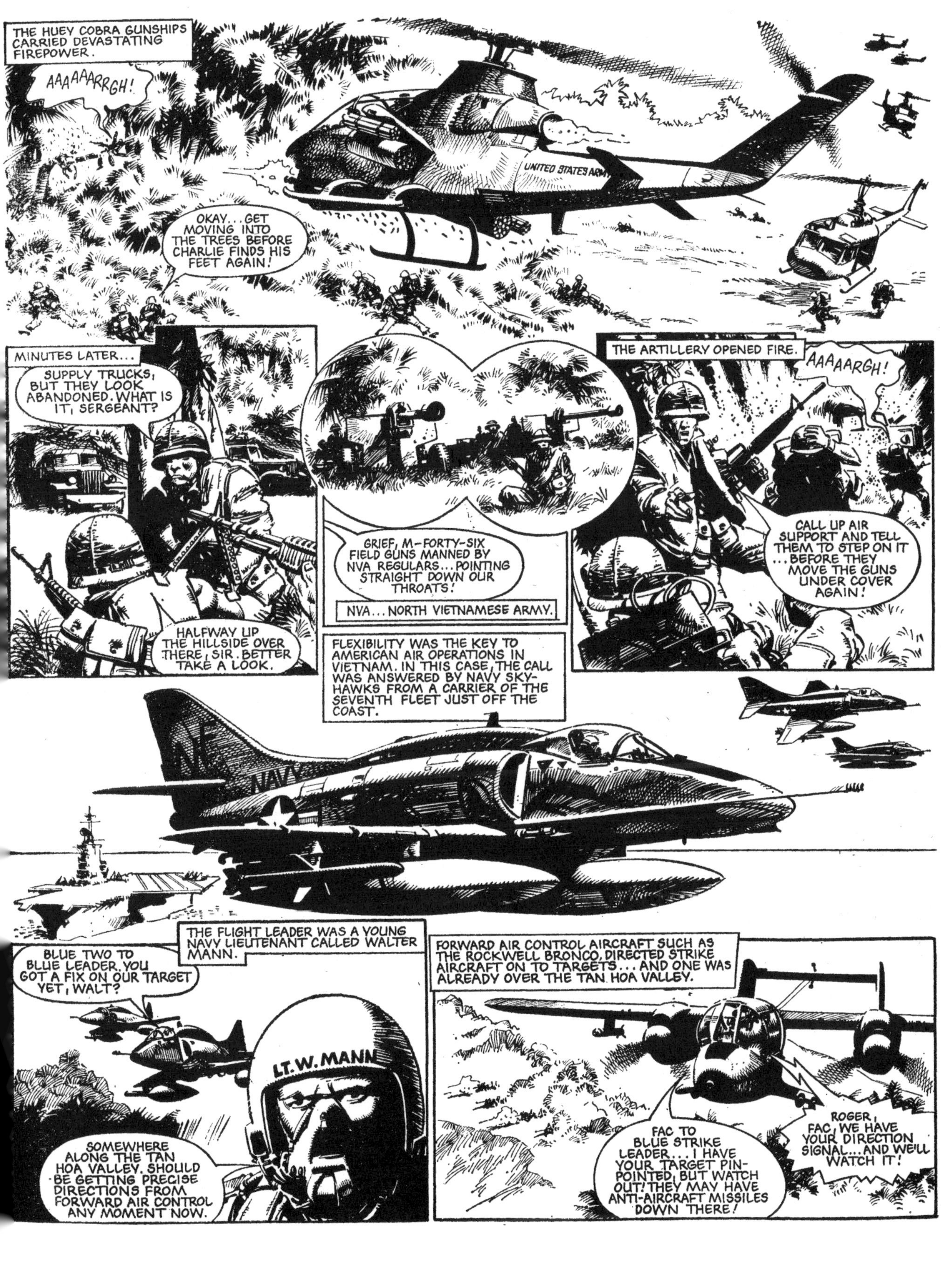

THE HUEY COBRA GUNSHIPS CARRIED DEVASTATING FIREPOWER.
AAAAAARRGH!
UNITED STATES ARMY
OKAY... GET MOVING INTO THE TREES BEFORE CHARLIE FINDS HIS FEET AGAIN!
MINUTES LATER...
SUPPLY TRUCKS, BUT THEY LOOK ABANDONED. WHAT IS IT, SERGEANT?
HALFWAY UP THE HILLSIDE OVER THERE, SIR. BETTER TAKE A LOOK.
GRIEF, M-FORTY-SIX FIELD GUNS MANNED BY NVA REGULARS... POINTING STRAIGHT DOWN OUR THROATS!
NVA... NORTH VIETNAMESE ARMY.
THE ARTILLERY OPENED FIRE.
AAAAARGH!
CALL UP AIR SUPPORT AND TELL THEM TO STEP ON IT ... BEFORE THEY MOVE THE GUNS UNDER COVER AGAIN!
FLEXIBILITY WAS THE KEY TO AMERICAN AIR OPERATIONS IN VIETNAM. IN THIS CASE, THE CALL WAS ANSWERED BY NAVY SKY-HAWKS FROM A CARRIER OF THE SEVENTH FLEET JUST OFF THE COAST.
NAVY
THE FLIGHT LEADER WAS A YOUNG NAVY LIEUTENANT CALLED WALTER MANN.
BLUE TWO TO BLUE LEADER. YOU GOT A FIX ON OUR TARGET YET, WALT?
LT. W. MANN
SOMEWHERE ALONG THE TAN HOA VALLEY. SHOULD BE GETTING PRECISE DIRECTIONS FROM FORWARD AIR CONTROL ANY MOMENT NOW.
FORWARD AIR CONTROL AIRCRAFT SUCH AS THE ROCKWELL BRONCO, DIRECTED STRIKE AIRCRAFT ON TO TARGETS... AND ONE WAS ALREADY OVER THE TAN HOA VALLEY.
FAC TO BLUE STRIKE LEADER... I HAVE YOUR TARGET PIN-POINTED, BUT WATCH OUT! THEY MAY HAVE ANTI-AIRCRAFT MISSILES DOWN THERE!
ROGER, FAC, WE HAVE YOUR DIRECTION SIGNAL... AND WE'LL WATCH IT!

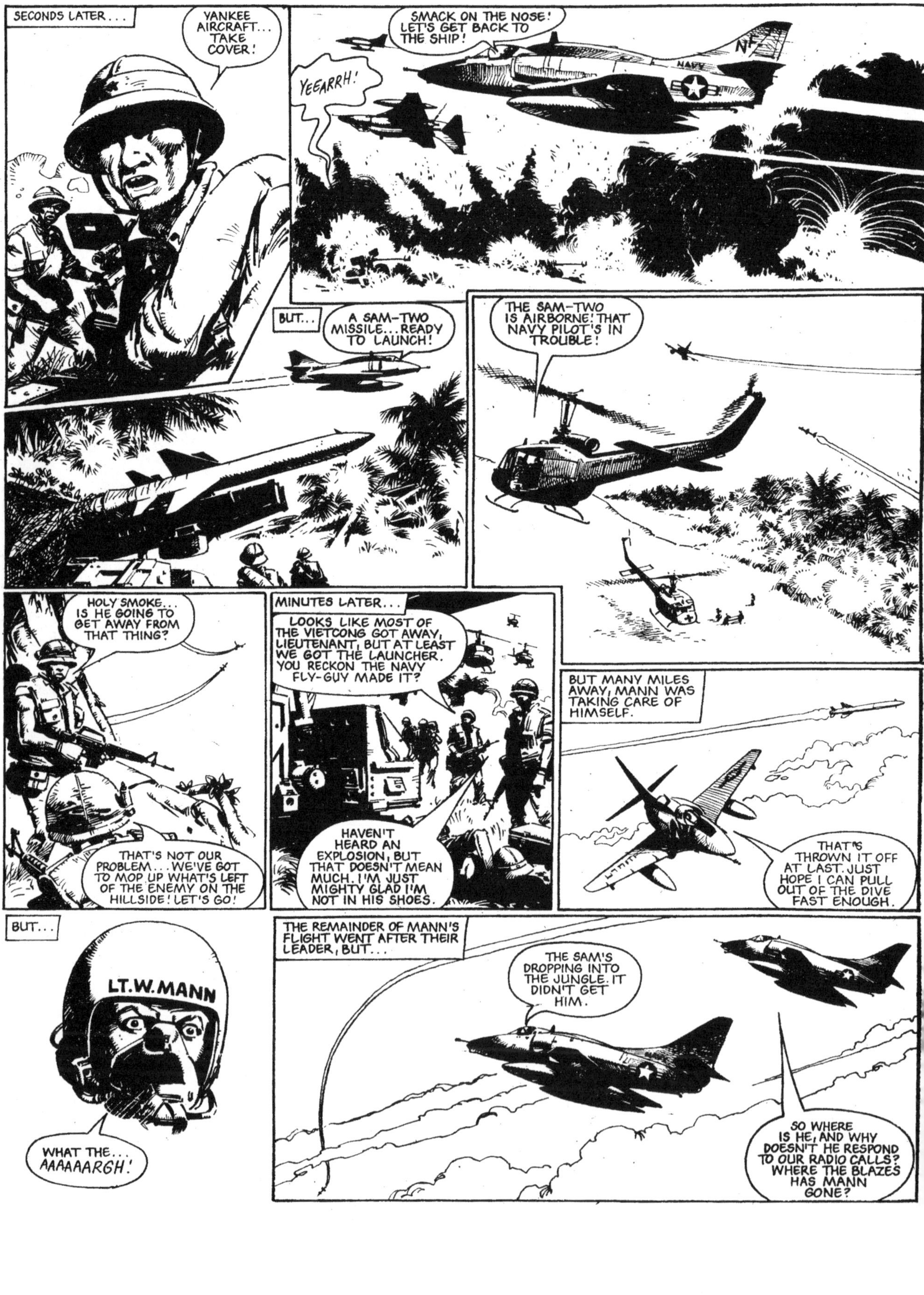
SECONDS LATER...
YANKEE AIRCRAFT... TAKE COVER!
SMACK ON THE NOSE! LET'S GET BACK TO THE SHIP!
YEEARRH!
BUT...
A SAM-TWO MISSILE... READY TO LAUNCH!
THE SAM-TWO IS AIRBORNE! THAT NAVY PILOT'S IN TROUBLE!
HOLY SMOKE... IS HE GOING TO GET AWAY FROM THAT THING?
THAT'S NOT OUR PROBLEM... WE'VE GOT TO MOP UP WHAT'S LEFT OF THE ENEMY ON THE HILLSIDE! LET'S GO!
MINUTES LATER...
LOOKS LIKE MOST OF THE VIETCONG GOT AWAY, LIEUTENANT, BUT AT LEAST WE GOT THE LAUNCHER. YOU RECKON THE NAVY FLY-GUY MADE IT?
HAVEN'T HEARD AN EXPLOSION, BUT THAT DOESN'T MEAN MUCH. I'M JUST MIGHTY GLAD I'M NOT IN HIS SHOES.
BUT MANY MILES AWAY, MANN WAS TAKING CARE OF HIMSELF.
THAT'S THROWN IT OFF AT LAST. JUST HOPE I CAN PULL OUT OF THE DIVE FAST ENOUGH.
BUT...
LT. W. MANN
WHAT THE... AAAAAARGH!
THE REMAINDER OF MANN'S FLIGHT WENT AFTER THEIR LEADER, BUT...
THE SAM'S DROPPING INTO THE JUNGLE. IT DIDN'T GET HIM.
SO WHERE IS HE, AND WHY DOESN'T HE RESPOND TO OUR RADIO CALLS? WHERE THE BLAZES HAS MANN GONE?

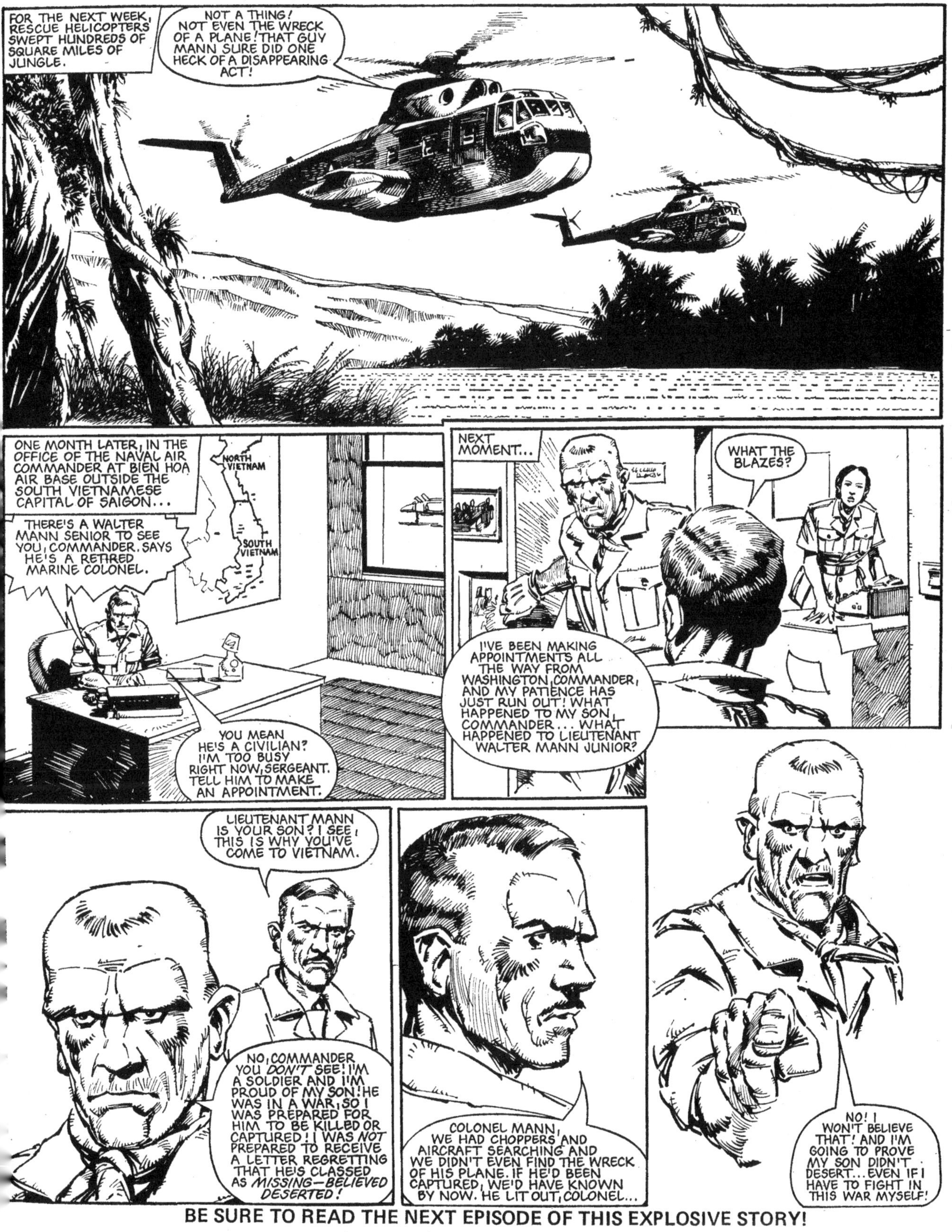

FOR THE NEXT WEEK, RESCUE HELICOPTERS SWEPT HUNDREDS OF SQUARE MILES OF JUNGLE.
NOT A THING! NOT EVEN THE WRECK OF A PLANE! THAT GUY MANN SURE DID ONE HECK OF A DISAPPEARING ACT!
ONE MONTH LATER, IN THE OFFICE OF THE NAVAL AIR COMMANDER AT BIEN HOA AIR BASE OUTSIDE THE SOUTH VIETNAMESE CAPITAL OF SAIGON...
NORTH VIETNAM
SOUTH VIETNAM
THERE'S A WALTER MANN SENIOR TO SEE YOU, COMMANDER. SAYS HE'S A RETIRED MARINE COLONEL.
YOU MEAN HE'S A CIVILIAN? I'M TOO BUSY RIGHT NOW, SERGEANT. TELL HIM TO MAKE AN APPOINTMENT.
NEXT MOMENT...
WHAT THE BLAZES?
I'VE BEEN MAKING APPOINTMENTS ALL THE WAY FROM WASHINGTON, COMMANDER, AND MY PATIENCE HAS JUST RUN OUT! WHAT HAPPENED TO MY SON, COMMANDER... WHAT HAPPENED TO LIEUTENANT WALTER MANN JUNIOR?
LIEUTENANT MANN IS YOUR SON? I SEE, THIS IS WHY YOU'VE COME TO VIETNAM.
NO, COMMANDER YOU DON'T SEE! I'M A SOLDIER AND I'M PROUD OF MY SON! HE WAS IN A WAR, SO I WAS PREPARED FOR HIM TO BE KILLED OR CAPTURED! I WAS NOT PREPARED TO RECEIVE A LETTER REGRETTING THAT HE'S CLASSED AS MISSING—BELIEVED DESERTED!
COLONEL MANN, WE HAD CHOPPERS AND AIRCRAFT SEARCHING AND WE DIDN'T EVEN FIND THE WRECK OF HIS PLANE. IF HE'D BEEN CAPTURED, WE'D HAVE KNOWN BY NOW. HE LIT OUT, COLONEL...
NO! I WON'T BELIEVE THAT! AND I'M GOING TO PROVE MY SON DIDN'T DESERT... EVEN IF I HAVE TO FIGHT IN THIS WAR MYSELF!

BE SURE TO READ THE NEXT EPISODE OF THIS EXPLOSIVE STORY!

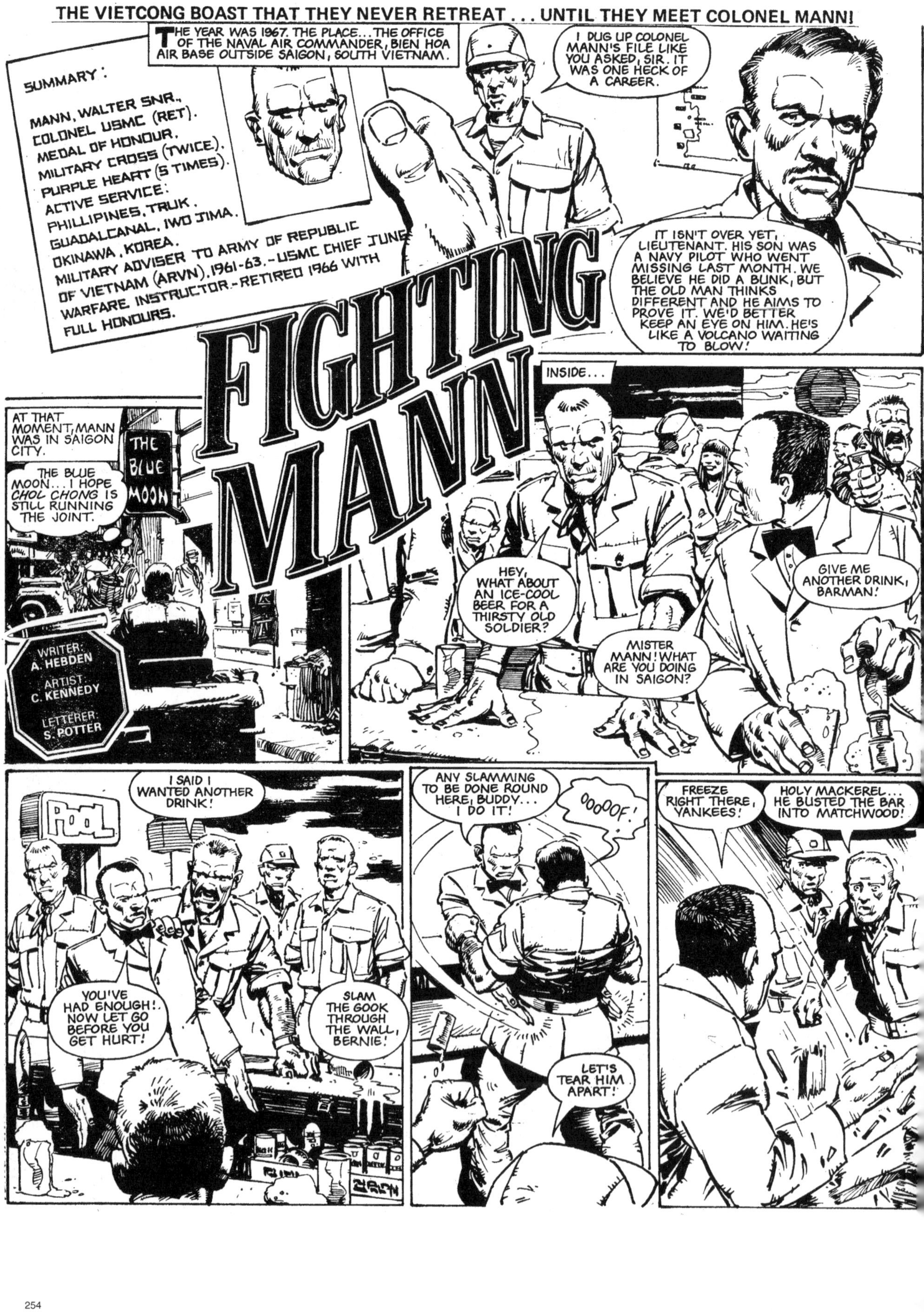

THE VIETCONG BOAST THAT THEY NEVER RETREAT . . . UNTIL THEY MEET COLONEL MANN!
THE YEAR WAS 1967. THE PLACE... THE OFFICE OF THE NAVAL AIR COMMANDER, BIEN HOA AIR BASE OUTSIDE SAIGON, SOUTH VIETNAM.
SUMMARY: MANN, WALTER SNR., COLONEL USMC (RET). MEDAL OF HONOUR. MILITARY CROSS (TWICE). PURPLE HEART (5 TIMES). ACTIVE SERVICE: PHILLIPINES, TRUK, GUADALCANAL, IWO JIMA, OKINAWA, KOREA. MILITARY ADVISER TO ARMY OF REPUBLIC OF VIETNAM (ARVN), 1961-63.-USMC CHIEF JUNGLE WARFARE INSTRUCTOR.-RETIRED 1966 WITH FULL HONOURS.
I DUG UP COLONEL MANN'S FILE LIKE YOU ASKED, SIR. IT WAS ONE HECK OF A CAREER.
IT ISN'T OVER YET, LIEUTENANT. HIS SON WAS A NAVY PILOT WHO WENT MISSING LAST MONTH. WE BELIEVE HE DID A BUNK, BUT THE OLD MAN THINKS DIFFERENT AND HE AIMS TO PROVE IT. WE'D BETTER KEEP AN EYE ON HIM. HE'S LIKE A VOLCANO WAITING TO BLOW!
FIGHTING MANN
AT THAT MOMENT, MANN WAS IN SAIGON CITY.
THE BLUE MOON
THE BLUE MOON... I HOPE CHOL CHONG IS STILL RUNNING THE JOINT.
WRITER: A. HEBDEN
ARTIST: C. KENNEDY
LETTERER: S. POTTER
INSIDE...
HEY, WHAT ABOUT AN ICE-COOL BEER FOR A THIRSTY OLD SOLDIER?
MISTER MANN! WHAT ARE YOU DOING IN SAIGON?
GIVE ME ANOTHER DRINK, BARMAN!
POOL
I SAID I WANTED ANOTHER DRINK!
YOU'VE HAD ENOUGH! NOW LET GO BEFORE YOU GET HURT!
SLAM THE GOOK THROUGH THE WALL, BERNIE!
ANY SLAMMING TO BE DONE ROUND HERE, BUDDY... I DO IT!
OOOOOF!
LET'S TEAR HIM APART!
FREEZE RIGHT THERE, YANKEES!
HOLY MACKEREL... HE BUSTED THE BAR INTO MATCHWOOD!

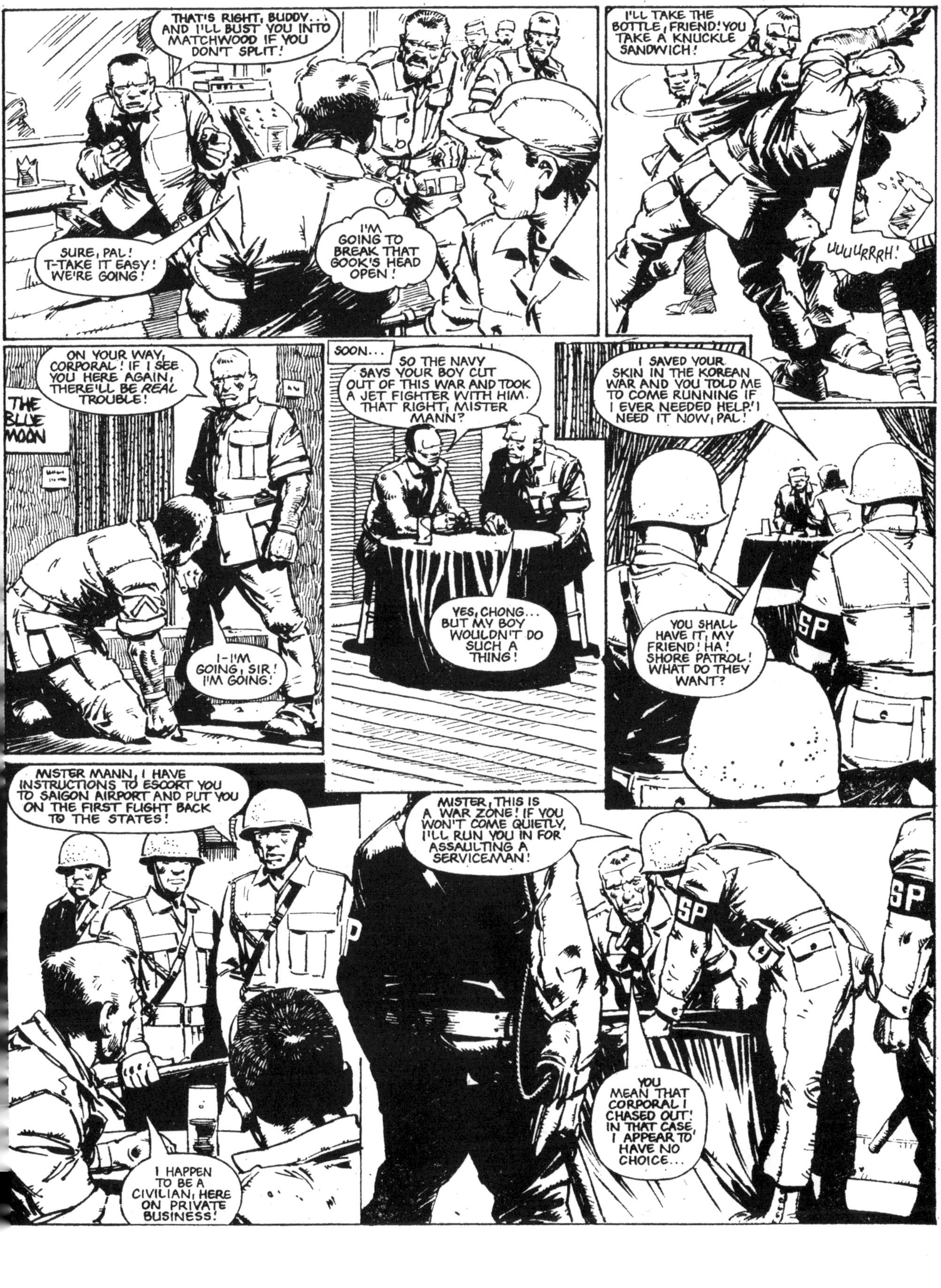
THAT'S RIGHT, BUDDY... AND I'LL BUST YOU INTO MATCHWOOD IF YOU DON'T SPLIT!
SURE, PAL! T-TAKE IT EASY! WE'RE GOING!
I'M GOING TO BREAK THAT GOOK'S HEAD OPEN!
I'LL TAKE THE BOTTLE, FRIEND! YOU TAKE A KNUCKLE SANDWICH!
UUUURRRH!
ON YOUR WAY, CORPORAL! IF I SEE YOU HERE AGAIN, THERE'LL BE *REAL* TROUBLE!
THE BLUE MOON
I-I'M GOING, SIR! I'M GOING!
SOON...
SO THE NAVY SAYS YOUR BOY CUT OUT OF THIS WAR AND TOOK A JET FIGHTER WITH HIM. THAT RIGHT, MISTER MANN?
YES, CHONG... BUT MY BOY WOULDN'T DO SUCH A THING!
I SAVED YOUR SKIN IN THE KOREAN WAR AND YOU TOLD ME TO COME RUNNING IF I EVER NEEDED HELP! I NEED IT NOW, PAL!
YOU SHALL HAVE IT, MY FRIEND! HA! SHORE PATROL! WHAT DO THEY WANT?
SP
MISTER MANN, I HAVE INSTRUCTIONS TO ESCORT YOU TO SAIGON AIRPORT AND PUT YOU ON THE FIRST FLIGHT BACK TO THE STATES!
I HAPPEN TO BE A CIVILIAN, HERE ON PRIVATE BUSINESS!
MISTER, THIS IS A WAR ZONE! IF YOU WON'T COME QUIETLY, I'LL RUN YOU IN FOR ASSAULTING A SERVICEMAN!
YOU MEAN THAT CORPORAL I CHASED OUT! IN THAT CASE, I APPEAR TO HAVE NO CHOICE...
SP
SP

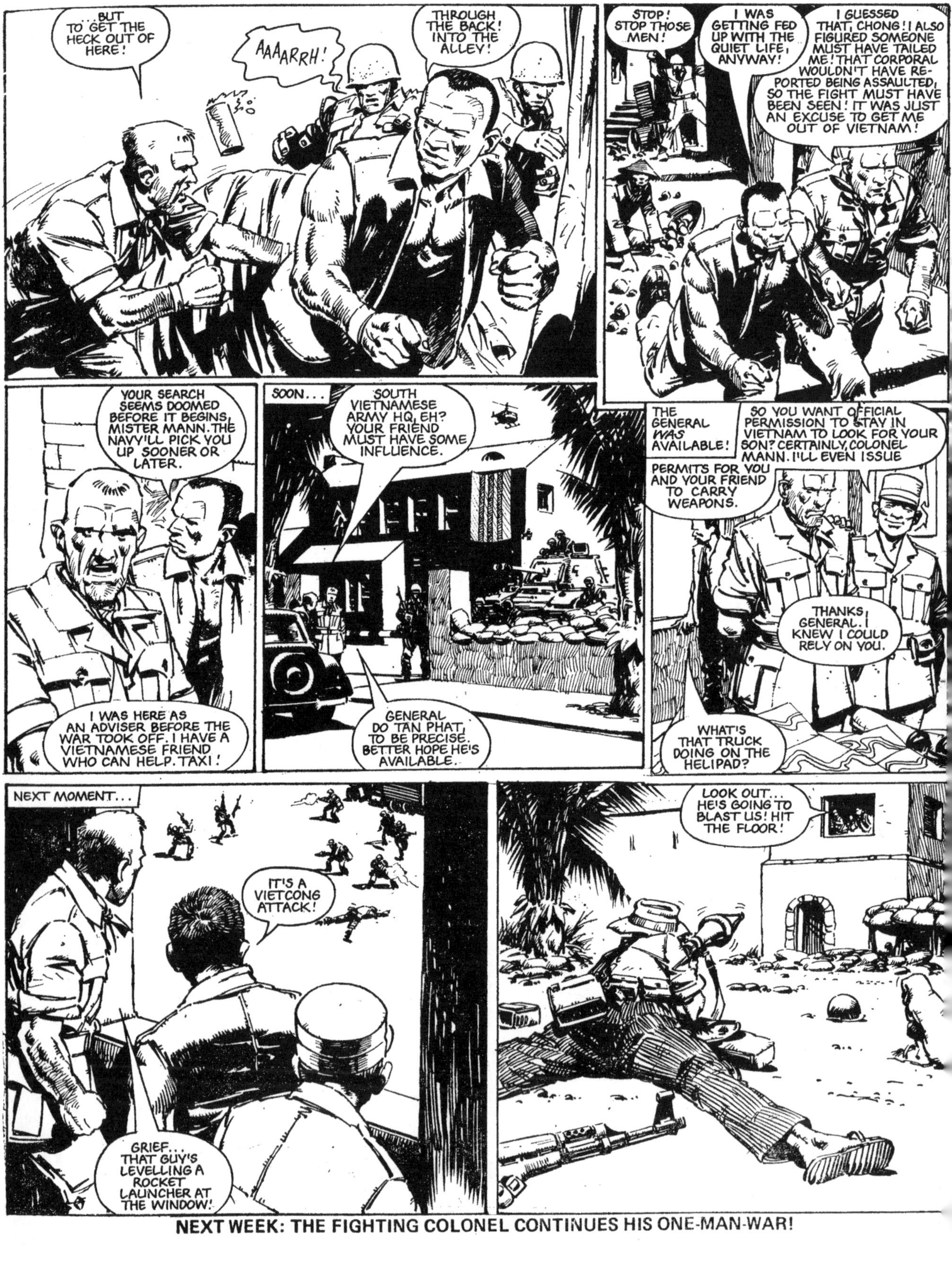
...BUT TO GET THE HECK OUT OF HERE!
AAAARRH!
THROUGH THE BACK! INTO THE ALLEY!
STOP! STOP THOSE MEN!
I WAS GETTING FED UP WITH THE QUIET LIFE, ANYWAY!
I GUESSED THAT, CHONG! I ALSO FIGURED SOMEONE MUST HAVE TAILED ME! THAT CORPORAL WOULDN'T HAVE REPORTED BEING ASSAULTED, SO THE FIGHT MUST HAVE BEEN SEEN! IT WAS JUST AN EXCUSE TO GET ME OUT OF VIETNAM!
YOUR SEARCH SEEMS DOOMED BEFORE IT BEGINS, MISTER MANN. THE NAVY'LL PICK YOU UP SOONER OR LATER.
I WAS HERE AS AN ADVISER BEFORE THE WAR TOOK OFF. I HAVE A VIETNAMESE FRIEND WHO CAN HELP. TAXI!
SOON...
SOUTH VIETNAMESE ARMY HQ, EH? YOUR FRIEND MUST HAVE SOME INFLUENCE.
GENERAL DO TAN PHAT, TO BE PRECISE. BETTER HOPE HE'S AVAILABLE.
THE GENERAL WAS AVAILABLE!
SO YOU WANT OFFICIAL PERMISSION TO STAY IN VIETNAM TO LOOK FOR YOUR SON? CERTAINLY, COLONEL MANN. I'LL EVEN ISSUE
PERMITS FOR YOU AND YOUR FRIEND TO CARRY WEAPONS.
THANKS, GENERAL. I KNEW I COULD RELY ON YOU.
WHAT'S THAT TRUCK DOING ON THE HELIPAD?
NEXT MOMENT...
IT'S A VIETCONG ATTACK!
GRIEF... THAT GUY'S LEVELLING A ROCKET LAUNCHER AT THE WINDOW!
LOOK OUT... HE'S GOING TO BLAST US! HIT THE FLOOR!

NEXT WEEK: THE FIGHTING COLONEL CONTINUES HIS ONE-MAN-WAR!

FEET AND FISTS FLY THIS WEEK WHEN MANN AND SONG TACKLE A HORDE OF VIETCONGS!

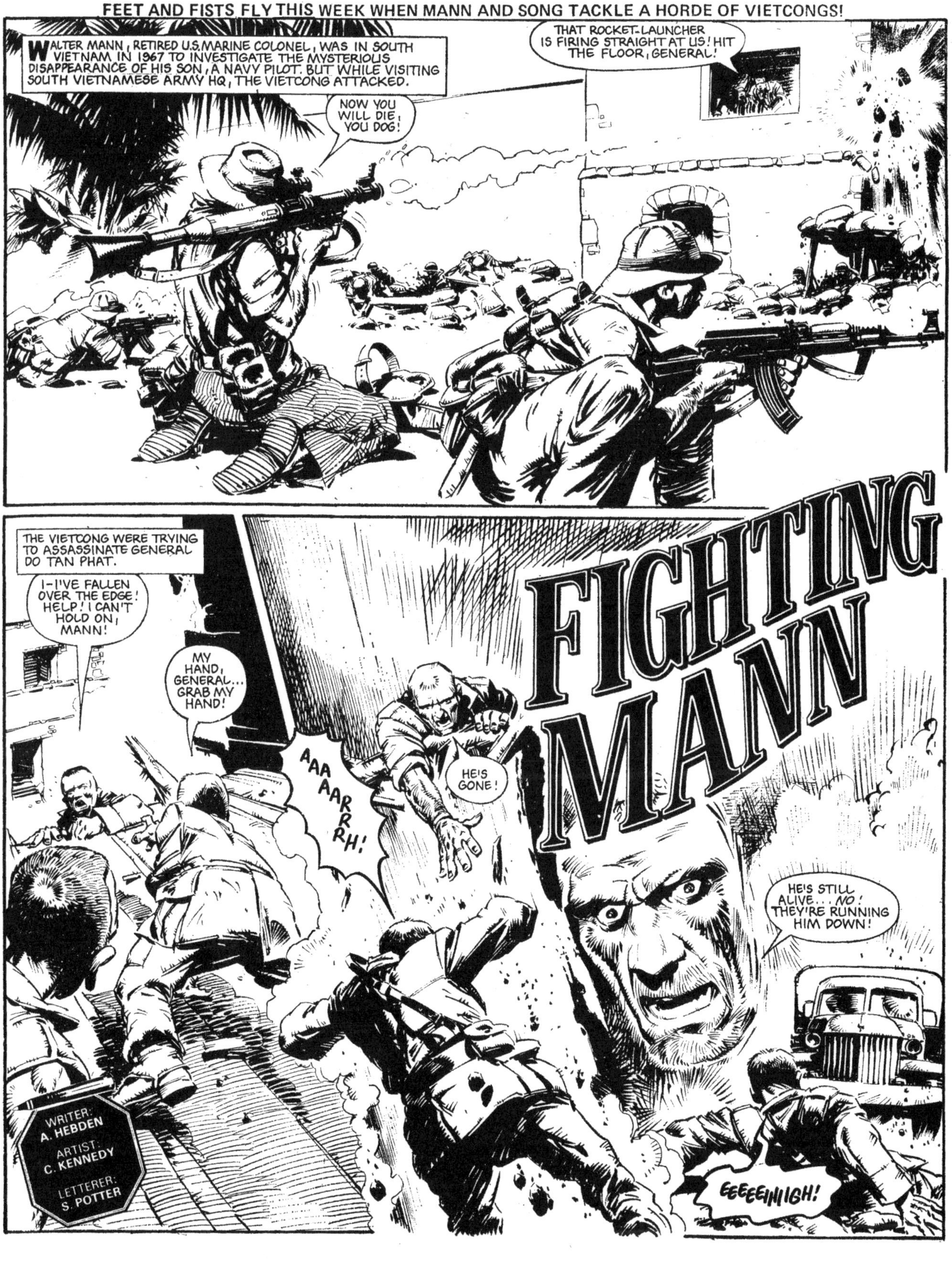

WALTER MANN, RETIRED U.S. MARINE COLONEL, WAS IN SOUTH VIETNAM IN 1967 TO INVESTIGATE THE MYSTERIOUS DISAPPEARANCE OF HIS SON, A NAVY PILOT. BUT WHILE VISITING SOUTH VIETNAMESE ARMY HQ, THE VIETCONG ATTACKED.
NOW YOU WILL DIE, YOU DOG!
THAT ROCKET-LAUNCHER IS FIRING STRAIGHT AT US! HIT THE FLOOR, GENERAL!
THE VIETCONG WERE TRYING TO ASSASSINATE GENERAL DO TAN PHAT.
I-I'VE FALLEN OVER THE EDGE! HELP! I CAN'T HOLD ON, MANN!
MY HAND, GENERAL... GRAB MY HAND!
AAAAAARRRH!
HE'S GONE!
FIGHTING MANN
HE'S STILL ALIVE... NO! THEY'RE RUNNING HIM DOWN!
EEEEEIIIIGH!
WRITER: A. HEBDEN
ARTIST: C. KENNEDY
LETTERER: S. POTTER

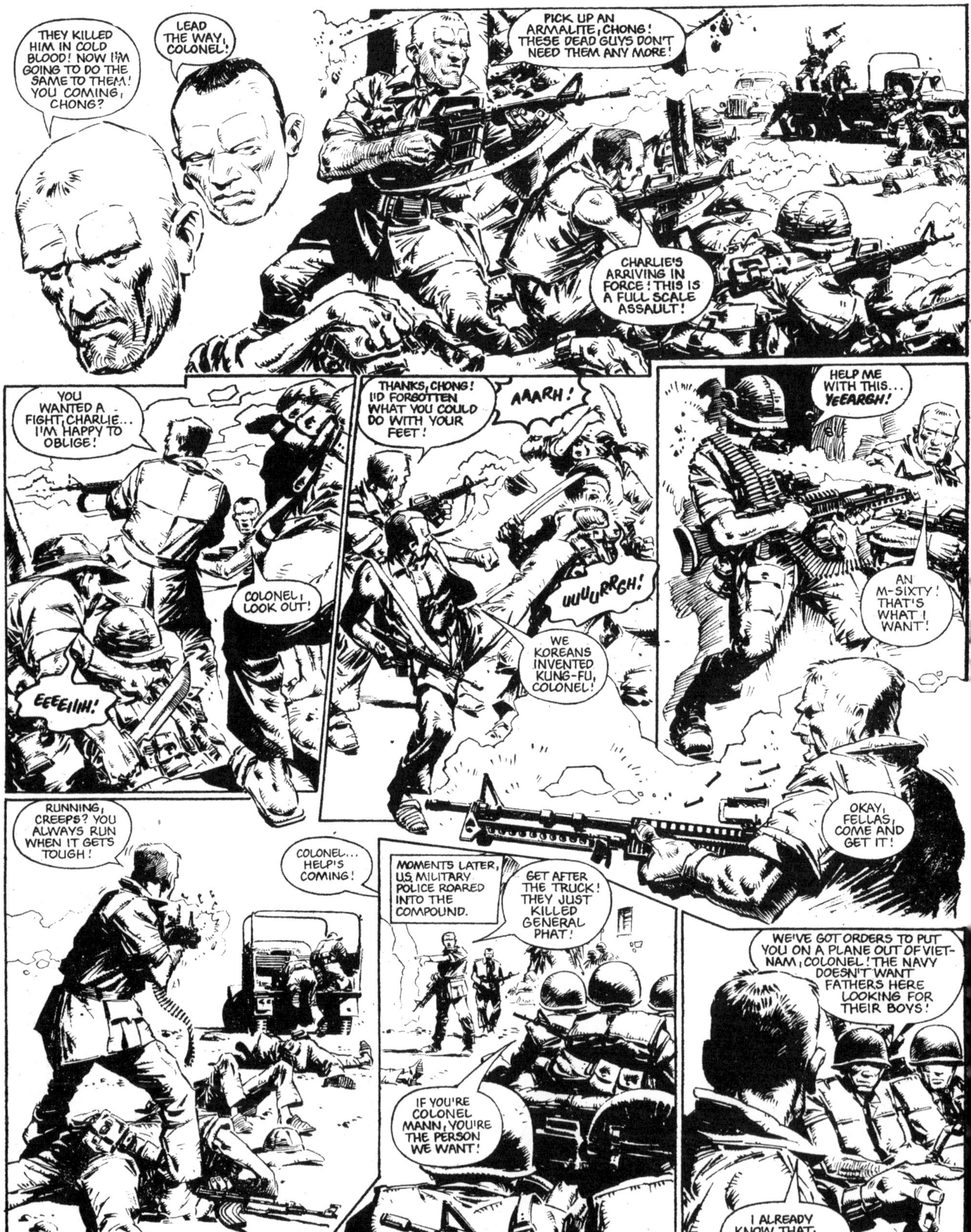

THEY KILLED HIM IN COLD BLOOD! NOW I'M GOING TO DO THE SAME TO THEM! YOU COMING, CHONG?
LEAD THE WAY, COLONEL!
PICK UP AN ARMALITE, CHONG! THESE DEAD GUYS DON'T NEED THEM ANY MORE!
CHARLIE'S ARRIVING IN FORCE! THIS IS A FULL SCALE ASSAULT!
YOU WANTED A FIGHT, CHARLIE... I'M HAPPY TO OBLIGE!
COLONEL, LOOK OUT!
EEEEIIIH!
THANKS, CHONG! I'D FORGOTTEN WHAT YOU COULD DO WITH YOUR FEET!
AAARH!
UUUURRGH!
WE KOREANS INVENTED KUNG-FU, COLONEL!
HELP ME WITH THIS... YEEARGH!
AN M-SIXTY! THAT'S WHAT I WANT!
OKAY, FELLAS, COME AND GET IT!
RUNNING, CREEPS? YOU ALWAYS RUN WHEN IT GETS TOUGH!
COLONEL... HELP'S COMING!
MOMENTS LATER, U.S. MILITARY POLICE ROARED INTO THE COMPOUND.
GET AFTER THE TRUCK! THEY JUST KILLED GENERAL PHAT!
IF YOU'RE COLONEL MANN, YOU'RE THE PERSON WE WANT!
WE'VE GOT ORDERS TO PUT YOU ON A PLANE OUT OF VIET-NAM, COLONEL! THE NAVY DOESN'T WANT FATHERS HERE LOOKING FOR THEIR BOYS!
I ALREADY KNOW THAT, MAJOR! BUT I'M STAYING!

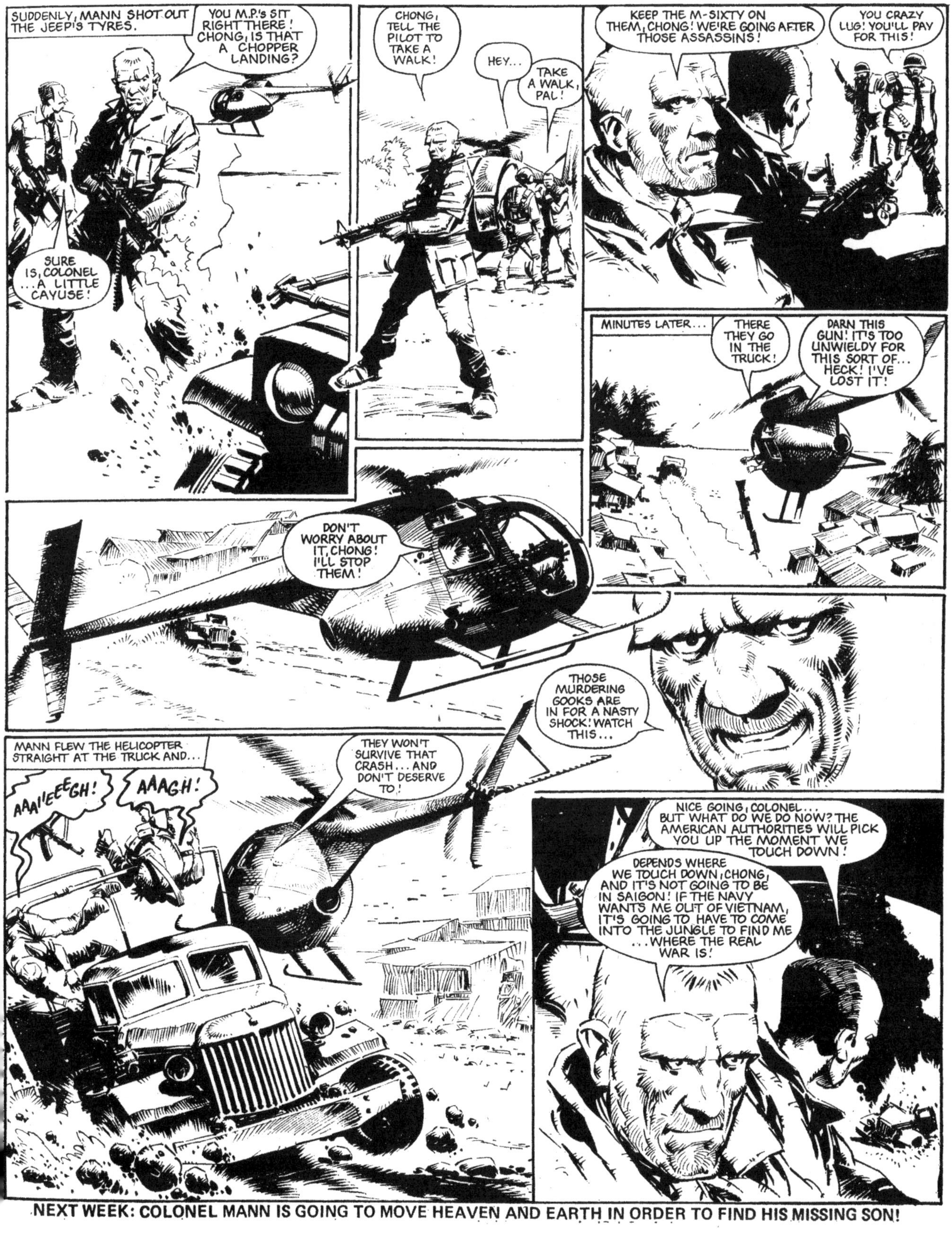

SUDDENLY, MANN SHOT OUT THE JEEP'S TYRES.
YOU M.P.'s SIT RIGHT THERE! CHONG, IS THAT A CHOPPER LANDING?
SURE IS, COLONEL ...A LITTLE CAYUSE!
CHONG, TELL THE PILOT TO TAKE A WALK!
HEY...
TAKE A WALK, PAL!
KEEP THE M-SIXTY ON THEM, CHONG! WE'RE GOING AFTER THOSE ASSASSINS!
YOU CRAZY LUG! YOU'LL PAY FOR THIS!
MINUTES LATER...
THERE THEY GO IN THE TRUCK!
DARN THIS GUN! IT'S TOO UNWIELDY FOR THIS SORT OF... HECK! I'VE LOST IT!
DON'T WORRY ABOUT IT, CHONG! I'LL STOP THEM!
THOSE MURDERING GOOKS ARE IN FOR A NASTY SHOCK! WATCH THIS...
MANN FLEW THE HELICOPTER STRAIGHT AT THE TRUCK AND...
THEY WON'T SURVIVE THAT CRASH...AND DON'T DESERVE TO!
AAAIEEEGH!
AAAGH!
NICE GOING, COLONEL... BUT WHAT DO WE DO NOW? THE AMERICAN AUTHORITIES WILL PICK YOU UP THE MOMENT WE TOUCH DOWN!
DEPENDS WHERE WE TOUCH DOWN, CHONG, AND IT'S NOT GOING TO BE IN SAIGON! IF THE NAVY WANTS ME OUT OF VIETNAM, IT'S GOING TO HAVE TO COME INTO THE JUNGLE TO FIND ME ...WHERE THE REAL WAR IS!

NEXT WEEK: COLONEL MANN IS GOING TO MOVE HEAVEN AND EARTH IN ORDER TO FIND HIS MISSING SON!

THE VIETCONG ARE TOLD "TAKE NO PRISONERS" . . . AND THAT INCLUDES COLONEL MANN!

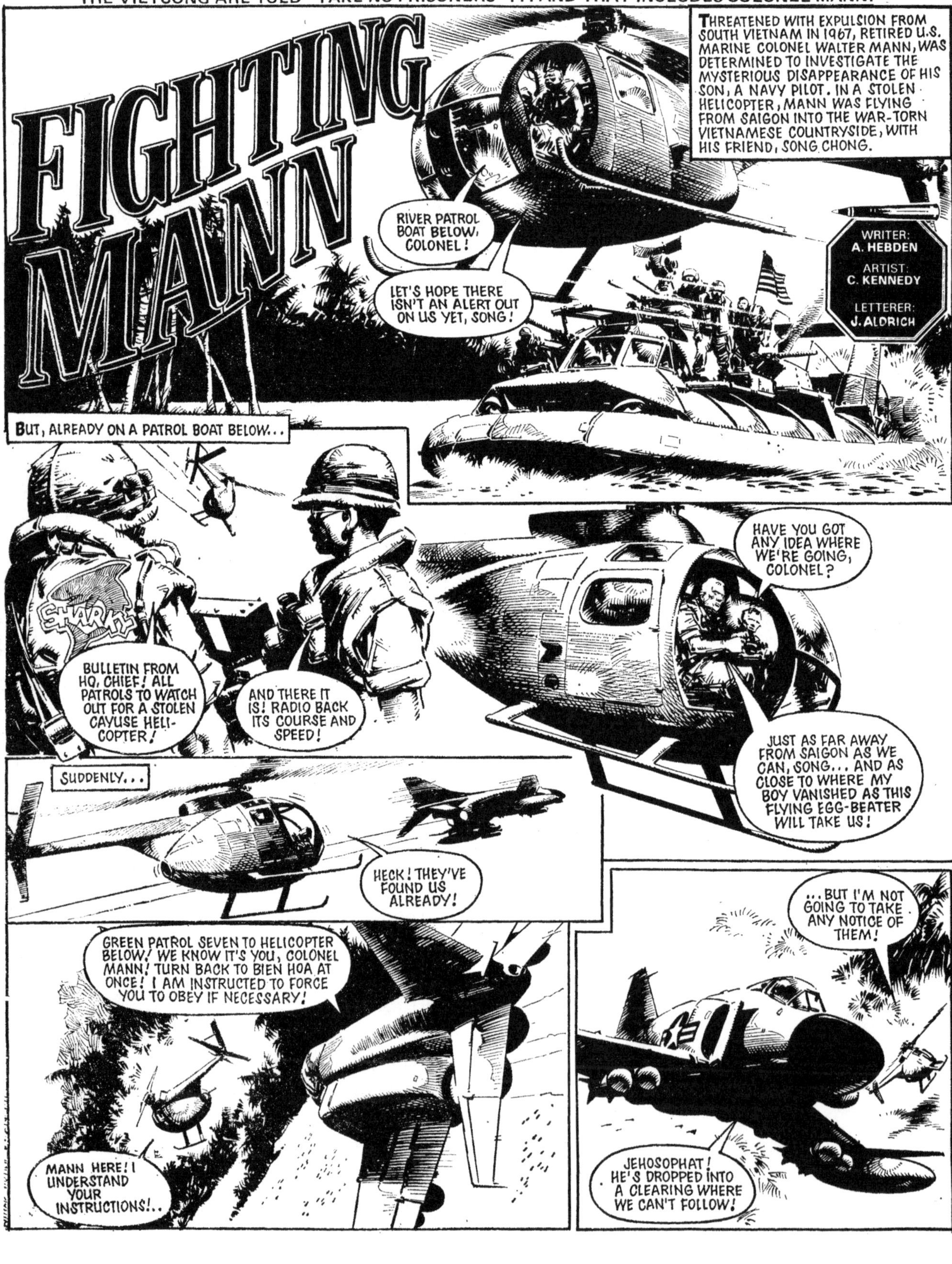

FIGHTING MANN
THREATENED WITH EXPULSION FROM SOUTH VIETNAM IN 1967, RETIRED U.S. MARINE COLONEL WALTER MANN, WAS DETERMINED TO INVESTIGATE THE MYSTERIOUS DISAPPEARANCE OF HIS SON, A NAVY PILOT. IN A STOLEN HELICOPTER, MANN WAS FLYING FROM SAIGON INTO THE WAR-TORN VIETNAMESE COUNTRYSIDE, WITH HIS FRIEND, SONG CHONG.
WRITER: A. HEBDEN
ARTIST: C. KENNEDY
LETTERER: J. ALDRICH
RIVER PATROL BOAT BELOW, COLONEL!
LET'S HOPE THERE ISN'T AN ALERT OUT ON US YET, SONG!
BUT, ALREADY ON A PATROL BOAT BELOW..
SHARKY
BULLETIN FROM HQ, CHIEF! ALL PATROLS TO WATCH OUT FOR A STOLEN CAYUSE HELI-COPTER!
AND THERE IT IS! RADIO BACK ITS COURSE AND SPEED!
HAVE YOU GOT ANY IDEA WHERE WE'RE GOING, COLONEL?
JUST AS FAR AWAY FROM SAIGON AS WE CAN, SONG... AND AS CLOSE TO WHERE MY BOY VANISHED AS THIS FLYING EGG-BEATER WILL TAKE US!
SUDDENLY...
HECK! THEY'VE FOUND US ALREADY!
GREEN PATROL SEVEN TO HELICOPTER BELOW! WE KNOW IT'S YOU, COLONEL MANN! TURN BACK TO BIEN HOA AT ONCE! I AM INSTRUCTED TO FORCE YOU TO OBEY IF NECESSARY!
MANN HERE! I UNDERSTAND YOUR INSTRUCTIONS!..
...BUT I'M NOT GOING TO TAKE ANY NOTICE OF THEM!
JEHOSOPHAT! HE'S DROPPED INTO A CLEARING WHERE WE CAN'T FOLLOW!

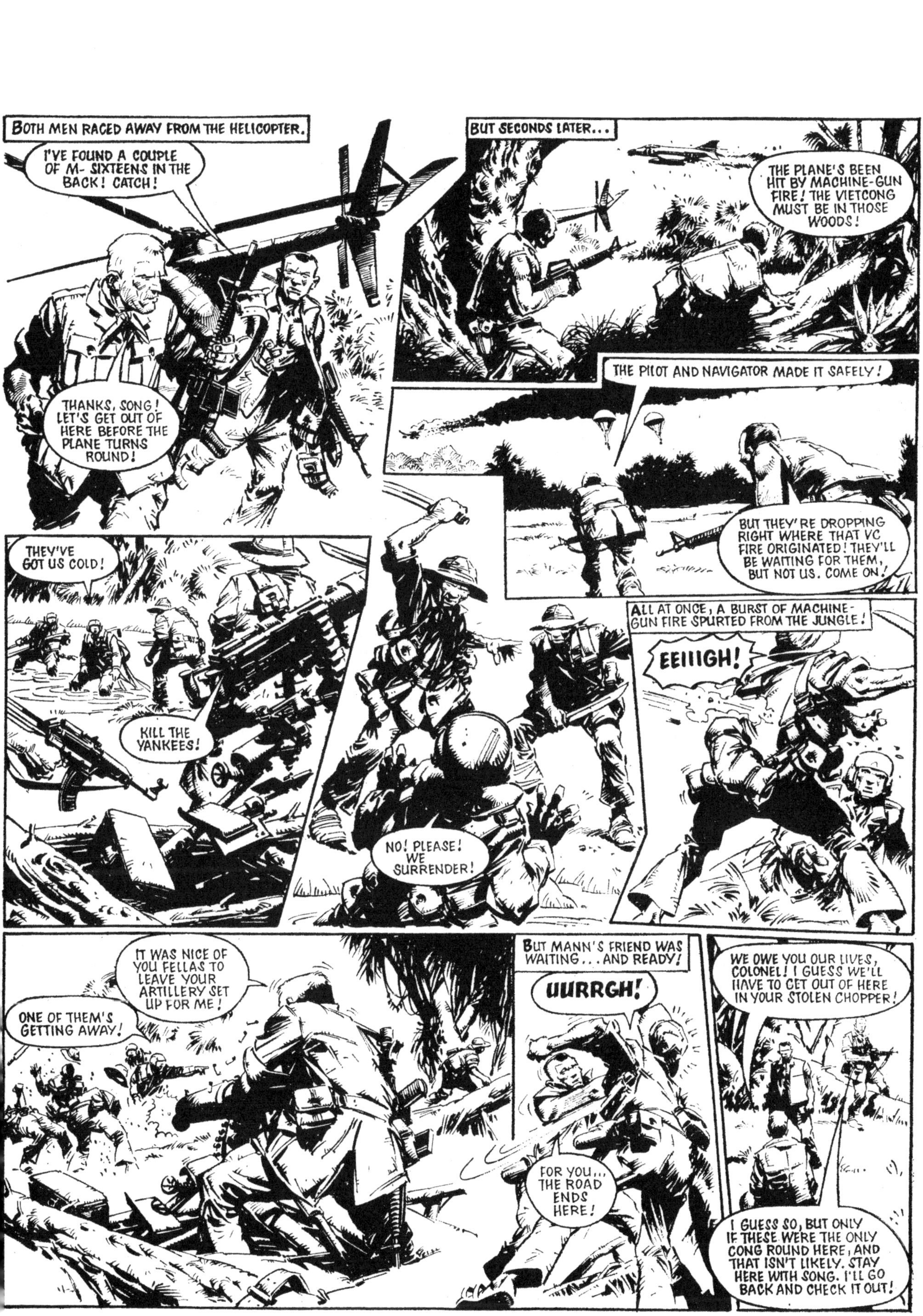
BOTH MEN RACED AWAY FROM THE HELICOPTER.
I'VE FOUND A COUPLE OF M- SIXTEENS IN THE BACK! CATCH!
THANKS, SONG! LET'S GET OUT OF HERE BEFORE THE PLANE TURNS ROUND!
BUT SECONDS LATER...
THE PLANE'S BEEN HIT BY MACHINE-GUN FIRE! THE VIETCONG MUST BE IN THOSE WOODS!
THE PILOT AND NAVIGATOR MADE IT SAFELY!
BUT THEY'RE DROPPING RIGHT WHERE THAT VC FIRE ORIGINATED! THEY'LL BE WAITING FOR THEM, BUT NOT US. COME ON!
THEY'VE GOT US COLD!
KILL THE YANKEES!
NO! PLEASE! WE SURRENDER!
ALL AT ONCE, A BURST OF MACHINE-GUN FIRE SPURTED FROM THE JUNGLE!
EEIIIGH!
IT WAS NICE OF YOU FELLAS TO LEAVE YOUR ARTILLERY SET UP FOR ME!
ONE OF THEM'S GETTING AWAY!
BUT MANN'S FRIEND WAS WAITING... AND READY!
UURRGH!
FOR YOU... THE ROAD ENDS HERE!
WE OWE YOU OUR LIVES, COLONEL! I GUESS WE'LL HAVE TO GET OUT OF HERE IN YOUR STOLEN CHOPPER!
I GUESS SO, BUT ONLY IF THESE WERE THE ONLY CONG ROUND HERE, AND THAT ISN'T LIKELY. STAY HERE WITH SONG. I'LL GO BACK AND CHECK IT OUT!

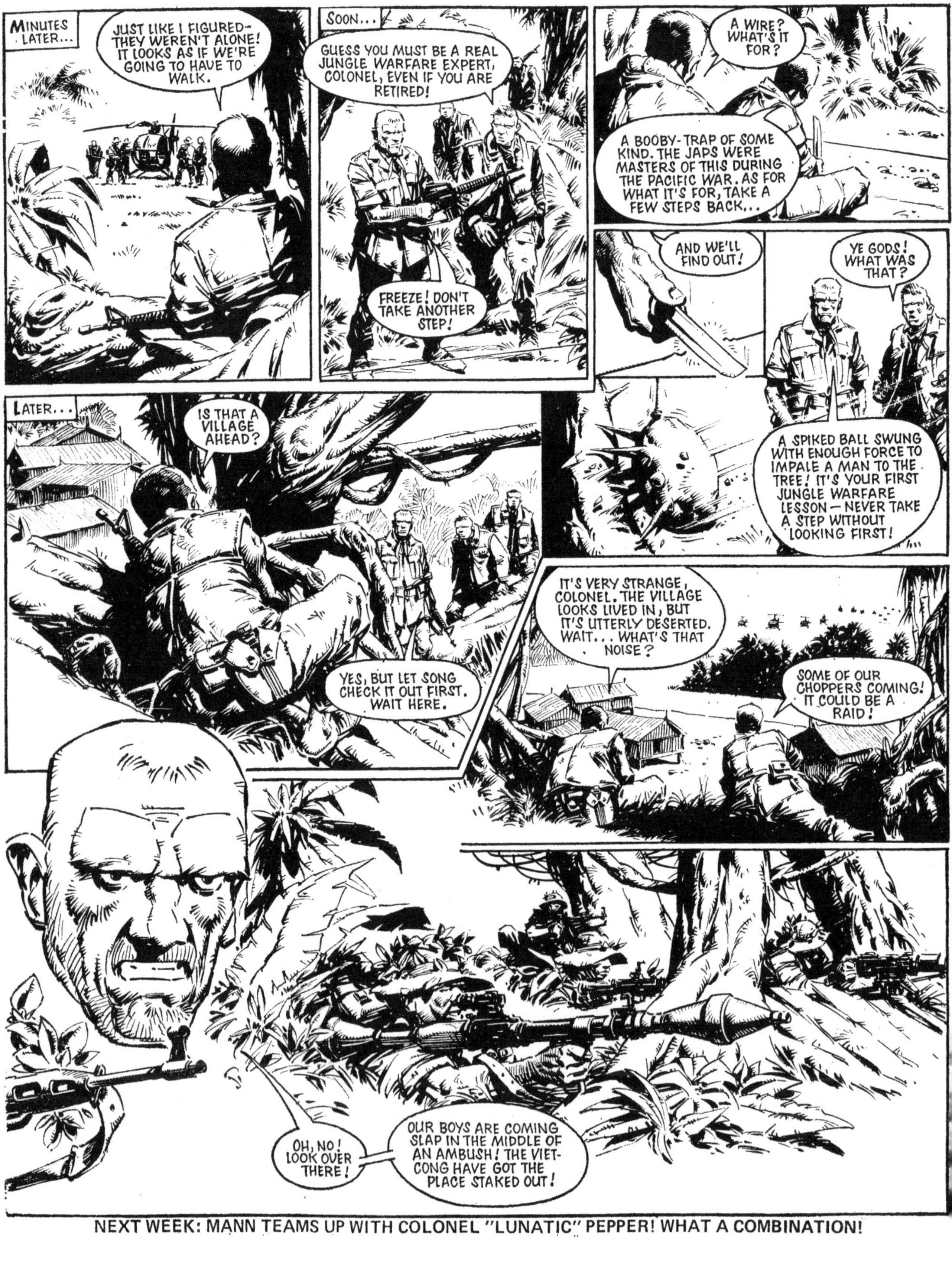

MINUTES LATER...
JUST LIKE I FIGURED- THEY WEREN'T ALONE! IT LOOKS AS IF WE'RE GOING TO HAVE TO WALK.
SOON...
GUESS YOU MUST BE A REAL JUNGLE WARFARE EXPERT, COLONEL, EVEN IF YOU ARE RETIRED!
FREEZE! DON'T TAKE ANOTHER STEP!
A WIRE? WHAT'S IT FOR?
A BOOBY-TRAP OF SOME KIND. THE JAPS WERE MASTERS OF THIS DURING THE PACIFIC WAR. AS FOR WHAT IT'S FOR, TAKE A FEW STEPS BACK...
AND WE'LL FIND OUT!
YE GODS! WHAT WAS THAT?
A SPIKED BALL SWUNG WITH ENOUGH FORCE TO IMPALE A MAN TO THE TREE! IT'S YOUR FIRST JUNGLE WARFARE LESSON — NEVER TAKE A STEP WITHOUT LOOKING FIRST!
LATER...
IS THAT A VILLAGE AHEAD?
YES, BUT LET SONG CHECK IT OUT FIRST. WAIT HERE.
IT'S VERY STRANGE, COLONEL. THE VILLAGE LOOKS LIVED IN, BUT IT'S UTTERLY DESERTED. WAIT... WHAT'S THAT NOISE?
SOME OF OUR CHOPPERS COMING! IT COULD BE A RAID!
OH, NO! LOOK OVER THERE!
OUR BOYS ARE COMING SLAP IN THE MIDDLE OF AN AMBUSH! THE VIET-CONG HAVE GOT THE PLACE STAKED OUT!

NEXT WEEK: MANN TEAMS UP WITH COLONEL "LUNATIC" PEPPER! WHAT A COMBINATION!

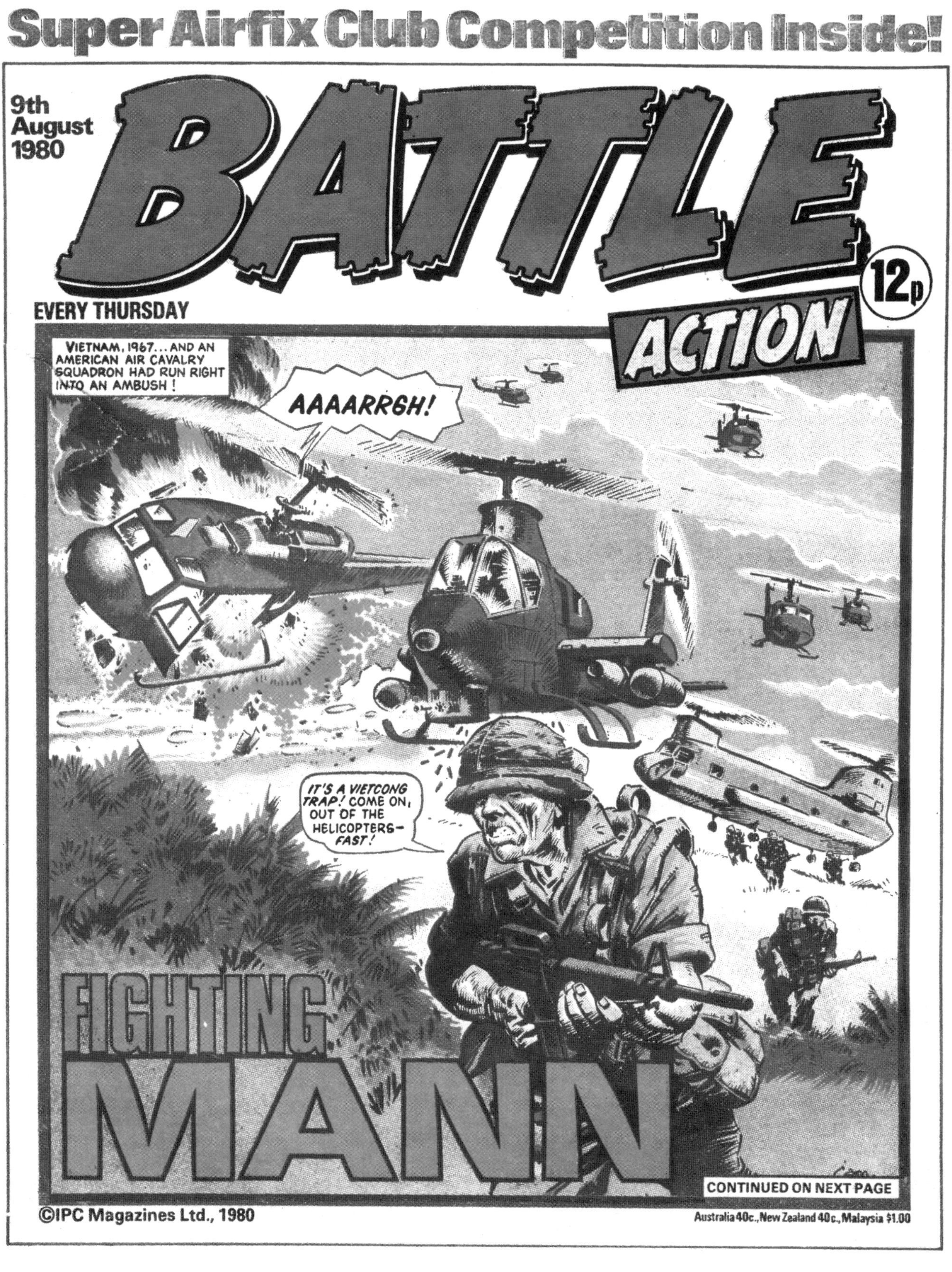
Super Airfix Club Competition Inside!
9th August 1980
BATTLE
12p
EVERY THURSDAY
ACTION
VIETNAM, 1967... AND AN AMERICAN AIR CAVALRY SQUADRON HAD RUN RIGHT INTO AN AMBUSH!
AAAARRGH!
IT'S A VIETCONG TRAP! COME ON, OUT OF THE HELICOPTERS — FAST!
FIGHTING MANN
CONTINUED ON NEXT PAGE
©IPC Magazines Ltd., 1980
Australia 40c., New Zealand 40c., Malaysia $1.00

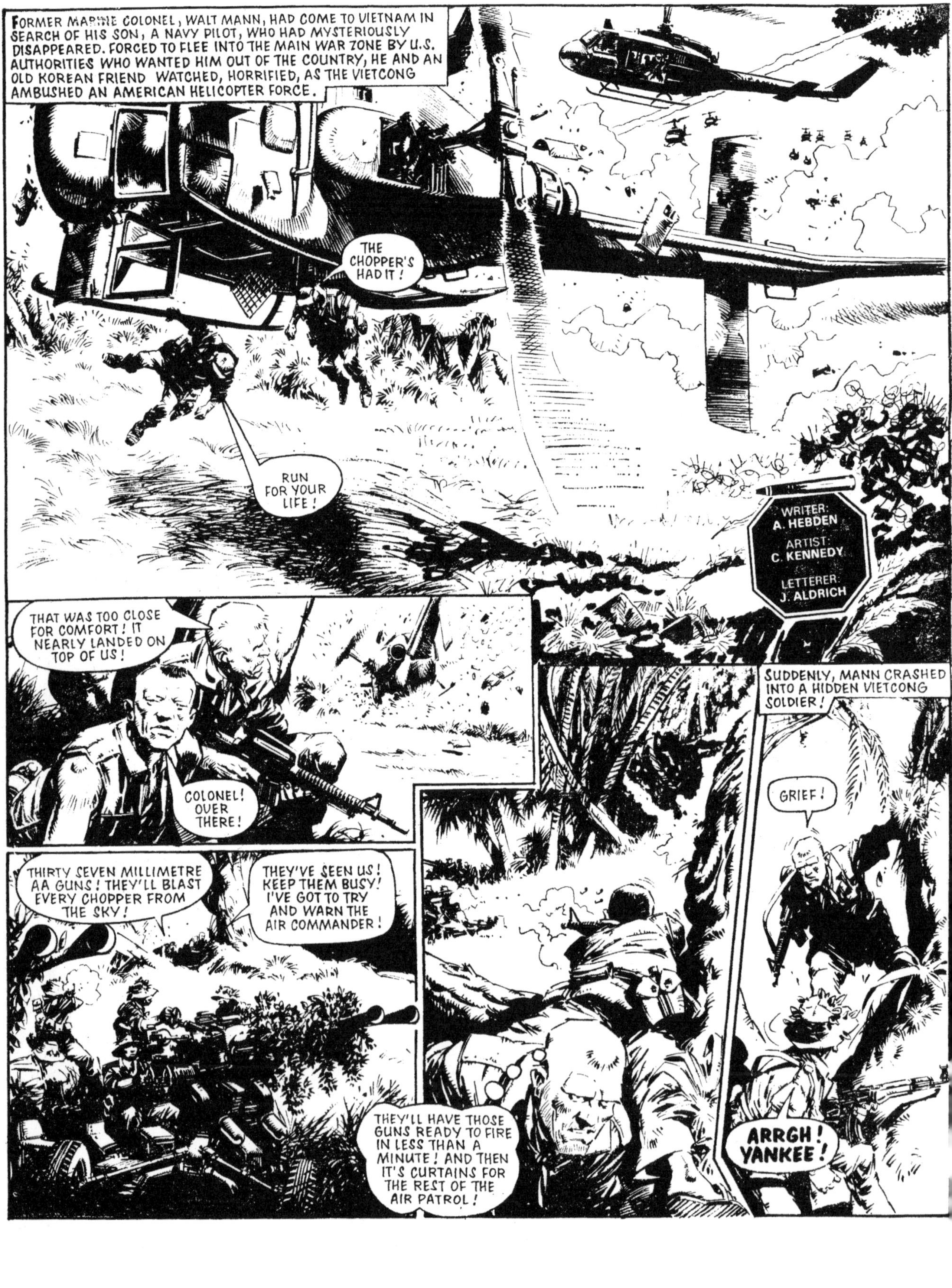
FORMER MARINE COLONEL, WALT MANN, HAD COME TO VIETNAM IN SEARCH OF HIS SON, A NAVY PILOT, WHO HAD MYSTERIOUSLY DISAPPEARED. FORCED TO FLEE INTO THE MAIN WAR ZONE BY U.S. AUTHORITIES WHO WANTED HIM OUT OF THE COUNTRY, HE AND AN OLD KOREAN FRIEND WATCHED, HORRIFIED, AS THE VIETCONG AMBUSHED AN AMERICAN HELICOPTER FORCE.
THE CHOPPER'S HAD IT!
RUN FOR YOUR LIFE!
WRITER: A. HEBDEN
ARTIST: C. KENNEDY
LETTERER: J. ALDRICH
THAT WAS TOO CLOSE FOR COMFORT! IT NEARLY LANDED ON TOP OF US!
COLONEL! OVER THERE!
THIRTY SEVEN MILLIMETRE AA GUNS! THEY'LL BLAST EVERY CHOPPER FROM THE SKY!
THEY'VE SEEN US! KEEP THEM BUSY! I'VE GOT TO TRY AND WARN THE AIR COMMANDER!
THEY'LL HAVE THOSE GUNS READY TO FIRE IN LESS THAN A MINUTE! AND THEN IT'S CURTAINS FOR THE REST OF THE AIR PATROL!
SUDDENLY, MANN CRASHED INTO A HIDDEN VIETCONG SOLDIER!
GRIEF!
ARRGH! YANKEE!

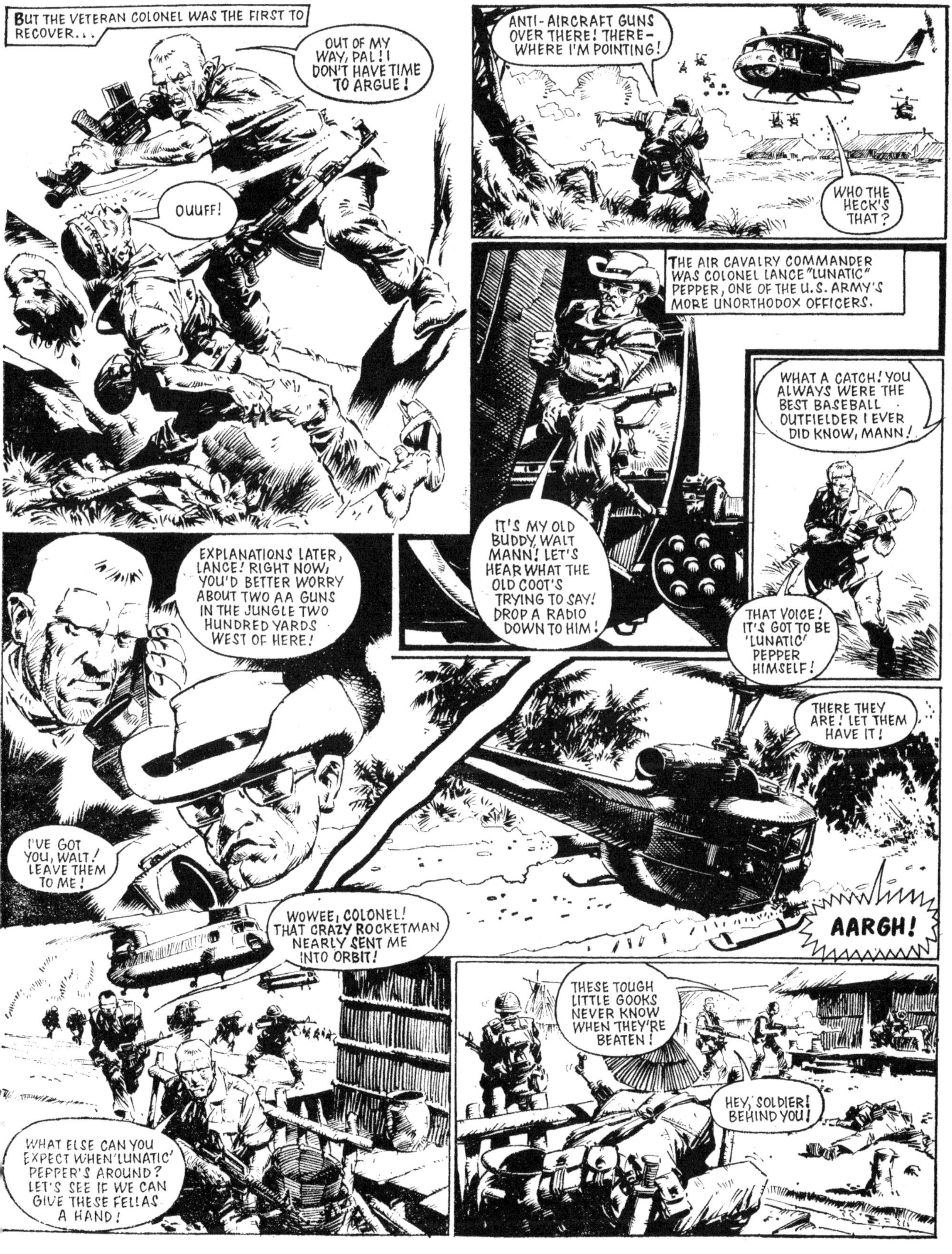
BUT THE VETERAN COLONEL WAS THE FIRST TO RECOVER...
OUT OF MY WAY, PAL! I DON'T HAVE TIME TO ARGUE!
OUUFF!
ANTI-AIRCRAFT GUNS OVER THERE! THERE-WHERE I'M POINTING!
WHO THE HECK'S THAT?
THE AIR CAVALRY COMMANDER WAS COLONEL LANCE "LUNATIC" PEPPER, ONE OF THE U.S. ARMY'S MORE UNORTHODOX OFFICERS.
IT'S MY OLD BUDDY, WALT MANN! LET'S HEAR WHAT THE OLD COOT'S TRYING TO SAY! DROP A RADIO DOWN TO HIM!
WHAT A CATCH! YOU ALWAYS WERE THE BEST BASEBALL OUTFIELDER I EVER DID KNOW, MANN!
THAT VOICE! IT'S GOT TO BE 'LUNATIC' PEPPER HIMSELF!
EXPLANATIONS LATER, LANCE! RIGHT NOW, YOU'D BETTER WORRY ABOUT TWO AA GUNS IN THE JUNGLE TWO HUNDRED YARDS WEST OF HERE!
I'VE GOT YOU, WALT! LEAVE THEM TO ME!
THERE THEY ARE! LET THEM HAVE IT!
AARGH!
WOWEE, COLONEL! THAT CRAZY ROCKETMAN NEARLY SENT ME INTO ORBIT!
WHAT ELSE CAN YOU EXPECT WHEN 'LUNATIC' PEPPER'S AROUND? LET'S SEE IF WE CAN GIVE THESE FELLAS A HAND!
THESE TOUGH LITTLE GOOKS NEVER KNOW WHEN THEY'RE BEATEN!
HEY, SOLDIER! BEHIND YOU!

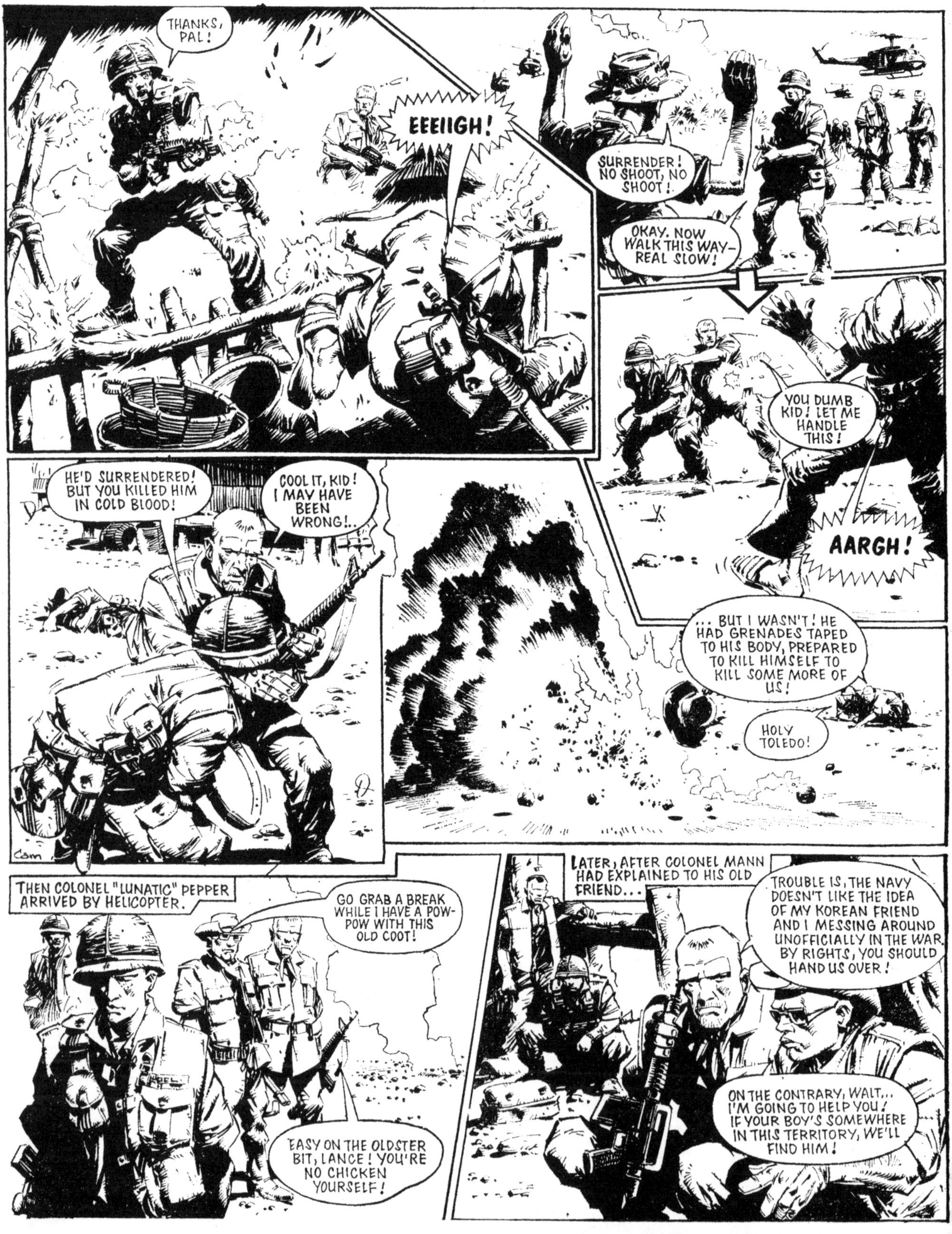
THANKS, PAL!
EEEIIGH!
SURRENDER! NO SHOOT, NO SHOOT!
OKAY. NOW WALK THIS WAY- REAL SLOW!
YOU DUMB KID! LET ME HANDLE THIS!
AARGH!
HE'D SURRENDERED! BUT YOU KILLED HIM IN COLD BLOOD!
COOL IT, KID! I MAY HAVE BEEN WRONG!..
... BUT I WASN'T! HE HAD GRENADES TAPED TO HIS BODY, PREPARED TO KILL HIMSELF TO KILL SOME MORE OF US!
HOLY TOLEDO!
THEN COLONEL "LUNATIC" PEPPER ARRIVED BY HELICOPTER.
GO GRAB A BREAK WHILE I HAVE A POW-POW WITH THIS OLD COOT!
EASY ON THE OLDSTER BIT, LANCE! YOU'RE NO CHICKEN YOURSELF!
LATER, AFTER COLONEL MANN HAD EXPLAINED TO HIS OLD FRIEND...
TROUBLE IS, THE NAVY DOESN'T LIKE THE IDEA OF MY KOREAN FRIEND AND I MESSING AROUND UNOFFICIALLY IN THE WAR. BY RIGHTS, YOU SHOULD HAND US OVER!
ON THE CONTRARY, WALT... I'M GOING TO HELP YOU! IF YOUR BOY'S SOMEWHERE IN THIS TERRITORY, WE'LL FIND HIM!

.MISSION ENDS...MISSION ENDS...MISSION ENDS...MISSION ENDS...MISSION ENDS...MISSION ENDS...MISSION ENI

DEATH SQUAD

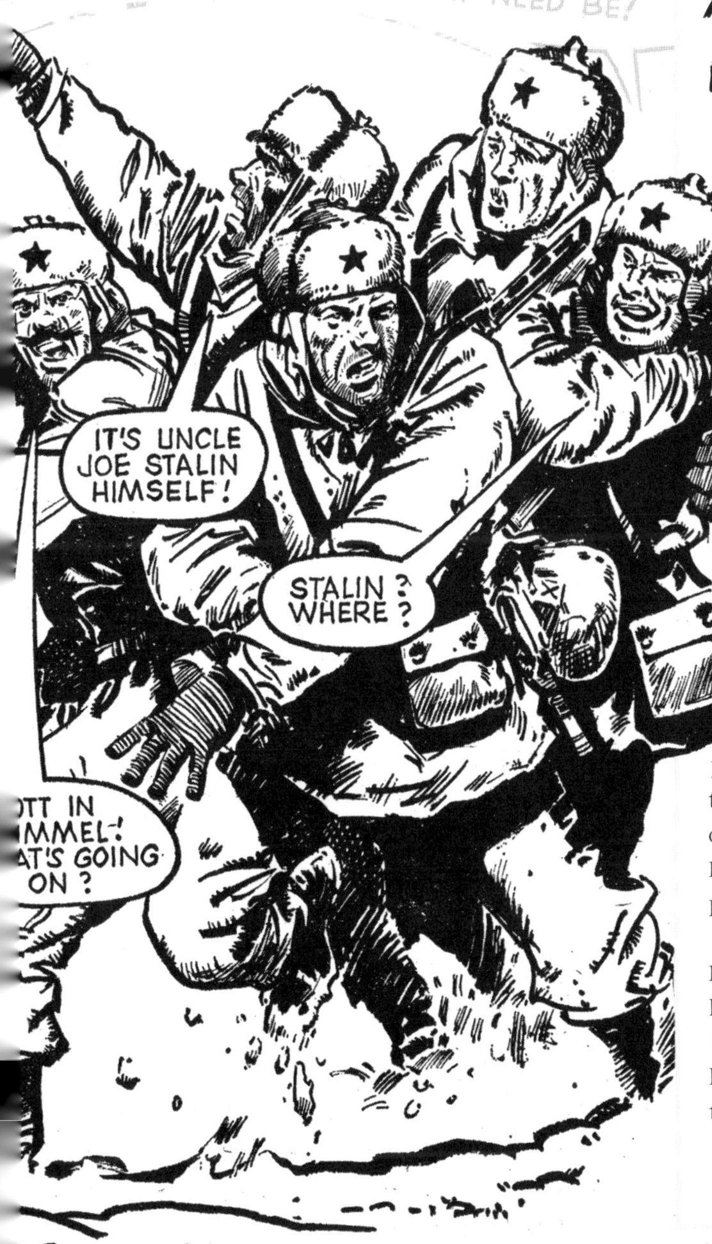
IT'S UNCLE JOE STALIN HIMSELF!
STALIN? WHERE?

"YOU'RE IN A WEHRMACHT PUNISHMENT SQUAD NOW... AND WE DON'T FIGHT BY THE RULES!"

They were known as the Swede, Licker, Gus, Frankie and Granda: German army rejects, no-hopers, conmen and criminals sentenced to fight on the brutally harsh Eastern Front in punishment battalions or die facing a Wehrmacht firing squad.

Led by volunteer and First World War veteran Feldwebel Halbritter, known to them all as "Grandad", they had no choice but to accept every suicide mission they were given, no matter how slim the odds of survival!

'Death Squad' debuted alongside 'Fighting Mann' and ran from December 1980 until April 1981, marking another attempt by *Battle's* editorial department to not only replace an old favourite but to flip an established format on its head — this time 'Rat Pack', but presented from a German perspective. As with all *Battle*'s German characters, the Death Squad often found themselves fighting not only the Allies but also the Nazis in the guise of Major Brandt, the sadistic S.S. officer in charge of the punishment squads.

Like Joe Colquhoun and Chris Western, Eric Bradbury is often described as one of the unsung heroes of British comics and was a master at capturing the gritty realism of the battlefield, where his meticulous and at times macabre artwork seemed to bring the war to hideous life.

WRITTEN BY Mark Andrew
DRAWN BY Eric Bradbury

IF YOU HAVE THE NERVE, START READING THIS POWERFUL NEW STORY TODAY!

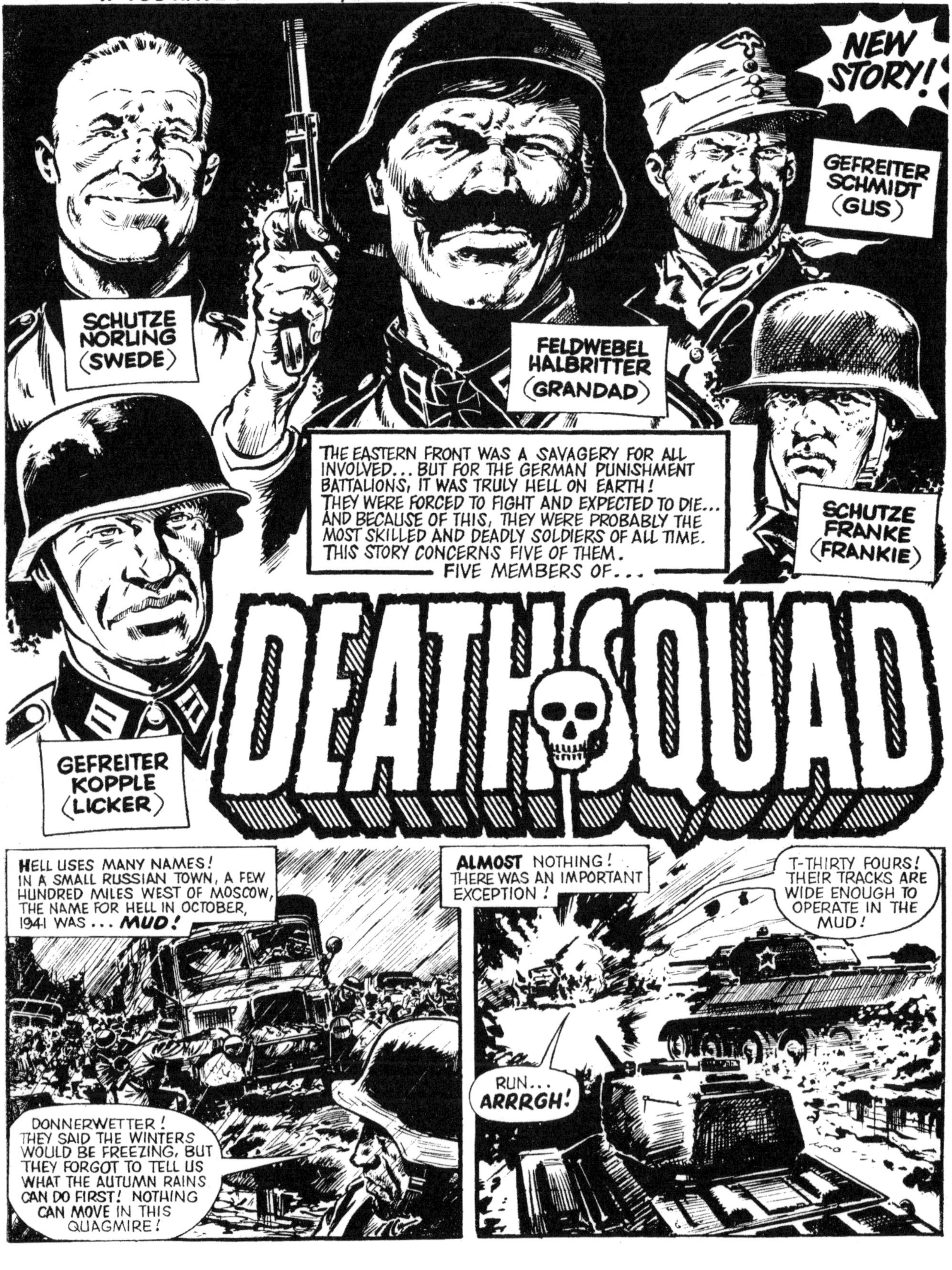

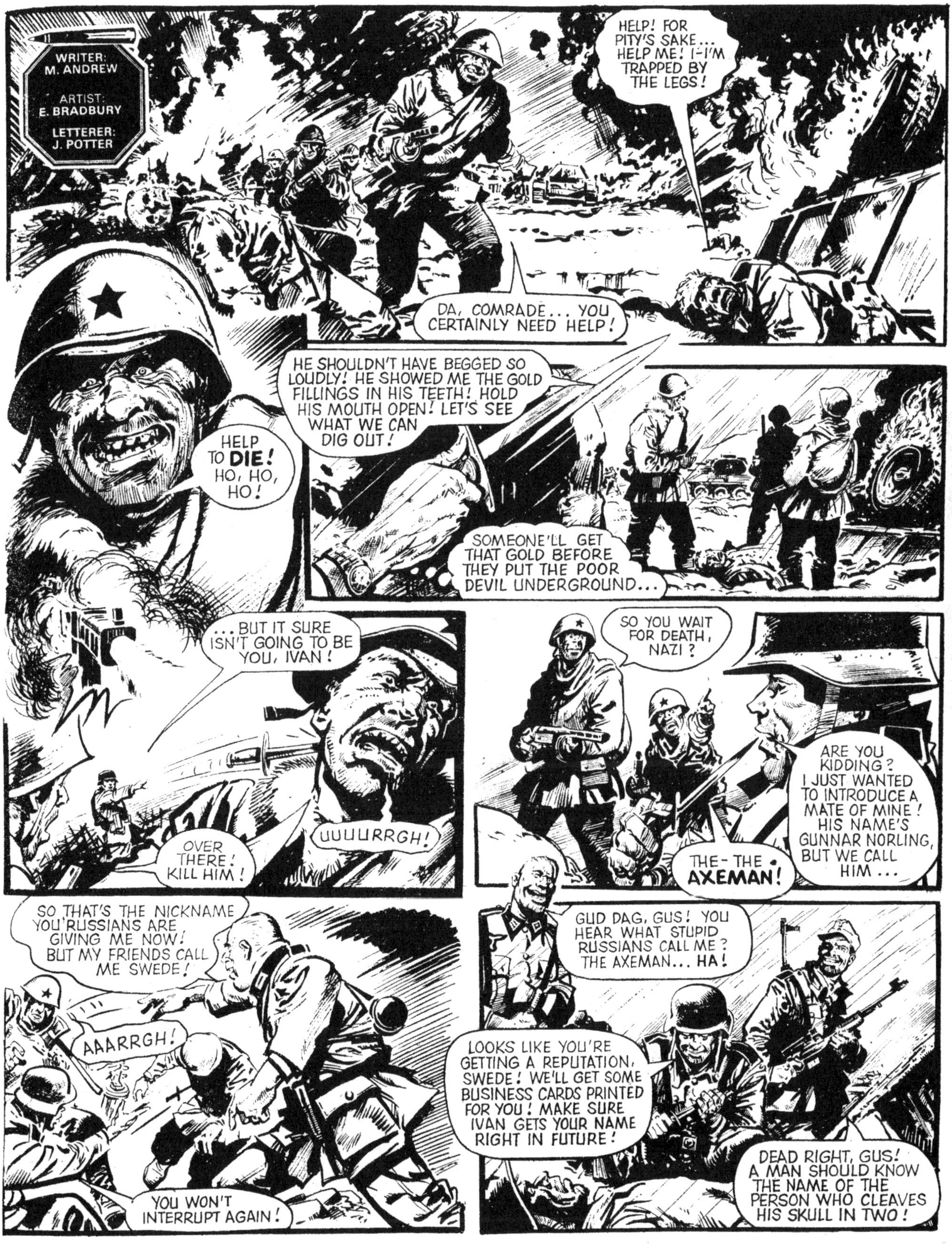
WRITER: M. ANDREW
ARTIST: E. BRADBURY
LETTERER: J. POTTER
HELP! FOR PITY'S SAKE... HELP ME! I-I'M TRAPPED BY THE LEGS!
DA, COMRADE... YOU CERTAINLY NEED HELP!
HELP TO DIE! HO, HO, HO!
HE SHOULDN'T HAVE BEGGED SO LOUDLY! HE SHOWED ME THE GOLD FILLINGS IN HIS TEETH! HOLD HIS MOUTH OPEN! LET'S SEE WHAT WE CAN DIG OUT!
SOMEONE'LL GET THAT GOLD BEFORE THEY PUT THE POOR DEVIL UNDERGROUND...
...BUT IT SURE ISN'T GOING TO BE YOU, IVAN!
UUUURRGH!
OVER THERE! KILL HIM!
SO YOU WAIT FOR DEATH, NAZI?
ARE YOU KIDDING? I JUST WANTED TO INTRODUCE A MATE OF MINE! HIS NAME'S GUNNAR NORLING, BUT WE CALL HIM...
THE- THE AXEMAN!
SO THAT'S THE NICKNAME YOU RUSSIANS ARE GIVING ME NOW! BUT MY FRIENDS CALL ME SWEDE!
AAARRGH!
YOU WON'T INTERRUPT AGAIN!
GUD DAG, GUS! YOU HEAR WHAT STUPID RUSSIANS CALL ME? THE AXEMAN... HA!
LOOKS LIKE YOU'RE GETTING A REPUTATION, SWEDE! WE'LL GET SOME BUSINESS CARDS PRINTED FOR YOU! MAKE SURE IVAN GETS YOUR NAME RIGHT IN FUTURE!
DEAD RIGHT, GUS! A MAN SHOULD KNOW THE NAME OF THE PERSON WHO CLEAVES HIS SKULL IN TWO!

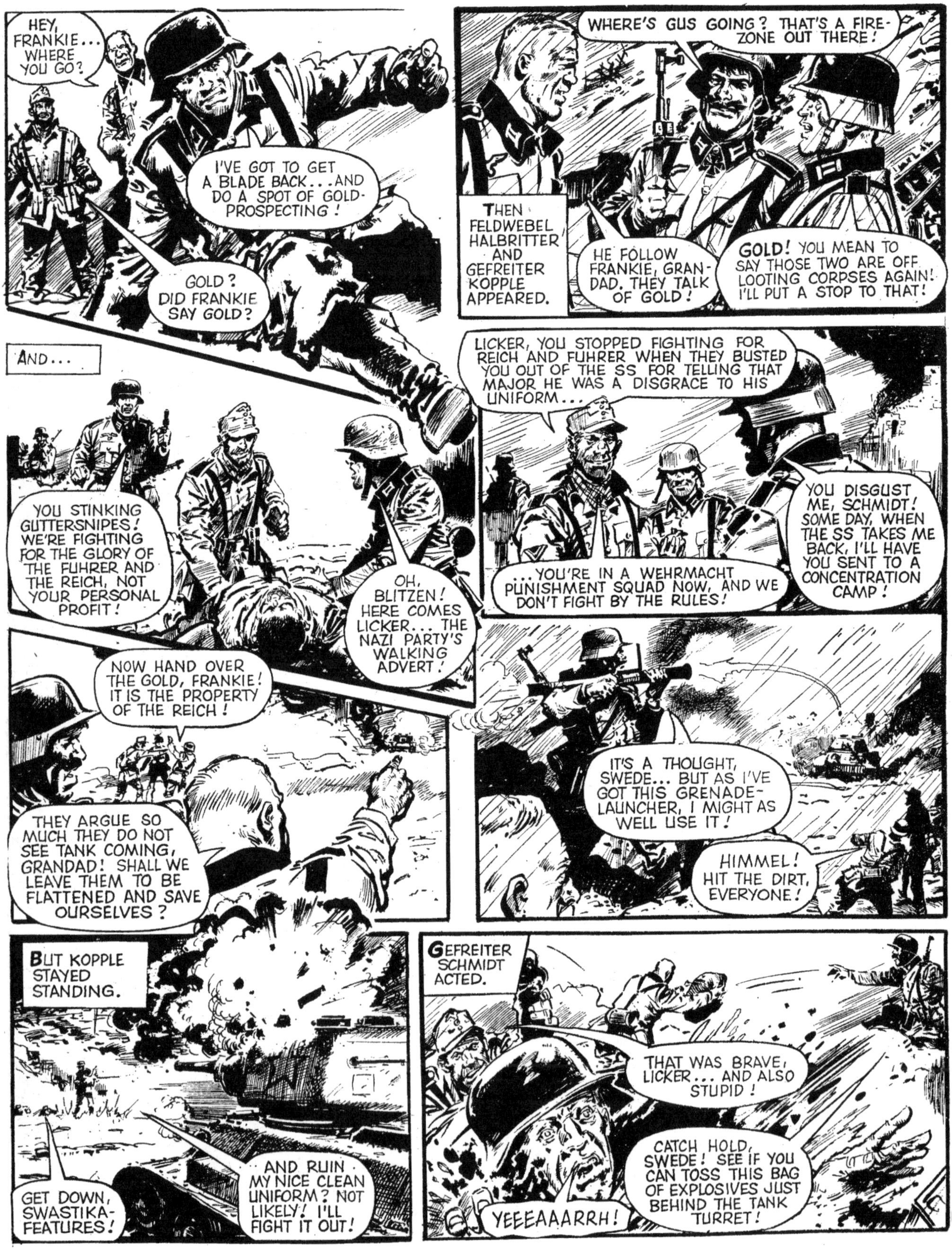
HEY, FRANKIE... WHERE YOU GO?
I'VE GOT TO GET A BLADE BACK...AND DO A SPOT OF GOLD-PROSPECTING!
GOLD? DID FRANKIE SAY GOLD?
WHERE'S GUS GOING? THAT'S A FIRE-ZONE OUT THERE!
THEN FELDWEBEL HALBRITTER AND GEFREITER KOPPLE APPEARED.
HE FOLLOW FRANKIE, GRANDAD. THEY TALK OF GOLD!
GOLD! YOU MEAN TO SAY THOSE TWO ARE OFF LOOTING CORPSES AGAIN! I'LL PUT A STOP TO THAT!
AND...
YOU STINKING GUTTERSNIPES! WE'RE FIGHTING FOR THE GLORY OF THE FUHRER AND THE REICH, NOT YOUR PERSONAL PROFIT!
OH, BLITZEN! HERE COMES LICKER... THE NAZI PARTY'S WALKING ADVERT!
LICKER, YOU STOPPED FIGHTING FOR REICH AND FUHRER WHEN THEY BUSTED YOU OUT OF THE SS FOR TELLING THAT MAJOR HE WAS A DISGRACE TO HIS UNIFORM...
...YOU'RE IN A WEHRMACHT PUNISHMENT SQUAD NOW, AND WE DON'T FIGHT BY THE RULES!
YOU DISGUST ME, SCHMIDT! SOME DAY, WHEN THE SS TAKES ME BACK, I'LL HAVE YOU SENT TO A CONCENTRATION CAMP!
NOW HAND OVER THE GOLD, FRANKIE! IT IS THE PROPERTY OF THE REICH!
THEY ARGUE SO MUCH THEY DO NOT SEE TANK COMING, GRANDAD! SHALL WE LEAVE THEM TO BE FLATTENED AND SAVE OURSELVES?
IT'S A THOUGHT, SWEDE... BUT AS I'VE GOT THIS GRENADE-LAUNCHER, I MIGHT AS WELL USE IT!
HIMMEL! HIT THE DIRT, EVERYONE!
BUT KOPPLE STAYED STANDING.
GET DOWN, SWASTIKA-FEATURES!
AND RUIN MY NICE CLEAN UNIFORM? NOT LIKELY! I'LL FIGHT IT OUT!
GEFREITER SCHMIDT ACTED.
THAT WAS BRAVE, LICKER... AND ALSO STUPID!
CATCH HOLD, SWEDE! SEE IF YOU CAN TOSS THIS BAG OF EXPLOSIVES JUST BEHIND THE TANK TURRET!
YEEEAAARRH!

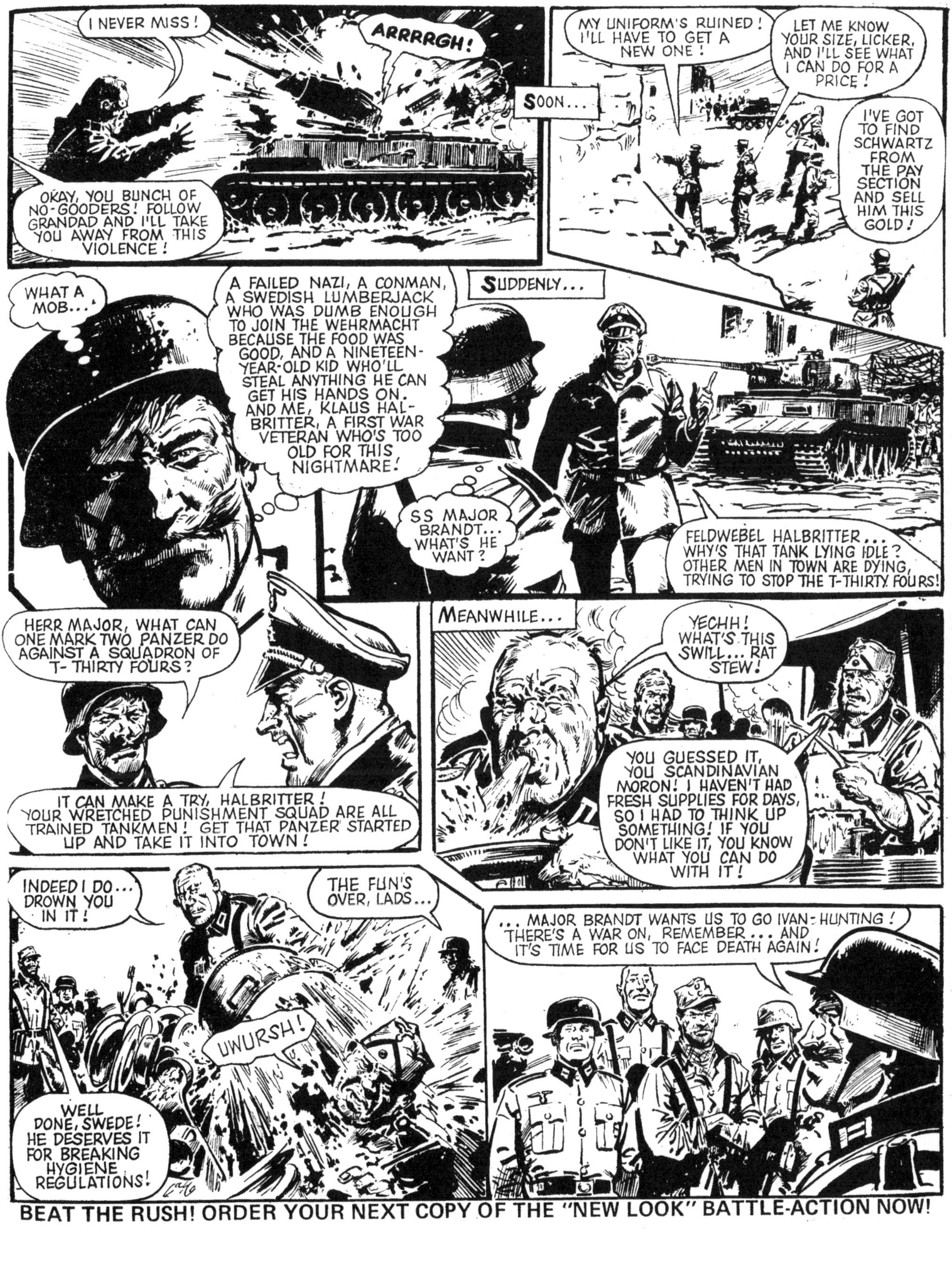

I NEVER MISS!
ARRRRGH!
OKAY, YOU BUNCH OF NO-GOODERS! FOLLOW GRANDAD AND I'LL TAKE YOU AWAY FROM THIS VIOLENCE!
SOON...
MY UNIFORM'S RUINED! I'LL HAVE TO GET A NEW ONE!
LET ME KNOW YOUR SIZE, LICKER, AND I'LL SEE WHAT I CAN DO FOR A PRICE!
I'VE GOT TO FIND SCHWARTZ FROM THE PAY SECTION AND SELL HIM THIS GOLD!
WHAT A MOB...
A FAILED NAZI, A CONMAN, A SWEDISH LUMBERJACK WHO WAS DUMB ENOUGH TO JOIN THE WEHRMACHT BECAUSE THE FOOD WAS GOOD, AND A NINETEEN-YEAR-OLD KID WHO'LL STEAL ANYTHING HE CAN GET HIS HANDS ON. AND ME, KLAUS HALBRITTER, A FIRST WAR VETERAN WHO'S TOO OLD FOR THIS NIGHTMARE!
SUDDENLY...
SS MAJOR BRANDT... WHAT'S HE WANT?
FELDWEBEL HALBRITTER... WHY'S THAT TANK LYING IDLE? OTHER MEN IN TOWN ARE DYING, TRYING TO STOP THE T-THIRTY FOURS!
HERR MAJOR, WHAT CAN ONE MARK TWO PANZER DO AGAINST A SQUADRON OF T-THIRTY FOURS?
IT CAN MAKE A TRY, HALBRITTER! YOUR WRETCHED PUNISHMENT SQUAD ARE ALL TRAINED TANKMEN! GET THAT PANZER STARTED UP AND TAKE IT INTO TOWN!
MEANWHILE...
YECHH! WHAT'S THIS SWILL... RAT STEW!
YOU GUESSED IT, YOU SCANDINAVIAN MORON! I HAVEN'T HAD FRESH SUPPLIES FOR DAYS, SO I HAD TO THINK UP SOMETHING! IF YOU DON'T LIKE IT, YOU KNOW WHAT YOU CAN DO WITH IT!
INDEED I DO... DROWN YOU IN IT!
THE FUN'S OVER, LADS...
UWURSH!
WELL DONE, SWEDE! HE DESERVES IT FOR BREAKING HYGIENE REGULATIONS!
... MAJOR BRANDT WANTS US TO GO IVAN-HUNTING! THERE'S A WAR ON, REMEMBER... AND IT'S TIME FOR US TO FACE DEATH AGAIN!

BEAT THE RUSH! ORDER YOUR NEXT COPY OF THE "NEW LOOK" BATTLE-ACTION NOW!

YOU HAVE TO BE TOUGH TO SURVIVE ON THE EASTERN FRONT AND THE DEATH SQUAD INTEND TO SURVIVE!

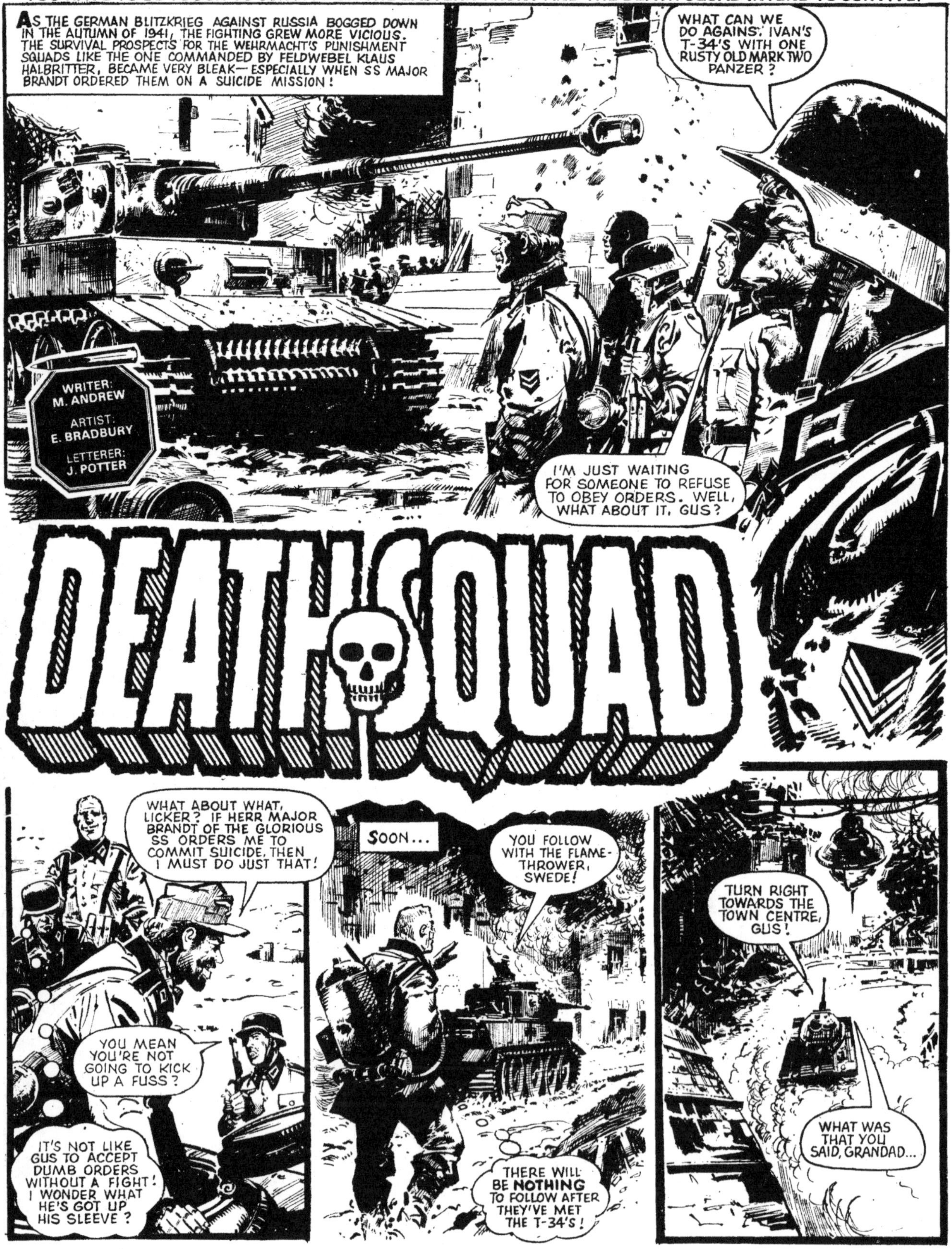

AS THE GERMAN BLITZKRIEG AGAINST RUSSIA BOGGED DOWN IN THE AUTUMN OF 1941, THE FIGHTING GREW MORE VICIOUS. THE SURVIVAL PROSPECTS FOR THE WEHRMACHT'S PUNISHMENT SQUADS LIKE THE ONE COMMANDED BY FELDWEBEL KLAUS HALBRITTER, BECAME VERY BLEAK— ESPECIALLY WHEN SS MAJOR BRANDT ORDERED THEM ON A SUICIDE MISSION!
WHAT CAN WE DO AGAINST IVAN'S T-34'S WITH ONE RUSTY OLD MARK TWO PANZER?
WRITER: M. ANDREW
ARTIST: E. BRADBURY
LETTERER: J. POTTER
I'M JUST WAITING FOR SOMEONE TO REFUSE TO OBEY ORDERS. WELL, WHAT ABOUT IT, GUS?
DEATH SQUAD
WHAT ABOUT WHAT, LICKER? IF HERR MAJOR BRANDT OF THE GLORIOUS SS ORDERS ME TO COMMIT SUICIDE, THEN I MUST DO JUST THAT!
YOU MEAN YOU'RE NOT GOING TO KICK UP A FUSS?
IT'S NOT LIKE GUS TO ACCEPT DUMB ORDERS WITHOUT A FIGHT! I WONDER WHAT HE'S GOT UP HIS SLEEVE?
SOON...
YOU FOLLOW WITH THE FLAME-THROWER, SWEDE!
THERE WILL BE NOTHING TO FOLLOW AFTER THEY'VE MET THE T-34'S!
TURN RIGHT TOWARDS THE TOWN CENTRE, GUS!
WHAT WAS THAT YOU SAID, GRANDAD...

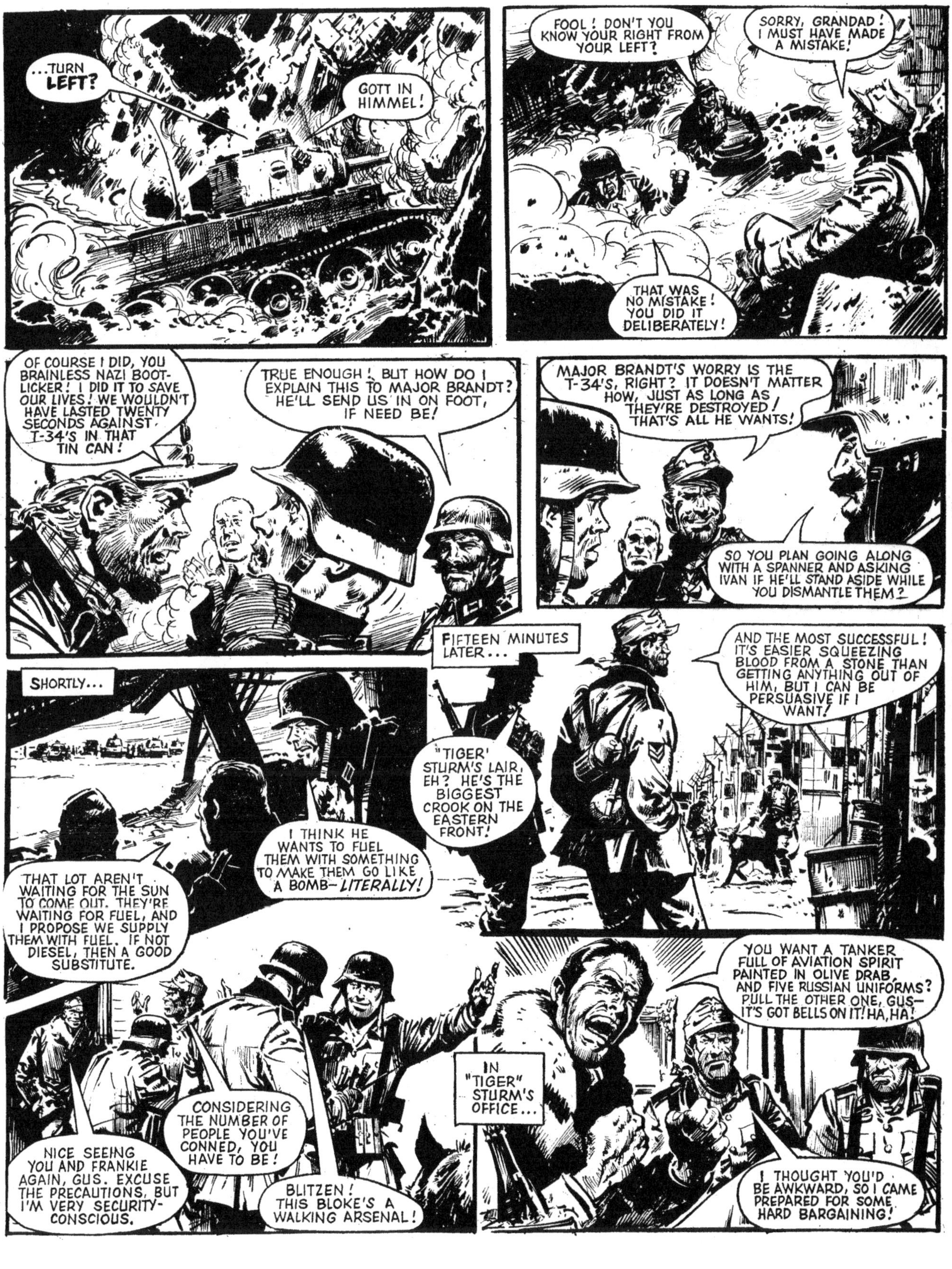

...TURN LEFT?
GOTT IN HIMMEL!
FOOL! DON'T YOU KNOW YOUR RIGHT FROM YOUR LEFT?
SORRY, GRANDAD! I MUST HAVE MADE A MISTAKE!
THAT WAS NO MISTAKE! YOU DID IT DELIBERATELY!
OF COURSE I DID, YOU BRAINLESS NAZI BOOT-LICKER! I DID IT TO SAVE OUR LIVES! WE WOULDN'T HAVE LASTED TWENTY SECONDS AGAINST T-34'S IN THAT TIN CAN!
TRUE ENOUGH! BUT HOW DO I EXPLAIN THIS TO MAJOR BRANDT? HE'LL SEND US IN ON FOOT, IF NEED BE!
MAJOR BRANDT'S WORRY IS THE T-34'S, RIGHT? IT DOESN'T MATTER HOW, JUST AS LONG AS THEY'RE DESTROYED! THAT'S ALL HE WANTS!
SO YOU PLAN GOING ALONG WITH A SPANNER AND ASKING IVAN IF HE'LL STAND ASIDE WHILE YOU DISMANTLE THEM?
SHORTLY...
THAT LOT AREN'T WAITING FOR THE SUN TO COME OUT. THEY'RE WAITING FOR FUEL, AND I PROPOSE WE SUPPLY THEM WITH FUEL. IF NOT DIESEL, THEN A GOOD SUBSTITUTE.
I THINK HE WANTS TO FUEL THEM WITH SOMETHING TO MAKE THEM GO LIKE A BOMB—LITERALLY!
FIFTEEN MINUTES LATER...
"TIGER' STURM'S LAIR, EH? HE'S THE BIGGEST CROOK ON THE EASTERN FRONT!
AND THE MOST SUCCESSFUL! IT'S EASIER SQUEEZING BLOOD FROM A STONE THAN GETTING ANYTHING OUT OF HIM, BUT I CAN BE PERSUASIVE IF I WANT!
NICE SEEING YOU AND FRANKIE AGAIN, GUS. EXCUSE THE PRECAUTIONS, BUT I'M VERY SECURITY-CONSCIOUS.
CONSIDERING THE NUMBER OF PEOPLE YOU'VE CONNED, YOU HAVE TO BE!
BLITZEN! THIS BLOKE'S A WALKING ARSENAL!
IN "TIGER" STURM'S OFFICE...
YOU WANT A TANKER FULL OF AVIATION SPIRIT PAINTED IN OLIVE DRAB, AND FIVE RUSSIAN UNIFORMS? PULL THE OTHER ONE, GUS—IT'S GOT BELLS ON IT! HA, HA!
I THOUGHT YOU'D BE AWKWARD, SO I CAME PREPARED FOR SOME HARD BARGAINING!

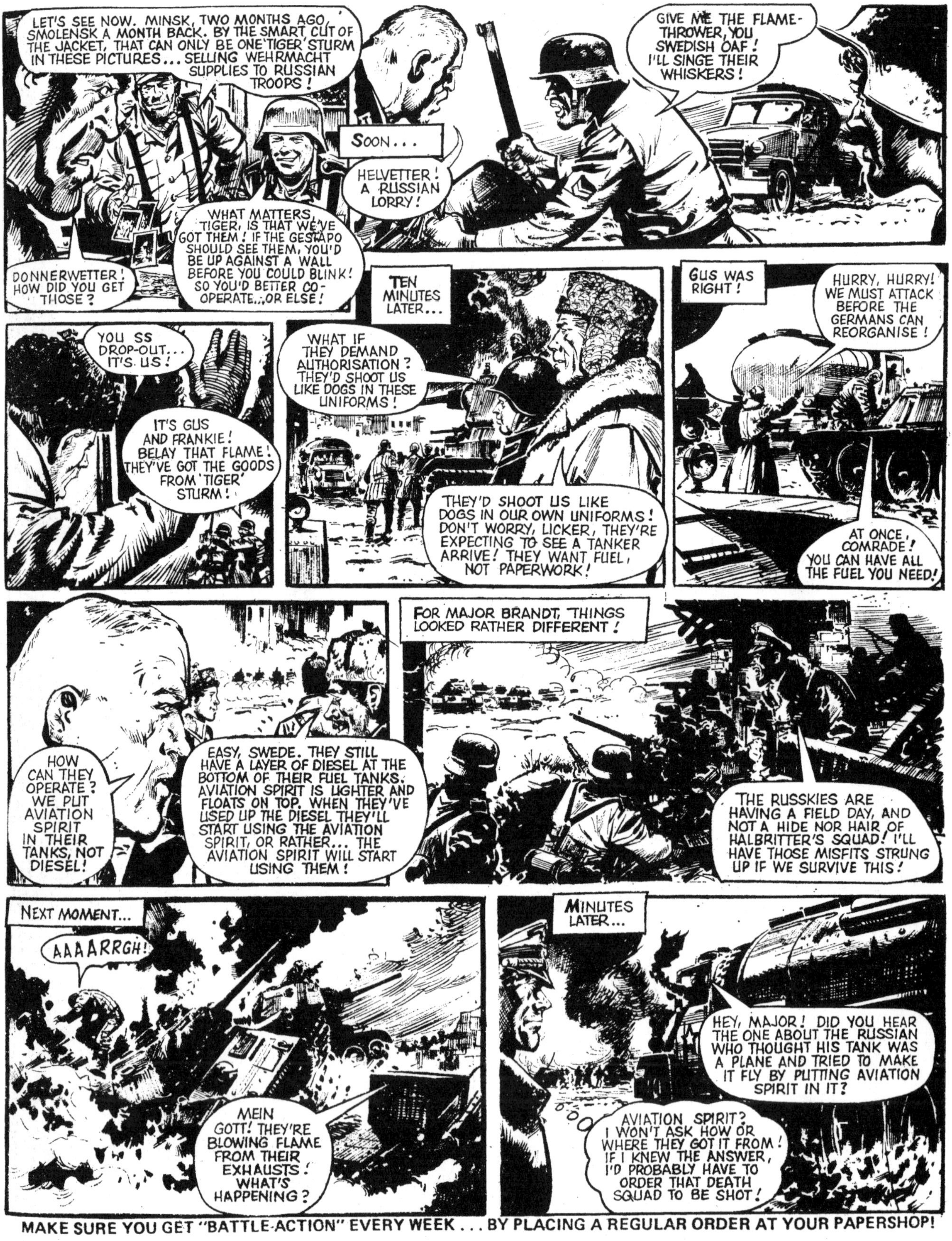
LET'S SEE NOW. MINSK, TWO MONTHS AGO, SMOLENSK A MONTH BACK. BY THE SMART CUT OF THE JACKET, THAT CAN ONLY BE ONE 'TIGER' STURM IN THESE PICTURES... SELLING WEHRMACHT SUPPLIES TO RUSSIAN TROOPS!
DONNERWETTER! HOW DID YOU GET THOSE?
WHAT MATTERS, TIGER, IS THAT WE'VE GOT THEM! IF THE GESTAPO SHOULD SEE THEM, YOU'D BE UP AGAINST A WALL BEFORE YOU COULD BLINK! SO YOU'D BETTER CO-OPERATE...OR ELSE!
SOON...
HELVETTER! A RUSSIAN LORRY!
GIVE ME THE FLAME-THROWER, YOU SWEDISH OAF! I'LL SINGE THEIR WHISKERS!
YOU SS DROP-OUT... IT'S US!
IT'S GUS AND FRANKIE! BELAY THAT FLAME! THEY'VE GOT THE GOODS FROM 'TIGER' STURM!
TEN MINUTES LATER...
WHAT IF THEY DEMAND AUTHORISATION? THEY'D SHOOT US LIKE DOGS IN THESE UNIFORMS!
THEY'D SHOOT US LIKE DOGS IN OUR OWN UNIFORMS! DON'T WORRY, LICKER, THEY'RE EXPECTING TO SEE A TANKER ARRIVE! THEY WANT FUEL, NOT PAPERWORK!
GUS WAS RIGHT!
HURRY, HURRY! WE MUST ATTACK BEFORE THE GERMANS CAN REORGANISE!
AT ONCE, COMRADE! YOU CAN HAVE ALL THE FUEL YOU NEED!
HOW CAN THEY OPERATE? WE PUT AVIATION SPIRIT IN THEIR TANKS, NOT DIESEL!
EASY, SWEDE. THEY STILL HAVE A LAYER OF DIESEL AT THE BOTTOM OF THEIR FUEL TANKS. AVIATION SPIRIT IS LIGHTER AND FLOATS ON TOP. WHEN THEY'VE USED UP THE DIESEL THEY'LL START USING THE AVIATION SPIRIT, OR RATHER... THE AVIATION SPIRIT WILL START USING THEM!
FOR MAJOR BRANDT, THINGS LOOKED RATHER DIFFERENT!
THE RUSSKIES ARE HAVING A FIELD DAY, AND NOT A HIDE NOR HAIR OF HALBRITTER'S SQUAD! I'LL HAVE THOSE MISFITS STRUNG UP IF WE SURVIVE THIS!
NEXT MOMENT...
AAAARRGH!
MEIN GOTT! THEY'RE BLOWING FLAME FROM THEIR EXHAUSTS! WHAT'S HAPPENING?
MINUTES LATER...
HEY, MAJOR! DID YOU HEAR THE ONE ABOUT THE RUSSIAN WHO THOUGHT HIS TANK WAS A PLANE AND TRIED TO MAKE IT FLY BY PUTTING AVIATION SPIRIT IN IT?
AVIATION SPIRIT? I WON'T ASK HOW OR WHERE THEY GOT IT FROM! IF I KNEW THE ANSWER, I'D PROBABLY HAVE TO ORDER THAT DEATH SQUAD TO BE SHOT!

MAKE SURE YOU GET "BATTLE-ACTION" EVERY WEEK . . . BY PLACING A REGULAR ORDER AT YOUR PAPERSHOP!

THIS WEEK THE DEATH SQUAD ARE ON THE PROWL! SO, RUSSKIES WATCH OUT!

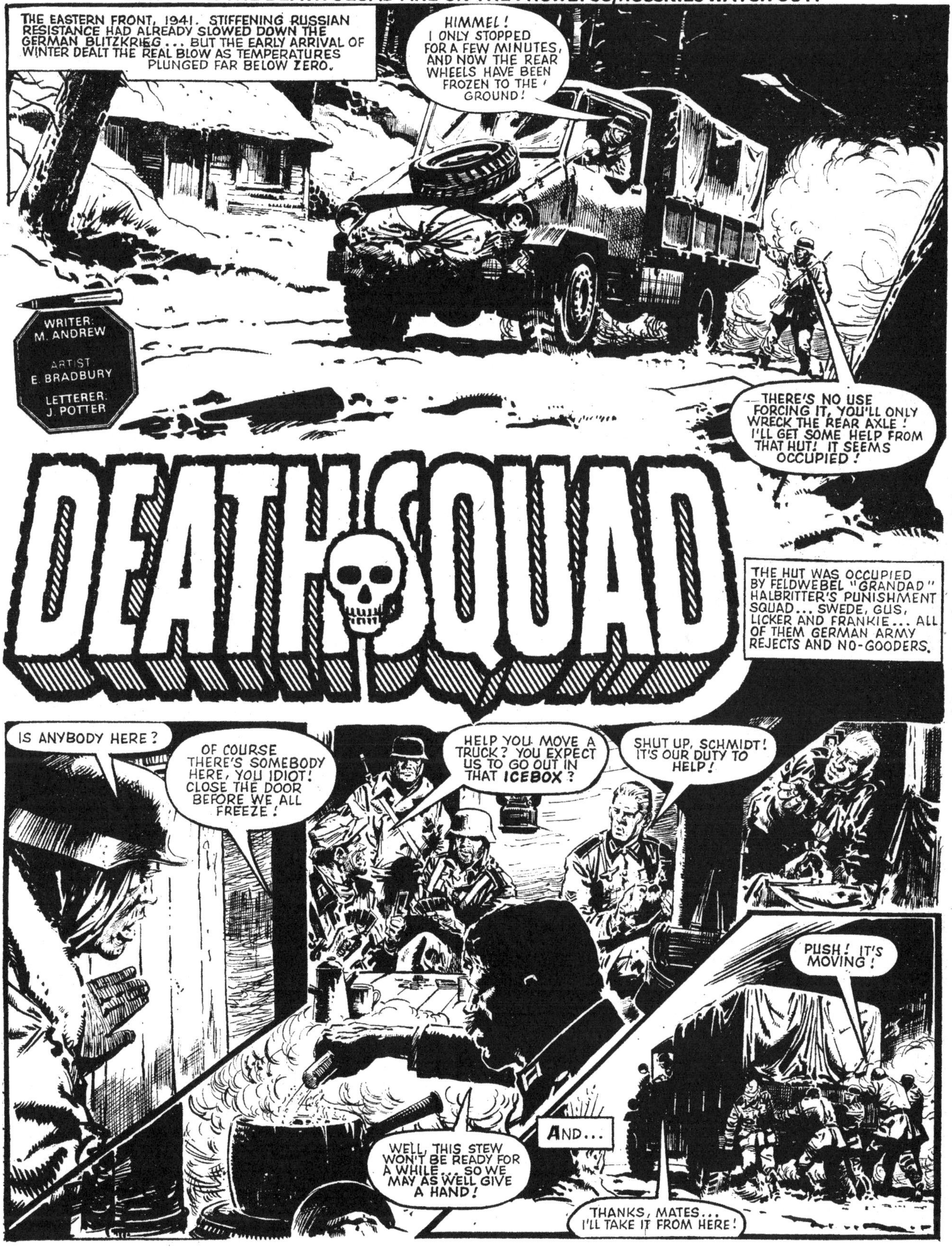

THE EASTERN FRONT, 1941. STIFFENING RUSSIAN RESISTANCE HAD ALREADY SLOWED DOWN THE GERMAN BLITZKRIEG ... BUT THE EARLY ARRIVAL OF WINTER DEALT THE REAL BLOW AS TEMPERATURES PLUNGED FAR BELOW ZERO.
HIMMEL! I ONLY STOPPED FOR A FEW MINUTES, AND NOW THE REAR WHEELS HAVE BEEN FROZEN TO THE GROUND!
WRITER: M. ANDREW
ARTIST: E. BRADBURY
LETTERER: J. POTTER
THERE'S NO USE FORCING IT, YOU'LL ONLY WRECK THE REAR AXLE! I'LL GET SOME HELP FROM THAT HUT! IT SEEMS OCCUPIED!
DEATH SQUAD
THE HUT WAS OCCUPIED BY FELDWEBEL "GRANDAD" HALBRITTER'S PUNISHMENT SQUAD... SWEDE, GUS, LICKER AND FRANKIE... ALL OF THEM GERMAN ARMY REJECTS AND NO-GOODERS.
IS ANYBODY HERE?
OF COURSE THERE'S SOMEBODY HERE, YOU IDIOT! CLOSE THE DOOR BEFORE WE ALL FREEZE!
HELP YOU MOVE A TRUCK? YOU EXPECT US TO GO OUT IN THAT ICEBOX?
SHUT UP, SCHMIDT! IT'S OUR DUTY TO HELP!
WELL, THIS STEW WON'T BE READY FOR A WHILE... SO WE MAY AS WELL GIVE A HAND!
AND...
PUSH! IT'S MOVING!
THANKS, MATES... I'LL TAKE IT FROM HERE!

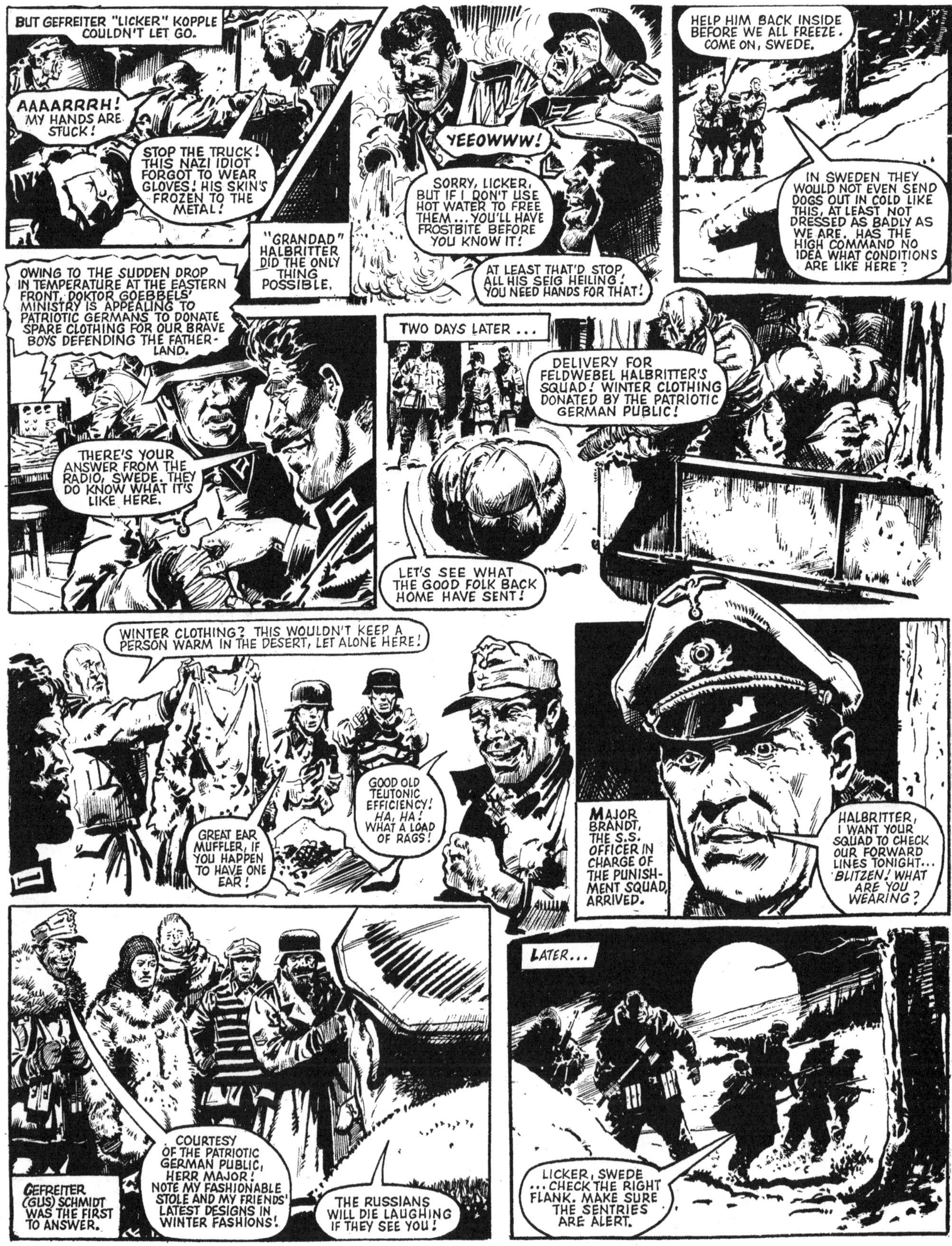
BUT GEFREITER "LICKER" KOPPLE COULDN'T LET GO.
AAAARRRH! MY HANDS ARE STUCK!
STOP THE TRUCK! THIS NAZI IDIOT FORGOT TO WEAR GLOVES! HIS SKIN'S FROZEN TO THE METAL!
"GRANDAD" HALBRITTER DID THE ONLY THING POSSIBLE.
YEEOWWW!
SORRY, LICKER, BUT IF I DON'T USE HOT WATER TO FREE THEM... YOU'LL HAVE FROSTBITE BEFORE YOU KNOW IT!
AT LEAST THAT'D STOP ALL HIS SEIG HEILING! YOU NEED HANDS FOR THAT!
HELP HIM BACK INSIDE BEFORE WE ALL FREEZE. COME ON, SWEDE.
IN SWEDEN THEY WOULD NOT EVEN SEND DOGS OUT IN COLD LIKE THIS, AT LEAST NOT DRESSED AS BADLY AS WE ARE. HAS THE HIGH COMMAND NO IDEA WHAT CONDITIONS ARE LIKE HERE?
OWING TO THE SUDDEN DROP IN TEMPERATURE AT THE EASTERN FRONT, DOKTOR GOEBBELS' MINISTRY IS APPEALING TO PATRIOTIC GERMANS TO DONATE SPARE CLOTHING FOR OUR BRAVE BOYS DEFENDING THE FATHERLAND.
THERE'S YOUR ANSWER FROM THE RADIO, SWEDE. THEY DO KNOW WHAT IT'S LIKE HERE.
TWO DAYS LATER...
DELIVERY FOR FELDWEBEL HALBRITTER'S SQUAD! WINTER CLOTHING DONATED BY THE PATRIOTIC GERMAN PUBLIC!
LET'S SEE WHAT THE GOOD FOLK BACK HOME HAVE SENT!
WINTER CLOTHING? THIS WOULDN'T KEEP A PERSON WARM IN THE DESERT, LET ALONE HERE!
GREAT EAR MUFFLER, IF YOU HAPPEN TO HAVE ONE EAR!
GOOD OLD TEUTONIC EFFICIENCY! HA, HA! WHAT A LOAD OF RAGS!
MAJOR BRANDT, THE S.S. OFFICER IN CHARGE OF THE PUNISHMENT SQUAD, ARRIVED.
HALBRITTER, I WANT YOUR SQUAD TO CHECK OUR FORWARD LINES TONIGHT... BLITZEN! WHAT ARE YOU WEARING?
GEFREITER (GUS) SCHMIDT WAS THE FIRST TO ANSWER.
COURTESY OF THE PATRIOTIC GERMAN PUBLIC, HERR MAJOR! NOTE MY FASHIONABLE STOLE AND MY FRIENDS' LATEST DESIGNS IN WINTER FASHIONS!
THE RUSSIANS WILL DIE LAUGHING IF THEY SEE YOU!
LATER...
LICKER, SWEDE ... CHECK THE RIGHT FLANK. MAKE SURE THE SENTRIES ARE ALERT.

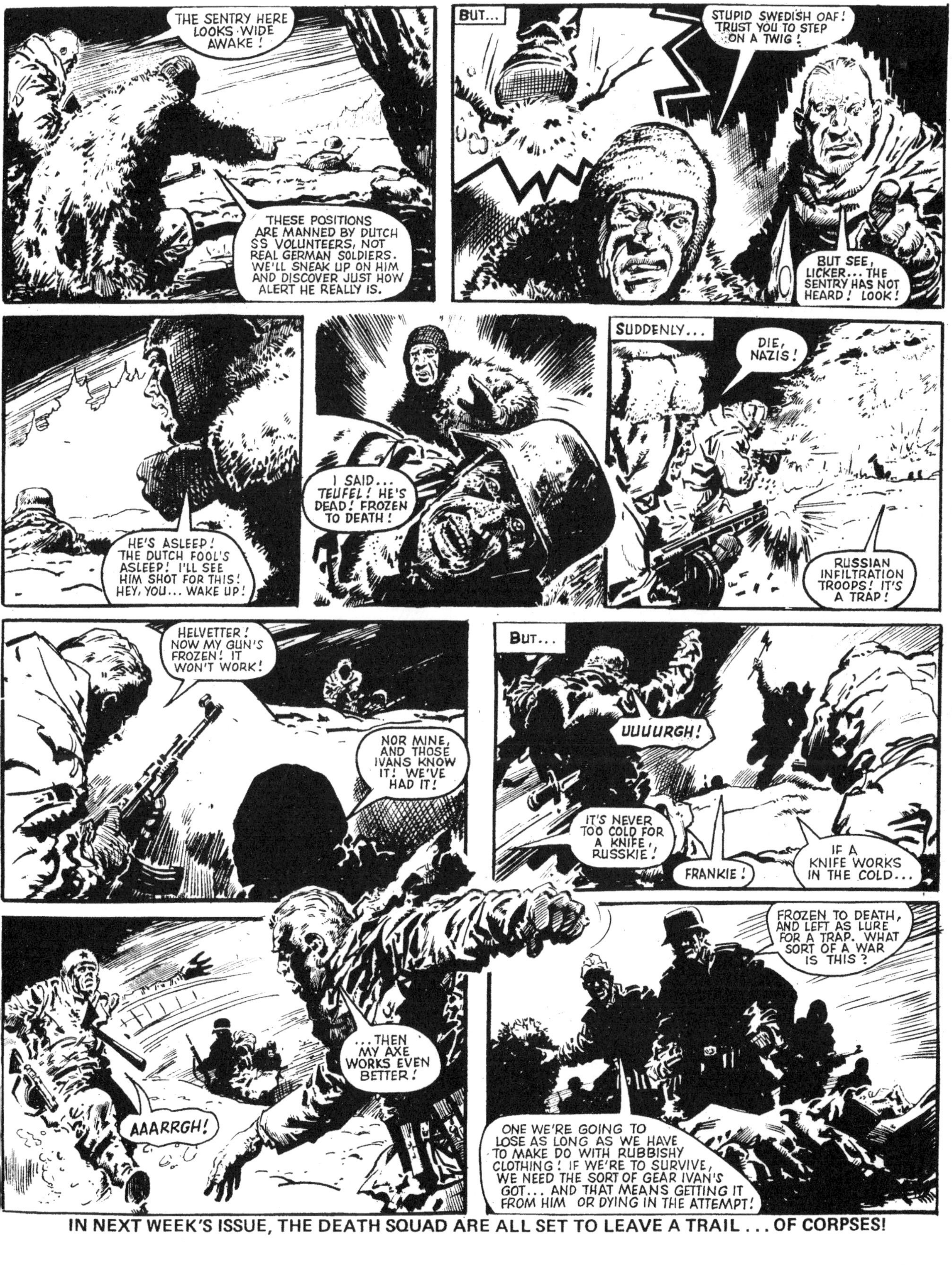
THE SENTRY HERE LOOKS WIDE AWAKE!
THESE POSITIONS ARE MANNED BY DUTCH SS VOLUNTEERS, NOT REAL GERMAN SOLDIERS. WE'LL SNEAK UP ON HIM AND DISCOVER JUST HOW ALERT HE REALLY IS.
BUT...
STUPID SWEDISH OAF! TRUST YOU TO STEP ON A TWIG!
BUT SEE, LICKER... THE SENTRY HAS NOT HEARD! LOOK!
HE'S ASLEEP! THE DUTCH FOOL'S ASLEEP! I'LL SEE HIM SHOT FOR THIS! HEY, YOU... WAKE UP!
I SAID... TEUFEL! HE'S DEAD! FROZEN TO DEATH!
SUDDENLY...
DIE, NAZIS!
RUSSIAN INFILTRATION TROOPS! IT'S A TRAP!
HELVETTER! NOW MY GUN'S FROZEN! IT WON'T WORK!
NOR MINE, AND THOSE IVANS KNOW IT! WE'VE HAD IT!
BUT...
UUUURGH!
IT'S NEVER TOO COLD FOR A KNIFE, RUSSKIE!
FRANKIE!
IF A KNIFE WORKS IN THE COLD...
...THEN MY AXE WORKS EVEN BETTER!
AAARRGH!
FROZEN TO DEATH, AND LEFT AS LURE FOR A TRAP. WHAT SORT OF A WAR IS THIS?
ONE WE'RE GOING TO LOSE AS LONG AS WE HAVE TO MAKE DO WITH RUBBISHY CLOTHING! IF WE'RE TO SURVIVE, WE NEED THE SORT OF GEAR IVAN'S GOT... AND THAT MEANS GETTING IT FROM HIM OR DYING IN THE ATTEMPT!

IN NEXT WEEK'S ISSUE, THE DEATH SQUAD ARE ALL SET TO LEAVE A TRAIL . . . OF CORPSES!

THE SWEDE KNOWS JUST HOW TO EXTRACT INFORMATION FROM A PRISONER! HE SHARPENS HIS AXE!

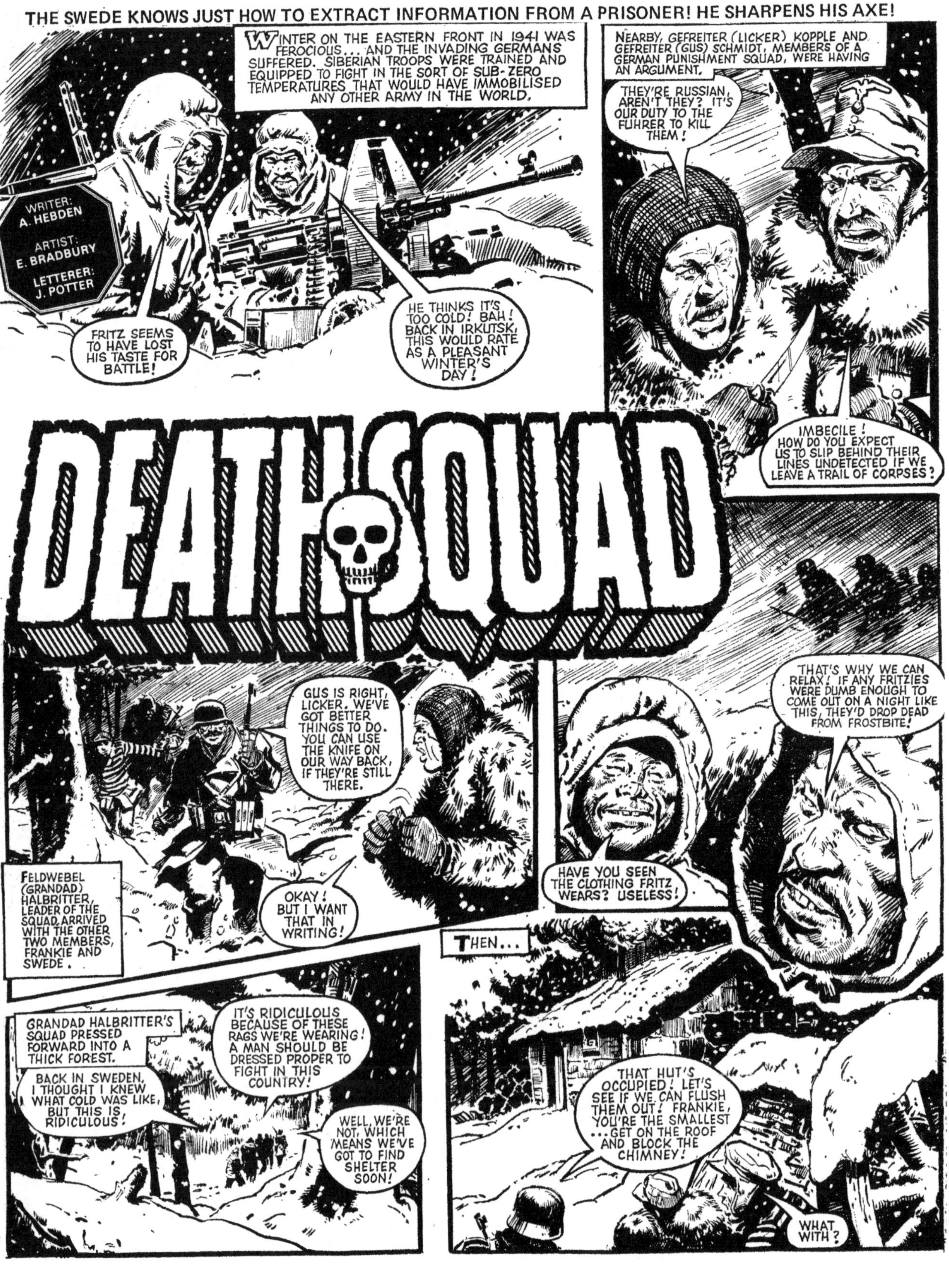

WINTER ON THE EASTERN FRONT IN 1941 WAS FEROCIOUS... AND THE INVADING GERMANS SUFFERED. SIBERIAN TROOPS WERE TRAINED AND EQUIPPED TO FIGHT IN THE SORT OF SUB-ZERO TEMPERATURES THAT WOULD HAVE IMMOBILISED ANY OTHER ARMY IN THE WORLD.
WRITER: A. HEBDEN
ARTIST: E. BRADBURY
LETTERER: J. POTTER
FRITZ SEEMS TO HAVE LOST HIS TASTE FOR BATTLE!
HE THINKS IT'S TOO COLD! BAH! BACK IN IRKUTSK, THIS WOULD RATE AS A PLEASANT WINTER'S DAY!
NEARBY, GEFREITER (LICKER) KOPPLE AND GEFREITER (GUS) SCHMIDT, MEMBERS OF A GERMAN PUNISHMENT SQUAD, WERE HAVING AN ARGUMENT.
THEY'RE RUSSIAN, AREN'T THEY? IT'S OUR DUTY TO THE FUHRER TO KILL THEM!
IMBECILE! HOW DO YOU EXPECT US TO SLIP BEHIND THEIR LINES UNDETECTED IF WE LEAVE A TRAIL OF CORPSES?
DEATH SQUAD
GUS IS RIGHT, LICKER. WE'VE GOT BETTER THINGS TO DO. YOU CAN USE THE KNIFE ON OUR WAY BACK, IF THEY'RE STILL THERE.
OKAY! BUT I WANT THAT IN WRITING!
FELDWEBEL (GRANDAD) HALBRITTER, LEADER OF THE SQUAD, ARRIVED WITH THE OTHER TWO MEMBERS, FRANKIE AND SWEDE.
THAT'S WHY WE CAN RELAX! IF ANY FRITZIES WERE DUMB ENOUGH TO COME OUT ON A NIGHT LIKE THIS, THEY'D DROP DEAD FROM FROSTBITE!
HAVE YOU SEEN THE CLOTHING FRITZ WEARS? USELESS!
GRANDAD HALBRITTER'S SQUAD PRESSED FORWARD INTO A THICK FOREST.
BACK IN SWEDEN, I THOUGHT I KNEW WHAT COLD WAS LIKE, BUT THIS IS RIDICULOUS!
IT'S RIDICULOUS BECAUSE OF THESE RAGS WE'RE WEARING! A MAN SHOULD BE DRESSED PROPER TO FIGHT IN THIS COUNTRY!
WELL, WE'RE NOT, WHICH MEANS WE'VE GOT TO FIND SHELTER SOON!
THEN...
THAT HUT'S OCCUPIED! LET'S SEE IF WE CAN FLUSH THEM OUT! FRANKIE, YOU'RE THE SMALLEST ...GET ON THE ROOF AND BLOCK THE CHIMNEY!
WHAT WITH?

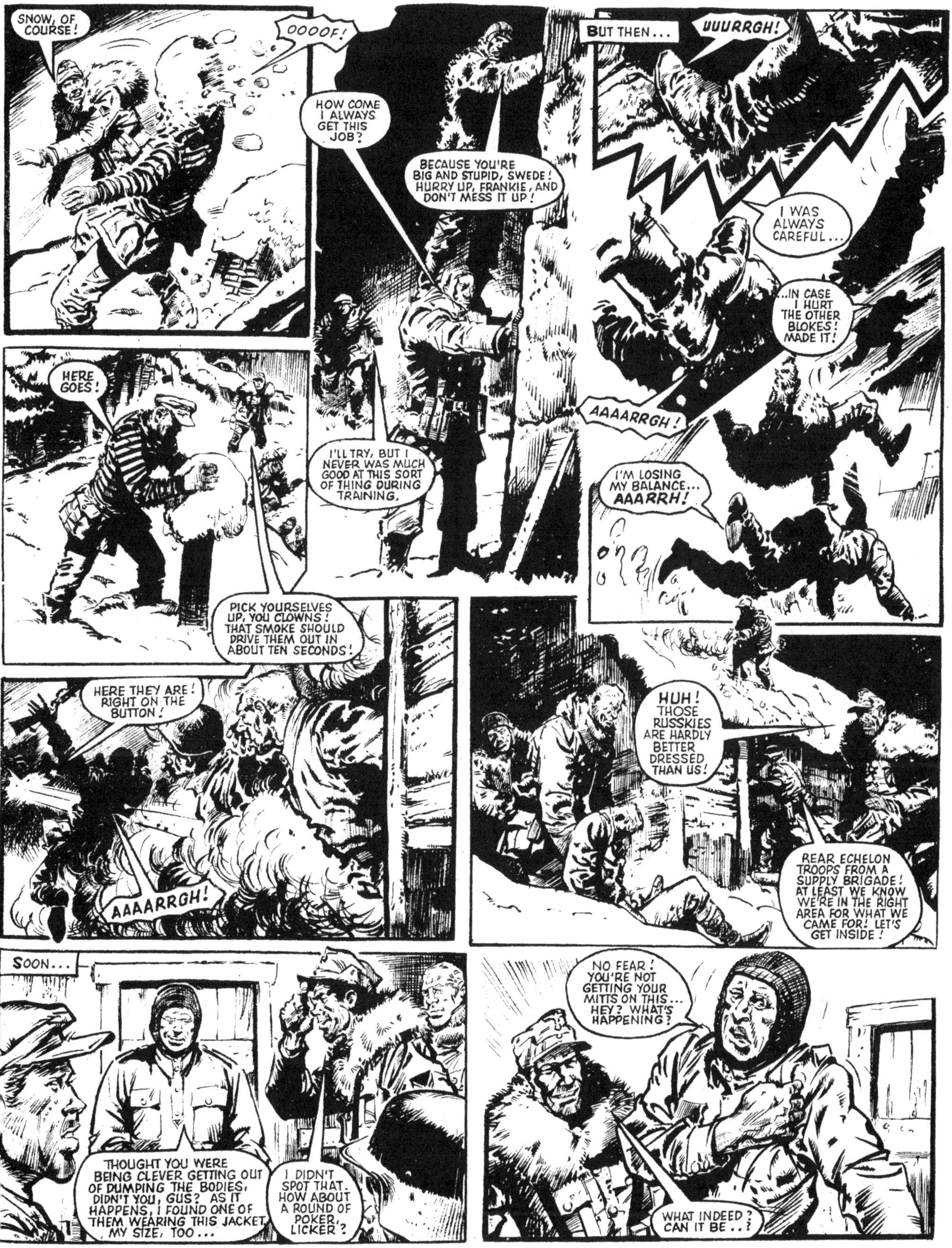

SNOW, OF COURSE!
OOOOF!
HOW COME I ALWAYS GET THIS JOB?
BECAUSE YOU'RE BIG AND STUPID, SWEDE! HURRY UP, FRANKIE, AND DON'T MESS IT UP!
BUT THEN...
UUURRGH!
I WAS ALWAYS CAREFUL...
..IN CASE I HURT THE OTHER BLOKES! MADE IT!
HERE GOES!
I'LL TRY, BUT I NEVER WAS MUCH GOOD AT THIS SORT OF THING DURING TRAINING.
AAAARRGH!
I'M LOSING MY BALANCE... AAARRH!
PICK YOURSELVES UP, YOU CLOWNS! THAT SMOKE SHOULD DRIVE THEM OUT IN ABOUT TEN SECONDS!
HERE THEY ARE! RIGHT ON THE BUTTON!
AAAARRGH!
HUH! THOSE RUSSKIES ARE HARDLY BETTER DRESSED THAN US!
REAR ECHELON TROOPS FROM A SUPPLY BRIGADE! AT LEAST WE KNOW WE'RE IN THE RIGHT AREA FOR WHAT WE CAME FOR! LET'S GET INSIDE!
SOON...
THOUGHT YOU WERE BEING CLEVER GETTING OUT OF DUMPING THE BODIES, DIDN'T YOU, GUS? AS IT HAPPENS, I FOUND ONE OF THEM WEARING THIS JACKET. MY SIZE, TOO...
I DIDN'T SPOT THAT. HOW ABOUT A ROUND OF POKER, LICKER?
NO FEAR! YOU'RE NOT GETTING YOUR MITTS ON THIS... HEY? WHAT'S HAPPENING?
WHAT INDEED? CAN IT BE..?

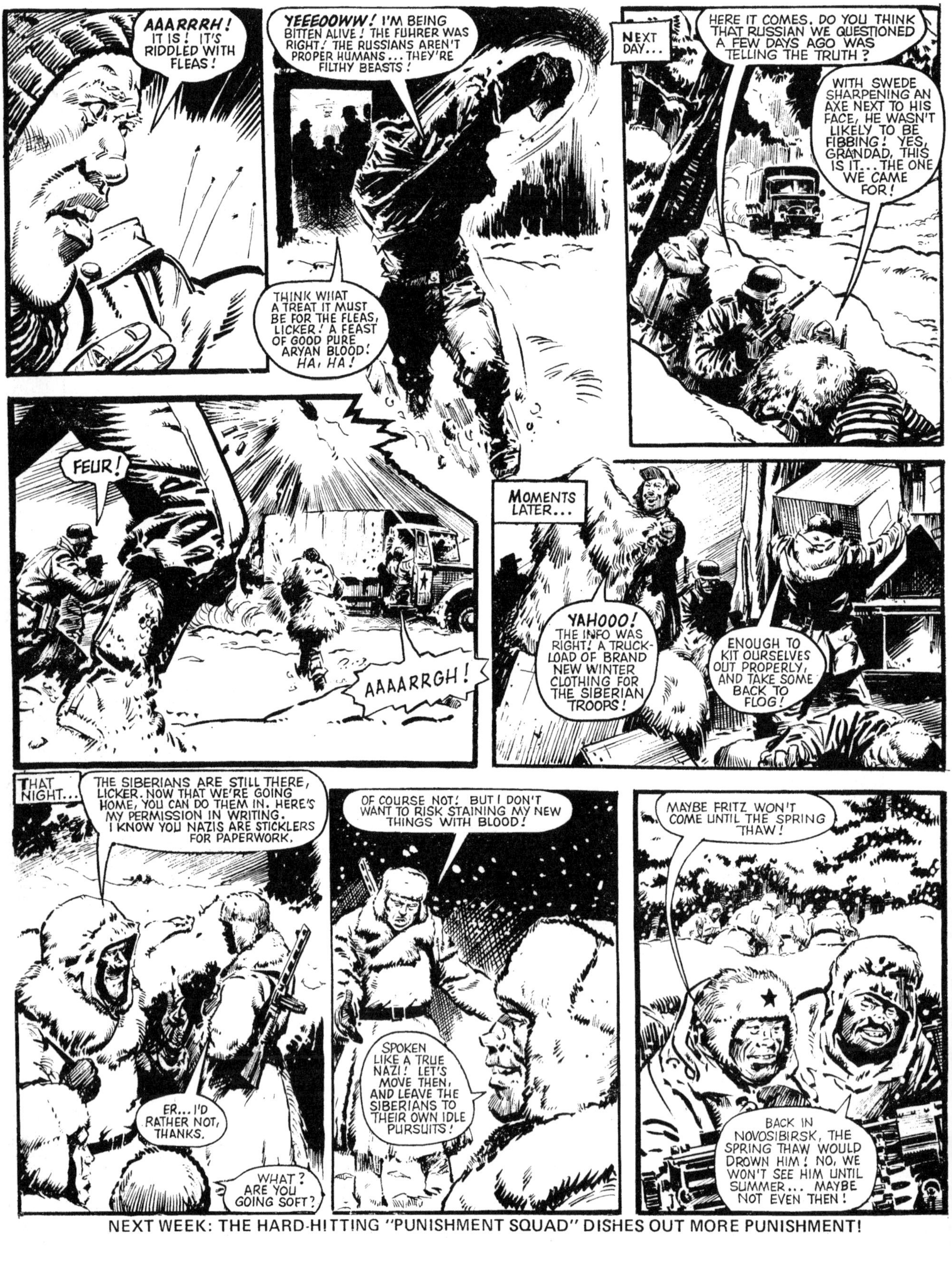
AAARRRH! IT IS! IT'S RIDDLED WITH FLEAS!
YEEEOOWW! I'M BEING BITTEN ALIVE! THE FUHRER WAS RIGHT! THE RUSSIANS AREN'T PROPER HUMANS... THEY'RE FILTHY BEASTS!
THINK WHAT A TREAT IT MUST BE FOR THE FLEAS, LICKER! A FEAST OF GOOD PURE ARYAN BLOOD! HA, HA!
NEXT DAY...
HERE IT COMES. DO YOU THINK THAT RUSSIAN WE QUESTIONED A FEW DAYS AGO WAS TELLING THE TRUTH?
WITH SWEDE SHARPENING AN AXE NEXT TO HIS FACE, HE WASN'T LIKELY TO BE FIBBING! YES, GRANDAD, THIS IS IT... THE ONE WE CAME FOR!
FEUR!
AAAARRGH!
MOMENTS LATER...
YAHOOO! THE INFO WAS RIGHT! A TRUCK-LOAD OF BRAND NEW WINTER CLOTHING FOR THE SIBERIAN TROOPS!
ENOUGH TO KIT OURSELVES OUT PROPERLY, AND TAKE SOME BACK TO FLOG!
THAT NIGHT...
THE SIBERIANS ARE STILL THERE, LICKER. NOW THAT WE'RE GOING HOME, YOU CAN DO THEM IN. HERE'S MY PERMISSION IN WRITING. I KNOW YOU NAZIS ARE STICKLERS FOR PAPERWORK.
ER... I'D RATHER NOT, THANKS.
WHAT? ARE YOU GOING SOFT?
OF COURSE NOT! BUT I DON'T WANT TO RISK STAINING MY NEW THINGS WITH BLOOD!
SPOKEN LIKE A TRUE NAZI! LET'S MOVE THEN, AND LEAVE THE SIBERIANS TO THEIR OWN IDLE PURSUITS!
MAYBE FRITZ WON'T COME UNTIL THE SPRING THAW!
BACK IN NOVOSIBIRSK, THE SPRING THAW WOULD DROWN HIM! NO, WE WON'T SEE HIM UNTIL SUMMER... MAYBE NOT EVEN THEN!

NEXT WEEK: THE HARD-HITTING "PUNISHMENT SQUAD" DISHES OUT MORE PUNISHMENT!

A PROMISE OF SAFE CONDUCT . . . FROM THE FUHRER HIMSELF! THERE'S GOT TO BE A CATCH SOMEWHERE!

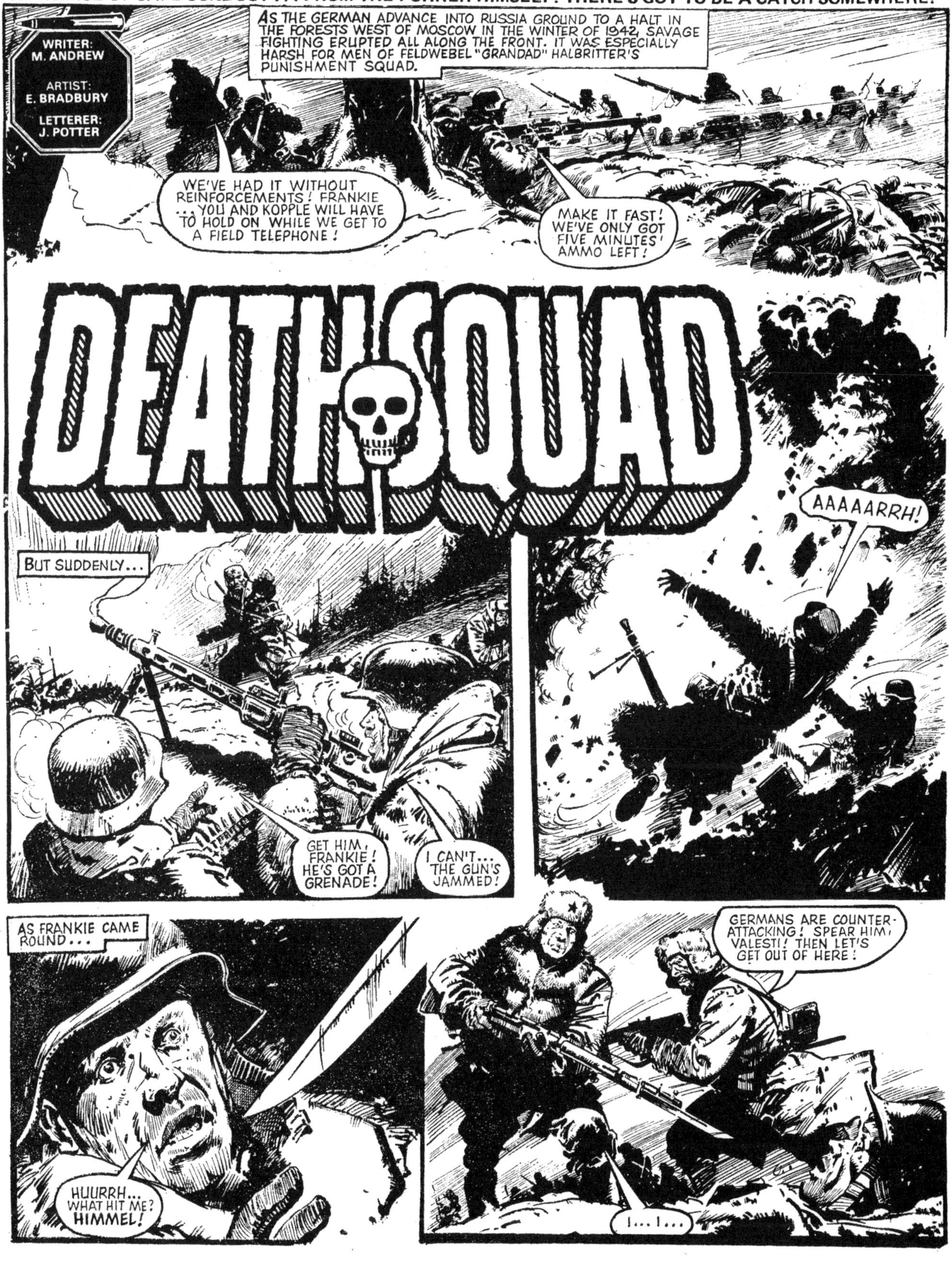
WRITER: M. ANDREW
ARTIST: E. BRADBURY
LETTERER: J. POTTER
AS THE GERMAN ADVANCE INTO RUSSIA GROUND TO A HALT IN THE FORESTS WEST OF MOSCOW IN THE WINTER OF 1942, SAVAGE FIGHTING ERUPTED ALL ALONG THE FRONT. IT WAS ESPECIALLY HARSH FOR MEN OF FELDWEBEL "GRANDAD" HALBRITTER'S PUNISHMENT SQUAD.
WE'VE HAD IT WITHOUT REINFORCEMENTS! FRANKIE ... YOU AND KOPPLE WILL HAVE TO HOLD ON WHILE WE GET TO A FIELD TELEPHONE!
MAKE IT FAST! WE'VE ONLY GOT FIVE MINUTES' AMMO LEFT!
DEATH SQUAD
BUT SUDDENLY...
GET HIM, FRANKIE! HE'S GOT A GRENADE!
I CAN'T... THE GUN'S JAMMED!
AAAAARRH!
AS FRANKIE CAME ROUND...
HUURRH... WHAT HIT ME? HIMMEL!
GERMANS ARE COUNTER-ATTACKING! SPEAR HIM, VALESTI! THEN LET'S GET OUT OF HERE!
I... I...

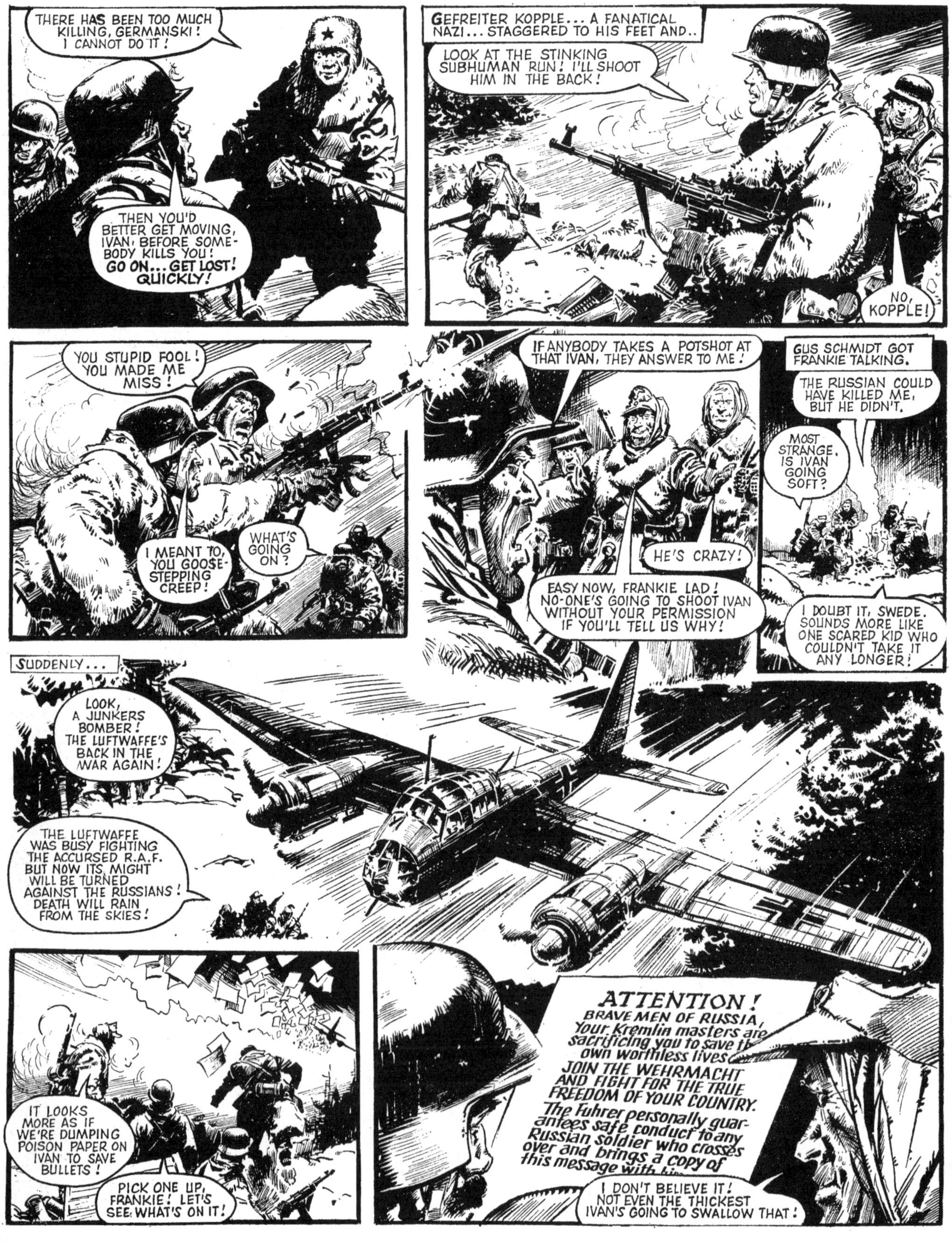

THERE HAS BEEN TOO MUCH KILLING, GERMANSKI! I CANNOT DO IT!
THEN YOU'D BETTER GET MOVING, IVAN, BEFORE SOMEBODY KILLS YOU! GO ON... GET LOST! QUICKLY!
GEFREITER KOPPLE... A FANATICAL NAZI... STAGGERED TO HIS FEET AND..
LOOK AT THE STINKING SUBHUMAN RUN! I'LL SHOOT HIM IN THE BACK!
NO, KOPPLE!
YOU STUPID FOOL! YOU MADE ME MISS!
I MEANT TO, YOU GOOSE-STEPPING CREEP!
WHAT'S GOING ON?
IF ANYBODY TAKES A POTSHOT AT THAT IVAN, THEY ANSWER TO ME!
HE'S CRAZY!
EASY NOW, FRANKIE LAD! NO-ONE'S GOING TO SHOOT IVAN WITHOUT YOUR PERMISSION IF YOU'LL TELL US WHY!
GUS SCHMIDT GOT FRANKIE TALKING.
THE RUSSIAN COULD HAVE KILLED ME, BUT HE DIDN'T.
MOST STRANGE. IS IVAN GOING SOFT?
I DOUBT IT, SWEDE. SOUNDS MORE LIKE ONE SCARED KID WHO COULDN'T TAKE IT ANY LONGER!
SUDDENLY...
LOOK, A JUNKERS BOMBER! THE LUFTWAFFE'S BACK IN THE WAR AGAIN!
THE LUFTWAFFE WAS BUSY FIGHTING THE ACCURSED R.A.F. BUT NOW ITS MIGHT WILL BE TURNED AGAINST THE RUSSIANS! DEATH WILL RAIN FROM THE SKIES!
IT LOOKS MORE AS IF WE'RE DUMPING POISON PAPER ON IVAN TO SAVE BULLETS!
PICK ONE UP, FRANKIE! LET'S SEE WHAT'S ON IT!
ATTENTION! BRAVE MEN OF RUSSIA, Your Kremlin masters are sacrificing you to save th own worthless lives JOIN THE WEHRMACHT AND FIGHT FOR THE TRUE FREEDOM OF YOUR COUNTRY. The Fuhrer personally guarantees safe conduct to any Russian soldier who crosses over and brings a copy of this message with
I DON'T BELIEVE IT! NOT EVEN THE THICKEST IVAN'S GOING TO SWALLOW THAT!

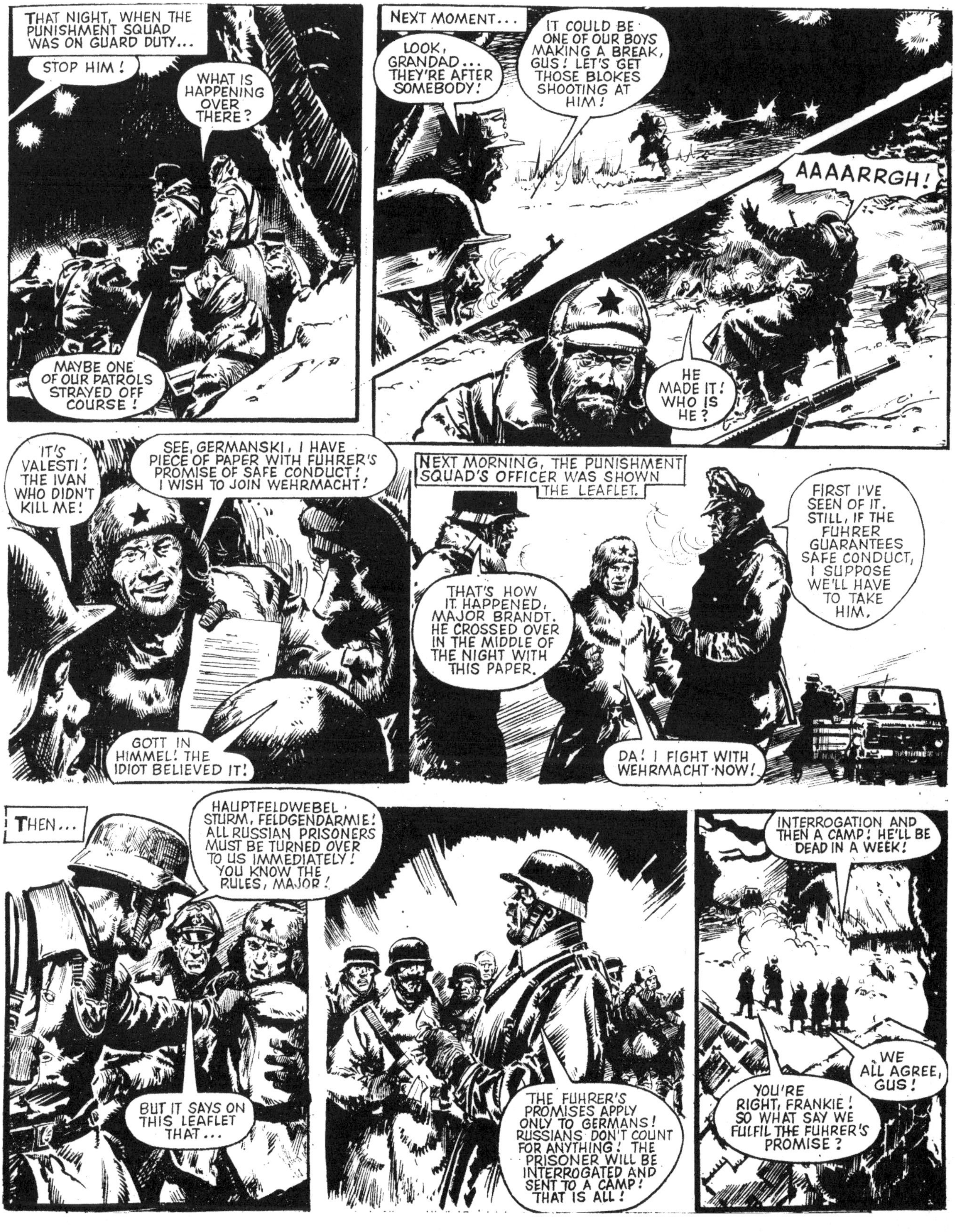
THAT NIGHT, WHEN THE PUNISHMENT SQUAD WAS ON GUARD DUTY...
STOP HIM!
WHAT IS HAPPENING OVER THERE?
MAYBE ONE OF OUR PATROLS STRAYED OFF COURSE!
NEXT MOMENT...
LOOK, GRANDAD... THEY'RE AFTER SOMEBODY!
IT COULD BE ONE OF OUR BOYS MAKING A BREAK, GUS! LET'S GET THOSE BLOKES SHOOTING AT HIM!
AAAARRGH!
HE MADE IT! WHO IS HE?
IT'S VALESTI! THE IVAN WHO DIDN'T KILL ME!
SEE, GERMANSKI, I HAVE PIECE OF PAPER WITH FUHRER'S PROMISE OF SAFE CONDUCT! I WISH TO JOIN WEHRMACHT!
GOTT IN HIMMEL! THE IDIOT BELIEVED IT!
NEXT MORNING, THE PUNISHMENT SQUAD'S OFFICER WAS SHOWN THE LEAFLET.
THAT'S HOW IT HAPPENED, MAJOR BRANDT. HE CROSSED OVER IN THE MIDDLE OF THE NIGHT WITH THIS PAPER.
FIRST I'VE SEEN OF IT. STILL, IF THE FUHRER GUARANTEES SAFE CONDUCT, I SUPPOSE WE'LL HAVE TO TAKE HIM.
DA! I FIGHT WITH WEHRMACHT NOW!
THEN...
HAUPTFELDWEBEL STURM, FELDGENDARMIE! ALL RUSSIAN PRISONERS MUST BE TURNED OVER TO US IMMEDIATELY! YOU KNOW THE RULES, MAJOR!
BUT IT SAYS ON THIS LEAFLET THAT...
THE FUHRER'S PROMISES APPLY ONLY TO GERMANS! RUSSIANS DON'T COUNT FOR ANYTHING! THE PRISONER WILL BE INTERROGATED AND SENT TO A CAMP! THAT IS ALL!
INTERROGATION AND THEN A CAMP! HE'LL BE DEAD IN A WEEK!
YOU'RE RIGHT, FRANKIE! SO WHAT SAY WE FULFIL THE FUHRER'S PROMISE?
WE ALL AGREE, GUS!

SSION ENDS...MISSION ENDS...MISSION ENDS...MISSION ENDS...MISSION ENDS...MISSION ENDS...MISSION ENDS...

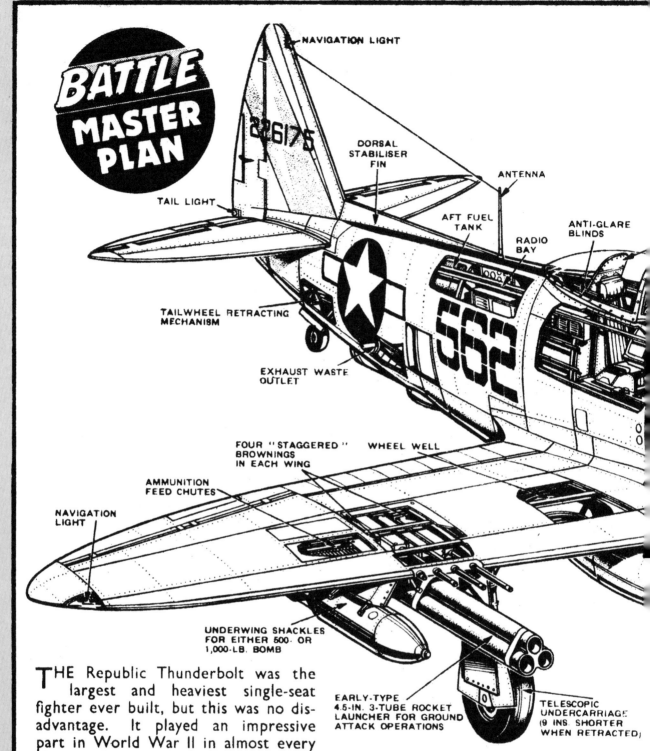

BATTLE MASTER PLAN

NAVIGATION LIGHT

DORSAL STABILISER FIN

ANTENNA

TAIL LIGHT

AFT FUEL TANK

ANTI-GLARE BLINDS

RADIO BAY

226175

562

TAILWHEEL RETRACTING MECHANISM

EXHAUST WASTE OUTLET

FOUR "STAGGERED" BROWNINGS IN EACH WING

WHEEL WELL

AMMUNITION FEED CHUTES

NAVIGATION LIGHT

UNDERWING SHACKLES FOR EITHER 500- OR 1,000-LB. BOMB

EARLY-TYPE 4.5-IN. 3-TUBE ROCKET LAUNCHER FOR GROUND ATTACK OPERATIONS

TELESCOPIC UNDERCARRIAGE (9 INS. SHORTER WHEN RETRACTED)

THE Republic Thunderbolt was the largest and heaviest single-seat fighter ever built, but this was no disadvantage. It played an impressive part in World War II in almost every theatre of war.

The Thunderbolt made its operational début with the U.S. Air Force in Britain in 1943, and proved itself as an efficient high-altitude escort plane. Luftwaffe pilots soon learnt to fear these stocky aircraft, which could absorb an immense amount of damage and still return to base.

On the way back from escorting the high-flying Liberators and Flying Fortresses, the Thunderbolts would fly very low and use their ammunition up on ground targets. In this way, almost by accident, the Thunderbolt discovered its most famous rôle : that of fighter-bomber.

With its load of bombs and rockets,

REPUBLIC P.47D "THUNDERBOLT"

LARGEST SINGLE-SEAT FIGHTER EVER BUILT

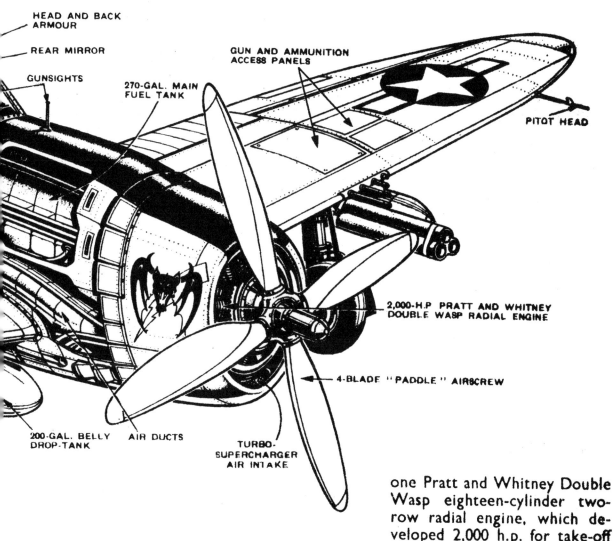

HEAD AND BACK ARMOUR

REAR MIRROR

GUNSIGHTS

270-GAL. MAIN FUEL TANK

GUN AND AMMUNITION ACCESS PANELS

PITOT HEAD

2,000-H.P PRATT AND WHITNEY DOUBLE WASP RADIAL ENGINE

4-BLADE "PADDLE" AIRSCREW

200-GAL. BELLY DROP-TANK

AIR DUCTS

TURBO-SUPERCHARGER AIR INTAKE

the Thunderbolt played a big part in softening up Hitler's European defences in preparation for D-Day. Between D-Day and the end of the War in Europe, Thunderbolts destroyed 86,000 railway coaches, 9,000 engines, 68,000 motor-cars and lorries, and 6,000 armoured vehicles in Germany alone !

The Thunderbolt was powered by one Pratt and Whitney Double Wasp eighteen-cylinder two-row radial engine, which developed 2,000 h.p. for take-off and 23,000 h.p. at 31,000 feet with turbo-supercharging.

Its maximum speed was 429 m.p.h. at 30,000 feet, and 350 m.p.h. at sea level. It had a service ceiling of 40,000 feet and a range of 950 miles.

The Thunderbolt carried an armament of six or eight Browning machine-guns, and 2,500 lb. of bombs or ten HVAR missiles.

FOLLOW THE COMPLETE STORY OF CHARLEY'S WAR IN THESE BEAUTIFUL COLLECTORS' EDITIONS

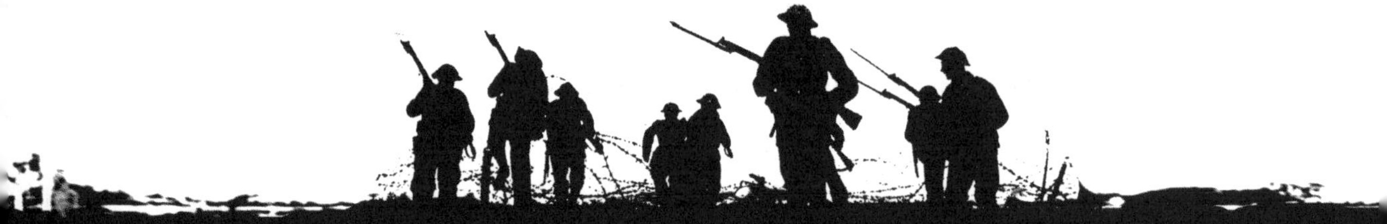

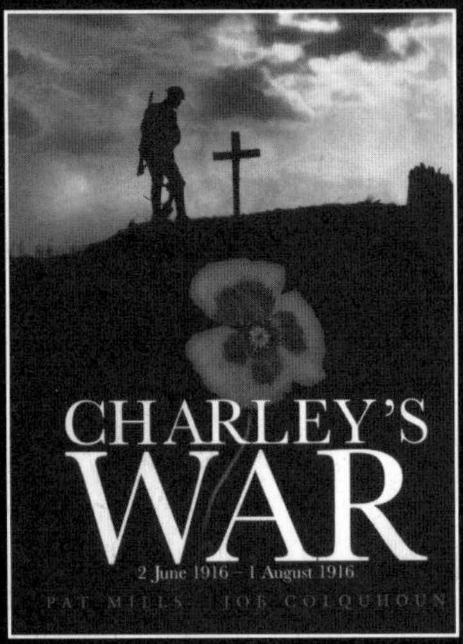
CHARLEY'S
WAR
2 June 1916 – 1 August 1916
PAT MILLS JOE COLQUHOUN

2 June – 1 August 1916
ISBN: 9781840236279

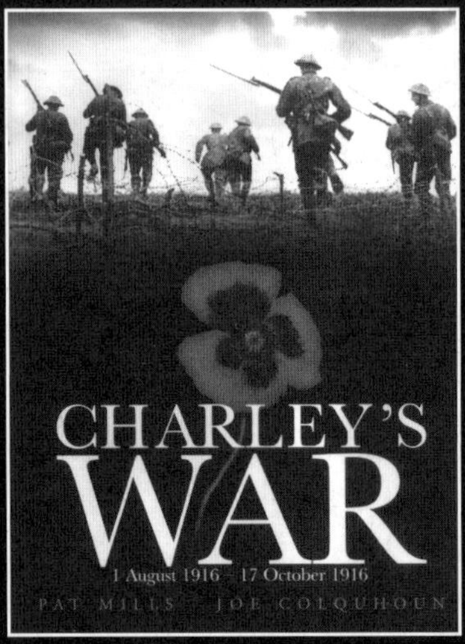
CHARLEY'S
WAR
1 August 1916 – 17 October 1916
PAT MILLS JOE COLQUHOUN

1 August – 17 October 1916
ISBN: 9781840239294

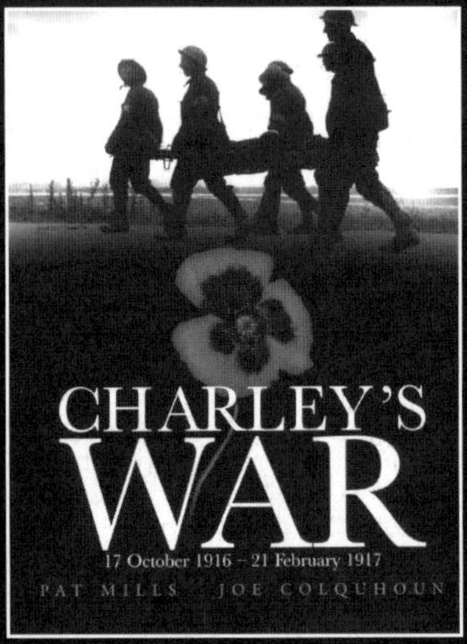
CHARLEY'S
WAR
17 October 1916 – 21 February 1917
PAT MILLS JOE COLQUHOUN

17 October 1916 – 21 February 1917
ISBN: 9781845762704

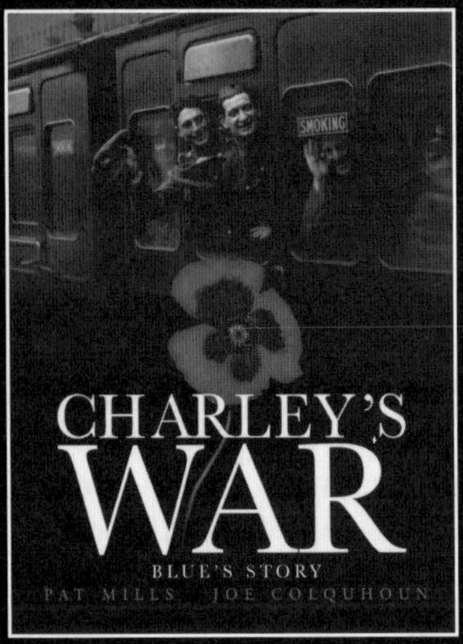
SMOKING
CHARLEY'S
WAR
BLUE'S STORY
PAT MILLS JOE COLQUHOUN

Blue's Story
ISBN: 9781845763237

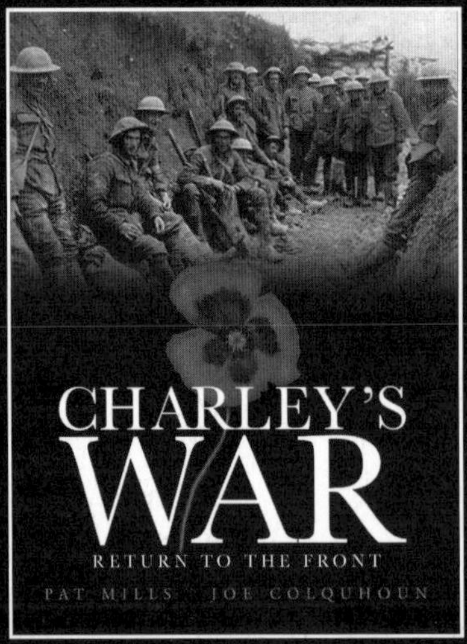
CHARLEY'S
WAR
RETURN TO THE FRONT
PAT MILLS JOE COLQUHOUN

Return to the Front
ISBN: 9781845767969

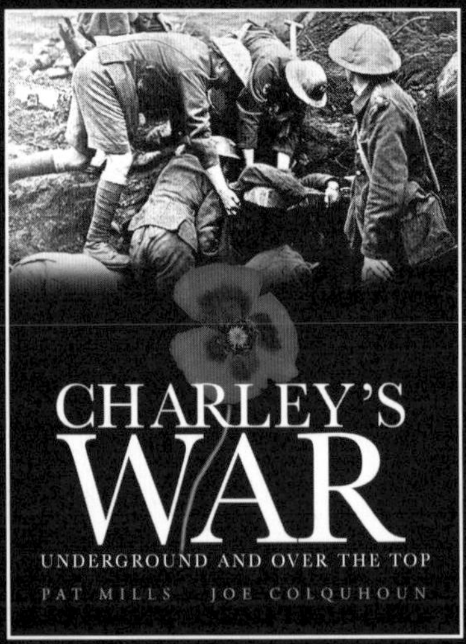
CHARLEY'S
WAR
UNDERGROUND AND OVER THE TOP
PAT MILLS JOE COLQUHOUN

Underground and Over the Top
ISBN: 9781845767976
AVAILABLE OCTOBER 2009

NOW AVAILABLE FROM TITAN BOOKS

WWW.TITANBOOKS.COM

THE *BATTLE* CONTINUES!

FOLLOW YOUR FAVOURITE CHARACTERS' ADVENTURES IN THESE ALL-NEW REPRINT COLLECTIONS!

FALCONS' FIRST FLIGHT
JOHNNY RED

NOT FINAL COVER

DARKIE'S MOB
THE ENTIRE BLOOD-SOAKED EPIC!!

NOT FINAL COVER

PLUS

RAT PACK

AND

MAJOR EAZY

COMING SOON!

WWW.TITANBOOKS.COM

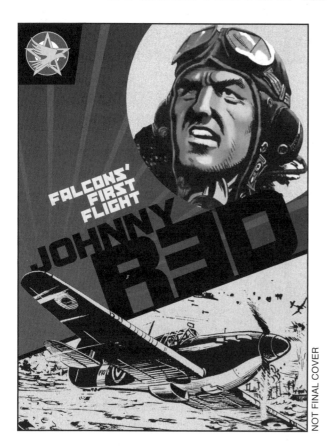

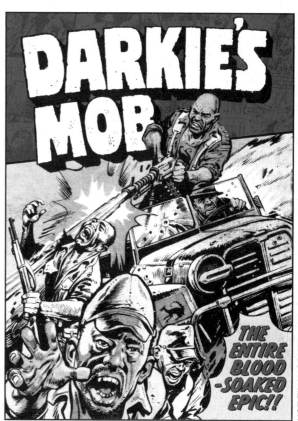

CLASSIC BRITISH COMICS FROM TITAN BOOKS

208 PAGES OF THRILLING FOOTBALL ACTION!
THE BEST OF ROY OF THE ROVERS
THE 1970s
WITH AN INTRODUCTION BY FRANK SKINNER

THE BUMPER BOOK OF
ROY OF THE ROVERS

JEFF HAWKE
OVERLORD
SYDNEY JORDAN
WILLIE PATTERSON

JEFF HAWKE
THE AMBASSADORS
SYDNEY JORDAN
WILLIE PATTERSON

GREEN COBRA
MODESTY
Blaise

MODESTY
Blaise
THE SCARLET MAIDEN

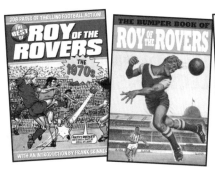

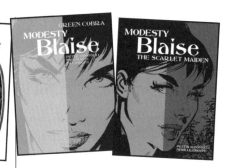

ROY OF THE ROVERS

- The Best of Roy of the Rovers: The 1980s
- The Best of Roy of the Rovers: The 1970s
- The Bumper Book of Roy of the Rovers: Volume 1
- The Bumper Book of Roy of the Rovers: Volume 2

DAN DARE
PILOT OF THE FUTURE
THE PHANTOM FLEET

DAN DARE
PILOT OF THE FUTURE
ROGUE PLANET

DAN DARE

- Voyage to Venus Part 1
- Voyage to Venus Part 2
- The Red Moon Mystery
- Marooned on Mercury
- Operation Saturn Part 1
- Operation Saturn Part 2
- Prisoners of Space
- The Man From Nowhere
- Rogue Planet
- Reign of the Robots
- The Phantom Fleet
- Trip to Trouble

JEFF HAWKE

- Overlord
- The Ambassadors

JAMES BOND 007
THE SPY WHO LOVED ME

JAMES BOND 007
THE MAN WITH THE GOLDEN GUN

JAMES BOND

- Casino Royale
- Dr No
- Goldfinger
- On Her Majesty's Secret Service
- The Man with the Golden Gun
- Octopussy
- The Spy Who Loved Me
- Colonel Sun
- The Golden Ghost
- Trouble Spot
- The Phoenix Project
- Death Wing
- The Girl Machine

MODESTY BLAISE

- The Gabriel Set-Up
- Mister Sun
- Top Traitor
- The Black Pearl
- Bad Suki
- The Hell-Makers
- The Green-Eyed Monster
- The Puppet Master
- The Gallows Bird
- Cry Wolf
- The Inca Trail
- Death Trap
- Yellowstone Booty
- Green Cobra
- The Lady Killers
- The Scarlet Maiden

FOR MORE INFORMATION ON THESE TITLES — AND MUCH, MUCH MORE — CHECK OUT OUR WEBSITE AT WWW.TITANBOOKS.COM!